Cases on Interactive Technology Environments and Transnational Collaboration:
Concerns and Perspectives

Siran Mukerji
IGNOU, India

Purnendu Tripathi
IGNOU, India

Information Science REFERENCE

INFORMATION SCIENCE REFERENCE
Hershey · New York

Director of Editorial Content:	Kristin Klinger
Director of Book Publications:	Julia Mosemann
Acquisitions Editor:	Lindsay Johnston
Development Editor:	Elizabeth Ardner
Publishing Assistant:	Deanna Jo Zombro
Typesetter:	Keith Glazewski
Production Editor:	Jamie Snavely
Cover Design:	Lisa Tosheff
Printed at:	Yurchak Printing Inc.

Published in the United States of America by
Information Science Reference (an imprint of IGI Global)
701 E. Chocolate Avenue
Hershey PA 17033
Tel: 717-533-8845
Fax: 717-533-8661
E-mail: cust@igi-global.com
Web site: http://www.igi-global.com/reference

Library of Congress Cataloging-in-Publication Data

Cases on interactive technology environments and transnational collaboration : concerns and perspectives / Siran Mukerji and Purnendu Tripathi, editors. p. cm.
Includes bibliographical references and index.
Summary: "This book provides a comparative and comprehensive analysis of technologically enabled educational environments and various issues concerning education and collaborations across the world besides focusing on best practices and experiences from a varied range of countries"--Provided by publisher.
ISBN 978-1-61520-909-5 (hardcover) -- ISBN 978-1-61520-910-1 (ebook) 1. Group work in education--Computer networks--Cross-cultural studies. 2. Computer-assisted instruction--Cross-cultural studies. 3. Educational technology--Cross-cultural studies. 4. Education and globalization--Cross-cultural studies. I. Mukerji, Siran. II. Tripathi, Purnendu, 1975- LB1032.C39 2010 371.33'4--dc22
2009040564

British Cataloguing in Publication Data
A Cataloguing in Publication record for this book is available from the British Library.

Table of Contents

Detailed Table of Contents

This case study by Karin Levinsen presents the three-year research and development IT Folder Project (PIF) of Denmark, which aims at facilitating the inclusion of young children with potential reading and writing difficulties in normal classes. The research focuses on everyday practice in schools and produces knowledge that gradually qualifies and consolidates a sustainable implementation strategy for the municipality involved regarding ICT as a change agent for inclusion.

In this chapter, Don Krug and Jenny Arntzen present the research that investigated the formation of ICT ecologies of learning in a Canadian teacher education program. This research paper looks critically at the Canadian educational contexts and how teacher candidates (TCs) are prepared to use ICT when entering the teaching profession. It highlights how a group of eight teacher candidate researchers (TCRs) engaged in *efficacious learning.*

This case by Trish Andrews elucidates the use of technology to support the delivery of common curriculum for mining engineering education in Australia which is struggling to meet the demand for highly trained professionals for the minerals industry. It outlines the challenges in such collaborations and discusses the range of corporate and open source technologies selected and adopted to overcome these challenges to enable collaborative teaching and learning activities in this trans-national program.

The present paper builds on Aissetou's personal initiatory experience in eLearning and highlights some specific challenges that traditional universities such as the University Abdou Moumouni (UAM) of Niamey in Niger face in their efforts to introduce eLearning and distance learning as a new mode of course delivery. The study shows that even though challenges are big, however political and institutional support can freshen up the perspectives and change opportunities into realities.

Kevin Downing in this case provides a comparative evaluation of two pilot online courses with their traditionally taught counterparts in one of the universities of Hong Kong. This case highlights the impact of adopting a blended learning approach to an undergraduate programme and studies the impact of online learning opportunities on the personality and behaviour of Asian students.

This chapter focuses on the influence of the Wiki environment on teachers who participate in teacher education programs. This study revolves around a multicultural group of teachers - younger and older, experienced and novices, Jews and Arabs who are examined while learning literature and its instruction with Wiki. The paper underscores various factors that influence the learning process and participants' attitude toward the use of Wiki.

The case study is on the use of a visual case "Henry Brubaker" in different subjects in the area of business organization to delve into the subject of design and implementation of organizational structures. While different methodologies are used for studying any subject, the authors in this case prove that the audiovisual case methodology substantially increases student motivation for attending the class sessions and for studying the subject.

Maria and Efstathios are of the opinion that at a time when mathematics and science provide essential knowledge tools and the foundations for lifelong learning skills, cross-national studies of student achievement in Europe indicate lack of mathematical and scientific competence for a considerable proportion of the student population. The present paper is on the EU-funded project *SMASH* which acknowledges the central role of parents in children's learning and aims to raise the educational standards of European youth in mathematics and science by cultivating underlying home cultures as springboards for learning. The paper based on this innovative project consortium focuses on how this project has developed an innovative intercultural parent-trainer training course that is delivered through combined use of e-learning and physical meetings while also devising related resources for professionals involved in parent education initiatives.

This exploratory case study tells about the technology enabled learning initiatives in education in Samoa, focusing on the developments taking place in a leading university in the Pacific Ocean island nation of Samoa and its Ministry of Education, Sports and Culture (MESC). The discussion includes an evaluation of the effectiveness of presently used technology/ technology mix used in e-learning and its effectiveness in facing the demands posed by STEP factors. It also discusses the various international partnerships/ collaboration fostered by the University and MESC to facilitate and enhance access to education for students.

The author of this chapter feels that the institutional effects of the technology enhanced performance assessment evidentiary demands on university programs which are undergoing review by national accrediting bodies have received lesser attention by the scholars. While addressing this, she examines the institutional dynamics of accreditation review experienced by faculty in a department offering graduate programs for educational leadership. The chapter outlines four phases of development of the essential elements of a web-based assessment system, and describes the questions raised by faculty about performance evidence, the assessment of that evidence, and the nature of measures of program outcome effectiveness.

The planning and elaboration of the Teaching-Learning Objects (T-LO) are gaining heightened importance in Brazil. Therefore, the researchers in this paper look towards presenting the conceptual singularities of the T-LO; the Instructional Design (ID) processes and the importance of the Instructional Project (IP) elaboration to guarantee a meaningful potentiality of the T-LO. On the basis of the results of the research study, attention is being centred on the contribution of a framework (called the T-LO List), which is used to analyze how the T-LO developed, implemented, and evaluated in a specific context of a didactic module elaboration.

Universiti Putra Malaysia's vision is to be fully online so as to enhance and encourage the culture of ICT in supporting teaching and learning. For achieving this goal, two strategies were put forth, one to implement the use of one learning management system (LMS) and secondly to enhance competency of academic staff in using the LMS. This paper reports on this endeavour and journey of UPM in adapting the use of LMS from the early 1990s until today.

This paper aims to present the findings of a comparative study of two different computer reading programmes with the overall objective of compiling a minimum set of requirements for such a programme in a third world educational environment. It also provides an insight into the challenges, benefits and limitations of implementing technology assisted reading on a wide scale. The results of this study are used to formulate strategies to best obtain results in reading difficulties.

This paper from Eastern part of Africa evaluates the initial phase of e-learning, the importance of rightful attitude, context, and instructional design in digital learning environments in the universities of three countries of this region, namely, Makerere University in Uganda, University of Nairobi, Kenya and University of Dar es Salaam, Tanzania. It discusses whether the learning environment created so

Foreword

We are living, working and educating in a defining era of human history. The impact of technology on our lives and on learning is unfolding with each fresh breakthrough and with each attempt by teachers and learners alike to integrate these changes into the repertoire of modalities labeled as pedagogy. Thanks to technology, we are learning how to educate in new ways, but with our "eyes on the prize," the effective preparation of the next generations of intellectuals and problem solvers, the business elites, professors and teachers alike, and the worlds' growing population who understand more fully with each passing day the vital importance of education to them and their families. We may be approaching a moment when there is broad consensus on the necessity for educating all in our national societies in order to achieve national and transnational economic and social goals.

We are also in a position to learn from one another as never before. The challenges we face leap across national borders and defy oceans. The global nature of the issues of our time requires global perspectives and solutions. We need each other. Pierre Teihard de Chardin was clairvoyant in the early twentieth century, at the apex of nation-state supremacy when he counseled that "The age of nations is passed. If we are not to perish, we must set aside our ancient prejudices, and build the earth."

Technology in multiple expressions makes it possible to connect far more efficiently and effectively than the occasional conference. We share the potential benefits of connection that technology facilitates. Technology invites collaboration if we fully understand the benefits of such relationships, not only to inform our individual projects, but to create a cadre of effective analysts and practitioners who can, like no time before, work in close association at what used to be considered great distances. We now work in virtual proximity.

Technology and collaboration are twin prisms through which to approach this work. While technology enables us to pursue our issues and interests with unprecedented autonomy, collaboration tempers the penchant to "go it alone" with the reminder that enhanced benefit can be reaped via partnerships in pursuit of answers to our queries. Collaboration is becoming more valued within and across societies as a successful strategy to address issues. Technology is not only facilitating collaboration, it is directly assisting in making collaboration a contemporary, preferred strategy. We learn separately and together, and utilize the power of technological connections to bolster the acceptability of this approach.

In many ways, this collaborative work by Professors Mukerji and Tripathi highlights the changing dynamic of education today. The focus of the selected cases contributed by their colleagues from across the planet is the presentation of learning scenarios rooted in technology. Not many years ago, such a perspective would have been limited and the process of change evolutionary. But the rate and pace of technological change have escalated exponentially in a surprisingly short time. Blackboards no longer signify a hard surface for writing with chalk, but a tech product designed to enhance teaching. Teaching was a relatively insular process with instructors creating their own pedagogical fiefdoms which they ruled often with impunity. There were extended periods of time when faculty would discuss the issues of their respective disciplines, but not usually the reality of teaching and learning in their classroom domains.

This eclectic work demonstrates just how significantly the milieu has changed. Technologies, rapidly changing and easily shared, are re-defining teaching and learning on a global scale. This volume offers the reader a broad view of work in this area which is global in perspective yet local in application. By engaging their colleagues to contribute and aggregating their latest research in one volume, Drs. Mukerji and Tripathi have methodically advanced the reader's awareness of the current confluence of educational technology and its collaborative use. They effectively demonstrate the salience of sharing best practices in the efficient and effective use of technology to enhance and advance learning.

The work presents a considerable list of education issues with global resonance and relevance. Within these carefully selected cases one discovers approaches to innovative learning supported by technologies that liberate rather than limit the learner. The authors encourage us to think and create not just "outside the box," but beyond national borders to discover and connect others equally devoted to the advancement of learning. Learning is rightly understood as an essential human right and as a transformer of people and societies. Access to learning, especially enhanced by technology, creates opportunities for personal and systemic growth, development and independence.

Importantly, the selected cases address real problems and advance our awareness of issues and encourage us to upgrade our knowledge and join the global conversation on the advancement of teaching and learning. The issues tackled run the full spectrum from the salience of faculty development to learning for children with serious communication challenges, from using e-learning in West Africa to personality profiles which adapt most readily to on line learning, from teaching styles in Norway to learning management in Malaysia. A clear strength of this compendium is the variety of examples drawn from colleagues on almost every continent, and the applicability of most of the cases to other global regions.

What is apparent from this well conceptualized work is the global, transformational prowess of access to learning. Personal and national goals are being re-framed by the myriad use of ever-changing technology as a powerful democratizing agent. As a species, we will only become more connected and more collaborative but, hopefully, more appreciative that we all face the challenges of accelerated change.

We should collaborate in this way to nurture the creative learning environments we will require in order to thrive in this intertwined, global century. Our authors have offered their readers a useful, diverse collection of relevant studies from across the world.

Don Betz
Northeastern State University

***Don Betz**, Ph. D. in International Studies from University of Denver, is presently the President of Northeastern State University and is a veteran educationist and administrator with more than 37 years of experience in higher education. Earlier, Prof. Betz was the Chancellor of the University of Wisconsin-River Falls. Prof. Betz's career began in higher education in 1971 as Assistant Professor of Political Science at Northeastern University where he served in various capacities, including Vice President for University Relations, Dean of Continuing Studies, Director of the Sequoyah Institute, Executive Director of the Educational Foundation, and Professor of Political Science. For five years he held the positions of Provost and Vice President for Academic Affairs at Palmer College, Davenport and Chief Academic Officer for the Palmer Chiropractic University System. In 1999, he took the post of Vice President for Academic Affairs and Professor of Political Science at the University of Central Oklahoma where he also served as Provost. Prof. Betz also has had long association with the United Nations where he held important positions and has served as an important connection between the United Nations and NGO's worldwide active on Middle East peace issues. He has been the Chairman of the International Coordinating Committee for NGOs on the Question of Palestine (ICCP) from 1985-2002 and of the United Nations-sponsored International NGO Meetings on the Question of Palestine for the past fifteen years. He has also been a chair, and/or speaker at more than 50 United Nations conferences, seminars and symposiums around the globe. He has been the recipient of numerous awards and authored articles and papers on the topics of international affairs, higher education, and leadership.*

Preface

Technology is essential for access to learning and development of a knowledge society. Imagine the two unique scenarios, wherein a learner in the far flung remote area of East African country of Uganda has access to technology enabled learning environment and in Denmark, technology being used for inclusion of children with special needs in the normal classrooms. Can we have collaborative strategies amongst the institutions to have interactive learning environment for the learners? How educational institutions in the developing and developed world are adaptable to innovations in technological environments through transnational collaboration for access to learning? How can we adopt the novel technologies and learn from the experiences of others so as to make customatized learning environment for our learners? The idea behind this book is to put forth international case studies to fetch answers for the above stated questions.

This book provides a comparative and comprehensive analysis of technologically enabled educational environments and various issues concerning education and collaborations across the world besides focusing on best practices and experiences from a varied range of countries. It showcases 19 case studies on the broad theme of Interactive technology environments and Transnational collaboration from Australia, Botswana, Brazil, Canada, Cyprus, Denmark, Hong Kong (People's Republic of China), Israel, Italy, Malaysia, Niger, Norway, Samoa, South Africa, Spain, Uganda and USA.

The readers will find an interesting account of collaborative efforts using technology enhanced learning environment for mining education, e-business management for Mediterranean countries, and initiatives of e-learning in Sub-Saharan Africa, East African countries, Samoa and Niger. Innovative approaches to use interactive learning environment are presented in cases of personality and online learning and young children with reading and writing difficulties.

How technology can effectively be used for training and development of teachers? This yet another vital issue has been discussed in the case studies of learning style and institutional barriers, ecologies of learning, teachers learning with wiki and web based performance assessment. Challenges for developing an information society, student retention in online learning environments, framework for analyzing Teaching-Learning Objects (T-LO), and blended approach for parent trainers training course on Mathematics and Science are some of the cases, which highlight the importance of technology integrated blended learning approach for addressing social and intellectual dimensions in knowledge society.

The first chapter of the book by Robson Marinho of Andrews University discusses the core issue of faculty development in the instructional technology and deliberates upon faculty's learning experiences and struggles they do in learning the instructional technology. This case in a very interesting manner addresses the core concerns of the influences that learning style and personal experiences have on faculty's learning experiences and also highlights the institutional barriers affecting the faculty members in dealing with instructional technology. While focusing on participant's personal approach and learning styles, it brings to light one dominant learning characteristic of each of the participant, compares it with the participant's result in the Index of Learning Styles Questionnaire and its potential implications for academic administrators in promoting the use of instructional technology by the faculty members.

The chapter "International Collaboration in Distance Education in Sub-Saharan Africa: Trends, Trials and Tomorrow's Thrusts" focuses on international collaboration initiatives undertaken in Sub-Saharan Africa (SSA) for utilizing technology in distance education. While highlighting a number of important collaborative endeavours, the authors Gbolagade Adekanmbi and Bopelo Boitshwarelo have observed a similar goal of pooling together ICT resources and know-how for the improvement of educational outcomes. They consider the African Virtual University (AVU) consortium as a viable approach to collaboration which has yielded significant results. The paper also brings to the fore various vital challenges facing technology-focused collaboration in the SSA and presents suggestions for bringing socio-institutional change in the African countries.

The third chapter by Karin Tweddell Levinsen titled "Effective use of ICT for Inclusive Learning of Young Children with reading and writing Difficulties" presents a case of Danish IT Folder Project (PIF), which is a research-based iterative intervention involving two primary schools and the local Pedagogic Development Centre (PDC) in the municipality, aiming at inclusion of young children with potential reading and writing difficulties in normal classes. The case presents initial results of the project on the quality of the children's inclusion process and the modifications of the screening tests, organizational changes in the municipality and the local schools due to these results.

The next chapter by Don Krug and Jenny Arntzen discusses the research that aimed to investigate the formation of ICT ecologies of learning in a teacher education program in Canada. The authors strongly believe the growth and development of ICT in Canada has placed tremendous responsibility on educators to be informed about not only acquiring ICT ICT literacies but, more importantly, to understand the consequences of emerging social, technological, economic, and political ICT issues that hinder and/or enhance student learning, health, and knowledge. This research project critically analyzes the Canadian educational contexts and deliberates on the procedure used for preparing those individuals who are entering the teacher profession in using ICT and also elucidates how a group of eight teacher candidate researchers (TCRs) engaged in *efficacious learning.*

In the fifth chapter, Trish Andrews of University of Queensland, Australia, discusses about a technology based collaborative approach used in a consortium of four mining schools in Australia, to develop and deliver a common curriculum for mining engineering education. The case further elucidates the challenges in the collaborative project and use of open source technologies to overcome these challenges towards an effective collaborative teaching and learning activities in this trans-national program.

This case study explores the development of E-Learning in Niger and attempts to identify the opportunities and challenges that traditional universities like University Abdou Moumouni faces in the pursuit of introducing online and distance learning as a new mode of course delivery in the higher education. The author Aissetou Drame Yaye believes that even though there are enormous challenges for these institutions but political and institutional support can re-vitalize and enrich the perspectives and help in transforming the opportunities into realities.

In the seventh chapter on Personality and Online Learning, Kevin Downing illustrates a comparative evaluation of two pilot online courses with their traditionally taught counterparts in one of the universities of Hong Kong. The case compares the students of both the different sets of programs and their satisfaction measures were taken from participants in both modes of delivery and then compared with student learning style. While highlighting impact of blended learning approach to an undergraduate programme, the findings of the case suggests change in the behavioural pattern of Asian students from Introverts to online Extraverts when given the opportunity to reflect on what they have learned and contribute to an online discussion forum.

Yael Poyas of Haifa University, Israel in the subsequent chapter discusses the influence of the Wiki environment on multicultural group of teachers - young and old, experienced and novices, Jews and Arabs, who were participating in teacher education programs. The outcome of the study suggests three main factors influencing the learning process and participants' attitude toward the use of Wiki i.e. Level of professional development and teaching experience, Culture and mother-tongue of the participants, and the Discord between academic norms and the Wiki environment's democratic norms.

The authors Xavier M. Triadó Ivern, Pilar Aparicio Chueca, Natalia Jaría Chacón and Amal Elasri Ejjaberi in this case study have presented the affect of audio-visual case methodology for teaching Business in virtual mode. They have also attempted to study the influence of using such a method for better understanding of the theoretical concepts by the students.

"SMASH: Blended Training for Parent Education in Mathematics and Science" by Maria Meletiou Mavrotheris and Efstathios Mavrotheris is based on the EU-funded project *SMASH* that provides an innovative intercultural parent-trainer training course and related resources for professionals involved in parent education initiatives with the objective of raising the educational standards of European youth in mathematics and science. This training course is provided in a blended mode i.e. by the combination of use of e-learning and physical meetings. The course equips the trainers with knowledge, techniques, and implementation tools for high-quality, culturally differentiated training in mathematics and science education required for educating the parents of elementary and middle school children (ages 6-15) in their communities.

The next case study on experiences, issues and challenges of introducing technology enabled educational initiatives in the Pacific Ocean island of Samoa by Ioana T. Chan Mow, presents an overview of the prevailing status of technology based learning in this island nation for education and development opportunities. While concentrating on solutions and recommendations for future strategies, the chapter also examines various international partnerships and collaborations advanced by a leading university and the Ministry of Education, Sports and Culture of Samoa for improving the access to education.

Hanne Mawhinney, the author of the next case study, feels that less scholarly attention has been paid to the institutional effects of the technology enhanced performance assessment evidentiary demands on university programs undergoing review by national accrediting bodies. She addresses this issue in this chapter, wherein she examines the institutional dynamics of accreditation review experienced by faculty in a department offering graduate programs for educational leadership.

In the thirteenth chapter, Carolyn Stevenson discusses the issue of retention of students in online learning environments. The author opines that a collaborative effort of instructors, administrators, and students is needed to promote student success. In the study, she also stresses on the need for fostering relationships in the community that is critical for academic success and student retention. The case makes an attempt to discuss strategies for retaining and motivating online students.

The chapter "Challenges in Aligning Pedagogical Practices and Pupils Competencies with Demands of the Information Society: The Case of Norway" by Hans Christian Arnseth and Ove Edvard Hatlevik try to determine the reasons behind the difficulty faced while changing the educational practices that makes it suited for providing the capabilities required for an information society and global economy. The authors, while providing an insight into the complexities involved in changing institutional practices, taking the instance of Norway as a case here, argue that new technologies must be cultivated over a period of time for innovative, productive and active learning and teaching.

The next chapter by Wael Assaf, Gianluca Elia, Ayham Fayyoumi, and Cesare Taurino discusses collaborative learning experiences in teaching of e-Business Management, aiming to create e-Business Capabilities through blended learning approach in Mediterranean Countries. The case elucidates the pedagogical approach "Learning-in-Action" together with some considerations on the effectiveness and the implications of the Problem-Based Learning (PBL) strategy in the program. It also ponders on the important role of this collaborative academic program in generating intellectual capital assets, Social Capital and Structural Capital.

In the sixteenth chapter, Ingrid Kleist Clark Nunes and Elena Maria Mallmann discuss how Teaching-Learning Objects (T-LO) are potentially meaningful in answering the principles of autonomy, interaction, interactivity, motivation and cooperation in hypermediatic didactic materials. The authors elaborate on the contribution of a framework (The T-LO List), which is used to analyze the T-LO developed, implemented, and evaluated in the specific context of a didactic module elaboration. The case concludes with the finding that it is important to realize that the usage of a framework to analyze the T-LO can orient theoretical methodological steps of planning, developing, implementing, observing, reflecting, and re-planning, all carried out by multidisciplinary teams.

The paper authored by Aida Suraya, Zaidan Abdul Wahab and Hamidah Meseran traces on the experiences of Universiti Putra Malaysia in using a Learning Management System from early 1990s and how it has evolved over the years, thus augmenting the culture of ICT supported teaching and learning. Through the case, it is evident that there has been a practice of each faculty deciding on its own platform for implementing e-Learning which resulted into the emergence of various LMSs. This gave rise to multiple difficulties hence a strategy was formulated to initiate and implement a single LMS for the University.

Gerda Van Wyk and Arno Louw through the paper, have attempted to present the findings of a comparative study between two different computer reading programmes, aimed at compiling a minimum set of requirements for such a programme in a developing country. They also identify the challenges, merits and demerits of implementing technology assisted reading on a larger magnitude. The paper here also suggests technology assisted measures for alleviating the reading difficulties.

The final chapter of the volume is a case study by Walimbwa Michael of Makerere University, Uganda, which attempts to evaluate the initial phase of e-learning, the importance of a rightful attitude, context, and instructional design in digital learning environments in three universities of the East African region. The case presents a crisis solving approach for stimulating a creative context for the meaningful introduction of e-learning and its impact on motivating institutions to integrate e-learning further. The findings of the study suggest that introduction of e-learning environment should be accompanied by an attitudinal change and empowering users with an authentic approach with less technological complexity. He also believes that review of curriculum, and assessment and training for acquaintance with e-learning environments are also essential for ensuring readiness towards accepting e-learning methods.

Through this case book, we have tried to bring to the readers the experiences, research studies, insights and challenges of the institutions across the globe, which when analyzed seem to highlight common concerns and perspectives for interactive technology and transnational collaborations in education. We hope through this endeavour, we will be able to get the institutions closer and enhance the accessibility of education.

Siran Mukerji
Purnendu Tripathi

Acknowledgment

We express our sincerest gratitude to the members of academia who have taken the time to contribute extremely thought provoking and insightful papers for this book, making it a truly international collection. Thank you so much for your effort, it is greatly appreciated. We are indeed grateful to the IGI Global Team for being so supportive and for giving us the much needed help at every stage of the project. Many thanks for the sustained cooperation.

Siran Mukerji
Purnendu Tripathi

Chapter 1
Faculty Development in Instructional Technology in the Context of Learning Styles and Institutional Barriers

Robson Marinho
Andrews University, USA

ABSTRACT

This chapter describes the within-case analysis of ten faculty members who agreed to share their learning experience and struggles in learning instructional technology. The case focuses on the in-depth description of each participant stressing their unique personal approach and learning styles, describing the main steps experienced and resources utilized by the participants during the learning process. It also highlights one dominant learning characteristic of each participant, which is compared with the participant's result in the Index of Learning Styles Questionnaire of North Carolina State University, with potential implications for academic administrators in promoting the use of instructional technology by faculty members of diverse profiles. The case also discusses the institutional barriers faced by faculty members while learning how to use instructional technology at a public university in the United States. Three institutional barriers were a major concern for the participants: Time, rewards, and cost. One hundred percent of the participants agreed that providing more time—along with financial and academic rewards—is critical to supporting the learning and implementation of instructional technology.

CASE BACKGROUND

Objectives

The purpose of this study was to collect and analyze information about the personal experiences of faculty members in learning to use instructional technology and to analyze how their learning experience was impacted by one professional development intervention. The main objectives of this study were:

1. Analyze the unique journey of individual faculty members in learning instructional technology and how their personal profiles and learning styles impacted their learning approach.

DOI: 10.4018/978-1-61520-909-5.ch001

2. Learn the story of faculty members describing their struggles, failures, achievements and successes in learning instructional technology.
3. Discuss the major difficulties and institutional barriers that prevent faculty from learning and using instructional technology.
4. Analyze which aspects of a technology workshop series the participants consider successful in promoting and facilitating learning in instructional technology.
5. Address possible suggestions of faculty for policy-makers on ways to overcome institutional barriers and increase the positive impact of professional development programs in technology.

Problem Statement

Many faculty members participate in professional development programs in instructional technology, but they may feel intimidated by the challenge of mastering the use of technological resources, and there is little information about the many factors influencing the way in which they learn about instructional technology. An in-depth look at how faculty approach this learning situation and the ways in which their learning can be successfully facilitated is an area that needs additional research.

Research Questions

The following research questions guided the study:

1. How do faculty cope with the fear and threat of failure in using instructional technology?
2. How do learning styles and personal experiences influence faculty learning experience?
3. What are the major difficulties and institutional barriers that prevent faculty from learning and using instructional technology on a regular basis?
4. How do professional development interventions impact faculty experiences in learning instructional

Theoretical Framework

Three major areas of literature are particularly useful in informing how the process of learning instructional technology is influenced by faculty personal styles in professional development programs: (1) Faculty attitudes towards change in technology, (2) learning styles models, and (3) Faculty Development Approaches. These areas are briefly addressed below.

Faculty Attitudes towards Change and Technology

Literature on faculty attitudes towards change and technology has direct implications for faculty development, because research suggests that the use of instructional technology by faculty members is intrinsically related to their attitudes and beliefs regarding the role of technology in education (Race, 2001; Mishra, Koehler & Zhao, 2007). The obvious implication for faculty development programs is that developmental interventions need to consider faculty attitudes and beliefs regarding instructional technology.

The adoption of instructional technology always involves a change process, and people will not always accept a change simply because others tell them of its practical advantages over an existing practice. In fact, the adoption process depends on a set of perceptions toward the change by the people involved in the desired change (Lee and Lawson, 2002), and this set of perceptions has been defined as the process by which people attach meaning to their experience (Eggan and Kauchak, 2004). In other words, without seeing real advantages to instructional technology, no one will actually change their teaching style to adopt technology in the classroom.

Like any other change process, the adoption of instructional technology faces different types of barriers and obstacles. Ertmer (1999) refers to two kinds of barriers: First-order barriers refer to extrinsic obstacles, which are factors external to the individual who are implementing the change, such as lack of equipment, time, training, or technical support; second-order barriers refer to intrinsic obstacles, which are related to the attitudes and beliefs of those involved in the change process, such as the challenge of traditional practices. According to her, "traditional approaches to change have focused on helping those involved in a change to overcome first-order barriers" (p. 151). However, as she says, the most effective approach to change is to focus on people's belief systems, and not only on the extrinsic obstacles.

Analyzing the intrinsic factors of a change process in the adoption of instructional technology, Lee and Lawson (2002) developed what they call a Concerns Matrix addressing two major dimensions of change: The degree to which change is compatible with the values and beliefs of the target audience, and the levels of the institution affected by the change process. They found that some faculty members who were skeptical of technology were not persuaded to use computers even five years after being exposed to a faculty development intervention. They concluded that a concern analysis must be conducted before any change is introduced.

This discussion about the effects of personal beliefs on a change process is supported by Rogers' (1995) Diffusion of Innovation Theory, according to which a technological innovation passes through four consecutive stages described as follows: (a) innovation, meaning the stage at which an idea is perceived as new, (b) diffusion or communication through channels within the social system, (c) time for adoption of the innovation, and (d) integration within the social system, a set of interrelated units sharing a common goal and including potential adopters. Innovation diffusion research explains how and why users adopt a new information medium, such as the Internet.

Rogers' theory also makes a distinction between different adopter categories, in which adopters are classified on the basis of their speed of adoption. Applying Rogers' description to faculty members, the categories can be identified as (a) innovators, characterized as venturesome faculty; (b) early adopters, described as those having more years of education and higher social status; (c) early majority, the deliberate ones; (d) late majority, the skeptical faculty; and (e) laggards, who are the most traditional and change resistant faculty members (Clarke, 1999).

The basic characteristics of each group of adopters can be described as follows:

1. Innovators: The risk takers willing to take the initiative and time to try something new and different.
2. Early adopters: People who tend to be respected group leaders, the individuals essential to adoption by the whole group.
3. Early majority: People who are careful, safe, deliberate individuals who do not want to risk time or other resources.
4. Late majority: People suspicious of innovations and resistant to change. They are hard to move without significant influence.
5. Laggards: These are people who are consistent and sometimes inflexible in resisting change. They only change under some kind of pressure (Rogers, 1995; Pacific University, 2002).

Learning Styles

The importance of considering learning styles in professional development programs in instructional technology is supported by current research that shows an increasing investment in innovative developmental interventions in instructional technology (Carliner & Shank, 2008; Garrison & Vaughan, 2008; Kidd and Song, 2007).

Research literature says that personal learning styles have an influence on the learning experience. Learning style is a generic term as an umbrella concept for recognizing individual learning differences. From different psychological and philosophical beliefs, a variety of authors have proposed different learning style models, and no one has a monopoly on the term or can claim to represent learning style in its entirety (Butler, 1987). In fact Dunn and Griggs (1998) explain that, despite differences in terminology, the models themselves overlap as they address different aspects of learning. Some researchers, for example, have focused on motivation and sociological traits, as well as on the structure of learning (Canfield and Lafferty, 1976; Dunn and Griggs, 1998; Gregorc, 1985; Hill, 1971; Ramirez and Castenada, 1974). Most of these researchers and Kolb (1984) have focused on the way learners perceive the world as a basis for developing their model, and all of them with the addition of Herrmann (1988) have addressed the way the human brain behaves and processes information. Listing all the learning styles models would be a very extensive task, therefore, this section briefly addresses a few models that focus on different learning dimensions and approaches.

Kolb's theory:. Based primarily on Dewey (1938), Lewin (1951), and Piaget (1977), Kolb (1984) developed a model called experiential learning as a four-step process, starting with immediate *concrete experience* with people or the environment, and then thinking about this experience through *reflective observations* looking to the meaning of things, from which learners engage in *abstract conceptualization* by analyzing ideas to understand a situation. In the final step, learners apply this analysis in *active experimentation*, getting things done and acting in new and more complex situations (Claxton and Murrell, 1987; Kolb 2000).

Gregorc's theory: The theory developed by Gregorc (1985; 1998) is similar to Kolb's dimensions, but identifies style in terms of the labels Concrete, Abstract, Sequential, and Random (Sarasin, 1998). Each combination of style describes a different type of learner and the way individuals relate to the world. In short, Gregorc proposes four types of mind styles: (1) concrete sequential, (2) concrete random, (3) abstract sequential, and (4) abstract random (Gregorc, 1998).

Felder-Silverman Learning Style Model: Synthesizing findings from Kolb (1984) and Gardner (1993), Felder and Silverman (1988) developed a learning style model at North Carolina State University, usually referred to as Index of Learning Styles Questionnaire developed (ILS). This model is based on four double dimensions: Sensing and intuitive, visual and verbal, active and reflective, sequential and global Felder (1993).

Herrmann Brain Dominance Instrument (HBDI): This model of brain dominance combines Sperry's (1975) split-brain concept with MacLean's (1978) triune brain concept to explain the thinking process by the right and left-brain hemispheres, as well as cerebral and limbic sections. The theory is based on the assumption that, wherever there are two of anything in the body, one is naturally dominant over the other, such as being right or left handed. It classifies learners according to their preferences for thinking and mode of knowing as a metaphorical interpretation based on the functions of different hemispheres of the brain. Nasmith, Schultz, and Williams (2003) summarize the four quadrants as distinct groups of activities as follows:

1. Quadrant A (left cerebral): Logic, analysis, mathematical, problem solving.
2. Quadrant B (left limbic): Organizing, planning, control, sequential.
3. Quadrant C (right limbic): Interpersonal, emotional, musical, spiritual.
4. Quadrant D (right cerebral): Imaginative, holistic, intuitive, and conceptual.

The application of the instrument associated with the theory (HBDI) indicates the degree of preference or lack of preference for the type of thinking represented by each quadrant by generating a score for each quadrant (Herrmann, 1988). As Nasmith et al. (2003) explain, "a primary preference for a quadrant indicates the greatest preference for its characteristic process" (p. 4).

The Myers-Briggs Type Indicator (MBTI): This instrument was designed to apply Carl Jung's theory in counseling, education, and business (Myers, 1976; Claxton and Murrell, 1987). According to the Jung's theory, the world can be perceived in two distinct ways, which are sensing and intuition. The theory also states that people use either thinking or feeling to come to conclusions and make judgments, employing two contrasting attitudes toward life, which is either a judging or a perceptive attitude, and using two contrasting preferences to deal with life: Extraversion and introversion. The main characteristics of each personality type can be described as follows:

1. Extraversion (E) versus Introversion (I): "This preference tells us how people 'charge their batteries'" (Brightman, 1998, p. 1). *Extraverts* focus on the outer world of people and find energy in things and people, while *Introverts* find energy in the inner world of ideas, concepts, and abstractions. They are motivated internally, and their minds are sometimes so active that they are "closed" to the outside world (Personality Pathways, 2003).
2. Sensing (S) versus Intuition (N): Sensing people are detail oriented and focus on facts and practical solutions, while Intuitive people seek out patterns and relationships among the facts they have gathered (Brightman, 1998; Personality Pathways, 2003).
3. Thinking (T) versus Feeling (F): Thinking students value analysis, logic, honesty, and principle. They focus on tasks and on the work to be accomplished and are most convinced by rational arguments. Feeling learners are diplomatic and tactful and make decisions by focusing on human values and needs. They appear warm and friendly and tend to be good at persuasion and facilitating differences among group members. They avoid arguments and conflicts and value harmony by seeking consensus and popular opinion (Brightman, 1998; Personality Pathways, 2003).
4. Judging (J) versus Perceptive (P): Judging people are decisive and like to plan the details in advance before moving into action. They focus on completing the task, like to act quickly, and prefer working with deadlines and schedules. Perceptive people are curious, adaptable, and spontaneous, but may have difficulty making decisions. They start many tasks, want to know everything about each task, and often find it difficult to complete a task. They are naturally tolerant of time pressure and work best as the deadlines approaches. They usually question the need for many rules and feel comfortable in extending deadlines (Brightman, 1998; Personality Pathways, 2003).

Dunn and Dunn model: This model is based on the theory that each person "has biologically and developmentally imposed characteristics that respond either positively or negatively to a variety of environmental, emotional, sociological, physiological, cognitive and instructional variables" (Dunn and Griggs, 1998). Here is how Dunn (2000) summarizes the individual's reaction to learning in different instructional settings:

1. Environmental preference: Learner's reaction to sound, light, temperature, and class design.
2. Emotional preferences: Influenced by motivation, persistence, responsibility and structure.
3. Sociological preferences: Learning alone or in group, working with peers or with either a collegial of authoritative adult. Includes a variety of approaches as opposed to patterns and routines.
4. Physiological preferences: Related to perception such as auditory, visual, tactual, or kinesthetic inclination. This level also includes time-of-day energy levels, such as the

preference for studying early in the morning or late in the night, and food intake (eating or not while studying), as well as mobility such as sitting still or moving around).

5. Psychological preferences: Related to global versus analytic processing, brain hemispheres, impulsive or reflective action.

Theory of multiple intelligences: Gardner (1993) took a more holistic approach in describing cognitive profiles by developing the theory of multiple intelligences. He performed interviews with hundreds of people and defined the first seven intelligences in 1983, adding the last two in 1999. According to Gardner, all human beings possess all nine intelligences in varying amounts, and each person has a different intellectual composition. Below are the nine intelligences proposed by Gardner (2000), as outlined by Disney Learning Partnership (n.d):

1. Verbal-Linguistic Intelligence: Well-developed verbal skills and sensitivity to the sounds, meanings and rhythms of words.
2. Mathematical-Logical Intelligence: Ability to think conceptually and abstractly, and capacity to discern logical or numerical patterns.
3. Musical Intelligence: Ability to produce and appreciate rhythm, pitch and timber.
4. Visual-Spatial Intelligence: Capacity to think in images and pictures, to visualize accurately and abstractly.
5. Bodily-Kinesthetic Intelligence: Ability to control one's body movements and to handle objects skillfully.
6. Interpersonal Intelligence: Capacity to detect and respond appropriately to the moods, motivations and desires of others.
7. Intrapersonal Intelligence: Capacity to be self-aware and in tune with inner feelings, values, beliefs and thinking processes.
8. Naturalist Intelligence: Ability to recognize and categorize plants, animals and other objects in nature.
9. Existential Intelligence: Sensitivity and capacity to tackle deep questions about human existence, such as the meaning of life, why do we die, and how did we get here.

Despite the popularity of the learning styles theories, it is important to mention that there is still a significant debate regarding the consistency of those theories. The strongest view against the existence of learning styles comes from Human Information Processing (HIP) theorists, who argue that learning style perspectives ignore the critical role that prior knowledge plays in a learning situation. Although agreeing with the importance of recognizing individual differences and providing students with personalized instruction, HIP theorists have the following disagreement with the learning styles theories: (a) confusion in the definition of the term "styles," (b) different learning style theories and instruments use different style categories to define learning style continuums, (c) weakness in reliability and validity of measurement instruments, and (d) identification of relevant characteristics in learners and instructional settings. According to those theorists, learners may react differently in different learning situations, and people have different ways of learning for particular tasks and for different contexts, so they recommend that teachers focus on the role that encoding, attention, motivation, and metacognition factors play in all learning situations. (Curry, 1990; Denzine, n.d.).

Faculty Development Approaches

Interrelated to faculty development theories, another segment of literature relevant to this study provides a consistent theoretical basis for general approaches to faculty development programs and interventions. Davis and Davis (1998) developed a model for professional development based on learning theories. As they say, "a training strategy is a theory-based effort to maximize a particular kind of learning" (p. 98). Table 1 summarizes what they call "the seven training strategies." The authors point out that each training strategy has its own strengths and weaknesses. Although it is tempting to select a training strategy that feels comfortable for the facilitator or is the preference of the participant, a trainer should make a rational choice of the strategy that best fits the desired learning outcomes.

These training strategies provide a framework for different faculty development interventions, which are intended to address both faculty beliefs and skills development. Based on different theoretical models, several experts propose a variety of approaches to faculty development programs and activities, but exploring those models is beyond the scope of this study. As a general concept, however, it is important to understand that there is a distinction between professional development and training. As Chism (1998) explains:

One reason for resistance to teaching preparation is the belief that such preparation will consist of skills training, which seems trivial. Formal attention to teaching preparation involves cultivating habits of reflection and developing conceptualizations and frameworks for practice to organize and evaluate skills and experiential knowledge gained prior to employment or on the job (p. 8).

This distinction makes professional development programs much more complex than a simple training session. This is the assumption underlining the faculty development intervention described in this study.

Methodology

As a multiple-case study, this research employed a qualitative approach, with an in-depth look at the many factors influencing the way faculty approach instructional technology and the ways in which their learning can be successfully facilitated.

Using a purposeful sample (Patton, 1990), ten participants were selected among faculty who attended a series of workshops and seminars in instructional technology, offered by the teaching center at a public university in the United States. In order to obtain a larger variety of data, the sampling strategy employed a maximum variation approach,

Table 1. The seven training strategies – side-by-side comparison

Strategy	Best Use	Facilitator
1. Behavioral	Skill development	Setting objectives Performing task analysis Providing feedback
2. Cognitive	Presentations and explanations	Selecting and presenting information
3. Inquiry	Critical, creative and dialogical thinking	Establishing climate Asking questions
4. Mental Models	Problem solving Decision making	Providing information Guiding discussion
5. Group Dynamics	Collaboration and working in teams	Composing groups Developing and using instruments
6. Virtual Reality	Dependence on competence and confidence in a simulated environment	Role playing Setting the scene Designing scripts and scenarios
7. Holistic	Personal learning and self discovery through experience	Identifying and matching experiences to participants Providing useful mechanisms for reflection

Note. From: Davis & Davis, 1998, 404-405.

including faculty from different disciplines and academic areas, and also from different levels of tenure and academic appointment.

Several different data collection methods were employed. The basic method consisted of in-depth face-to-face semi-structured interviews with the participants, supported by follow-up email interviews (Flick, 1998). The data included results of a learning style assessment obtained through participants' completion of the Index of Learning Styles Questionnaire developed at North Carolina State University. This inventory it is easily accessible on the web and provides immediate automatic results without requiring any registration or fee payment. As far as validation, Zywno (2003) collected 557 valid questionnaires for a psychosomatic analysis and found that the ILS instrument has relatively high test-retest reliability in repeated measurements over time, and concluded that the ILS is an appropriate and statistically acceptable for characterizing learning preferences (Zywno, 2003).

In addition, samples of handouts, descriptions of content, and copies of the actual agenda of the workshops were gathered for document analysis. Finally, the data collection included non-participant observations of the environment during one offering of the technology workshop (Marshall & Rossman, 1995).

After transcribing the interviews, the data was stored and classified into different categories. This categorical aggregation was the first one of a four-step process (Creswell, 1998) in which a collection of statements was put together, along with ideas, and examples by the participants about their experience in learning and interacting with instructional technology. The participants' statements were classified to find relevant and meaningful points common to different cases.

The second step was developing direct interpretations of specific statements by the participants to draw meaning from the participants' experiences. The following step established patterns and looked for a correspondence between the different categories, in order to find common topics across cases. Finally, the written report put together several conclusions based on the major themes of the study.

SETTING THE STAGE

The Organization

This case study describes the experience of 10 highly motivated faculty members who participated in a technology workshop series at a large public university in the United States. Offering more than 200 degree programs, this university enrolls around 30,000 students with a high representation of international students from over 100 countries. The institution has a faculty development center that offers continuous support for faculty in developing instructional technology skills. All the faculty members participating in this case study agreed to share their learning experiences, motivation, and personal struggles in the journey to learn instructional technology. Each participant was assigned a pseudonym in order to maintain confidentiality.

Case Players

Carol has a Ph.D. in Theater, with a master's degree in Reading and English Language Studies. She has been teaching in higher education for 25 years and is still in love with her career choice.

Diana is an assistant medical physiologist and has practiced as a medical technologist. She graduated from the School of Medicine with a Ph.D. in Physiology and Biophysics and did her postdoctoral work in Pediatric Immunology and Oncology. Her background includes 25 years of teaching in the medical school.

Jennifer has a Bachelor's degree in Nursing and a doctorate in Nursing Science. She has specializations in Nursing Administration and Operating Room Nursing, and has taught nursing education for more than 35 years.

Ellen has a Ph.D. in Musicology and Music History, and began teaching at the college level in 1990. She is passionate about online teaching.

Karen worked in art museum administration for about ten years, and moved to an academic career after earning her Ph.D. in American Civilization. She has taught Art History for more than a decade.

Roy earned his Ph.D. in Urban Technological Environmental Planning and has worked in Social Work Policy and Technology. His career includes over 22 years teaching and researching social work at three different universities.

Steve has a Master's degree in Physical Education and got his Ed.D. in Higher Education Administration, with a concentration in Human Performance (Physical Education). He has taught sports management courses over the last 30 years.

Nicole earned her Ph.D. in Anthropology and has been teaching this subject for over 12 years. Lately, she has been working in both teaching and faculty development.

Lisa has a background in Occupational Therapy and a master's degree in Applied Gerontology. She is finishing her doctorate in Education and has had a teaching career for more than eight years.

Bryan has a Ph.D. in Sociology and teaches courses in the sociology of religion, sociology of work, sociology of education and methodology. His research area is the scholarship of teaching and learning, but he also does some research on the intersection of religion and pop culture. He has taught Sociology for more than 13 years.

Table 2 shows the basic profile of each participant.

CASE DESCRIPTION

Introduction

With a clear sense of frustration, you may have had sometimes the same feeling expressed by a faculty member who said:

I find that the people who teach technology generally are good people, but I think they are really bored in teaching somebody like me... it is really painful for them to go at the speed that I catch things. They are repeating, but at the time they get to step four, I forgot what I did, and when they say, do it again, I may not remember anymore... Some of them are very patient, but I just sense in their

Table 2. Profile of participants

Pseudonym	Degree	Academic Discipline	Status	Teaching Experience
Carol	Ph.D.	Theater	Non Tenure	25 years
Diana	Ph.D.	Medical Physiology	Tenure	25 years
Jennifer	D.N.S.	Nursing Science	Tenure	30 years
Ellen	Ph.D.	Music History	Tenure	11 years
Karen	Ph.D.	Art History	Tenure	8 years
Roy	Ph.D.	Social Work	Tenure	19 years
Steve	Ed.D.	Physical Education	Tenure	29 years
Nicole	Ph.D.	Anthropology	Non Tenure	12 years
Lisa	M.A.	Applied Gerontology	Non Tenure	8 years
Bryan	Ph.D.	Sociology	Tenure	13 years

spirit that they are kind of thinking that I am dumb, or that I am taking too much of their time.

Like this person admitted, many faculty members with high levels of expertise in different areas may feel intimidated when challenged to learn and use instructional technology. This multiple case study describes different learning stories emphasizing personal characteristics of the participants, their personal learning styles, and their struggles facing personal and institutional barriers.

Case 1: Carol, the Emotional Learner

The Journey to Technology

To sum up her experience with technology, Carol says: "Technology did not crush in on me." All the schools she has worked at were Historically Black Colleges and Universities, which had no money. She recalls that her first experience with technology was when she received a National Endowment for the Humanities summer research grant on oral literature in Missouri in 1991. This is how she describes her emotions in her first encounter with technology:

There was a lady in the course who kept saying every day, "I got to go and check my email." I had never heard of it. And she was so excited, and in every break we had, she would go and check her email. Then when I came here, I was working for a top administrator, who kept sending me messages by email, and I was not getting them because I didn't want to. So he said, "You just have to learn this, because I am not going to send you messages in any other way! So, I learned enough to do email."

But this was just the beginning for Carol. As she was still struggling to use email in an effective way, her boss sent her to a workshop off campus to learn enough to get his messages. And as the campus became more and more involved in the online revolution, Carol could not avoid it anymore.

Learning Styles Analysis

Carol is a very unique type of technology learner. Her emotional way of doing things became clear as she told her story. In fact, her scores in the learning styles inventory reflect her emotional approach to learning, as she scored very high as an intuitive learner (9 points on an 11-point scale) as opposed to being a sensor or concrete learner. She also scored high (9 points) as a global/random learner as opposed to sequential learner. Carol scores are shown on Table 3.

Both the intuitive and the global learning characteristics have more to do with emotions than with logical reasoning: in fact, intuitive learners are described in the literature as people who like creativity and dislike repetition (Felder, 1996; Kolb, 2000; Kolb, 2007). They also "don't like 'plug-and-chug' courses that involve a lot of memorization and routine calculations" (Felder, 1996, p. 2), and usually prefer discovering possibilities and relationships, which describes how Carol described her learning experience with technology. The fact that Carol is also a global/random learner helps explain her struggles with technology, as Gregorc (1985) describes abstract-random learners as people who globally evaluate the learning experience atmosphere. They are attracted to nuances of mood and atmosphere, and tend to associate the medium with the message and relate the presenter's personality with the content of the presentation. They have preference

Table 3. ILS scores for Carol

Carol scores (11-point scale)			
Active	3		Reflective
Sensing		9	Intuitive
Visual	5		Verbal
Sequential		9	Global

for unstructured information and multisensory activities with no rules or guidelines.

Discussing her experience with technology, Carol does not disguise the force of her negative feelings towards technology, as in this example:

Sometimes I was typing up a newsletter for the community organization I was working for, and I would spend hours and hours typing the newsletter and I would hit a button and it would all be gone, and I wanted to die because I didn't save it. So it was an awful, awful, awful experience for me. I hated technology, and I hated anybody who used technology, and anybody who talked about it.

In spite of this negative feeling toward technology itself, Carol has a very positive attitude toward her technology instructors in the workshop setting: "What I liked the most was the attitude of the teachers. It was not in any way insulting. They never ever made me feel inadequate, which I knew I was."

Asked to relate her learning style with the technology experience, Carol proposes a formula for an ideal learning situation:

For me it is hands-on. I think that for my learning style the critical thing is the teacher-student ratio, and it almost will be like one-to-two or one-to-three. With any more than that, like 12 or 17 students, or whatever, instructors will be too busy with the other 12 and I am going to get lost.

A comparison of Carol's experience in learning technology with her natural learning style seems to imply the Carols' emotional nature has a direct impact on her learning process, thus explaining at least in part some of the difficulties that she has faced in her experience of learning technology. Her strong emotional reactions tend to make her more vulnerable to feelings of inadequacy for being slower than others, which results in anxiety and impatience with herself. In fact, she says she feels upset when she cannot perform as well as she would like, and she explains her disappointment: "If I press the wrong key I am upset because I didn't get it right. So it is frustrating for the instructors and it is frustrating for me, because I want it, but I just cannot." In other words, Carol's emotions and variations of mood and sentiments affect her learning performance.

Case 2: Diana, the Risk-taker

Diana's story is marked by a sequence of challenges and risks. Many episodes in her life stress how challenge and risk played an active role in her experience of learning instructional technology.

The Technology Challenge

Diana summarizes her story of learning instructional technology in a very short statement: "I am a risk taker, but I don't approach suicidal." She explains, for instance, that she did take some precautions to protect herself in the very first online class that she taught when she was still learning how to teach online courses. She decided to be part of a teaching team, with another instructor who was eager to learn and use technology, so, as she says, "we helped each other."

But her journey to technology began many years before. Referring to her very first experiences with instructional technology, Diana still remembers spending an entire week to prepare for a one-hour lecture using slides, tapes and handouts. Years later, Diana challenged herself to attend an intensive program in faculty development including interactive video and computer-based teaching. At the beginning, she went just to try it out, but in the next year she went with the express purpose of teaching an interactive video course, which she did, starting with a few students in the freshman level. Now she talks about the success of this course with a bit of unabashed pride: "This last fall when I taught the course, I had 229 students on seven sites of classrooms. So that tells you how little by little I expanded the course. I still use the statewide system."

Learning Styles Analysis

Diana admits that learning technology took a lot of hard work and persistence. Usually someone would show her how to do something and then she would go and do it, and when she got stuck, she would call a consultant to help her. Diana explains that her achievements with technology are due mostly to her willingness to take risks:

I was able to do that only because I used to try difficult things, even having minimal computer and technical knowledge. I think a lot of people get into it because they really love to work with computers, and computers are not a challenge for them. I have said more than once, if I can learn this technology, anybody else can.

Diana's scores on the Index of learning styles inventory show a high level of an intuitive/abstract learner (9 points on an 11-point scale) as opposed to being a sensor or concrete learner. She also scored high (9 points) as a global/random learner as opposed to sequential learners. She does admit that her favorite learning style is that of the abstract learner. Table 4 shows the Diana scores on the ILS inventory.

Diana does not see the learning styles theory as playing a direct role in her experience of learning technology. In fact her major characteristic as "risk-taker" does not fit well in any of the main theories of learning styles discussed in this study. On the contrary, Kolb (1993) refers to risk-takers as an example of learners who are in the concrete-active quadrant of his diagram, which is not the case with Diana. This discrepancy in itself seems to imply that, in some cases, other characteristics may be more relevant to the experience of learning technology than those assessed through learning styles inventories. Although this particular case does not necessarily contradict the learning styles theory, it does not support it either. As a result, it seems more appropriate to look at Diana's experience of learning technology as requiring a major characteristic or attitude of her personality, which is not necessarily her personal learning style in other areas. In other words, while the experience of learning technology sometimes may be explained by someone's learning style, in some other cases it may be better explained by another major personality characteristic.

Table 4. ILS scores for Diana

Diana scores (11-point scale)			
Active		3	**Reflective**
Sensing		9	**Intuitive**
Visual		5	**Verbal**
Sequential	.	9	**Global**

Case 3: Jennifer, the Visionary Learner

Envisioning Technology

A visionary of instructional technology, Jennifer started using glass slides 30 years ago, and has had all her lectures on overheads for more than 10 years. Although there was no technology department as she began, she took as much advantage as possible of the medical education resources group at her institution, which then was the department responsible for providing instructional resources for faculty members. Back in the 70s, Jennifer envisioned teaching some components of nursing skills in a video format, and started developing videotapes to be presented in the classroom. With little support, it was very difficult at the beginning, but in 1980, thanks to a research grant, she developed a series of teaching modules using video for classroom presentations.

The process of production, image-taking, editing, and selection of "actors and actresses" for her instructional "movies" was something totally unconventional and may resemble the early ages of the Hollywood industry. As unusual as it may seem, Jennifer was at the same time the producer, director, cameraperson, editor, and distributor of the movies. In addition, the site for recording her pictures was something much more "real" than any scene produced by Hollywood. This is how she describes the adventure of producing those videotapes:

We actually videotaped live surgery in the Emergency Room, and I did most of the editing in a very primitive way. We used to go at midnight to the Emergency Room (ER). We had one student as a cameraman on the ladder to shoot inside, and I also had a camera as I was standing down to shoot when the patient was coming. We didn't put over any sound track, so we had the actual sound of the patient and nurses' activities, and we really saw a lot of real blood!

Even using these primitive methods, Jennifer was always very careful with ethical concerns—asking permission before releasing a film. It was not easy, but she did respect the patient's privacy. She says, "We didn't really release it until after the patient was treated, and we would contact the family for release only for teaching purposes."

The times have changed and Jennifer no longer produces instructional materials in the same way. One of the reasons is because the grant elapsed. Another major reason is that the curriculum has changed, and the school does not have the Emergency Nursing module anymore. She feels that she does not need those materials as much as she did in the past. She actually gave the tapes to a hospital, and they are using them for teaching purposes as well.

Today, Jennifer does not use the old movies, overheads, or 35 mm pictures anymore. She says that now everything is in the PowerPoint format. She is now equipped with a digital camera, which she bought with grant funds, and takes advantage of digital pictures for her presentations. And she is always looking for new advancements in instructional technology.

Learning Style Analysis

Jennifer was a visionary of technology more than 30 years ago, a time when most faculty and institutions had no concern at all with instructional technology. It seems that a visionary personality goes along with a visual style in Jennifer's case. Even at a moderate level, her higher scores were as a visual learner (5 out of 11) and also as a sequential learner (5 out of 11). Table 5 shows how Jennifer scored on the ILS inventory.

The sequential aspect does not appear to be much applicable in Jennifer' story, but commenting on her favorite learning style in technology, Jennifer refers to the multiple intelligences theory in the following words:

The visual style appears to be most applicable as I reflect on my experiences and the learning path I took related to technology. I think the visual-spatial intelligence is my strongest intelligence related to instructional technology, especially in the development of course materials.

Jennifer's comments support the theoretical description of Gardner (2000), according to whom such learners develop the capacity to think in images and pictures, to visualize accurately and abstractly. Her comments also support Felder and Silverman (1988), as they state that visual

Table 5. ILS scores for Jennifer

Jennifer scores (11-point scale)			
Active		1	**Reflective**
Sensing	1		**Intuitive**
Visual	5		**Verbal**
Sequential	5		**Global**

learners get different information from visual images (pictures, diagrams, graphs, schematics, demonstrations) than from verbal material, which was very much the case in Jennifer's experience producing videotapes and pictures for her class presentations.

Case 4: Ellen, the Hard-working Learner

From the very beginning of her academic career, Ellen had to face a lot of hard work, as she began teaching a class with about 70 students, and had only one week for preparation after she knew she would teach that class. This is how she recalls the beginning of her teaching career:

I was a little bit intimidated, but I also had an extensive performance background, so I called on some of that performance background to help me at least get through the first two days, until the students realized that I was the teacher!

Hard Work in Technology

Before starting a new teaching assignment at another university, Ellen had a part-time job where she was asked to help maintain the company's website. She explains that she had no knowledge of HTML code at all, so she had three classes that lasted eight hours each, which was the full extent of her knowledge of computers, other than using word processors and everyday software. At the university, her new boss found out that she had the 24-hour HTML training from the previous job, and he challenged her to be in charge of the Internet distance-based classroom for Music Appreciation. Not very much aware of the enormity and urgency of the task, Ellen agreed to teach the class, only to realize later that she was facing a huge problem. This is how she narrates the conversation with her boss:

The way this class started was somewhat humorous. The head of the School of Music came to me and said, "We think you can have an online Music Appreciation class." Then I said, all right. It was the end of June and beginning of July, and I was thinking that I would have the summer and at least a year to do it, but he said: "Oh no, we have offered it for starting this August, so you have until August to have it up and running. So I had about a month and a half to prepare.

Ellen had to work very hard to accomplish the task. She describes herself as typically a traditional in-front-of-the-classroom type of lecturer at that point in time, and the idea that she would not even see the students scared her, and she was not sure of what really she was going to do. So, she learned to use the course management system on the web, and had to handle all of this new technology plus teach four other classes at the same time. She says that the staff in the teaching center was very instrumental in supporting and helping her not to panic when something went wrong.

Recalling her experience, Ellen summarizes the hard work she had to face to learn and make progress in technology with a sense of pride, as follows:

I started with minimal knowledge, no confidence at all, and a feeling that the computer was a tool of terror. Now I realize it is simply a tool like a pencil or a pen, the programs can or cannot work, depends on what I input.

Learning Styles Analysis

Ellen's scores on the learning styles test reflect her systematic way of doing things. She scored 9 out of 11 as a sequential learner, and 7 out of 11 as a sensing or concrete learner. Table 6 displays Ellen scores on the ILS inventory.

According to Gregorc (1985) this combination makes concrete-sequential learners prefer direct and hands-on experience. They like concrete and touchable tasks and step-by-step directions to follow. Felder (1993) refers to sensing learners as being very practical persons who don't mind detailed work and prefer to solve problems using well-established procedures. Supporting the same idea, Myers (1976) and Brightman (1998) describe sensing people as detail-oriented learners who focus on facts and practical solutions and prefer specific and orderly instructions.

Ellen's reflections about her personal style match the results of the learning styles inventory. This is how she describes herself:

I tend to learn more as a concrete, active, and reflective learner. I combine all these learning styles in my own approach to education, particularly instructional technology. I have used a hands-on approach with looking at a variety of possibilities and attempt to solve problems on my own.

This combination of learning styles supported by Ellen's self-analysis may explain her major characteristic of "hard work" when learning technology. As she says, she didn't mind staying long hours in the teaching center to learn how to set up an online class with just a month and a half of preparation. She had the task with a deadline, and she worked hard through all the steps to accomplish the task. And she did succeed in completing the work, which is very typical of a concrete-sequential learner.

Table 6. ILS scores for Ellen

Ellen scores (11-point scale)			
Active		3	**Reflective**
Sensing	7		**Intuitive**
Visual		1	**Verbal**
Sequential	9		**Global**

Case 5: Karen, the Dependent Learner

As it seems natural and usual for someone in the areas of history and museums, Karen has a very conservative teaching background. The irony of this area though, is that history and technology are mixed together as part of the teaching style of Art History, although in a conservative way. This is how Karen explains the marriage between technology and Art History:

I just don't know how otherwise I would teach Art History without a visual image. It is just the standard in the discipline, so everybody does that, and I learned Art History with slides.

From Conventional to Digital Imagery

Willing to enter the digital era, Karen went to a technology workshop on PowerPoint in order to learn the basics. She says she can see that the future is going to be digital, so she decided to learn at any cost. But it was not easy. Although the instructors in the workshop did a great job trying to make it user-friendly, she felt overwhelmed as it just seemed like such a huge task for her. But Karen did not give up and found her own way to learn by hiring somebody else on whom she could depend while learning. She says: "I am not sure I would have gone any farther without having a teaching assistant who is pretty knowledgeable." Taking advantage of this new alternative, Karen has regular appointments with her teaching assistant once a week to learn how to do PowerPoint.

Besides PowerPoint, Karen is also exploring the resources of the web and is now regularly using the course management system on the web, which she had never used before. At first she was simply posting pictures online. Now she has posted the syllabus, the study terms, and also study guides for tests. But again, she counts on her teaching assistant to scan the slides and post them on the web, so students can study for tests.

Learning Styles Analysis

Describing her personal approach to learning technology, Karen sees herself as dependent on someone else's help and support all the time. This major characteristic as a dependent learner makes all the difference for Karen. She says:

My feeling about the whole technology is that having one person sitting down just with me, so that whatever particular problem or questions I have, that person can be right there at my elbow to help me immediately.

Based on the learning styles inventory, Karen has a well balanced combination of learning styles, as she did not score high in any of the styles. In fact, she scored only 3 points out of 11 in three different styles: Active, sensing/concrete, and sequential, which is not enough to characterize one dominant style of learning. Table 7 shows Karen scores on the ILS inventory.

According to Kolb (1993) and his theory, the concrete-active combination may explain her major characteristic as dependent on somebody else for learning technology, as this type of learner tends to rely on other people's analysis rather than on their own, and enjoy applying learning in real life situations. Also, they are primarily the "hands-on" type of learner (Algonquin, 1996). Karen's assessment of her own style of learning technology seems to agree with this explanation:

I learn the computer best by the hands-on use of it, even though this is not a kind of learning that comes easily to me. Besides, I learn instructional technology quite well if I have someone by my side who is articulate and knows the programs, who is willing to verbally walk me through it, and assist if I get stuck.

Table 7. ILS scores for Karen

Karen scores (11-point scale)			
Active		3	**Reflective**
Sensing		3	**Intuitive**
Visual		1	**Verbal**
Sequential	3		**Global**

In other words, the inventory did not show a dominant learning style for Karen, therefore the connection between her personal characteristic and learning style offers little evidence to support the theory. Based on her own reflection, however, it seems that she has explored her personal learning characteristic as a dependent learner to learn what she needs in instructional technology.

Case 6: Roy, the Pragmatic Learner

Technology Expertise

Roy has had an easy time with technology since he has been a user. Even when using different technology applications, he didn't have problems, as he states: "I didn't have any difficult time actually. I am probably very technologically-minded, so I really didn't have major problems to do what I needed."

"Technologically-minded" is an apt self-description of Roy's experience using technology, since he started using web pages very extensively in 1994 and wrote a book on how to use the web in practical social work. He also wrote a tool-book and designed a series of exercises on developing websites.

Learning instructional applications of technology was not hard for Roy either, as he has been basically self-taught. In summarizing his journey, Roy describes his attachment to technology as a lifelong experience in the following terms:

I have been interested forever. Actually I have been interested for fun. It was interesting and cutting edge, so I enjoyed it very much. There is the recreational dimension to it. Part of that too is that, in terms of Social Work, it is very easy to get behind the cutting edge, because Social Work is very reluctant to use technology.

Learning Styles Analysis

On the Learning Styles test, Roy had his higher scores both as a visual and as an intuitive/abstract learner (7 out of 11), and also scored 5 as an active learner. Table 8 presents the scores of Roy on the ILS inventory.

Roy does agree with the visual aspect of his style, and says that he has "the ability to grasp and understand very complex systems easily and visualize them in an effective way." In addition, Kolb's theory describes the abstract-active learners as people who like solving problems and finding practical solutions and uses for learning (Algonquin, 1996; Kolb, 2000; Kolb, 2007), which matches the pragmatic aspect of Roy's personality. One difference, however, is that Roy thinks of himself as a concrete learner instead of the intuitive one shown in the test result, but he admits that his combination of styles has some differences from the pattern stated by some theorists. This is how he analyzes his personal style:

I tend to be a concrete-active and reflective learner. The difference is that I usually take the hands-on approach when learning instructional technology and am prone to trust my own analysis rather than someone else's.

In summary, although Roy's combination of styles somewhat differs from the standard of the theories, which makes it difficult to establish a relationship between his personal characteristics and learning style, his major characteristic of being pragmatic and utilitarian in part supports the description of Kolb's theory as addressed above (Algonquin, 1996).

Table 8. ILS scores for Roy

Roy scores (11-point scale)			
Active	5		Reflective
Sensing		7	Intuitive
Visual	7		Verbal
Sequential		1	Global

Case 7: Steve, the Social Learner.

The Social Adventure of Learning Technology

Steve got involved in instructional technology early on, when he chaired a symposium on teaching excellence back in the 70s and 80s, and technology was one of the teaching strategies discussed in the symposium. Inspired by the idea of technology as a teaching strategy, Steve wrote a grant and got enough money to buy technology equipment for the Physical Education Performance Lab. Such technology would allow instructors to put markers on people and videotape them, so the software would track the markers and do all the compilation of the movements. This is how Steve describes his excitement with the new equipment:

When we got the equipment, and I could take my class and show them a device that would draw a picture to show the movement, store the data, measure the strength, resistance, and speed of movement, this suggested to me that there is a lot more about technology that we can use.

Steve always found encouragement in other people and their experiences. For instance, he refers to a book on successful stories of faculty members using technology, where people discuss methods and programs they are using in their classes. Steve also recalls that he had good mentorship from a very trusted colleague who was a role model for him and helped him understand more about technology in the classroom. As he says, "I am not as technologically savvy as some, so I like to hang around with people who are."

Learning Style Analysis

On the learning styles inventory, Steve scored the maximum as an active learner (11 out of 11), and very high as a visual learner (9 out of 11). Table 9 displays the scores of Steve on the ILS inventory.

The visual aspect does not appear much when analyzing his style of learning technology, but the active component sounds like the perfect description of his style. According to Kolb's theory, a high score in the active category indicates individuals who have an orientation to experimentation and who learn best when they can engage in such things as projects, group discussions, and peer feedback. Usually they tend to be extroverts. They are also described as "hands-on" learners who tend to rely on other people's analysis rather than on their own and enjoy applying learning in real life situations (Algonquin, 1996; Claxton and Murrell, 1987; Kolb, 2007). Steve says he has no doubt that this is his style:

Clearly this is how I learn. From an IT standpoint, I've spent too little time reading the manual and probably too much time with trial and error. I've enjoyed all that I've learned from my IT colleagues because I could let them do the analysis and then I could do the application.

In addition, Felder (1993) states that active learners tend to learn while doing something active, like trying things out, sharing ideas and working in groups, which may explain Steve's major characteristic as a social learner. In fact, Steve agrees that his interpersonal intelligence plays a major role in his learning experience: "This is also something I'm good at. The IT application is that, when I'm really stuck on a problem, I can easily tap into the available human resources because I understand their motivations and desires."

His active learning style makes Steve interact with many people and learn from his colleagues, which determines his major characteristic as a social learner.

Table 9. ILS scores for Steve

Steve scores (11-point scale)			
Active	11		Reflective
Sensing	1		Intuitive
Visual	9		Verbal
Sequential	5	.	Global

Case 8: Nicole, the Skeptical Learner

Slow Involvement with Technology

Nicole started using technology in the classroom when she was teaching as a graduate student. She showed videos and used the overhead projector.

She recalls that one of her classrooms once had a multimedia tower with a VCR, a DVD, a computer, a cassette player, a CD player, and internet access. By having that in the classroom, she could easily do anything by just hitting a button and playing a CD, a DVD, or showing a video on the screen, and then turning it off. But, what really made a difference for her was that she could still use all her transparencies accumulated over the years, but instead of using the overhead projector, she used the document reader. Actually, she could bring in a book and just put the book on the document reader, or she could show a graph, a picture, or even an artifact."

Most of the times, however, Nicole would prefer using real objects to illustrate her classes, rather than using technology devices. Usually she would try technology when artifacts were not available.

Nicole recognizes that her weak relationship with technology has been affected by her skepticism towards it. As she admits, she is not quite convinced about online education and of all its benefits. In addition, she says she is not sure if her students will have the equipment that will make it look great and work well, or if they will hate it like she did as a student, because students don't have the access to the same level of technology as the faculty members do on campus. So she confesses being still a little bit hesitant and willing to let other people forge the pathway, and "when it becomes much smoother," she says, "then I will go."

In summary, Nicole can see the benefits and the potential, but technology has not attached itself to her in a way that she would go out and seek to learn and use it all the time.

Learning Styles Analysis

Nicole describes her experience of learning technology as a trial-and-error process, like setting up the computer and playing around. Except for one technology workshop, she had no other classes and no consultation at all. This is how she evaluates her learning process: "It was me sitting there by myself, trying something, and trying again, and when it didn't work I would get frustrated and say, "What the hell is that?" So it was trial and error, very much. No textbooks, no how-to books, no *PowerPoint for Dummies.*"

Nicole's self analysis totally matches the results of her learning styles test, as she scored higher both as an active and as a visual learner (7 out of 11 in both styles). Table 10 shows the scores of Nicole on the ILS inventory.

Kolb (1993) states that active learners rely heavily on experimentation, and are primarily "hands-on" people who tend to rely on the ability to get things done, and usually use trial and error to solve problems (Algonquin, 1996; Claxton and Murrell, 1987), very much like Nicole described above. On the other hand, Felder (1993) refers to visual learners as people who get more information from visual images than from verbal material, while Gardner (1993) describes the visual-spatial intelligence as the capacity to think in images and pictures, and the ability to visualize accurately and abstractly. Referring to her experience in learning technology, that is precisely how Nicole describes the visual side of her learning style:

Table 10. ILS scores for Nicole

Nicole scores (11-point scale)			
Active	7		**Reflective**
Sensing		5	**Intuitive**
Visual	7		**Verbal**
Sequential		5	**Global**

I am thinking that my experience with technology tends to be not so much text-based. I have to see it, I have to feel it, I have to feel what the key strokes are, and visualize what I have to do, where I have to click, where the button was, and in which side of the screen the menu was.

In short, while she is not very excited about technology, Nicole has a learning style that works best by visualizing things and doing something through a long trial and error process.

Case 9: Lisa, the "Watching" Learner

Enjoying Technology

Usually suspicious of technology, Lisa tended to always be afraid that things that she fears will not work. Therefore, when doing something on the laptop, for example, she would bring the laptop to project on the screen, but she would also make overheads too, just in case the projection would not work. She recalls that her first experiences with technology had to do with using an overhead projector and trying to figure it out how to turn it on and off.

Lisa describes her experience with technology as "exciting." The more she found out about the variety of technology applications, the more she wanted to implement those different things in the classroom. As she says, "When I was able to take that technology and get the students excited, that made sense to me. I was dealing with this MTV generation and was able to make connections with them. That was when I got excited and when the big connection was for me."

Lisa learned the very basics from her fellow faculty members. Usually she had someone in the department set up a manual that would explain step by step how to use a specific technology application. She also had other training opportunities such as classes or technology workshops taken through the teaching center. Other than that, she just experimented on her own and played around with different media.

Learning Style Analysis

Describing her learning process as a journey full of excitement and frustrations, Lisa stresses her preferred learning characteristic:

Watching other people use the technology was my favorite way of learning, and then seeing my instructors in the graduate school use the technology made me excited about it. Usually I had an instructor who would demonstrate it first, but until I actually tried it on my own, at times frustrating, I would not feel safe using it.

The preference of Lisa to learn technology by watching other people may be explained by her results in the learning styles inventory, as her dominant learning preference is the visual style. In fact she scored very high in only this category (9 points out of 11), showing a low and balanced combination of all other categories. Table 11 presents Lisa scores on the ILS inventory.

Taking Gardner's (1993) theory of visual-spatial intelligence as the capacity to think in images and pictures, and the ability to visualize accurately and abstractly, plus Felder's (1993) concept that visual learners get more information from visual images, we would have a framework to understand Lisa's learning preference. Commenting on her experience with technology, Lisa says that more than simply watching other people, she likes to visualize ideas:

The visual style relates to my learning experiences in IT in that I was able to picture and understand the overall process schemes and ideas, play with them mentally and apply them to the task. I like visualizing the background technical stuff as it helps me understand how the program works, and then manipulate it to meet my needs.

In addition, she says her visual style works best when assisted by continuous technical support, to deal with trouble and difficulties.

Case 10: Bryan, the Self-Taught Learner

Teaching Himself

During his 13-year teaching career, Bryan had used overheads and video occasionally, but most of his teaching was the traditional "chalk on the chalkboard." It was the use of a course management system on the web that really got him started with technology.

Bryan came up with the brilliant idea of putting partial notes online to be completed by students. He found that students responded very favorably to it, and they really appreciated having those online notes. So he got pretty positive feedback from students, both on the midterm and on the final course evaluation.

After one semester with this new experience, Bryan realized that he still had to write on the chalkboard a whole lot to help students get everything plugged in there. So in the next semester, Bryan came up with his brilliant solution number 2: He

Table 11. ILS scores for Lisa

Lisa scores (11-point scale)			
Active		1	Reflective
Sensing		5	Intuitive
Visual	9		Verbal
Sequential		5	Global

decided to convert his lectures into PowerPoint presentations. But not everything was in PowerPoint. Here is how Bryan describes the solution he found: "Sometimes I put questions and force them as a class to offer some examples."

Gradually, Bryan kept adding new features every semester, such as putting up practice exams on the web, as well as students' own notes on the web. As he explains, "students email their notes to me and I put it on the web. When the exam time goes around, every student should have their own notes from the discussion, but they also have their classmate's notes."

To make sure his methodology is effective, Bryan surveyed all his students at the end of the semester and found that 95% of the students strongly or greatly appreciated having the lecture notes available.

Learning Styles Analysis

It was hard to classify Bryan's learning style, especially because the result of his Learning Styles test was a well-balanced combination of styles, with only a slight predominance of the intuitive/abstract style (5 out of 11, as compared to 3 points for the active and global/random categories). Table 12 presents Bryan scores on the ILS inventory.

Based on Bryan's learning experience, however, it does make sense to apply the intuitive style to him. Kolb (1984) describes intuitive and abstract learners as concise and logical people, for whom abstract ideas and concepts are more important than people issues. They like to assimilate diverse data into an integrated whole, and they focus not so much on the practical application of ideas but on the soundness of ideas, and a good logical explanation is more important than practicality (Claxton and Murrell, 1987; Kolb, 2007). According to Myers (1976), intuitive people seek out patterns and relationships among the facts they have gathered. They trust their intuition and look for the big picture. They feel comfortable with ambiguous and imprecise data and with guessing their meaning (Brightman, 1998; Personality Pathways, 2003).

Table 12. ILS scores for Bryan

Bryan scores (11-point scale)			
Active	3		Reflective
Sensing		5	Intuitive
Visual	1		Verbal
Sequential		3	Global

The experience of Bryan in surveying the students to gather facts and data, then his successive application of different teaching ideas, all reflect his concern with logical ideas and sound solutions for his teaching problems. In fact he sees himself related to this category, according to his self-analysis:

I'm probably closest to the abstract-reflective learner. I don't know how this learning style impacted my use of learning technology. I had to stretch myself a bit to figure out how to use course management on the web, and I tried to think conceptually about how it might be used in my courses without creating too much work for myself.

Bryan also describes his learning process as being mostly a case of self-teaching with trial and error. This may relate to both the active and the random aspects of his learning style, although in low scale. According to Kolb (2000), active learners like experimentation, and Gregorc (1985) describes random learners as having an experimental trial and error attitude, as they like to find their own way in intuitive leaps and avoid step-by-step procedures. This description is close to the way Bryan analyzes his experience: "I taught myself to use PowerPoint and course management on the web. I had attended a couple of demonstrations of PowerPoint, but that was about it. It was a slow learning process of trial and error."

According to his comments, Bryan is always trying to find his own way of improving teaching and learning by testing different ideas and logical reasoning, which is typical of an intuitive learner, who tends to trust his intuition by teaching himself.

Faculty Struggles and Institutional Barriers

Most participants in this case felt that learning instructional technology has two opposite dimensions: the sense of accomplishment, and the sense of struggle and fear of failure. In fact, technology itself poses a lot of challenges for faculty who are not familiar with the technical details of computers and software. However, even worse than facing their own limitations is the frustration of missing the necessary support from the very institution they are willing to serve. Focusing on their personal learning experience with technology, participants in this case describe their major struggles and difficulties with institutional barriers such as system failure, lack of technical structure, and lack of academic and administrative support.

Equipment and System Failure

Most participants pointed to equipment and system failure as their main source of trouble and fear when using instructional technology. Seven out of ten participants have had negative experiences and feel that failure seems to be usual when dealing with technology. Nicole says:

It breaks down, it fails. And then, what do we do? When we go to a committee and have to use a PowerPoint, it is always wise to bring transparencies as a backup. Or if we have transparencies, bring handouts as a backup. Any kind of technology and machinery is going to break down.

According to Nicole, even a small failure of the technology is enough to make people hate it. In her opinion, everybody knows technology will, at some point, break down and fail. As a result, technology can very easily get a bad reputation, and she thinks it is very hard to overcome that reputation once it is there.

Karen has the same struggle in her classes and feels like failure with equipment is pretty normal. This is how she describes her troubles when using slides projectors in her classes of Art History:

I am always afraid of technology. Even with the slide projector, like if the bulb burns out in the middle of a test, then we have to go back and change it, but we can't because it is too hot. Or when the slides get stuck in the projector, or things like that.

It took time for Karen to overcome the fear of failure, since she was always scared with the risk of failure. However, one positive thing about Karen's experience is that the equipment failure does not decrease her willingness to use it. As she says, she never thinks of giving up.

Lisa feels frustrated when she has problems getting an image to show up on the screen, and setting up the hardware. And she remembers one of the most embarrassing situations in her technology adventure:

I had a guest speaker who came into my classroom, and I felt responsible because the equipment didn't work. Then I said to myself, let me go back to overheads and something like that.

Because she was afraid that things would not work, she always had an alternative, like bringing the laptop and also the overhead projector, in case something did not work.

The experience of Diana is a little different. In fact, teaching with technology does not bother her at all. She says that she likes to teach and she does it well. Although technology is challenging, she knows she has help available in the teaching center. One problem, though, does bother her. She says

The huge problem of failure, the things that terrify me more than even the technology, is having students not be able to access the medical library because the password does not work. They are registered for the course, but sometimes their password is not activated at a distance. I have been dealing with the registrar and the admissions office, and those are the tough parts, those are the things that keep me awake at night.

Those are the most difficult aspects of online education, from Diana's perspective. She thinks this is the real issue faculty have to be worried about. The technical support is no big deal, she says, because there is help available in the support center, and students are prepared to deal with that.

Bryan has had similar disappointments. He says that one thing that is really frustrating is when he goes to the classroom and the system is not working. This is his frustration: "When I try to login and I cannot access the server on campus. It really annoys me."

Another frustration that Bryan mentions is that sometimes things are out of control. There have been semesters when the demands on the course management on the web overwhelmed the system, so students could not get on the system to print out lecture notes, and they were coming to class aggravated, and Bryan was annoyed as well. Bryan feels that when technology is not reliable and consistent, when it does not work well, it tends to make everybody bothered.

Roy stresses the fact that technology is never one hundred percent reliable, because something always goes wrong. And like Nicole and Lisa, he usually prevents himself from being stopped by those failures, as he says: "I always have a plan B. When I get students taking quizzes online, I always know that a small percentage of them will be shut out or drop out of the system. Anyway, it is getting more reliable."

In other words, system failure is a permanent threat to technology users. In fact, Ellen says that struggles and fears are a continuous source of worries for her. She thinks sometimes the problem may be beyond the local network system. There are problems with the web system as well, and she reports a frustrating example:

Couple of weeks ago, when a virus attacked the internet, I had an online test going, and we lost all of our sound and real media files that had all of our musical examples that were on the test.

There are moments when Ellen feels it is total failure, and sometimes she thinks she will never have another student in this class again. But she feels encouraged when she gets emails back from students saying things like, "I know you didn't cause it, as you are doing the best job you could." In other words, it seems that no faculty member is free of equipment or system failure, and if they want to keep using the resources of technology they must be willing to deal with failures and frustrations.

Lack of Technical Support

But equipment or system failure is far from being the only source of disappointment when dealing with technology. For Roy, the problem was the lack of institutional interest and support. He says he had political struggles in his career because one institution where he worked did not want to invest in technology at all, so he could not do much at that time. Jennifer also reports her struggles because of the lack of equipment and support in her department. She says, "In my own unit in the school of Nursing, I did fear to fail, because we didn't have equipment and technology. We didn't have support for that, and it was very discouraging."

But Jennifer says it became very easy after she found support from the teaching center. She purchased a notebook with money from a grant, and used it in her school along with the few computers available there. However, she worried that after she discovered advanced ways of doing things in the teaching center, she would be unable to use the same methods in her department because of lack of support.

But this specific struggle is in the past already, as there is now equipment and support available. Jennifer explains that five years ago the department did not have any kind of help, not even a scanner to scan pictures for the web. She remembers that to get the school equipped was very hard. However, through this entire struggle, she says she never thought of giving up, because she was working in an area that she really likes.

Jennifer thinks that faculty in her institution now have reasons to celebrate, because everybody is encouraged to use technology throughout the campus system, and part of the excellence in teaching component for tenure and promotion is explaining how faculty incorporate technology in their teaching. She says, "It is very new and has been done in the last two or three years."

Time Commitment

If there is any issue in which all the participants agreed one hundred percent it is that the time commitment is a major barrier that interferes in their process of learning instructional technology. In other words, ten out of ten participants unanimously said that this is a big issue for them. Bryan says there is a lot of frustration when he looks at how much time he needs to perform some basic tasks. For example, he reports:

It takes a lot of time to convert lectures to PowerPoint, for example, particularly because I want to use some visual images. So we got to go hunting through the clipboard and on the web to find a picture of something. It is a time-consuming task.

Spending that much time with technology makes some faculty members worry about other roles they are neglecting in their career because of technology. Bryan says there were times when he was shaking his head thinking that he would not get any research done because he was spending so much time dealing with technology. He was worried that in some ways he would be penalized for doing it, because it was a time that he was not spending doing research. He thinks one reason is that he is not technologically savvy, as he does not know too much about computers and web pages. However, he says he is making progress, and eventually playing with PowerPoint gets easier the more he uses it. But using instructional technology has been very time-consuming because he had to figure out many things on his own.

Ellen has the same struggle with the time issue. She explains that there were brief moments when she thought the online class was not worth the amount of time it was taking, so she felt overwhelmed, as she describes:

I felt that was a failure on my part that I couldn't pick it up fast enough to know how to keep up with what I needed to do, because I have a lot of different ideas in my head, but I didn't know how to make them come to completion on a timely basis.

Sometimes Ellen wondered if she would even benefit the students enough to make it worth the effort. After a lot of frustration, however, she says she talked to the students, and they made her change her mind. As she says, suddenly she sees the light go on, as students get excited and involved in the learning process. Jennifer also struggles with the time issue. She says that sometimes she is scared because it takes a lot of time to learn something new, and she feels she does not have that much time available.

In turn, Nicole says she has a different problem about spending time. Because there were some students who refused to use the web to access course materials, she ended up having a two-way status among the students in class, those who used the web to a full degree, and those who refused to use it. That is how she describes her struggle:

I felt that I was doing double the work, because I had to do things on the web, but I still had to go back and do all the old way things on top of that to reach those students who didn't do it. And that is my hesitancy about technology.

Besides, Nicole thinks that for any faculty member it is going to be a matter of how many classes they teach and how much service they do. And she is very honest in addressing this issue:

Unless there is some reason why I have to know and do this, otherwise I would lose my job, so to speak, I would not spend much of my time on this. If I was a tenure track person, and my department chair told me that I should be spending my time on my research, and not playing around and putting up a nice website for my students, I mean, the dilemma research versus teaching, I would not do it.

So, for Nicole, it is either a matter of being forced into it in someway or just a matter of personal interest. And as she says, it is not a personal interest for her. So she thinks it is easy to find an excuse not to do it because of the time commitment it requires.

Bryan thinks the time commitment is an issue not only in the creation of online materials, as there is also an ongoing time commitment. As he reports: "After every class, somebody is emailing me stuff that I have to take the time to put it on the web. So the time I spend on my teaching has increased with the use of instructional technology."

Ellen is convinced that learning technology is a matter of time management, and she says she has spent long hours and days to do what she has done with technology so far. This is the way she sees this issue:

I have found myself waking up in the middle of the night, thinking of new ideas, but I don't have time for doing that. So, the biggest barrier is time. There is never enough for me to either teach, to continue my own learning, to do my research, which is necessary, or to sit on the committees and do the committee work.

Ellen thinks faculty members willing to learn about technology have to face the dilemma of taking time from other activities and still keep up with all their responsibilities, which is not easy, she says.

In her experience, Lisa felt how hard this time management issue is, and she describes how she faced the time dilemma to produce only small pieces of course materials:

When I think about creating activities and including that technology in the classroom, I feel big time constraints. When I know it took me a long time to edit a video and burn it on to a DVD, and produce only ten minutes of information. . .

Because it takes too much time, and it is not an essential responsibility, Karen says it is easy to keep doing things that are more "urgent," thus relegating technology as a secondary task. Referring to the time required preparing PowerPoint presentations, this is what Karen says:

In my case I have to get the slides scanned and digitized, and it is either my time or somebody else's time.. . If it is my time, I always tend to give my time for things that are due tomorrow or the next day.

As the preparation of her classes is a top priority in her job, Karen says that the PowerPoint stuff becomes an extra task, therefore, secondary.

Diana has her own conclusion about why many faculty members never get involved with technology. She thinks the time commitment is the main reason why technology is not a priority for faculty. This is her opinion:

Most faculty resist because it is time consuming, and faculty time is precious. The institution loves technology and supports it, but time is still an issue. But personally, I don't let barriers get on my way. If I really want to do something, I just go ahead.

The attitude of Diana seems to be typical of those who are successful in using instructional technology. Like Diana, people willing to teach with technology do not let barriers get on their way. That is how Steve thinks about time commitment as well. He sees the barriers and time requirements, but he says everything depends upon the willingness of faculty, even if the schedule is tight."

Jennifer and Roy agree with the others and refer to time as a big constraint. Jennifer mentions one example of how technology takes time from faculty and students: "Some students didn't have the latest version of the Real Player software to play a video clip that I posted on the web. I had the same problem on my laptop, and I had to spend 45 minutes to download it from the web. It is free, but there is also the time constraint."

Examples like this show that faculty must make it a priority in order to incorporate technology in their teaching routine. And that is exactly Carol's problem, as technology is not her high priority. In fact, she associates the time issue with her own reluctance to use technology. This is how she combines both things:

Time is the main thing. And so is my basic resistance to technology. I think that it slows down. If the time were available, I don't think I would pick it up as fast as I would like to believe I am capable of picking it up, because of this little resistance.

Despite her natural resistance, Carol wants to learn about technology, and she compensates her resistance by exploring an alternative learning method, which is having regular consultations in the teaching center. In short, she thinks that anybody who wants to use technology must be willing to spend enough time with it, as this is the only way to get proficiency and prepare consistent material.

The Rewards Issue

Another barrier addressed by the participants is the lack of rewards for faculty who spend time and effort dealing with instructional technology. Five participants mentioned that if institutions want faculty to use technology, they have to be rewarded in the promotion and tenure system. For Bryan, this is a basic concern, and this is his point of view:

I think many faculty worry that, if they spend a lot of time doing this, they will actually be punished for it, or that it may work against them when it comes to promotion and tenure, or when it comes to the annual review. And maybe the colleagues in the department or the university will look at this and say that they should have done more in publishing articles. So there is a concern that this sort of effort is not rewarded within the system.

For Carol, this is a matter of institutional priority. She thinks that, if the university really believes that instruction can be improved by technology, the institution should encourage faculty members to use technology in their work by including this issue as a part of the annual review for promotion.

Nicole thinks time and rewards are related issues. She guesses that at least three quarters of all faculty would say that they don't have the time to learn and use instructional technology. Nicole thinks faculty should be guaranteed not only the time, but also the support, like not teaching a class for one semester but getting paid for that time, in order to develop new online courses or strategies.

Commenting on her experience, Jennifer feels lucky that her institution encourages the use of technology throughout the whole campus. She explains that part of the "excellence in teaching" component for tenure and promotion is achieved by reporting how faculty members incorporate technology in their teaching. As she clarifies, this is something very new that has been done in the last two or three years. Steve also refers to his experience to stress the fact that technology did help him to be rewarded with promotion and tenure. He thinks institutions should make it official to all faculty members.

The Cost Issue

Three participants referred to cost as another barrier for implementing instructional technology. Jennifer says that cost is a big institutional barrier. She points to the fact that some students do not have computers at home. And even when they do, they may not have the appropriate software. For Karen, the problem of cost has to do with paying additional people like her teaching assistant. Whenever she needs somebody else's time, she has to pay the person. This of course is an institutional resources problem, but she has no choice but to hire knowledgeable people to help her continue using instructional technology.

Nicole also sees cost as a barrier, and she says that sometimes students complain about their computer at home, or they didn't have a computer at home, and this problem compromises student's access to the online environment. She thinks this will always be a problem in classes with diverse students, as some students will benefit from online materials while others will not. She thinks it gives an unfair advantage to some students over others who do not have a computer, or do not have the right program, or the right memory, or just are not familiar with the web environment.

The Technology Workshop Series

Willing to deal with their personal struggles and to develop their technology skills, all the participants in this case accepted the invitation to participate in a very innovative technology workshop series, as an initiative intended to foster faculty development in instructional technology and strengthen their motivation and technical skills. The workshop series called "Tech Camp," was designed in a creative way as intensive immersion experience to provide faculty with a rich technology environment supported by full technical and pedagogical assistance provided by faculty developers and technology expert. After the technology workshop series, participants were asked to share the impact of their learning experience described below.

More specifically, Tech Camp is a faculty development workshop series offered by the teaching center of a public university in the US and includes four different levels of seminars offered annually, ranging from basic to advanced content. Each level of seminar consists of a three-day workshop, in which the participants alternate training sessions in a computer lab with personal project presentations, exchange of personal experiences in using technology, and social interactions, including having breakfast and lunch together every day. The first three levels of workshop are taught every year during the summer, and the fourth level is taught the following spring. In order to make them more attractive and enjoyable, each workshop is structured under an illustrative theme related to sports or adventure. The basic content and features of the workshop are summarized below.

Level 1: The Summer Scout Camp

The first level of the technology workshop series is structured under the theme of a summer camp, with the classroom decorated with trees, tents, and a campfire. The participants, called campers, are invited to spend time around the campfire while learning instructional technology techniques and resources to be used in the classroom. Each camper receives a "Camper Survival Kit," which is the workshop handbook with printouts of all the lessons. This workshop is designed for faculty who are just beginning to work with online tools, have basic word processing skills, and are familiar with Internet browsing. The content of this workshop includes: Using course management system on the web and creating basic course materials online; creating basic PowerPoint slide shows; transferring files into an Internet server and linking them to a course environment; effective use of email, chat, and conferencing tools; linking electronic library resources; constructing an online quiz; and using the online grade book feature of the course management system.

Level 2: The Chateau Techneau Lodge

This level focuses on web page design, including planning and layout, along with basic creation, conversion, and enhancement of digital images for the web. The theme of this workshop is a winter ski resort called Chateau Techneau Lodge, where a series of exercises is designed to help participants to conquer the technology "slopes." Every day, participants enjoy lunch and sip hot chocolate by the "lodge" fire, and are challenged to experience the thrill of designing their very own course on the web. This workshop is designed for faculty members with intermediate technology skills.

Level 3: The Technology Cruise

Under the theme of a cruise, participants of this workshop "embark" as passengers aboard the S.S. Digital Divide with the mission of calming the stormy seas of technology by developing multimedia skills and navigating the basic technology tools for constructing online course materials. This level is designed to teach participants how to incorporate audio and video source material into web-based courses, which includes shooting, digitizing and editing audio and video media. Participants also get notions about the appropriate length of clips and on how to optimize media for better images.

Level 4: The Tech Olympics

Using the theme of the Olympic Games, campers are transformed into Olympians as they compete with themselves to achieve gold, silver, and bronze medals by finishing successive personal projects. In this workshop, the participants learn the basics of Web, CD-Rom authoring, DVD burning, and Flash web animation, using common authoring programs for each form of content distribution. This level is designed to build confidence in technological proficiency in an extremely hands-on learning environment.

General Workshop Structure

The workshop structure can be exemplified by the *Tech Olympics*, program. At the first day, participants entered the site to find a large painting of an Olympic stadium full of people on the front wall, while both an American flag and the five-intersecting- rings Olympic symbol were hanging from the ceiling. A table on the left-hand side of the room displayed all sorts of balls and sporting gear for tennis, baseball, golf, basketball, volleyball, football, soccer, and so on. Numbered sprint tracks were designed on the floor, and another table at the back of the room covered with breakfast foods, such as fruit salad, orange juice, toast, cookies, coffee, milk, banana nut muffins, and chocolate chip muffins. Participants were sitting in groups around five tables dispersed in the middle of the room.

At the opening ceremony, after welcoming the participants, the coordinator of the workshop lighted an electronic simulation of the Olympic torch, thus officially starting the workshop. The coordinator introduced the "team" of instructors, dressed in athletic clothes, and made jokes with each of them. Then he asked the participants to introduce themselves in a very informal atmosphere. All participants received a folder with the schedule of activities and the workshop material, plus a badge on which they were to write their names using colorful markers. After receiving the instructions for the day, participants recited the tech pledge in unison. It reads as follows:

On my honor, I will try to incorporate technology wherever appropriate into my teaching, my presentations, and classroom discussions. I will post my syllabus online and will develop interactive strategies for my students as I pursue excellence while exploring technology resources.

After the pledge, participants went downstairs to the computer lab for technology exercises. In the lab, every participant sat in front of a computer previously set up with the required software, while one instructor walked the participants through the content in a step by step presentation. While one instructor was presenting, another three or four instructors were circulating the room to answer questions and help the participants.

Theme Strategy

The reaction of almost all participants to the technology workshop was highly positive. Six out of the ten participants referred to the workshop strategy as "relaxing," and four of them found it "fun" and very attractive. Expressions like, "they made it very relaxing," or "I knew soon it would be fun," were repeated quite a few times by the participants during the interview. In fact, nine out of ten participants said they found the theme strategy a very powerful resource to make the workshop interesting and more attractive. Most of them said they enjoyed the different themes, which helped enhance their learning experience.

Some participants went to the workshop fearing that it would be very difficult, but the theme strategy made them feel comfortable at the very beginning. Jennifer says she was afraid: "I was pretty apprehensive that it would be so advanced. But in the first day, they made it very relaxing." Lisa described her feelings like this: "No way will I be able to do this! I said, Oh my gosh, this is never going to make sense! So it was a little intimidating at first, but it was fun."

A few comments by the participants are typical of their reaction to the theme strategy. Talking about their first impression of the workshop, some participants related the theme strategy to their learning experience. This is how Ellen reacted:

Oh my gosh! Things like fire and trees within this air conditioned environment, I think these people have lost their mind! But it added to the atmosphere and added relaxation because the first thing we all did was introducing ourselves and laughing.

After being afraid at the beginning, Lisa says the themes enhanced the peer interaction. She described her experience as a learning trip in the following words:

To me the cruise theme made all the difference. Each day we had a different work and a different place to sail, and when I came back from the workshop, I asked the faculty member I worked with: Where did you cruise to today?

Nicole also felt that the relaxing sense of vacation was helpful to her learning process:

Even though we were still on campus, we had a sense of being removed on retreat, so we were not on campus because we were in Cancun, or in the Olympics, or in the forest, so themes helped us feel like we were on vacation. So it was relaxed, and not do or die, or so serious like another workshop might be.

Attitude of the Instructors

Eight out of ten participants referred to the attitude of the instructors as one of the most positive aspects of the workshop. Bryan has his own explanation for why the attitude of the instructors is crucial for the success of the workshop. This is his opinion:

I think faculty come to the workshop a little worried that they are going to feel stupid, as they don't know how to do things and the technology people will look down their noses at them because they are not as well versed in using this technology as they are, but I found that not be the case at all.

According to Bryan, the fact that faculty have prestige and expertise in many different areas makes them very sensitive, as they don't like feeling disadvantaged in a learning situation. That is why the role of the instructors is decisive in making faculty feel comfortable. Diana thinks the environment was comfortable and encouraging because the instructors were willing to help with deference and respect. This is how she addressed this point:

The instructors are wonderful and have a respect for faculty and faculty expertise. They also know that faculty who come for help are very vulnerable, and they are supportive without being condescending and such. I think that the personnel are probably the strongest part of the workshop.

Impact on Learning

The impact of the workshop on the process of learning technology was different for each participant. They were asked to estimate which percentage of their learning of technology could be attributed to the workshop itself, and they came up with different levels of learning impact. Four out of ten participants estimated that 50% or more of their learning of technology could be attributed to the workshop, which means a very strong impact on their learning process. Three participants estimated that the impact on their learning of technology was between 25% and 50%, which could be considered a medium impact. Three other participants estimated the impact was less than 25%, meaning a low impact on their learning of technology.

Karen sounded very realistic describing how she felt about the impact of the workshop on her learning of technology, and this is her explanation:

For me it was a huge part. I would say that maybe 50% of my learning so far is due to the workshop, but I have a teaching assistant, and she may represent 40%, and I am only 10% of my improvement in technology.

Only Roy says the impact was as low as five percent. He is very experienced in technology, so the workshop was only an additional resource. But overall, the majority of the participants were very satisfied with their gains in learning technology through the workshop experience.

Regarding the way the workshop best facilitated their learning, six participants referred to the "hands-on" approach to learning as the most helpful methodology, as they appreciated the opportunity to watch the instructors and practice at the same time. To say that in the words of Roy, "the organizational pattern was pretty busy, transparent, so I understood what was going to happen. Methodology was good, mostly hands-on, quite professional."

Both the hands-on approach and the time available to work on their personal projects helped the participants develop technical skills and produce useful material for their classes.

Impact on Teaching

Commenting on their teaching experience with technology as a result of the workshop, six out of ten participants stressed that the workshop had a strong positive impact on their teaching routine.

They referred to this impact with expressions such as, "I had never used course management on the web before," or "I had never done a full PowerPoint presentation before." Some said things like, "it helped me a lot to use technology," or "there was an immediate change when I took the workshop." These participants sounded excited in describing some of their new experiences with technology.

Four participants said they didn't use the technology applications that they learned about at the workshop much. Bryan says that he used very little of what he learned because he was already using it. The other three participants said that the workshop did not make any impact on their teaching as they didn't change anything in the classroom. They have different reasons for that. Carol says she did not do anything different in part because of her subject area, which is Theater, and she feels that she does not have much to apply. Roy says he did not have time to produce the material he needs. This is how he analyzed it:

No changes. I haven't produced any streaming video for teaching yet. As far as the use of Flash and animations, I have one animation distributed on the web, and that is probably the only one I generated so far. The same with Dreamweaver, as I am probably using only 15 percent of it.

In other words, the majority of the participants did feel a strong impact of the workshop on their teaching and applied a great deal, but some others did not make any significant change in implementing instructional technology after the workshop participation.

Overview of Findings and Conclusions

Based on the participants' descriptions of their learning experiences with instructional technology, one major characteristic of each participant was identified and helped understand better how the learning process worked for each faculty member. In most cases, this dominant personal characteristic of the participants seemed to be consistent with the theoretical description of their learning styles, but in one specific case it was not consistent with the theory, and in three other cases there was little evidence to support the learning styles theories. Table 13 displays a comparison between the descriptions of the participants' dominant characteristics and their learning styles, as well as the theoretical support found for each dominant characteristic. Columns two and three of the table describe the relationship found between the dominant characteristic of each participant and their personal learning style as assessed by the ILS instrument, and column four presents the learning style theory that offered support for such relationship.

The last column of Table 13 applies the adoption categories of Rogers' (1995) diffusion of innovation theory to the participants in this study. Diana, Roy and Jennifer were classified as innovators, given their experience as risk takers willing to take the initiative and time to try something new and different. Ellen and Steve can be classified as early adopters since, to certain extent, they served as role models for their peers by being channels to help others to adopt innovations in instructional technology. Lisa and Karen fit in the early majority category, as they are careful, safe, deliberate, and do not want to risk much on the innovation process. Carol fits in the late majority because, even being suspicious of innovation and resistant to change, she keeps moving slowly influenced by peers and the environment. Nicole describes her experience as a laggard, since her skeptical attitude keeps her somewhat inflexible in resisting innovations in instructional technology.

From the data analysis, another theme that emerged was the positive impact of the technology workshop in the format it was presented. Faculty in this study identified seven major features of the workshop format that made a strong impact on their process of learning technology. These key features of the workshop were: (1) the theme

Table 13. A comparison of personal characteristics and learning styles

Participant	Dominant Characteristic	ILS Learning Style	Theoretical Support	Adoption Category
Carol	Emotional	Intuitive, Random	Gregorc, Felder	Late majority
Diana	Risk-Taker	Intuitive, Random	No theoretical support	Innovator
Jennifer	Visionary	Visual, Sequential	Gardner, Felder	Innovator
Ellen	Hard-worker	Concrete, Sequential	Gregorc, Myers, Brightman	Early adopter
Karen	Dependent	Concrete, Active, Sequential (low scores)	Kolb (little support)	Early majority
Roy	Pragmatic	Visual, Intuitive, Active	Kolb (little support)	Innovator
Steve	Social	Active (maximum score), Visual	Kolb	Early adopter
Nicole	Skeptical/ Trial-and-Error	Visual, Active	Kolb, Gardner (little support)	Laggard
Lisa	Watching	Visual	Gardner, Felder	Early majority
Bryan	Self-taught	Intuitive	Kolb, Myers	Early adopter

strategy of illustrating the workshop as a sportive adventure; (2) the respectful and caring attitude of the instructors in making participants feel comfortable; (3) the "hands-on" approach in using a computer lab for the participants to apply the content of the workshop; (4) the peer interaction in the classroom and also in social opportunities; (5) the time available for practice after each lesson and presentation by the instructors; (6) the opportunity to develop their own projects during the workshop; and (7) the continued assistance available to them as they worked for three days surrounded by instructors.

The way in which the technology workshop series was designed seems to include the concepts underlying the above approaches and strategies. Some functions such as modeling, skill training, intensive help, and a user-friendly environment, were mentioned by the participants as an effective part of the workshop format. In summary, participants approved the workshop format and they think faculty development programs should explore more the strategies used in this technology workshop series.

Based on the above discussion, the following conclusions seem to be evident:

1. In order to attract faculty members with different backgrounds, beliefs, and motivations, technology workshops need to be creative, dynamic, and involve participants in a presentation style that includes active learning strategies and a hands-on approach.
2. The theme strategy of illustrating the workshop as an adventure was found to be a powerful resource to break the natural fear many faculty members feel towards technology, and made them feel comfortable and relaxed enough to enjoy a real learning experience.
3. A prolonged immersion approach is crucial to make participants "live" in a technology environment with full support and tutoring available, so no participant will get stuck without solving the common problems technology presents for beginners.
4. A friendly, respectful, and patient attitude on the part of the instructors is essential for making faculty feel encouraged to participate. Being experts in many different areas,

faculty do not feel comfortable being treated as inferior for not knowing the basics of some programs or software.

5. The social interactions promoted by sharing food and participating in group discussion, as well as the peer teaching opportunities, are a powerful learning resource that make faculty encourage each other and exchange learning experiences.

The experience of the participants in this study provided helpful information on different aspects of the process of learning to use instructional technology. Putting together the relationship between the several different factors, the following findings and conclusions seem to be evident from this study:

1. From a practical perspective, this study found that the lack of time and rewards made it harder and more difficult for faculty to learn and use instructional technology. In other words, most faculty claim that they need more time and rewards from the institution.
2. From an institutional perspective, the study found that all the participants felt under stress because of the time commitment, since instructional technology was an addition to their already busy schedules. Therefore, most participants claim that the preparation of instructional technology materials should be included and rewarded as part of the regular work load. Faculty also fear compromising the promotion and tenure process by spending time with IT.
3. The participation of these faculty in professional development interventions such as the technology workshop series was very helpful to equip and develop faculty skills in instructional technology, thus enhancing the participants' learning experience.

According to this study, the learning process in instructional technology works as a cycle in two opposite directions. Faculty who have high levels of motivation, positive beliefs, and some background in technology take the most advantage of professional development programs in instructional technology, have a growing learning experience, and are successful in developing teaching strategies that involve students in an active learning experience. The cycle is repeated as the more they learn, the more they increase the background, motivation, and positive beliefs. In the opposite direction, faculty who have low levels of motivation, negative attitudes, and no background in technology take less advantage of professional development programs, have a slow learning experience, and do not use much instructional technology in the classroom. Figure 1 displays this double cycle describing the relationship between the different factors influencing the learning process of faculty members in instructional technology based on the experiences of the participants in this study.

Practical Implications and Recommendations

The findings of this study present practical implications for faculty development in instructional technology, both from an institutional perspective related to policy issues and from the personal perspective of individual faculty members who want to learn from the experience of fellows who have struggled and walked the journey of learning instructional technology. Based on these findings, the following recommendations seem relevant to address the needs of the participants from an institutional perspective:

1. Institutions and departments should restructure their academic reward system to compensate faculty members who develop successful teaching activities and strategies

Figure 1. Cycle of faculty learning experience in instructional technology

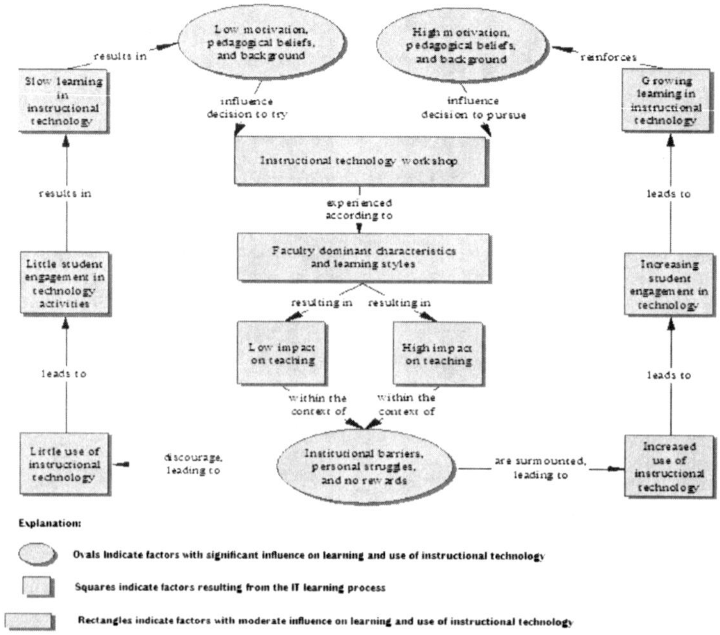

using instructional technology and the online environment. The promotion and tenure process should include and consider instructional technology as a relevant part of the teaching excellence component of promotion and tenure.

2. Institutions and departments should restructure their financial reward system to accommodate different criteria for assessing teaching load and instructional costs. The traditional model of measuring instructional costs based mostly on student/faculty ratio, average faculty salary, and student credit hours (Paulsen and Smart, 2001), must be reviewed to allow room for the time-consuming task of producing online courses and materials, thus providing a fair reward for faculty involved with instructional technology.
3. Institutions and departments should design both a short-term and a long-term pilot-plan for the implementation of faculty development programs in instructional technology, with a wide range of developmental interventions to reach faculty members at different levels of motivation and attitudes, as well as technology expertise and experience.
4. Based on the participants' descriptions of their dominant learning styles and characteristics, faculty development programs should address the needs of different types of learners and focus on different target audiences to reach faculty members with different profiles by promoting workshops with a wide variety of learning approaches including creative strategies like online games, instructional video clips, group discussions, and online case studies of pedagogical experiences using technology.

CONCLUSION

In summary, whether teaching instructional technology to an emotional learner, to a risk-taker or to a skeptical learner, it is always challenging to meet the needs and expectations of faculty with different learning styles, different technology backgrounds, different pedagogical beliefs, different attitudes towards technology, and who have their own pace and their own preferences in dealing with teaching and instruction.

Regarding the faculty development intervention, overall this innovative workshop series seems to have made a positive impact on the learning experience of most faculty members in instructional technology. However, even acknowledging the support of the institution in terms of providing faculty development opportunities, technical assistance and equipment available, one hundred percent of the participants agreed that institutional barriers such as time commitment and the lack of rewards are major barriers in terms of learning instructional technology. As a result, most participants tend to be under stress to accommodate all the demands of their professional appointment, such as teaching, research, service and participation in committees, and still be able to get involved with instructional technology. Many participants felt that instructional technology is an addition to their already heavy workload.

REFERENCES

Algonquin College. (1996). *Learning styles.* Retrieved August 28, 2003, from Algonquin College Website: http://www.algonquinc.on.ca/edtech/gened/styles.html

Brightman, H. (n.d.). *GSU master teacher program: On learning styles.* Retrieved July 3, 2003, from Georgia State University Website: http://www.gsu.edu/~dschjb/wwwmbti.html

Butler, K. (1987). Learning and teaching style: In theory and practice. Columbia, CT: The Learner's Dimension.

Canfield, A., & Lafferty, J. (1976). Learning style inventory. Detroit, MI: Humanics Media.

Carliner, S., & Shank, P. (2008). The e-leraning handbook. San Francisco: Pfeiffer.

Chism, N. (1998). Preparing graduate students to teach: Past, present, and future. In M. R. Clarke (Ed.), *A primer in diffusion of innovation theory.* Retrieved April 20, 2009, from http://www.anu.edu.au/people/Roger.Clarke/SOS/InnDiff.html

Claxton, C., & Murrell, P. (1987). *Learning styles: Implications for improving educational practices.* ASHE-ERIC Higher Education Report No. 4.

Creswell, J. (1998). Qualitative inquiry and research design. Thousand Oaks, CA: Sage.

Curry, L. (1990). A critique of the research on learning styles. *Educational Leadership, 48,* 50–56.

Davis, J., & Davis, A. (1998). *Effective training strategies: A comprehensive guide to maximizing learning in organizations.* San Francisco: Berrett-Koehler Publishers. Denzine, G. (n.d.). *The existence of learning styles: Myth or reality.* Retrieved September 17, 2003, from http://star.ucc.nau.edu/~dlk/Learn.styles.html

Dunn, R., & Griggs, S. (1998). Learning styles: Link between teaching and learning. In R. Dunn, & S. Griggs (Eds.), Learning styles and the nursing profession (pp. 9-23). New York: NLN Press.

Dziuban, C., Moskal, P., Juge, F., Truman, B., Sorg, S., & Hartman, J. (2002, February 15). *Developing a web-based instructional program in a metropolitan university.* Paper presented at University of Central Florida.

Eggan, P., & Kauchak, D. (2004). Educational Psychology: Windows on Classrooms. 7th Ed. Upper Saddle River, NJ, Merrill Prentice Hall.

Ertmer, P. A. (1999). Addressing first- and second-order barriers to change: Strategies for technology integration. *Educational Technology Research and Development*, *47*(4), 47–61. doi:10.1007/BF02299597

Felder, R. (1993). Reaching the second tier: Learning and teaching styles in college science education. *Journal of College Science Teaching*, *23*(5), 286–290.

Felder, R., & Silverman, L. (1988). Learning styles and teaching styles in engineering education. *English Education*, *78*(7), 674–681.

Flick, U. (1998). An introduction to qualitative research. Thousand Oaks, CA: SAGE Publications.

Gardner, H. (1993). Multiple intelligences: The theory in practice. New York: Basic.

Gardner, H. (2000). Intelligence reframed: Multiple intelligences for the 21st century. New York: Basic.

Garrison, R., & Vaughan, N. (2008). Blended learning in higher education. San Francisco: Jossey Bass.

Gregorc, A. (1985). An adult's guide to style. Columbia, CT: Gregorc Associates, Inc.

Gregorc, A. (1998). Mind Styles Model: Theory, Principles and Practice. Columbia, CT: Gregorc Associates, Inc.

Heinich, R., Molenda, M., Russell, J., & Smaldino, S. (2002). Instructional media and technologies for learning, 7th Ed. Columbus, OH: Prentice-Hall.

Herrmann, N. (1988). The creative brain. Lake Lure, NC: Brain Books.

Hill, J. (1971). Personalized education programs: Utilizing cognitive style mapping. Bloomfield Hills, MI: Oakland Community College.

Keeton, C. L. (2000). *Institutional structures that influence faculty to participate in distance education*. Dissertation Abstracts International, A-61 (10), 3840. (UMI No. AAT 9993226).

Kidd, T., & Song, H. (2007). Handbook of research on instructional systems and technology. Hershey, PA: IGI Global.

Kolb, D. (1984). Experiential learning: Experience as the source of learning and development. New York: Prentice-Hall.

Kolb, D. (2000). Facilitator's Guide to Learning. Philadelphia: Hay Group Transforming Learning.

Kolb, D. (2007). Kolb Learning Style Inventory. Philadelphia: Hay Group Transforming Learning.

Kolb, D. A. (1993). LSI-IIa: Self scoring inventory and interpretation booklet. Boston: McBer & Company.

Lee, H., & Lawson, A. (2002). What do the faculty think? The importance of concerns analysis in introducing technological change. *To Improve the Academy, 20,* 150-161.

Malinski, R. M. (2000). An examination of the experiences which university teachers have in the process of incorporating computer-mediated instruction techniques into their courses. *Dissertation Abstracts International, A-61*(06), 2270. (UMI No. AAT NQ50018).

Marincovich, M., Prostko, J., & Stout, F. (Eds.). The professional development of graduate teaching assistants. Bolton, MA: Anker.

Marshall, C., & Rossman, G. B. (1995). Designing qualitative research. Thousand Oaks, CA: Sage.

Middendorf, J. K. (1998). A case study in getting faculty to change. In M. Kaplan (Ed.), To Improve the Academy (Vol. 17, pp. 203-224).

Mishra, P., Koehler, M., & Zhao, Y. (2007). Faculty development by design: integrating technology in higher education. Charlotte, NC: Information Age Publishing.

Montgomery, C. J. (1999). Faculty attitudes toward technology-based distance education at the University of Nevada, Las Vegas. *Dissertation Abstracts International, A-60*(09), 3222. (UMI No. AAT 9946518).

Myers, I. (1976). *Introduction to type.* Gainesville, FL: Center for the Application of Psychological Type. Nasmith, G., Schultz, A., & Williams, T. (n.d.). *Thinking styles and impact on military leadership practices.* Retrieved July 1, 2006, from Canadian Defence Academy Website: http://www.cda-acd.forces.gc.ca/cfli/engraph/research/pdf/47.pdf

Pacific University. (2002). *Learning, technology and educational transformation: Examining the ed. tech. metamorphosis: Emerging butterfly or deleterious root worm?* Berglund Center Summer Institute. Retrieved April 26, 2009, from http://education.ed.pacificu.edu/bcis/workshop/adoption.html

Patton, M. Q. (1990). Qualitative evaluation and research methods. London: Sage.

Paulsen, M. B., & Smart, J. C. (2001). *The finance of higher education: Theory, research, policy & practice.* New York: Agathon Press. Personality Pathways. (n.d.). *What is your Myers-Briggs Personality Type?* Retrieved July 3, 2003, from http://www.personalitypathways.com/type_inventory.html

Race, S. P. (2001). Instructional technology preparation of pre-service teachers at Widener University: A descriptive case study (Pennsylvania). *Dissertation Abstracts International, A-60*(10), 3962. (UMI No. AAT 3003357).

Ramirez, M., & Castenada, A. (1974). Cultural democracy, bidognitive development, and education. New York: Academic Press.

Rogers, E. M. (1995). Diffusion of Innovations. New York: The Free Press.

Sorg, S., Truman, B., Dziuban, C., Moskal, P., Hartman, J., & Juge, F. (2002, February 15). *Faculty development learner support, and evaluation in Web-based programs.* Paper presented at University of Central Florida.

Zywno, M. (2003). A contribution to validation of score meaning for Felder-Soloman's index of learning styles. In *Proceedings of the 2003 American Society for Engineering Education Annual Conference & Exposition.*

ADDITIONAL READING

Bonk, C. J., & King, K. S. (1998). Electronic collaborators: Learner-centered technologies for literacy, apprenticeship, and discourse. Mahwah, NJ: L. Erlbaum Associates.

Chichering, A. W. (1981). The Modern American College: Responding to the New Realities of Diverse Students and a Changing Society. San Francisco: Jossey-Bass.

Chism, N. (2008). Faculty at the Margins: New Directions for Higher Education. San Francisco: Jossey-Bass.

Chism, N., Lees, N., & Evenbeck, S. (2002, Summer). Faculty development innovation for teaching. *Liberal Education, 88*(3), 34–41.

Dunn, R. (2000). Learning styles: Theory, research, and practice. *National Forum of Applied Educational Research Journal*, *13*(1), 3–22.

Epper, R. M., & Bates, A. W. (2001). Teaching faculty how to use technology: Best practices from leading institutions. Westport, CT: American Council on Education and Oryx Press.

Tileston, D. W. (2005). Ten Best Teaching Practices: How Brain Research, Learning Styles, and Standards Define Teaching Competencies. Tyler, TX: Corwin Press.

KEY TERMS AND DEFINITIONS

Instructional Technology: The art and science of designing, producing, and using solutions to instructional problems, using different media and systems that facilitate learning efficiently (Heinich, Molenda, Russell, and Smaldino, S., 2002)

Learning Styles: A generic term as an umbrella concept for recognizing individual learning differences and preferred ways of interacting or processing new information. No one has a monopoly on the term or can claim to represent learning style in its entirety (Butler, 1987; Kolb, 2000).

Faculty Development: A wide range of interventions, programs and resources intended to support faculty in developing expertise in specific subject-areas, such as mastering technologies for learning.

Teaching Strategies: A broad concept referring to the planning, implementation, assessment and management of educational activities, with the goal of producing learning.

Institutional Barriers: Lack of institutional support, resources or academic and financial rewards, thus discouraging faculty of learning and using instructional technology.

Faculty Rewards: Academic and financial recognition of faculty work with technology for learning, including the promotion and tenure process.

Pedagogical Attitudes: Faculty positive or negative reaction, including beliefs or disbeliefs regarding the benefits of technology applications for teaching and learning.

Chapter 2
International Collaboration in Distance Education in Sub-Saharan Africa:
Trends, Trials and Tomorrow's Thrusts

Gbolagade Adekanmbi
University of Botswana, Botswana

Bopelo Boitshwarelo
University of Botswana, Botswana

ABSTRACT

This chapter examines international collaboration in distance education in Sub-Saharan Africa (SSA), focusing on efforts aimed at utilizing technology. It identifies a number of significant collaborative endeavors. The collaborative efforts observed have a similar goal of pooling together ICT resources and expertise towards improving educational outcomes. The prevalence of teacher education and training across the initiatives, in the context of the Millennium Development Goals, is noted. Institutions outside Africa are actively involved in the funding and provision of expertise. Also, the AVU consortium model seems to be a viable approach to collaboration, with notable results seen. With the challenges facing technology-focused collaboration, such as a lack of enabling policies and the digital divide, the chapter suggests that African countries and institutions should pursue a culture of change and be more flexible. More formal training in distance education, utilizing Africans in the Diaspora and promoting dialogue across international spectrums are also recommended.

BACKGROUND

The main motivation for the introduction of distance education in sub-Saharan Africa in the early 19th century, apart from the sub continent's problem of unsatisfied educational demands, was the need to utilize an available international educational innovation. In this early thrust, distance education institutions which awarded the first set of qualifications were based on foreign soil, the tutors and the

DOI: 10.4018/978-1-61520-909-5.ch002

content of instruction were mostly foreign, and the course materials were developed outside the continent. Even when local initiatives were first seen, in the activities of individual entrepreneurs and university centres and departments, external organizations and outside agencies provided the needed technical and technological support, and helped in organizing training programmes for the personnel involved (Adekanmbi, 2002). Government involvement in distance education did not reduce the thrust of international activities. Rather, it assisted in the establishment of the Commonwealth of Learning in 1988. Over the years, international collaboration has taken new turns, with collaboration addressing such issues as programme development, research and publications, technology-based collaborative initiatives and among others, the promotion of digitization.

This paper examines the trends observable in distance education development in Africa. It discusses the nature of international collaboration in distance education in Africa and examines the trials and challenges it faces. It also investigates the extent to which international collaboration could have an impact on the use of technology in distance education on the continent. The paper further explores the rationale for integrating ICTs in distance education and identifies some of the existing collaborative efforts in the area of ICT-supported Open and Distance Learning (ODL). Of particular interest, among others, is the African Virtual University (AVU) and the role it has played in increasing access to quality ICT-supported ODL programmes through its unique collaborative model. The paper further analyses the nature of these efforts and identifies what the challenges and prospects are. It also examines future directions for collaborative initiatives in distance education on the continent, against the backdrop of problems which affects many collaborative initiatives. This is with a view to suggesting strategies through which Africa could further benefit from international collaboration in ICT-supported distance education.

The thesis of this paper is that international collaboration plays a major role in the development of distance education in sub-Saharan Africa and can influence, among others, the desire for ICT integration in distance education practices on the continent.

SETTING THE STAGE

Distance Education: Trends and Trials in Africa

The initial global attempts in tertiary distance education in Africa had its landmark in the early days of distance education in the UK (1840's), Canada (1919), Australia (1914), USA (1728) France and Germany (1856), and other parts of the developed world. From about 1915, British journals circulated the advertisements of leading British colleges such as Wolsey Hall, University Correspondence College, Rapid Results College, Foulks and Lynch and others (Harris, 1971). The colleges helped Africans to prepare for university based examinations set by the Universities of London, Oxford and Cambridge. Then known as colonial examinations, nationalists were later to query such offerings, referring especially to the foreign content as "problems of possible indoctrination and mental enslavement." Such was the nature of the beginning of distance education and the internationalization of higher education in many African countries.

Although the initial entry of tertiary distance education reflected the promotion of foreign content, the emergence of conventional universities in the new African states affected the nature of programmes offered. At the Ahmadu Bello University in Nigeria in 1967, the focus was on teacher education, and in other places, the liberal arts were common. The model of instruction was generally dual or integrated and conventional course offerings were generally replicated. At a later stage, open universities emerged in Nigeria,

Tanzania, and Zimbabwe, although it must be noted that many decades earlier, the University of South Africa (UNISA) was established as Africa's first open university.

It is noteworthy though that since its first African University Day celebrations in 1995, the Association of African Universities (AAU) has dedicated two themes to distance education, with universities organizing seminars around such themes. *Distance Education and African Universities* and *Cross Border Provision of Higher Education* were themes in 2003 and 2004 respectively (AAU, 2007). The Association for the Development of Education in Africa (ADEA) Working Group on Distance Education has also been active while the African Council for Distance Education (ACDE) is also making strides in the promotion of distance education.

On programme thrusts, teacher training initiatives at a distance have been prevalent. The findings on Zimbabwe (Chivore, 1992), Kenya (Kinyanjui, 1992), Tanzania (Chale, 1992), Nigeria and other parts of former British West Africa (Omolewa, 1978; 1982); reflect this assertion. Also, Adekanmbi's submissions (Adekanmbi, 2008; 2002; 1998), Aderinoye's writings (Aderinoye, 1992), and a host of others on Anglophone Africa, give some insight into the use of this field for teacher training. This has had its indirect impact on the promotion of basic education, which the World Bank has championed over the years. While distance education has helped to open up access, its use in the promotion of science and technology was late in coming.

The use of distance education as a strategy for promoting education for refugees, has been discussed by Thomas (1996). In this respect, its use at primary, secondary, tertiary, technical, professional, vocational education and training levels, including non-formal education and training are noted. Thomas (1996) also provides bibliographic details and advice on various institutional providers.

The examination of the development orientation of distance education programmes in Africa shows that the field appears to replicate old paradigms while its development orientation has been limited (Adekanmbi, 1998). Distance education may have emphasized entrance qualifications common in conventional education and not specifically addressed alternative routes to social development.

On training and development in the field, most formal training routes for practitioners have for a long time relied extensively on foreign programmes and Internet-based courses. The work of the Commonwealth of Learning (COL), since its establishment has however been significant in promoting the training of practitioners. Also, in-house training programmes, supported occasionally by outside agencies are also growing in the distance education departments and units in tertiary education institutions. There has also been a great reliance on foreign publications and research aimed at promoting development in the field.

A convergence of commercialization, technology use and the impact of globalisation on the fortunes of distance education is being observed. For example, many African universities may have started using distance education to improve their revenue base. In a submission, Bennel (1998) has noted that tertiary distance education in Africa is becoming an internationally tradable commodity, and this, in the context of an increasingly competitive global market (cited by Saint, 1999). In the context of globalization, courses are now moving from being limited to the traditional teacher training turf to include science, engineering, vocational and computing courses among others. Methods and media are slowly adopting a digital frame, open universities are increasing and cross border education is growing. In 1996, a third of all tertiary level enrolments in South Africa were distance education students (Saint, 1999).

Related to the above, some developments aimed primarily at improving the quality of operations and attempting to utilize new technology have been noted. A few examples reflected in Adekanmbi (2007) include the following:

- Publication of a Code of Ethics by National Association of Distance Education Organisations (NADEOSA) for its member institutions (NADEOSA, 2005)
- Establishment of the African Council for Distance Education

The research and collaborative initiatives of the Distance Education Association of Southern Africa (DEASA)

- Publication of the *Quality Criteria for Distance Education in South Africa* (Welch and Reed, 2005) with specific expectations relating to policy and planning, learners, quality assurance, information dissemination and results, among others.
- The drive by staff of distance education institutions to obtain the International Computer Drivers' Licence
- The case of Namibian College of Open and Distance Learning (NAMCOL) and Botswana College of Distance and Open Learning(BOCODOL) who have carried out Quality Assessment Audits of each institution's activities between them.
- The setting up of free toll lines by distance education organizations for students, a practice being utilised by NAMCOL for its students.
- UNISA's practice of distributed messages to its students
- The University of Botswana's utilisation of video conferencing, and in its conventional programmes, the partial use of web-based instruction.
- Development of vital policy documents to enhance practices and synergy between mainstream providers and conventional faculty practices. To this end, the University of Botswana Council has approved the University's *Distance Education Mainstreaming Policy* while the University of Namibia's Centre for External Studies now has a Policy Document on Open and Distance Learning in place.
- International conferences, especially technology-based conferences geared towards developing distance education practitioners have been reported (Wright 2007).

There have been a variety of challenges facing distance education in Africa. Two are worth highlighting here as they hint at the need for some degree of collaboration.

The first is the problem of staff retention in African universities, the subject of a major submission by Tettey (2006) to the World Bank. In the report, the loss rate of African university intellectuals is in the neighbourhood of 23000 a year, with countries such as Egypt, Kenya, Nigeria, Ghana and South Africa greatly affected (The Chronicle of Higher Education, November 2, 2001:A63). The report covers the Universities of Botswana, Ibadan, Kwazulu Natal, Ghana and the Makerere University. Among the difficulties cited are staff recruitment, attrition due to poor service conditions, the problem of an ageing professoriate, and the fact that many of the universities operated below capacities. Tettey (2006) also notes that appointment procedures were cumbersome, with the resultant loss of potential employees. Procedures for promotion were also stressful. Workload problems were due to mostly large classes which reflect an enrolment expansion policy without an accompanying capacity. The result is that very often, the gaps have been difficult to fill.

The second challenge generally facing tertiary education in Africa, but more so, facing distance education, is that of digital divide. Adekanmbi (2008) while citing the International Telecommunications Union (2004) notes:

- The digital divide between the developed countries and the developing nations was 11 times more in 1994 with respect to fixed telephones lines per 100 inhabitants. In 2004, it was only 4 times more.
- For mobile phone subscription, the divide was 27 times more in 1994, but in 2004 it was 4 times more.
- For Internet users per 100 inhabitants, the divide in 1994 was 73 times more, but in 2004, it was 8 times more.
- The overall Internet penetration by region in 2004 was 1.8% for Africa while Europe enjoyed a 30.6% position and the Americas had 30.5.

Digital divide refers to the gaps between individuals, communities and nations in their capacity to utilize, and the extent to which they have access to or own various forms of Information and Communication Technologies (ICTs). This also refers to imbalances which occur as a result of the availability or non-availability of resources or skills which individuals require to operate new technologies (Wikipedia, 2007). Selwyn et al (2006) have observed that these gaps may often be based on class, gender, age levels, socio-economic groupings, poverty and other disparities in knowledge or opportunities to educational facilities, means or structures. It has been seen that the digital divide in Africa has 'a spatial dimension, an educational dimension, a social dimension, and an income dimension' (Nwuke, 2003: p.36). The writer also cites the ITU, which reports that 80% of phone users in Africa are located in only six countries. For those who have the Internet, a great probability exists that 'a substantial number of computers in Africa is owned by the expatriate community' who, probably, account for 'much of the Internet usage' (Nwuke, 2003, p.36). No doubt, this has posed a major challenge to Africa's drive to utilize new technology in its distance education operations.

Given these and other challenges, collaboration becomes a useful strategy for moving the fortunes of distance education forward in the Continent.

CASE DESCRIPTION

International Collaboration in Distance Education

Collaboration is the pooling together of resources, human, material and physical, with the aim of building capacity, promoting efficiency, meeting institutional goals and ensuring a fair distribution of meager available resources. It has been seen to facilitate opportunities for local, regional and international cooperation as well increase clientele participation in activities. Adekanmbi (2004) has identified the following as problems which collaboration further addresses, especially in African distance education institutions: course material development, limitation in library and information resources, programme implementation delay, obsolescence in knowledge, inadequate training capacity, and copyright issues. In addressing these, collaboration thus takes various forms, including direct intervention, shared market, shared resources, association and the eclectic models, among others (Adekanmbi, 2004).

Distance education institutions in Africa also collaborate to address the problems of production delays, inappropriate expertise, inadequate technical training, conversion of programmes and aiding of other technology-oriented applications. Also addressed are resource sharing, space utilisation, adoption and adaptation of courses and joint research and publication initiatives. Perhaps a major area is the mitigation of the effects of low technology as most distance education outfits in Africa still wear predominantly a 'print gown'.

Over the years various organizations have promoted practices and sponsored distance education in the region. Examples include the

International Extension College, British Council, Commonwealth of Learning (COL), USAID, and the German Foundation for International Development. For advocacy, organisation of conferences and the promotion of training, the International Council for Open and Distance Education (ICDE), Distance Education Association of Southern Africa, National Association of Distance Education Organisations in Southern Africa, the West African Distance Education Association, and of course COL, among others, have been actively involved. For documentation, material development and research, the International Centre for Distance Learning, and the COL have been very active. For example, COL has sponsored initiatives for DEASA members in media related training and the Certificate for Practitioners in Distance Education programme, among other local collaborative efforts within the region.

It is appropriate to say that COL is one of the most active, if not the most active organizations providing access to and support for training in distance education in Africa. Apart from publishing a *Directive of Courses and Materials for Training in Distance Education* (COL, 1995), the level of documentations available through its web site is very high (see, for example, the COL website/ col. org.). Also, the level of involvement of COL in making available information on courses across the globe is high. Since inception, COL has had sponsored numerous fellowships through the assistance of the Government of British Columbia. This has enabled many university lecturers to benefit from educational exchanges across Commonwealth countries, thus improving the standards of distance education practice in local institutions. Also, through COL, many professionals have traveled overseas from the British Columbia to make their skills available through consultancy work. Information available on COL website shows new developments in this area. Notably too, a lot of research support has been indirectly provided by the International Centre for Distance Learning, an arm of the Open University of the UK, through its documentation services.

Challenges to International Collaboration

Elliot (2001) warns against the rhetoric of collaboration, suggesting that so often, there is much talk about collaboration with little actual success seen on the ground. This perhaps is why Woodrow et al (cited in Woodrow and Thomas, 2002:3) write:

Collaboration is widely perceived as an essential component of policies to widen participation by under represented groups, but evidence on the relative merits of different forms of collaboration is not easy to find. Almost there is an impression that to collaborate at all is the most important thing and that how it is done is largely incidental. Hence the structures and strategies employed sometimes appear to have developed almost incidentally, rather than as the result of any conscious and informed choice between alternative patterns of collaboration.

Also, other writers have explored the nature of bottlenecks collaboration faces which must be avoided if it is to achieve desired results. For example, Moran and Mugridge (1993) and King (1996) have noted such issues as lack of mission clarity of organizations involved, absence of a clear funding policy, and the lack of effective leadership, among others.

Although there are sometimes problems in collaboration, a concept Johnston (1997) has noted to be 'full of uncharted territories, ambiguities and institutional complexities' (cited in Schultz and Abbey, 2001, p.160), the gains far outweigh the problems. Based on the foregoing, collaboration will enhance learner success in programmes; distance education professionals would be able to work out minimum standards of practice; and the possibility of the utilisation of technology for collaborate training, would be greater. Dialogue between practitioners will also grow.

Technology Concerns

Rationale for ICT Use in Distance Education

In the various collaborative initiatives on the continent, the one linked to technology use has been of great concern. One major reason is that technology-oriented collaboration appears geared towards addressing the stigma that sub-Saharan African distance education systems wear a predominantly print gown. Thus recent moves to pursue a technology-oriented distance education provision in various parts of Africa have been reported in the literature (Adekanmbi, 2008; Saint, 1999; Daniel, 2005). While some distance education organizations have been attempting to adapt to technology-oriented changes to improve their practices, there are questions to which answers are required. For example, what rationales drive technology use in higher education in Africa, what forms has international collaboration taken in the promotion of technology in distance education? What challenges are faced in the process? How can these challenges be reduced to ensure proper utilization of technology in distance education?

There are a variety of reasons why information and communications technologies are used in education, particularly ODL. Debande and Ottersten (2004) identify four rationales for integrating technology in education in general. The first, *social rationale* is concerned with the role that ICTs play particularly with regards to communication and interaction between people. Second, the *economic and vocational rationale* is based on the requisite of ensuring that learners are prepared for the job market which requires ICT skills. Third is *pedagogical rationale* which recognizes the role ICT plays in improving the quality of teaching and learning. Fourth, the *cost effectiveness rationale,* which recognizes that ICT can reach far and wide even to the most disadvantaged communities in a cost-effective way. With specific reference to distance education in Africa, all these rationales apply. However, it seems the reasons that feature prominently are the fact that ICTs can increase access to distance education and the quality thereof (Mackintosh 2005; Lewin, 2003; Daniel & Menon, 2005). In other words the cost-effectiveness and pedagogy rationale reign supreme.

Following from the above, international collaboration in distance education in Africa is therefore driven mainly by these two notions of increasing access to and enhancing quality of education. As a result, initiatives that are geared towards integrating ICTs in education have grown in recent years both from within and outside Africa. An investigation into the literature reveals a few notable examples and these are discussed in the next sub-section.

African Initiatives of Collaborative ICT Utilization in Education

There is generally a consensus that ICTs hold a tremendous hope for the African continent in terms of educational development hence the growing numbers of projects and initiatives geared towards harnessing their potential (Mackintosh, 2005). For example, in its advertisement for its first ever-international conference on ICT for Development held in May 2006, E-learning Africa (2005) recognised the efforts that were already being made by the various stakeholders to take up e-Learning. It acknowledged the emergence of an African community of practitioners in e-Learning which has begun to "address the issues that are related to the efficient use of advanced modern technologies..." Specifically, the initiatives briefly discussed here are those with an international collaborative dimension, comprehensive in nature, widespread in reach and having a degree of impact regarding STEP factors.

SchoolNet Africa

SchoolNet Africa (SNA) is one notable initiative which provides support to practitioners, education policy makers, teachers and learners in a significant number of African counties (E-learning Africa, 2005). It is an African learning network set up to support national schoolnets to enhance learning and teaching through effective use of ICT. SNA which was founded in July 2000 has at least 10 SSA countries participating in it to date. It is an Africa-led initiative and is non-governmental in nature. It is driven by the philosophy that ICTs have a significant potential to enhance education in Africa (ThinkQuestAfrica, 2002). One of the significant projects of SNA is the African Teachers Network (ATN) whose aim is to be an active community of practice of teachers from all over Africa (http://www.schoolnetafrica.org/english/at_centre.html). The network's mission includes building capacity through collaborative projects, sharing resources, participation in different forums, and organization of professional development programmes of a diverse nature. The ATN envisions an improved teaching practice in the continent of Africa. Through its other various programs, the SNA has reportedly managed to:

- Facilitate many African schools' access to the Internet and other ICT tools,
- Continuously build and reinforce capabilities on the use of ICTs among teachers and students,
- Organise campaigns to promote ICT use at different teaching levels as well as develop activities that bring together different sectors and stakeholders into partnerships with the education community,
- Develop educational materials and,
- Carry out other projects that include the Global Teenager Project (GTP) which gets pupils and teachers to discuss contemporary issues online. It currently involves at least 20 countries (SchoolNet Africa, 2007).

DFID Imfundo Project

Recognizing that the use of technology in education is imperative for Africa's economic growth, the British government through the Department for International Development (DFID) set up a millennium education initiative in 2000 called the Imfundo*: Partnership for IT in Education* (Selinger, 2002). This is '...an initiative in DFID which considers ways in which Information and Communication Technology can be used to support Education in Sub-Saharan Africa (Info Dev. 2009).' This is with the view that ICTs can play a major role in extending information and knowledge to the poor and marginilised of the continent. Its major role is to create partnerships to contribute to the delivery of universal primary education and gender equality in Africa. The programme had a particular focus on teacher training and improving the professional development in general (Selinger, 2002) but with a more specific emphasis on improving access to and quality of primary education. A key feature of this project was to invite and coordinate contributions of resources from various stakeholders in different sectors. It was also to develop a Resource Bank and identify, through *liaison partners,* activities in the concerned African countries where these resources could be efficiently utilized (Unwin, 2005). In addition the project worked with *local partners* to ensure that appropriate and sustainable activities are implemented meaningfully and in context. This initiative ran in Ethiopia, Ghana, Kenya and South Africa. While this project was short-lived apparently due to its ambitious nature which went beyond the core agenda of the DFID, it received accolades from its beneficiaries in Africa. It also provided a useful framework for partnerships involving the used of ICTs in education. One of the significant achievements of the project is the Knowledge Bank of reference materials which is used to share information on the use of ICTs in education in Africa. Additionally, the Resource Bank mentioned above brings together all kinds of resources including expertise and ideas from the business community (Department for International Development, 2009).

COL Initiative of VUSSC

The Virtual University for Small States of the Commonwealth (VUSSC) can be traced back to a meeting of the Commonwealth Ministers of Education that was held in Halifax, Nova Scotia, Canada in 2000. At that Conference, ministers from small states expressed a common concern about the lack of critical mass in expertise and resources to engage with online learning in an autonomous fashion. This challenge emanated from the fact that these countries were small either territory-wise or demographically. Consequently, they either have limited resources and/or limited skilled manpower. While this initiative involves a number of countries from a number of regions of the world a significant number of countries from mainland Africa and islands states from around the continent are part thereof. Specifically, the countries from SSA are Botswana, The Gambia, Lesotho, Namibia, Sierra Leone, and Swaziland. Details of this initiative are contained in a document developed by COL and Government interlocutors (2007). The plan for the VUSSC was approved in 2003, and in 2005, representatives from 22 countries agreed to form the VUSSC. As a consortium, VUSSC would "develop capacity, develop and share learning content and courses, and work toward establishing a standards and credit transfer mechanism". This would be underpinned by the following:

- Members would share resources, expertise and experiences towards quality education and training for learners of various needs;
- COL would handle coordination, quality assurance and facilitate networking; and
- Members would have regular consultations as they developed and implemented their programmes as well as participating and availing resources towards quality learning environments.

Rather than attempt to create a new institution, the intention of this initiative was to augment efforts in the various post-secondary institutions so as to combat the challenges faced by the member states. The VUSSC initiative was to ensure that member countries build capacity to provide quality educational programmes using various technologies.

Membership has since increased quite significantly and to date, the VUSSC has engaged extensively in cooperative material development using online technologies where countries like Botswana and Namibia have participated (West, 2007; Daniel & West, 2008). This is done through training and materials development workshops called "boot camps". However, increasingly online collaborative methods of development are being used as capacity grows. Additionally, the VUSSC has decided to establish a Transnational Qualifications Framework (TQF) which will assist in formalising the working arrangements among member states and their respective institutions as well as ensure credibility of courses and programmes internationally. As the VUSSC looks ahead, the member states are encouraged to adapt and meaningfully make use of VUSSC initiatives by putting in place local institutional arrangements to reach their goals (Daniel, 2008). The latest information on VUSSC is that it now has several courses in a variety of areas and other materials, toolkits, resources and guides (VUSSC, 2009).

The African Virtual University

The African Virtual University (AVU) was established in 1997 in response to the problems facing the higher education sector (Shrestha, 2000). It is geared towards promoting alternative modes of the delivery of tertiary education with a view to complementing the efforts of existing institutions of higher learning. The AVU is described in its website as a "Pan African Inter-governmental organisation whose aim is to increase access to higher education and training through the innovative use of Information and communication technologies" (www.avu.org). The AVU headquarters are situated in Nairobi and it currently operates in about 27 countries, with a total of 55 technology-based learning centres. These centres are equipped with the necessary cabling and hardware and receive digital satellite transmissions. The AVU offers certificate, diploma and degree programs in a variety of programmes, particularly science and technology, IT and business studies. Specifically sponsored by the African Bank, teacher education and training has also become part of its menu. The AVU is essentially a network of ICT e-learning meant to avail educational resources and content in specific areas to partner institutions in Africa. These resources come from other universities in the continent and also from top universities overseas. In addition to educational resources, the AVU seeks to improve e-learning capacity in training ODL professionals and as well as physical resources. Courses are predominantly done through either asynchronous videotaped classes or synchronous satellite video feeds where students can ask questions telephonically. Essentially AVU is a kind of open university run in consortium style and as mentioned in its website it "builds and manages large consortia".

A detailed analysis of a specific case of AVU operations is done by Juma (2006) where the author describes the experience of Kenyatta University's participation in this initiative. This Kenyan University which started its partnership with the AVU in 1997, is one of the most notable examples and as such its experience offers a number of lessons. These are discussed by Juma and they include the need:

- To promote University ownership of AVU;
- To have community awareness campaigns about the AVU, including the business community;
- To have adequate learner support materials and equipment particularly ICT facilities;
- For skilled manpower;
- To have committed leadership for both the project and the partner university;
- To increase capacity building particularly in ICT skills and
- For delivery of quality academic programmes so that they can attract higher enrolments and have value for money.

Overall, the AVU has been successful with the number of partner institutions still on the rise. However, there is reportedly more uptake in Anglophone than Francophone Africa due to lower use of ODL methods in the latter (Juma, 2006).

Observation and Analysis

From the four cases above a number of observations seem to emerge. First, it is clear that international collaboration in Africa with regard to educational ICTs has only emerged, in a serious way, in the last twelve years. The AVU has been the first notable initiative to be developed. This is clearly understandable as around the time of setting it up, ICTs were becoming increasingly available in Africa.

Second, a similar set of aims run through these "collaborative endeavours". This is their objective of bringing together ICT resources and expertise for improving the quality and quantity of educational outcomes, particularly in post-secondary education. There is also the added objective of building capacity in the area of e-Learning for the region. This resonates with the pedagogical and the cost effectiveness rationale for using ICTs in education. However, it also, perhaps indirectly, touches on the other rationales: vocational/economic rationale as using modern technologies to educate learners prepares them for the global work market and; social because collaborative methods of learning foster the social dimension of education and prepares learners to function in society in a cohesive way. Thus there is clear indication that these efforts have sought to meet Social, Technological, Economic and Political (STEP) demands to varying extents.

Third, an emphasis on teacher education and training is evident. This seems to be a consequence of a response to the Millennium Development Goals (MDGs) on education by sponsoring organizations. By training teachers using modern technologies, these initiatives and others recognize the role of teachers in preparing the current generation of young people for technology-driven economies. A fourth observation is that these collaboration initiatives, except perhaps SNA, are initiated, funded or coordinated by international institutions and/or governments. This may be attributable to the fact that financial, technological and appropriate human resources reside predominantly outside the African continent.

Lastly in all these collaborative endeavours the consortium approach to collaboration is clearly visible with the AVU standing out prominently in this regard on several counts: The AVU is:

- Pan African and intergovernmental in nature;
- Has the highest membership of countries participating and benefiting from it;
- Brings together both institutions from within and without Africa and
- Has a strategic focus making it a sustainable endeavour; to date it has trained thousands of students in various fields particularly at the Kenyatta University.

The AVU has thus played a significant role over the last decade in increasing access to quality ICT-supported ODL programmes through its unique collaborative model.

CURRENT CHALLENGES

With particular reference to AVU, the Kenyatta University case, though a success story has reportedly faced a number of challenges (Juma, 2006). First, there are administrative challenges which emanate from the fact that the administration and management of a virtual university is different from a face-to-face university. Decision-making processes are usually slow and inflexible in the conventional institution while dealing with a virtual educational environment requires quicker, more creative and flexible decision-making processes. Secondly, capacity building, particularly with reference to academic staff's need to appreciate and use ICT in learning is a challenge as massive change such as this is never easy. Thirdly, owing to the fact that bureaucratic procedures of conventional systems are usually slow, cooperation can be difficult to formalize.

As a general observation, the over dependence of collaborative endeavors on external sponsors has generally led to non-sustainability as the programmes tend to stall if the support stops. It would seem therefore that strong partnerships with local institutions can ensure a high degree of sustainability. The AVU has generally been successful as its approach has been to integrate its interventions into the strategic intentions of the local partner institutions and focus on building capacity. This is a demand driven approach which is widely advocated for by Unwin (2005). Unwin in his exploration of partnerships for ICT for Development in Africa came to the following conclusion that partnerships, particularly of an international nature should concentrate not just on the supply aspects of the collaborative relationship but also on the demand side (the local implementation environment). This approach allows for initiatives to sufficiently appreciate the realities of the demand side with all its complexities and constraints.

Unwin (2005) also places emphasis on transparency among partners in terms of their contributions and what they expect to benefit from the partnership. The Imfundo project was exemplary as it outlined ethical guidelines, benefits framework and memorandums of understanding. This way, its activities were guided by a set of core principles and an acknowledgement of the different interests of the partners in terms of what they will contribute and benefit.He further recommended that partnerships should be multi-sector in nature involving partners from different sectors rather just having numerous stakeholders from a single sector.

In a study on e-learning, commissioned in 2004 by SNA in partnership with other organisations such as COL, the use of ICT in both pre-service and in-service teacher education in African countries was examined. Menon and Daniel (2005) have identified the following as one of the significant challenges: the lack of a comprehensive pan-African framework to inspire the development of local technological models and local teacher training content for building teachers' ICT capabilities.

SOLUTIONS AND RECOMMENDATIONS

As we envisage the future of collaboration, the following should further assist in ensuring the full utilization of collaborative initiatives in African distance education practices, especially in the context of promoting technology oriented distance education practices.

As evident from the discussion thus far, ICTs are necessary for the realization of wider access to quality tertiary education in Africa. However, given the challenges of infrastructure and limited capacities, international collaboration in ICT-use in education becomes imperative. The continent therefore will need to strengthen existing partnerships and if needs be create new and more innovative ones. The AVU has proved to be a viable initiative which many SSA countries can use to widen provision of quality higher and professional education. However institutions will need to be flexible in their operations, innovative in their thinking and generally have a culture that welcomes change if they are to fully benefit from such an endeavour. Similarly the VUSSC can be tapped into by African member states. While the VUSSC has promoted a bottom-up approach to its operations, it is also formalizing its arrangements so that the courses and programmes it helps develop will have a local relevance while having credibility at an international level. Seeing that a consortium arrangement seems to have good prospects in terms of sustainability and effectiveness similar initiatives in the context of ODL that address a variety of educational needs are possible. Apart from consortium arrangements, other initiatives and activities can be carried out to promote collaboration in the region, as further discussed below.

During international conferences, distance education practitioners in Africa can exchange ideas, collaborate with colleagues and develop new synergies which assist them in utilizing their best ideas. In recent times, the University of Pretoria and the University of Botswana engaged in the sharing of expertise and experience in joint organization of digital scholarship conferences. To date, two of such conferences have been held, in 2007 and 2008 in Gaborone and Pretoria respectively, while a third one is in the process of being planned for 2010. The DEASA is also encouraging and promoting technology-oriented collaboration among its members through its conferences and workshops. In West Africa, East Africa and Central Africa, this idea can be further promoted in the various regional associations. It is also right to call attention to the wide range of international conferences on educational technology, with a long list of such provided every year by Clayton Wright (Wright 2007). Such collaborative initiatives will no doubt enhance the development of useful ideas in ICT integration in distance education.

The absence of technology policies in many countries in Africa is a major hindrance to the contextual use of technology in distance education. Among other things, clear policies help to identify users, provide opportunities for linkages and identify possible areas of collaboration among many users within regions and local educational landscape. Such policies not only provide useful contexts for distance education to thrive, they also enhance the extension of pedagogical information access to rural areas. In addition, they encourage the collaboration of various stakeholders within national contexts to derive the best benefits from policy implementation. Related to this, Government provision of electricity to rural areas in Africa will also facilitate the growth of technology-enhanced educational initiatives, with distance education benefiting in the process. It is therefore imperative that all African countries develop ICT policies.

African scholars in Diaspora can be encouraged to return home on occasions and help utilize new skills in technology in local distance education projects. Ite (2004) used the term 'Return to sender' in a chapter on globalization, where he suggests that scholars from the African continent who have benefitted from exposure to new ways of doing things should from time to time return to their countries or institutions of origin. This is to provide needed assistance. ICT use is one way where such assistance is greatly needed, especially in distance education. The Federal Government of Nigeria has actually taken the 'Return to sender' phenomenon to a new level where its National Universities Commission has developed a system that facilitates the return of citizen lecturers from their places of abode abroad to Nigeria for short terms of academic engagement. Such interventions not only allow for the use of the expertise of the citizen concerned, but may open up new opportunities for institutional collaboration in distance education.

The promotion of the discipline of distance education is another area worth exploring. The training of practitioners in distance education, at the beginning was late in coming. Initial reliance on training was limited to the use of trainers from the International Extension College in the UK, local training initiatives and at a later stage, the participation in Masters and higher degree programmes where distance education was carried out by research. Recently, a Certificate Programme for Practitioners in distance education collaboratively done by the Commonwealth of Learning and DEASA has been used to promote skills development in the field. The enhancement of the curriculum of such programmes by incorporating technology based units of instruction will further promote the use of ICTs in distance education. For collaborative purposes, joint development of programmes between institutional providers of distance education is also needed. Related to this, the identification of centers of excellence in various parts of Africa, especially of institutions that have achieved more in technology-oriented practices will further help the new institutions which lag behind further promote their distance education practices.

It has been observed that many business corporations have adopted successful technological practices that help enhance corporate practices for broad financial gains. Collaboration between the institutional providers of distance education and the corporate sector should be encouraged to promote growth in the field. The sharing of such experiences with local tertiary institutions will further ensure that technology is used to maximum benefit.

Most distance education institutions in Africa are working towards widening the access and promoting the growth of student numbers. The growth of open universities in the region is a realisation of this, in some measure. But access also has to be widened with respect to the offering of courses in technology related programmes for students in distance education programmes.

Generally, its is expected that institutions offering distance education must be in the fore front of innovation promotion, ICT policy implementation, promotion of a vibrant mentoring scheme for staff and students and the pursuit of collaborative research in various areas of their operation, especially in the field of ICT. The provision of support for distance learners through the use of technology enhanced practices is also crucial.

REFERENCES

Abramson, M., Bird, J., & Stennet, A. (1996). Introduction. In M. Abramson, J. Bird, & A. Stennet (Eds.), Further and higher education partnerships: The future for collaboration (pp.1-3). Buckingham, UK: Open University Press.

Adekanmbi, G. (1998). Development orientation of distance education programmes in Africa: A preliminary submission. *Ghana Educational Media and Technology Association (GEMTA). Journal*, *2*, 59–70.

Adekanmbi, G. (2002). A comment on the education and training of distance education practitioners in Africa. Open and Distance Learning Association of Australia (ODLAA) Papers, (pp. 1-11).

Adekanmbi, G. (2004). Collaborative strategies for implementing continuing education programmes in Botswana. In D. Sanders & K. Brosnan et al. (Eds.), Learning transformations: Changing learners, organizations and communities (pp. 87-95). London: FACE.

Adekanmbi, G. (2007). Quantitative aspirations, qualitative considerations and technological imperatives: Collaborating for progress in African distance education. *Journal of Sociology and Education in Africa*, *6*(1), 1–12.

Adekanmbi, G. (2008). The neo liberal ideology and the future of higher education in Africa: Lessons for Nigeria. The Second Annual Professor (Mrs) Grace Mbipom Foundation Lecture, University of Calabar, Nigeria, 4 June 2008.

Aderinoye, R. (1992). *Retention and failure in distance education: the experience of the National Teachers' Institute, (NTI) Kaduna*. Unpublished Doctoral Thesis, University of Ibadan, Nigeria.

Chale, E. M. (1992). Application and cost effectiveness of distance education in teacher preparation: A case study of Tanzania. In P. Murphy and A. Zhiri (Eds.), Distance Education in Anglophone Africa (pp.123-136). Washington, DC: The World Bank.

Commonwealth of Learning. (1995). Directory of courses and materials for training in distance education. Vancouver: Commonwealth of Learning.

Commonwealth of Learning and the VUSSC government interlocutors. (2007). *A business strategy for the Virtual University for small states of the Commonwealth (2007– 2013)*. Retrieved June 7, 2009, from http://www.col.org/sitecollectionDocument/VUSSC.Business_Plan_20070220.doc

Daniel, J. (2005). Open and distance learning in Africa. In 15 CCEM mid-term review for Africa and Europe, Freetown, Sierra Leone, 14 November 2005.

Daniel, J., & Menon, M. (2005). *ODL and ICTs for teacher development in Sub-Saharan Africa: The experience of the Commonwealth of Learning*. Retrieved 12 November, 2005, from http://www.col.org/speeches/JD_0509BOCODOL.htm

Daniel, J., & West, P. (2008). *The virtual university for small states of the Commonwealth: What is it for? How is it doing? Where is it going?* Retrieved June 7, 2009, from http://www.col.org/resources/speeches/2008presentations/2008-VUSSC/Pages/articleVUSSC.aspx

Debande, O., & Ottersten, E. K. (2004). Information and communication technologies: A tool for empowering and developing the horizon of the learner. *Higher Education Management and Policy*, *16*(2), 31–61. doi:10.1787/hemp-v16-art15-en

Department for International Development. (2009). *Imfundo: Partnership for IT in education.* Retrieved September 20, 2009, from http://imfundo.digitalbrain.com/imfundo/

eLearning Africa. (2005). *1st International conference on ICT for development, education and training, UNCC, Addis Ababa, Ethiopia May 24-26, 2006.* Retrieved 12 November, 2005, from http://www.elearning-africa.com/conference.php

Elliott, A. (2001). Introduction. In M. Richards, A. Eliot, V. Woloshyn, & C. Mitchell (Eds.), Collaboration uncovered: the forgotten, the assumed, and the unexamined in collaborative education. Westport, CT: Bergin and Garvey.

Harris, W. J. A. (1971). Education by post (England). In O. Mackenzie & E.L. Christensen (Eds.), The changing world of correspondence study (pp. 299-302). University Park, PA: Pennsylvania State University Press.

InfoDev. (2009). *Quick guide: ICT and education at DFID.* Retrieved 07 June, 2009, from http://74.125.77.132/search?q=cache:i8YkiIxFsalJ:www.infodev.org/en/Publication.146.html

Ite, U. (2004). *Return to sender: using the African intellectual disapora to establish academic links.*

ITU, International Telecommunications Union. (2007). *Measuring Village ICT in Sub-Saharan Africa.* Retrieved December 11, 2007, from http://www.itu.int/ITU-D/ict/statistics/material/Africa_Village_ICT_2007.pdf

Juma, M. N. (2006). Kenyatta University-African Virtual University, Kenya. In D. Antoni (Ed.), The virtual university: Models and messages/ lessons from case studies. Paris: UNESCO.

King, R. (1996). Competition or co-operation? In *Universities in the Twenty-first Century, Education in a Borderless World Conference*, Singapore, 13-14 August, IDP Education Australia.

Kinyanjui, P. (1992). The organization of teacher training at a distance with particular reference to Kenya. In P. Murphy and A. Zhiri (Eds.), Distance education in Anglophone Africa: Experience with secondary education and teacher training (pp. 117-122). Washington, DC: The World Bank.

Lewin, K. M. (2000). New technologies and knowledge acquisition and use in developing countries. *Compare, 30*(3), 313–321. doi:10.1080/713657464

Mackintosh, W. (2005). Can you lead from behind? Critical reflections on the rhetoric of e-learning, open distance learning and, ICTs for development in Sub- Saharan Africa (SSA). In A. A. Carr-Chellman (Ed.). Global Perspectives on e- learning: Rhetoric and reality (pp.222-240). Thousand Oaks, California: SAGE Publications.

Moran, L., & Mugridge, I. (Eds.). (1993). Collaboration in distance education: International case studies. New York: Nicholas Publishing.

Nwuke, K. (2003). Higher education, economic growth, and information technology in Africa: some challenges and issues. In Beebe, M., Kouakou, K., Oyeyinka-Oyelaran, B. & Rao, M. (Eds.), Africa Dot Edu: IT opportunities and higher education in Africa (pp.17-42). New Delhi: Tata McGraw-Hill Publishing Company Limited.

Omolewa, M. (1978). Oxford University Delegacy of Local Examinations and Secondary School Education in Nigeria, 1929-1937. *Journal of Educational Administration and History, 10*(2), 39–44. doi:10.1080/0022062780100205

Omolewa, M. (1982). Historical antecedents of distance education in Nigeria, 1887-1960. *Adult Education in Nigeria, 7*(December), 7–26.

Saint, W. (1999). Tertiary distance education and technology in sub-Saharan Africa. Washington, DC: The World Bank.

Saint, W. (1999). Tertiary distance education and technology in sub-Saharan Africa. Washington DC: The World Bank.

SchoolNet Africa. (2007). *African education knowledge warehouse*. Retrieved on July 20, 2009, from http://www.schoolnetafrica.org/english/index.htm

Schutz, A., & Abbey, S. (2001). Collaborative mentoring: insights from a university research centre. In M. Richards, A. Elliott, V. Woloshyn, & C. Mitchell (Eds.), Collaboration uncovered: the forgotten, the assumed, and the unexamined in collaborative education (pp.219-235). Westport, CT: Bergin and Garvey.

Selinger, M. (2002). *Education and skills development in sub-Saharan Africa.* Paper presented at the ASET Conference on Untangling the Web: Establishing Learning Links, 7-10th July, Melbourne, Australia.

Selwyn, N., Gorard, S., & Furlong, J. (2006). Adult learning in the digital age. London and New York: Routledge.

Shrestha, G. (2000). Utilization of information and communications technology for education in Africa. Addis Ababa, Ethiopia: UNESCO, IICBA.

Tettey, W. (2006). Staff retention in African universities: elements of a sustainable strategy. Washington DC: The World Bank.

Thinkquest. (2002). *About SchoolNet Africa.* Retrieved November 14, 2005, from http://www.thinkquestafrica.org/about_sna.shtm

Thomas, J. (1996). Distance education for refugees: The experience of using distance and open learning with refugees in Africa, 1980-1995 with guidelines for action and a directory of information. Cambridge, UK: International Extension College.

Unwin, T. (2005). Partnerships in development practice: Evidence from multi-stakeholder ICT4D partnerships practice in Africa. Paris: UNESCO.

VUSSC. (2009). *A virtual university for small states of the Commonwealth (VUSSC).* Retrieved on 24 July 2009 from http://www.vussc.info/

West, P. G. (2007). The virtual university becomes a reality. *Educational Technology, 67*(6), 38–40.

Wikipedia. (2007). *Digital divide*. Retrieved December 11, 2007, from http://en.wikipedia.org/wiki/Digital_divide

Woodrow, M., & Thomas, L. (2002). Pyramids or spiders? Cross-sector collaboration to widen participation, learning from international experiences. In L. Thomas, M. Cooper, & J. Quinn (Eds.), Collaboration to widen participation in higher education (pp. 3-28). Stoke on Trent: Trentham Books.

Wright, C. (2007, June 15). *Educational technology conferences for 2007-2008.*

Zeleza, P., & Olukoshi, A. (Eds.). African universities in the twenty-first century Vol. 1. Dakar, Senegal: CODESRIA.

ADDITIONAL READING

Adei, S. (2004). Overview of university level education in Africa. In M. Beebe, K. Kouakou, B. Oyeyinka-Oyelaran & M. Rao (Eds.), Africa Dot Edu: IT Opportunities and Higher Education in Africa (pp. 90). New Delhi: Tata McGraw-Hill Publishing Company Limited.

Altbach, P. (2008). Globalization and forces for change in higher education. *Industry and Higher Education, 50*(Winter), 2.

Ayoubi, R. M., & Al-Habaibeh, A. (2006). An investigation into international business collaboration in higher education organizations. *International Journal of Educational Management, 20*. Retrieved 18 May 2009 from http://www.emeraldinsight.com/Insight/ViewContentServlet?Filename+Published

Eastmond, D. (2000). Realizing the promise of distance education in low technology countries. *ETR & D, 48*(2), 100–111. doi:10.1007/BF02313405

Farrell, G. (Ed.). (2003). A virtual university for small states of the Commonwealth. Vancouver, Canada: The Commonwealth of Learning.

Hanna, E., Donald, , & Latchem, C. (2002). Beyond national borders: Transforming higher education institutions. *Journal of Studies in International Education, 6*, 115–133. doi:10.1177/1028315302006002003

Isaacs, S., Broekman, I., & Mogale, T. (2004). Contextualizing Education in Africa: the role of ICTs. In T. James (Ed.), Information and communication technologies for development in Africa: Volume 3, Networking institutions of Learning --SchoolNet (Vol. 3, pp. 1-23). Ottawa, Canada: CODESRIA/IDRC.

Naidoo, V. (April 2003). *ICT in education policy-Reflecting on key issues.* Paper presented at the Pan-African workshop focusing on using ICT to support the education systems in Africa, organized by the Ministry of Education (Botswana), SchoolNet and Commonwealth of Learning in partnership with other agencies, Gaborone, Botswana.

Oduaran, A., & Bhola, H. (2006). Widening access to education as social policy: essays in honor of Michael Omolewa. Dordrecht: Springer.

Organization for Economic Cooperation and Development. (2007). Qualification Systems: bridges to lifelong learning. Paris: OECD.

Selwyn, N., Gorard, S., & Furlong, J. (2006). Adult learning in the digital age. London and New York: Routledge.

UNESCO. (2005). Global education digest. Montreal: UNESCO Institute for Statistics.

UNESCO. (2006). Education for all global monitoring report. Paris: UNESCO.

Varghese, N. (Ed.). (2006). Growth and expansion of private higher education in Africa. Paris: International Institute for Educational Planning (IIEP).

KEY TERMS AND DEFINITIONS

Collaboration: The working together of two or more entities, governments or institutions, with the aim of sharing resources to achieve common goals.

Digital Divide: The gap between individuals, contexts or sections of the population that have access to, or ability to utilize the Internet and other digital technologies and those that do not.

Diaspora: A dispersion or movement of any population sharing a common ethnic identity from their territory to other far removed areas

Globalization: A phenomenon in which nations and people become more interlinked, with broad implications for political, social, economic and technological integration.

Information and Communication Technologies: Technologies used to create, manage and distribute information as well as facilitate communication.

Sub-Saharan Africa: The African countries located south of the Sahara Desert. The term is used in opposition to North Africa which is mostly inhabited by Arabs.

Virtual University: A tertiary institution that provides higher education programs through electronic media.

Chapter 3
Effective Use of ICT for Inclusive Learning of Young Children with Reading and Writing Difficulties

Karin Tweddell Levinsen
Aarhus University, Denmark

ABSTRACT

This case presents the three-year research and development IT Folder Project (PIF), which has been aimed at facilitating the inclusion of young children with potential reading and writing difficulties in normal classes. The research focuses on everyday practice in schools and produces knowledge that gradually qualifies and consolidates a sustainable implementation strategy for the municipality involved regarding ICT as a change agent for inclusion. The children with potential difficulties are identified though tests and the adults and the classes involved "accompany" the children into the project. Thus, the adults involved are not necessarily passionate about ICT; they are representative of the average Danish schoolteacher. The case presents the first year and a half of the project and the initial results regarding the quality of the children's inclusion process along with modifications of the screening tests and organizational changes in the municipality and the local schools based on these results.

ORGANIZATION BACKGROUND

The IT Folder Project (PIF) differs from previous Danish projects on ICT implementation in two ways. First, the project involves teachers who can be described as early and late majority adaptors of ICT (Rogers, 1995), while previous projects have worked with voluntary innovators and early adaptors. The experience has been that projects involving innovators and early adopters tend to fade away as soon as the special conditions that have made the project possible are withdrawn or if the innovators who drive the process change job. Therefore, PIF produces valuable knowledge of the conditions for implementing ICT in everyday practice in Danish schools. Second, as an explorative and design-based study, PIF is carried out as an iterative collaborative process that aims to use and share knowledge as it is produced and at all levels in the municipal organization. PIF is based on iterative principles of

DOI: 10.4018/978-1-61520-909-5.ch003

project management and project design derived from the field of Interaction Design (Sharp, Rogers & Preece, 2007). Thus, PIF is a research-based iterative intervention that involves two primary schools, including both the teachers and the school administration, as well as the local Pedagogic Development Centre (PDC) in the municipality, the local politicians and decision makers.

The processes and everyday practices that PIF intends to change are the organizational structures within the school system that deals with children who are identified as having reading- and writing difficulties. The present practice in Denmark is that children who are observed by their teachers to have problems are tested in third grade. If they are diagnosed as dyslexic they are offered special needs education from fourth grade. The special needs education can take place either by letting the children remain and in their class most of the time and giving them segregated lessons some of the time, or by transferring the children to a dyslexic school. Often these children, who are in general able-minded, have lost both their confidence and their desire for learning because they feel they have failed many times. They have developed a repertoire of strategies to hide their difficulties and additionally, they are seriously left behind in school subjects.

In addition to bringing about change in organizational structures, PIF also intends to impact the way the teachers and other resource persons think about reading and writing difficulties. This is done by introducing a PIF philosophy according to which the children's difficulties are perceived as contextual conditions. The idea is to move the focus of agency away from the traditional approach by which the difficulties are treated as personal defects. On the contrary, the PIF philosophy focuses on changes in the everyday context that remove barriers for the children's inclusion in the normal classes. According to Holmgaard (2007) and the Danish Ministry of Education (Undervisningsministeriet, 2003), reading is traditionally understood as the relation between a person and a text. According to the traditional view, reading and writing are understood as the ability to code and decode content represented as signs, e.g. letters, syllables and sentences. Reading and writing difficulties are seen as problems with coding and decoding signs. The problems become a handicap – a personal disability – that requires intervention in terms of special needs initiatives. This discourse revolves around persons *with* reading and writing disabilities. Holmgaard's research demonstrates that children experience their own *reading difficulties* when they observe other children's *reading abilities* (Ibid: 8). The children experience that they are different from other children. However, the nature of the children's social experience depends on how *being different* is handled by the child and by others. According to Holmgaard, adults' reactions are pivotal for the child's self-esteem: whether they think they *have* a disability or whether they think they *are in* a difficult situation. When difficulties become a situation a person *is in*, the focus for possible interventions becomes the context and the practice, *not* the person. This interpretation emancipates reading and writing from being defined solely as the ability to code and decode signs. On the contrary, the PIF philosophy is based on the assumption that modification of context and practice may remove barriers and allow the person *in* difficulties to participate on equal terms and be included in the normal class. Thus, according to the PIF philosophy:

- to read may mean to use *text-to-speech* applications that transform text to synthetic voice
- to write may mean to use *speech-to-text* applications that transform spoken words into text or applications for dyslexics that support spelling and generation of words.

Using these tools, the child can participate and work with the same subject as the other pupils, but not necessarily at the same level (Tetler, 2000).

Therefore, inclusion depends on the participants' attitudes and the ongoing negotiation of identity that is performed in the community of learning.

A final dimension of the PIF philosophy is the assumption that part of changing the context is to work with the ways that the stakeholders at all levels in the organization think about ICT. In the minds of the adults who belong to the generation that Prensky (2001) names the digital immigrants, a computer is an advanced typewriter with access to an unlimited web-based dictionary. Therefore, ICT is traditionally understood as a tool and accordingly, ICT literacy is understood as the skills that are required to perform functional and basic actions when undertaking particular operations using that tool. In contrast, the PIF philosophy takes its point of departure in the present condition that society is e-permeated and that digitalization impacts all aspects of our lives as the Internet is the fabric of our lives (Castells 2001). Thus the PIF philosophy understands ICT as multi-dimensional: a tool, an environment, a form of personal identification, a social context, an actor, etc. and ICT literacy draws closer to the cultural concept of *buildung*. As a consequence, a basic assumption of the PIF philosophy is that the way actors understand ICT has an impact on the way they practice ICT, e.g. in relation to reading and writing difficulties. The traditional position sees ICT as a tool that is designed to reduce the consequences of a handicap and compensate for the person's disability (Florian & Hegarty 2004, Sheehy 2005). This is called compensational ICT, which *changes the user*. In contrast, according to the PIF philosophy, ICT is a preventive and substitutional continuation of the person, just like glasses (Tetler 2000). Substitutional ICT *changes the practice and the context* and not the user. From the substitutional perspective, technology takes on several appearances or existential forms:

- *Artifact*: ICT is a tool that the person uses
- *Attribute*: ICT is a personal attribute that involves negotiation of identity
- *Social actor*: ICT is an actor in the social context

Compensational ICT is something we always notice and think about while substitutional ICT is just there as an everyday dimension of the context and practice. Using Heidegger's distinction between *Zeug* and *dasein* (Heidegger, 1996) we may say that compenstational ICT is *zeug* and always consciously *ready-to-hand* while substitutional ICT is *dasein* and just there, *present-at-hand* when needed.

PIF is a three-year project that runs from 2007 to 2010. PIF is designed as a collaborative research and development project involving the Danish University School of Education, Aarhus University; the municipal government of a suburb of the Danish capital, Copenhagen; the Pedagogic Development Centre of that municipality; and the management of two local schools. The research is financed by the Danish Ministry of Education while the local activities and ICT support are financed by the municipality. The hardware and software involved in the project are partly donated by companies.

SETTING THE STAGE

The Salamanca Statement on Special Needs Education in 1994 called attention to the issue of inclusion in Europe. The statement addresses the problems and rights of learners who for different reasons are excluded or segregated from ordinary education. As a consequence of the Salamanca Statement, the concept of *the inclusive school* is now widely accepted and international organizations (UNESCO's Institute for Information Technologies in Education (IITE) and the independent Centre for Studies on Inclusive Education (CSIE)) work politically for inclusion and support a wide range of initiatives related to research and development of everyday practice in educational institutions (Kotsik & Tokareva 2007).

Dyson (1999) argues that the Salamanca Statement does not define inclusion and leaves the concept open for a variety of interpretations. Dyson identifies four dominant discourses which he groups into two meta-discourses. The meta-discourses are: 1) politics-ethics and 2) economics-pragmatics, which Dyson argues are mutually incompatible because they are based on entirely different grounds and target groups as summarized in Table 1 below.

The UK government tries to embrace this ambiguity by supporting "… the 'strong educational as well as social and moral grounds' for students learning together in the mainstream" and by declaring "…inclusion as the 'keystone' of its education policy" (Rustemier 2002, chap. 2). In Denmark, *the spacious school*-concept substituted *the inclusive school*-concept by around 2000. However, the new concept still encompasses the original ambiguity of the Salamanca Statement (Holmgaard, 2004). Therefore, it is difficult to distinguish between interpretations of inclusion in the Danish discourse. In some contexts inclusion means the same as in the CSIE definition based on the political-ethical discourse: 'Inclusive education means disabled and non-disabled children and young people learning together in ordinary pre-school provision, schools, colleges and universities, with appropriate networks of support' (Rustemier, 2002). In other contexts, inclusion is part of the economic-pragmatic cost-benefit solution and tends to mean integration. Integrated learners are not included in the political-ethical sense. On the contrary, they do not participate in the shared activities but have a parallel existence within the same space as the other learners (Tetler 2000) or, as is more common, they receive special needs education segregated from the ordinary class (Egelund, 2004).

In the same period, European societies have become increasingly e-permeated and social existence is continuously challenged by a broad variety of internet, Web 2.0 services and mobile solutions. The world economy has become an intertwined, dynamic network based on global scale digitalization. This development has forced international society and international organizations to address the challenges of the emerging network society and to formulate frameworks for the development of future competences and education (Castells 2000 & 2001, G8, OECD). Since the mid-90s, ICT and education have been promoted at EU and national levels through ambitious plans of action and research and development programs along with substantial economic resources. In 1995, the Danish Government formulated an ICT and Education Strategy and began to fund a massive implementation of hardware and digital infrastructure in Danish schools.

Because of the heavy national investment in ICT and education, the results of the OECD PISA study from 2000 created shockwaves in Denmark (Undervisningsministeriet, 2004). The PISA study established that 1 – 1½ million adult Danes did not read well enough to complete a professional training program (PISA, 2000). The government's reaction was to implement the so-called ITMF Project (IT and Media in primary schools) from 2001 to 2004. ITMF merged the idea of inclusion with the idea of using ICT as a lever or change agent

Table 1. Meta discourses

	Political – ethical discourse	Economic – pragmatic discourse
Basic question	What the inclusive school IS	What the inclusive school CAN DO
Ontology	Philosophical and ideal arguments: Human rights, democracy, justice What we OUGHT to do	Arguments resting on empirics and measurability: Effectiveness What is COST-EFFECTIVE to do
Target-group	Minorities of all kinds	Groups with special education needs

for inclusion. Among the 105 projects that were performed at one third of all Danish schools and supported with DKK 340 million, ITMF encompassed projects in which learners with diagnosed reading and writing disabilities were integrated through *the IT backpack.* The IT backpack is a real backpack that contains a laptop PC with e.g. text-to-speech applications; a spell checker, and an OCR scanner. The group of children who received the IT backpack was limited to fourth to seventh grade pupils, that is, the age group that dominates special education efforts in Denmark (Haven & Nielsen, 2004). However, the initiatives focused primarily on cost effective efforts to produce good readers and the IT backpack was introduced as a compensational tool. The IT backpack learners acquired their compensational skills in segregated reading classes, which, in combination with the IT backpack, allowed them to be integrated rather than included.

At the same time, and partly because of the PISA study, the Danish Education Act was changed in 2003. The vision of the inclusive school and the idea of inclusion became central to the Act (Undervisningsministeriet, 2003), but when the ITMF projects were concluded in 2004, the demand for special needs education in Denmark exploded and in spite of the new Act, the cost for special needs education kept on growing. As late as 2005, the Minister of Education stated that 'weak reading skills may constitute the most serious social problem in Denmark' (Undervisningsministeriet 2005). In 2006, the Education Act was changed again, this time stressing the implementation of the inclusive school vision with a direct focus on inclusion. The 2005 Act states that weak learners should remain in and be included in the ordinary classes and that special needs education should be avoided. At present, the IT backpack is implemented in primary schools all over the country but, as described above, the interpretation of *the spacious school* is still ambiguous. Most practitioners speak from the political-ethical position while the government and local decision makers speak from the economic-pragmatic position. The gap between practitioners and decision makers' discourse and the impact on the inclusive practice has been – as described in the following section - an important driver in the initiation and formation of the present case.

CASE DESCRIPTION

The consultants at the participating municipality's Pedagogic Development Centre (PDC) and the manager of the local dyslexia school are all involved in the nationwide IT backpack project. During the implementation of the project, they became gradually aware of the ambiguity in the discourse and saw the mutual incompatibility of the meta-discourses mentioned above. They understood how this ambiguity left the decision makers and the practitioners divided by the gap between the two meta-discourses. They wanted to bridge the gap and focus on the benefits for the individual child without denying the perspective of cost effectiveness. They also realized that the available knowledge of how to actually implement inclusion and how to use ICT as a change agent or lever in the process was scarce. Also, the available knowledge appeared to be prescriptive rather than process oriented or aimed at individual benefits. The PDC group began to ask how inclusion could help ensure that individual children overcome their potential reading and writing difficulties and get the necessary strength (political-ethical perspective) to acquire the key competencies of the future (economic-pragmatic perspective) as defined by the OECD (Rychen & Salganik, 2003). In addition to this, the PDC group believed that young children in the first through third grades with identified potential reading and writing difficulties could benefit from ICT-supported integration. They hypothesized that early intervention with ICT could prevent a negative individual development until the children were old enough to participate in the IT backpack initiative and the available special needs offers starting in fourth grade. Some published research confirms this assumption (Bladt 2006 & 2008). Due to these reflections, the PDC group contacted the Danish School of Education and proposed a joint research and development project. In the following section, the framework of the project is presented.

As the standard methods of visitation are aimed at children who are nearing the end of third grade, the PDC has modified the method in order to identify potential reading and writing difficulties among young children. This method is implemented in two primary schools and the identified children are referred to PIF. ICT as a change agent or lever for inclusion means that inclusion is *done in practice.* Accordingly, we have designed special workshops that challenge both the participants' understanding of what it means to read and write, of reading and writing difficulties, and of ICT in general and specifically as a change agent for inclusion. Both the visitation method and the workshops are subject to iterative modifications throughout the project.

Technology Concerns

As a future-oriented development project, PIF is continuously affected by technological development both in terms of ICT as an artifact and as a multi-dimensional cultural aspect. Consequently, the IT Folder is not an object or thing. In PIF, the IT Folder is perceived as a conceptual model and therefore, the IT Folder is not equivalent to the current tablet PC solution. In other words, although the IT folder has a core definition, its realization is changing and dependent on the technological development and the actual context in which it is realized. According to Connolly's definition (1974, pp. 10-44), *essentially contested concepts,* although they possess a core *notion,* are always relative to the concrete use in a changing and fluid context. We understand the IT Folder as a concept that is continuously fluid and essentially contested. Therefore, the concept can never avoid interpretive, contextual and opinion driven argument about what might be the best *realization* of the shared notion. *Figure 1* displays three successive versions or appearances of the conceptual IT Folder. Two years ago, the IT Folder version 1.0 was an IT Backpack; today, version 2.0 is a tablet PC with a touch screen, a scanner pen, an A4 format OCR scanner and a headset. The next version 3.0 may be a mobile device, e.g. a mobile phone or an iPod, which includes the promising new technology that directly translates digital photos of text into digital speech.

One aim of PIF is to explore how the change and modification of practice and designs for learning may support the IT Folder as *dasein - presence-at-hand* existence - that allows it to function as both inclusive and as a substitutional continuation of the person. In the concrete realization of the project, the PIF philosophy implies the following choices and assumptions regarding the three existential forms:

- *The conceptual model as an artifact:* The target group in PIF is young children who do not profit from version 1.0 of the IT Folder. It is simply too heavy and may attract attention in a negative way as a personal attribute. For the artifact to become *present-at-hand* it must be easy to carry around and use. Therefore, version 2.0 of the IT Folder is small and handy – a tablet pc. The software must meet the users' needs, but as PIF is an entirely new approach, we start from scratch and implement the same software as in the IT backpack. Identification of users' needs and software requirements is part of the action research.
- *The conceptual model as a personal attribute:* For the ICT attribute to become *present-at-hand*, the user must accept it as an integrated continuation of his/her personality. The others – the class, teachers, the parents etc. - must also ascribe positive

Figure 1. The successive versions of the IT folder

connotations to the ICT attribute, its properties and the user. Accordingly, the teachers and other resource persons have to be introduced to the PIF philosophy.

- *The conceptual model as a social actor:* For the ICT social actor to become *present-at-hand,* the practice, that is, the complexity of designs for learning, learning activities, social interaction and the interaction design of the artifact must be thought of and carefully designed in order to create a participative social space for the user of the IT Folder. Therefore, the project must challenge current practice and inspire and develop new practices.

The IT Folder's various forms of existence are interdependent. They can be distinguished as analytical units but they cannot be separated in practice. The PIF philosophy, which understands substitutional ICT and inclusion as *presence-at-hand* thus implies that the main effort lies in the social and pedagogical implementation of ICT in specific contexts and with specific people, rather than in a general implementation of technology as such. Of course, the quality and nature of hardware, software, functionality and organizational IT support are very important. This is demonstrated by the choice of the version 2.0 artifact. However, if ICT is only thought of as an object or a tool – *ready-to-hand* – the transformation of ICT from being a change agent that supports compensation and integration to becoming a change agent for substitution and inclusion cannot occur.

Management and Organizational Concerns

As a consequence of the PIF way of understanding reading and writing and technology, the project rests on the basic assumption that inclusion using ICT is not a product that can be issued by decree; on the contrary, inclusion is a process and is *done in practice*! Therefore, the aim of the PIF philosophy and intervention in practice is to change the ways that participants handle *being different* and how they speak about, perform and *do inclusion*. Accordingly, the PIF research unit (see Figure 3) is the complexity of relations and agency including both human and non-human actors that exist around a child in reading and writing difficulties. That is: the everyday practice;

the physical set-up at the school; the designs for learning; the available tools and resources; and the child's social network (teachers, school friends, parents and resource persons). Additionally, PIF explores how new designs for learning and teaching can meet the full complexity in ways that allow inclusion to become an ongoing and sustainable practice in the municipality's school organization at all levels.

Research into inclusion of learners in reading and writing difficulties is scarce and mainly concentrated on curriculum access and ICT as an instructional tool for learning. There is no previous knowledge or experience to lean on and therefore, PIF is designed as collaborative action research involving the PDC, teachers, children, families, the researcher and the organizational levels in the municipality. The long-term perspective in the project allows for observation of phenomenological representations of emerging interrelation between the three existential forms of ICT (artifact, attribute, social actor) and inclusion and for identifying e.g. possibilities and barriers, the gradual transformation from integration to inclusion; changes in designs for learning; involvement of the children's social environment; and perspectives that are not anticipated. The iterative design of PIF allows everyday practice to benefit from growing insight and from continuous knowledge sharing among the participants throughout the progression of the project.

The project is designed as three steps moving iteratively from the pilot phase towards a large-scale implementation in the municipality after phase 2 (Figure 2).

The pilot was used to develop and test various data collection methods and ways of performing interventions in practice, e.g.:

- The standard visitation method aims at children in late third grade. Thus, PDC had to modify the method to fit younger children.
- ICT as a change agent for inclusion means that inclusion is *done in practice.* Accordingly, we designed special workshops that challenge both the participants' way of speaking about ICT and inclusion, their understanding of reading and writing and reading and writing difficulties as well as their understanding of ICT in general and specifically as a change agent for inclusion.

Both the visitation method and the workshops are subject to iterative modifications throughout the project. The pilot also experimented with organizational forms, e.g. the structural organization of knowledge sharing workshops, in order to initiate and ground the development of sustainable organizational models that anchor implementation and support the establishment of a local culture of knowledge sharing and practice in the municipality. PDC also offers knowledge sharing activities that are addressed at children and their parents in both PIF and the IT Backpack project. Phase

Figure 2. The overall project plan

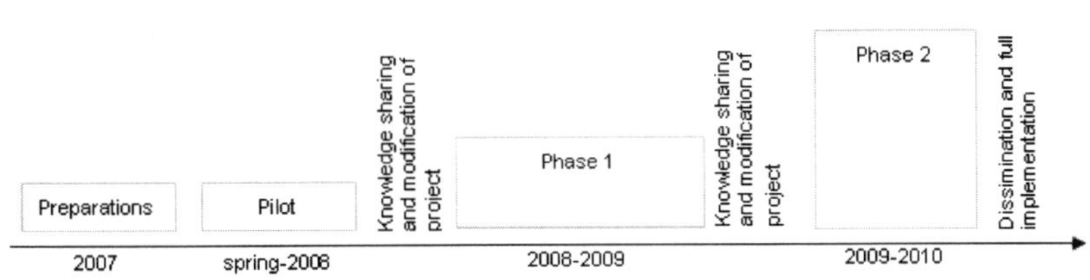

1 iterates the same activities, but teachers who participated in the pilot are now ready to extend their inclusive activities when new children and teachers are admitted to the project. As the project runs until 2010 we cannot predict phase 2, that is, how or to what extent inclusion may be implemented in the municipality. However, the experiences and the knowledge produced in the previous phase constitute a basis for the design of learning recommendations, as well as a generalized description of cases and scenarios.

Each phase begins with a workshop at which the PIF philosophy is introduced to new participants. In specially designed role-play scenarios, participants explore the interrelationship between the three forms of ICT existence using the tablet PC and software. For example, five participants may act out a scenario in which one participant plays a second grade math teacher while the four others play a group of children, one of whom gets to use the IT Folder. The rest of the participants observe the role play from instructed perspectives, focusing on aspects such as body language, consistency of dialogue, how the actor using the IT Folder is included, etc. The role play confronts the participants' understanding of inclusion, reading and writing and technology as well as of reading and writing difficulties as either a personal disability or a contextual matter. The participants' experience of performing the role play and the observers' descriptions of their observations form a basis for critical discussions and reflections and support the emergence of new ideas of how to *do inclusion in practice* and how to deal with *being different*. That is, how to modify everyday practice in order to make inclusion possible. In order to anchor the process locally, PIF organizes knowledge sharing as regular meetings among the project participants. This approach has two functions: 1) the inclusive practice is a real life experiment that integrates ICT into the three forms of existence and involves children that may be vulnerable. Therefore, it is important to share knowledge and to develop a sensitivity and ability to act and adjust practice and negotiate identity on the fly; 2) the meetings are repeated throughout the project and are part of the PDC's organizational long-term strategy, which aims at consolidating knowledge sharing and exploration as a sustainable culture and practice in the municipality after the project has ended.

The object of research in PIF is everyday practice, which embraces the complexity of the interrelated interaction between the single user of the IT Folder artifact, who bears the attributes related to the IT Folder artifact on the one hand,

Figure 3. The model shows the complex interaction of the emerging practice and the action research and how changes within the research unit continuously affect the process

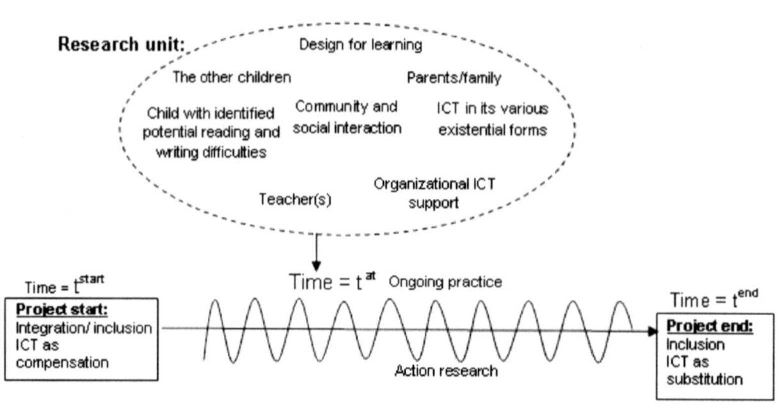

and the *communities of practice* in which the user participates (Wenger, 1998) on the other, together with the IT Folder as a social actor. Thus, data collection focuses on everyday life in the school and at home as well as the on the changes that occur over time in relation to the IT folder attribute, e.g.: the learner's role and self-understanding; the teacher's work; the practice of the communities of practice; the parents' role and understanding of the project; users' ICT demands. The scope of PIF is to capture the complexity and describe the essential conditions that influence the quality of the process of change from integration to inclusion that PIF intends to implement. Additionally, the workshops and the knowledge sharing activities are both part of the data collection and contribute to the organizational dimension in the project.

The data are collected through qualitative, anthropology inspired methods. Participant observation in the school focuses on the single learner in reading difficulties and on practice and interaction in the class. The observation is documented through video recordings and thick description (Geertz 1973). Qualitative interviews with learners, teachers, children and parents focus on the informants' understanding of inclusion as a process and their experience of the inclusive practice. The action research produces data during the workshops where the PIF philosophy is introduced and during the knowledge sharing meetings. But action research also means that the researcher interferes in the everyday practice during visits to the classes. Thus, the qualitative data collection and the action research are not separate but integrated research activities, both contributing to the continuing dialogue and development of the project.

CURRENT CHALLENGES FACING THE ORGANIZATION

Since the project is running until 2010 and only the data from the pilot phase have been subjected to deep analysis, the following section presents some of the emerging challenges that face the project itself as well as muncipalities trying to implement ICT supported inclusion in a sustainable way.

The Visitation Method

In the pilot phase, eight children were visited from the two schools and of these, six continued into Phase 1 (Table 2). Two girls from 3 b in school 2 left the project. The new visitation for phase 1 identified five new children who were taken into the project. The test is performed during the spring and the intervention takes place in the following grade. Therefore, the children are tested in first and second grade and are taken into the project and followed by the researcher during the second and third grade.

The visitation process is a challenge for PIF for several reasons. In Denmark, nobody has ever before tried to diagnose children younger than the end of third grade for potential reading- and writing difficulties, and during the pilot, the test teachers used the official test method. The idea of the early test is that potential reading and writing difficulties may be exactly that – *potential*. This

Table 2. Visitation

	School 1		School 2	
pilot	1 Boy – 3 a 1 Girl – 3 b		4 boys – 2 a 2 girls – 3 b	
Phase 1	1 Boy – 4 a 1 Girl – 4 b	1 boy – 2 a 1 girl – 2 a	4 boys – 3 a	1 girl – 1 b 2 boys – 2 b
Phase 2	Visitation starts in april 2009			

means that the difficulties may go away during the course of the project. Therefore, this test is not part of the large and official test and intervention program and accordingly, no psycologist is involved and no official reports are written. However, during the subsequent period in which the children were involved in the project, the test teachers who followed the children in the everyday school practice became aware that the standard method seemed to have severe flaws in relation to young children. They found that other children in the classes who may have benefitted from PIF had slipped though the test without being diagnosed. On the other hand, the two girls in the pilot from 3 b in school 2 turned out to be in less difficulties than the test had diagnosed, and both girls rejected the IT Folder as they found it inconvenient rather than helpful.

The test teachers presented their observations and reflections at a knowledge sharing meeting and during the discussions it became evident that the concept of *potential reading and writing difficulties* and the corresponding phonomenological appeerences are to a large degree socially constructed and therefore weakly structured as opposed to well-structured concepts and phenomena (Feltovich et al., 1996). That is, their meaning is inherently ambiguous and interpretive rather than clear and measurable. Consequently, the meaning of genuinely weakly structured concepts and phenomena is always negotiated and they can never – no matter how much knowledge we may produce and share – become well stuctured. Further, the concept of *potential reading and writing difficulties* is also essentially contested as the interpretation is entirely dependent on the ever-changing context in which it is realized and socially constructed (Connolly, 1974). The ambiguous and fluid nature of these central dimensions in the PIF project and in the everyday school practice produces a major challenge for the actors in terms of finding ways of ongoing negotiation of meaning and dealing with the inherent fluidity of practice (de Laet & Mol, 2000).

Further, the test teachers identified some major differences between testing third graders as opposed to first and second graders. When the children are tested at the end of third grade, they have already developed a repertoire of compensational strategies in order to hide their reading and writing difficulties and try to cope with the school life and they have become really good at faking. A typical strategy is that the child develops the ability to memorize an immense amount of text. They are able to learn a text by heart when others read it aloud and they are able to reproduce the text perfectly without actually reading anything. If the child is asked to read from an abitrary point in the text, they are unable to do so. In fourth grade, the content becomes too complex and the stategy collapses. Additionally, these strategies place a huge cognitive load on the child who begins to fall behind in relation to school subjects such as history, nature and math. When the official test is performed, the children, who are in general able minded, have lost both their self-esteem and the desire to learn because they have fallen short too many times and are seriously left behind in their school subjects. In order to ensure the most accurate diagnosis, the official test is designed to get behind both the compensational strategies and the rejection of cooperation that is the product of the children's low self-esteem. In contrast to children at the end of third grade, the younger children have not yet developed and consolidated these kinds of behavioral patterns and are therefore at risk of being misinterpreted and misdiagnosed by the official test. Another important aspect is that the official test method has been developed to diagnose reading and writing difficulties as a personal disability rather than a contextual situation.

The test teachers, PDC and the reasearcher are currently using the knowledge sharing structure of PIF and the iterative design of the project to develop a deeper understanding of what it means to be in *potential reading and writing difficulties* as well as to produce descriptions of how potential reading and writing difficulties may be operationalized as observable phenomena. This work has a twofold potential. First, it can help develop and refine a test method to identify young children's potential reading and writing difficulties. Second, due to the iterative project design and changing nature of the project, the same activity may help identify important indicators PIF teachers can use to recognize progress in the children's potential reading and writing difficulties

The Interpretation of Reading and Writing Difficulties

Another aspect of the visitation methods that challenges PIF and especially the vision of a long-term sustainable implementation of early test and intervention in the everyday school practice is the differing views on reading and writing difficulties among professionals. Within the community of special needs teachers and experts, the discussion revolves on whether it is acceptable to view reading and writing difficulties as contextional challenges rather than a personal disability. Some experts purely reject the idea of a contextual approach and therefore also reject the notion of *potential* in relation to reading and writing difficulties. At present, there is no consensus in the professional and research communities. The differing views can be described as a struggle between paradigms as described by Latour and Woolgar (1979).

As mentioned above, the current official approach is to deal with *actual* reading and writing difficulties as a disability and to intervene from fourth grade. However, if the contextual approach becomes accepted as a method for dealing with young children's *potential* reading and writing difficulties, then the borderline and the grey zone between *being in a difficult situation* and actually *having a learning disability* must be identified and described. In contrast, the official approach has no need to deal with a gray zone as everybody with reading and writing difficulties is on the special needs and intervention side of the line. The ongoing struggle between the reading-writing paradigms may produce a serious challenge to the project. The risk of unreflecting dissemination and implementation of the PIF philosophy and the PIF approach is that children, who – from the contextual approach perspective – are in the grey zone, may become exposed to the ambiguity of the political-ethical and the economic-pragmatic meta-discourses. The boy and the girl from school 1 who started in the PIF pilot are cases that exemplify this challenge. They are now at the end of third grade and are both diagnosed as dyslexics and have been transferred to the dyslexic school.

Even though both children have been included in many aspects of the learning activities in their classes during the project, their teachers and the special needs teachers agree that their difficulties are severe and have to be described as a disability that has to be compensated for rather than substituted. Thus, the teachers speak from the political-ethical position and accept that *potential* means that the children are in the grey zone and that it takes time to diagnose whether the *potential difficulties* will go away or not. They conclude that PIF has been a success for these children as they have a repertoire of appropriate strategies and their self-esteem intact when they come to the dyslexic school. The girl comes from a Pakistani and Urdu speaking immigrant background. Instead of being seen as one more integration problem, her problems in reading and writing Danish have been acknowledged as a struggle to learn and she is now successfully identified as a dyslexic Danish girl with an immigrant background. In the meantime, her spoken Danish has improved considerably as she uses the synthetic speech in the IT Folder to listen to and practice Danish words. The teachers expect that she will return to the normal class after one or two years. The boy comes from a challenging divorce background and he has been understimulated during his early childhood. When he started school he had almost no spoken language and at the beginning of the project he spoke in single words and only when he was directly addressed. Now, he "reads" by having digital text read aloud at five times the normal speed and he is included in the everyday learning activities. He asks questions about how to interpret abstract concepts and likes to play with words and is good with numbers and math. However, he cannot read at all and he needs support to keep on fighting. The teachers expect that he will have to stay in the dyslexic school for the rest of his time in primary school. Both children were confident and eager to learn when the started at the dyslexic school. As the boy says: "I can't wait to begin at the dyslexic school because, you know, I can't read."

The municipal authorities view these children and the project from the economic-pragmatic position and do not acknowledge the gray zone. They interpret the project with regard to the new Danish Education Act, which stresses the importance of inclusion, but only as intervention that aims at inclusion here and now and with the aim of reducing the cost for special needs education. Therefore, as the municipality has supported the project with substantial founding, they expected a ROI (return of investment) in terms of reduced costs due to a decrease in the number of children transferred to the dyslexic school. From this position, they saw the transfer of the two children to the dyslexic school as a PIF failure. Since the children had been given an IT Folder and the teachers were trained to cope with modifications of the everyday practice, why, they asked, had these children not learned to read and write? Why had they not been cured of their reading and writing difficulties? And why were they not included?

Consequently, the original ambiguity of the Salamanca Statement becomes visible in a concrete case along with the scientific struggle between the reading-writing paradigms. The challenge is twofold: 1) How to balance the political–ethical analysis of personal growth and advantage with the economic-pragmatic cost benefit analysis of ROI; and 2) How to persuade authorities that it is relevant to accept both the notion of *potential* reading and writing difficulties and the notion of the *grey zone*. Of course, if the children are transferred to the dyslexic school after participating in PIF, the immediate inclusion has not succeeded. As a cost benefit calculation, this is a short-term evaluation. On the other hand, if these children stay in the normal class, the risk is high that inclusion may turn inside out and become severe and damaging social exclusion as the children will face increasingly higher cognitive stress and demands in order to stay included. Therefore a possible arena where the opposing paradigms, interpretations and discourses may meet could be in the convergence of ROI and a long-term evaluation of these children's chances of becoming included and productive citizens when they grow up.

The Interpretation of Reading and Writing

The professionals have differing opinions of what it means to read and write. The teachers in the project have modified their views and accept that reading letters and listening may be equally acceptable ways of acquiring knowledge, just as writing and constructing words with the help of digital tools may be equally acceptable ways of producing text. However, parts of the professional community as well as the official Danish evaluation system do not accept alternatives to text when it comes to mediating a subject. The children may produce alternative mediations during the learning activities, but when it comes to the official summative evaluations they are not allowed to use any substitutional ICT.

In the project we found that the children produced alternative material that demonstrates an acceptable level of understanding of subject matters. For example, most of the children have passed formative reading and writing tests using their IT folder and have produced results that place them in the middle to upper half of their classes. Without the IT folder, most of them drop to the lowest level. This is a clear indicator that the IT folder functions as intended. Another example comes from the subject of religion in second grade at school 1 (PIF, phase 1). The theme was the parable of the Good Samaritan and the class was introduced to the parable by the teacher. After the introduction, the class and the teacher talked about the meaning of the parable and produced drawings. Then the class went to the computer room where the children's task was to produce an individual PhotoStory about what it would mean to act like the Good Samaritan if there were a physically disabled child – e.g. in a wheelchair – in the class. PhotoStory is a freeware application from Microsoft. PhotoStory has an accessible and intuitive interface and the application is designed to produce "movies" out of still images, speech and text. The children, a boy and a girl, had their story outline sketched as a cartoon on paper. They sat together discussing images they had found on Google image search. The next step was to arrange the images in a sequence in PhotoStory and write sentences to tell the story. They used their word construction tool to produce small and rather primitive sentences. Finally, both children used the sound feature in PhotoStory and recorded their narrative in spoken words. They did not reproduce the written text but spoke in long, complex and dramatized sentences to each image. Both stories demonstrated that the core aspects of the subject matter were present and that the children were able to reflect on the parable in relation to a given scenario.

Thus, when children are allowed to substitute written text with an alternative means of expression, they may demonstrate a subject understanding at the same level as the other children in the class. The challenge is to persuade the authorities that in some cases, this is acceptable also when it comes to the official summative evaluations.

How to Catch the Small Signs that may Lead to Major Changes

As mentioned earlier, one result of the pilot phase is the emerging awareness of the necessity of being able to recognize and identify any progress in the children's *potential reading and writing difficulties*. This represents a major challenge to the PIF philsophy in terms of sustainability and dissemination. The teachers are trained to identify progress in terms of indicators that correspond with the cognitive development as defined by e.g. Jean Piaget and Jerome Bruner, together with the subject-related descriptions of the learning objectives that are fixed by the Education Act for primary schools. However, the children in PIF are *in* reading and writing difficulties that impact on their subject-related learning process. Therefore, one cannot expect that the first observable indicators are subject-related in the traditional sense as changes that can be measured through formative or summative evaluation.

Research observations of the classes have shown that the changes may be subtle and that they are closely related to the self-protecting behavior that most of the PIF children are already practicing. This means that it is hard to define what exactly to look for and it is impossible to produce a list of typical observations. The indicators are closely related to the context and to the individual child and the challenge is how to inspire teachers to develop a sensitivity towards the subtle and non-subject-related indicators. Further, these small signs are both the fragile seeds that the teacher may "cultivate" in order to support the child's move towards inclusion and learning and at the same time, the incidents that can severely demotivate the child if they are misinterpreted or ignored. One way to approach this challenge is to articulate the finding of indicators as a sensitivity towards fields of awareness that relate to the individual child. Gregory Bateson claimed that what matters in research and observation is the difference

(Bateson 1991, s. 188). PIF uses Bateson's claim as it is extended by Levinsen (2005):

What matters is the difference that makes a difference in a time perspective

As the research is preliminary, some specific cases may illustrate the meaning *of fields of awareness* and *sensitivity towards differences that makes a difference* over time.

The boy from school 1 who was transferred to the dyslexic school did three things that the teachers did not grasp as important when they happened. But as the incidents were discussed at the knowledge sharing meeting, the teachers acknowledged the importance of these incidents as indicators of progress. The first incident appeared when the-boy-without-a-language explained to the researcher how to access homepages with online games and how to play the games. Apparently, he possessed a rather complex language when he felt on safe ground. He knew about the games and he knew he was good at using the computer. Therefore, he felt superior and had no barriers to overcome. It had never occurred to any of the teachers to talk with him about something that he found relevant and soon he began to help his classmates when they had problems with the computers, logins, navigation etc. The second incident appeared one day when he worked in a group where they had to sort words into categories. He asked: "Is 'newspaper' a concept or an object?". This was the first time ever he took an initiative in a learning process. The third time, he talked with the teacher about a story he had "read" by listening to the synthetic voice. In the story, the main character could not sleep at night. During the conversation the boy elaborated and concluded that the main character's concrete feeling is an instance of the general condition *fear of darkness*. That is, he demonstrates that he is able to distinguish between a concrete phenomenon and the abstract notion of a concept even though he cannot read or write anything.

Another interesting case is the girl in second grade in school 1 (PIF phase 1). The class is working on syllables and the assignment is to figure out the number of syllables in various words. The girl – as usual – uses her IT Folder and listens to the words, mumbles to herself and counts on her fingers. She gets *mo-bil-te-le-fon* (mobile phone) right and writes 5. However, two words in the assignment have only one syllable and here the results are as follows (Table 3):

The teacher sees the error and wants to correct and explain to the girl that *bjerg* only has one syllable. The researcher wonders how the difference came about as the girl obviously understands the principle. The girl is a listener and what happens is that she first listens to the synthetic voice and then repeats the words for herself. In Danish the word *skridt* is a short and unmistakably one-syllable sound and she writes "1". In contrast, the word *bjerg* may be pronounced as *bje-erg,* which produces two syllables for the listener. Now, the girl remembers that in Danish there is a rule saying that syllables are often marked after a vocal, resulting in *bje-e-rg*. This chain of reflection leads her to the reasonable conclusion that *bjerg* is a three-syllable word. In this situation, the teacher's interpretation could easily have demotivated the girl. When the teacher realizes that the girl's reasoning makes perfect sense for a listener, she also sees how she can encourage the girl. In this case, the girl would fail in both a formative and a summative test, but as an individual who relies on listening, she actually solves the assignment correctly.

The above-mentioned cases are examples drawn from a large and as yet unpublished body of research observations that represent *differences that*

Table 3. Word and syllables

The word	How many syllables
Bjerg (mountain):	3
Skridt (step):	1

makes a difference. However, based on the initial results from PIF, we recommend that PDC implement a strategy where the workshops that prepare practitioners and resource persons for the inclusive practice are carefully followed and documented in order to allow for a meta-reflective perspective that produces the necessary insight to continuously develop and refine the workshop design and activities in relation to the actual and ever-changing practice in schools. This is important as teachers and other resource persons need to develop their sensitivity towards the subtle indicators of emerging progress in the children's *potential reading and writing difficulties*. Further, we recommend that the test teachers are supported in their experiments with and development of the test method. The PDC has already implemented an organizational model that supports and sustains knowledge-sharing practice among the various layers in the municipal organization. However, based on our experiences of the gap between decision makers' and practitioners' discourses on inclusion, we recommend that the PDC implement a strategy that encourages decision makers and practitioners to negotiate the meaning of inclusion and gradually produce a mutual understanding of inclusion and inclusive practice. We find that this recommendation is crucial for the success of any other initiative in the process, in order to move economic and organizational efforts towards everyday practice rather than focussing solely on technological issues.

REFERENCES

Bateson, G. (1991). A Sacred Unity. In Donaldson (Ed.), Further Steps to an Ecology of Mind. HarperCollins Publishers.

Bladt, K. (2006). It-støttet undervisning udvikler børns selvværd og fremmer inklusion [ICT supported teaching develops childrens self esteem and promote inclusion]. *Kognition &Pædagogik*, *61*(16), 56–69.

Bladt, K. (2008). It-støttet undervisning fremmer ligeværdig deltagelse [ICT supported education promotes equal participation]. *Viden om læsning, 3*, 16-19.

Castells, M. (2000). Materials for an exploratory theory of the network society. *The British Journal of Sociology*, *51*(1), 5–24. doi:10.1080/000713100358408

Castells, M. (2001). The Internet Galaxy: Reflections on the Internet, Business and Society. London: Oxford University Press.

Connolly, W. E. (1974). Essentially Contested Concepts in Politics. In W.E. Connolly (Ed.), The Terms of Political Discourse (pp. 10-44). Lexington, MA: Heath.

Dyson, A. (1999). Inclusion and Inclusions: Theories and discourses in inclusive education. In H. Daniels & P. Garner (1999), World yearbook of education 1999: Inclusive education (pp. 36-54). London: Kogan Page.

Egelund, N. (2004). Specialpædagogisk praksis – indspil og udspil (Special needs pedagogic practice). København: Danmarks Pædagogiske Universitets Forlag.

Feltovich, P. J., Spiro, R. J., Coulson, R. L., & Feltovich, J. (1996). Collaboration Within and Among Minds: Mastering Complexity, Individually and in Groups. In T. Koschmann (Ed.), CSCL: Theory and practice of an emerging paradigm (pp. 25-44). Mahwah, NJ: Lawrence Erlbaum Associates, Publishers.

Florian, F., & Hegarty, J. (2004). ICT and Special Educational Needs. UK: Mcgraw-Hill Education, Open University Press.

Geertz, C. (1973). The Interpretation of Cultures. NY: Basic books.

Haven, D., & Nielsen, H. (2004). *Ordblindhed - Rapport over spørgeskemaundersøgelsen: Kommunale tilbud til ordblinde elever* [Dyslexia – Report from the survey: municipal offers to dyslexic students]. Dansk Videnscenter for Ordblindhed, Virum 2004. Retrieved January 20, 2009, from http://www.dvo.dk/fileadmin/lavervi/publik/pprrapport/index.html

Heidegger, M. (1996). Being and Time. (J. Stambaugh trans.). Albany, NY: State University of New York Press.

Holmgaard, A. (2004). Hvordan blev inklusion til rummelighed? – en analyse af rummelighedsbegrebets oprindelse (How inclusion became spaciousness). *Psykologisk Paedagogisk Rådgivning*, 2.

Kotsik, B., & Tokareva, N. (2007). UNESCO IITE Contribution to e-Inclusion Policy Development for Education of Students with Disabilities. In *The first International Conference on ICT & Accessibility,* Hammamet, Tunesia. Retrieved January 20, 2009, from http://www.esstt.rnu.tn/utic/tica2007/index96b6.html?pId=5

de Laet, M., & Mol, A. (2000). The Zimbabwe Bush Pump: Mechanics of a Fluid Technology. *Social Studies of Science*, *30*(2), 225–263. doi:10.1177/030631200030002002

Latour, B., & Woolgar, S. (1979). Laboratory Life: the Social Construction of Scientific Facts. Los Angeles, CA: Sage.

Levinsen, K. (2005). Virtuel Uddannelsespraksis. Master i IKT og Læring - et casestudie i hvordan proaktiv proceshåndtering kan forbedre praksis i virtuelle læringsmiljøer [Virtual educational practice. Master in ICT and Learning – a case study of how proactive process management may improve practice in virtual learning environments]. Copenhagen: Samfundslitteratur.

Prensky, M. (2001). Digital Natives, Digital Immigrants. *On the Horizon, 9*(5). Lincoln, NE: NCB University Press.

Programme for International Student Assessment. (2000). Retrieved January 20, 2009, from http://www.sfi.dk/sw198.asp

Rogers, E. M. (1995). Diffusion of Innovations. New York: The Free Press.

Rustemier, S. (2002). *Inclusion Information Guide.* Retrieved January 20, 2009, from http://inclusion.uwe.ac.uk/csie/studnts02.htm

Rychen, D., & Salganik, L. (2003). Key Competencies for a Successful Life and Well-Functioning Society. Cambridge, MA: Hogrefe & Huber.

Sharp, H., Rogers, Y., & Preece, J. (2007). Interaction Design: Beyond Human-Computer Interaction. Chichester, UK: John Wiley & Sons Ltd.

Sheehy, K. (2005). ICT and Special Educational Needs: a Tool for Inclusion. *British Journal of Learning Disabilities*, *33*(4), 206–207. doi:10.1111/j.1468-3156.2005.00366.x

Statement, S. (1994). Retrieved January 20, 2009, from http://www.inclusion.com/artsalamanca.html

Tetler, S. (2000). Den inkluderende skole – fra vision til virkelighed (The inklusive school – from vision to realization). København, Danmark: Nordisk Forlag A/S.

Undervisningsministeriet. (2003). *Skolens rummelighed - fra idé til handling* [The spacious school – from idea to action]. Retrieved January 20, 2009, from http://pub.uvm.dk/2003/rummelighed/

Undervisningsministeriet. (2004). OECD-rapport om grundskolen i Danmark – 2004. [OECD-Report on the primary school in Denmark]. *Uddannelses-styrelsens temahæfteserie,* 5. Retrieved January 20, 2009, from http://pub.uvm.dk/2004/oecd/

Undervisningsministeriet. (2005). *National handlingsplan for læsning* [National plan of action for reading]. Retrieved January 20, 2009, from http://www.uvm.dk/05/documents/national_handlingsplan.pdf

Wenger, E. (1998). Communities of practice - Learning, meaning, and identity. Cambridge, UK: Cambridge University Press.

ADDITIONAL READING

Abbott, C. (2007). E-inclusion: Learning Difficulties and Digital Technologies, REPORT 15: FUTURELAB SERIES, Kings College, London.

Florian, L., & Hegarty, J. (Eds.). (2004). ICT and Special Educational Needs: a Tool for Inclusion. Maidenhead: Open University Press.

Goodison, T. A. (2002). Learning with ICT at primary level: pupils' perceptions. *Journal of Computer Assisted Learning, 18*, 282–295. doi:10.1046/j.0266-4909.2002.00240.x

Jacobson C., Heindorff H., & Björn, M. (2007). *ICT in Teaching.* WR06 Report of CallDysc Project: Växjö University.

Management, R. (2006). *E-learning Nordic 2006.* Retrieved from:http://www.skolutveckling.se/it_i_skolan/undersokningar_rapporter/enordic2006/

Silvernail. (2004). *The impact of Maine's One-to-One Laptop Program on Middle School Teachers and Students.* University of Southern Maine. Retrieved from http://www.usm.maine.edu/cepare/Reports/MLTI_Report1.pdf

Swedish National Agency for School Improvement. (2008). *Effective use of ICT in schools Analysis of international research. Retrieved from*http://www.skolutveckling.se

KEY TERMS AND DEFINITIONS

Inclusive Education: It means disabled and non-disabled children and young people learning together in ordinary pre-school provision, schools, colleges and universities, with appropriate networks of support' (Rustemier, 2002).

Compensational ICT: It is a tool that is designed to reduce the consequences of a handicap and compensate for the person's disability (Florian & Hegarty 2004, Sheehy 2005) i.e. it *changes the user.*

Substitutional ICT: Substitutional ICT *changes the practice and the context* and not the user.

IT Backpack: It is a real backpack that contains a laptop PC with e.g. text-to-speech applications; a spell checker, and an OCR scanner. Today, version 2.0 is a tablet PC with a touch screen, a scanner pen, an A4 format OCR scanner and a headset. The next version 3.0 may be a mobile device, e.g. a mobile phone or an iPod, which includes the promising new technology that directly translates digital photos of text into digital speech.

Chapter 4
Ecologies of Learning:
Efficacious Learning and ICT Pedagogical and Technological Adaptability

Don Krug
University of British Columbia, Canada

Jenny Arntzen
University of British Columbia, Canada

ABSTRACT

In this chapter the authors present research that investigated the formation of ICT ecologies of learning in a Canadian teacher education program. The growth and development of ICT in Canada has placed tremendous responsibility on educators to be informed about not only acquiring ICT skills and knowledge (ICT literacies) but, more importantly, to understand the consequences of emerging social, technological, economic, and political ICT issues that hinder and/or enhance student learning, health, and knowledge. The authors' research project looked critically at Canadian educational contexts and how teacher candidates (TCs) are prepared to use ICT when entering the teaching profession. The authors highlight how a group of eight teacher candidate researchers (TCRs) engaged in efficacious learning.

ORGANIZATION BACKGROUND

The proliferation of Information and Communication Technologies (ICT) is challenging how and when learning occurs as well as the ways we live and think (Schofield, 1995; Turkle, 1996; Tapscott, 1998; Dexter, Anderson & Becker, 1999). ICT encompasses many different forms of digital media and technologies. For the purposes of this research, our focus was on educational hardware and software for facilitating pedagogical processes of communication, curriculum and research. Educators in Canada face emerging social, technological, economic, and political (STEP) issues as digital technologies infuse everyday experiences and impact people's abilities to construct meaningful and relevant understandings of the world in which we live (Anderson, 2000: Mayer, 2002, 2003: Spiro, et al., 1991). We view ICT ecologies of learning as conceptual positions that acknowledge that all contextual issues are multi-dimensionally and multi-directionally articulated by experiences, human socially interested agency, and environmental conditions. Research shows that ICT has increased the complexity of people's

DOI: 10.4018/978-1-61520-909-5.ch004

ways of living (culture), saturating experiences with profound challenges of pedagogical and technological adaptability (Foucault, 1982; Hall, 1981; Kirsh, 2000). In this chapter, we provide an overview of Canadian technology enabled learning within educational organizations in British Columbia (BC). We bring forward some of the core issues of ICT advancement in Canada. The growth and development of ICT in Canada has placed tremendous responsibility on educators to be informed about not only acquiring ICT skills and knowledge (ICT literacies) but, more importantly, to understand the consequences of emerging social, technological, economic, and political ICT issues on school cultures (Fullan, 1993; Schofield, 1995) that affect student learning, health, and knowledge (Maeroff, 2003).

SETTING THE STAGE

Our research project looked critically at Canadian educational contexts and how teacher candidates (TCs) prepared to use ICT when entering the teaching profession. We have completed the second-year of a three-year study that focused on how one cohort of thirty-six elementary TCs accepted, resisted or opposed using ICT during their teacher education program (TEP) at the University of British Columbia (UBC). We wanted to know if TCs could study their own evolving pedagogical self-efficacy, as a means to increase their ICT knowledge and leadership in educational situations (Lorsbach & Jinks, 1999). According to Bandura (1995) self-efficacy is "the belief in one's capabilities to organize and execute the courses of action required to manage prospective situations" (1995, p. 2). We hypothesized that pedagogical self-efficacy might enable TCs to make informed decisions about ICT pedagogical and technological adaptability, as well as eventually prepare K-7 students for an ever-changing knowledge-based society.

In 1994 Ross reviewed 88 studies of teacher efficacy in pre-college settings and identified potential connections with a teachers' sense of efficacy and their practices. Ross stated that teachers with a strong sense of efficacy are more likely to (1) learn and use new approaches and strategies for teaching, (2) use management techniques that enhance student autonomy, (3) provide special assistance to low achieving students, (4) build students' self-perceptions of their academic skills, (5) set attainable goals, and (6) persist in the face of student failure. There are several studies that examined teacher efficacy, however we did not assume that the findings from one study would transfer into our situation.

In this chapter, we briefly describe articulation(s) as a collaborative and reflexive research counter-methodology. We used articulation(s) to examine ICT, cultural, and educational relationships and to unsettle taken-for-granted assumptions, perspectives, and practices within the dynamic forces of change in the TEP at UBC. We follow with a discussion of Canadian (federal) and British Columbia (provincial) educational agencies in relation to social accessibility, economic viability, political engagement, and technological adaptability. Our research case is about the formation of ecologies of learning and ICT pedagogical and technological adaptability. We highlight how a group of eight teacher candidate researchers (TCRs) engaged in efficacious learning. Conceptual cycles of critical inquiry were introduced to the TCRs to help mediate the ICT challenges facing educators in their day-to-day teaching in BC. We provided professional education for the TCRs to enhance their ICT skills and confidence. We wanted to enable them to challenge their own, and other teacher's, conceptual and practical use of ICT within the contextual conditions of educational ICT policies. These opportunities were offered over and above the instruction they received in the UBC teacher education program. In our research we found that critical inquiry supported their examination of connections between their teaching and learning experiences (pedagogy) and how technological adaptability affected conditions associated with educational environments. In the conclusion characteristics of efficacious learning are articulated with examples drawn from our examination of the TCRs experiences in the TEP at UBC.

CASE DESCRIPTION: ARTICULATIONS

Before introducing the case study, it is important to have a sense of how, and why, we drew together several seemingly diverse philosophies, theories, and concepts through a counter methodology of articulation(s). Articulation(s) are acts of connecting that can make a unity of two or more different elements, under certain forces of human agency and contextual conditions. They are linkages, which are not necessary, determined, absolute, or essential for all time. As researchers, we wanted the TCRs to ask, "Under what circumstances can or should educational connections be forged or made with ICT?" With the TCRs, we talked about critical inquiry as a practical process of learning about diverse philosophies, theories, and concepts as applied to everyday life experiences both in formal and informal educational settings. We also relied on poststructural interpretations of language to investigate intersecting dimensions of philosophies, i.e., phenomenology and constructivism, as well as constructed unities we identified from theories within cognitive science, systems theory, complexity studies, and cultural studies.

The eight TCRs (5 male, 3 female) who volunteered to participate in the research project underwent a series of introductory technology and preparatory inquiry sessions over the course of their TEP (see Figure 1). These experiences were based on critical inquiry as an *assemblage* (Deleuze & Guattari, 1987) of efficacious learning.

Research activities began in the first term of the first year with graduate research assistants (GRAs) joining the TCs in their program for in-class observations of TEP instructors' use of ICT. In the second term of the first year, in consultation with the TCs two Faculty Advisors, we taught technology sessions to the whole cohort. These were 30 – 40 minute bi-weekly sessions in a computer lab. The focus of these technology sessions was "global citizenship." The TCs learned to use multi-media applications, Internet

Figure 1. Data collection timeline (Krug & Arntzen 2009)

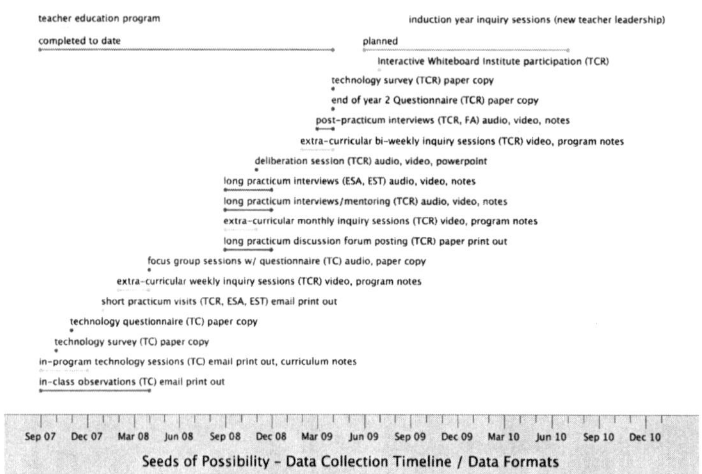

resources, and an online presentation application (wiki). Their projects were available for teaching later in the program, as an online resource, during the long practicum the following fall. In the process of participating, the TCs acquired ICT and pedagogical literacies. The sessions culminated with group presentations on their topics e.g. e-waste, cyber bullying, Internet safety, etc. (GRA, Notes 1).

At the conclusion of the first term, an invitation was extended to the entire TC cohort to become voluntary co-researchers. Once the TCRs were accepted as research participants, they were issued a laptop computer, LCD projector, and digital video camera. The laptops were provisioned with educational software and a class set of digital cameras and a secure server with social networking software was also available.

We met regularly as a group to discuss teaching and learning with ICT. These inquiry sessions prepared the TCRs to teach using ICT during their long practicum. They also provided TCRs with ICT literacies they needed to contribute to the research: 1) design and produce a lesson using ICT; 2) video record themselves teaching; 3) manage multiple files; 4) edit their teaching video; 5) produce an annotated presentation; 6) present their teaching video and 7) engage in critical discourse about its content. Surveys, video, interviews, photographs, and documents were collected of their participation and learning through these experiences.

CURRENT CHALLENGES FACING THE ORGANIZATION: A CANADIAN CONTEXT

In our discussion of the Canadian contexts of ICT in education with the TCRs, we looked generally at social accessibility, technological adaptability, economic validity, and political engagement. Canada does not have a federal governing organization for education. Each province and territory has exclusive jurisdiction over education. Leadership for national interests across public and private education is provided through a number of organizations. The Council of Ministers of Education, Canada (CMEC) is an intergovernmental body founded in 1967 by Ministers of Education. Ministers consult and act on matters of mutual interest, but the CMEC does not have a mandate to regulate federal or provincial educational policy. In 2008 the CMEC issued a joint declaration, "Learn Canada 2020". This report provided a framework for Canadian provinces and territories to enhance Canada's educational systems, learning opportunities, and overall education outcomes. Learn Canada 2020 called for a well-educated population be linked with: 1) a vibrant knowledge-based economy in the 21st century; 2) a socially progressive, sustainable society; and 3) enhanced personal growth opportunities for all Canadians. Conspicuously absent was any mention of ICT in the report.

The Canadian Teachers' Federation (CTF) is the national labor organization that defends the rights of teachers and advocates for a strong public education system by initiating dialogue in Canada and influencing public policy issues in education. In 2003 Industry Canada and the Canadian Teacher Federation (CTF), sponsored *An Investigation of the Integration of Information and Communication Technology into Canadian Schools and Classrooms: Feasibility Study, Phase 1*. They reported that while more teachers use ICT, public elementary and secondary teachers expressed a sense of disconnect, a lack of ICT skill and confidence, no participation in ICT decisions, and no shared vision of the future of education. The study found teachers accepted using ICT in their classes and lessons and a majority perceived computers as important. A majority of teachers reported using the Internet and instructional CD-ROMS in their classes and up to half of them used desktop publishing, spreadsheets, computer games and simulations, and presentation software.

Regionally, each provincial and territorial government agency enacts ICT curricula and policy through its own Ministry of Education (Alberta, British Columbia, Manitoba, New Brunswick, Newfoundland and Labrador, Ontario, Saskatchewan), Department of Education (Nova Scotia, Nunavut, Prince Edward Island), Department of Education, Culture and Employment (Northwest Territories, Yukon), or Ministère de l'Éducation, du Loisir et du Sport (Quebec). The BC Ministry of Education developed BC Performance Standards for voluntary use in BC schools. ICT was listed as a key area of learning along with reading, writing, numeracy, and social responsibility. They state, "Information and Communications Technology is an essential component of schooling today. In our knowledge-based society, ICT is ubiquitous. Growing dependence on technology in all aspects of society emphasizes the importance of ensuring that students develop information literacy skills and understandings they need to live and work in an ever-changing environment" ("Information and communications technology integration performance standards," 2009). The BC ICTI Performance Standards are organized around four aspects of how students can use ICT to collect, organize, analyze and interpret, and present information. The Ministry of Education writes, "The emphasis is not on information sources or software applications associated with specific technologies but on the student's representation of their learning and the steps they used to construct their knowledge" ("Aspects of information and communications technology integration," 2009).

The BC College of Teachers is the professional self-regulatory body for more than 70,000 licensed educators in British Columbia. The BCCT "set and enforce standards for professional educators, assess applicants to the profession, and issue teaching certificates" ("Welcome to the BC College of Teachers," 2009). The BC Confederation of Parent Advisory Councils (BCCPAC) represents the collective activities of Parent Advisory Councils (PAC) operating at the school level, and District Parent Advisory Councils (DPAC) who represent PACs at the district level. BCCPAC is a charitable non-profit organization that advocates at the provincial level on behalf of the PACs and DPACs. These are just a few of the more prominent educational organizations in the province that deal directly or indirectly with ICT and education.

ICT Social Accessibility

ICT social accessibility in Canada continues to be based primarily on economic, geographic, and social (ethnic) factors. Canada is listed in the 2009 International Telecommunication Union's, "Measuring the Information Society: ICT Development Index" as having an economy that includes a high level of ICT access and use with a population with high ICT skills. In British Columbia, rural communities have the lowest connectivity, while 92% of the province has access to broadband networks. The provincial government recently announced over $30 million support for broadband connectivity and capacity building to help bridge the digital divide for First Nations communities (Premiers Technology Council Report, 2009, p. 7). A survey by the Canadian Internet Project indicates that BC has the highest rate of high-speed connectivity in Canada.

With regards to distributive learning, the Virtual School Society (VSS) is an independent, non-profit entity founded in 2006 to enhance the use of distributive learning in British Columbia. This group helped to modify BC provincial legislation so students can use technology to individualize their education programs and to provide equitable access to education for students with restricted options. Virtual education enrollment has grown with nearly 50,000 students taking online courses in 2007/08. To facilitate broader accessibility, the BC Ministry of Education established the British Columbia Enterprise Student Information System (BCeSIS) that allows educators to access information about students.

Economic Viability

Canada is one of 33 economies with a high degree of ICT investment, and together accounted for 15 per cent of the world's population in 2007, which included twenty-one European countries, ten Asia & Pacific economies, as well as Canada, and the United States (Premiers Technology Council Report 2009 p. 46). BC's technology sectors include ICT, New Media and Life Sciences that comprise over 7,000 companies, $12 billion in revenues, and employ over 63,000 people. The BC government has added financial support in research, research facilities, and graduate schools. BC had the highest ICT growth in Canada between 1997 and 2004, in employment, R&D spending, and software and computer services revenue. Between 2004 and 2007, Industry revenue topped $1 billion.

Despite these statistics, the technological infrastructure of BC educational institutions, K-12 and post-secondary institutions are struggling to provide adequate hardware, software, human infrastructure and professional development. BC PACs play a critical role in provisioning schools with digital technology. These parent groups are eligible to apply for grant funding to augment core curriculum. PACs are purchasing computers, for self-contained and mobile labs, along with interactive whiteboards and digital cameras because district funding to individual schools is insufficient to meet the need.

Political Engagement

The BC government reports (Premiers Technology Council Report 2009) investing to ensure that the education system has excellent infrastructure that provides the best technologies for K-12 education, post secondary education and associated research. The report suggested that ideally technology infrastructure should:

- Provide a platform for research collaboration in universities;
- Support and enhance the delivery of education services;
- Provide options for students to receive educational services that meet learning styles and access requirements; and
- Enhance opportunities for teachers to participate in professional development.

In Canada, virtual education (VE) or e-learning provides Canadians the flexibility to learn at their own pace at any age and in almost any location. VE has been a contentious issue in BC as school boards draw funding from the Ministry of Education for student enrollment. But participation in virtual education reduces physical and geographical barriers and also allows for more educational options to learners with disabilities and those living in remote areas. The proportion of VE courses delivered online in Canada is one of the highest among countries; however, research suggests that Canadian post-secondary institutions have been slower than those in many other countries to incorporate significant online components into their programs (Paris, 2005).

Technological Adaptability

Since personal computers were introduced in schools in the mid 1970s, educational agencies and faculty members have invested significant resources in developing the means for students to use ICT as an integral part of learning. Initially the focus was on the acquisition of clusters of stand-alone personal computers to provide access and instruction for students in specialized facilities or computer labs. As the power of these digital machines grew rapidly, educators were caught up in efforts to upgrade and replace equipment that would run new applications. These new applications required increased computer processing speed and memory. During the 1990s, the educational focus shifted to networking computers, first in local area networks for instructional purposes within schools and later to wide area networks to provide connections to the Internet. Most recent efforts are concentrated on increasing the speed or bandwidth of fiber optic cable and wireless networks required to expand communications beyond classrooms and schools, and to provide access to video and audio content required to realizing the full learning potential of the technology. The penetration of ICT throughout the school system means that technological adaptability has become more complex, putting increased pressure on school organizations and operations.

In British Columbia, teacher candidates learn to use ICT through one of nine TEP in the province: Vancouver Island University, Simon Fraser University, Trinity Western University, Thompson Rivers University, University of the Fraser Valley, University of British Columbia, University of Northern British Columbia, University of Victoria, University of British Columbia – Okanagan. Of the nine TEP, none of them have an articulated ICT integration plan or course of study. All TEPs offer only one or two courses in the use of computers in education, and this/these course(s) is/are a requirement at six of the nine institutions. Of the remaining three TEP, one has a one-credit course requirement at the end of the program to digitally represent the BCCT teaching standards as an efolio using Wordpress, and the other two list no ICT requirement or courses in their program information on their website.

At the University of British Columbia (UBC), the Faculty of Education does not have an educational technologies plan for its undergraduate and graduate programs. Nor does it provide policy or leadership to guide students, staff, instructors, faculty members, or administrators learning about and the use of ICT in professional teaching practice. Individual faculty members, instructors, and support staff spearhead the infusion of ICT within curricula. Below we describe some solutions and recommendations based on our ecologies of learning research.

SOLUTIONS AND RECOMMENDATIONS: ECOLOGIES OF INQUIRY AND TEP

In this section we bring together theoretical and methodological approaches with anecdotal data from our case study. We integrate STEP issues in BC and Canada with some theoretical concepts and data from the lived experiences of our TCRs. Our approach to critical inquiry integrated conceptual, iterative, learning processes that included: (1) direct experiences, (2) observations and reflections, and (3) deliberation and dialogue (Kolb, 1984; Birt, Krug, and Sheridan, 1997). This assemblage of critical inquiry processes is not a linear narrative (presented here for the sake of efficiency). Critical inquiry processes are temporal and spatial "moments of arbitrary closure" (Slack, 1996, p.115) that mark historical, social, political, ethical, and cultural contextual conditions. While a record of critical inquiry can mark moments of learning about cultural practices, it can also be used to partially document the co-emergence of cognitive and experiential learning. Lakoff and Johnson (cited in Lakoff, 1988) argued that,

Meaningful conceptual structures arise from two sources: (1) from the structured nature of bodily and social experience and (2) from our innate capacity to imaginatively project from certain well-structured aspects of bodily and interactional experience to abstract conceptual structures. Rational thought is application of very general cognitive processes—focusing, scanning, superimposition, figure-ground reversal, etc.—to such structures. (p. 121)

In recent years there has been growing acceptance of findings from neuroscience about relationships amongst cognition, learning, and social and cultural experiences (Varela, Thompson, & Rosch, 1991; Thompson, 2004). Varela, Thompson, & Rosch (1991) argued convincingly that the mind should be understood as coupled with the body through human experiences and environmental situations. In other words, inquiry processes are articulated with what we can directly experience, observe and reflect on, deliberate and discuss, and collaboratively participate in and act on in the world in which we live.

Our critical inquiry was conducted with TCRs to encourage deliberation of observations from their day-to-day ICT experiences in the TEP. We discussed how these experiences had shaped their perceptions as educators using ICT. These inquiry sessions sensitized the TCRs to be more observant of their contextual conditions.

Direct Experiences

Our research began by meeting and talking with TCs in a two-year elementary TEP at UBC. Several years ago, Varela, Thompson, & Rosch (1991) called for a disciplined examination of direct experiences and their relationship to cognition and learning. In *Embodied Mind*, they argued that past scientific notions of cognition have been limited because they failed to reconcile a sense of common ground with human experiences. Eisner (2002) reminds us that,

In 1901 Dewey wrote an article titled 'The Educational Situation,' in which he discussed the constructed character of experience. That construction was not only activated by the prior experience the child brought to the situation; it was also the result of the child's interactions with the social and material conditions in which he or she worked. In this view, learning and culture were inseparable. (p. 94)

We found it was important to examine what constitutes the contextual conditions of the TCs' social situations when studying the impact of ICT in education. Through an investigation of direct experiences, we wanted to learn about a great variety of cultural practices that, too often, fall outside certain notions of cognitive science. These conceptual inquiry processes mediated our multisensory perceptions (Valera and Thompson, 1991).

As we began our research, we were curious to know if course instructors would positively or negatively act as role models when it came to using ICT within their courses. We had no avenue to mentor instructors prior to the school year. Instructors could volunteer to participate and fortunately, all 33 accepted our invitation. Based on past research, we knew that the TCs course experiences could influence how they eventually conceptualized and valued ICT in relationship to their own pedagogical practices (Krug, et al.; Arntzen, 2007; Krug, 2006). We had a GRA attend all of the courses in the TEP along with the TCs to establish common shared direct experiences.

We collected data on active and passive learning and technological adaption, as well as other pedagogical and ICT concepts. Our data indicated that TCs experienced a wide and diverse range of exposure to ICT within their TEP. For example, in music education, TCs were required to use ICT to complete several assignments: 1) weekly video activities; 2) learning to use a music production application, 3) video tape and edit a performance and a final video project, 4) submit all work for assessment on a DVD (Syllabus 1). The course instructor was a former music teacher who was unfamiliar with these applications and who wasn't confident with her technology skills. She told the GRA that she was pleased to have technology support and couldn't see how she would be able to deal with both teaching the content of the course and building her ICT skills (GRA, Notes 2). She struggled to use ICT in the presence of the TCs. Fortunately, one of the TCRs volunteered to teach a music authoring application (Garageband) to other students in the course. The GRA and TCR mentored the course instructor reversing the roles of instructor and learner. After the lesson, the instructor told the GRA that the Garageband lesson was exactly what the student's needed. (GRA, Notes 3).

Later, when asked to describe one anxiety provoking use of digital technology in any of their courses, one TC replied, "iMovie. This was a huge point of frustration for many of us dealing w/ the complexities and incompatibilities of Macs and PCs – did not help that our professor [instructor] had no concept of how this worked." (TC, Survey 2). This frustration appeared in other research surveys, "Almost every time one of our instructors tried to use technology for a lesson something went wrong and we had to wait for 10-15 minutes for it to be fixed..." (TC, Survey 3) This same respondent admitted to being turned off to using ICT in her long practicum, "The one time that I was going to use the Internet for a lesson my teacher said that it was unreliable in the school." Twenty-eight TCs in the cohort did not volunteer for the three-year study. A few of them were opposed to using ICT in education because of e-waste, social justice issues (i.e., inequality (digital divide), safety, intellectual property rights, and a general lack of time. Several others already felt comfortable using ICT but were too busy. Some of them just resisted using ICT within their pedagogical practices because they did not see any advantage for themselves or the students. A few TCs believed their ICT skills and confidence were sufficient for teaching and they did not need support in this area (TC, Survey 3).

The TCRs participated in several critical inquiry sessions that linked direct experiences, observation and reflection, deliberation and discussion, and collaborative actions in an iterative cycle of learning. Direct experiences were viewed and discussed as nested in fluid cycles of social, technological, economic, and political contexts. Therefore, when an instructor or TC encountered a technical problem, many of the TCRs were able to mediate their own frustration by recalling the larger complexity of the situation. They viewed problem solving as a dynamic process to reach one solution among many possibilities. For example, TCR 6 favorably discussed the Garageband lesson, "[TCR 7] and I were doing a drum lesson captured via a digital video camera. [We] used iMovie to edit significant tracks of the video reel. [We] presented it to the [TC] cohort in class [and] burned a final DVD-R to hand in. [We] used a multimodal method: Mindmap, story, pictures, classical and improvised musical notation." (TCR 6, Survey 4). This TCR was able to adapt technologically to the situation and recognized that he could learn from fellow classmates as well as the course instructor.

Observations and Reflections

Conducting critical inquiry provided ways to represent (i.e., writing, drawing, video, audio) observations of, and reflections on, particular cultural practices. Kolb (1984) writes, "If the education begins by bringing out the learner's beliefs and theories, examining and testing them, and then integrating the new, more refined ideas into the person's belief systems, the learning process will be facilitated" (p. 28). Kolb stressed reflexive learning and conducting inquiry by building on what the learner already knows.

As the TCRs progressed through the TEP, we met to talk and consider the choices they made about their teaching practices using ICT. We encouraged them to question why they chose or rejected to examine certain information more carefully. We asked them why they remembered certain detailed accounts of their experiences (Van Maanen, 1988; Emerson et al, 1995). Through these processes multiple views of using ICT were identified, and the TCRs learned about diverse ways of teaching. They had opportunities to observe each other using ICT, to talk with one another, listen to one another, and re-tell stories about their experiences.

For example, TCR 4 described how ICT was used in his science education course, "...our final assignment ...we had to pick a unit, for a grade, and he [the instructor] had a system to make sure no one did the same one. ...[the instructor] burned [CDs] ...and gave them all out. So, right now, if I was called into a grade four class, maybe I got a two-week sub [substitute teacher]... there are 16 different lessons on the area these kids would be learning" (TCR 4, Interview 2).

TCRs had opportunities to discuss the challenges of teaching during their long practicum, including sharing their observations about students' responses to technology. For instance, two TCRs were discussing the challenge of planning lessons for special needs students. "...there is one kid in my class... [who] has behaviour issues and he's in his last year and he's at a grade 4 reading level [in a grade 7 class]...But when I bring out technology he's totally into it and he does way better." TCR 7 asked, "Does that mean he could be doing his writing assignments on the computer in the library?" TCR 1 responded, "Yeah..." "Well, ...let's go for it..." (TCR 1, 7, Inquiry Session 2). These TCRs discussed a common challenge in education, a student's literacy skills are insufficient to meet grade level expectations. They chose to adapt their lessons and use ICT so it was possible for the student to accomplish course tasks and provide a social space for the student to succeed in school. In this situation, technological adaptability was a condition of social accessibility of ICT and learning. During another session, we had a guest presenter come in to show how interactive whiteboards were being used in her elementary school. Later, TCR 4 described why he was unable to use an interactive whiteboard in his practicum classroom because there was no projector permanently installed. The projector couldn't be installed during the time of his practicum because union protocols did not allow it. This TCR struggled to find pedagogical relevance for using an interactive whiteboard because it was not accessible (TCR 4, Interview 2).

The TCRs observed and reflected on their different ICT experiences in the TEP. Through these shared experiences they questioned their beliefs and theories in relation to their learning. They learned about technological adaptation from each other and as they began to research additional information on using ICT from books, online resources, and empirical evidence. They shared information in an online discussion forum, over email, and at inquiry sessions. Their experiences led to examining different perspectives to those views expressed in our sessions. Each cycle of inquiry contributed to previous knowledge and to increasing ability to adapt to situations.

Deliberation and Dialogue

During the first term of the second year, we facilitated TCR deliberation and dialogue about TEP experiences, bringing concepts to the surface about ICT, pedagogy, and contextual conditions through language-use. We discussed the ubiquitous use of the term "tool" when referring to digital technologies in educational discourse and examined ICT knowledge and pedagogy as affected by active, efficacious, and collaborative learning. We made time for the TCRs to not only reflect on, but also to deliberate and engage in dialogue about their ICT experiences and observations of their TEP and during their long practicum (McCutcheon, 2001).

We emphasized that critical inquiry processes needed to be viewed within specific contextual conditions as a way for us to mark "moments of arbitrary closure" (Slack, 1996, p.115). These arbitrary moments of closure enabled us to critically consider related meanings and values associated with language used to represent ecologies of learning. Eisner (2002) said,

> *Language is a way to make distinctions, and distinctions promote differences and separation. It is important to remember that these modes of thought are empirically inseparable. The senses feed ideas, and ideas focus one's senses. We find what we seek — and often more than we seek. At the same time imagination is moderated by what we believe we have the skill to create. What we have is a complex, integrated, and mutually determining array of cognitive processes interacting. Language and the theories that are used to describe them are ways of highlighting these processes so they are inspectable. They are not intended to assign them an independent existence. (p. 100)*

During our inquiry processes, we used deliberation and dialogue to analyze observations and experiences. Arbitrary moments of closure (moments) provided a means to "inspect" ideas and language in relationship with contextual conditions (i.e. books, websites, architecture, cultural formations). These ideas and contextual conditions were re-presented to support the telling of an informed narrative (Denzin, 1996; Stuhr, Krug, & Scott, 1995).

We theorized that ecologies of learning were important for TCRs to learn about in order for them question, analyze, and interpret the complexity of contextual conditions. We discussed ways to create opportunities to analyze the TCRs' experiences. Our lively inquiry exchanges made it possible for TCRs to debate their views with us, and each other. We required TCR discussions be based on direct experiences, and observations and reflections, from the TEP and extended practicum. We looked for moments that could be interpreted from multiple points of view. We were aware that moments of ICT practice relied on articulations of various forms of information and interpretations. Re-presenting experiences through multiple discourses provided for moments of reflexive deliberation. We studied the language used to deliberate about experiences and contextual conditions. The process of examining language challenged meanings associated with taken-for-granted perspectives. Sharing deliberations encouraged analysis of ICT practices and contextual relations as multiple and changing, rather than fixed within an individual experience.

Deliberations on ICT "Tools"

Discussions about the ubiquitous use of the term "tool(s)" took place as an integral part of ICT instructional sessions, inquiry sessions, interviews, and focus groups. Throughout the research, whenever the term "tool(s)" was used in the context of education and ICT, we would call attention to this use and ask the TCRs to consider alternate, more specific descriptive terms.

The term "tool" also appeared frequently in TCs use of language, "Even though it is the computer age, true teaching lies in the facilitator and not the tool. Computers are tools and like all tools, can be misused." (TC Survey 1) "I think they are valuable because they can be fun educational tools." "I don't think it should be central, but it's one more tool." "It would be useful as a communication tool & different form of expression." (TC, Survey 2).

We discussed the curricular conundrum posed by the use of the term "tool(s)" in education, arguing language can mislead and reduce, as well as open and clarify, conscious perceptions and perspectives (Arntzen, Krug, Wen 2008). The problem with using tool to represent all forms of ICT is that this language deskills teachers to learn about the complex technological, pedagogical, and cultural realities associated with ICT in professional teaching practice. Eventually, TCRs discussed learning about, and with digital technologies in their professional teaching practice, "[inquiry sessions]...taught me how to think about and position ICT in a classroom to be more than a tool." "I am convinced ICTs, digital tech, (call it what you want) are not mere tools." (TCR 7, 4 Survey 4) "I am pleased to say that I now know the difference between using ICT as a tool and using ICT in the classroom to enhance learning!!!" (TCR, Survey 5).

Deliberations on Active and Passive Learning

Deliberations on building pedagogical knowledge of active, efficacious, and collaborative learning occurred throughout the research program. We drew on shared experiences from observing in the TEP and expanded moments of discussion to include observations of pedagogy from the short and long practicum. These concepts of pedagogical knowledge, although familiar to the TCRs, were not modeled by instructors in the TEP. There are several differences in an active versus a passive learning approach. For example, active learning focuses on the learning process, whereas passive learning focuses on content. Below are a few other comparisons (See Figure 2).

Active learning was not regularly practiced within the TEP. Passive learning had a profound effect on many of the TCs sense of agency and engagement (Tan, 1997). A common comment we heard during the focus group sessions was they were going through "hoop jumping" (TCR 4 Interview 2), "There were a lot of make work activities and assignments that didn't really feel essential to good teaching." (TC Survey 3). These perceptions and experiences extended to the use of ICT, "Learning to use another website and using the functions on that site just added more technology anxiety." (TC, Survey 3)

We facilitated 18 inquiry sessions with the TCRs and at least 4 in-class ICT sessions with the whole cohort from January 1, 2008 until April 30, 2009. We attempted to engage TCRs in deliberation and dialogue about an active learning approach to teaching. We asked them what role student learning should play in teaching. (GRA Notes 4). The TCRs were introduced to different aspects of critical inquiry processes from action research and video ethnography. An assemblage of knowledge was posted on a discussion forum and TCRs led conversations on the topics they had researched. (TCR 4, Inquiry Session 1).

The TCRs were responsible for designing curricula that actively engaged learners with ICT. This development produced ICT experiences that could be taught and videotaped later in their practicum. The TCRs worked in groups of three, brainstorming ideas, discussing active learning and ICT, and they produced online resources for these educational experiences. One TCR had flown over Mt. St. Helens and wanted to provide this perspective for her students when teaching an earth science lesson. She asked another TCR to help her use Google maps and video to create an interactive game that would give her students the sensation of flying over Mt. St. Helens. TCR 6 was an experienced gamer, and he showed her how the controls on Google Maps were similar to gaming operations. She used this knowledge to learn to navigate in Google Maps (TCR 7, Inquiry Session 1).

Deliberations on Teaching with ICT

The TCRs taught an ICT lesson during their long practicum, made a video recording of that experience, and edited the video for deliberation and discussion by the group. Some of the lessons video taped included: learning about a cultural holiday tradition using a blog to post pictures and research students collected from the Internet; teaching long division using a Smartboard and

Figure 2. Active vs. passive learning, (Sinclair, McClaren, & Griffin, 2006)

ACTIVE Learning	PASSIVE Learning
Focus on Learning Processes	Focus on Content Presentation
Focus on Communication & Interactions	Focus on Access & Download
Co-developed with Learners &	Fixed or Static Design
Instructors shaping Design	Individualized
Customized/Personalized	Teacher-Directed
Cooperatively Activated	Static
Evolving Knowledge & Understanding	Information/Content
Learning-paced	System-paced
Collaborative & 1:1 many:many	1:many
Contribute, Tag, and Share (Folksonomy)	Search and Retain
Demonstrations and Prototypes	Tests and Examinations
Negotiated and Contracted	Prescribed
Feedback rich	Feedback limited

an animated software application; researching government and politics using a webquest with students; and learning about extreme weather by having students write, perform, and video record a weather report.

The TCRs reviewed their video recordings in relative privacy and wrote about why the seven particular moments they selected were significant. During the annotation process the TCRs discussed their teaching experiences. Although their review, selection, and representation were ostensibly done privately, they openly shared their experiences. The TCRs were comfortable sharing their triumphs and challenges, even as they considered moments from their practicum that were decidedly uncomfortable (TCR, Inquiry Session 3).

An inquiry session was devoted to public discussion of their annotated presentations. Prior to beginning the presentations, we reminded the TCRs to respect one another. We said, "We really think of this group as a team, and not as the two of us [PI and GRA] and you guys are the participants. We like to think of you guys as being part of a research group that is doing this…" (PI, Inquiry Session 4) "…to start with [we would like to have] each of you present your deliberation that you put together, and have a brief conversation afterwards about some of the things you present and talk about … there have to be some ground rules… the ground rules are, if you say anything to someone, and there is the potential of hurting their feelings, that you think twice before you say it, and, the person who is hearing what is being said, realize that nobody here is actually trying to do that, to say something that will hurt your feelings." Conceptually, the TCRs were guided toward, "The idea here is to be …as honest and open as possible about what it is you are presenting, and what it is we're responding to, it's going to benefit all of us, not just the person who is presenting. The idea is to have an open conversation knowing well that people's feelings have the potential of being hurt, and also trying to respect one another. …If we are not open and honest with each other, there isn't going to be any kind of development… …we want you to think about your thinking …when you had to look at your video you had to think about why you decided what you decided to do… when you are presenting, we are going to be talking about what it is you were thinking at this particular time… the deliberation is on seeing yourself, and your relationship to that." After this, the TCRs proceeded to share their deliberations and discuss their experiences, thoughts, conundrums, and solutions.

Afterwards, several TCRs conveyed that deliberation and dialogue was helpful. TCR 1 said, "I really thought the video-stills reflection was a valuable way to look at our use of digital technologies. I wished I could have video'd myself teaching on more occasions." (Survey 3). TCR 3 pointed out, "This is ongoing. These practices help decide what to use and how much time to invest into using ICT at any given time. In addition, I believe these practices have been useful in thinking about ways to use newer web 2.0 functions in the classroom." (Survey 3). TCR 2 stressed "My reflections help me change things for the next time and make it run more smoothly." (Survey 3), TCR 6 expanded on several points, "Deliberation made me realize that digital technology needs to be supplemented with appropriate instructional practices. It has the potential to fall short of content. Like a reflection of a lesson plan, deliberating on tech use can help me figure out what was and was not effective and also route out possible fallacies of my thinking about tech use. If I did not deliberate, I might become discouraged using ICTs if I hit a minor snag, which is totally unfair, and unproductive." (Survey 3), TCR 8 provided another view, "Reflection is always occurring. It was good to reflect weekly on the blog [discussion forum] to almost force myself to think of the goods and the struggles of technology. Communicating as a group is great to discuss and share information about technology." (Survey 3)

Collaborative Action

The TCRs learned about why and how meanings are struggled over when engaging in collaborative actions. Professional education should include opportunities to pose problems, specify those paths that can be traveled for solutions and work together to enact solutions (Varela, Thompson, Rosch 1991). This view of critical inquiry acknowledges that there is no one process or absolute articulation of human consciousness and experiences. An ecology of learning is nested in multiple perspectives that embody the tensions and ambiguities of everyday lives. Our collaborative actions included examining ICT issues from historical and contemporary perspectives and politically engaging the TCRs in "making-public" their views about ICT issues. At this point in time, TCRs have voiced their views primarily within the safety of our group inquiry sessions. As this study progresses we anticipate that collaborative actions will include local and national conferences.

As part of collaborative actions we asked the TCRs to journal about their experiences while doing their extended practicum using a secure, online discussion forum. One posting revealed evolving ICT knowledge of TCR 2 in her sponsor school. She was attending a staff meeting at her practicum school and observed staff members using an interactive whiteboard to present information to the group. The teacher using the interactive whiteboard was having difficulty and needed to re-calibrate the board. TCR 2 observed the instructions the librarian gave the teacher to, "press on the crosses with her finger." TCR 2 also remembered the interactive whiteboard session she had attended in a research inquiry session and, "...thought to myself, she should really be doing this with the pen so that it's very precise." (TCR 2, Online Posting 1) As a student teacher, the TCR did not feel confident to interrupt the proceedings, but she noted in her discussion forum posting, "When the teacher finally started writing things on the board I could tell it was a little off... and moving quite slowly." (TCR 2, Online Posting 2). This example represents a moment when collaborative action was actually no action because the TRC realized it would be inappropriate to intervene at the time. Instead the TCR waited until later to convey the information to her colleague in a more personal and professional space.

Making public can also mean sharing ICT knowledge about pedagogical and technological adaptability with new colleagues. The TCRs learned to ask each other for help, and, eventually, became support for others in the program and at their practicum schools, "I would often help with AV setup for assemblies." (TCR 4, Survey 4), "I was very persistent about getting the two in-class computers [in sponsor teacher's classroom] debugged and updated so that they could be used as resources." (TCR 7, Survey 4). "I toggled with my SA's [sponsor teacher's] computer and networking devices until Internet was available." (TCR, 6 Survey 4). "Right before an assembly the principal asked me to set up my laptop in the gym to show a slideshow of pictures. So I brought my laptop, the projector and some speakers down on a trolley and set them up in the gym. The school got to see the photos and the principal was happy I could help." (TCR 2, Survey 4). ICT leadership takes time and active collaboration can help to build comfort and confidence that is needed to participate in school change.

Ecological and Efficacious Learning

In this Chapter we reported on our research that examined if and how TCs could study their own evolving ICT pedagogical self-efficacy, as a means to increase their ICT knowledge and leadership in educational situations. We introduced a group of eight TCRs to critical inquiry as a way to directly experience, observe and reflect on, deliberate and discuss, and take collaborative action, with regards to their evolving ecologies of learning. We used the concept of ecology as a philosophical position of inquiry conditioned in time and space that articulate connections among knowledge, cultures, contexts, and diverse experiences. Our orientation to ecology emerged out of the conceptual positioning of phenomenology and constructivism into articulated moments of language. Experiences are a human construction of multiple realities situated within evolving social, technological, economic, and political contextual forces of human agency, organizational structures and policies. Our perception of our ontological and existential positions in the world creates both possibilities and restrictions when trying to act or imagine beyond historically established social, technological, economic, political contexts, and cultural conditions. Understanding the formation of experiences through language calls for conscious effort and awareness to perceive and communicate. This continual reconstruction of multiple forms of realities discloses the world into particular perceptions.

In this chapter we focused on the technological adaptability of a small group of TCs in the TEP at UBC. Given the limitations of our study sample size, we will not attempt to over-generalize our findings. We did however find that there is merit in using critical inquiry for assisting TCs in transitioning from the role of student in a TEP into the roles of learner, teacher, researcher, and leader.

In our research, during their critical inquiry the TCRs had opportunities to collaboratively examine ways to influence students/colleagues engagement and learning with ICT. For example, there was the time in our study when the GRA and the TCR mentored the course instructor on how to book a computer lab and teach Garageband. This experience reversed the roles of the instructor and instructed on how to teach with and about ICT.

The TCRs sense of self-efficacy provided a conscious perception that they could deal with unmotivated students and situations that were difficult. For example, two TCRs discussed the challenge of planning lessons for special needs students. Together they found a solution for the student to accomplish learning tasks using ICT and providing the student an opportunity to succeed in school.

The TCRs developing sense of efficacy provided them with confidence to plan and organize educational experiences using ICT and make decisions when the use of ICT was not necessary or intrusive. For example, one TCR described how difficult it was to use the interactive whiteboard in his practicum classroom because there was no projector permanently installed. The projector couldn't be installed during the time of his practicum because union protocols did not allow it. When asked how these combined experiences affected his perception of himself as a teacher who uses technology, he said, "well, it's okay... we've got the rolling Mac Lab" (TCR 4, Interview 2). He was able to adapt pedagogically and technologically his interests to the schools political situation.

Many times these TCRs were open to trying unfamiliar pedagogical practices and willing to work with these methods to understand them better. These initiatives increased the demand placed on them and their commit to teaching. The TCRs brought a wide variety of learning activities back for deliberation. During one inquiry session, they reviewed their teaching video recordings and selected a minimum of seven significant moments. They proceeded to share their deliberations and discuss their experiences, thoughts, conundrums, and solutions. One TCR said, "This is ongoing. These practices help decide what to use and how much time to invest into using ICT at any given time. In addition, I believe these practices have been useful in thinking about ways to use newer web 2.0 functions in the classroom" (TCR 3, Survey 3). Pedagogical and technological adaptability takes patience and persistence. Self-efficacious learning instills a desire to persevere.

The TCRs persisted when their practicum and course experiences were frustrating and demonstrated resilience in the face of adversity. For example one TC said a huge point of frustration for many of us dealing w/ the complexities and incompatibilities of Macs and PCs – did not help that our professor [instructor] had no concept of how this worked." (TC, Survey 2). However, one of the TCRs favorably discussed the Garageband lesson, "[TCR 7] and I were doing a drum lesson captured via a digital video camera. [We] used iMovie to edit significant tracks of the video reel. [We] presented it to the [TC] cohort in class [and] burned a final DVD-R to hand in. [We] used a multimodal method: Mindmap, story, pictures, classical and improvised musical notation." (TCR 7 Survey 4). TCR 7 was able to adapt technologically to the situation and recognized that he could learn from fellow classmates as well as the course instructor. In even the most frustrating situations there is usually a glimmer of hope. Finding this can provide reassurance that a solution is possible.

In addition, as their sense of self-efficacy grew stronger they were able to be less critical of students/colleagues struggling and able to help those who demanded more attention and patience. If you recall, the TCR observed a staff members who had difficulty calibrating an interactive whiteboard. She "...thought... she should really be doing this with the pen so that it's very precise... When the teacher finally started writing things on the board I could tell it was a little off... and moving quite slowly." (TCR 2, Online Posting 3). Rather than disrupt the session or embarrass the librarian and teacher, the TCR showed patience in waiting until later to share this information at a more opportune time.

As the 21st Century begins, teachers (as well as students) need ways to engage with complex cultural issues and contextual conditions. Cultural practices are contextually situated within socially interested points of view. Teacher education programs need to prepare teacher candidates to become active, efficacious, and collaborative learners. We believe studying ecologies of learning and critical inquiry can provide ways to adapt and integrate pedagogical and technological practices into educational situations.

NOTE

In this chapter we do not differentiate between different forms of educational hardware and software, such as wireless laptops, desktop computers, interactive whiteboards, social networking software, video conversion software, etc. We focused on the technological adaptability of a small group of teacher candidates in using critical inquiry for assisting them in transitioning from the role of student in a teacher education program into the roles of learner, teacher, researcher, and leader. We were less interested in how they used a particular type of ICT in a particular way, than how they developed a sense of efficacy to plan and organize educational experiences using ICT.

REFERENCES

Anderson, J. R. (2000). Learning and memory. New York, NY: Wiley & Sons.

Arntzen, J. (2007). Mentoring information and communication technologies within teacher education: Synthesizing Research Practice with Research Literature. In C. Montgomerie & J. Seale (Eds.), *Proceedings of World Conference on Educational Multimedia, Hypermedia and Telecommunications 2007* (pp. 2383-2386). Chesapeake, VA: AACE.

Arntzen, J., Krug, D. H., & Wen, Z. (2008). ICT literacies and the curricular conundrum of calling all complex digital technologies Tools. *International Journal of Educational Development*, *4*(4).

Aspects of information and communications technology integration. (2009). Retrieved June 5, 2009, from http://www.bced.gov.bc.ca/perf_stands/icti/content.php?page=aspectsict

Bandura, A. (1995). Self-efficacy in changing societies. Cambridge, UK: Cambridge University Press.

Birt, D., Krug, D. H., & Sheridan, M. (1997). Earthly matters: Learning occurs when you hear the grass singing. *Art Education, 50*(6), 6–14. doi:10.2307/3193682

Canadian Teachers' Federation. (2003). *An investigation of the integration of information and communication technology into Canadian schools and classrooms*.

Deleuze, G., & Guattari, F. (1987). A thousand plateaus: Capitalism and schizophrenia. Minneapolis, MN: University of Minneapolis Press.

Denzin, N. (1996). The facts and fictions of qualitative inquiry. *Qualitative Inquiry, 2*(2), 230–241. doi:10.1177/107780049600200207

Denzin, N. (2004). The war on culture, the war on truth. *Cultural Studies Critical Methodologies, 4*(2), 137–142. doi:10.1177/1532708603256627

Dexter, S. L., Anderson, R. E., & Becker, H. J. (1999). Teachers' views of computers as catalysts for changes in their teaching practice. *Journal of Research on Computing in Education, 31*(3), 221–239.

Dryburgh, H. (2002). Learning computer skills. *Canadian Social Trends, 64*(4), 20–24.

Eisner, E. W. (2002). The arts and the creation of mind. New Haven and London: Yale University Press.

Emerson, R., Fretz, R., & Shaw, L. (1995). Writing ethnographic fieldnotes. Chicago: University of Chicago Press.

Foucault, M. (1982). The subject and power. *Critical Inquiry, 8*(4), 777–795. doi:10.1086/448181

Fullan, M. (1993). Change forces: Probing the depths of educational reform. Bristol, PA: Falmer Press.

Information and communications technology integration performance standards. (n.d.). Retrieved June 5, 2009, from http://www.bced.gov.bc.ca/perf_stands/icti/content.php?page=overview

Kirsh, D. (2000). A few thought on cognitive overload. *Intellectica, 30*, 19–53.

Kolb, D. (1983). Experiential learning: Experience as the source of learning and development. New York: Prentice Hall.

Krug, D. (2006). Seeds of possibility: Mentoring K-7 educators' ICT ecology of cognition. Social Sciences and Humanities Research Council.

Krug, D., Echols, F., Wynston, G., & Seeds Graduate Mentors (2005-06). *Report: The Seeds of Possibility: Integrating ICT into the Teacher Education Two-year Elementary Program.* Faculty of Education Dean's Learning Technology Funds, The University of British Columbia. 1-12.

Krug, D. H, & Arntzen, J. (2009). *Seeds of Possibility: Timeline of research activities.*

Lakoff, G. (1988). Cognitive Semantics. In U. Eco, M. Santambrogio & P. Violi (Eds.), Meaning and mental representations. Bloomington: Indiana University Press.

Lorsbach, A. W., & Jinks, J. L. (1999). Self-efficacy theory and learning environment research. *Learning Environments Research, 2*, 157–167. doi:10.1023/A:1009902810926

Maeroff, G. I. (2003). A classroom one: How online learning is changing our schools and colleges. New York: Palgrave Macmillan.

Mayer, R. E. (2002). The promise of educational psychology: Teaching for meaningful learning (Vol. 2). Upper Saddle River, NJ: Prentice Hall.

Mayer, R. E., & Moreno, R. (2003). Nine ways to reduce cognitive load in multimedia learning. *Educational Psychologist, 38*(1), 43–52. doi:10.1207/S15326985EP3801_6

McCutcheon, G. (2001). Developing the curriculum: Solo and group deliberation. Troy, NY: Educator's International Press, Incorporated.

Measuring the information society: The ICT development index. (2009). Geneva, Switzerland: International Telecommunications Union.

Organisation for Economic Co-operation and Development. (2005). E-learning in tertiary education: Where do we stand? Paris: OECD.

Plante, J., & Beattie, D. (2004). Connectivity and ICT Integration in Canadian Elementary and Secondary Schools: First Results from the Information and Communications Technologies in Schools Survey, 2003-2004. Ottawa: Statistics Canada.

Premier's Technology Council: 10th report. (2007 September). Vancouver, BC: Premier's Technology Council.

Ross, J. A. (1994). *Beliefs that make a difference: The origins and impacts of teacher efficacy*. Paper presented at the Annual meeting of the Canadian Association for Curriculum Studies.

Schechter, C. (2005). Communal deliberation: The art of learning schools. *International Journal of Educational Management*, *19*(3), 197–206. doi:10.1108/09513540510590986

Schofield, J. W. (1995). Computer and classroom culture. New York: Cambridge University Press.

Seely Brown, J. (1999). *Learning, working and playing in the digital age: Creating learning ecologies*. Retrieved June 8, 2009, from http://serendip.brynmawr.edu/sci_edu/seelybrown/

Sinclair, G. McClaren, & Griffin, M. (2006). *E-learning and beyond: A discussion paper prepared as part of the Campus 2020 process for the British Columbia Ministry of Advanced Education*. Retrieved June 8, 2009, from www.aved.gov.bc.ca/campus2020/documents/e-learning.pdf

Slack, J. D. (1996). The theory and method of articulation in cultural studies. In D. Morley & K.-H. Chen (Eds.), Stuart Hall: Critical dialogues in cultural studies. New York: Taylor & Francis.

Spiro, R. J., Feltovich, P. J., Jacobson, M. J., & Coulson, R. L. (1991). Cognitive flexibility, constructivism, and Hypertext. Hillsdale, NJ: Lawrence Erlbaum Associates.

State of e-learning in Canada. (2009). Ottawa, ON: Canadian Council on Learning.

Stuhr, P., Krug, D. H., & Scott, A. P. (1995). Partial tales of three translators: An essay. *Studies in Art Education*, *37*(1), 29–46. doi:10.2307/1320490

Tan, M. (1997). Multi-agent reinforcement learning vs. cooperative agents In M. N. Huhns & M. P. Singh (Eds.), Readings in Agents (pp. 487). San Francisco: Morgan Kaufmann.

Tapscott, D. (1998). Growing up digital: The rise of the net generation. New York: McGraw-Hill.

Thompson, E. (2004). Life and mind: From autopoiesis to neurophenomenology. A tribute to Francisco Varela. *Phenomenology and the Cognitive Sciences*, *3*, 381–398. doi:10.1023/B:PHEN.0000048936.73339.dd

Thompson, E. (2007). Empathy and enculturation Mind in life: Biology, phenomenology and the sciences of the mind. Boston: Harvard University Press.

Turkle, S. (1996). Life on the screen. Cambridge, MA: MIT Press.

Van Maanen, J. (1988). Tales of the field: On writing ethnography. Chicago: University of Chicago Press.

Varela, F. J. (1992). Ethical know-how: Action, wisdom and cognition. Stanford, CA: Stanford University Press.

Varela, F. J., Thompson, E., & Rosch, E. (1991). The embodied mind: Cognitive science and human experience. Cambridge, MA: The MIT Press.

Welcome to the BC College of Teachers. (2009). Retrieved June 5, 2009, from http://www.bcct.ca/

ADDITIONAL READING

Bandura, A. (1997). Self-efficacy: The exercise of control. New York: W.H. Freeman.

Bawden, D. (2001). Information and digital literacy: A review of concepts. *The Journal of Documentation*, *57*(2), 218–259. doi:10.1108/EUM0000000007083

Boekaerts, P., Pintrich, R., & Zeidner, M. (2000). (Eds.), Handbook of self-regulation. San Diego, California: Academic Press.

Boles, K., & Troven, V. (1996). Teacher leaders and power: Achieving school reform from the classroom. In G. Moller and M. Katzenmeyer (Eds.). Every Teacher as a Leader, New Directions for School Leadership, No. 1, Fall 1996. San Francisco, CA: Jossey-Bass.

Building student ICT in teacher education expertise. Retrieved June 8, 2009, from http://www.uoregon.edu/~moursund/ICT-planning/building-expertise.htm

Governer issues executive order supporting digital literacy efforts in California (2009). Retrieved June 8, 2009, from http://www.ictliteracy.info/Executive%20Order%20S-06-09.htm

Helleve, I. (2007). In an ICT-based teacher-education context: why was our group 'the magic group? *European Journal of Teacher Education*, *30*(3), 267–284. doi:10.1080/02619760701486118

Karagiorgi, Y., & Charalambous, K. (2006). ICT in-service training and school practices: in search for the impact. *Journal of Education for Teaching*, *32*(4), 395–411. doi:10.1080/02607470600981995

Moursand, D., & Bielefeldt, T. (1999). Will new teachers be prepared to teach in a digital age? International Society for Technology in Education & Milken Exchange on Education Technology, U.S.A.

Past experience is invaluable for complex decision making, brain research shows (2009). Retrieved June 8, 2009, from http://www.sciencedaily.com/releases/2009/05/090513130930.htm

Rogers, P. L. (2000). Barriers to adopting emerging technologies in education. *Journal of Educational Computing Research*, *22*(4), 455–472. doi:10.2190/4UJE-B6VW-A30N-MCE5

Roschelle, J. (1995). *What should collaborative technology be? A perspective from Dewey and situated learning*. Available online at: ACM Digital Library http://portal.acm.org/ dl.cfm?collportal&dl ACM&CFID 28918368&CFTOKEN 76631710 (accessed 5 October 2004).

Saltiel, I. M., Sgroi, A., & Brockett, R. G. (1998). (Eds.). The power and potential of collaborative learning partnerships. San Francisco: Jossey-Bass Publishers.

Scho¨ n, D. A. (1987) *Educating the reflective practitioner*, San Francisco, CA: Jossey-Bass.

Schunk, D. H., & Zimmerman, B. J. (1998). (Eds.). Self-regulated learning and performance. Hillsdale, N.J.: Lawrence Earlbaum Associates.

Wenger, E. (1998). Communities of practice. Learning, meaning and identity. Cambridge, UK: Cambridge University Press.

Zeichner, K., & Liston, D. (1998). Reflective teaching. NJ: Lawrence Erlbaum.

KEY TERMS AND DEFINITIONS

Arbitrary Moments of Closure: Temporal and spatial moments of closure that mark historical, social, political, ethical, and cultural contextual conditions.

Articulation: An act of connecting two or more different elements of certain forces of human agency and contextual conditions to make a temporary unity.

Assemblage: When the multiple is treated as substantive, "multiplicity", ceasing to have one subject or object, but is considered a momentary composite of diverse elements: participants, histories, purposes, contexts.

Critical Inquiry: A cyclical, experiential learning process that includes direct experience, observation and reflection, deliberation and dialogue and collaborative action.

Deliberation: A socially interactive process to "inspect" ideas and language in relationship with contextual conditions.

Ecologies of Learning: A philosophical position of inquiry conditioned in time and space to articulate connections among knowledge, cultures, contexts, and diverse experiences.

Efficacious Learning: Understanding the reciprocal relationship between the learning environment (learning ecologies; see Seely Brown, 1999) and a sense of confidence to perform tasks.

ICT: Information and Communication Technologies: a diverse, continuously evolving collection of hardware devices, software applications and online (Internet) environments that are formed, and forming to enact, enable and enrich human interaction.

ICT Literacies: Acquiring ICT skills and knowledge to be able to manipulate digital devices, software applications and online resources, manage multiple files, produce multi-media content, and design interactive learning activities.

Tool: Device for making material changes on other objects, as by cutting, shearing, striking, rubbing, grinding, squeezing, measuring, or other processes. Tools are the main means by which human beings control and manipulate their physical environment.

Chapter 5
Mining Education Australia:
Adapting Technology to Support a Collaborative Approach to Transnational Teaching for Mining Professionals

Trish Andrews
The University of Queensland, Australia

ABSTRACT

Due to a range of social and economic factors, Australian institutions have struggled to meet the demand for highly trained professionals for the minerals industry in recent years. In order to address this issue, Mining Education Australia, a consortia of four of Australia's mining schools was established to develop and deliver a common curriculum for mining engineering education.. The use of technology to support the delivery of this common curriculum is integral to the success of this initiative. This chapter outlines the challenges in such collaborations and discusses the range of corporate and open source technologies selected and adopted to overcome these challenges to enable collaborative teaching and learning activities in this trans-national program.

INTRODUCTION

Mining Education Australia (MEA) was established to address the need to develop a sustainable approach to the provision of a higher education program for minerals industry professionals through the development and delivery of a national curriculum. This chapter outlines the development of MEA and in particular will focus on:

- An outline of the social and economic issues facing minerals education in Australia.
- A discussion of the approach to curriculum design adopted by MEA to support the development of a national curriculum, including the theoretical considerations.

DOI: 10.4018/978-1-61520-909-5.ch005

- An outline of the issues involved in establishing a common teaching and learning program across four institutions and the ways in which adapting technologies have helped to address these issues.
- A description of the blended approach to teaching and learning implemented to support the large face-to-face cohorts in partner institutions in some subject areas and to address shortfalls in academic expertise in partner institutions in particular specialist areas.
- A discussion of the technologies adapted to support cross institutional teaching and learning activities including Moodle, interactive teaching and learning rooms, lecture recording and videoconferencing.
- A discussion of the implementation of an online peer review system to support high quality project based activities across the partner institutions.
- An explanation of the development of an online database to provide a common and accessible repository for all MEA materials, processes and policies.
- An outline of future developments including the adoption of an e-portfolio approach for MEA.

BACKGROUND

Australia is one of the world's leading mining countries (Australia Bureau of Statistics, 2008) with the minerals industry contributing significantly to Australia' s prosperity. In 2005-2006 the mining industry contributed 7% to Australia's gross domestic product (Australia Bureau of Statistics 2008). The industry is Australia's second largest exporter, accounting for 37% of total exports in 2006-2007 (Australia Bureau of Statistics, 2008). The mining industry also contributed 17% to total national expenditure on research and development (R&D) in 2006 – 2007 (Australia Bureau of Statistics, 2008). However, despite its significant contribution to Australia's wealth, the cycle of 'boom and bust' that affects the minerals industry has a significant impact on the capacity of universities to maintain educational programs for mining professionals. In times of downturn, institutions struggle to attract sufficient student numbers to minerals education programs to remain viable. Conversely, during peak boom periods, institutions can be swamped with enrolments in these programs but struggle to attract high quality PhD students. As financial rewards are considerably higher in the minerals industry than in education professions, few are attracted to the academic world, resulting in challenges in providing sufficient academic staff to support these programs. Additionally, the educational environment is one where many higher education institutions and programs in Australia are struggling to maintain their economic viability. Consequently, many courses and programs are being closed down as institutions implement minimum student enrolment figures as indicators of feasibility.

In the mid to late nineties, during a period of downturn in the minerals industries and lacking sufficient enrolments to meet institutional requirements for financial viability, organizations in Australia and internationally closed many mining education programs. This resulted in a serious worldwide shortage in the number of highly qualified people for the minerals professions (The University of New South Wales, 2006). In order for the Australian minerals industry to maintain its contribution to economic and social outcomes for the country, it is considered essential that the higher education system is able to provide and support the kind of high quality education required to provide professional staff capable of enabling the industry to continue to compete in a global environment and to "maintain its social license to operate" (The University of New South Wales, 2006).

Much of Australia's mining industry is located in rural and remote areas of Australia. In addition to the considerable contributions to GDP, export earnings and R&D expenditure outlined above, mining companies have been a major influence in the development of communities in the remote regions where mining activities are commonly undertaken. The minerals industry:

- is responsible for significant infrastructure development – since 1967, the industry has built 26 towns, 12 ports, 25 airfields and over 2,000 kilometres of railway line;
- is often the sole provider of social infrastructure – health, education and welfare – in remote areas of Australia – infrastructure that often endures long past the cessation of mining activities; and
- directly and indirectly employs more than 320,000 Australians, many of whom are located in sparsely populated, remote and regional Australia; (The University of New South Wales, 2006).

In 1998 a discussion paper *Back from the Brink* identified that the minerals industry was facing a crisis in its capacity to employ high quality professionals as both nationally and internationally there was significant shortage of minerals professionals with the required skills, available to meet the rapidly growing demand for such. At the time:

- Only four universities in Australia offered comprehensive 4-year undergraduate degree programs in mining engineering
- The number of academics teaching mining engineering was continuing to decline, while the median age of remaining academics was increasing
- The number of students enrolling in PhDs was and remains at a low level severely restricting Australia's capacity to maintain a viable number of academics to provide education for the minerals industry (The University of New South Wales, 2006).

To address this problem, MTEC establishing a national, collaborative mining education school called Mining Education Australia (MEA) in 2005, which aimed to:

- Develop and deliver a national curriculum for the third and fourth year of the mining engineering degree
- Provide high quality graduates with the skills and abilities to meet the requirements of the minerals industry both in Australia and overseas
- Address 'shortfalls' in academic expertise in individual partner universities by judicious use of technology (The University of New South Wales, 2006).

At the time of its inception, institutions wanting to join MEA needed to be currently providing a full four-year undergraduate program. The initial partners in the MEA collaboration were the Curtin University of Technology (Western Australian School of Mines), The University of New South Wales (School of Mining Engineering) and The University of Queensland (Faculty of Engineering – Discipline of Mining Engineering and Minerals Process Engineering). Only one major Australian mining school, located at the University of Wollongong, opted not to join MEA. In 2009, the university of Adelaide commenced offer of a four-year mining engineering degree and joined as a full partner of MEA. MEA now provides more than 90% of Australia's minerals professionals to the industry.

MEA was aware that considerable funding would be required to support the development of a national curriculum. While significant funding was provided by MTEC, the intention to integrate technology extensively required more funding. MEA applied for and was successful in being awarded 1.3 million dollars from the Commonwealth Collaboration and Structural Reform fund to support the development of the collaboration.

DEVELOPING A NATIONAL CURRICULUM TO MEET IDENTIFIED INDUSTRY NEEDS

Developing a national curriculum across a number of widely dispersed universities, located in different Australian states, created particular challenges both in terms of working collaboratively and in how to deliver the program effectively across the partner institutions. Academics traditionally work independently and have little interaction with others in the course development process. Higher Education institutions generally are equally unused to the notion of collaborative course development and cross-institutional teaching and learning. Consequently, there are many barriers to developing successful cross-institutional educational collaborations (e.g. Kezar, 2005).

MEA's intention to develop a common curriculum required a completely different approach than that previously practiced by the MEA partner universities. The teaching of mining education has generally taken a fairly traditional path with a strong lecture /tutorial approach combined with projects in the final year. The development of the new program included input from an industry advisory group that consisted of representatives of major employers. This group identified the need for integrating professional skills or graduate attributes as part of the overall program and provided a set of graduate skills they considered essential to the mineral's industry (see Figure 1).

In order to be more responsive to the identified industry needs outlined in Table 1, it became clear that MEA needed to consider an approach to curriculum design that would provide greater opportunity for the integration and development of skills such as team work, communication, problem solving and critical thinking. Consequently, it was decided to adopt more constructivist and social constructivist approaches to teaching and learning. Thus, constructivist approaches to teaching and learning take the view that learners bring knowledge and experience to the learning process and that learning is an active process (Mayer, 1999). Constructive approaches to learning are designed to enable students to build on existing knowledge and understanding to negotiate new understandings and knowledge. Social constructivist approaches to teaching and learning commonly include more social interactions as part of learning activities and draw on the work of Vygotsky (1978), who took the view that social interactions are a key part of the learning process. Social constructivist approaches to teaching and learning commonly include such strategies as

Figure 1. Essential graduate skills to the mineral's industry

Attribute	Knowledge	Skill	Awareness	Behaviour	Comments
Understand core Engineering & Mining Engineering	♉♉♉	♉♉♉			Content
Recognise, define & solve problems	♉♉♉	♉♉♉			Critical
Access, evaluate & synthesise information		♉♉♉			Important
Think critically, laterally and creatively		♉♉♉		♉♉	Valued
Communicate effectively		♉♉♉		♉♉	Important
Work in teams		♉♉♉		♉♉	Important
Understand sustainability & cultural diversity , I'national issues	♉		♉♉♉		Value added
Working in remote environments			♉♉♉	♉♉♉	Career
Lifelong learning & personal development	♉	♉		♉♉♉	Attitude
Integrity				♉♉♉	Personal
Manage ambiguity, tough & resilient			♉	♉♉♉	Attitude
Basic business and mgt skills	♉	♉			Basics

reciprocal teaching, opportunities for peer learning, problem based learning and other activities that involve people learning from the experience of others (Schunk, 2000). While MEA integrated more active, project, case-based and collaborative learning approaches into the new program as a way of meeting identified industry needs and requirements it also extended the notion of socio constructivist learning to the curriculum design process itself.

CROSS INSTITUTIONAL COURSE DEVELOPMENT PROCESS

Creating genuine collaboratively developed courses where academics work together to develop the course and program is difficult to achieve. In previous attempts to work more collaboratively with Australian mining schools, MTEC had engaged a number of mining academics to develop materials around key topic areas. These materials were of a high quality and included many active and interactive learning activities consistent with the more social constructivist teaching and learning approach MEA was now actively adopting. However, academics did not work in a truly collaborative fashion to develop these materials, taking more of a co-operative approach (Panitz, 1996) with individual academics taking responsibility for particular tasks, but with little discussion of the whole task (Wiersema, 2000). Consequently, academics lacked ownership of these materials. Additionally, in many cases these materials were difficult for individual academics to integrate and use in their courses. The materials lacked a relationship to specific course outcomes and assessment tasks, and although comprehensive and containing good teaching and learning activities, were often difficult for staff and students to navigate.

To foster a more collaborative development process and encourage ownership and use of the planned courses, MEA introduced both a team approach to course development and a more rigorous approach to curriculum design. A program leaders committee (PLC) consisting of an academic representative from each partner institution was established to oversee the academic development of the program. Wherever possible, all courses were developed by a team that included a representative from each partner university. This approach resulted in a pool of expertise being available to each course, allowing for a much richer and deeper course from a content perspective. This approach also meant that all members of the team were required to work together to establish and agree all aspects of the curriculum including learning objectives, learning activities and assessment. The curriculum design approach was based on Biggs (1999) model of an aligned curriculum with an identifiable relationship between the different aspects of the curriculum. A table to demonstrate the relationship between learning outcomes and assessment is required to be included in all course profiles as per Table 1.

As a consequence of the collaborative development process, this common curriculum is well understood by all team members and provides unique opportunities for cross-institutional or reciprocal teaching (Schunk, 2000). It also provides opportunities for cross-institutional small group student projects.

BLENDED LEARNING APPROACH

In order to support the teaching and learning activities of MEA and enable true collaborative teaching and learning across the partner institutions, it was recognized at all levels of management that a blended learning approach would be required and that technology would be integral to the success of this intention. Each partner institution had quite large cohorts in some core courses, and a commitment to face-to-face teaching supported by technology. On the other hand, some elective courses such as advanced ventilation could be

Table 1. Relationship between learning outcomes and assessment

Learning outcomes	Assessment Methods
1. Describe and illustrate the given surface mining systems and related equipment and support infrastructure.	• Presentation • Final group project report
2. Design and evaluate the given surface mining systems	• Presentation • Final group project report
3. Identify and evaluate core risks in the mining system	• Presentation • Final group project report
4. Appraise the given mining systems with respect to safe, efficient, economic and environmentally and socially responsible operations	• Presentation • Final group project report
5. Demonstrate awareness of major technological trends.	• Presentation • Final group project report

made viable by pooling student numbers across the partnership. MEA also had staff shortages in some areas that required filling by staff from other partner institutions. Previous to MEA, staff had travelled to other institutions where required to provide face-to-face teaching. MEA was committed to integrating more technological solutions to address this requirement. Technologies under consideration included a learning management system, an online peer assessment tool, lecture recording, videoconferencing and webconferencing. The use of these tools was made feasible by the existence of national and institutional infrastructure although it was recognized by MEA senior management that some capital expenditure would also be required by participating institutions.

IMPLEMENTING AND MANAGING MEA TECHNOLOGY DECISIONS

MEA has several layers of management including a board of directors, an executive committee, a director and the PLC who all have different degrees of input into technology decision making processes. MEA has also instituted an IT subcommittee which has responsibility for investigating suitable technologies to support the academic program. The IT subcommittee consists of the educational consultant and a representative from each partner university. Issues and challenges relating to the use of technology to support the collaboration are referred to the IT subcommittee who identify and explore workable solutions. The IT subcommittee refers their suggestions and recommendations to the PLC. Decisions about the use of technology to support the program are primarily made at the program leaders level, although some direction and agreement, particularly in relation to large capital expenditure also comes from the director and the executive committee. All decisions to adopt a technology are first trailed by selected staff and then agreement is sought from the staff to implement the technology across the program. MEA has subsequently adopted a number of open source and corporate technologies to support the design, development and delivery of the program.

AVAILABILITY OF TECHNOLOGY INFRASTRUCTURE

The university sector in Australia has access to high quality broadband internet access provided by AARNET http://www.aarnet.edu.au/aarnet3.aspx. The AARNET backbone extends to all capital cities and some major regional centers and provides the infrastructure for universities to use a range of technologies at high bandwidth rates, including the internet and videoconferencing.

All partner universities have existing infrastructure and tools relating to the provision and support of teaching and learning activities. All partner universities have learning management systems (LMSs) videoconferencing equipment and lecture recording tools. However access to these tools is not always easily accessible or financially viable for programs such as MEA. Institutional priorities can create barriers to effective use of technology for transnational teaching, requiring innovative solutions.

IMPERATIVES AND BARRIERS TO CROSS-INSTITUTIONAL COLLABORATION

MEA's intention to integrate technology across the program was deemed critical to its success. However, it soon became apparent that there were significant issues to be overcome to implement this effectively. While the use of technology to support the MEA collaboration was seen as offering many benefits to both staff and students in terms of sharing academic expertise and enhancing the learning opportunities and outcomes for students, (Strieter & Blalock, 2006: Kezar, 2005: Keats, 2003) individual institutional arrangements created significant hurdles. As Kezar notes, institutions 'are generally not structured to support collaborative approaches to learning' (2005, p. 833).

Interacting with other institutions is a complicated activity, with many barriers to inter-institutional interaction inherently in place, particularly in relation to security. Institutions necessarily have a focus on their own students and generally have limited provision for non-institutional students and staff to participate in teaching and learning activities and it was quickly recognized that a workable solution needed to be found if the use of technology to support the collaboration was going to be successful.

As well as the difficulties in interacting across institutions created by polices around institutional security, other institutional policies and procedures also created challenges in utilizing technologies for MEA. While IP videoconferencing has cut the cost of videoconferencing considerably (Caladine et al, in press), room hire rates in some institutions can still make this unaffordable. Facilities vary considerably in their technological setup, which can also create challenges in cross-institutional interactions. Additionally many of these facilities are centrally managed and access can be difficult particularly if the spaces are being utilized for a variety of teaching and learning applications, not just for videoconferencing activities. Lecture recording can also be difficult to access, depending on the extent to which institutions have adopted technologies such as this. For instance, at the time MEA initially sought to use the lecture recording technology at UQ, only lecture theatres holding 200 or more students had been fitted with technology, making it inaccessible to MEA whose classes are usually less than a hundred students, and were thus allocated to other teaching spaces.

UTILISING LEARNING MANAGEMENT SYSTEMS

Despite these challenges, MEA initially sought to support cross-university teaching and collaboration through utilizing a Learning Management Systems (LMS). From the outset this was problematical as each of the MEA partner universities had different learning management systems. When the first MEA courses were offered in first semester 2007, each individual partner university took responsibility for offering one or two courses, with the intention that all students could access the course from the one website regardless of their location. While this seemed feasible in principle, in reality this was an unworkable solution with many problems and delays encountered in obtaining cross-institutional enrolments and a lack of support for students who did not belong to the hosting institution for any technical problems that arose. MEA then provided the courses on all of the partners' websites but this duplication was seen as both inefficient and time consuming. In particular it created issues in ensuring that everyone was using the same version of the materials and that all materials were updated routinely. In order to resolve this issue, MEA actively began to explore alternatives (Andrews & Daly, 2008).

Shibboleth Technology

In order to find a workable approach to this dilemma of a suitable LMS, during the all-staff workshop held at the end of semester I, 2007 the MEA staff were unanimously supportive of exploring a solution to cross-institutional teaching. In order to get this exploration underway, the MEA IT subcommittee was charged with the responsibility of investigating alternative solutions.

One possible solution initially explored by the project team was the use of Shibboleth technology. The advantage of Shibboleth technology is its ability to move secure identity information between organizations. It is widely used in the UK and considered a viable and secure solution to the seamless supporting of cross-institutional enrolments (more information on Shibboleth can be found at http://shibbbboleth.internet2.edu/). However, while it could be easily envisaged that Shibboleth technology could solve the issue of cross-institutional enrolment it did not provide a solution to cross-institutional collaboration (Andrews & Daly, 2008).

Open Source Tools

In considering a corporate solution such as Blackboard, it was quickly realized that this was untenable from a financial perspective. While MEA enrolments of 300 plus per year are healthy for a minerals education program, they are not sufficient to support the license fees corporate LMS companies charge institutions.

The IT subcommittee sought the assistance of the director of the Teaching and Learning Centre at UNSW who suggested we investigate an open source tool such as Moodle, to address our issues. Open source is commonly defined as any program whose source code is made available for use or modification as users or other developers see fit (Bacon & Dillon, 2007). This flexibility means that software tools can be easily adapted to the specific needs of individual organizations.

There are both pros and cons to using open source tools in higher education. Some of the advantages of open source software tools include:

- Lower software costs
- Simplified licence agreements
- Potential for scaling/consolidation
- No vendor 'lock-in"
- High quality, flexible software (Williams, Clegg & Dulaney, 2005).

However there are also recognized disadvantages, which MEA needed to carefully consider. These included:

- Lack of transparency in relation to costs such as training, implementation, etc
- Little or no service and support
- Many versions of the software
- 'unfinished nature' of the software
- difficulties in accessing appropriate training access to training (Williams, Clegg & Dulaney, 2005

Many of these disadvantages have been addressed by open source software developers in recent years (Andrews & Daly 2008). Currently, many such companies are maintaining their financial viability through the provision of support and training services to clients. Issues around software versions have been addressed through better project management approaches and users can select from the different versions of the software to meet their own particular institutional needs (Andrews & Daly, 2008).

Adopting Moodle

Moodle has been widely adopted across the sector (http://moodle.org/stats/) both nationally and internationally and in 2008 had more than half the market share of LMS systems worldwide. This strongly indicated that Moodle was both a stable and appropriate LMS for an educational organization. Further it is being successfully used by several significant distance education organizations such as the UK Open University to support their students, further supporting its feasibility as a LMS for MEA. Philosophically, Moodle had been built from a social constructivist perspective with a focus on engaging students in the teaching and learning process. This fitted well with MEA, although there was some concern with the need for hosting and supporting the service and how this would be best addressed.

In order to pursue a cost effective solution, MEA investigated services run by Netspot (http://www.netspot.com.au/moodle.htm) who are heavily involved in developing and supporting Moodle. Fees for this service were well within Mean's means and considerably lower than the fees required for a corporate solution. Netspot also provides training and support services including extensive help desk support for both staff and students.

Based on this it was decided to trial Moodle using the Underground Mining Systems course in 2007. This course was a project based course with approximately 100 students enrolled. The course had few lectures and staff were willing to experiment with Moodle, making it suitable for a trial (Andrews & Daly 2008). Staff also trialed the use of lecture recording, videoing the lecture and adding the PowerPoint's later. Feedback from both staff and students in relation to the trial was favorable and demonstrated that Moodle would support collaborative teaching across the partner institutions.

At the next MEA all-staff workshop it was decided that Moodle would be adopted as the LMS for the program. An approach to implementation and moving all courses onto Moodle was put in place. Inspite of this agreement there has been considerable resistance to this. Many staff have continued to use the LMS in their home institution particularly where staff have not been engaged in cross-institutional teaching, perpetuating problems of different versions of materials and other issues relating to duplication. Direction and intervention by the PLC has now addressed this and all courses are now using Moodle for their LMS.

INTEGRATING A CONTENT MANAGEMENT SYSTEM

Effective management of documents and materials across four institutions requires processes that will support standardization, version control and ease of access to materials. Issues with different versions of documents being used, lack of standardization, and uncertainty about polices and processes to be implemented by current staff influenced the decision to implement a content management system in 2009. Additionally, MEA was conscious of the need to provide information on the background to MEA and polices, procedures and processes for incoming staff.

There are many content management systems on the market. For MEA, ease of interface with Moodle and hosting of the system, along with the system's capability to meet MEA's needs were prime determiners in the selection process. Given its ability to interface with Moodle, along with the support of Netspot for hosting the service and its fit in meeting MEA requirements, a decision was made to implement EQUELLA as the content management system (see http://www.thelearningedge.com.au/products.php **for** more information on EQUELLA).

In order to integrate EQUELLA into MEA, an approach to organizing the documents as part of the process of developing the content management system was required. This was particularly challenging to both MEA and the EQUELLA staff as this development was not driven by library staff as is usually the case in the development of content management systems. An initial two day meeting was convened which included academic staff with strong technical backgrounds and an understanding of content management systems as well as the IT subcommittee. This meeting also involved the project manager, an EQUELLA consultant and admin staff responsible for inputting information into the system.

During this initial workshop staff sought to identify how best to organize the content, which required identifying what 'collections' would provide the most effective way of organizing the MEA materials. It was decided that two collections were needed: MEA background, polices and procedures and teaching and learning. This workshop also discussed in some detail how best to organize the material in the collections.

EQUELLA itself takes a train the trainer approach and has a focus on building capacity in client organizations. The educational consultant and an academic from Adelaide attended an intensive two-day training course then organized basic training for the academic staff in each of the partner universities. This is intended to provide staff with sufficient basic skills to add information relating to their courses and to search the database to fin the materials to meet their needs both for teaching and learning and in relation to MEA's policies and procedures. It is recognized that an administrative person is required to manage the day-to-day running of the database and this person will be appointed in the second half of 2009. The system is currently being established for use in late 2009.

INTEGRATING AN ONLINE PEER REVIEW PROCESS

The adoption of more project based teaching and learning was challenging to staff, many of whom were concerned with the need to mark students work in a way that reflected the real performance of each individual group member. This is an issue which has received some attention in the literature (Herbert, 2006; Kennedy, 2005). It is recognised that a common and problematical aspect of group work is that of individual students exaggerating their marks inaccurately. In these situations group members agree to give equal marks, whether or not this reflects individual activity, in order to avoid discord within the group. MEA students had also commented on the smallness of their industry and the impact this had on not upsetting other group members, so agreeing to allocate equal marks for group work, regardless of individual input. This issue was of great concern to MEA staff and finding a workable solution was a key priority for the MEA team (Andrews & Lind, 2007).

As a consequence of these concerns, in the first instance MEA decided to investigate and implement an approach to ensure group work standards across the program which included an approach to peer assessment.

Initially MEA decided to adopt an approach that had been successfully developed in the engineering program over several years (Crosthwaite & Cameron, 2006). The approach utilized by the chemical engineers was not a technologically supported approach. The success of the approach included active staff intervention in groups where members appeared to be having difficulties with functioning, support for developing group processes and regular mentoring. Using this approach, each group member is asked to:

- Reflect on each team members performance and allocate a score that reflects this,
- Write a comment on each group member's performance.

Using a mathematical formula, each group member's scores are calculated, and this score is included in the consideration of the final grade awarded to individual students. The intent of this approach was to discourage those group members who did not contribute equally to group activities and took a 'free-ride' on other group members' work (Crosthwaite, 2006).

MEA adopted this approach in part, using only the scoring aspect of the approach, as this method had been previously used successfully by a lecturer at one of the partnership universities. Given the low staffing numbers, lack of tutors and relatively large class sizes, MEA staff were concerned with their ability to support the mentoring aspects of the peer review approach as implemented in the chemical engineering program.

Unfortunately this initial peer review approach was unsuccessful and it became clear that some ability to mentor students and to provide constructive feedback as well as an individual score was necessary to a successful peer review approach. Workload considerations and the ability for students to comment truthfully on each other's contributions were also seen as necessary, but there was no consensus within MEA as to how that might be achieved.

A presentation by MEA representatives at a national assessment conference in 2007 (Andrews & Lind, 2007) led to suggestions from Keith Willey, one of the developers of SPARK, an open source online self and peer assessment tool, to consider adopting an online tool to address peer assessment issues. It was his view that a tool such as SPARK would be able to address MEA's issues not just in relation to group assessment but also its need for cross-institutional validity and standardisation. SPARK had been progressively developed by engineering schools at the University of Technology Sydney and The University of Sydney and successfully integrated into their engineering and other programs over several years. It is now a highly sophisticated and usable tool, with enormous capacity.

Given the outcomes reported by the SPARK team on improvements to group learning that were supported by the tool (Willey & Freeman, 2006), it was decided to explore the option of open source online peer assessment tools further. As for adopting Moodle there are strong arguments for considering open source tools for small programs such as MEA for both pedagogical and financial reasons. A team consisting of the chair of the program leaders committee and the IT subcommittee reviewed a number of tools including iPeer, WebPA and SPARK. iPeer (http://ipeer.apsc.ubc.ca/home/) developed by the University of British Columbia was already in use in the first year of the undergraduate mining engineering program at UNSW. However an in-depth analysis of the tool felt that it was not comprehensive enough to address the peer assessment and moderation requirements of the MEA program. Another open source tool WebPA (http://webpaproject.lboro.ac.uk/) developed by JISC was still in developmental stages and it was also considered that this tool was not suitable for the needs of the MEA program at its then stage of development. The team felt the SPARK tool was most suited to their needs and arrangements were made to further investigate its use.

Several MEA staff attended an intensive workshop Sydney in December 2007. Staff were impressed by its capabilities and a decision was made to implement SPARK in 2008. Academics found the tool to be useful, although were dissatisfied with some aspects. However the open source nature of the tool meant that required adjustments could be quickly implemented. MEA staff are now using SPARK widely across the program with good outcomes in relation to group work and some staff have become highly sophisticated users. These staff are great champions of the tool and are increasingly taking on training and mentoring of other staff.

LECTURE RECORDING AND PODCASTING

Podcasting, including lecture recording is a useful tool for extending expertise beyond the classroom. In the case of MEA, particularly for some elective courses in 2008, lecture recording enabled courses to be delivered at all partner universities by one lecturer, who was the only one with a high level of expertise in that particular area across all the partner institutions. While the lecture recording system, lectopia, (http://lectopia.com.au) was available at the lecturer's home institution (UQ), the lecturer was not able to access it as it was only installed at that stage in lecture theatres of 200 or larger, as discussed previously. Notwithstanding, the lecture used a portable recorder to record the lectures for delivery to the other partner institutions. The recorded lectures were made available both on line and in class-time. Lecturers at the other institutions presented the recorded lecture and engaged in learning activities with students based on these recordings. This approach was deemed suitable by both staff and students who felt that recorded lectures meet the needs of both lecturers and students.

The use of lecture recording to support cross-institutional teaching is increasing with more courses electing to use this approach for some aspects of the teaching. As the integration of tools such as lectopia expands into smaller classrooms, these tools also become more available to MEA.

DEVELOPING TECHNOLOGY-RICH INTERACTIVE TEACHING AND LEARNING SPACES

MEA's commitment to more social and interactive approaches to teaching and learning and the desire to engage in reciprocal teaching (Schunk, 2000) between the partner universities extended to the design of new teaching and learning spaces at the participating institutions. It is acknowledged that traditional teaching and learning spaces (Brown & Long, 2006) can inhibit the types of teaching and learning that occur in those spaces. The development of these new spaces was aimed at designing technology enriched learning environments that would support collaborative approaches to teaching and learning both internally and externally.

To date the University of New South Wales and the University of Queensland have redesigned and refurbished existing spaces as interactive teaching and learning spaces. The UQ space was funded by UQ infrastructure funding, while the UNSW space was funded by competitive national infrastructure development funds. Plans are at place at WASM and the university of Adelaide to construct spaces for use in 2010 and 2011 respectively.

The University of Queensland is an acknowledged national and international leader in innovative learning space design and has developed a number of technology-rich collaborative teaching and learning spaces in recent years. In developing the interactive teaching and learning spaces, MEA staff consulted with UQ staff involved in the development of the collaborative teaching and learning spaces at UQ, particularly in relation to technologies to support both internal and external collaborations. Computers along the walls support individual work, while the wheeled chairs enable ease of interaction for group activities. This room is also fitted with a Polycom (http://www.polycom.com/products/index.html) videoconferencing system to support external collaboration with the other MEA partners. In the absence of an interactive teaching and learning space at WASM in the short term, the school has purchased a Polycom PVX (http://www.polycom.com/products/index.html) desktop videoconferencing system and ran it from his office PC using a web cam. This created a successful link to UNSW and effectively supports cross-institutional teaching

The space at the University of Queensland seeks to support collaborative approaches to teaching and learning. Circular workstations fitted with computers, allow students to interact with each other and with a range of learning materials including mining specific software tools to complete collaborative learning tasks (See Figure 2).

The space at the University of New South Wales has a particular focus on external collaboration and to support cross university teaching and learning, videoconferencing facilities using Polycom videoconferencing systems are integrated into the room. The videoconferencing system is dual channel enabling participants to see and interact with presenters, presentation materials and other participants. Microphones suspended from the ceiling allow for ease of interaction with remote teachers and students. The room is also wireless enabled and students can engage in collaborative teaching and learning activities using laptops and other mobile devices (See Figure 3).

OTHER TECHNOLOGIES

Virtual Mine UNSW

MEA also utilize a range of other technologies including specialized software packages to support the program. Additionally, the mining school at the University of New South Wales had long been involved in developing a virtual mine (http://www.mining.unsw.edu.au/index.html). This is an immersive environment developed using icenema where students can engage in a variety of activities around mine safety and other issues relating to mining. Scenario based learning activities are utilized to assist students to develop understandings of the safety issues in mines and how these might be most effectively addressed. Student response system (SRS) technology has also been integrated in to these environment, to support learning through providing feedback and guiding students to develop desired learning outcomes. Ways of linking these technologies to other partner institutions will be explored in the future. The Table 2 summaries the current use of technologies across the MEA program.

Figure 2. University of Queensland interactive teaching and learning space

Figure 3. Interactive teaching and learning space, University of New South Wales

APPLICATION SERVICE PROVIDERS

The notion of application service providers is one that is increasingly being investigated by Higher education, particularly in relation to hosting services such as content management systems and learning management systems. For MEA, providing hardware in the form of servers and technical support for tools such as Moodle is financially unviable. Equally these kinds of services are not necessarily supplied by home institutions who in many cases have corporate arrangements in place to support products such as Blackboard. In order to provide a solution hosting and supporting its LMS as outlined previously, MEA investigated application service providers, Netspot, located in Adelaide, who provide hosting and user support for both staff and students at a fraction of the cost of a commercial license. This means that MEA does not need to invest in technical support, difficult to provide in a financially viable fashion across the four partner institutions. Netspot provides a helpdesk accessible for extended hours during weekdays and for some hours on weekends for both staff and students.

Table 2. Technology use by course

Course Name	Technologies utilized for teaching and learning
Socio-Environmental Aspects	Moodle; SPARK
Mine Planning	Moodle ; SPARK
Mine Ventilation	Moodle Cross university interactive tutorials using interactive teaching spaces
Rock breakage	Moodle; Online quizzes
Surface Mining systems	Moodle; SPARK
Underground Mining Systems	Moodle; SPARK; Some lecture recording
Hard Rock Mine Design and Feasibility	Moodle; SPARK Online lectures and software training between universities
Coal Mine Design and Feasibility	Moodle ; SPARK Online lectures and software training between universities
Mine Geotechnical Engineering	Moodle; Lecture recording
Mining Research Project 1	Moodle
Mining Research Project 2	Moodle
Mine Management	Moodle; lecture recording
Mining in a global Environment	Moodle Virtual interaction with mining personnel in a mixed reality environment using web conferencing tools. This includes deep investigation of sustainability issues at a remote site
Mining Asset Management	Moodle; lecture recording
Advanced Mine Ventilation	Moodle On-site ventilation activity Cross-university teaching using the interactive teaching space in 2009 Cross –university interactive tutorials using the interactive teaching spaces
Advanced Geotechnical Engineering	Moodle Virtual Reality Module for Advanced Geomechanics

The provision of the server by the hosting organization was also a cost-effective solution, avoiding the need to invest in expensive hardware that would require continual upgrading. Additionally, Netspot also provides training services, further addressing MEA needs. As MEA has adopted other technologies such as EQUELLA and SPARK, Netspot is also providing hosting services for these technologies.

DEVELOPING AND SUPPORTING STAFF

Apart from mostly minimal use of learning management systems, the majority of MEA staff were used to teaching in face-to-face classrooms and had little understanding of the technologies proposed to support collaboration across the program and how these might be best utilized to support cross university teaching and learning. In most cases where staff adopt technologies for teaching they are driven not only by institutional priorities but also by their own interests and beliefs in how the technology might support their teaching and learning activities. While there were exceptions, for most MEA staff this was not the case. In order to assist MEA staff to develop an understanding of the possibilities offered by the technologies, several workshops were conducted, highlighting these technologies, but there was little interest expressed in pursuing these technologies further.

In attempt to encourage take-up of videoconferencing, web conferencing and podcasting the educational consultant identified one staff member at each of the original partner institutions and asked them to develop a short lesson relating to mining education to present to staff at the next all staff workshop. Staff were asked to complete a feedback form on what they thought were the strength sand weaknesses of the technologies and how they might be able to use them in their own teaching and learning practice. This approach was quite successful in getting staff to understand the affordances of the technologies and stimulated some initial use of podcasting and videoconferencing. Bandwidth and other operational considerations relating to webconferencing tools such as Elluminate (http://www.elluminate.com/) and Wimba (http://www.wimba.com/) have limited use of these tools by MEA staff to date.

Moodle Masters, SPARK Masters

In order to support the technological innovations that enable many of the collaborative aspects of MEA it was recognized that MEA needed to build capacity within the organization form both a technological and pedagogical perspective. Further to provide training and pedagogical support for the technologies adopted by MEA, it was decided to implement a mastery approach to staff development and support. Interested academics from each university were invited to develop skills in each of the technologies, Moodle, SPARK, Quizzes and EQUELLA. In some cases this was the same person. These individuals attended intensive workshops run by the tool developers in the case of SPARK and the hosting organization in the case of Moodle. Their responsibilities include:

- to be the first point of contact in their institutions in relation to the technologies they are supporting
- to develop a high level of competency in the use and applications of the technologies,
- to provide basic training
- to liaise with organizations /developers in regards to any issues relating to the tools.

FUTURE DIRECTIONS

MEA is constantly reviewing its technology needs in response to maintaining and expanding its collaborative teaching and learning activities, meeting individual academic needs and maintaining a sustainable transnational educational environment in a global financial downturn. With these factors in mind, new and emerging technologies will be added to the mix to meet identified needs including student response system technology.

However, the next technology that MEA intends to adopt to support collaboration across the program to respond to ongoing industry needs is an ePortfolio system. ePortfolios are recognized for providing many benefits for students, staff and institutions (Miller, 2009). Miller outlines the following possible impacts on student learning:

- build learners personal and academic identities as they complete complex projects and reflect on their capabilities and progress,
- facilitate the integration of learning as students connect learning across courses and time,
- be focused on developing self-assessment abilities in which students judge the quality of working using the same criteria exports use,
- help students plan their own academic pathways, as they come to understand what they know and are able to do and what they still need to learn (p. 9).

Given the nature of ePortfolios and the many opportunities they provide, institutions need to carefully consider what the intended outcomes of integrating an ePortfolio are and what they hope to achieve from adopting such a technology. For

MEA this is an important discussion that will be part of the all-staff workshop in late 2009, with investigations into an appropriate system commencing in 2010. There are a number of both open source and corporate tools available and MEA will make its selection based on the tool's ability to meet MEA's needs in this area.

CONCLUSION

Many existing and emerging corporate and open source technologies are available and accessible for supporting transnational teaching and learning collaborations. These technologies can support constructivist and social constructivist approaches to teaching and learning and create a truly collaborative learning environment where expertise is shared across participating institutions. Selection of the tools needs to be made on their ability to meet the organizations' educational needs and financial considerations. The use of technology to support the transnational teaching and learning program within MEA is constantly evolving, driven by both internal and external factors. Appropriate support from all levels of management is an important part of the successful use of technology to support transnational teaching and learning activities.

ACKNOWLEDGMENT

The development of MEA has been supported by finds from MEA and CASR.

REFERENCES

AARNET home page. (2009). Accessed May 10, 2090, from http://www.aarnet.edu.au/aarnet3.aspx

Andrews, T., & Daly, C. (2008). Using Moodle, an open source learning management system, to support a national teaching and learning collaboration. In *Proceedings of the 19th Conference of the Australasian Association for Engineering Education,* Yeppoon, Australia.

Andrews, T., & Lind, G. (2007). Evaluation and assessment of problem-based and case-based learning in the Mining Education Australia (MEA) collaborative initiative. In *Proceedings ATN Assessment and Evaluation Conference,* QUT, Brisbane.

Australian Bureau of Statistics. (2008). *Year Book Australia*. Retrieved May 10, 2009, from http://www.abs.gov.au/AUSSTATS/abs@.nsf/7d12b0f6763c78caca257061001cc588/76282812C4583EB5CA2573D20010CC8A?opendocument

Bacon, S., & Dillion, T. (2007). *Opening education: The potential of open source approaches for education*. Future Lab. Retrieved May 5, 2009, from http://www.futurelab.org.uk

Biggs, J. B. (1999). Teaching for quality learning at university: What the student does. Buckingham, UK: Society for Research in Higher Education and Open University Press.

Boud, D., Cohen, R., & Sampson, J. (1998). Peer learning and assessment. *Assessment & Evaluation in Higher Education, 24*(4), 413–426. doi:10.1080/0260293990240405

Brown, M., & Long, P. (2006).Trends in Learning Space Design. In D. Oblinger (Ed.), *Learning Spaces*. Retrieved April 15, 2007, from www.educause.edu/learningspaces.

Caladine, R., Andrews, T., Tynan, B., Symth, R., & Vale, D. (in press). New communications Options: A renaissance in IP use. In Veletsianos, G. (Ed.), Using Emerging Technologies in Distance Education. Athabasca, Canada: Athabasca University Press.

Crosthwaite, C. (2006). *Team projects: facilitating successful student teams and project centred learning*. Presentation to MEA staff, Brisbane, 14th July.

Crosthwaite, C., & Cameron, I. (2006). Changing a culture: Project centered curriculum, creativity, challenge, change: partnerships in engineering education. In *Proceedings 17th Conference of the Australasian Association of Engineering Education (AAEE)*, Auckland, New Zealand.

Dooley, B. (2006). *Open Source E-Learning: Alternatives to Proprietary Tools, Systems and Courseware.* Brandon Hall Research. Retrieved March 10, 2008, from http://www.brandon- hall.com/publications/opensource/opensource.shtml

Elluminate. (n.d.). Retrieved May 5, 2009, from http://www.elluminate.com

EQUELLA. (n.d.). Retrieved May 5, 2009, from http://www.thelearningedge.com.au/products.php

Herbet, N. (2006, September). *Peer Assessment: is it fair?* Paper presented at Uniserve Science Assessment Symposium Proceedings, The University of Sydney.

ipeer. (n.d.) Retrieved July 17, 2008, from http://ipeer.apsc.ubc.ca/home/

JISC. (2006). *Shibboleth: Connecting People and Resources Briefing* (version 2). Retrieved July 17, 2008, from http://www.jisc.ac.uk/publications/publications/pub_shibboleth.aspx.

Keats, D. (2003). Collaborative Development of Open Content: A Process Model to Unlock the

Kennedy, G. J. (2005). Peer assessment in group projects: Is it worth it? *Proceedings of the Seventh Australian Conference on Computing Education*. Newcastle, Australia.

Kezar, A. (2005). Redesigning for Collaboration within Higher Education Institutions. *Research in Higher Education*, *46*(7), 831–860. doi:10.1007/s11162-004-6227-5

Lectopia homepage. (n.d) Retrieved May 5th 2009 from http://lectopia.com.au.

Mayer, R. E. (1999). Designing instruction for constructivist learning. In C.M. Reigeluth (Ed.), Instructional design theories and models (pp 141-159). Mahwah, NJ: Lawrence Erlbaum.

Miller, R. (2009). The Benefits of E-portfolios for Students and Faculty in Their Own Words. *Peer Review, 11*(1). Retrieved May 5, 2009, from http://www.aacu.org/peerreview/pr-wi09/pr-wi09_benefits.cfm

Minerals Council of Australia national Tertiary Education Taskforce. (1998). *Back From the Brink: Reshaping Minerals Tertiary Education.* Discussion paper, February 1998.

Moodle. (n.d.). Retrieved May 18, 2009, from http://moodle.org/.

Moodle statistics. (2008). Retrieved May 18, 2009, from http://moodle.org/stats/

Netspot homepage. (n.d.). Retrieved May 5, 2009, from http://www.netspot.com.au/moodle.htm

Panitz, T. (1996). A definition of Collaborative versus Cooperative learning. *Deliberations.* Retrieved May 18, 2009, from http://www.londonmet.ac.uk/deliberations/collaborative-learning/panitz-paper.cfm

Polycom home page. (2009). Retrieved May 4, 2008, from http://www.polycom.com/products/index.html.

Potential for African Universities. *First Monday*, 8 (2). Retrieved May 2, 2008, from http://firstmonday.org/issues/issue8_2/keats/index.html.

Schunk, D. H. (2000). Learning Theories: An Educational Perspective (3rd edition). Upper Saddle River, NJ: Merrill.

Shibboleth. (2008). Retrieved July 17, 2008, from http://shibbbboleth.internet2.edu/

Strieter, L., & Blalock, L. B. (2006). Journey to successful collaborations. *Journal of Extension, 44* (1). Retrieved May 4, 2008, from http://www.joe.org/joe/2006february/tt4p.shtml

The School of Mining Engineering. *UNSW home page*. (2009). Retrieved May 4, 2009, from http://www.mining.unsw.edu.au/index.html

The University of New South Wales. (2006). Application for a CASR grant. Implementation of Mining Education Australia.

Vgotsky, L. (1978). Mind in Society. London: Harvard University Press.

Web, P. *A*. (n.d). Retrieved May 4, 2009, from http://webpaproject.lboro.ac.uk/

Wiersema, N. (2000). How does Collaborative Learning actually work in a classroom and how do students react to it? A Brief Reflection. *Deliberations*. Retrieved June 11, 2008, from http://www.londonmet.ac.uk/deliberations/collaborative-learning/wiersema.cfm

Willey, K., & Freeman, M. (2006). Improving teamwork and engagement: the case for self and peer assessment. *Australasian Journal of Engineering Education, 2*. Retrieved from http://www.aaee.com.au/journal/2006/willey0106.pdf

Willey, K., & Gardner, A. P. (2009 July). *Investigating the capacity of self and peer assessment to engage students and increase their desire to learn.* Paper presented at SEFI 37th Annual Conference, Rotterdam, The Netherlands.

Williams, J., Clegg, P., & Dulaney, E. (2005). *The Advantages of Adopting Open Source Software.* Retrieved July 17th 2008, from http://www.informit.com/articles/article.aspx?p=376255

Wimba. (n.d.). Retrieved May15, 2009, from http://www.wimba.com/

ADDITIONAL READING

Amey, M., Eddy, L., & Ozaki, C. (2007). Demands for partnership and collaboration in higher education: A model. *New Directions for Community Colleges, 139*, 5–14. doi:10.1002/cc.288

Boswell, C., & Cannon, S. (2005). New horizons for collaborative partnerships. *Online Journal of Issues in Nursing, 10*(1), 75–80.

Bottomly, J. (2005). Recionfiguring Institutional strategies for flexible learning and deliver. In V. Jackupec & J. Garrick (Eds.), Flexible learning, human resource and organisational development: Putting theory to work. London: Routledge.

Courant, C., & Griffiths, R. (2006). Software and collaboration in higher education: A study of open source software. *Online report*. Retrieved from http://www.ithaka.org/saved-pages/strategic-services/oss/OOSS_Report_FINAL.pdf

Gatlif, B., & Wendel, F. (1998). Inter-institutional collaboration and team teaching. *American Journal of Distance Education, 12*(1), 26–37. doi:10.1080/08923649809526981

Jackupec, V., & Garrick, J. (Eds.). (2000). Flexible learning, human resource and organisational development: Putting theory to work. London: Routledge.

Kawatchi, P. (2008). Future Directions for Distance Education 'Researching and Promoting Access to Education and Training. In The Role of Distance Education and e-Learning in Technology-Enhanced Environments' EDEN / UNESCO 5th Research Workshop: Plenary Session Paris. Retrieved July11, 2009, from AJDE2008_Kawachi_EDEN.pdf

Keats, D. (2003). Collaborative Development of Open Content: A Process Model Potential for African Universities. *First Monday, 8*(2). Retrieved May 2, 2008, from http://firstmonday.org/issues/issue8_2/keats/index.html

Malik, N. (2005). Framework of Collaborative Research and Development on Distance Learning Technology for Asia. In *Proceedings, 19th AAOU Annual Conference*. Jakarta: Indonesia.

McCurdy, S., & Schroder, R. (2006). Achieving Diversity Through Online inter-institutional collaborations. *Journal of Asynchronous Learning Networks*, *10*(1).

OECD. (2007). *Giving knowledge for free: The emergence of open educational resources.* Website. Retrieved July 10, 2008, from http://213.253.134.43/oecd/ pdfs/browseit/9607041E.pdf

Pauwels, A. (2007). Collaborative Structural Reform Research Project: Innovative approaches to the provision of Languages other than English in Australian Higher Education. *DASSH*. Retrieved May 20, 2008, from http://www.dassh.edu.au/casr/casr_projects.html

Reed, G., Cooper, J., & Young, L. (2007). A partnership in flux: The demise of a program. *New Directions for Community Colleges*, *139*, 79–90. doi:10.1002/cc.295

Smith, M. S., & Casserly, C. M. (2006). The promise of open educational resources. *Change*, *38*(5), 8–17. doi:10.3200/CHNG.38.5.8-17

Stein, R., & Short, P. (2001). Collaboration in Delivering Higher Education Programs: Barriers and Challenges. *The Review of Higher Education*, *24*(4), 417–435. doi:10.1353/rhe.2001.0010

Tripathi, P., & Mukerji, S. (2008). Access and equity to education in India through synergy of conventional and ODL systems: A step towards democratization of education. *Open Praxis*, *9*(9). Retrieved 20 June, 2008, from http:// www.distanceandaccesstoeducation.org/contents/OP2008-IGNOU.pdf

Tynan, B., & Smyth, R. (Eds.). (2007). Collaborations to offer small courses forum, final report. University of New England.

Wang, X., Dannenhoffer, J., Davidson, B., & Spector, J. (2005). Design Issues in a Cross-Institutional Collaboration on a Distance Education Course. *Distance Education*, *26*(3), 405–423. doi:10.1080/01587910500291546

Wheeler, D. A. (2007). *Why Open Source Software / Free Software (OSS/FS, FLOSS, or FOSS)? Look at the Numbers!* Retrieved July 17, 2008, from http://www.dwheeler.com/oss_fs_why.html

Wiley, D. (2007). *On the sustainability of open educational resource initiatives in higher education.* OECD Publication: Center for Educational Research and Innovation CERI. Retrieved 20 June, 2008, from http://www.oecd.org/dataoecd/33/9/38645447.pdf

Willey, K., & Gardner, A. P. (2008). *Using self and peer assessment for professional and team skill development: do well functioning teams experience all the benefits?* Paper presented at ATN Assessment Conference 2008: Engaging Students in Assessment, University of South Australia, Adelaide.

Willey, K., & Gardner, A. P. (2008). *Improvements in the self and peer assessment tool SPARK: do they improve learning outcomes?* Paper presented at ATN Assessment Conference 2008: Engaging Students in Assessment, University of South Australia, Adelaide.

Willey, K., & Gardner, A. P. (2008). Using self assessment to integrate graduate attribute development with discipline content delivery. In *Proceedings of the 36th Annual Conference of SEFI.* SEFI 36th Annual Conference. Denmark:Aalborg.

Willey, K., & Gardner, A. P. (2009). *Self and Peer Assessment: A Necessary Ingredient in Developing and Tracking Students' Graduate Attributes*. Paper presented at Research in Engineering Education Symposium, Queensland, Australia.

Willey, K., & Gardner, A. P. (2009, July). *Changing Student's Perceptions of Self and Peer Assessment.* Paper presented at Research in Engineering Education Symposium, Queensland, Australia.

Wilson, T. (2008). New ways of mediating learning: Investigating the implications of adopting open educational resources for tertiary education at an institution in the United Kingdom as compared to one in South Africa. *International Review of Research in Open and Distance Learning, 9*(1), 1-4. Retrieved, June 20, 2009, from Jhttp://www.irrodl.org/index.php/irrodl/article/view/485/1000

Wong, D. (2008). Online distance learning provides additional learning opportunities and improves the socioeconomic status of working adults in Malaysia. *Asian Journal of Distance Education, 6*(1), 5-14. Retrieved from www.AsianJDE.org/2008v6.1.Wong.pdf

Zondiros, D. (2008). Access, inequality and exclusion. *European Journal of Open, Distance and E-Learning.* Retrieved from http://www.eurodl.org/index.php?keyword=distance%20education&article=302

Zondiros, D. (2008). Online, distance education and globalisation: Its impact on educational access, inequality and exclusion. *European Journal of Open, Distance and E-Learning, I* (January to June). Retrieved June 25, 2009, from http://www.eurodl.org/materials/special/2008/Dimitris_Zondiros.htm

KEY TERMS AND DEFINITIONS

MEA: Mining Education Australia.: A collaboration of four Australian mining schools to provide a common national curriculum for the 3rd and 4th year of the Mining Engineering Degree.

EQUELLA: A learning content management system, EQUELLA is a digital repository where materials can be stored and accessed.

LMS: Learning management system – a software package for delivering teaching and learning activities and materials and for managing some of the administrative aspects of teaching and learning activities.

MOODLE: An open source learning management system widely used around the world.

SPARK: Self and peer assessment kit. SPARK is an online tool designed to support self and peer assessment for team-based activities.

Open Source Tools: Open source tools are software programs which provide their source c ode free of charge for development or adaptation by users

Lecture Recording: Lecture recording refers to automatic taping of face-to-face lectures using software such as Lectopia.

Interactive Teaching and Learning spaces: These spaces are technology rich teaching and learning spaces that use technology to support interaction for both face-to-face and distance learning activities.

PLC: Program leaders committee. This team consists of a representative of each of the partner institutions of MEA and oversees the academic program.

Application Service Providers: Application service providers are organizations that provide services for a range internet and other technologies. These services include hosting, training and end-user support.

Chapter 6
Development of E-Learning in Niger: Opportunities, Challenges and Perspectives

Aissetou Drame Yaye
African Network for Agriculture, Agroforestry and Natural Resources Education (ANAFE), Kenya

ABSTRACT

The University Abdou Moumouni (UAM) of Niamey in Niger mainly focused on traditional face to face learning, and even the existence of the African Virtual University since the years 1999 did not change the situation. It is only after the official opening at the University of the Francophone Digital Campus in December 2003 that lecturers and students started overseeing and taking advantages of all the benefits of e-Learning and distance learning. The present paper builds on the author's personal initiatory experience in e-Learning to highlight some specific challenges that traditional universities such as the UAM face in their efforts to introduce e-Learning and distance learning as a new mode of course delivery. The study shows that even though challenges are big, political and institutional support can freshen the perspectives and change opportunities into realities.

ORGANIZATIONAL BACKGROUND

Niger is a vast West African country of 1,267000 km^2 locked between Burkina Faso, Benin, Mali, Chad, Nigeria, Algeria and Libya (Figure 1). On 25% of the surface area live two third of the populations while the remaining 75% is occupied by the Sahara Desert. Agriculture employs three quarters of the population and accounts to 40% of Niger's GDP (Agyeman, 2007). Statistics from a World Bank study (World Bank, 2006) give some socio economic indicators (Figure 2). The demographic growth in Niger is one of the world's highest with a fertility rate of 7 live births per woman. A recent study from the Ministry of Finance projected that the current population of about 13 million inhabitants will grow to 55 million by 2050 (Cabinet Premier Minister, 2003). Uranium contributes 31% to the country's total export earning, but sixty percent of the population live below the poverty line (Agyeman, 2007).

DOI: 10.4018/978-1-61520-909-5.ch006

Figure 1. Map of Niger (http://www.lonelyplanet.com/maps/africa/niger/)

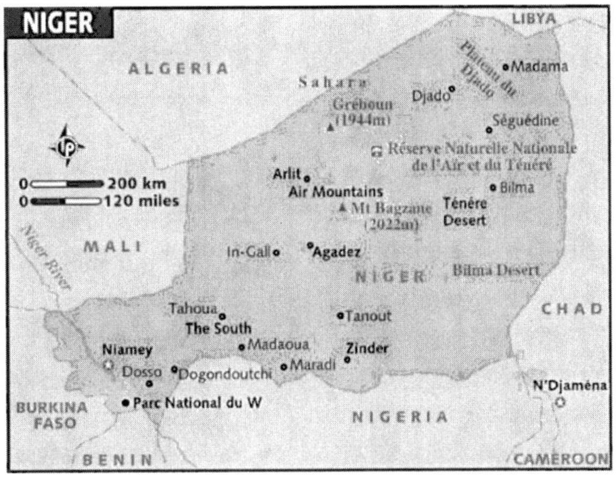

Figure 2. General statistics on Niger (World Bank, 2006)

Indicator	Value
Total population	13 499 000
Annual population growth rate (%)	2.9
Population of age 0 – 14 (%)	49
Rural population (%)	78
GDP per capita (US $)	835
Total fertility rate (%)	7.1
Infant mortality rate (‰)	154
Live expectancy at birth (years)	45
HIV rate (%) in adults of 15 – 49	1.2
Primary school enrollment for girls (%)	32
Primary school enrollment for boys (%)	46
Secondary school enrollment for girls (%)	5
Secondary school enrollment for boys (%)	8

Niger's education system consists of six years of primary school, four years of junior secondary school, and three years of senior secondary school and two to four years of tertiary education. Primary school enrollments for both boys and girls are less than 50%, while less than 10% of the children attend secondary schools. Tertiary enrollment concerns only 1% of the population having finished secondary school (Salmi, 2000).

Until 2004 there was only one university in Niger. It was created as a public training institution in 1971 under the name of High Education Center of Niger. In 1973, it became the University of Niamey, and in 1992, it received the name of University Abdou Moumouni (UAM) of Niamey in memory of the first Nigerien physicist and former University President. Created under a governmental law, the University Abdou Moumouni (UAM) of Niamey is a public institution almost entirely financed by the Niger government despites some assistance received through bilateral and multilateral cooperation. It is administered by the Ministry of Secondary and Higher Education, Science, Research and Technology (MESSRT).

Like the majority of tertiary agricultural education institutions in Sub Saharan Africa, the University Abdou Moumouni (UAM) of Niamey was created as a pure traditional university using talk and chalk with the main objective of providing the government with graduates to fill up the public sector positions left vacant by departing colonial personals. This happened in a context where the telecommunication network was largely undeveloped and regulated by the Ministry of Communication. Since 1996 the only Internet service provider was the National Telecom SONITEL through fiber connectivity.

In favor of the globalization occurring in a knowledge-based developing world, and confronted to the numerical divide, the University Abdou Moumouni, like the other Sub Saharan African Tertiary Education institutions, is in the process of developing new ways of delivering higher education programmes. Under the supervision of CAMES (Le Comité Africain et Malgache sur l'Enseignement Superieur), deep reforms are being introduced through the Licence- Master-

Doctorat principle to harmonize programmes, methodologies and teaching strategies within all French speaking African universities. Training networks such as the African Network for Agriculture, Agroforestry and Natural Resources Education (ANAFE) engaged in curriculum review and development, are also struggling for more relevant and contextualized course content, and for finding innovative ways to attract more students into tertiary agricultural education. In this process, Information and Communication Technologies (ICTs) are more and more seen as a driving tool for Internet based learning that can improve the quality, flexibility and accessibility of education.

Enhancing the use of ICTs, and particularly e-Learning can be a big challenge in a country like Niger which is capable to provide for only 10% of its population with electricity. However, to show its engagement, the government of Niger, with the assistance of the Economic and Monetary Union of West Africa (UEMOA) finalized its ICT development plan that was presented to the Assembly in May 2005. Further the Niger High Commission for New Technologies in Information and Communication (HCNTIC) was established to support the process through development of legal, regulatory and institutional framework including the harmonization of policies with the neighboring countries (Agyeman, 2007). The HCNTIC is located at the Prime Minister's Office and is also responsible for policy promotion and technology development at the national level. All these developments at the regional and national policy levels supported the leaders at the UAM in their efforts to enhance use of ICTs and e-Learning facilities and competencies into the Faculties. Training of lecturers in the use of ICFs in education was one of the main focuses.

This paper will draw from the personal learning experience in open distance education of a Lecturer of the University Abdou Moumouni of Niamey to highlight the opportunities and new perspectives but also the challenges linked to the introduction of e-Learning at UAM of Niamey.

SETTING THE STAGE

Since 2000, the UAM is composed of six faculties and three research institutes which are:

- The Faculty of Sciences
- The Faculty of Human Sciences
- The Faculty of Economic and law Sciences
- The Faculty of Health Sciences
- The Faculty of Agriculture
- The Faculty of Pedagogy
- The Institute on Radio Isotopes
- The Institute of Research on Mathematics Sciences
- The Institute of Research on Human Sciences

Faculties deal with teaching and research while the institutes' main area is research and technology development. Since 2000 the majority of the Faculties and Institutes were only concerned with undergraduate training. Post graduate level studies were introduced only recently. The University curricula at the faculties have been changed several times to reflect the emerging needs and challenges deriving from the society and the globalized economical situation. Faculty Lecturers are hired after their MSc or PhD without any pedagogical training. However since 1990, the first requirement for a candidate lecturer is to hold a PhD.

Students' enrollment records gathered by the Registrar's Offices showed that the student enrollment rate is 4% since a decade, leading to 6,596 students for the academic year 2003/2004, and about 8,000 students in 2006/2007. This increase in student enrollment combined with insufficient funding is the root cause of the difficulties that the National Centre for Social affairs faced in dealing with students' scholarships, housing and transportation. The overall number of male students is almost three to four times higher than that of females (Figure 3). Out of the 8000 students enrolled in 2006/2007, over 6000 were males. There is a constant increase in male students' enrollment, while at the same time little improvement is observed in the female situation. However, since 2004, there seems to be a slight increase in the number of females, which is still much lower than what is observed with males.

There are more than 250 male lecturers, compared to less than 50 females (Figure 4). The situation varies within faculties: The Faculties of Letters and Human Sciences, the Faculty of Sciences and the Faculty of Medicine and Health Sciences have each only about 5 to 6 women lecturers, while there are only two at the Faculty of Agriculture and four at the Faculty of Education.

A much better situation is found with the support staff (Secretaries, laboratory technicians, cleaners, etc.) counting almost as many females than males, with even a tendency of women taking over men in number (Figure 5). Laboratories, training and research facilities were built in all these faculties but very few computers were part of the equipment.

The liberalization of the telecommunication sector in 2005 through the partial privatization of the national Telecom operator SONITE led to the improvement of the Internet services through the installment by SONITEL of 2 MB bandwidth

Figure 3. Male and female students enrolled at the Abdou Moumouni University (Niger) from 1998 - 2005

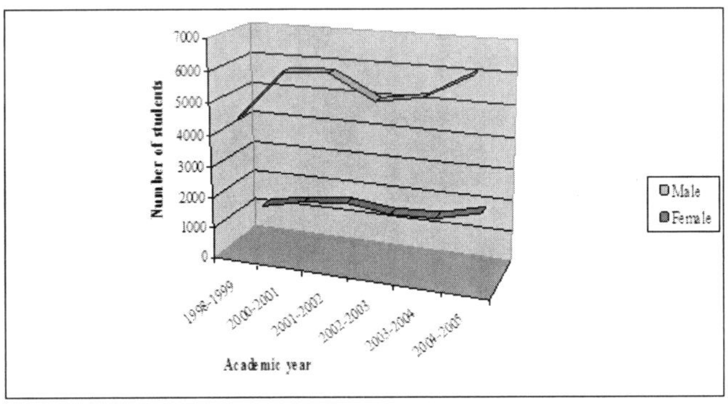

Figure 4. The Percentage of students enrolled in the various Faculties of the AMU of Niamey

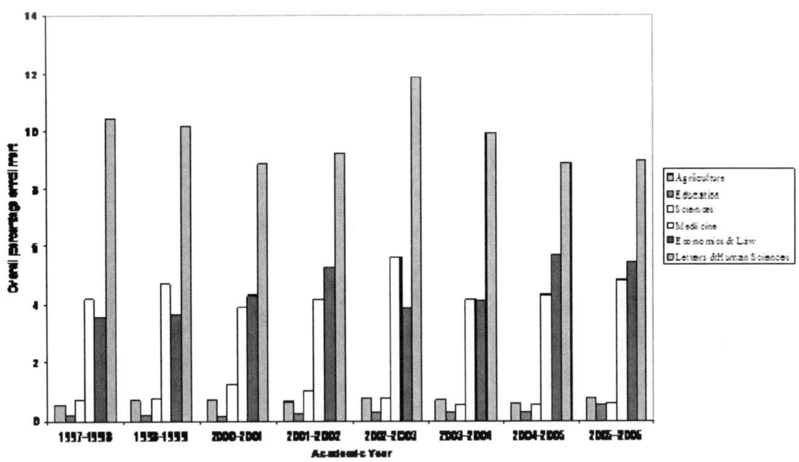

Figure 5. Male (blue) and female (red) faculty support staff

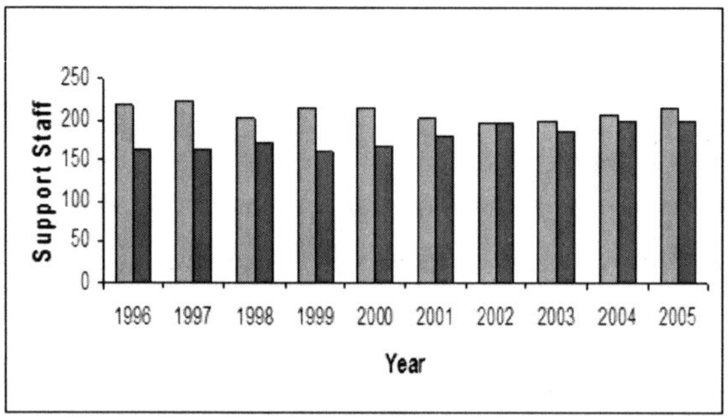

connectivity. New operators providing Internet and cellular telephony services also came in with many of them connected to the VSAT service using wireless connectivity (Wi-Fi). Some of them established their Internet communication through dial-up connection or telephone lines.

CASE DESCRIPTION

E-learning Opportunities at UAM: The Francophone Campus Network

The University Agency for Francophonie (Agence Universitaire pour la Francophonie: AUF) was created in 1961 in Montreal (Canada) by the Heads of States of French speaking countries. AUF is an association of 524 French speaking tertiary education institutions in 60 countries disseminated throughout all the five continents (AUF, 2003). The main objective of the AUF is to enhance scientific exchanges, promote international cooperation and reinforce the institutional and individual competencies of the member institutions. This interuniversity partnership is done mainly through financial and technical support to lecturers, scientists and students from Southern universities to create research networks participate to scientific conferences and exchange programmes, and benefit from specific degree and non degree training courses.

In its efforts to popularize the use of Information and Communication Technologies (ICTs) in education, the AUF created a network of 24 Francophone Numerical Campuses within French speaking universities to bring ICT infrastructure and techniques closer to lecturers and students. The overarching objective of the Francophone Numerical Campuses (CNF) is to enhance the appropriation of ICTs in the training institutions. This will be achieved through training, production of pedagogical contents, networking and distribution of scientific and technical information. The specific objectives are to:

- Facilitate inter-university partnerships that will allow deployment and spreading of e-Learning and distance learning settings based on use of ICTs in education.
- Promote the introduction of education technologies in lecturers' pedagogical practices, particularly through assistance in the development of online courses.
- Reinforce and modernize classical modes of teaching by progressively introducing course modules using digital supports.

The Francophone Numerical Campus of Niamey is hosted by the Faculty of Agriculture on a surface area of 200 square meters. It counts 70 computers connected through two servers to an internet speed of 128 kilobits per second (Refer, 2006).

It was officially opened on 12 December 2003 in the presence of about 400 people. The government of Niger showed its endorsement of the CNF by delegating four Ministers to attend the opening ceremony. These ministers were the Minister of Higher Education, Research and Technology, the Minister of Basic Education and Alphabetization, the Minister of Equipment and Infrastructure and the Minister of Youth and Professional Insertion of Young People. The Rector of the University Agency for Francophonie (Agence Universitaire pour le Francophonie: AUF) based in France, the

Director of AUF for West Africa based in Dakar (Senegal), the Rector, Deans, Heads of Departments, Lecturers, technical staff and students of University Abdou Moumouni, and many Ambassadors among whom the French Ambassador, attended the opening ceremony.

The public was composed of University lecturers and technical staff, research scientists, graduate and post graduate students. This public was enthusiastic to be offered possibilities of easier access to emails and scientific and technical information. The resource centre composed of two training rooms each equipped with 20 computers, is mainly used for distance learning, development of e-contents and distance learning projects.

Training courses offered at the CNF include short training of five to seven days on the use of ICTs in academic environment, and two semesters to two years Master degree courses in various Agriculture, Science, Education and health fields. The short term training workshops are called Transfer Workshops and they build capacity of lecturers in particular areas of ICTs such as the use of search and access tools to scientific documentation, management of online public scientific writing, Conception, development and use of online courses, Tutoring in Open Distance Learning courses, etc.

One of the first distance learning Master Degree programmes offered to lecturers at the Abdou Moumouni University was the Master UTICEF (Utilization des Technologies de l'Information et de la Communication dans l'Enseignement et la Formation) called "Use of ICTs in Teaching and Training" and developed by the University Agency for Francophonie in collaboration with the University Louis Pasteur of Strasbourg (France). Like all the AUF activities, this collaboration was officialized through a tripartite convention linking AUF, its Southern university members and a particular French speaking Northern institution delivering the activity. This tripartite convention allowed AUF to partially sponsor students from the South to register online for the Master UTICEF offered by the University of Strasbourg and to receive their diploma through the AUF regional officers.

The Master UTICEF is a blended course composed of 40 weeks of distance learning on Internet, starting with 50 hours of face to face course taken during one week in the Francophone Numerical Campus (CNF) of one of the beneficiaries' countries. Students are registered on second year Professional Master at the Louis Pasteur University which delivers the diploma. In all CNFs, training rooms are made available for registered students who have unlimited access during working hours from Monday to Saturday. Students' evaluation is a continuous process based on grading of individual and team work in each of the six virtual modules called Teaching Units, but also two face to face exams (a mid-term and a final) which are taken under supervision in the CNFs and using computers not connected to Internet. The final evaluation relates to the distance learning course project that the students developed under the distance- assistance of a tutor.

The course was delivered through the ACOLAD (Apprentissage COL laboratif A Distance, 2006) platform (ACOLAD, 2006). ACOLAD is a virtual environment which graphical interface is based on a metaphorical representation of a university environment making available various learning spaces such as the class and group discussion rooms, the library, the lectures' offices, and the student's personal desk. Tools for synchronous and asynchronous discussions such as chat, emails, forum discussions and pager are also available. The course also makes good use of various open source knowledge management systems such as Moodle and Claritine, and platforms like WIKI, and the students are encouraged to enhance their skills in some technical tools such as Mot 2 and Inspiration. Throughout the course, learning is facilitated and supported by experienced tutors who are very effective in breaking the learners' feeling of isolation what result in very limited abandonment.

The Master UTICEF course starts with one week face to face gathering that aims to develop the participants' procedural competences. This first week's objective is to build participants' skills in using the different tools, particularly the learning platform "ACOLAD". It also presents the course programme, the different learning environments and the students' first draft projects which consist in developing a distance learning course which should be finalized and defended by the end of the semester.

Like many distance learning programmes, the Master UTICEF course has lots of value-adding characteristics which make it attractive for Universities. These include:

1. The first week face to face course: it allows participants from the same geographic region to meet and know each other. Having seen each other and being able to put a face on a name appearing during a chat made the synchronous and asynchronous sessions friendlier. It also helps a lot during personal work when one requires peer support and can freely call upon a colleague for help.
2. The virtual platform ACOLAD: It is built on a university architecture, what makes it easy to familiarize with the environments such as the library where resources could be found, the class rooms for synchronous group discussions, the lecturers' room where students have no access, and the social centre, a free discussion place where participants can exchange ideas in privacy without any chat recording device. Another space available on ACOLAD in the student's desk where the student's personal project is located. Apart from the owner of the desk, only the tutors can access it to view and comment on the different versions of the project. All these virtual environments /spaces are equipped with virtual working facilities such as tables, cupboards to store documents, notebook, mailing box, microphone, etc.
3. The facilitation by competent tutors: The hardest part in distance learning is the frustration deriving from isolation. Isolation could be experienced when working alone without any hope of getting assistance for example on a totally new area, when using an ICT tool we are not familiar with, or when trying to understand a new concept or theory. Many agricultural scientists like me had problems with educational theories such as behaviorism, cognitive principles, constructivism, etc. The HTML language also gave me hard time and I would certainly have abandoned if the modules were not facilitated by good proactive tutors. These tutors were able to detect on time students in difficulties and to bring their interest back by proactively backstopping and helping them understand assignments that seemed difficult.
4. The peer assistance: Traditional learning reinforces competition since each student is evaluated based on his/her personal work. Trying to be the best student involves lots of personal and individual investment to gain more knowledge than the others, and also to hide and not share this knowledge with the others. When students graduate in such an environment, they particularly lack one of the most needed modern time skills: working in team. Distance learning courses like the Master UTICEF reinforces collaborative work and information sharing. Learning in small teams of 2 to 3 with clearly established responsibilities and deadline develops creativity, responsiveness and willingness to interact with others. The problem solving approach adopted in team work is another way of forging critical thinking, tolerance and respect for others.
5. The flexibility in learning: The January 2005 promotion was composed of 24 students from different geographical locations: Sub Saharan and Tropical Africa (Burkina Faso, Niger, Senegal, DRC), Northern

Africa (Morocco, Tunisia and Algeria), and Northern and Eastern Europe (France, Belgium, Switzerland, Bulgaria). This caused often issues of time zone during synchronous discussions or for respecting deadlines in posting activities, but all participants managed to adapt to that. Flexibility of the programme, linked with the existence of the network of Francophone Numerical Campuses, allowed me to sit for my mid-term exam outside my country, in the CNF of Bamako in Mali where I was on official university mission. The flexibility of the programme also permitted me to defend my Master thesis on the phone from my house in Niger and in front of a silent but cheering public composed of my husband and my three sons. The two investigators during this phone defense were my project supervisor located in France, and another tutor member of the jury who was based in Tunisia. Fortunately no power cut off disturbed the one-hour defense that day.

CURRENT CHALLENGES FACED BY NIGER IN INTRODUCING E-LEARNING IN THE UNIVERSITIES

Like all the lecturers at the University, I received the announcement for the January 2005 Promotion of the Master UTICEF, which applied to all lecturers no matter their disciplines. The programme started in 2004 with two promotions a year, but until 2005, only two lecturers from Niger applied and benefited from the sponsorship offered by the UAF. I was the third lecturer, and the first woman sponsored in Niger. From the beginning, I was confronted to the reality of introducing distance learning in a traditional institution, which translated into the following challenges:

1. *The need for personal financial investment not affordable to all*: the course was a partial sponsorship from the AUF and the beneficiaries have to contribute CFA 500,000, which corresponded to about USD 1000 or one month salary for an Associate Professor at the University Abdou Moumouni. Other personal costs necessary for a proper follow up of the course was having an Internet connection at home or paying for US $ 1 per hour connection in the cybercafés to follow seminars and group discussions during non working hours. For example my telephone bills at home increased from CFA 30,000 (about US $ 60) to almost US $ 200 per month during the first semester of the course.
2. *The need for high investment in time and energy due to limited support from institution's leaders*: As required by the sponsoring agency, all selected participants provide a letter from their institution stressing that their teaching and other academic duties shall be reduced by half to allow them to follow the course properly. However, this engagement even though signed was difficult to fulfill in African Universities due to insufficient staffing and lack of money to hire temporary lecturers. As a consequence, participating lecturers had the same responsibilities as before but could however make arrangement with their colleagues to plan their lecturing activities in a more flexible way. Therefore, instead of the 15 hours investment per week officially required from participants, I ended up adding up to 28 h of extra work per week to my official University assignments.
3. *The lack of direct technical support within the University*: The majority of Faculties at the UAM except the Faculty of Sciences lack official computer science personals. Therefore, all technical issues were referred to the CNF of Niamey which has only one computer technician who was dealing with the two Internet servers, and also with all the requests for technical support coming from the users of the campus.

4. *The lack of basic computer knowledge of many lecturers and students*: My e-Learning project was an Agro-forestry course for 4th Year students of the Faculty of Agriculture of the UAM of Niamey. The course was tested for 4 weeks during the academic year 2006 – 2007 by a group a 20 volunteer fourth year students of the Faculty of Agriculture of the UAM. The online facilitation was provided by two colleagues who attended respectively the 2004 Master UTICEF and Transfer sessions on tutoring. The University Louis Pasteur of Strasbourg (France) allowed me as the content developer for the course, to use the UTICEF project testing platform "ACOLAD Project" where I register the tutors and the students who could freely access with their login and passwords. The director of the CNF of Niamey kindly allocated one of the training rooms to the students who thus could access the computers and Internet at any time during opening hours, and for the whole duration of the programme. The programme started with 4 hours of face to face orientation that I used to explain the programme, and the platform. Two additional hours were however necessary to familiarize some students with the basic use of computer.
5. *The other challenges directly linked to agricultural and natural resources management sciences*: these include the low competences of lecturers in developing iterative digital exercises based on local realities and in incorporating contextualized illustrations into e-Learning content. It seems that success of distance programmes varies with disciplines and that content and pedagogy of some subjects in Mathematics, science and technology are easier to develop using ICTs than others (Davesh and Crowley, 2008).

PERSPECTIVES IN INTRODUCING E-LEARNING AT THE UAM

The World Summit for Information Society held in Geneva (Switzerland) in December 2003 has defined the new society as "a society where everyone has the possibility to create, receive, use and share information and knowledge in order to promote sustainable development and to improve quality of live" (WSIS, 2003, SICNF). During the Summit the reduction of the unequal access to the New Information and Communication Technologies (NTICS) between the North and the South, called digital divide has been defined as a global priority goal (Galy and Dane, 2005). Despite the known fact that the UAM doesn't have sufficient bandwidth per PC to allow for example for video conferencing, and no wireless links available in the campus, the students who have evaluated the above described course strongly recommended that distance learning should be an option to introduce in the UAM modes of learning. Even though the UAM needs more expertise in e-Learning design and in knowledge management system, various perspectives of introducing e-Learning into course programmes exist and are built on the following observations:

- Strong political support expressed through the elimination of license fees and monopoly pricing for educational bandwidth. From 2007, the liberalization of the telecommunication sector enhanced competition for more efficient Internet connection with the arrival of private Internet providers such as Orange, Celtel/Zain, Telecel and Sahelcom. As a result, the rate of telephone penetration rose from 0.2% in 2002 to 2.4% in 2005 and 8% in 2007 (African Economic Outlook, 2009). With support from the World Bank, the Economic and Monetary Union of West Africa (UEMOA) and the French Development Cooperation the government also developed the

National Information and Communication Infrastructure (NICI) plan and its implementation plan for 2005 – 2010.

- University leaders are more and more sensitized on the importance of ICTs in education what makes them more supportive of ICT related projects linked to tertiary education. Following this change of mindset, the University authority increased computer density on campus in 2008 by providing each of the 270 lecturers with a new laptop, by connecting all the offices to Internet and by equipping all the Faculties with a computer room connected to Internet for use by students from third year. Some Deans were also very effective in lobbying international organizations for support in equipping libraries and lecturers' offices with computers.
- Plans exist at the national level to implement some ICT initiatives such as:
  - The improvement of the connectivity through very Small Aperture Terminal (VSAT) for a higher bandwidth
  - The expansion of the campus networks (Intranet) to extend Internet access to all students
  - The shared purchasing of online distance education tools through the AUF network.
  - The intensification of the training of lecturers and students in the use of ICTs.

Perspectives for e-Learning exist for UAM, but this will take time and it might be necessary to first reinforce and modernize classical modes of teaching by progressively introducing course modules using digital supports.

CONCLUSION

The above described experience shows that e-Learning can be successfully incorporated into the programme of a traditional Faculty and University. This needs however institutional and political support. It also needs high technical support of specialists such as computer technicians, graphic designers and e-content developers. Mindset of certain lecturers who did not want to change their ways of teaching is also been favorably changed. Since attitude change is a major hurdle, the move from traditional classrooms to e-learning can be made in small steps making change easier to accept. Blended learning environments for example enable resource persons and instructional designers to develop the skills needed for e-learning in small increments (Beniest et al., 2008).

At the UAM of Niamey, the increasing number of lecturers, other education professionals and graduate students applying for and registering for distance learning programmes offered through the Francophone Numerical Campus of Niamey in Niger, highlights the growing interest for distance learning in Niger. The resource Centre of the CNF is always full of people coming to consult their mails, to search for documentation or to look for training opportunities. E-Learning and distance learning have already gained institutional support at UAM, with almost all the Faculties looking for funding to pay for their lecturers and technicians to be trained in using ICTs in education. In 2008, the Rector's office equipped all lecturers of the UAM with their individual laptops. Many Faculties, like the Faculty of Agriculture also made available free internet access in all their offices, their libraries and in their students' computer rooms.

Agricultural e-Learning content and course development requires strong collaboration between specialists, and between academicians and researchers, the only way of producing high quality and contextualized online courses for African training institutions. Before we fulfill our dreams of introducing e-Learning mode at the University Abdou Moumouni of Niamey, we probably need to start step by step, by reinforcing and modernizing our classical modes of teaching and progressively introducing course modules using more ICTs and digital supports.

REFERENCES

ACOLAD. (2006). Retrieved from http://www.paris4.sorbonne.fr/e-cursus/texte/acolad.htm

African Economic Outlook. (2009). *Niger: Innovation and ICT*. Retrieved from http://africaeconomicoutlook.org/en/countries/westAfrica/niger/

Agyeman, O. T. (2007). *Survey of ICT and Education in Africa. Niger country report*. Retrieved from http://www.infodev.org

AUFP4. (n.d.). *Programme « Technologies de l'information et de la communication et appropriation des savoirs » de l'Agence universitaire de la Francophonie*. Retrieved from http://www.auf.org/programmes/ programme4/

Beniest, J., Vandenbosch, T., & Drame Yaye, A. (2008). *E-Learning for Agriculture and Natural Resources Management Education: Some Experiences and Future Directions*. Paper presented at the Second Symposium of ANAFE on Mainstreaming Climate Change into Agricultural Education: Tools, Challenges and Perspectives, Lilongwe, Malawi.

Cabinet du Premier Ministre. (2003). *Ministère des Enseignements Secondaires et Supérieur, de la Recherche et de la Technologie*. Document portant Politique Nationale d'Enseignement Supérieur et de Recherche au Niger.

Galy, K. A., & Dane, E. (2005). *Obstacles et solutions à l'appropriation des NTICs au Sud: leçons sur l'expérience de l'Université Abdou Moumouni du Niger.*

Kapur, D. M., & Crowley, M. (2008). *Beyond the ABCs: Higher Education and Developing Countries*. Working paper Number 139, February 2008, Center for Global Development.

Refer. (2006). Retrieved from http://www.refer.ne

Salmi, J. (2000). Tertiary Education in the Twenty-first Century: Challenges and Opportunities. The World Bank Latin America and Caribbean Regional Office.

SICNF. (2004). *Les enjeux de la Société de l'Information – le dispositif du Campus numérique*. Présentation du CNF de Niamey aux différents publics cibles. Retrieved from http://ftp.refer.ne/Documents/CNFNy/CNFNy_presentation-2004-02-11_html/presentation.html

SMSI. (2003). *Sommet Mondial sur la Société de l'Information, première phase*, Genève, 10-12 décembre 2003. Retrieved from http://www.itu.int/wsis/index-fr.html

World Bank. (2006). Annual Report: Health, Nutrition and Population.

ADDITIONAL READING

ACOLAD. (2006). Retrieved from http://www.paris4.sorbonne.fr/e-cursus/texte/acolad.htm

African Economic Outlook. (2009). *Niger: Innovation and ICT*. Retrieved from http://africaeconomicoutlook.org/en/countries/westAfrica/niger/

http://www.auf.org (n.d.).

http://www.refer.ne (n.d.).

KEY TERMS AND DEFINITIONS

Bandwidth Connectivity: Rate of data transfer, i.e. the capacity of the Internet connection being used.

Dial up Connection: This involves connecting a device to a network via a modem and a public telephone network. Dial-up access is just like a phone connection except that the parties at the two ends are computer devices rather than people.

e-Learning: (Use of new multimedia technologies and the Internet in traditional learning.

ICTs: Information and Communication Technologies.

Fiber Connection: Connection that uses fiber optic cables to communicate.

VSAT: Very small Aperture Terminal. Receivers and transmitters installed at dispersed sites and connecting to a central hub via satellite.

Chapter 7
Personality and Online Learning

Kevin Downing
City University Hong Kong, People's Republic of China

ABSTRACT

This chapter provides a comparative evaluation of two pilot online courses with their traditionally taught counterparts in one of the universities of Hong Kong. As part of a natural experiment, students enrolled on two online courses were compared with their peers who were enrolled on the equivalent classroom based courses. Student satisfaction measures were taken from participants in both modes of delivery and compared with student learning style. This case highlights the impact of adopting a blended learning approach to an undergraduate programme, and suggests that Asian students who behave like Introverts in the classroom environment are likely to behave as online Extraverts when given the opportunity to reflect on what they have learned and contribute to an online discussion forum.

ORGANISATION BACKGROUND

City University of Hong Kong is one of eight Government funded universities in the Special Administrative Region (SAR). It has three Colleges (Science and Engineering, Humanities and Social Science, and Business) and two Schools (Law and Creative Media) with a total undergraduate and postgraduate student population of approximately 20, 000 students. Despite, being a relatively young institution, only receiving university status in 1994, it is ranked 18th in Asia and 147th in the world by The Times Higher/QS World University Rankings (2008).

DOI: 10.4018/978-1-61520-909-5.ch007

SETTING THE STAGE

Introduction

Online learning is now generally accepted as an effective method of instruction. Much recent educational research has focused on examining the purposes and situations for which online education is best suited. Typically, this research has concentrated on five main areas:

- What are the particular characteristics of effective online students and teachers?
- Is online learning and teaching as effective as traditional face-to-face teaching?
- What factors determine the most appropriate use of technology in an online teaching situation?
- How important is teacher-student and student-student interaction in the online learning process?
- What cost factors should be considered when planning or implementing distance education programs and how are those costs offset by benefits to the learner?

This chapter concentrates on the first two of these five areas and provides a comparative evaluation of two pilot online courses with their traditionally taught counterparts. As part of a natural experiment (an experiment where the conditions observed occur naturally and require no manipulation of variables), students enrolled on two online courses were compared with their peers who were enrolled on the equivalent classroom based courses. Student satisfaction measures were taken from participants in both modes of delivery and compared with student learning style measured using the Honey and Mumford Learning Style Questionnaire (2000).

Learning Style and Online Learning

Terrell & Dringus (2000) investigated the effect of learning style on student success in an online learning environment and concluded that institutions offering online education programmes should give consideration to the different learning styles of their students because these could impact significantly on academic achievement. The effect of learning style on student success in online learning has been extensively researched and so does not form the focus of this study (Dille & Mezack, 1991; Souder, 1993; Ridley & Sammour, 1996; Diaz, 2000a). However, the relationship between learning style and student satisfaction in two online applied psychology courses is investigated because research into the link between learning styles and student satisfaction, in Asia in particular, remains rare. In concluding that online students were more independent and on-campus students were more dependent, Diaz & Cartnal (1999) demonstrated that health education students enrolled in an online class were likely to have different learning styles than equivalent on-campus students. The study reported in this chapter further investigates the learning styles of online and traditional students and correlates these factors with students' reported satisfaction with the learning experience.

Acknowledging their debt to Kolb's (1984) work on learning and the identification of learning styles, Honey & Mumford (1986) identify a different four stage process from Kolb's Converger, Diverger, Assimilator and Accommodator which involves four styles which they call Activists, Reflectors, Theorists and Pragmatists. For a full description of each learning style, see Honey and Mumford (1982). These learning style preferences appear particularly appropriate for a comparative study of this type because they are based on the idea that students pick up habits in relation to learning which they regularly utilise. According to the theory, the authors would expect the characteristics of Reflectors and Theorists to be most suited to online learning, and therefore to produce the highest satisfaction levels. Activists and Pragmatists might be expected to produce the highest satisfaction levels in the traditional mode of learning. These are the correlations primarily tested in this research.

Other Key Factors

A summary of key research studies in this area yields some conflicting findings relevant to the current research. Riding (2002) and Downing et al., (2007) identify some key issues related to creating and maintaining interaction in online learning environments, with the latter suggesting that the timing and nature of both formative and summative assessments have a significant impact, at least among Asian students, on levels and type of online interaction. Wenger (1998) and Lieberman (2000) consider the relative value of networks as learning communities for teacher training and development and identify a number of advantages to this mode of learning grounded in social learning theory. Downing et al., (2009) even consider the impact that gender might play in the formation and development of blended learning environments suggesting that there might be differences between male and female students in terms of preferences and practices in online learning environments. Egan et al. (1991) concluded that conventional instruction is generally perceived to be better organised and more clearly presented than online education. However, Martin and Rainey (1993) found no significant difference in positive attitudes towards course material between online and traditional education. In addition, research by Souder (1993) indicates that achievement on various tests administered by course instructors tends to be higher for 'distant' as opposed to 'traditional' students. Perhaps one key factor inherent in all of these seemingly contradictory findings is the design of the instructional material, irrespective of whether it is delivered online or through more traditional means. Many teachers and researchers (E.g. Wood, 1997; Littlejohn et al. 1999) point out that the organisation and reflection necessary to effectively teach online often improves an instructor's traditional teaching. This is a theme continued by Downing, (2001) who identifies the eventual success or failure of online teaching as largely due to the same factors that have always been central to the provision of a quality learning experience. These factors include the energy, commitment and imagination of those responsible for providing the teaching and learning environment, whether it is virtual or actual. However, another key factor has also been reported and that is the demographic differences between online and traditional students. Online students are generally older, have completed more college credit hours and more degree programmes, and tend to have a higher all-college prior GPA (grade point average) than their traditional counterparts (Gibson & Graff, 1992; Thompson, 1998).

The study reported here avoids some of the potentially confusing effects of these two factors because the same author designed both the traditional courses and their online counterparts, and the sample of students was allocated to either mode of delivery on the basis of quota. In other words, because of local university-based administrative reasons, students were more or less randomly allocated to either the online or traditional mode. This provided an ideal opportunity to reduce the potential effects of the two key factors identified above.

CASE DESCRIPTION

Method

A comparative evaluation of two pilot online applied psychology courses with their traditionally taught counterparts was undertaken at City University of Hong Kong. Students enrolled on two online courses were compared with their matched peers who were enrolled on the equivalent classroom based (traditional) courses. Student satisfaction measures were taken from participants in both modes of delivery and correlated with student learning style measured using the Honey and Mumford Learning Style Questionnaire (2000). The two courses, 'Psychology for Everyday Life' and 'Behaviour in Organisations' were developed by the same author for associate degree students from Hong Kong in both traditional and online mode.

Classification Rationale

According to Gandell et al. (2000), the extent of Web use can be described in terms of the impact it has on learning relevance to the course. They categorised the extent of use according to the relevance and importance of learning goals appropriately addressed. Consequently, they identify five categories that represent a continuum of extent of use:

- **Minimal:** Use of the Web that is neither relevant nor necessary to achieve any explicitly stated course learning goals and therefore has no impact on course-related learning.
- **Supplemental:** Use of the Web that is relevant but not necessary to achieve a few explicitly stated course goals and therefore does not have much impact on related student learning.
- **Integral:** Use of the Web that is relevant and contributes to achieving some of the learning goals in the course, and would have a fair impact on student learning.
- **Central:** Use of the Web that is relevant and necessary to achieve most learning goals in the course, and would have a substantial impact on student learning.
- **Exclusive:** Use of the Web that is relevant and necessary to achieve all learning goals in the course, and would have a major impact on student learning.

Gandell et al's (2000) classification system has been adopted for the comparisons made in this research. The two online Applied Psychology courses in this research are categorised in the Central/Exclusive mode, but also make use of what has become known as 'blended' learning. According to Valiathan (2002), blended learning is used to describe learning that mixes various event-based activities, including face-to-face classrooms, online learning, and self-paced learning. The main tool for accessing the two online courses is the learning management system, Web CT.

Traditional (Classroom-Based) Mode of Delivery

Students enrolled for this mode of delivery experience two hours of face-to-face lectures/tutorials each week for thirteen weeks. All learning material is presented using these lectures, tutorials, and problem based learning activities. There is a ratio of one teacher to around thirty students per class and the course is largely teacher-centred. The instructors mainly use overhead projectors, PowerPoint or hard copies of notes to deliver the teaching, and arrange tutorial small group exercises. The extent of Web use is largely minimal (Gandell et al, 2000) and is primarily to allow students the option of downloading copies of lecture notes and tutorials.

Online Mode of Delivery

The extent of Web use for the online mode of delivery is in the exclusive category in which the use of the Web is both relevant and necessary, and would have a major impact on student learning. However, the online courses in this study are blended learning, which combines the three major formats of learning. Blended learning seeks the optimum blend of self study, teacher-led events and group collaboration, each deployed in a blend of asynchronous or synchronous modes, appropriate for the leaning outcomes. The main tool for accessing these courses is, once again, the online learning management system Web CT and each three credit course is constructed of ten units of learning material with students being recommended to spend ten hours to study each unit. Teaching and learning materials are presented in a variety of formats and include video clips, audio clips, images, animations, url links to websites, PowerPoint presentations, and formative and summative quizzes. A total of 7 hours and 40 minutes of face-to-face contact is provided via five tutorials which take place in weeks one, three, six, nine and twelve of a thirteen week semester. Each of the first four tutorials are 1 hour and 20 minutes in duration with the last tutorial lasting two hours and 20 minutes to allow for students summative small-group presentations. A bulletin board is provided on the Web CT platform for each online version of the course to allow students to engage in discussion and collaboration with fellow students and teachers. The objective here was to foster the formation of a virtual learning community for the online courses and this objective was achieved. (For a more detailed look at some detailed aspects of forming a virtual community see Wenger (1998), Lieberman, (2001), Riding (2002) and Downing et al. (2007)). The extent of Web use is in this case is therefore exclusive (Gandell et al, 2000) because the online materials (units) are both relevant and necessary to achieve the learning and assessment outcomes.

Participants

All participants were first year City University of Hong Kong associate degree students.

Students enrolled in the two traditional and the two equivalent online applied psychology courses were asked to voluntarily participate in this study. A total of 160 students were selected at random from the volunteers (N=160). 80 of these were taken from the two traditional courses and 80 from the two online courses. All participants were of similar academic background evidenced by their successful application to study at associate degree level at City University of Hong Kong. Participants were therefore matched for education, age, gender, and life experience across the two conditions, traditional and online. Therefore, this is a related (matched) pairs design, and the data was analysed using a Wilcoxon Matched Pairs Signed Ranks test. The data presented in this paper is related only to the matched pairs (n=32 pairs or N=64) who were assessed as 'Reflectors' after completing the Honey and Mumford (2000) questionnaire because this group produced the most significant and interesting results.

Procedure

The Honey & Mumford Learning Styles Questionnaire (2000) was administered to all students in the third week of the semester in order that it was administered face-to-face at the same stage for all groups. The classes were allocated an additional hour to complete the questionnaires, and assistance was available to clarify words and sentences, which caused difficulty in interpretation. A Teaching Feedback Questionnaire (TFQ), in regular use at City University of Hong Kong, was administered to the students during week twelve in order to ascertain the level of student satisfaction for each of the four courses and each of the two conditions. Follow up interviews were conducted with 12 matched pairs who volunteered to give their time for this purpose. Questions were asked about what aspects of the online and traditional modes of delivery most suited their style of study, and which aspects they found most problematic.

Instruments

LSQ: The Honey and Mumford (2000) Learning Style Questionnaire (LSQ) was used to ascertain student learning styles. The questionnaire contains eighty questions designed to differentiate between four main learning 'styles'. Participants are asked to tick or cross to indicate whether on balance they agree or disagree with a statement. This instrument was chosen because it has been standardised, is in wide use in academic institutions around the world, and substantial norm data is in existence to allow some triangulation. The vast majority of items are behavioural in the sense that they describe an action that someone might or might not be seen to take, although occasionally an item probes an area of preference or belief rather than a manifest

Table1. Matched pairs TFQ distribution of scores for reflectors

Mode of Delivery	TFQ Score 7: Excellent	6: Very Good	5: Good	4: Average	3: Below Average	2: Poor	1: Very Poor
Traditional	2	8	15	7	0	0	0
Online (Blended)	15	17	0	0	0	0	0

(N=32 Matched Pairs)

behaviour. In common with most questionnaires of this type, the LSQ is designed to elicit general trends or tendencies running through a person's behaviour, and does place undue significance on any one item. The eighty questions are distributed equally over the four learning styles: Activists, Reflectors, Theorists and Pragmatists. These trait descriptions are detailed in the Appendix. There are no right or wrong answers. Respondents put a tick if they agree more than disagree and put a cross if they disagree more than agree.

TFQ: The Teaching Feedback Questionnaire (TFQ) is a fairly standard course feedback questionnaire. It is submitted anonymously and online for most courses taught within City University of Hong Kong. This questionnaire was designed by City University of Hong Kong for identifying levels of student satisfaction with particular courses. It is usually administered towards the end of each semester to all students within a group or cohort. Most of the questions provide simple ordinal data on a 7-point Likert scale of strongly agree, agree, neutral, disagree, and strongly disagree. The data produced is ordinal.

Table2. Wilcoxon signed ranks test

		N	Mean Rank	Sum of Ranks
Condition B (traditional) Condition A (online)	Negative Ranks	25 [a]	13.76	344.00
	Positive Ranks	1 [b]	7.00	7.00
	Ties	6 [c]		
	Total	32		

a) Condition B (traditional) < Condition A (online)
b) Condition B (traditional) > Condition A (online)
c) Condition A (online) = Condition B (traditional)

Results

Following administration of the Honey and Mumford Learning Styles Questionnaire, 32 matched pairs were identified as primarily reflectors in their learning style and their Teaching Feedback Questionnaire data was analysed using the Wilcoxon Matched Pairs Signed Ranks Test. The results for this group were highly significant and are reported in the Table 1, Table 2, and Table 3.

The results from the other learning style groups (Activists, Theorists, Pragmatists, and combinations) are not reported here because their data yielded no significant relationships between learning style and student satisfaction. However, the results for the students with a clear preferred style of Reflector are presented and discussed because the Reflectors in this study showed a highly significant preference (as measured by satisfaction levels) for the model of online (blended) learning presented.

Table3. Test statistics [b]

	Condition B (traditional) - Condition A (online)
Z	-4.363 [a]
Asymp. Sig. (2-tailed)	.000

a) Based on positive ranks.
b) Wilcoxon Signed Ranks Test

DISCUSSION

Salmon (2001) refers to Activists and Pragmatists as 'online extraverts'. An Extravert is an outgoing, gregarious, sensation-seeking personality type who seeks stimulation to raise levels of cortical arousal to an optimum for efficient functioning (Eysenck, 1959, 1963, 1991). In other words, they are often seen as sociable and open when compared with their Introvert colleagues.

Activists and Pragmatists

Honey and Mumford (1982, 1986, and 2000) describe Activists as liking a wide range of different activities, and immersing themselves fully and without bias in new activities. They are gregarious people, constantly involving themselves with others but in doing so, they tend to be seen as 'hogging the limelight'. They are the life and soul of the party and seek to centre all activities on themselves. This description appears to describe the archetypal Extravert and it is clear that involving Activists in learning activities (both traditional and online) should not be too difficult. Honey and Mumford describe Pragmatists as keen on trying out new ideas to see if they work in practice. They like to experiment with the applications of these ideas. They like to get on with things and act quickly and confidently, responding to problems and opportunities as a 'challenge'. They are essentially practical down to earth people who like making practical decisions and solving problems. Whilst this description is less like an extreme Extravert, nonetheless it does contain factors which would suggest that these individuals would also find traditional and online activities equally stimulating.

Theorists and Reflectors

Salmon (2001) also describes Theorists and Reflectors, the other two learning styles identified by Honey and Mumford, as 'online Introverts'. An Introvert is at the other end of the continuum from the Extravert. Eysenck (1991) describes Introverts as experiencing high levels of cortical arousal, and consequently they avoid additional external stimulation to reduce their levels of cortical arousal to optimum levels. They prefer quiet reading and appear to avoid social settings or situations where they might find themselves in large groups. In other words, these are often the individuals that sit quietly in traditional classroom settings and find it difficult to interact when compared with their Extravert colleagues. Honey and Mumford (1982) describe Theorists as thinking problems through in a vertical, step by step logical way. They like to analyse and synthesise, and tend to be detached, analytical and dedicated to rational objectivity rather than anything subjective and ambiguous. This is their 'mental set' and they rigidly reject anything that doesn't fit with it. They tend to be perfectionists who won't rest easy until things are tidy and fit into their rational scheme. They need time to explore links between ideas and structure their thinking. These individuals often feel frustrated and find it difficult to speak up in the traditional classroom. Some studies (Terrell & Dringus, 2000; Souder, 1993) have suggested that online learning is a more effective means of teaching those with this learning style although the present research identified no significant differences in teaching feedback scores in both traditional and online delivery modes for Theorists. Reflectors like to stand back and ponder experiences and observe them from many different perspectives. They collect data and think deeply about it before coming to any conclusions. This thorough collection and analysis of data about experiences and events is what counts for them, so they tend to postpone coming to conclusions for as long as possible. This means that they do not contribute greatly to traditional classroom discussion because they are still collecting data and ruminating over its value. Their philosophy tends to be cautious, so they prefer to think deeply about concepts and activities before giving considered responses. Consequently, they often feel left out in traditional classroom settings.

Reflectors amongst Asian Students

In addition, Barron (2002) points out that the Reflector learning style is much more prevalent among Asian students studying degree courses in Australia than amongst Western students, and that whilst this might not significantly impact upon completion of the educational programme, it does influence student satisfaction levels. This is borne out by the highly significant results reported in this chapter, whereby all participants could be classed as Asian students, and a large proportion of them, 32 matched pairs (64 students from a total of 160 = 40%) were identified as strong Reflectors after completing the Honey and Mumford Learning Styles Questionnaire. These matched pairs of reflectors demonstrated a marked preference for the online (blended) mode of delivery (see Table 1 above), and some of the potential reasons for this were highlighted during a follow-up interview conducted by a non-teaching colleague of the author.

Follow up interviews with 24 volunteers (12 matched pairs) from the two conditions revealed that invariably Reflectors found that they had not had time to process the information in the traditional mode of delivery before they were expected to enter into classroom discussion, and that often other student colleagues had already commented on what they would have liked to have said. More than half of these students reported that this left them feeling unable to contribute fully and feel a part of the learning experience, although they reported still enjoying the course. Conversely, 10 of the 12 Reflectors in the online mode said that the use of the Bulletin Board function in Web CT had allowed them to participate in discussions about both online and tutorial material over a period of weeks. And all 12 reported that having tutorial material available in the Web CT Download Centre one week in advance of the tutorial had allowed them to think about what was coming, and make more of a contribution either online via the Bulletin Board or in the face-to-face tutorials.

CONCLUSION

Reflectors as Online Extraverts

Results from this study contradict the findings of Salmon (2001) reported above. Far from Reflectors being 'online Introverts', it would appear that the time given for reflection, and the opportunity to engage in discussion with the teacher and fellow students via the online Bulletin Board, allows those students with this learning style to behave in a more Extravert and active way. This is in stark contrast to feelings of being unable to contribute fully, or having been 'beaten to the comment' reported by Reflectors in the traditional mode of delivery. Therefore, the authors of this paper argue than Reflectors at least are 'online Extraverts', and that the use of online (blended) learning significantly improves student satisfaction levels for Reflectors. Furthermore, given the reported prevalence of this style of learning amongst Asian students, this is clearly an important factor to be considered by those responsible for the design and delivery of programmes to Asian students, particularly in 'Western' universities. International student recruitment, particularly from Asia is changing the student profile in these universities (Dobson et al., 1998) and the pressure is on to manage this student diversity and provide appropriate support for international students. The impact of what is sometimes called Confucian heritage culture (Lee, 1999) is often underestimated because Asian students are generally viewed by Western educators as diligent note-takers, well-disciplined, hard-working, quiet, respectful, and good attendees (Barron, 2002; Adam et al., 1999; Volet and Renshaw, 1999; Bradley and Bradley, 1984). Whilst these students might be successful in completing the programmes they are following, this study suggests that the traditional classroom-based learning experience might not be as satisfying for Asian Reflectors as an online blended mode of delivery, and Western universities would be well-advised to consider this when planning programmes with an internationally diverse student population in mind.

Whilst it is now largely accepted that social and cultural factors have a significant impact on cognitive development with Piaget (1977) himself acknowledging the impact of social factors and peer interaction on cognitive development, there remains relatively little work on the impact of modes of delivery on metacognitive development in university students. Reflectors already possess many of the metacognitive skills (Downing et al., 2007 and 20082008) required for success in higher education but are clearly often left feeling out of touch with purely classroom-based traditional modes of learning because they do not provide the opportunity to appropriately reflect before responding to what they learn. Vygotsky's (1986) view was that in order to subject a function to intellectual and voluntary control, we must first possess that function. In other words, metacognition and self-reflection will develop first as a skill which needs to be practiced before it can be used as a series of consciously controlled strategies. It would appear from the study presented in this chapter that the online mode of delivery provides Reflectors with a means of practicing this essential skill, and therefore developing their metacognitive abilities, which is not provided by more traditional learning approaches and it is this which probably underlies their online Extravert tendencies.

REFERENCES

Adam, M., Maxwell, G. A., Pooran, J., & Scott, B. (1999). *South East Asian Students Learning Styles*. Paper presented at the CHME Hospitality Research Conference, Surrey, pp. 9-21.

Barron, P. E. (2002). Providing a More Successful Education Experience for Asian Hospitality Management Students Studying in Australia: A Focus on Teaching and Learning Styles. *Journal of Teaching in Travel & Tourism*, *2*(2), 63–88. doi:10.1300/J172v02n02_04

Bradley, D., & Bradley, M. (1984). Problems of Asian Students in Australia: Language, Culture and Education. Canberra: Department of Education and Youth Affairs.

Diaz, D. P. (2000a). *Comparison of student characteristics, and evaluation of student success. In an online health education course*. Unpublished doctoral dissertation, Nova Southeastern University, Fort Lauderdale, Florida

Diaz, D. P., & Cartnal, R. B. (1999). Students' learning styles in two classes: Online distance learning and equivalent on-campus. *College Teaching*, *47*(4), 130–135. doi:10.1080/87567559909595802

Dille, B., & Mezack, M. (1991). Identifying predictors of high risk among community college telecourse students. *American Journal of Distance Education*, *5*(1), 24–25. doi:10.1080/08923649109526729

Dobson, I. R., Sharma, R., & Calderon, A. J. (1998). *The Comparative Performance of Overseas and Australian Undergraduates*. Paper presented at the 12th Australian International Education Conference, Canberra, 3-18.

Downing, K. (2001). Information Technology, Education and Health Care: constructivism in the 21st Century. *Educational Studies*, *27*(3), 229–235. doi:10.1080/03055690120076510

Downing, K., Chan, S.-W., Downing, W. K., Kwong, T., & Lam, T. F. (2008). Measuring gender differences in cognitive functioning. *Multicultural Education & Technology Journal*, *2*(1), 4–18. doi:10.1108/17504970810867124

Downing, K., Ho, R., Shin, K., Vrijmoed, L., & Wong, E. (2007). Metacognitive development and moving away. *Educational Studies*, *33*(1), 1–13. doi:10.1080/03055690600850347

Downing, K., Kwong, T., Chan, S., Lam, I., & Downing, W. K. (2009). Problem-based learning and the development of metacognition. *Higher Education*, *57*(5), 609–621. doi:10.1007/s10734-008-9165-x

Downing, K., Lam, T., Kwong, T., Downing, W. K., & Chan, S. (2007). Creating interaction in online learning: a case study. *ALT-J*, *15*(3), 201–215. doi:10.1080/09687760701673592

Egan, M. W., Sebastian, J., & Welch, M. (1991, March). Effective television teaching: Perceptions of those who count most...distance learners. *Proceedings of the Rural Education Symposium, Nashville*, TN. (ERIC Document Reproduction Service No. ED 342 579).

Eysenck, H. J. (1959). Manual of the Maudsley Personality Inventory. London: University of London Press.

Eysenck, H. J. (1963). On the dual nature of extraversion. *The British Journal of Social and Clinical Psychology*, *2*, 46.

Eysenck, H. J., & Eysenck, S. B. G. (1991). Manual of the Eysenck Personality Scales (EPS Adult). London: Hodder and Stoughton.

Gandell, T., Weston, C., Finkelstein, A., & Weiner, L. (2000). Appropriate use of the web in teaching higher education. In B.L. Mann (Ed.), Perspectives in web course management (pp. 61-68). Toronto: Canadian Scholar's Press.

Gibson, C. C., & Graff, A. O. (1992). Impact of adult's preferred learning styles and perception of barriers on completions of external baccalaureate degree programs. *Journal of Distance Education*, *VII*(1), 39–51.

Honey, P., & Mumford, A. (1982). The Manual of Learning Styles. UK: McGraw Hill.

Honey, P., & Mumford, A. (1986). The Manual of Learning Styles. Maidenhead: Peter Honey Publications

Honey, P., & Mumford, A. (2000). The Learning Styles Questionnaire. Maidenhead: Peter Honey Publications

Kolb, D. (1984). Experiential Learning: Experience as the Source of Development. Englewood Cliffs: Prentice-Hall.

Lee, W. O. (1999). The Cultural Context for Chinese Learners: Conceptions of Learning in the Confucian Tradition. In D.A Watkins & J.B. Biggs (eds.), The Chinese Learner: Cultural, Psychological and Contextual Influences (pp. 22-42). Hong Kong: Centre for Comparative Research in Education/Camberwell, Victoria: Australian Council for Educational Research.

Lieberman, A. (2000). Networks as learning communities-Shaping the future of teacher development. *Journal of Teacher Education*, *51*(3), 221–227. doi:10.1177/0022487100051003010

Littlejohn, A. H., & Stefani, L. J. (1999). Effective use of communication and information technology: bridging the skills gap. *ALT-J*, *7*(2), 66–76. doi:10.1080/0968776990070208

Littlejohn, A. H., Stefani, L. J., & Sclater, N. (1999). Promoting effective use of technology, the pedagogy and the practicalities: a case study. [Oxford CTISS.]. *Active Learning*, *11*, 27–30.

Piaget, J. (1977). The development of thought: Equilibrium of cognitive structures. New York: Viking Press.

Riding, P. (2002). On-line teacher communities and continuing professional development. *Teacher Development*, *5*(3).

Ridley, D. R., & Sammour, H. Y. (1996). Viable alternative means of instructional delivery: Online courses as an alternative teaching method. *College Student Journal*, *30*, 337–339.

Salmon, G. (2001, February). *Psychological and Group Learning Perspectives*. Paper presented at the E-Learning Conference, London.

Souder, W. E. (1993). The effectiveness of traditional vs. satellite delivery in three management of technology master's degree programs. *American Journal of Distance Education*, *7*(1), 37–53. doi:10.1080/08923649309526809

Terrell, S. R., & Dringus, L. (2000). An investigation of the effect of learning style on student success in an online learning environment. *Journal of Educational Technology Systems*, *28*(3), 231–238. doi:10.2190/R53M-BVBD-UGV5-77EH

Thompson, M. M. (1998). Distance learners in higher education. In C. Gibson (Ed.), Distance learners in higher education: Institutional responses for quality outcomes (pp. 9-24). Madison, WI: Atwood.

Volet, S. E., & Renshaw, P. (1999). Chinese Students at an Australian University: Adaptability and Continuity. In D. A. Watkins & J. B. Biggs (Ed.), The Chinese Learner: Cultural, Psychological and Contextual Influences (pp. 205-220). Hong Kong: Centre for Comparative Research in Education/ Camberwell, Victoria: Australian Council for Educational Research.

Vygotsky, L. S. (1986). Thought and language. Cambridge MA.: MIT Press.

Wenger, E. (1998). Communities of practice learning, meaning and identity. Cambridge: Cambridge University Press.

Wood, J. (1997). Staff development for the virtual campus: a matter of teacher's first re-skilling as learners? Presented at Alt C, University of Wolverhampton.

ADDITIONAL READING

Bandura, A. (1965). Influence of model's reinforcement contingencies on the acquisition of imitative responses. *Journal of Personality and Social Psychology*, *1*, 589–595. doi:10.1037/h0022070

Biggs, J. (1999). Teaching for quality learning in university. London: The Society for Research into Higher Education & Open University Press.

Boaz, M., Elliott, B., Foshee, D., Hardy, D., Jarmon, C., & Olcott, D. (1999). Teaching at a distance: A handbook for instructors. Mission Viejo, CA: League for Innovation in the Community College.

Boettcher, J. (1999). Another look at the tower of WWWebble. *Syllabus Magazine*, *13*(3), 50–52.

Bourne, J. R., McMaster, E., Reiger, J., & Campbell, J. O. (1997). Paradigms for on-line learning: A case study in the design and implementation of an asynchronous learning networks (ALN) course. *Journal of Asynchronous Learning Networks*, *1*(2), 38–56.

Brown, R. E. (2001). The process of community building in distance learning classes. *Journal of Asynchronous Learning Networks*, *5*(2), 18–35.

Carver, C. S., Scheier, M. F., & Weintraub, J. K. (1989). Assessing coping strategies: A theoretically based approach. *Journal of Personality and Social Psychology*, *56*(2), 267–283. doi:10.1037/0022-3514.56.2.267

Chou, C. C. (2001). Formative evaluation of synchronous CMC systems for a learner centered online course. *Journal of Interactive Learning Research*, *12*(2/3), 170–188.

Cook, K. (2000). Computer conferencing really makes the Web interactive. In E. J. Leach (Ed.), A collection of practices from the league's conference on information technology. Mission Viejo, CA: League for Innovation in the Community College.

De Laat, M., & Lally, V. (2004). It's not so easy: Researching the complexity of emergent participant roles and awareness in asynchronous networked learning discussions. *Journal of Computer Assisted Learning, 20*, 165–171. doi:10.1111/j.1365-2729.2004.00085.x

Downing, K. J., & Shin, K. (2006, November). *Developing metacognition with LASSI online.* Paper presented at International Conference of the Asia-Pacific Educational Research Association, Hong Kong Institute of Education, Hong Kong.

Garrison, D. R., & Anderson, T. (2003). E-learning in the 21st century: A framework for research and practice. London: Routledge Falmer.

Gilbert, P. K., & Dabbagh, N. (2005). How to structure online discussions for meaningful discourse: A case study. *British Journal of Educational Technology, 36*(1), 5–18. doi:10.1111/j.1467-8535.2005.00434.x

Grady, D. B. (2003). Mapping online discussions with lexical scores. *Journal of Interactive Learning, 14*(2), 209–229.

Grundy, J. (2002 December). Flexible learning and the flexible worker [White Paper]. London: British Telecom.

Henri, F., & Pudelko, B. (2003). Understanding and analysing activity and learning in virtual communities. *Journal of Computer Assisted Learning, 19*, 474–487. doi:10.1046/j.0266-4909.2003.00051.x

Hron, A., & Friedrich, H. F. (2003). A review of web-based collaborative learning: factors beyond technology. *Journal of Computer Assisted Learning, 19*, 70–79. doi:10.1046/j.0266-4909.2002.00007.x

Hwang, W. Y., & Wang, C. Y. (2004). A study of learning time patterns in asynchronous learning environments. *Journal of Computer Assisted Learning, 20*, 292–304. doi:10.1111/j.1365-2729.2004.00088.x

Kay, R. H. (2006). Developing a comprehensive metric for assessing discussion board Effectiveness. *British Journal of Educational Technology, 37*(5), 761–783. doi:10.1111/j.1467-8535.2006.00560.x

Lally, V., & Barrett, E. (1999). Building a learning community on-line: Towards socio academic interaction. *Research Papers in Education, 14*(2), 147–163. doi:10.1080/0267152990140205

McGregor, D. (1967). The professional manager. New York: McGraw-Hill.

McNaught, C., & Lam, P. (2005). Building an evaluation culture and evidence base for e-learning in three Hong Kong universities. *British Journal of Educational Technology, 36*(4), 599–614. doi:10.1111/j.1467-8535.2005.00538.x

Meyer, K. A. (2003). Face-to-face versus threaded discussions: The role of time and higher order thinking. *Journal of Asynchronous Learning Networks, 7*(3), 55–65.

Muirhead, B. (2001). Enhancing social interaction in computer-mediated distance education, *United States Distance Learning Association Ed at a Distance Magazine and Ed Journal, 15*(40). Retrieved April 3, from: www.usdla.org/html/journal/APR01_Issue/article02.html

Nash, S. S. (2004). New quality benchmarks for online courses: Meshing technology and conceptual underpinning. In *Selected Papers from the Fifteenth International Conference on College Teaching and Learning,* Jacksonville, Fl., U.S.A. 29th March-2nd April 2004 (pp. 195-222).

Nicol, D. J., Minty, I., & Sinclair, C. (2003). The social dimensions of online learning. *Innovations in Education and Teaching International, 40*(3), 270–280. doi:10.1080/1470329032000103807

Poole, D. M. (2000). Student participation in a discussion oriented online course: a case study. *Journal of Research on Computing in Education, 33*(2), 162–177.

Robertson, T. J., & Klotz, J. (2004). How can instructors and administrators fill the missing link in online instruction. *Online Journal of Distance Learning Administration, 5*(4). Retrieved April 3, 2007 from http://www.westga.edu/~dist ance/ojdl a/winter54 /roberson54.htm

Salmon, G. (2000). eModerating: The key to teaching and learning online. London: Routledge Falmer.

Schallert, D. L., & Reed, J. H., & D-Team, T. (2003). Intellectual, motivational, textual, and cultural considerations in teaching and learning with computer-mediated discussion. *Journal of Research on Technology in Education, 36*(2), 103–118.

Seabolt, B., & Arends, B. (2000). *Remaining real in a virtual world.* Retrieved April 3, 2007, from http://www.web ct.com/service/viewcontentframe?contentID=2385 857&pageName=index.html

Selwyn, N. (2000). Creating a 'connected' community? Teachers use of an electronic discussion group. *Teachers College Record, 102*(4), 750–778. doi:10.1111/0161-4681.00076

Son, J. (2002). Online discussion in a CALL course for distance language teachers. *CALICO Journal, 20*(1), 127–144.

Valiathan, P. (2006). *Blended learning models.* Retrieved April 3, 2007 from http://www.learningcircuits.org/2002/aug2002/valiathan.html

Vygotsky, L. S. (1978). Mind in society: The development of higher psychological processes. Cambridge, MA: Harvard University Press.

Wickstrom, C. D. (2003). A funny thing happened on the way to the forum. *Journal of Adolescent & Adult Literacy, 46*(5), 414–423.

Yukselturk, E., & Top, E. (2006). Reconsidering online course discussions: A case study. *Journal of Educational Technology Systems, 34*(3), 341–367. doi:10.2190/6GQ8-P7TX-VGMR-4NR4

KEY TERMS AND DEFINITIONS

Reflectors: Reflectors like to stand back and ponder experiences, observing them from many different perspectives before passing judgment or asking further questions. They tend to postpone reaching conclusions until they feel they have all the relevant information.

Extraverts: An Extravert is an outgoing, gregarious, sensation-seeking personality type who seeks stimulation to raise levels of cortical arousal to an optimum for efficient functioning. In other words, they are often seen as sociable and open when compared with their Introvert colleagues.

Activists: Activists are gregarious and like a wide range of different activities, immersing themselves fully and without bias in new activities in particular. They are sometimes seen as hogging the limelight.

Pragmatists: Pragmatists are keen on trying out new ideas to see if they work in practice. They like to experiment with the applications of these ideas, and to get on with things and act quickly and confidently, responding to problems and opportunities as a 'challenge'.

Minimal: Use of the Web that is neither relevant nor necessary to achieve any explicitly stated course learning goals and therefore has no impact on course-related learning.

Supplemental: Use of the Web that is relevant but not necessary to achieve a few explicitly stated course goals and therefore does not have much impact on related student learning.

Online Introverts: An online introvert is someone who displays introverted characteristics when in an online environment. Introverts experience high levels of cortical arousal, and consequently they avoid additional external stimulation to reduce their levels of cortical arousal to optimum levels. They prefer quiet reading and appear to avoid social settings or situations where they might find themselves in large groups.

Chapter 8
Teachers Learning with Wiki: Factors Influencing Behaviors and Outcomes

Yael Poyas
Oranim – College of Education and Haifa University, Israel

ABSTRACT

Wiki implementation in education has been thoroughly researched over the past few years, particularly due to the use of this technology in higher education institutions. One unique branch of this research is the influence of the Wiki environment on teachers who participate in teacher education programs. A multicultural group of teachers - younger and older, experienced and novices, Jews and Arabs – was examined while learning literature and its instruction with Wiki. Satisfaction with the learning process and its outcomes, as well as with relations among learners and between them and the lecturer, was high. Three main factors influenced the learning process and participants' attitude toward the use of Wiki: (a) level of professional development and teaching experience, (b) culture and mother-tongue of the participants, and (c) discord between academic norms and the Wiki environment's democratic norms.

INTRODUCTION

The aim of this chapter is to present the impact of teachers' professional level, their culture and learning habits on their behaviors while learning with Wiki, and on the outcomes of this learning activity. The chapter begins with a brief review of the literature regarding Wiki-enhanced teaching, including its use in teacher education. It then describes phenomena uncovered by a study which examined a group of multi-aged and multicultural teachers with diverse professional experience, who learned in a Wiki environment. At the end, challenges for teacher education are discussed.

DOI: 10.4018/978-1-61520-909-5.ch008

Teaching and Learning in a Wiki Environment

Wiki technology allows participants to share the writing and editing of varied documents according to the writers' goals. Every participant may write, add, edit, change or erase paragraphs or expressions in the edited document as needed (Leuf & Cunningham, 2001). This is a multi-modal, hypertextual, transparent environment, with a relatively user-friendly interface, and few limitations on text dimensions. Among its advantages are the 'archive' and 'history' features, allowing one to follow the process of document development and the relative contributions of the different participants, as well as reconstruct and improve previously rejected versions (Read, 2005; Ravid, 2006). These characteristics invite teachers and educators to adopt this social technology in order to extend the learning process beyond the classroom walls. Studies examining Wiki-assisted learning have shown its advantages, noting its support of constructivist learning processes (Farabaugh, 2007; Wand & Beasley, 2008); group planning and implementation of tasks; strengthening interactions among learners and between them and their teacher as compared with the interaction taking place in traditional learning environments, as well as exposing the knowledge accumulated by a group of learners to the entire group and its assessment throughout the learning process (Morgan, 2004; Watson, Boudreau, York, Greiner & Wynn, 2008). Wiki is one of the tools available for constructing an effective connection between the concept of "writing for learning" (Emig, 1977) and active learning, using cooperation which was found to be effective for learning and knowledge construction (Salomon & Perkins, 1998; Slavin, 1996). Additional studies have shown that learning with Wiki strengthens and improves the participants' efforts to contribute to the group's document creation and improve it, through constant exposure to the other participants and external readers (Ravid, 2006). Writing in the Wiki environment has been found to encourage, if based on appropriate pedagogy, complex processes of reading comprehension, multiple interpretations, dialogue among interpreters and free creative writing (Desilets & Paquet, 2005; Farabaugh, 2007).

Satisfaction with learning with Wiki depends on the application of appropriate pedagogy, which may foster efficient usage of the environment's advantages. The literature shows that participants' knowledge and trust of each other have a positive effect on cooperation and minimize harmful competition. Learning tasks best suited to this environment are characterized by having a wide perspective and openness to different points of view (Meshar-Tal & Tal-el-Hasid, 2006). In addition, familiarity with and respect towards the rules of working, behavior and politeness in the environment, minimize tension among participants (Ben-Zvi, 2007). It has been shown that it is important to inform participants regarding the characteristics of writing in a hypertext environment, as these are different from the rules of normative academic writing. It is also important to present criteria for assessment of both process and product in advance (Meshar-Tal & Tal-el-Hasid, 2006; Morgan, 2004).

Teaching with Wiki influences teachers' work, since they are required to be facilitators, managers and orchestrators simultaneously (Schneider, Synteta & Girardin, 2003). Discussion by learners regarding the written documents is essential for the promotion of learning, and its contribution is enhanced when the teacher deals in his/her comments with critical thinking, not only with linguistics, quantitative or content-based issues (Wang & Beasley, 2008). Documents or products constructed on Wiki pages become part of the data resources for discussion, research or processing, growing from the contribution of all partners in the learning project. Therefore, in order to mindfully use the developing content and ongoing process, teachers are required to apply flexible teaching.

Alongside the advantages of Wiki technology for teaching and learning, Wiki has some limitations as well. Research shows that the culture of teaching and learning the various domains affects the level of effectiveness of using Wiki. It was found, for instance, to be effective in the learning of text-based or interpretive domains, but less effective for the learning of technical ones (Rick & Guzdial, 2006). Research also reports teachers' difficulties in assessing each learner's contribution to the written product and the processes students undergo while learning with Wiki (Trentin, 2009).

Cultural Aspects and Learning with Wiki

Culture, as a set of epistemological and philosophical perceptions, beliefs, behaviors and patterns of actions influences its members' ways of thinking and interpreting (Branch, 1997; Matsumoto, 1996). Different cultures have different symbolic systems and ways of coding and decoding knowledge (Wild, 1999). Various studies proposed a variety of models to explain the variance between cultures, for instance the differences between individual and collectivist cultures, cultures capable of accepting ambiguity and those avoiding it, and cultures with high-level context-dependent communication as opposed to cultures with low-level context-dependent communication (Gunawardena, Wilson & Nolla, 2003; Hall, 1966, 1976; Hofstede, 1986; Matsumoto, 1996). Learning in multicultural groups in a social technological interactive environment such as Wiki, may cause participants various problems, owing to different cultural codes, culture-dependent information processing and expression, as well as culture-dependent networks of relationships and norms of interpersonal communication (Gunawardena, Wilson, & Nolla, 2001; Hall, 2006). Studies show that students from cultures avoiding ambiguity find online learning environments more frustrating than students from cultures accepting ambiguity (Downey, Wentling, Wentling & Wadsworth, 2005). The culture's attitude toward language also influences distance communication through social interactive technologies. There are cultures in which language is perceived as a tool conveying a precise meaning, and other cultures, like the Arab culture, where it is perceived as a system of linguistic forms, arousing feelings and visual images. Thus, while one culture pursues functional, exact and unambiguous use of language, another prefers affective language, rich in imagery (Dwairy, 2006; Zaharna, 1995).

It is also reported that while developing their pages in Wiki, many learners find it difficult to cope with the task of knowledge construction based on the norms they had become used to, in which the teacher not only provides them with the required knowledge but also determines the framework for its organization and presentation (Farabaugh, 2007; Wang & Beasley, 2008). Such difficulties become acute when individuals, partaking in a collaborative interactive multicultural learning group, are accustomed to traditional ways of teaching and learning, i.e. spoon-feeding, thus face tremendous difficulties in attempting to adapt to the self-directed environment (Alsunbul, 2001).

The characteristics of academic culture were also found to affect activity in the Wiki environment: accepted academic norms, which honor ownership of knowledge and copyright laws, minimize learners' willingness to allow peers to edit their Wiki pages and their own willingness to evaluate others' work (Lindsey, 2006; Wang & Beasley, 2008; Wheeler, 2009).

Wiki Environments and Teacher Education

Implementation of new educational technology in schools faces many difficulties due to economic, political, organizational, and pedagogical obstacles (Pelgrum, 2001). A crucial factor affecting implementation is teachers' attitudes toward the benefits of technology for everyday school instruction (Becker, 2000; Cuban, 2001). Teachers indicate the clash between schools' time allocation for learning specific topics and the time-consuming constructivist mode of learning needed for learning with technology; they also perceive technology as a motivating, refreshing device rather than an on-going learning mode. Moreover, many of them still hold the traditional mode of teaching – chalk and talk, face-to-face with their students – as the efficient way to achieve school demands (Lim & Khine, 2006). Although studies concerning the ability of teachers to innovatively implement educational technology in their teaching found that experienced teachers manage it successfully, relying on their rich pedagogical content knowledge, while novice teachers need more support (Hughes, 2005), other studies concerning teachers' attitudes toward school reforms found that the most experienced teachers were the most anxious and had the lowest endorsement for the changes to come (Butler-Williams & Kpo, 1990).

Research in the domain of teacher education repeatedly emphasizes the difficulty of bridging the theoretical knowledge learned in the training program and the innovative, experimental teaching methods sometimes implemented in these programs on the one hand, and traditional reality which draws the novice teachers into it in many of the existing educational frameworks on the other (Black & Halliwell, 2000; Ethel & McMeniman, 2000; Goodlad, 1990; Korthagen & Brouwer, 2005; Korthagen, & Kessels, 1999; Leinhardt, Young, & Merriman, 1995). Assimilation of technology in a teacher education program as a strategy for enlarging the teachers' toolbox is important today, in light of the growing usage of educational technology in school organization, assessment and teaching:

If teachers are to develop a curricular vision with respect to the use of technology for learning, teacher education programs need to think of their responsibilities as including the production of technically literate teaching professionals who have a set of ideas about how their students should be able to use technology within particular disciplines. (Darling-Hammond, Banks, Zumwalt, Gomez, Gamoran Sherin, Griesdorn, & Finn, 2005, p.199)

Different studies have examined student teachers' and teacher educators' willingness, affinity and opinions vis-a-vis educational technology, and it seems that in many cases support of technology assimilation stems from marketing, organizational and administrative reasons, and less from pedagogical and teaching reasons (Mills, Yanes & Casebeer, 2009; Schneider, 2009). Willingness to reach the necessary standards in technological literacy was found to be affected mostly by the student teachers' former experience and to a lesser degree by their viewpoints, interest in the field and the level of support provided (Kadijevich & Haapasalo, 2008). Other studies emphasize the need to deliberately implement mindful use of educational technology in teacher education programs from a curricular point of view, in order to increase preservice teachers' awareness of its advantages rather than a sporadic nondeliberate experience with it (Collier, Weinburgh, & Rivera, 2004).

Research regarding the potential of the Wiki environment for teacher education and teacher educators' opinions of it is at a very early stage, but growing fast due to spreading use of this technology (e.g. Wheeler, 2009; Wheeler, Yeomana & Wheeler, 2008). Research in this field is particularly important in light of the fact that teaching in teacher education programs allows students to experience varied teaching models which they may use in their own teaching in the future. If this experience undergoes reflective processing and is integrated with the future teachers' curricular thinking it may be translated into effective use in the planning of teaching, working together with colleagues and actual classroom instruction (Darling-Hammond et al., 2005).

TEACHERS' INTRODUCTION INTO WIKI WORLD

Two Israeli multicultural groups of teachers (n=36) participated in a blended-learning activity

(Graham, 2005; Heinze & Procter, 2004) in the domain of Literature and its instruction using the Wiki environment. One group included experienced teachers from all school levels (n=19) and the other was comprised of novice teachers experiencing their first steps in teaching alongside learning in a teacher education program (n=17). In the novices group, there were 14 Arabs and three Jews, and in the experienced group 9 Arabs and 10 Jews. As expected, the novices were much younger from the experienced teachers (average age of 24 years vs. 38 years). The language of learning and writing in both groups was Hebrew, therefore allowing the Jewish teachers to write in their mother-tongue and compelling the Arabs to write in their second language. Multi-directional and open tasks, appropriate to the professional level of the students, were administered. They aimed at (a) developing a body of knowledge concerning literary texts, their interpretations and instruction, and (b) introducing the participants to the Wiki environment's potential in encouraging democratic, constructivist, collaborative learning and shared processes of constructing knowledge. For instance, participants were asked to write an entry on a topic related to the novel they were reading in class; describe, analyze and interpret the issue from various perspectives, or discuss a story and construct a well rationalized teaching unit for its instruction. For both groups it was their first experience of learning with Wiki.

The Wiki environment provided data regarding the products being constructed, their structure, language and content, as well as regarding the process of construction: dates of entry, different versions, comments, and feedback and requests noted in the 'discussion' section. Documented oral and written responses of the participants' reactions and their lecturer's reflections allowed examination of social and individual attitudes towards the experience of learning with Wiki.

LESSONS DRIVEN FROM THE EXAMINATION OF TEACHERS' BEHAVIORS

The next section will focus on the similarities and differences between the two groups in light of their characteristics.

It should be noted that in spite of some difficulties which are discussed later, learners' and the lecturer's satisfaction was found to be high in both groups, and most learners reported in their feedback that they enjoyed the learning process and had experienced feelings of vitality, constant activity, development and gradual improvement in their interpretations, their writing and their interactions with peers throughout the process.

Experienced and Novice Teachers in the Wiki Space

Pace

The experienced teachers were more hesitant in their pace of entering the Wiki environment and getting accustomed to writing in a hypertext environment. In the first two weeks nothing was written. From then on some responses started to appear slowly, and were encouraged by the lecturer. Only in the last third of the learning project did meaningful work become apparent, linked and growing richer every week. These teachers were conservative regarding the development of their work and the organization of their writing, and tended to remain longer with the characteristics of traditional academic writing before adopting the hypertext environment link-related writing style. This phenomenon may be explained by the difficulty to adjust to changes that shake long-established thinking and working frames and habits. On the other hand, the novice teachers demonstrated quick learning of the technology and writing in a hypertext environment.

Sharing Work-in-progress with Peers

Most of the novice teachers (75%) perceived the Wiki environment as a digital variation of a 'draft' from the first moment of entry, and as an open space for conversing with the text and with colleagues. They did not hesitate to present work in progress, erase, change, move, argue and add. In fact, these teachers used all the possibilities the tool afforded them, including links, attachment of documents, pictures, etc. However, some of them were very 'silent' and their presence in the Wiki space was hardly noticed throughout the learning project. They preferred exposing a consolidated document which was a result of face-to-face meetings and writing on a word processor. The expert teachers demonstrated an opposite picture. Most of them said clearly and unequivocally that they refuse to show their work in progress. Most of them (80%) preferred writing their ideas privately on a word processor, and only when the work was completed, uploaded it to the site for all to see. Some of them mentioned that as teachers and adults they could not exhibit incomplete work, unfinished thoughts or disorganized paragraphs. For them the Wiki was the last clean version, the page you 'hand over to the teacher' for evaluation. As a result, the site became alive and fully active only in the last third of the learning project.

No doubt the mode of using the Wiki (i.e. an on-going draft until reaching the desired product or a clean completed hand-out) affected their lecturer's and peers' ability to contribute, assist or criticize the constructed products. The 'discussion' pages reflected the learners' mode of usage: those of the experienced teachers were dull and lacked mutual interactions.

Attitudes towards Learning with Wiki in a School Context

The participants' opinions regarding Wiki implementation in a school context were greatly influenced by their professional identities. Generally, the experienced teachers expressed more positive attitudes concerning Wiki's contribution towards teaching and learning in school context, and could portray learning situations with Wiki in their classrooms, while the novices were more reserved and hesitant and could not imagine themselves using Wiki in their classrooms.

The experienced teachers' professional identity was reflected in their reactions, comments and behaviors as though it constituted the prism through which they evaluated their experience in the Wiki environment: "As a learner, as well as a teacher, I find the linkages among our pages and the need to read others' documents an efficient way to 'keep everyone in the picture'; it sucks you in, you are more involved." These teachers were able to fluently explain, at the end of the project, whether or not they would integrate Wiki in their teaching and why, considering Wiki's advantages and disadvantages from a teacher's point of view: "It's wonderful. Imagine an entire class creating such a data base, which preserves their work over time for everyone. The parents can see it and respond; other pupils can see, respond and learn. We practice ongoing writing while learning, and that's simply wonderful," or, "I decided I would like to work with my students to enrich the Arabic Wikipedia. I find it poor and in need of more enrichment. It is an exciting, educating experience, which also addresses the need to develop linguistic skills." Side by side with these, one could also hear other voices: "I had a hard time reading all the material every week and following developments on the site. Wiki might be a wonderful thing, but it uses up time I don't have as a teacher." The writing experience and the need to be updated and react to their peers proved to some of the participants that teaching with Wiki demands continuous investment and much time on the part of the teacher, who is usually overloaded. As shown above, the experienced teachers acknowledged Wiki's advantages, but at the same time were aware of the extra load it might impose on the teacher.

On the other hand, the novice teachers demonstrated a general agreement as to Wiki's advantages, and expressed pleasure and interest in working with it. There was no recorded professional insight as to their ability to use this environment for teaching. Some of them mentioned that the Wiki environment may enhance the motivation of the Internet and 'zapping generation' pupils. Other responses tended to connect the questions of future usage of Wiki with three types of factors: (a) political-economic factors, such as the availability of the technology at school; (b) perception of their roles as teachers in the school system, such as coping with time allocation and demands to teach all the material for final exams; (c) perception of their position at school as novice teachers, needing to comply with the subject-matter coordinator's attitudes. It seems that mere experience with a particular learning environment during the teacher education program is not enough to construct a model of its efficient application in future teaching. In this sense, the novices' attitudes correspond with research findings concerning the gap between principles, strategies and tools taught in training programs and novices' ability to mindfully implement them later in practice.

Cultural Differences - Arabs and Jews – and their Impact on Learning with Wiki

Language and Pace of Writing

Differences were observed between Arabs and Jews in the pace of entering the writing process in the Wiki environment. The experienced Arab teachers took longer to begin than their Jewish counterparts. This may be explained by their fear of writing in a faulty style, making linguistic and spelling mistakes for all to see (as mentioned above, the Arabs wrote in Hebrew, their second language). Although they claimed, during the lessons, that the language of writing, Hebrew, did not cause any problems as they were fluent in it, their informal conversations with the lecturer (which were documented in her notes) revealed another picture. One of the Arab teachers pointed out: "When I saw that I wasn't the only one to write with mistakes, and that my Jewish colleagues also make them, I felt sufficiently confident to start writing as well." This phenomenon corroborates others' findings which show that writing in the Wiki environment in a foreign or additional language may weaken the writers' confidence (Yildiz & Bichelmeyer, 2003). However, Arab novice teachers, who constituted the majority of the group, showed no hesitation in their writing and were the first to write, while the Jewish novices took longer to start their writing. This might be due to the fact that in the latter case, language factors did not hold back the beginning of the writing process since most group participants were Arabs (14 out of 17), shared the same difficulties, and felt secure enough within the group of learners.

Those who were part of the majority, or part of the more vocal group, felt safe even in a linguistically foreign environment, and found the inner resources to be the first to write. However, participants who were part of the minority in the group, or felt as a minority, preferred to wait and see "where the wind blows" before expressing themselves.

While considering the level of language mastery as well as the participants' position in the group, one may conclude that linguistic weakness may reduce participants' confidence and slow the pace of writing in the public sphere of the Wiki environment, when they feel less dominant and less secure in the group. It probably has a stronger impact in adult, professionally and linguistically self-aware groups, as shown in the case of the experienced teachers' group.

Difficulties in Autonomous, Self-governing Knowledge Construction

An additional explanation to the pace differences mentioned above may be related to feelings of insecurity regarding the lecturer's intentions, hesitations and doubts due to the openness of the task and the fact that it relies to a great extent on personal autonomous interpretation and a personal voice. Sentences such as "I did not really understand what you expected me to write" or "I wanted to see how others write before beginning" appeared in different ways and at different levels. Some of the experienced Arab teachers approached the lecturer in the middle of the learning project, asking her to assist them by supplying some guidelines and opening sentences. These hesitations and the sense of getting lost may result from cultural factors characterizing Arab society in Israel. This society is characterized by more collectivist tendencies than Jewish society; communication among its members is context-dependent, and it is regarded as tending to avoid ambiguity (Al-Haj, 1988; 1989; 1999; Dwairy, 2006). Authorities are highly respected as the main source of information, and when facing the challenges of the modern world members of the community frequently seek solutions in the traditional literature and vast past experience, leaving minor room for personal judgment and creative thinking (Dwairy, 2006). Since the tasks the learners had to perform in the Wiki space were wide-open and mostly interpreter-dependent, they posed a hindrance to learners, especially Arabs, and triggered a sense of insecurity among them. Upon starting and receiving help in their initial steps they grew independent, and eventually participated like the rest.

As mentioned above, the Arab novice teachers were not hesitant at the beginning of the process of writing their pages, and their pages were developed rapidly, bringing information about the authors of the text studied, experts' interpretation and didactic suggestions for teaching these texts retrieved from the Internet or from textbooks. But later on, when they had to independently evaluate interpretations of the literary texts, choose between them, and construct a defensible teaching unit concerning the texts, they faced more difficulties than their Jewish counterparts, and as can be learnt from the 'discussions', asked for support more frequently.

The difficulty of coping with the demands of self-governed tasks typical of the Wiki environment learning processes may hinder group performance and raise frustration when the group is more blended and multicultural, since it slows down the pace of some individuals in the group while others push forward, and because weaknesses and difficulties become public due to the Wiki's transparency.

Difficulties in Applying Critical Thinking

Both groups, the experienced teachers and the novices, Jews and Arabs, faced difficulties applying critical thinking while writing in their pages concerning both content and frames of organization. Naturally, at the beginning the pages included factual data and some experts' interpretations, as well as opinions retrieved from Internet sites. After a while it became clear that the pages lacked organization and a reasonable sequence. Later, when the participants had to conclude, articulate their own interpretation, and relate to the topic from a holistic point of view, while conversing with others' pages, many expressed frustration and helplessness by asking for help through their 'discussion' pages. Arab participants experienced this difficulty more than their Jewish counterparts and needed more assistance from the lecturer to accomplish the task. Most Jewish participants said they understand the problem in their entries but they do not know how to apply a critical lens. As a result they asked for massive help and guidance. However, most of the Arab participants had difficulties in understanding the problem. Some of them expressed confusion and disappointment when facing the lecturer's critical comments, not realizing what she meant by asking to hear their personal voice and to read their broader interpretation. This phenomenon may be explained by cultural factors, which attribute much respect to traditions and authorities and consider the critical personal voice as inappropriate (Dwairy, 2006). It may also be a result of traditional instruction modes which are still prevalent in many Arab schools, in which students have fewer opportunities to academically and critically explore and express their own voice (Eilam, 2002; Toren & Iliyan, 2008).

Participants' Awareness of Cultural Factors through Wiki

A growing awareness of the role of cultural characteristics and cultural factors in text interpretation and instruction was evidenced during the learning process development in both novices and experienced teachers' groups. The experienced teachers exhibited great curiosity concerning their peers' life stories. The interaction between the national-religious make-up of the group, the novel learnt, and the tasks raised great interest in the 'other' culture. The novel studied (*The Day Lasts more than a Hundred Years* by Chinghiz Aitmatov) presented a Muslim culture in confrontation with the ruling culture, which attempted to impose a total ideology and annihilate religious, cultural and traditional expressions. The cultural-religious knowledge of the seven Muslim students in the experienced teachers' group contributed to the comprehension of the behavior of some of the characters in the novel, knowledge which was presented in some of the Wiki pages, informing Jewish and Christian writers in the group. As a result, participants requested to hear more about the traditions involved and about their peers' family stories during the group meetings. These oral conversations continued outside the classroom, and as the learning process unfolded participants were observed sitting in culturally blended groups rather than mono-cultural ones.

The written responses in the Wiki 'discussions' of the novices group elicited inter-cultural considerations concerning the appropriate corpus of texts for teaching in high-school classrooms. Considerations revealed religious factors: Moslems, Jews and Christians responded differently to the same text: "I will not teach this story, because the dominant role of the pig in it makes me feel uncomfortable" (a Moslem teacher); "Every child has a pig bank. It's only a bank" (a Christian teacher). The transparency of such written remarks in the Wiki 'discussion' raised the learners' and the lecturer's awareness of the issue of cultural factors which affect the selection of literary works for teaching, and induced the lecturer to deal with it also face-to-face.

In this sense the Wiki environment allowed the construction of an interactive "common interpretive space" (Sumara, 2002) which encouraged cross-cultural discussions between participants.

Learning with Wiki in the Academic Sphere

Ownership of the Written Documents

Sensitivity regarding ownership of the written document, a prominent phenomenon, which was also described in the literature (e.g. Wang & Beasley, 2008) was evidenced in both groups. The experienced teachers opposed any peer involvement in editing others' texts. Some of them admitted that it is part of the Wiki's immanent nature to invite interference for the sake of improvement, but for them it is a type of invasion of privacy, rudeness and impoliteness. In this case, comprehension of the principle of knowledge sharing and editing was not translated into agreement and acceptance of this principle.

In the novice teachers' 'discussion' one could find angry comments regarding erasing sentences written by another learner and changes made to them: "I am asking you to plllllllllease not change things without letting me know. I am really really asking. Add as much as you like, but do not change things. It is disrespectful. I am working with you, which means I am a partner in this work, so don't take such initiatives and erase without telling me." This quote from one of the 'discussions' testifies to the difficulty the writer has accepting changes and erasure of her words. She welcomed additions, but opposed changes and erasure. Clearly this safeguarding of the honor and value of the text, which represents not only its content but also the writer, is related to the group's success or failure in setting acceptable norms of cooperative work in the Wiki environment.

Request for Lecturer Evaluation and Reluctance to Evaluate Peers' Work

Both groups requested lecturer evaluation on an on-going basis. When participants thought this was not forthcoming enough, they would email the lecturer, asking for her evaluation of their work: "Hello, doctor, I would like to know what you think about the page I have done." Or, "Since we talked I have changed quite a lot, I would appreciate some feedback." On the other hand, only rarely did peer evaluation receive a response, sometimes only following a clear, intentional comment made by the lecturer. The experienced teachers found much interest in reading the 'discussions' of their peers and the conversations between them and the lecturer. These exchanges provided them with new directions of thought or guidance and direction. At the same time, writing their own evaluation of a colleague's work in his/her 'discussion' page was perceived as 'invasion of someone's private study', thus they did not tend to write feedback. This is an interesting approach - perceiving feedback as an act taking place between two people: the one critiquing and the one being critiqued, and not as a learning space for all learners. The novices were also asked to assess the teaching units written by their colleagues, and most of them did so meticulously, but this assessment was only partially related to by the unit's authors. Feedback earning a response was written by students with a high social status in the group (i.e., those who were more popular and more successful). Feedback written by students who were not considered by their peers to be knowledgeable did not receive any response, despite the fact that they mostly called important problems to the writers' attention. That is, the evaluators' social status within the group greatly affected acceptance or rejection of their evaluation.

In both groups the learners did not hesitate to say in feedback discussions that the lecturer's evaluation was much more important than peer evaluation, as ultimately she was the one giving them a grade for the course, a grade which was heavily based on the quality of their written products in the Wiki. This fact strengthens the discrepancy between the cooperative democratic character of Wiki and the reality of hierarchic evaluation norms common in educational institutions.

CONCLUSION AND RECOMMENDATIONS

Learning with Wiki encourages a multi-voiced community of learners. It creates a technological-organizational home for multiple voices, which can converse with each other directly in order to construct a rich body of knowledge. The activities described in this chapter were constructed in this spirit in the two teacher education frameworks.

The study described above confirms the findings of former research which testify to the contribution of writing in the Wiki environment within the context of blended learning, when supported by appropriate pedagogy. This contribution is bigger than the sum of the written products found on the site constructed during the learning process, and includes insights regarding social processes, involvement in the process, acquisition of editing and rewriting habits, and motivation for deep exploration. The blended learning model reduced tension and anxiety which might have stemmed from the cultural characteristics of the participants. The aligned development of the face-to-face meetings and the process of writing in the Wiki environment were found to be effective in neutralizing technological, professional and cultural problems on the one hand, and strengthening the relevance of the written products through constant discussion on the other.

Three factors were found to influence the learners' activity on the Wiki site and their insights from this activity:

Teachers' Professional Experience

Professional expertise is the basis on which experience in the Wiki environment gains its meaning. It was found that the professional development stage of the learners in the Wiki environment is significant regarding their ability to analyze, generalize and come to conclusions regarding the Wiki technology's possibilities and limitations in teaching in K-12 schools. Experienced teachers, whose pedagogical content knowledge is rich and complex, view almost every experience through the lens of their teaching experience, and are thus able to relate to the options and/or constraints of this technology in teaching in varied contexts. On the other hand, pre-service teachers, who are at the stage of acquiring the profession and do not yet fully comprehend the essence of teaching nor the relations between educational goals, curriculum demands and modes of instruction, perceive writing in Wiki as an academic learning task, and have difficulty connecting it to teaching. Thus, sporadic experiences with Wiki during the pre-service education program are insufficient. It is recommended to implement it more systematically throughout the program and accompany it with mindful reflection on the process in order to understand the adequate pedagogies for utilizing its advantages, and to develop a positive perception toward the challenges it poses to teachers.

Cultural and Linguistic Characteristics

Writers writing not in their mother tongue might find the transparency of the Wiki environment intimidating, since it might reflect their linguistic deficiencies for all to see. Furthermore, when collaborating from a distance, cultural differences may result in misunderstandings due to different cultures' perceptions of personal voice and independent interpretation within the community. As described above, most Arab participants faced difficulties constructing their own texts and voicing individual reasoned interpretations. It was found that blended learning in a secure environment, in which participants are acquainted with each other and may explain themselves face-to-face, may reduce frustration and apprehensions. However, when the majority of the group constitutes of one culture, its members feel free and secures enough to participate whatever their mother-tongue is, while the minority is more hesitant.

Modes of Evaluation

Academic norms of evaluation were found to hinder the democratic collaborative and formative mode of evaluation afforded and encouraged by Wiki features. These norms reduce attention to peers' feedback and motivate participants to avoid critiquing their peers' texts. The Wiki's ability to become a common space for constructing knowledge while constantly editing, advising, changing and consulting is transformed into a net of discrete conversations between the lecturer and each individual participant, while the others watch from the sidelines. It becomes apparent that the constructivist, explorative nature of learning with Wiki calls for appropriate assessment modes, which take into account the level of interactions between peers and modes of responding to feedback.

To sum up, it is important to continue the research on teachers' and teacher-educators' attitudes toward teaching with Wiki, and their use of it. In turn, this will lead to the construction of pedagogies enhancing the Wiki's contribution, and acquaint all users with suitable new ways of teaching which might minimize the friction with academic norms and university culture. It is necessary to study the cultural aspects of learning in the Wiki environment, particularly in a world of widening globalization trends, side by side with persistent cultural-national struggles. It is of particular importance to focus the research regarding use of Wiki in teacher education programs, as these teachers will be the ones integrating this tool into their teaching in the future, or preferring another tool to it: "... the university should take on the task of helping learners integrate and transform their knowledge by theorizing practice and particularizing theory" (Leinhardt, Young, & Merriman, 1995, p. 404). In this sense, teacher education programs (i.e., pre-service and in-service) should take on the task of theorizing and reflecting on teachers' experiences with Wiki as well as particularizing teaching and learning theories while using educational technology in diverse contexts.

REFERENCES

Aitmatov, G. (2006). *Ve Ha Yom Einenu Cale (The day lasts more than a hundred years)*. (D. Marcon & A. Porat, Trans.). Tel-Aviv: Am-Oved.

Alsunbul, A. (2001). Education in the Arab world in the outset of the third millenium. Alxandria, Egypt: University Library.

Becker, H. J. (2000). *Findings from the teaching, learning and computing survey: Is Larry Cuban right?* Retrieved May, 8, 2009, from http://www.crito.uci.edu/tlc/findings/ccsso.pdf

Ben-Zvi, D. (2007). Using Wiki to promote collaborative learning in statistics education. *Technology Innovations in Statistics Education, 1*(1), Article 4. Retrieved May, 3, 2009, from: http://repositories.cdlib.org/uclastat/cts/tise/vol1/iss1/art4

Black, A. L., & Halliwell, G. (2000). Assessing practical knowledge: How? Why? *Teaching and Teacher Education, 16*, 103–115. doi:10.1016/S0742-051X(99)00045-1

Butler-Williams, L. A., & Kpo, W. (1990). *A Study of Teachers' Attitudes toward School Reform.* Paper presented at the Annual Meeting of the American Educational Research Association, Boston, MA.

Collier, S., Weinburgh, M., & Rivera, M. (2004). Infusing Technology Skills into a Teacher Education Program: Change in Students' Knowledge About and Use of Technology. *Journal of Technology and Teacher Education, 12*(3), 447–468.

Cuban, L. (2001). Why are most teachers infrequent and restrained users of computers in their classrooms? In J. Woodward & L. Cuban (Eds.), Technology curriculum and professional development. Thousand Oaks, CA: Corwin Press.

Darling-Hammond, L., Banks, J., Zumwalt, K., Gomez, L., Gamoran Sherin, M., Griesdorn, K., & Finn, L.-E. (2005). Educational goals and purposes: Developing a curricular vision for teaching. In L. Darling-Hammond & J. Bransford (Eds.), Preparing teachers for a changing world (pp. 169-200). San Francisco, CA: Jossey-Bass.

Désilets, A., & Paquet, S. (2005). Wiki as a tool for web-based collaborative story telling in primary school: A case study. In *EdMedia 2005, World Conference on Educational Multimedia, Hypermedia & Telecommunications*, Montréal, Québec, Canada. June 27-July 2, 2005.

Downey, S., Wentling, R. M., Wentling, T., & Wadsworth, A. (2005). The Relationship between National Culture and the Usability of an E-learning System. *Human Resource Development International*, *8*(1), 47–64. doi:10.1080/1367886042000338245

Dwairy, M. A. (2006). Counseling and psychotherapy with Arab and Muslims: A culturally sensitive approach. New York: Teachers College Press.

Eilam, B. (2002). Passing Through Western-Democratic Teacher Education: The Case of Israeli Arab Teachers. *Teachers College Record*, *104*(8), 1656–1701. doi:10.1111/1467-9620.00216

Emig, J. (1977). Writing as a mode of learning. *College Composition and Communication*, *28*(2), 122–128. doi:10.2307/356095

Ethel, R. G., & McMeniman, M. M. (2000). Unlocking the knowledge in action of an expert practitioner. *Journal of Teacher Education*, *51*(2), 87–102. doi:10.1177/002248710005100203

Farabaugh, R. (2007). 'The Isle is Full of Noises': Using Wiki Software to Establish a Discourse Community in a Shakespeare Classroom. *Language Awareness*, *16*(1), 41–56. doi:10.2167/la428.0

Goodlad, J. I. (1990). Places where teachers are taught. San Francisco: Jossey Bass.

Graham, C. R. (2005). Blended learning systems: Definition, current trends, and future directions. In C. J. Bonk, & C. R. Graham (Eds.). Handbook of blended learning: Global perspectives, local designs (pp. 3-21). San Francisco, CA: Pfeiffer.

Hall, A. (2006). Who's learning? Responding to the needs of a culturally diverse world of online learners. In *Proceedings of the 23rd annual ascilite conference,* The University of Sydney.

Heinze, A., & Procter, C. (2004). Reflections on the use of blended learning. In *Conference Proceedings Education in a Changing Environment,* 13Th-14th September, 2004. Retrieved April, 30, 2009, from http://www.ece.salford.ac.uk/proceedings/papers/ah_04.rtf

Hughes, J. (2005). The Role of Teacher Knowledge and Learning Experiences in Forming Technology-Integrated Pedagogy. *Journal of Technology and Teacher Education*, *13*(2), 277–302.

Kadijevich, Dj., & Haapasalo, L. (2008). Factors that influence student teachers' interest to achieve educational technology standards. *Computers & Education*, *50*(1), 262–270. doi:10.1016/j.compedu.2006.05.005

Korthagen, F., & Brouwer, N. (2005). Can teacher education make a difference? *American Educational Research Journal*, *42*(1), 153–224. doi:10.3102/00028312042001153

Korthagen, F., & Kessels, J. P. A. M. (1999). Linking theory and practice: Changing the pedagogy of teacher education. *Educational Researcher*, *28*, 4–17.

Leinhardt, G., Young, K. M., & Merriman, J. (1995). Integrating professional knowledge: The theory of practice and the practice of theory. *Learning and Instruction*, *5*, 401–408. doi:10.1016/0959-4752(95)00025-9

Leuf, B., & Cunningham, W. (2001). The Wiki Way: Collaboration and Sharing on the Internet. Reading, MA: Addison-Wesley.

Lim, C. P., & Khine, M. S. (2006). Managing teachers' barriers to ICT integration in Singapore schools. *Journal of Technology and Teacher Education*, *14*(1), 97–125.

Lyndsay, G. (2006). Using Wikis in schools. *Futurelab innovation in education.* Retrieved May, 3, 2009, from http://www.futurelab.org.uk/resources/documents/discussion_papers/Wikis_in_Schools.pdf

Meshar-Tal, H., & Tal-el-Hasid, E. (2006). Collaborative assignments in Wiki-based environment academic courses. *Al Ha Gova, 6*, 44–47.

Mills, S. J., Yanes, M. J., & Casebeer, C. M. (2009). Perceptions of distance learning among faculty of a college of education. *MERLOT Journal of Online Learning and Teaching, 5*(1), 19–28.

Morgan, M. (2004). *Notes towards a Rhetoric of Wiki.* Paper presented at CCCC 2004, San Antonio TX. Retrieved May, 3, 2009, from: http://mcmorgan.org/academics/papers_and_presentations/notes_towards_a_rhetoric_of/

Pelgrum, W. J. (2001). Obstacles to the integration of ICT in education: Results from a worldwide educational assessment. *Computers & Education, 37*, 163–178. doi:10.1016/S0360-1315(01)00045-8

Ravid, G. (2006). Wiki: New challenges in higher education. [Hebrew]. *Al Ha Gova, 6*, 40–43.

Read, B. (2005). Romantic poetry meets 21st century technology. *The Chronicle of Higher Education, 51*(45).

Rick, J., & Guzdial, M. (2006). Situating CoWeb: a scholarship of application. *International Journal of Computer-Supported Collaborative Learning, 1*(1), 89–115. doi:10.1007/s11412-006-6842-6

Salomon, G., & Perkins, D. N. (1998). Individual and social aspects of learning. *Review of Research in Education, 23*, 1–24.

Schneider, D. K., & Synteta, P. Frété, C., & Girardin, S. (2003). Conception and implementation of rich pedagogical scenarios through collaborative portal sites: Clear focus and fuzzy edges. *Paper presented at ICOOL – International Conference on Open and Online Learning, University of Mauritius*. Retrieved May, 3, 2009, from: http://tecfa.unige.ch/proj/seed/catalog/docs/icool03-schneider.pdf

Schneider, R. (2009). Examining the Instructional Design of a Technology Enhanced Course for New Mentor Teachers. *Journal of Technology and Teacher Education, 17*(1), 85–107.

Slavin, R. E. (1996). Research for the future: Research on cooperative learning and achievement: What we know, what we need to know. *Contemporary Educational Psychology, 21*, 43–69. doi:10.1006/ceps.1996.0004

Sumara, D. J. (2002). Why reading literature in school still matters. Mahwah, NJ: Lawrence Erlbaum Associates.

Toren, Z., & Iliyan, S. (2008). The problems of the beginning teacher in the Arab schools in Israel. *Teaching and Teacher Education, 24*, 1041–1056. doi:10.1016/j.tate.2007.11.009

Trentin, G. (2009). Using Wiki to evaluate individual contribution to collaborative learning projects. *Journal of Computer Assisted Learning, 25*, 43–55. doi:10.1111/j.1365-2729.2008.00276.x

Wang, L. C., & Beasley, W. (2008). The wiki as a Web 2.0 tool in education. *International Journal of Technology in Teaching and Learning, 4*(1), 78–45.

Watson, R. T., Boudreau, M.-C., York, P. T., Greiner, M., & Wynn, D. E. (2008). Opening the classroom. *Journal of Information Systems Education, 19*(1). Retrieved May, 3, 2009, from: http://202.116.45.198/kcyjxl/jxtj/pdf/9/3.Opening%20the%20Classroom.pdf

Wheeler, S. (2009). Using Wikis to promote quality learning in teacher education. *Learning, Media and Technology, 34*(1), 1–10. doi:10.1080/17439880902759851

Wheeler, S., Yeomana, P., & Wheeler, D. (2008). The good, the bad and the wiki: Evaluating student-generated content for collaborative learning. *British Journal of Educational Technology, 39*(6), 987–995. doi:10.1111/j.1467-8535.2007.00799.x

Yildiz, S., & Bichelmeyer, B. A. (2003). Exploring electronic forum participation and interaction by EFL speakers in two web-based graduate-level courses. *Distance Education, 24*(2), 175–193. doi:10.1080/0158791032000127464

Zaharna, R. S. (1995). Understanding cultural preferences of Arab communication patterns. *Public Relations Review, 21*(3), 241–255. doi:10.1016/0363-8111(95)90024-1

ADDITIONAL READING

Bonk, C. J., & Graham, C. R. (Eds.) (2006). Handbook of Blended Learning: Global Perspectives, Local Designs. San Francisco, CA: Pfeiffer Publishing.

Garrison, D. R., & Kanuka, H. (2004). Blended learning: Uncovering its transformative potential in higher education. *The Internet and Higher Education, 7*(2), 95–105. doi:10.1016/j.iheduc.2004.02.001

Means, B. (2008). Technology's role in curriculum and instruction. In M. Connelly, F.H. He, & J. Phillion (Eds.), The Sage handbook of curriculum and instruction. Thousand Oaks, CA: Sage Publications, Inc.

Parker, K. R., & Chao, J. T. (2007). Wiki as a teaching tool. *Interdisciplinary Journal of Knowledge and Learning Objects, 3*. Retrieved May 1, 2009, from http://www.scribd.com/doc/167120/Wiki-as-a-Teaching-Tool

Ravid, G., Kalman, Y., & Rafaeli, M. S. (2008). Wikibooks in higher education: Empowerment through online distributed collaboration. *Computers in Human Behavior, 24*(5), 1913–1928. doi:10.1016/j.chb.2008.02.010

KEY TERMS AND DEFINITIONS

Wiki: A website that allows users to design, write and edit its content (add, omit or modify the text).

Teacher Education: Programs for teacher training and professional development.

Higher Education: Educational programs beyond 12th grade.

Cultural Factors: Culture-dependent characteristics.

Educational Technology: Technology which initiates and supports teaching and learning.

Critical Thinking: Mental processes involving mindful examination, analyses, and substantiated evaluation of ideas, as well as social and cultural phenomena.

Linguistic Characteristics: Characteristics and modes of language use.

Chapter 9
Audio-Visual Case Methodology for Teaching Business in Virtual Campus:
The Henry Brubaker Case

Xavier M.Triadó Ivern
Universitat de Barcelona, Spain

Pilar Aparicio Chueca
Universitat de Barcelona, Spain

Natalia Jaría
Universitat de Barcelona, Spain

Amal Elasri
Universitat de Barcelona, Spain

ABSTRACT

Henry Brubaker is a visual case used in different subjects in the area of business organization to delve into the subject of design and implementation of organizational structures. The projection to the students has been conducted by using different methodologies. The authors have already proven that the audiovisual case methodology is substantially related to the increases of student motivation not only to attend the lesson, but also to study the subject. It is not significant, moreover, that there is also a strong evidence for a positive correlation between the audiovisual case methodology used and improvements in the learning process. Likewise, the observations that the authors have collected so far suggest that this way of teaching fosters a better understanding of the theoretical concepts explained in the classroom.

DOI: 10.4018/978-1-61520-909-5.ch009

ORGANIZATION BACKGROUND

The Henry Brubaker case is based on the 1969 book *Accomplices to the Crime: The Arkansas Prison Scandal*, by Tom Murton and Joe Hyam. The film that reproduces the case scenes is titled *Brubaker*, directed by Stuart Rosenberg and produced in 1980.

In 1967, Winthorp Rockefeller composed a report about the penitentiary system in Arkansas where he detailed the horrific conditions in which the inmates lived. In addition to several humiliating cases, the quality and quantity of food given to them was very poor in a prison where several types of vegetables were grown and dairy goods were produced which yielded an average 1.4 million dollars profit in the 1960's.

Given this situation, Rockefeller decided to reform the system with Murton's help, who was already experienced in similar cases in the Arkansas region. In February 1968, Murton, as the new warden, ordered the land in Cummins penitentiary to be dug and the corpses of various inmates who had been buried in strange circumstances were found. Later on, it was discovered that they had lived a decadent slave-like situation in the prison. These facts demanded a radical change in the organization of the penitentiary and the system. This is the basis of the case we are presenting: the organizational change and the structural forms that allow it.

In reference to this, and to the visual case here presented, the aim of this study is the type of organization that exists in Wakefield penitentiary, based on the organization of an actual fact. At the same time, Tom Murton, Brubaker in the film, proves, from an inmate's perspective first, and as the prison warden later, that the prisoners suffer all kinds of abuses, in addition to the corruption of all the high-ranking officials.

The case makes it possible to address different aspects of an organization: the organization of functions, the formal and informal organizational systems, team work development, delegation, confidence in the organization, power use, the role of authority in the leader and unjust use of power among others, as well as the ethical aspects of the organization. Naturally, the teacher must select which aspects he or she wants to deal with in the course by means of this case and focus attention and questions on them.

SETTING THE STAGE

Our students' learning is a matter of constant concern for many teachers. It has been observed that, in various areas of knowledge, this learning is sometimes seriously hindered by the difficulty in associating the theoretical notions explained in the classroom to the real life of an organization. Students usually associate the conceptual definitions given in class with an abstract reality distant from their own. The lack of work experience –especially in the morning groups– aggravates the problem.

In view of this situation, the possibility of using more than the traditional pedagogic methods was valued. There exists the need to create a teaching methodology that not only helps in the learning process by bringing the theoretical classroom world closer to the practical world of real life, but that also increases student motivation and performance.

The era of global technology in which we are living is also defining university life. During the last years, the majority of the universities have adopted an open-source method called Moodle. It is a **virtual campus**[1] where students and teachers can share a virtual space to work and which offers many possibilities to learn in useful and diverse ways.

The case methodology starts at the beginning of the last century, as a teaching tool for executive formation programs carried out in the Harvard Business School. Each case introduces situations and problems (cases), habitually obtained from real organizations. Each group of people have to investigate and find solutions, and discuses about its effectiveness. (Pujol i Fons, 1981, p.151). The intention of this activity is learn concepts, as they have to apply, in the real world.

The case methodology is very appropriate and important in the "teaching-learning" process in the courses, since not only does it make it possible to deal with fundamental learning aims, but it also helps to reduce the existing distance between the classroom and the real world. The realistic character of this methodology makes it a useful tool to bring the students closer to the actual problems of the companies, since it allows a better understanding not only of their complexity and multidimensionality, but also of the difficulty to analyze it.

Although, we can consider the usefulness of cases for educational proposes. Case studies cut across a range of companies, industries and situations, providing an exposure far greater than what students are likely to experience otherwise. They can increase knowledge of many management subjects by dealing intensively with problems in each field (Corey, 1976).

Paul R. Lawrence of the Harvard Business School offered the following advice in his book "the preparation of Case Material" in the late 50's. He said then a good case has to:

- Be a vehicle by which a chunk of reality is brought into de classroom to be worked over by the class and the instructor,
- Keeps the class discussion grounded on some of the stubborn facts that must be faced up to in real-life situations,
- An anchor on academic flights of speculation,
- Record of complex situations,
- Target for the expression of attitudes in ways of thinking brought into the classroom,
- And represents a job of good reporting.

In spite of this, case study does not intend to substitute theoretical lectures, but it constitutes a good complement because it is an intermediate method between traditional theoretical teaching and actual practical training in companies. In fact, the case method has an unquestionable pedagogic value, since it accomplishes that the students actively participate in the learning process. It helps improve the following aspects (Easton, 1992, p. 7-9):

- Developing analytical abilities: classifying, sorting and evaluating the data the case presents.
- Adequately applying concepts, principles and techniques. It must be taken into account that these do not solve problems by themselves, because of which it is necessary to determine when and where to use them.
- Stimulating creative capability, for instance, in the search of alternative solutions, in the very determinations of the problems or for the later presentation of the conclusions.
- Developing communication capabilities when presenting the case, discussing and arguing with others, defending an opinion or writing a reasoned report.
- Carrying out a knowledge self-diagnostic or self-evaluation.

Below, the explanation focuses on the existing connection between the theory explained in the classroom and the situation observed in Henry Brubaker's visual case.

Classroom theory is explained within the subject of "Organic structure of organization". The aim is for the students to observe the type of organizational structure that occurs in Wakefield penitentiary in two situations: the first one, while Brubaker is posing as an inmate and identifies the current formal and informal structure of the organization; and the second one, when he unveils himself as the new warden to everybody and carries out the organizational change in the prison.

A fundamental question that must not be overlooked is why using the case of such a conditioned organization as a prison. Why using an organization where people are deprived of freedom? A case where the positions are extreme can be a good teaching resource for the students to understand it clearly and take positions about what can and cannot be done. At the same time, trying to provoke a change in a structure that seems unchangeable is a challenge. Frequently the students see it as an "impossible" challenge. At the same time, when they are "shown" –and the visual case is helpful here– that another organization is possible, their eyes open. This change of mentality, this openness to new concepts, this way to structure reality is what the case intends to provoke in the students.

With Henry Brubaker's unveiling as the new warden of Wakefield penitentiary, the former officials lose power. This is due to their unjustified use of it, in addition to the fact that some of them, like trusted inmates, make a useless use of it.

With his managing style, Brubaker decides to delegate authority by dividing responsibilities among the different jail workers, and he personally takes care of supervising the different activities and fixing whatever problems arise due to the actions of his subordinates.

At the same time, he creates a new position which involves a revolutionary measure that had not existed in the prison up to that time: the "Prisoner Committee", thus decentralizing the organization. This committee is made up by a group of inmates who –as a group– are assigned a specific task.

They meet in order to coordinate activities, exchange information and making decisions about different subjects. What Brubaker intended with this committee was to foster the penitentiary's organizational synergy, as well as to increase his acceptance as a warden by the largest group in the prison and to prevente power abuse from some of the trusted inmates.

All these changes provoke unfavourable reactions in the very actors who must come to terms with them and understand them. Little by little, a different way to organize the same reality is born. It does not seem possible, it improves organization and it makes it more just and effective.

CASE DESCRIPTION

Technology Concerns and Components

In order to start working with this methodology, it is necessary to highlight, firstly, that the classroom where it is going to be applied must be equipped with a computer, a projector and a screen to display the visual case, whereas the students must have a computer, or access to one, to carry out the virtual campus tasks. No additional technological items are required.

To prepare the case, as regards the scene selection, it may be advisable to rescue scenes from the DVD format to a format that is more computer-friendly. Converting a DVD is a very simple process that any teacher can carry out with some computer skills. We recommend using the HandBrake open-source freeware. It is an open-source, GPL-licensed, multiplatform, multithreaded video transcoder, available for MacOS X, Linux and Windows. The output file format can be MP4, MKV, AVI or OGM. It is available at http://handbrake.fr/. Figure 1 exemplifies the aforementioned process. An alternative is to use a similar programme called Need4 Video Converter 6.0 downloadable at http://need4video.com/.

Once the software has been installed, we can open HandBrake and select the "VIDEOTS" folder which contains the original DVD footage. Once the folder has been selected, the programme is now ready to convert the formats automatically. In case of doubt about the use of the software, the reader should consult the programme's help website.

Figure 1. Handbrake software example

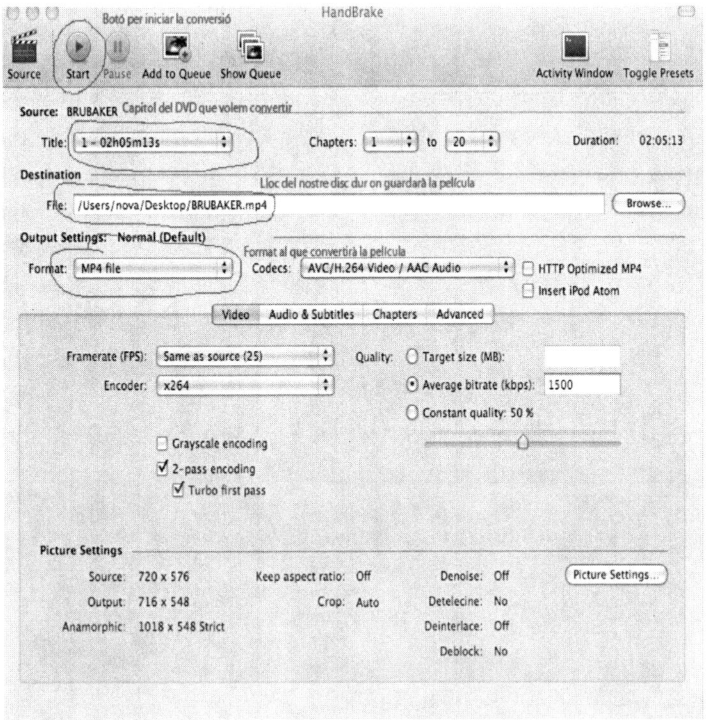

Next, the sequence to be used must be extracted. In order to prepare the clips, we recommend using the QuickTime software (http://www.apple.com/quicktime/download/). In its free version, it plays films. However, in order to work with the files, a licence must be purchased, at a reasonable cost. An alternative programme is RealMedia, available at http://www.real.com/.

QuickTime has a simple option to mark the beginning and ending of the scene we wish to use, copy it on the memory as with other documents and create a new QuickTime document with only the selected scene. These files can be saved in different formats and qualities, so they can be uploaded to the Virtual Campus without excessively loading the server. A 10-minute video can weigh about 10 Mb, with a very good quality for a computer screen.

They can also be used in a classroom presentation, or else they can be played one by one at the teacher's convenience, according to the previously established guideline. There is also the possibility to create a DVD with the selected material if the students have no access to a computer or access to the servers cannot always be guaranteed.

In order to upload a video to the Virtual Campus, the software's help may be consulted, since the instructions might vary depending on the version installed. As a general rule, it is very much like uploading a document, file or link to a website. The first step is to upload the video to the Campus, trying to keep the file size reasonable.

Management and Organizational Concerns

The phases followed for the case follow-up and visualization are explained below (Figure 2). The procedure breaks up into four phases: planning the case in the teaching plan, making up the visual case, the teaching-learning strategies in the virtual campus and, finally, starting up the audiovisual case. The attached figure displays this methodology.

First of all, we would like to emphasize that we firmly recommend the teachers to start with prior planning of every case they will use in class, and it is only then that they should start making up the visual case.

Phase 0: Planning the Case in the Teaching Plan

In order to initiate Henry Brubaker's visual case, it should have been previously reflected on the teaching plan of the course that will incorporate it. It must be highlighted that visual cases are not independent or complementary tools, neither can they be used at convenience or according to unforeseen opportunities, nor outside the course's previously defined theoretical framework (see theme framework in figure 3). Each visual case is

Figure 2. Protocol of action for starting up visual cases [Self-made]

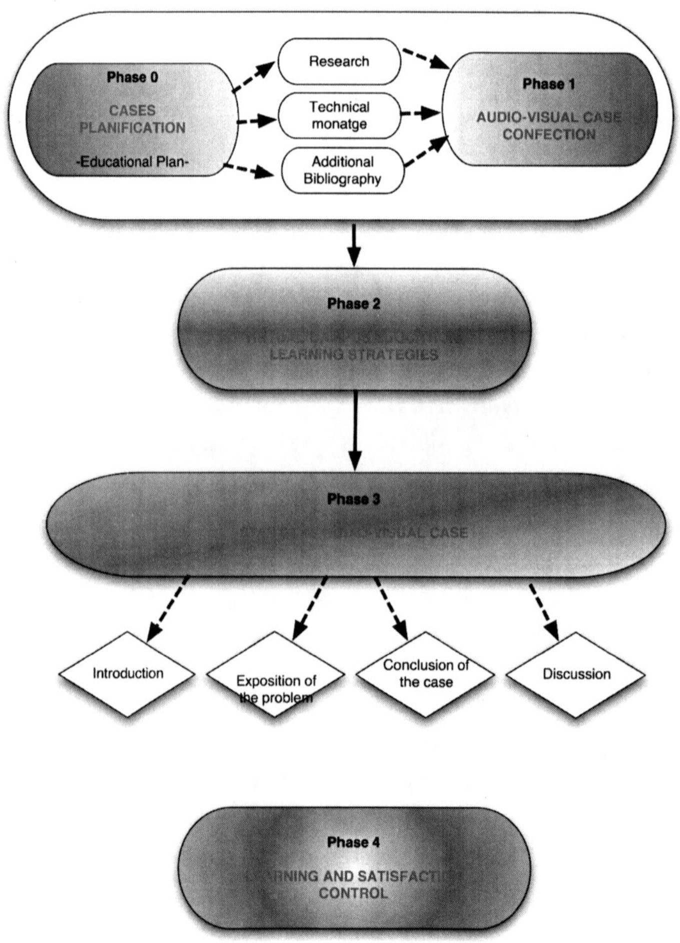

an opportunity to apply theory, helping the students to incorporate it and favouring reflection. As we have just mentioned, everything starts by compiling the basic material. The sources are diverse: a fragment from a film, a documentary that deals with the subject, recording scenes at a laboratory, in demonstrations, commemorative exhibitions, etc. All these materials are useful, but they are a draft and they need to be worked.

The teacher must prepare a calendar at the beginning of the year and temporize it, i.e. reflecting the volume of the course and the time he or she will dedicate to each lesson, as well as in which lessons and moments he or she intends to apply and reflect on what he or she is conveying to the students through theory. Following this guideline, Henry Brubaker's visual case has been framed inside the theoretical subject "Organic structure of organization", although it may be used in other subjects, according to the scenes chosen and the edited.

When using it, we recommend adapting the case to the type of students, given that the characteristics of each group may differ between turns, work experience or ages. We also recommend determining the most adequate workload for them, adapting it to the group's dimension type.

Phase 1: Making up the Visual Case

Once the case has been planned, as well as the moment where it will take place, it must be made up. Specifically, the most adequate scenes for the problem we intend to address must be selected and a guideline for the case must be established. In addition to selecting the teaching material, we will attach the case, the bibliography and relevant reading documents that will provide the students with complementary items in order to acquire the knowledge and the reflexion, so we can subsequently discuss the case.

Figure 3. Aspects of the visual cases [Self-made]

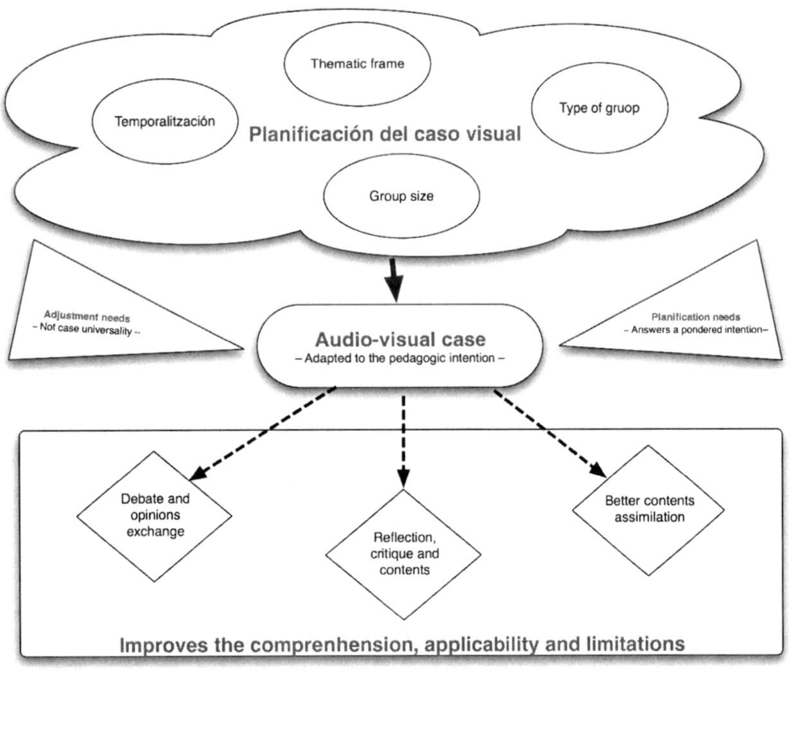

As has been mentioned above, it all starts by compiling the basic material. The sources are diverse: a fragment from a film, a documentary that deals with the subject, etc. All these materials are useful, but they are a draft and they need to be worked. The documentary sources are diverse and can yield different types of cases. Some films, like the Henry Brubaker film presented in this chapter, are a living reflection of reality and can constitute good work material.

We also recommend working with reports taken from television shows, websites with visual contents, demonstrations or commemorative expositions among others. They can be very useful. Their advantage is that they are based on actual facts which the reporter has witnessed or investigated him- or herself. Even interviews that deal with these subjects can be used. It is usually easy to obtain the permits to use the material for teaching purposes. Some laws grant generic permits if only brief scenes are compiled and used for teaching purposes. In order to guarantee it, it is recommendable to protect the virtual campus through a password to keep visitors from freely gaining access to these contents.

The first step after choosing the material is to consider the argument that will follow the case exposition. The people who will watch the case may not necessarily have the same interest and focus that we have when making it up. Therefore, it must contain an introduction, an approach to or definition of the problem, a conclusion to the problem and a proposal of resolutions or debate.

As has been previously pointed out[2], it is recommendable to edit the material with different sequences, since it allows us to interrupt the playback as interesting footage appears. This makes it possible for the students to contribute new reflections. Moreover, the teacher can channel all these reflections him- or herself through new questions that actually delve into the visual case.

The sequence of scenes must follow a guideline and can be interrupted by some questions –such as a PowerPoint presentation or some activities from the virtual campus– in order to help the students reflect.

Phase 2: Teaching-Learning Strategies at the Virtual Campus

The methodology of all the visual cases aims to be a tool that favours reflection on the concepts and situations the students must learn, acquire and generate skills about. In this sense, as has just been mentioned, the virtual campus can help each student to take his or her time to reflect and enrich his or her classmates.

The scene, or scenes, of the visual case uploaded to the virtual campus will be worked individually by each student, regardless of whether the aim is to foster later group debates or other cooperative activities. The teacher may ask the students to complete the tasks of the virtual campus after watching the case or the corresponding scene.

To make this section understandable and not merely a list of possible strategies, the most studied ones are explained in detail. To take advantage of the tools the virtual campus offers and work the case being shown to the students, there exist different strategies. It must be highlighted that at the virtual campus, the tools are diverse, and like all tools, some are more adequate for some things than for others. By themselves, tools are instruments that may help the teacher to plan or reflect the planning (calendar), control and qualify tasks, questionnaires, etc. On the other hand, by following a tidy coherent sequence, the teacher will take advantage of the tools at his or her disposal in order to make the virtual space a planned global learning strategy for the students.

Bearing in mind the aforementioned differentiation, one of the most useful tools offered by the virtual campus is the calendar option. It allows the teacher to carry out his or her organization strategy and course planning: days devoted to theory, practice, mid-term exams, reminders, deadlines, important dates or classroom changes among others. It is important to comment that, both in the calendar and in the rest of tools available to carry out the different teaching strategies, the virtual campus offers the possibility to prepare activities differentiated by groups –morning and evening, small work groups in one course– and marking each group's planning separately on the calendar.

Once the case has been shown in class, the teacher can write a questionnaire at the virtual campus to verify it has been properly interpreted by the students. As far as student work is concerned, this strategy is individual. The questionnaire may contain all kinds of questions: open, closed, true/false, multiple-choice, etc. It is a very useful choice for large groups, since closed questions are much easier to correct for the teacher. The teacher him/herself must decide what will be asked, how and when, since he or she can also decide from what day and time the questionnaire will be open, as well as the date of availability.

It is a valid strategy too for small and medium-sized groups. The variety of questions being so broad, the teachers can adapt the questionnaire to their needs.

In a teaching-learning environment, the retroaction offered to the students is important. By following this initial strategy that helps the teacher check the initial level of interpretation of the visual case, he or she will be able to clarify the students' ideas in the next lesson, or at the virtual campus, and guide them in the right direction.

In order to foster work group and interactions, chatrooms can be created where the students talk online in real time. Fluid interaction is thus stimulated among them. Another interesting possibility is the teacher using this tool to establish specific hours to solve doubts on the spot.

Still on cooperative work, which is the part is that requires most efforts in large groups, a very interesting choice is the workshop. This kind of strategy favours learning among peers in addition to fostering a positive interdependence through inter-student evaluation. A new critical spirit is thus stimulated, this time allowing the teacher less leeway. In any case, the teachers are aware at all times of the workshop comments. This makes it easier to evaluate the students' interventions.

If technical vocabulary has been used in the visual case, a very useful original strategy to share knowledge is to create a glossary. This activity allows the participants to create and maintain a list of definitions of the concepts that appeared in the case. It is a way for the students to become familiar with the specific jargon of the course they are studying and to be able to interpret texts with specific concepts of the field. The students can thus get closer to the professional world that awaits them after the university.

All these strategies offered by the virtual campus are intended to grant the students the possibility to apply a specific situation individually and thus opposing their opinions with respect to the work previously done in class. This way to work provides the students with new ideas, so that they can observe from a different point of view, and in an environment without pressure, such as being outside the academic environment, new concepts of which they had not been aware in class.

Phase 3: Starting up the Visual Case

To start up the case, there are three differentiated phases: first, the case introduction, then, the definition of the problem and, last, the conclusion of the case.

a) Case Introduction

As has been remarked, in communication and publicity, the beginning is the key moment to get attention on the message to be conveyed (Saperas, 1998). Therefore, introducing Henry Brubaker's case is one of the most essential points in order to obtain the students' acceptance. It is necessary for the teacher to define the problem to solve and establish a connecting thread with the subject being studied in class. One of the strategies used to do so is finding, from the beginning, a group of students willing to work the case in depth and presenting ideas and final arguments to their classmates.

The "Organic structure of organization" theoretical subject is being presented in class through explanations and reflections lectured by the teacher. They can ask questions that will subliminally prepare the students' minds for the subjects they will debate later regarding the Brubaker case. This teacher presentation is often carried out through the traditional teaching system and it usually takes between four and six hours of class, depending on the group, the students' level and how deep the subject will be dealt with. Once this part is over, the teacher will notify the students the date when the case will be played in the classroom.

Thanks to this introduction and the later notification of the playback date in class, the teacher gets the students to revise the theory and finding, in addition to more detailed information on the subject being studied. It is then that the visual case methodology becomes a good tool to consolidate the concepts brought forward by the teaching plan.

The same information that has been conveyed in class is also given through the Virtual Campus, where a detailed notice is published with the visual case aim and playback date. This initiative is intended to keep contact with the students who are repeating the course and who, for whichever reasons, cannot attend some of the lessons.

In this sense, it is necessary to give some technical advice from experience. The first piece of advice is to play a few initial scenes that introduce the context of the problem to be dealt with, along with some context questions that get the students thinking in the same direction. The mission of this introduction is basically to make all the students think in one direction, arouse interest in the problem and contextualize it for further discussions.

b) Defining the Problem

After introducing the case and arousing the students' interest, the problem must be defined and we must get the students to identify it and acquire it.

To accomplish that, the teacher makes a more detailed presentation of the visual case and defines a series of problems and questions before playing it. In the case of Henry Brubaker, the problem defined is "A real case to analyze organizational change", making the students reflect on questions about identifying a structure, like Wakefield penitentiary. All these questions are reflected on a guideline that gives the students additional material to their previous notes. Next, a debate is held with the whole group with the help of the handed out guideline.

The students discuss the problem, analyze it, suggest solutions and rectify their classmates' initial opinions, so that the group as a whole reaches a final reflection. The reason to carry out this exercise is enabling the students to apply the concepts discussed after watching the case, having formulated other situations and having debated the different viewpoints.

c) Conclusion of the Case and Comments to Bear in Mind

After the initial discussion, the teacher projects the different scenes of the visual case –small fragments into which the case has been subdivided to focus on the specific concepts of each part–. Henry Brubaker's case has been divided into five scenes whose titles are:

- Short 1: Understanding how this organization works.
- Short 2: Clarifying responsibilities in the organization.
- Short 3: Brubaker's management style.
- Short 4: A change in the organization: how can it be possible?
- Short 5: Final considerations.

We recommend three sessions –not necessarily exclusively for the case– to let the students work and discuss the concepts that we want to convey. The two first sessions are dedicated to actual work, while the third one is dedicated to conclusions and summary of what has been learned.

Once the first scene has been played in class, where the students should understand Wakefield penitentiary's initial organization, the group answers questions that were a guide for them and which, after the first playback, they are ready to answer. This first scene is important and it requires a more active role from the teacher, since he or she must frame the problem, i.e. give the students a context so they can understand the problems of the organization and give coherence to the scenes that will come next. During this first session, the teacher must conduct the debate leading the students to a correct reflection on the subject. This discussion lasts about 20-30 minutes, depending on how large the group is.

Next, in the very classroom, and once the students have understood the context and identified who the actors are and what roles they play within the organization, the second scene is played, "Clarifying responsibilities in the organization", which lasts 11 minutes in our case. At the same time, as we have mentioned in the previous paragraph, new questions are asked to provoke reflection. Here the possible organizational change taking place at Wakefield penitentiary becomes apparent with the arrival of the new warden, Henry Brubaker, risen from amongst the inmates. The new structure is thus also defined and whether it can work or not remains unknown. The discussion of this scene is brief, about 10-15 minutes, and the point is to make the students identify how the organization is structured and what changes should be made. It is advisable to write down, on the blackboard or the students' personal notes, the following lines so they can be recovered when discussing the next scene.

In order to answer this question, the third scene is played –the last scene played in the classroom that day–, "Brubaker's management style", and subsequently the discussion on the case continues. This scene proves how Henry Brubaker completely changes the previous management style.

Now we have reached the culminating point of the case, since it is now that the students have to suggest, think, justify and reason the changes to be proposed to Henry Brubaker. It is now that the students can identify the kind of problems Brubaker will find in the prison and which will yield the recommendations of the group for his new organizational structure to work out.

It may be advisable to leave the students thinking about the case and finish the first case session here. The students will leave the classroom with questions and suggestions on their minds to work in teams and present solutions for the case.

The next session may begin with several teams' proposals about how to organize, in our case, the penitentiary. The debate may last up to 30-40 minutes. Afterwards the fourth scene can be played. It is called "A change in the organization: how can it be possible?" This scene shows the organizational changes since Henry Brubaker's arrival as a warden and how life changes within the organization.

There is still one brief extract that shows the final conclusion of the case and how the organization and the environment respond to the changes fostered by the warden. This scene must be worked individually through the Virtual Campus, where other questions are also proposed. The students must solve them and upload them to the "Tasks" section before the next session. As homework, the students are asked to identify the kind of structure that has prevailed, as well as whether it can work. The teacher can then analyze and classify these individual papers and give the students feedback on their answers.

As will be detailed in the next sub-section, "Discussion", during the third and last in-house session, once all the students have already turned in their task and they have received the teacher's comments, he or she will discuss the general results and his or her impressions. In the very classroom, the teacher makes a final reflection on the case studied so that all the students become aware of facts they did not notice initially. However, this reflection does not intend to provide one exclusive solution to the problem, but an orientation guide for every student.

To instigate debate, discussion and reflection, the students make groups of 4 to 6 people. Each of them starts a debate on the studied sequence at the Virtual Campus for approximately 20 minutes. The object of this activity is to achieve mutual enrichment through the constant exchange and contrast of information with all that has been done individually. The goal is to make the students identify the different organizational problems, make them work cooperatively in the classroom, suggest solutions to the problems. If the teacher deems it necessary, the groups may be required to hand in a report with the solutions they propose to the company's problems.

After a reasonable time span, with the whole class present, the groups share their different solutions as well as all the other aspects of the sequence they have worked on their own and those played in the previous session.

Once all the papers have been corrected, the contributions to the virtual campus as well as the individual paper and the group report, the teacher makes a final report with all the group's marks which reflects the result of applying the visual case methodological protocol in a virtual campus environment.

DISCUSSION

To instigate debate, discussion and reflection, the students make groups of 4 to 6 people. Each of them starts a debate on the studied sequence at the Virtual Campus for approximately 20 minutes. The object of this activity is to achieve mutual enrichment through the constant exchange and contrast of information with all that has been done individually. The goal is to make the students identify the different organizational problems, make them work cooperatively in the classroom, suggest solutions to the problems. If the teacher deems it necessary, the groups may be required to hand in a report with the solutions they propose to the company's problems.

After a reasonable time span, with the whole class present, the groups share their different solutions as well as all the other aspects of the sequence they have worked on their own and those played in the previous session.

Once all the papers have been corrected, the contributions to the virtual campus as well as the individual paper and the group report, the teacher makes a final report with all the group's marks which reflects the result of applying the visual case methodological protocol in a virtual campus environment.

In the experiences carried out in groups from several studies, they were asked to answer a questionnaire that made it possible to measure and validate how efficient this methodology is.

CURRENT CHALLENGES FACING THE ORGANIZATION

This section focuses on describing the changes that take place throughout the visual case, how they are perceived by the students and how they should find solutions to the problem formulated by means of the theory explained during the previous session, as has been pointed out.

An interesting point in this visual case is to understand a specific organization, its determining factors, its possibilities, its organizational culture, the agents that make it up and the relationships of power and authority. This first point gives way to a debate and exemplification of theoretical concepts that are necessary in behaviour and organizational strategy courses.

Another very interesting aspect is the organizational change: identifying how it can be fostered, the strategies that should sustain it, the choice of key people in the change and the implications in the organization. Within this point, the perception of the initial impossibility to carry out a change in the organizational structure of a penitentiary is an aspect to be highlighted, as well as one the case's own characteristics. It does not seem that such an organization as this can be organized in a way that is not the hierarchical structure, with freedom-deprived inmates who should be helped to get reinserted in the society.

The possibility of organizing a prison more horizontally or collaboratively is not usually an initial proposal among the students. They tend to promote another structure of alternative power that replaces the previous one. The question is how long the reform will last if the previous one got corrupted. Who guarantees justice among the weak, those deprived of freedom and those inclined to accept abuse because the prison is an organization enclosed in itself?

The possibility to establish committees that bring the problems forward and guarantee a minimum of justice and equity for the inmates, as promoted by Henry Brubaker, is usually shocking for the students. They discover the sense and the possibilities of organizational flattening, as well as the difficulties and dangers it may cause if it is not done properly.

The case shows, as mentioned above, an organization dominated by the medium-ranked officials' power abuse and the high-ranked officials' tolerance. In this organization, everybody tries to abuse the weak one, the inmate. The power structure is based on prize and punishment and on the unjust use of power that guarantees individual benefits for those who hold that power. To this environment comes a reformer, Henry Brubaker, who has been commissioned to change the prison, unknowing of the magnitude of the corruption. He comes from the military career and has got leadership qualities.

The diverse aspects of change can be studied as well as the internal and external strategies that an organization needs to implement in order to adopt it. It makes it possible to work with the students, the choice of the human group that should enable the change and the resistance of those whose "status quo" is modified. Along with these aspects, the use and abuse of power can be discussed, as well as responsibility and commitment in the organization, the officials' motivation or the informal languages that arise in the institutions among others.

One last aspect to discuss about this case is leadership, its characteristics, the need to foster change and the difficulties to replace it within the organization.

SOLUTIONS AND RECOMMENDATIONS

The solutions of the visual case have already been mentioned above. Still, we will summarize the points that may be studied in this case.

Despite that, because of the possibility to fit together different theoretical subjects, such as power and authority or organizational structures among others, there is not one solution to the problem, but different aspects play a role and they depend on each teacher's point of view.

The first strong aspect of the case is acknowledging that an organization can be organized in more than one way and that change is possible, but not at all easy to implement. This leads us to teach the students the connection between structure and organizational strategy.

Another strong point of the case is understanding that all organizations, when they reach a certain size, can either maintain a centralized power or else foster delegation. They can be structured vertically or horizontally.

A third aspect of the case focuses on the use of power and the behaviour of individuals in their job. Discussing power will easily lead to develop authority and leadership aspects. This usually provokes and interesting conceptual debate that

Table 1. Feedback of the students

Question	Mean	Std. Dev.
The visual cases helped me apply my knowledge to practice.	7.55	1.276
The cases have helped me realize the applicability of the theoretical concepts studied in class.	7.49	1.609
I would like more activities like this in other courses of the degree.	7.41	2.111
My study improves because I understand the concepts of the course.	6.98	1.548
I a more motivated to attend the course sessions.	6.8	2.309

will have to end in the specific application to the case to try and help Henry Brubaker.

As for the recommendations of the case, the first and essential one is to define properly how we wish to use it. It is a case that is open enough so as to need the teacher's previous delimitation so that the students know on what to focus at every moment.

A recommendation with respect to the students comes from the very methodology we are proposing. It is important for the case's success to form balanced groups of students where all of them participate. They should discuss the possible organizational change structure and promotion alternatives internally. In order to assess the students individually and keep them from staying aside, we recommend an individual assignment and a later group presentation and discussion.

With the aim to obtain the learning of the pupils is very important that the teacher can control the different groups, fostering a critical vision and balancing participation, preventing any group from monopolizing the discussion.

Table 1 summarizes the advantages obtained from a 64-student sample in a course where four visual cases were used –one of them, Henry Brubaker– and four written cases similar to Harvard's. The scores are on a scale from 1 to 10. As it can be seen, the audio-visual cases helped, with 7.55 point of average, the students to apply the knowledge to the practice, as well as, with a similar average, 7.49, the used cases have served to see the applicability of the theoretical concepts explained in class.

Another of the advantages that the students value notably, is they would like to do more similar activities in other courses of the degree. Although, they think their study improves because they understand the concepts of the course and for that reason, they are motivated to attend the course sessions.

Regardless of this data, the students claim this methodology helped them participate more in the sessions and it fostered more regular attendance to class. The attendance percentage, which is not mandatory, is 93%.

REFERENCES

Aparicio, P., & Castán, J. Mª, Espluga, C.Mª, Gallardo, E., Guitart, L., Miravitlles, P., Nuñez, A., Rimbau, E., Triadó, X.Mª., & Viu, M. (2004). *Desarrollo de casos audiovisuales para el aprendizaje en organización de empresas.* Paper presented at III Congreso Internacional de Docencia Universitária e Innovación (CIDUI), Gerona, Spain.

Burgos, D., & Corbalan, G. (2006). Modelado y uso de escenarios de aprendizaje en entornos b-learning desde la práctica educativa. En *III Jornadas Campus Virtual*, September, Madrid (Spain), University Complutense of Madrid. Retrieved June 30th, 2006, from http://dspace.learningnetworks.org

Burgos, D., Tattersall, C., & Koper, R. (2005). Utilización de estándares en el aprendizaje virtual. En II Jornadas Campus Virtual, May 2005. Madrid: Universidad Complutense de Madrid

Castro, E. (2004). Manual del Profesor de Moodle. Retrieved from http://download.moodle.org/docs/teacher-Cole, J. (2006). *Using Moodle. Teaching with the Popular Open Source Management System.* Retrieved October 19, 2006, from http://docs.moodle.org/en/Using_Moodle_book

Corey, E. R. (1996). The use of cases in management education. Teaching note 9-376-240. Harvard Business School.

Easton, G. (1992). Learning from case studies. London: Prentice Hall.

Gallardo, E., Aparicio, P., & Triadó, X. (2008). *Adapting an audiovisual case methodology to a virtual campus in business organization lessons.* Paper presented at INTED 08. International Technology, Education and Development Conference, València, Spain.

Lawrence, P. R. (1953). The preparation of Case Material. In K. R. Andrews (Ed.), The Case Method of Teaching Human Relations and Administration (p.215). Cambridge, MA: Harvard University Press.

Martin, J. (2006). *Manual del Profesor de Moodle 1.5.* Retrieved from http://www.lasalle.es/descargas/ManualMoodle2006.zip

Molist, M. (2006). Institutos y universidades apuestan por la plataforma libre de 'e-learning' Moodle. *EL PAÍS.* Retrieved from http://www.elpais.es/articulo/portada/Institutos/universidades/apuestan/plataforma/libre/e-MOODLE. (n.d.). Retrieved from http://moodle.org/

Pujol, i Fons. (1981). *Los métodos en la enseñanza universitaria.* Pamplona, Spain: Eunsa.

Saperas, E. (1998). Manual básico de teoría de comunicación. Barcelona, Spain: CIMS.

Triadó, X. (2008). El aprendizaje en ciencias sociales mediante el uso de casos audiovisuales. Un instrumento de aprendizaje, motivación y mejora de la comprensión conceptual. *Revista Didáctica, Innovación y Multimedia. Núm 11.* Retrieved from http://dewey.uab.es/pmarques/dim/revistaDIM11/revcentro1.htm

Triadó, X. (2008). El uso de casos audiovisuales como instrumento de aprendizaje, motivación y mejora de la comprensión educativa en el ámbito de las ciencias sociales. *Revista de Innovación e Investigación Educativa, 18*, 213–222.

ADDITIONAL READING

Accino Domínguez, J. A. (2002). Un entorno de componentes para enseñanza virtual basado en software libre. *Novatica, 156*, 55–60.

Cole, J. (2006). *Using Moodle. Teaching with the Popular Open Source Management System.* Retrived October 19, 2006, from http://docs.moodle.org/en/Using_Moodle_book

Daft, R. L. (2003). Organizational theory and design 8 Ed. Boston: South Western College Publishing.

Hayes, N. (2002). Managing Teams. A strategy for success. Cengage Learning EMEA.

Hodge, B. J., Anthony, W. P., & Gales, L. M. (2002). Organizational Theory. A Strategic Approach. Upper Saddle River, NJ: Prentice Hall Inc.

Murton, T., & Hyams, J. (1970). *Accomplices to the Crime: the Arkansas Prison Scandal* Publisher: Grove Press, Inc.

Ostroff, F. (1999). The horizontal organization. New York: Oxford University Press.

Rees, W. D., & Porter, C. (2008). Skills of Management. Cengage Learning EMEA.

Robbins, S. P. (2003). Organizational Behaviour. Upper Saddle River, NJ: Pearson Education.

Robertson, M., & Collins, A. (2003). OPEN SOURCE INITIATIVE (OSI). The Open source definition: The video role model as an enterprise teaching aid. *Education+Training, 45*(6), pp. 331-340. Retrieved from http://www.opensource.org/docs/definition.php

Silverman, R. (Producer), & Rosenberg, S. (Director). (1980). *Brubaker* [Motion Picture]. USA: Fox.

Stoner, J., Daniel, R., & Gilbert, Jr. (1999). *Management 6 Ed.* Upper Saddle River, NJ: Prentice Hall.

Triadó, X. (2008). El uso de casos audiovisuales como instrumento de aprendizaje, motivación y mejora de la comprensión educativa en el ámbito de las ciencias sociales. *Revista de Innovación e Investigación Educativa, 18*, 213–222.

Triadó, X. (2008). Revista Didáctica, Innovación y Multimedia. Núm 11. *El aprendizaje en ciencias sociales mediante el uso de casos audiovisuales. Un instrumento de aprendizaje, motivación y mejora de la comprensión conceptual.* Retrieved from http://dewey.uab.es/pmarques/dim/revistaDIM11/revcentro1.htm

KEY TERMS AND DEFINITIONS

Audiovisual Case: Presentation of situations or problems (cases) obtained from real situations by the use of extracts from films, television reports or interviews. Using them enables a greater interaction and dynamism in the classroom.

Organizational Structure: Ways into which work can be divided and grouped within an organization to later coordinate it orienting it to goal achievement. There are six basic elements that the administrators address when designing their organization's structure: work specialization, departmentalization, chain of command, span of control, centralization and decentralization and formalization. [Robbins, S.P.; *Organizational Behaviour*]

Organizational Change: The set of structural variations that organizations undergo and which translate into a new organizational behaviour.

Organizational Leadership: Leadership has been described as the process of social influence to others in the accomplishment of a common goal. In our case, we use this term to manage change in an organization and create a new structure better fitted with their objectives and goals.

Teaching Metholology: It is a way of doing something, especially in a systematic way; it implies an orderly logical arrangement (usually in steps).

Team Management: Use of the techniques, processes and instruments that aim to organize and coordinate a work group which is part of an organization.

Moodle Cases: It is a free open-source e-learning software platform, also known as a Course Management System, Learning Management System or Virtual Learning Environment. Moodle is designed to help educators create online courses with opportunities for rich interaction. We propose to use this platform to watch, answer and work interactively with students for visual cases.

ENDNOTES

1. From this point on, when we speak of Virtual Campus, we will be referring to the aforementioned platform.
2. According to our experience, it is recommendable to convert a DVD or a video to QuickTime format. Other software can also be used, but the one mentioned is very easy to use and provides good footage treatment. The way to do so has been explain in the Technology Concern section.

Chapter 10
SMASH:
Blended Training for Parent Education in Mathematics and Science

Maria Meletiou-Mavrotheris
European University Cyprus, Cyprus

Efstathios Mavrotheris
Open University of Cyprus, Cyprus

ABSTRACT

At a time when mathematics and science provide essential knowledge tools and the foundations for lifelong learning skills, cross-national studies of student achievement in Europe indicate lack of mathematical and scientific competence for a considerable proportion of the student population. Acknowledging the central role of parents in children's learning, the EU-funded project SMASH aims to raise the educational standards of European youth in mathematics and science by cultivating underlying home cultures as springboards for learning. The project consortium has developed an innovative intercultural parent-trainer training course and related resources for professionals involved in parent education initiatives. The course, which is delivered through combined use of e-learning and physical meetings, provides these professionals with current knowledge, techniques, and implementation tools for the provision of high-quality, culturally differentiated training in mathematics and science education to parents of elementary and middle school children (ages 6-15) in their communities. Online multilingual resources support and promote the program's activities and objectives by offering open access to the parent-trainer training course content and tools.

BACKGROUND TO THE PROJECT

In technology-based society, where mathematics and science provide essential knowledge tools and the foundations for more advanced or specialized training either in higher education or through lifelong learning, several studies indicate the lack of mathematical and scientific competence of a considerable proportion of both the adult and student population around Europe (IALS, PISA, TIMSS). Research also indicates that pupils with poor quantitative skills are likely to have fallen behind by the age of ten. Thus, if the European Union is to achieve the objective set by the European Council for a

DOI: 10.4018/978-1-61520-909-5.ch010

considerable increase in the number of European college-level students graduating in mathematics, science and technology and pursuing technical careers, it should put more focus on improving student achievement in mathematics and science at a young age (Commission of the European Communities, 2007). The Joint Interim Report "Education and Training 2010" adopted by the Council and the Commission in 2004, highlights the need for accelerated reforms and calls on Member States to take action in order to motivate young people to take a greater interest in science and mathematics, and to undertake scientific and technical studies and careers (Council of the European Union, 2004). Several of the Lisbon Education & Training Indicators measure progress towards improved recruitment and performance of students in mathematics and science.

Significant reform efforts in mathematics and science education are occurring at both the European and national levels. It has been recognized that the core of school mathematics and science should no longer be the teaching of techniques and calculations that computers can do much faster and more reliably, but the development of problem-solving skills that students will need to effectively live and function in a highly complex society. Numerous initiatives are underway aimed at raising the quality of teaching and learning through the development and implementation of pedagogically sound, technology-based tools and curricula. Despite their usefulness, these initiatives tend to focus on formal education systems and to underestimate the influence of the informal learning occurring outside school. In particular, while teachers are being offered professional development opportunities on pedagogical and technology trends in mathematics and science education, no analogous opportunities are being offered to the other important stakeholder in improved education - parents. In its December 2004 progress report, Working Group D "Increasing Participation in Mathematics, Sciences and Technology" notes the general lack of initiatives in the EU that aim to involve parents (European Commission, 2004). The report points out that stronger and more and effective partnerships between schools and parents are an important area for policy makers to consider.

Parents are the central contributors to a child's education, thus having them involved and engaged in the educational process of their children is of paramount importance to their academic achievement in mathematics and science. The research literature indicates a very strong positive relationship between school performance and a conducive to learning home environment (Kellaghan et al., 1993; Huntsinger et al., 1999; Carter, 2002; Chen, 2001; Downey, 2005). Given the fundamental changes that have occurred in both the content and pedagogy of mathematics and science, the majority of parents do not have the needed knowledge to create an environment within the home that fosters their child's development and is coordinated with classroom work. The vast majority of parents encountered school mathematics and science as drill-oriented subjects, made up of rules and procedures to be memorized, thus many of them maintain a very algorithmic approach and, often, negative attitudes towards the subjects. Moreover, most parents lack the necessary knowledge to guide their children towards constructive uses of technology in support of their learning and developmental needs (Becta, 2001). As a result, although the majority of children in Europe have access to a computer at home (Mavrotheris et al., 2004; Ramboll Management, 2006) and spend far more time using ICT than they do at school (Becta, 2001; Ramboll Management, 2006), computers are not utilized constructively. Rather, children often use technology at home for non-educational purposes such as playing computer games (Mavrotheris et al., 2004).

Parent education is considered an "essential component" of successful parental involvement (Freedman and Montgomery, 1994; Covarrubia, 2000; DiCamillo, 2001). To spur reform in mathematics and science education, parents should be provided with guidance on how to enhance their children's learning experiences.

SETTING THE STAGE

SMASH (**S**uccess in **MA**th and **S**cience at **H**ome), a project funded by the European Union under the Lifelong Learning Program/Grundtvig action, was proposed in response to the need for reaching out to parents and informing them about new developments in mathematics and science education. The overall aim of the program, which has a 2-year duration (December 2007-November 2009), is to offer high-quality training to parent educators around Europe that will equip them with the required knowledge, skills, and resources to provide professional guidance to parents of elementary and middle school children (ages 6-15) in how to best support their child's development in mathematics and science. More specifically, the project consortium, comprised of seven partner institutions in five European countries (Cyprus, Greece, Spain, Czech Republic, and UK), has the following objectives:

a. Develop, pilot test, and offer an intercultural parent-trainer training course for European teachers, school administrators, representatives of parent associations, and others involved in training activities for parents, that will prepare them through combined use of e-learning and physical meetings to implement in their communities culturally differentiated parent-training programs for supporting children's development in mathematics and science.
b. Develop, pilot test, and distribute to parent educators for use in their parent-training programs a culturally differentiated training pack for parents offering technology-enhanced, research-based educational aids and resources for parents to support the development of their children's mathematical and scientific knowledge and skills.
c. Design and develop a multilingual information base to support and promote the program's activities and objectives by offering open access to the parent-trainer training course content and pedagogical approach, to the parent training pack, and to various other links and resources.
d. Initialize networking among parent educators across Europe by building an online community for the exchange of ideas, content, tools, and didactic approaches relating to parent education in mathematics and science. The long-term objective is to sustain and, if possible, to expand this community into a pan-European network of communication.

CASE DESCRIPTION

In this section, we provide an overview of the *SMASH* project. First, we describe the key activities taking place during the project lifetime. Next, we outline the SMASH parent-training course design. Finally, we discuss the quality assurance processes used in the project to ensure the provision of a high-quality distance education course that delivers its stated aims, satisfying all interested stakeholders in the educational system that could benefit from the project outputs.

Key Stages of Program Development

In the two-year timeframe of the SMASH program, the following activities have/will take place in order to achieve the project objectives:

- *Development of a pedagogical framework for parent training in mathematics and science:* At the outset of the project, the consortium worked towards developing a framework for best practices in parent training programs in mathematics and science education, through combined use of e-learning and physical meetings. The preliminary design of the framework, which guided the design of the parent-trainer training course was based on desk research into the different approaches to parent education used across Europe and internationally, and after taking into account cultural differences in teaching and learning methods, as well technical considerations regarding online course delivery (e.g. current limitations in terms of equipment, software, protocols, and network bandwidth). The pedagogical framework was validated during the pilot delivery of the parent-trainer course and was revised accordingly.

- *Development of parent-trainer training course and accompanying parent training pack:* The consortium designed the parent-trainer training course pack and the accompanying parent-training pack, based on the guidelines set in the pedagogical framework. The parent-trainer training course pack provides a state-of-the-art overview of new pedagogical methodologies and didactical routes in parent education. It aims at equipping parent educators with the most up-to-date knowledge, skills, and technologies to successfully implement high-quality parent training in mathematics and science education. The parent-training pack offers technology-enhanced, research-based and culturally adapted educational aids and resources to support children's development in mathematics and science at home, to be adapted and used by parent educators in their parent training programs. Material has been developed in English and translated into the partners' national languages (Greek, Czech, and Spanish). It is culturally differentiated to accommodate local conditions in each participating country.
- *Design and development of information base infrastructure and services:* In parallel to the development of the instructional material, the team worked on the technical design and development of an online information base to support the project activities and outputs. The information base, implemented as an interactive multilingual web portal, supports anytime, anywhere education and collaboration of parent educators and parents around Europe. It includes the parent-trainer and parent training packs developed through the project and a variety of other distance learning tools and resources for parent educators and parents, including forums for discussion and networking between parent educators and parents (e.g. email, chat rooms, discussion forums, wikis, etc.).
- *Pilot testing and validation of the parent-trainer course and accompanying parent training pack:* A pilot delivery of the parent-trainer training course took place during the spring of 2009. Before being offered to the EU educational community, the parent-trainer training course and its accompanying parent training pack were pilot tested locally in three of the partner countries (Cyprus, Spain and Czech Republic), on groups of 15-20 parent educators per country. Upon completion of the parent-trainer training course, some of the course participants ran parent training workshops in their respective communities, using the parent training pack developed by the consortium. Instructional materials and services were revised based on the feedback received from the pilot delivery of the course and the follow-up parent training workshops.
- *Offering of Grundtvig parent-trainer training course:* The revised parent-training course has entered the EU Lifelong

Learning Program Training Database for increasing visibility and access to parent educators across Europe. It will be offered as a Grundtvig training course targeting school and/or adult mathematics and science teachers, school administrators, counselors, representatives of parent associations, or other professionals involved in training activities for parents. The SMASH course has been scheduled for offering twice during the fall of 2009, in two of the partner countries (Cyprus and the Czech Republic). After completion of the project, the consortium will continue to offer the parent-trainer training course as a Grundtvig course, thus increasing access to large numbers of educators involved in parent education.

- *Information base Content and Services Enrichment:* At the end of the project, final revisions and enhancements to the project information base content and services will be made and it will then be opened not only to the parent-trainer training course participants, but to all interested parents and parent educators. The information base will integrate a variety of resources and distance learning and communication tools. It will include:
  - i. *A "hypertextbook"* with the content of the *parent-trainer training course*, to be used as a self-paced course, in a facilitated online mode, or as part or all of the material used in a face-to-face course or workshop;
  - ii. The accompanying *parent training pack*, which could be used by distance-learning organizations delivering training to groups of parents and/or other adult end-users, or for independent study by individual parents;
  - iii. *Collaboration tools* supporting dialogue and exchange of ideas between European parents and parent educators, such as forums of discussion, chat rooms, and application sharing;
  - iv. *Mathematics and Science Family Kits* that will include culturally and developmentally appropriate educational games and technology-enhanced and hands-on activities parents can do at home with their children to strengthen their learning;
  - v. *Reports and articles* developed through the project;
  - vi. *Links to mathematics and science education resources* available on the Internet.

The open access to the project outcomes and the information published through the information base by users outside the consortium will help improve the collective knowledge of the mathematics and science parent and parent educator communities by supporting the sharing of multiple, multinational perspectives, and by facilitating easier flow of information among stakeholders. It will also ensure sustainability of the system after the completion of the project.

Design of SMASH Parent-Trainer Training Course

The main outcome of the SMASH project is the intercultural parent-trainer training course that will be offered to the European educational community. We next provide an overview of the *SMASH* course design: course objectives, principles guiding course design, pedagogical and didactical approach, and course content and structure.

Objectives of the Parent-Trainer Training Course

Parent educators trained through the program will gain expertise in how plan, design, and facilitate an effective parent training course in mathematics and science education. They will:

- Develop effective strategies for parent training by getting acquainted with the main principles of adult mathematics and science learning, and of parent education;
- Gain better understanding of informal mathematics/science education and inquiry, and of ways to encourage family-based informal mathematics/science education practices;
- Get familiarized with innovative methodologies, tools and technologies that parents can employ at home to facilitate their children's learning;
- Get familiarized with the rationale and content of the parent-training pack prepared by the consortium, and with ways to facilitate its use during the parent-training course;
- Develop strategies for promoting parental engagement and learning, and particularly for increasing the involvement of "hard to reach families";
- Learn how to convey complicated scientific ideas in a simple language that families can understand; and
- Learn how to effectively communicate with parents coming from different cultural and/or socio-economic backgrounds.

Thus, parent educators completing our course will be equipped with the necessary knowledge, tools and resources to provide high-quality training in mathematics and science education to parents in their communities. Consequently, we expect that these professionals will, in turn, offer parent training programs that will help the parents:

- Increase their awareness of the value and importance of mathematics and science literacy for their children's future;
- Better appreciate how mathematics and science are connected to everyday experiences, and learn how to help their children to make the connection;
- Gain a better understanding of informal mathematics and science education and inquiry;
- Become more skilled and confident in nurturing their child's (and their own) learning and growth in mathematics and science;
- Learn how to foster their children's natural curiosity about the world, how to appropriately address their informal mathematics and science inquiries, and how to assist them in exploring the world around them;
- Get familiarized with a variety of innovative methodologies, tools, and technologies they can employ at home to support their children's informal mathematics and science learning;
- Learn more about educational programs and how the school works; and
- Become better equipped to support and monitor their children's mathematics and science learning at school.

Principles Guiding Parent-Trainer Training Course Design

- All parents care deeply about their children and want the best for them. A 'blaming' approach does not work and is inappropriate;
- All parents have strengths and are important, and can contribute to their child's education;
- All parents can learn how to help their children in school;
- All parents have useful ideas and insights about their children;
- All decisions about how to involve parents should be made only after consulting with them;
- We need to treat parents as equal partners – to share cultural insights and traditions, and to enrich and connect school learning and family life experiences;
- Our services should be equally accessible to all parents, including those hard-to-reach groups (e.g. parents living in remote areas,

parents who have developed a mistrust of schools due to their own education experience, etc.); and

- We need to continually challenge our methods of practice and be open to change.

Course Pedagogical and Didactical Approach

The theory of learning underlying SMASH is social constructivism. The design of the parent-trainer training course has been based on the importance of dialogue and collaboration between parents, parent educators, and researchers, and of inquiry and exploration as a process of knowledge construction (Ponte, 2001). The course has been jointly designed by a multinational consortium of educators, representatives of parents' and teachers' organizations, experienced distance learning instructors, authors of technology supported courses, and technicians, in order to ensure consideration of all different perspectives into the integrated pedagogical framework. Particular care has been taken to build on parents' knowledge and experiences and to respect cultural differences in parenting approaches (Onikama et al., 1998). Educators participating in the parent-trainer training course developed through the project will be trained to provide parent training that goes beyond the transfer of knowledge and development of skills, but is rather based on dialogic learning (Flecha, 2000), viewing parents as valuable intellectual resources to the learning process (Civil, 2002).

A central conviction underlying the *SMASH* design is that learning is a social act best supported through collaborative activities (Vygotsky, 1978; McConnell, 2000). While the project employs innovative technological tools and resources to support educationally useful human-computer interactions, its focus is on exploiting technology to support human-human interactions (Barab et al., 2001). The SMASH parent-trainer training course promotes intercultural awareness and exchange of experiences and ideas, by providing a virtual space where European mathematics and science parent educators with a broad range of experiences and expertise can come together to reflect upon relevant education theory and practice, and build collaborations. Course participants will be encouraged and expected to engage in joint discussions and to work collaboratively in completing projects and other assignments. The aim is to build relationships and construct a multinational community that will support best practices and innovation in parent training in mathematics and science education.

SMASH course participants will be provided with ample opportunities for interactive and collaborative learning through use of a wide array of tools, artifacts and resources (Gordon et al., 2007). They will engage in authentic educational activities such as projects, experiments, group work, and discussions. The strategies employed will include open-ended investigations, use of real-data, simulations, visualizations, collaboration and reflection on one's own and on others' ideas and experiences. These strategies are based on current principles of learning and are endorsed by professional organizations in mathematics and science education. Through use of these strategies, we will provide a learning environment that will help participating parent educators gain better understanding of informal mathematics and science education and inquiry. Moreover, the learning environment will serve as a model to the parent educators as to the type of training they should provide to parents, in order to increase their scientific interest and knowledge and their ability to promote family-based informal mathematics and science education practices.

Course Content and Structure

Course Content

The project consortium has designed the parent-trainer training course pack and the accompanying parent-training pack based on the guidelines set in the project pedagogical framework developed at the beginning of the program. The parent-trainer training course pack provides a state-of-the-art overview of new pedagogical methodologies and didactical routes in parent education. It explores a broad range of topics of interest to mathematics and science parent educators, including the following: (i) Principles of child psychology and mathematics and science learning; (ii) Computer-supported teaching and learning; (iii) Principles of adult mathematics and science learning; (iv) Parental involvement and student achievement; (v) Basic principles of parent education; (vi) Recommended practices for promoting parental engagement and learning (e.g. family mathematics and science nights, family involvement case studies, etc.); and (vii) Evaluation of parent education programs. Special emphasis has been paid to EU transversal policy issues, such as promoting participation of females, integration of disabled people, and inclusion of socially and economically excluded families.

The parent-training pack offers technology-enhanced, research-based and culturally adapted educational aids and resources to support children's development in mathematics and science at home, to be adapted and used by parent educators in their parent training programs. It consists of multimedia based training modules, to be delivered as a series of mini-workshops, that familiarize parents with some general principles of learning, with learning theories specific to mathematics and science, as well as with the use of learning technologies (e.g. use of state-of-the-art mathematics and science educational software as well as general-purpose software like Excel, guidelines for selecting appropriate educational software and for making internet surfing conducive to learning, etc.).

An isomorphic approach has been adopted for the development of course material targeting parent educators and parents. The program aims at educating parent educators and parents in the same principles and common language, to ensure the sharing of similar understandings regarding the ways in which parents can reinforce children's learning of mathematics and science at home. The intent is not to remediate or compensate for skills taught in school, but to spark children's scientific interest and to stimulate their informal learning of mathematics and science.

The teaching strategies employed in both the parent-trainer and the parent-training course to educate parent educators and parents about ways to promote informal mathematics and science learning at home, include the following:

- Project-based Learning
- Inquiry-based learning
- Case-based Learning/ Scenario based learning
- Role playing

Material has been developed in English and has been translated into the partners' national languages (Greek, Czech and Spanish). It has been culturally differentiated to accommodate local conditions in each participating country. The content is in digital form and will be available online via the project information base.

Course Structure

Parent educators will receive training through combined use of e-learning and physical classroom meetings. The course is made up of three parts:

i. *One-week Intensive training seminar:* At the beginning of the course, parent educators from all over Europe will gather together to attend the seminar. Course participants will be familiarized with the course and its objectives, and with the facilities offered by the course e-Learning system. More importantly, they will get the chance to meet and interact with one another, share issues and problems, as well as exploit the tutors' presence to ask questions about things they are unsure of (Simpson, 2002). We believe that this initial in-person meeting will reinforce parent educator online engagement (Kavanaugh et al., 2005) since it could mitigate the problem of trust and social presence online (Ardichvili et al., 2003).

The seminar will consist of a combination of mini-workshops that will include technology-based and hands-on activities in small groups (5-6 persons), presentations by experts, role-play, videos documenting learning activities of parents with children, and discussions. During the seminar, there will be particular emphasis on enhancing parent educators' skills in adapting the provided parent training material based on the context-specific needs and interests of parents in their community. Language of tuition will be English.

ii. *ICT-mediated instruction using the project information base:* The second part of the course will be delivered online utilizing the interactive information base built specifically for this project. Parent educators will review the material that was provided to them during the Intensive Training Seminar and prepare for their guided field practice. Online moderated discussions– both asynchronous and synchronous – will allow participants to share content, ideas, and instructional strategies.
iii. *Guided field practice:* At a final stage, parent educators will undertake a teaching experiment. They will customize and expand upon the parent-training materials provided to them, and apply them in their own communities. Partners will act as mentors, providing their support to parent educators using online communication tools. Parent educators will write up their experiences, including a critical analysis of their work and that resulting from parents. This will help them to reflect on their practice and apply self-criticism constructively. Once the guided field practice is completed, they will report on their experiences to the other parent educators, and exchange ideas and insights as to how to further improve their parent training practices.

Upon successful completion of the course, participants will get certification as authorized trainers to run the parent training program developed through this project.

Building Quality Assurance into the SMASH project

Here we present the Quality Assurance (QA) System underlying SMASH. QA has become a prominent issue, as an effective method and tool to respond to the challenge of quality in online education (Belawati and Zuhairi). A QA system is a set of systematic management and assessment procedures adopted in order to monitor performance against objectives, and to ensure achievement of quality outputs and quality improvements (Harman, 2000). QA systems ensure that an effective, efficient and satisfying experience is provided for learners (Lockwood, 2005), and thus play a critical role in allaying stakeholder concerns regarding the quality of online education. They serve public accountability purposes, help inform learner choice, contribute to improved teaching learning and administrative processes, and help disseminate best practices with the goal of leading to overall improvement of distance education systems (Belawati and Zuhairi, 2007).

Evaluation plays a major role in a QA system, since it is the process by which the quality of content, teaching effectiveness and administrative efficiency of an online learning environment are assessed (Lockwood, 2005). Evaluation is not an abstract research exercise but an essential tool of good management that needs to permeate and influence all aspects of a course or program from conception to final review (Calder, 1994). It can contribute to the quality of online courses at the design, development and presentation stages. It can help meet both internal and external needs for information, feedback, and insight into the nature and quality of a teaching/training provision.

The SMASH consortium is made up of a multinational group of established educators, researchers, representatives of parents' and teachers' organizations, distance learning instructors, authors of technology supported courses, and technicians, who have extensive experience in transnational cooperation through participation in numerous EU-funded projects. Undoubtedly, this synergy of collaboration among partners with complementing expertise and specialization contributes to improved quality in each area of the parent-trainer training course production and delivery process (Rowntree, 2005). Nonetheless, there are still a number of possible risks that could adversely affect the quality of the *SMASH* course. We next discuss some management and organizational concerns, and some technology concerns addressed by the SMASH QA system in order to avoid such risks, and to ensure the provision of a high-quality distance education course. We also outline the evaluation processes employed to assess the project effectiveness in delivering its stated aims.

Management and Organizational Concerns

The SMASH project consortium is comprised of seven partners originating from five different European countries, who have been selected due to their complementing interests and expertise. While this cross-fertilization of cultures and expertise contributes towards increasing the volume of co-operation between organizations involved in adult/parent education initiatives throughout Europe, and can lead to higher quality outputs compared with a purely national approach, there are at the same time several complexities to managing a transnational team of partners. Issues of intercultural competence and cultural differences can become roadblocks to the success of the project. One pitfall often experienced by multinational teams is the danger of an assumed 'common' language while in reality there is differential interpretation due to cultural differences and/or linguistic difficulties. Also, the physical separation of partners might lead to problems in the timely and effective management of the project activities. To prevent such problems, and ensure successful collaboration and efficient handling of the consortium's schedule and cost commitments, the SMASH consortium set at the outset of the project a clearly defined, formal methodology for executing, monitoring and reporting the different project tasks. Setting an effective project management plan was necessary for reducing misunderstandings and aiding efficient co-operation.

Several project management techniques have been employed by the SMASH consortium to make the project run more smoothly and deliver its desired results, on time and to budget. Each partner institution's role is defined in the project work plan and in the partner agreements signed at the beginning of the project between the coordinating institution and each partner. The partner agreements aim to facilitate communication and collaboration among the partners and ensure that activities are conducted by the partners as specified in the proposal and to resolve disputes that may arise. They outline the obligations of each party: allocation of funds based on obligations and the work plan, grant transfer procedures, reporting, liabilities, damages for non-performance, confidentiality agreements, intellectual property rights handling, etc. In the unfortunate case that disputes do occur and cannot be resolved amicably, they will be resolved according to the rules outlined in the partner agreement.

The project work plan is made up of nine workpackages, organized around specific actions/aspects of the project: (1) Project Management; (2) Definition of End-User Requirements; (3) Development of pedagogical framework and instructional content; (4) Design and development of information base infrastructure and services; (5) Pilot testing and validation of the parent-trainer course and accompanying parent training pack; (6) Offering of Grundtvig parent-trainer training course; (7) Evaluation; (8) Dissemination; (9) Post Project Exploitation and Sustainability Strategy. Each workpackage requires specific technical and pedagogical expertise, and workpackage leaders have been selected based on the required experience for the respective actions. Workpackage leaders monitor progress on specific tasks, i.e. implementation milestones, intermediate, and final deliverables of workpackages, by setting short and longer-term goals leading to their completion.

Management of the project activities is being achieved through ongoing communication and collaboration among participating institutions. The consortium meets twice a year to plan and monitor work progress by setting interim implementation goals and evaluating interim results based on work plan. Additional meetings at a smaller scale may be scheduled for the completion of subtasks. Further, online tools were set up when the project started in order to facilitate communication and collaboration among the partners between consortium meetings. They include mailing lists, forums, file sharing portals for the exchange of documents, a member-only area in the project web-site with confidential information (e.g. meeting agendas, meeting minutes, interim reports, implementation goals, partner agreements, report forms, etc.), video-conferences to take place among partners at least on a monthly basis, forums, and chat rooms. This ongoing discussion and mutual commenting is stimulating and helps to improve the quality of the project outcomes and results.

Technology Concerns

With the exception of the physical gathering of the parent educators during the one-week intensive training seminar, the remainder of the course will be offered online by utilizing the instructional content and services of the dedicated information base developed through the project for teaching, support and coordination purposes. The financial and logistic difficulties of engaging parent educators in face-to-face professional development opportunities for a long period of time, as well as the need for training that can draw on powerful resources often not available locally, have encouraged the adoption of a blended-learning approach. Offering the biggest part of the course online will give parent educators flexibility and convenience, allowing them to determine their own place, pace, and time of study (Bregar et al., 2002). At the same time, however, distance education posits special challenges that ought to be met in order to provide an effective learning environment that motivates and supports learners. *The SMASH* QA system had to incorporate several strategies in order to ensure the provision of a supportive, knowledge-building and sharing environment that fosters sustained parent educator participation and collaboration.

An important issue of concern has been how to design a course that meets the needs and goals of a group of parent educators characterized by diversity in a number of different parameters. The distance learning portion of the *SMASH* parent-trainer training course had to be designed to meet the needs of a fairly specialized audience:

- Participants will belong to different professions (e.g. school and/or adult mathematics and science teachers, school administrators, counselors) and will work under fairly diverse environments
- Participants will be busy adults working full-time jobs
- Participants will be fairly demographically diverse, across several time-zones

Another issue of concern has been the appropriate selection and use of teaching media (Lockwood, 2005). Although all of the parent educators will have access to a computer and

Internet connection at home (this will be a course requirement), we do expect a great variety in participating parent educators':

- Experience and comfort with technology;
- Expertise in using Internet-based services;
- Previous experience in taking on online course;
- Expertise in the use of mathematics or science education software, applets, etc;
- Type of computer technology, and educational software they have available for the support of the teaching and learning process;
- Supporting equipment they have available for teaching and learning purposes: VCR's, DVD's, audio devices, digital blackboards, AV/Data communication equipment etc; and
- Bandwidth they have available for deploying AV/Data communication.

A number of pedagogical, but also technical issues have been incorporated into the design of the *SMASH* course and its related services (adopted from Meyer and Thille, 2006) in order to meet the needs of this diverse group of parent educators and to best help them meet the challenges of distance education:

- Choice of accessible media in terms of reasonable cost and time taken;
- Use of a variety of media in order to appeal to individual learner circumstances, needs and preferences;
- User-friendly interface and navigation services;
- User friendly content addressing workplace educational needs;
- Multimedia content presentation (audio, video, text, images, etc) to ensure effective knowledge transfer;
- Activities and resources (simulations, animations, video clips, etc.) that stimulate and engage parent educators participating in the course, and address a variety of teaching and learning styles;
- Access to multiple distance collaboration tools that promote interaction with peers and with course facilitators;
- Use of a variety of approaches towards content so that participants can "pick and choose" what works best for them;
- Regular assessments for course facilitators to monitor progress and provide feedback, and for participants to monitor their own progress;
- Careful scheduling of course activities to accommodate for the main national or religious holidays in different countries, to offer parent educators flexibility, and to accommodate different time zones;
- Setting of realistic work expectations – ensuring that the workload associated with the course is not overwhelming so as not to overburden parent educators; and
- Follow-up procedures to help parent educators apply what they learn in the course to a real parent-training session.

To offer parent educators flexibility and to accommodate different time zones, the largest portion of the course will be delivered asynchronously. Asynchronous means of communication and collaboration will include discussion forums, mailing lists, blogs, and wikis. There will also be some synchronous communication through use of technologies such as digital blackboards, audio/video streaming, and chat rooms. One-way informational postings such as articles and videos will also serve as objects for supporting interaction (Barab et al., 2001).

In addition to being available on the project e-Learning system, the course material will also be available in CD/DVD format to overcome potential bandwidth limitations, and ensure maximum accessibility of learning materials.

Role of Evaluation

Evaluation is an integral part of the SMASH project design. It is an ongoing process carried out at every stage of the project, in order to ensure that all key activities are carried out on time and effectively by the consortium partners, and that necessary revisions or improvements to the project's methodologies, products, and outcomes are timely identified. It includes both formative and summative assessment tools and protocols for evaluating the quality of the project products and services.

The project evaluation strategy was developed early in the project to ensure that all key activities are carried out on time and effectively. Measurable criteria of success defined according to the project plan have been set to serve as a basis for evaluating the program's success in attaining its objectives. The evaluation strategy integrates both technical and instructional design principles. It covers fields such as cost-efficiency of this type of training, level of knowledge and skills obtained by participant parent educators and parents, demonstration of efficiency and/or limitations in technology and quality of services provided, and the extent to which the developed parent-trainer training course and its accompanying resources offer suited pedagogical frameworks adapted to a realistic level in various types of cultural and educational contexts.

Two complementary types of evaluation are utilized to provide constant feedback on the project's development process and impact: internal evaluation and external evaluation:

Internal evaluation is an ongoing process for monitoring the implementation progress based on the work plan, and for generating objective feedback among partners aiming at the continuous improvement of project products and services. To ensure timely internal feedback generation and integration, demonstrations of interim results (pedagogical methodologies, instructional content, project information base services and tools etc.) are scheduled during the consortium meetings, but also using online communication between meetings. This process ensures that the interdisciplinary expertise available in the consortium is fully exploited as work progresses.

External evaluation is being achieved through the engagement of end-user groups unrelated to the consortium. Its goal is to generate unbiased feedback on the products developed, aiming at the continuous improvement of the project products i.e. the content and services, and the parent-trainer training course itself. To ensure that evaluation results arrive early enough for integration into the project outputs, an *initial evaluation phase* aimed at the validation of user requirements, and the provision of informal reviews on the content and services under development has been taking place through the engagement of user groups of parents and parent educators in all the participating countries. The *main external evaluation phase* took place during the pilot testing of the parent-trainer training course and its accompanying parent-training pack. As already noted, there was a pilot delivery of the course in the participant countries, and follow-up parent training workshops organized and run by participant parent educators in their communities with the support of the project team. Various forms of assessment tools and protocols were used to collect and document evidence of changes in parent educators' pedagogical and content knowledge of mathematics and science, attitudes towards the subjects and teaching practices, and the impact that these changes have on their ability to provide effective parent training, including (i) web-based surveys administered to parents and parent educators at the end of the SMASH course; (ii) videotaping of classroom episodes, (iii) interviewing of small groups of parents and parent educators, (iv) self-reports and course evaluations by parent educators; (v) postings in discussion forums; and (vi) quantitative statistics automatically collected by the system (e.g. number of parent educators participating in a discussion forum, or successfully completing group assignments, number of postings by each participant, etc.) The pilot testing in different countries also allowed the consortium to check for possible cultural bias of the program tools and resources. The analysis of these data informed the revision of the course pedagogical frameworks, instructional and curricular materials, as well as the tools and resources of the course information base.

CURRENT CHALLENGES FACING THE CONSORTIUM

In a technology-based society, mathematics and science literacy are among the key competencies that all individuals need for employment, inclusion, subsequent learning, as well as personal fulfillment and development (Commission of the European Communities, 2002). These competencies should be acquired by the end of compulsory schooling, since they are a prerequisite for participation in lifelong learning.

Recognizing the crucial role of mathematics and science education in achieving sustainable development and fulfilling the personal aspirations of European citizens, the SMASH project aspires to raise the educational standards of European youth in these disciplines through building European parents' capacity to contribute towards raising their children's achievement in mathematics and science. Taking into account best practices in mathematics and science education, adult education, parent education, and distance learning, the project aims to enrich European elementary and middle school children's learning of mathematics and science through cultivating underlying home cultures as springboards for learning. The parent-trainer training course developed through the project goes far beyond traditional adult training practices. It builds parent educators' knowledge and skills through a hands-on, inquiry-based approach that seamlessly combines best pedagogical practices with contemporary technologies, including the Internet for maximum flexibility.

As already noted, the SMASH parent-trainer training course and its related resources were pilot tested in three partner countries (Cyprus, Spain, Czech Republic) and were revised based on feedback received from the pilot delivery. After final revisions and updating of the information base with the latest version of all content, the SMASH course entered the EU Lifelong Learning Program-Grundtvig database for European wide recruitment. The first offerings of the course have been scheduled for the Fall 2009 semester, in Cyprus and in the Czech Republic.

The overall feedback from the target user groups from all three partner countries participating in the *SMASH* course pilot delivery, as well as from external experts regarding the course content, services, and didactical approaches has been very positive. Key conclusions from the analysis of the data obtained during the pilot parent-trainer training course delivery were that *SMASH* was quite successful in providing course participants with the required knowledge and tools to plan, and design, and implement effective parent training seminars in mathematics and science education. The follow-up parent-training seminars organized by some of the parent educators trained through the program were met with great enthusiasm by parents. The vast majority of parents participating in these seminars rated them very positively, agreeing that their participation in the seminars increased their awareness of the many ways in which they could promote their children's mathematical and scientific development through informal, family-based practices.

Since the SMASH course has now been opened to the Europe education community, it could be attended by parent educators around Europe. Thus, parent educators enrolled in the SMASH Grundtvig course could originate from any European country, and thus be geographically, culturally, and linguistically heterogeneous. Also, unlike the pilot course which was mainly conducted through face-to-face meetings with local parent educators, the biggest part of the Grundtvig course will be offered via distance education. Thus, there are special challenges currently facing the consortium that did not exist during the pilot course delivery. One important issue of concern is the danger of a low completion rate. While in the pilot course delivery, all the course participants managed to successfully complete the course, we cannot assume that the same will happen during the actual course offering. As the research literature indicates, Open and Distance Learning (ODL) institutions tend to experience much higher rates of student attrition than conventional institutions (Barolli et al., 2006), with often unacceptably low completion rates (Mayes, 2001). Of course, the SMASH course participants will be educated, adult learners, who are themselves in the teaching profession (Evans, 1994), and who voluntarily participate in the course. Consequently, we expect the majority of them to be sufficiently self-disciplined and self-directed learners, who are intrinsically interested in mathematics and science parent education. Still, different parent educators will have different backgrounds, different goals, and different learning styles and approaches. Given their overburdened schedules, they will be willing to invest time on the course only if it stimulates and engages them, and addresses their specific educational needs and preferences (Rowntree, 2005).

Another difficulty we anticipate is in achieving the successful building of a European online community of parent educators, which is a main objective of the project. The SMASH course design has given special emphasis to the building an online community for the exchange of ideas, content, tools, and didactic approaches among European mathematics and science parent educators. We recognize, however, that given the diversity in parent educators' cultural and professional backgrounds, social context, comfort with technology, experience with distance education etc., the establishment of a functional online community of practice will be quite challenging. An online community does not automatically take shape through the availability of the online space (Rourke and Kanuka, 2007). The existing research literature highlights several difficulties in building and maintaining online communities involving shared professional learning. Despite the benefits reported by proponents of online communities of practice, such communities are notably difficult to form and maintain. There is strong research evidence indicating that many distance learners join discussion forums, read messages, but do not contribute to discussions (Simpson, 2002). As a result, while online education holds the potential for vibrant interaction and rich dialog, "online instructional experiences can become quite wooden and lifeless at times" (Muirhead, 2007).

SOLUTIONS AND RECOMMENDATIONS

Early attempts of Internet-based instruction assumed that setting up an attractive Web site with interesting online and multimedia applications was adequate for learning to take place (Simpson, 2002). It is now recognized that the level of success of a distance learning course is determined by multiple factors –underlying theory, design, technologies, teaching strategies, effectiveness of such technologies, and support for learners available (Robson, 2000). Learner support, in particular, assumes a vital role in distance education given the isolation from peers, their tutor, and the institution often experienced by online learners (Simpson, 2002). While there are multiple interacting factors determining learner success or failure in distance education, some of which are beyond the control of the institutions, research does indicate that the very low rates of course completion experienced in many systems of ODL are associated with low levels of learner support (Thorpe, 2005), and that some institutional interventions can contribute towards learner success if appropriately targeted (Robinson, 1995). Distance education students who fail to establish support networks are more likely to withdraw (Simpson, 2002). Interaction between supporters and learners, as well among learners, is essential for high-quality learning. Although there are some learners who choose distance education because they "do not want interaction with other people" (Thorpe and Pettit, 2001), the vast majority do value contact with instructors and other learners, even if they do not always use the services provided. Learner support can help strengthen student motivation and reduce the drop-out rate (Barolli et al., 2006). In particular, what happens in the early stages of student recruitment and enrolment appears to have a significant effect on later success or failure (Robinson, 1995).

The SMASH consortium recognizes the fact that learner support is not a compensatory, but an essential component of the instructional process, which in distance learning assumes an even more important role than in conventional instruction. In *SMASH*, learner support is an integral component of the course design, and has been designed as part of the course participants' experience. It is seen as "a necessary and cost-effective way of retaining students as well as an essential humanizing element of any open and distance learning system" (Simpson, 2002).

The SMASH QA system includes several strategies to ensure quality of learner support which will maximize learner participation and progress. For example, each parent educator participating in the course will be assigned a personal tutor who will offer them guidance and support throughout the course. They will also have access to technical experts for advice on problems of a technical nature. To ensure timely response to learners, a set of rules on learner service levels has been developed, such as responding to email enquiries from course participants within a 24-hour period and providing feedback on assignments within seven days after submission (Chua and Lam, 2007).

Monitoring of parent educator participation will be done both at the course level, and the learner level. Monitoring at the course level will allow the consortium to detect problems that might affect learners as a whole (e.g. a very high drop-out rate, a much lower average learner performance on a specific assignment). It will also allow them to find out whether the actual profile of parent educators registering for the course matches the expected parent educator profile based on which the course is being designed. If this is not the case, then changes will need to be made to either the recruitment procedure or the course itself (Calder, 1994).

The *SMASH* QA system will also monitor the individual progress of learners in order to determine whether they need additional help or support. A number of tools will be used to track learner participation and progress, including statistics automatically generated by the course learning platform (e.g. level of frequency and duration of login for every learner, turn-around time for an assignment, number of assignments completed to date against target etc.).

The SMASH QA system also includes several strategies to promote dialogue and transnational collaboration among parent educators participating in the course, thus contributing towards the establishment of a functional online community of practitioners. Realizing that collaborative learning environments require carefully crafted designs – both technical and social (Collazos et al., 2006), we will employ pedagogical and technology structures that encourage communication and cooperation, and support the community's shared purpose. A number of strategies will be used to ensure that all course participants actively contribute to course activities, including the following:

- Participation in discussion forums, wikis, and other collaborative activities will be a compulsory element of the course;
- A clear set of criteria will be established in the course syllabus to help parent educators better understand the academic expectations and increase the intellectual depth of their contributions (Muirhead, 2007);

- Participants will be assigned to small groups, and each group will be facilitated by a tutor;
- Participating groups will receive periodic milestone group assignments which they will jointly complete using social software tools such as wikis;
- Sufficient time will be provided for group members to make meaningful interpersonal connections before the assignment of the first cognitive task (Beuchot and Bullen, 2005);
- Monitored bulletin board forums will allow the groups to exchange ideas and help each other. In addition, instructors will use the bulletin board to facilitate discussions on pedagogical techniques, and to encourage parent educators to think more deeply about concepts;
- Each member of a discussion group will be assigned to serve as moderator at least once during the course duration; and
- Parent educators will be asked to self-assess their contributions to the online discussions by first filling out a self-assessment form that includes a scale response, and to substantiate the score they receive with evidence from their discussion postings (Kayler and Weller, 2007).

Delivery of the course will be facilitated by members of the consortium from all participating countries with expertise in mathematics and/or science education. Since the course will be designed to be a community-based learning experience, the facilitators' role will be to guide the discussions and encourage full, thoughtful involvement of all participants, and to provide feedback. Facilitators will help to deepen the learning experience for course participants by encouraging productive interaction and critical reflection on parent education practices (Gray, 2004). They will employ moderating strategies for promoting the building of social connections that will extend beyond the level of social interaction and sharing of information.

An important motivational factor influencing the success of an online community of practice is the nature of the tasks in which the learners engage. Merely forming a discussion forum and providing the technology will not automatically lead to the development of a community of practice that supports well-managed, conducive to learning conversations (Doolan et al., 2006). Similarly, mere provision of social software such as a wiki will not be adequate to generate collaborative co-creation and shared learning (e.g. Kennard, 2007; Bruns and Humphreys, 2007). In the SMASH course, both the dialogue and the assignments will be based on experiential learning, i.e. they will make use of the parent educators' own experiences as learning resources (Aalto and Jalava, 1995). They will be structured so as to explicitly make ties among theory and practice, in order to help parent educators make new connections between the course readings and theory and their personal and professional experiences.

REFERENCES

Aalto, P., & Jalava, M. (1995). Implementing experiences from small-scale courses to large education systems. In F. Lockwood (Ed.), Open and Distance Learning Today (pp. 255-264). London: Routledge.

Ardichvili, A., Page, V., & Wentling, T. (2003). Motivation and barriers to participation in virtual knowledge-sharing communities of practice. *Journal of Knowledge Management*, *7*(1), 64–77. doi:10.1108/13673270310463626

Barab, S. A., Makinster, J. G., Moore, J. A., & Cunningham, D. J. (2001). Designing and Building an On-line Community: The Struggle to Support Sociability in the Inquiry Learning Forum. *Educational Technology Research and Development*, *49*(4), 71–96. doi:10.1007/BF02504948

Barolli, L., Koyama, A., Durresi, A., & De Marco, G. (2006). A web-based e-Learning Efficiency by Stimulating Learner's Motivation. *Information Systems Frontiers*, *8*, 297–306. doi:10.1007/s10796-006-9004-5

Becta. (2001). *ImpaCT2 – Emerging Findings from the Evaluation of the Impact of Information and Communications Technologies on Pupil Attainment.* Retrieved from http://www.becta.org.uk/research/reports/impact2

Belawati, T., & Zuhairi, A. (2007). The Practice of a Quality Assurance System in Open and Distance Learning: A case study at Universitas Terbuka Indonesia (The Indonesia Open University). *The International Review of Research in Open and Distance Learning, 8*(1), 1-15. Retrieved July 29, 2007, from http://www.irrodl.org/index.php/irrodl/article/view/340/782

Beuchot, A., & Bullen, M. (2005). Interaction and interpersonality in online discussion forums. *Distance Education*, *26*(1), 67–87. doi:10.1080/01587910500081285

Bregar, L., Ograjensek, I., & Bavdaz, K. (2002). Statistical Education and the Workplace: Present State of Affairs and Future Challenges. In B. Phillips (Ed.), *Proceedings of the Sixth International Conference on Teaching Statistics (ICOTS6)*. Cape Town, South Africa: IASE.

Bruns, A., & Humphreys, S. (2007). Building Collaborative Capacities in Learners: The M/Cyclopedia Project Revisited. In *Proceedings of International Symposium on Wikis*, Montréal, Canada.

Calder, J. (1994). Programme Evaluation and Quality. London: Kogan Page.

Carter, S. (2002). The Impact of Parent/Family Involvement on Student Outcomes: An Annotated Bibliography of Research during the Past Decade. Eugene, OR: Consortium for Appropriate Dispute Resolution in Special Education.

Chen, H. (2001). Parents' attitudes and expectations regarding science education: Comparisons among American, Chinese-American, and Chinese families. *Adolescence*, *36*, 305–313.

Chua, A., & Lam, W. (2007). Quality assurance in online education: The Universitas 21 Global approach. *British Journal of Educational Technology*, *38*(1), 133–152. doi:10.1111/j.1467-8535.2006.00652.x

Civil, M. (2002). Everyday Mathematics, Mathematicians' Mathematics, and School Mathematics: Can We Bring Them Together? In M. Brenner & J. Moschkovich (Eds.), Everyday and academic mathematics in the classroom. Journal of Research in Mathematics Education Monograph #11 (pp. 40-62). Reston, VA: NCTM.

Collazos, C. Guerrero, L., Pino, J., Ochoa, S., & Stahl G. (2006). A Model and a Game for Investigating and Designing Collaborative Learning Environments. In *Proceedings of 8th International Symposium on Computers in Education*, SIIE'06, León, Spain.

Commission of the European Communities. (2002). *European benchmarks in education and training: follow-up to the Lisbon European Council.* COM(2002) 629 final, Brussels, Belgium. Retrieved June 2008, from http://ec.europa.eu/education/policies/2010/doc/bench_ed_trai_en.pdf

Commission of the European Communities. (2007). *A Coherent Framework of Indicators and Benchmarks for Monitoring Progress Towards the Lisbon Objectives in Education and Training*. Retrieved February 2008, from http://eur lex.europa.eu/LexUriServ/site/en/com/ 2007/com2007_0061en01.pdf

Council of the European Union. (2004, February 26). *Joint Interim Report of the Council and the Commission on the implementation of the Detailed Work Programme.* Retrieved from http://europa.eu.int/comm/education/policies/2010/doc/jir_council_final.pdf

Covarrubia, J. (2000). Family literacy: Sharing classrooms with parents. *Principal, 80*(1), 44–45.

DiCamillo, M. P. (2001). Parent Education as an Essential Component of Parent Involvement Programs. In D. B. Hiatt-Michael (Ed.), Promising Practices for Family Involvement in Schools (pp. 153-183). Greenwich, CT: Information Age Publishing.

Doolan, M., Hilliard, A., & Thorton, H. (2006). Collaborative Learning: Using technology for fostering those valued practices inherent in constructive environments in traditional education. *Journal for the Enhancement of Learning and Teaching, 3*(2), 7–17.

Downey, D. B. (2005). When Bigger is Not Better: Family Size, Parental Resources, and Children's Educational Performance. *American Sociological Review, 60*, 746–761. doi:10.2307/2096320

European Commission, Directorate-General for Education and Culture. (2004). *Working Group D 'Mathematics, Science and Technology' Objective 1.4 Increasing recruitment to scientific and technical studies Interim report.* Retrieved from http://ec.europa.eu/education/policies/2010/doc/math2004.pdf

Evans, T. (1994). Understanding Learners in Open and Distance Education. London: Kogan Page.

Flecha, R. (2000). Sharing words: Theory and practice of dialogic learning. Lanham, MA: Rowman & Littlefield Publishers.

Freedman, E., & Montgomery, J. F. (1994). Parent Education and Student Achievement. *Thrust for Educational Leadership, 24*, 40–44.

Gordon, S., Petocz, P., & Reid, A. (2007). Tools, artefacts, resources and pedagogy—stories of international statistics educators. In P. L Jeffery (Ed.), *Australian Association for Research in Education 2006 Conference Papers*, AARE, Adelaide. Retrieved March 25, 2008 from http://www.aare.edu.au/06pap/gor06358.pdf Gray, B. (2004). Informal Learning in an Online Community of Practice. *Journal of Distance Education, 19*(1), 20-35.

Harman, G. (2000). Quality assurance in higher education. Bangkok: Ministry of University Affairs & UNESCO PROAP.

Huntsinger, C. S., Jose, P. E., & Ching, W. D. (1994). *Ethnic differences in early math learning: A comparison of Chinese-American and Caucasian-American families.* Presented at the Annual Symposium of the Jean Piaget Society, Chicago, IL. (ERIC Document Reproduction Service No. 375940).

Kavanaugh, A., Carroll, J. M., Rosson, M. B., Zin, T. T., & Reese, D. D. (2005). Community networks: Where offline communities meet on-line' [Electronic Version]. *Journal of Computer-Mediated Communication, 10.* Retrieved June 2008 from http://jcmc.indiana.edu/vol10/issue4/kavanaugh.html

Kayler, M., & Weller, K. (2007). Pedagogy, Self-Assessment, and Online Discussion Groups. *Educational Technology & Society, 10*(1), 136–147.

Kellaghan, T., Sloane, K., Alvarez, B., & Bloom, B. S. (1993). Home Environment & School Learning: Promoting Parental Involvement in the Education of Children. San Francisco: Jossey-Bass.

Kennard, C. (2007). Wiki Productivity and Discussion Forum Activity in a Postgraduate Online Distance Learning Cours. In C. Montgomery C., & J. Seale (eds.), *Proceedings of World Conference on Educational Multimedia, Hypermedia and Telecommunications 2007.* Chesapeake, VA: AACE.

Lockwood, F. (2005). Quality Assurance and Evaluation (Overview Essay 4). H804 Implementing Online, Open and Distance Learning. Milton Keynes: The Open University.

Management, R. (2006). *E-learning Nordic 2006: Impact of ICT on Education.* Retrieved February 2008, from http://wwwupload.pls.ramboll.dk/eng/Publications/PublicAdministration/ StudyOnInnovative-learningEnvironments.pdf

Mavrotheris, E., Meletiou-Mavrotheris, M., & Maouri, C. (2004). Towards a More Constructive Use of Technology in Mathematics and Science. In *Proceedings of the 1st International Conference on Information & Communication Technologies*.

Mayes, J. T. (2001). Quality in an e-University. *Assessment & Evaluation in Higher Education, 26*(5), 465–473. doi:10.1080/02602930120082032

McConnell, D. (2000). Implementing Computer Supported Cooperative Learning. London: Kogan Page.

Meyer, O., & Thille, C. (2006). Developing Statistical Literacy across Social, Economic and Geographical Barriers Using a Stand-Alone Online Course. *Proceedings of the 7th International Conference on Teaching Statistics*. Retrieved January 2007 from http://www.stat.auckland.ac.nz/~iase/publications/17/ 6C3_MEYE.pdf

Muirhead, B. (2007). Integrating Creativity into Online University Classes. *Educational Technology & Society, 10*(1), 1–13.

Onikama, D. L., Hammond, O. W., & Koki, S. (1998). Family Involvement in Education: A Synthesis of Research for Pacific Educators. Honolulu, HI: Pacific Resources for Education and Learning.

Ponte, J. P. (2001). Investigating in Mathematics and in Learning to Teach Mathematics. In F. L. Lin & T J. Cooney (Eds.), Making Sense of Mathematics Teacher Education (pp. 53-72). Dordrecht: Kluwer.

Robinson, B. (1995). Research and Pragmatism in Learner Support. In F. Lockwood (Ed.), Open and Distance Learning Today (pp. 221-231). London: Routledge.

Robson, J. (2000). Evaluating On-line Teaching. *Open Learning, 15*(2), 151–172. doi:10.1080/713688394

Rourke, L., & Kanuka, H. (2007). Barriers to online critical discourse. *IJCSCL, 2*(1), 105–126.

Rowntree, D. (2005). Designing ODL Courses and Programmes (Overview Essay 2). H804 Implementing Online, Open and Distance Learning. Milton Keynes: The Open University.

Simpson, O. (2002). Supporting students in online, open and distance learning. London and New York: Taylor and Francis Group.

Thorpe, M. (2005). Preparing for course development in ODL (Overview Essay 3). H804 Supporting Learners in ODL Systems. Milton Keynes, UK: The Open University.

Thorpe, M., & Pettit, J. (2001). Choices and costs for course designers. H804 Implementing Online, Open and Distance Learning. Milton Keynes, UK: The Open University.

Vygotsky, L. S. (1978). Mind in society: The development of higher psychological processes. Cambridge, MA: Harvard University.

ADDITIONAL READING

American Association for the Advancement of Science. (2004). Science & Everyday Experiences: A Parent Educator Manual. Washington, DC: Delta Research & Educational Foundation

Baker, D., Street, B., & Tomlin, A. (2002). *Understanding relationships between home and school numeracy practices: Examples from the field.* Paper presented at AERA Annual Conference, New Orleans, April 1-5.

Barab, S. A., & Duffy, T. (2000). From Practice Fields to Communities of Practice. In D. Jonassen, & S. M. Land (Eds.), Theoretical Foundations of Learning Environments (pp. 25-56). Mahwah, NJ: Lawrence Erlbaum Associates.

Carter, S. (2003). Educating Our Children Together: A Sourcebook for Effective Family-School-Community Partnerships. Consortium for Alternative Dispute Resolution in Special Education (CADRE).

Civil, M., & Andrade, R. (2002). Transitions between home and school mathematics: rays of hope amidst the passing clouds. In G. de Abreu, A.J. Bishop, & N.C. Presmeg (Eds.), Transitions between contexts of mathematical practices (pp. 149-169). Dordrecht: Kluwer.

Crawford, K. (2004). E-Learning and Activity: Supporting Communication, Cooperation and Co-Invention. In *Proceedings of the 2nd IEEE Workshop on Wireless and Mobile Technologies in Education (WMTE '04)*. JungLi, Taiwan: IEEE Computer Society.

Epstein, J. L., Sanders, M. G., Simon, B. S., Salinas, K. C., Rodriguez Jansorn, N., & Van Voorhis, F. L. (2002). School, family, and community partnerships. Your handbook for action (2nd ed.). Thousand Oaks, CA: Corwin Press.

Greening, T. (1998). Building the constructivist toolbox: An exploration of cognitive technologies. *Educational Technology*, *38*(2), 23–35.

Hannafin, M. J., Hannafin, K.M., & Land, S, M., & Oliver, K. (1997). Grounded practice and the design of constructivist learning environments. *Educational Technology Research and Development*, *45*(3), 101–117. doi:10.1007/BF02299733

Hannafin, M. J., & Land, S, M. (1997). The foundations and assumptions of technology-enhanced student-centered learning environments. *Instructional Science*, *25*, 167–202. doi:10.1023/A:1002997414652

Henderson, A., & Mapp, K. L. (2002). A new wave of evidence: The impact of school, family, and community connections on student achievement. Austin, TX: National Center for Family and Community Connections with Schools.

Hoyles, C., Wolf, A., Molyneux-Hodgson, S., & Kent, P. (2002). Mathematical Skills in the Workplace. Final report to the Science, Technology and Mathematics Council. London: Institute of Education.

Kilpatrick, S., Field, J., & Falk, I. (2003). Social capital: an analytical tool for exploring lifelong learning and community development. *British Educational Research Journal*, *29*(3), 417–433. doi:10.1080/01411920301859

Koschmann, T. D., Myers, A. C., Feltovich, P. J., & Barrows, H. S. (1994). Using technology to assist in realizing effective learning and instruction: A principled approach to the use of computers in collaborative learning. *Journal of the Learning Sciences*, *3*(3), 227–264. doi:10.1207/s15327809jls0303_2

Lunds, A. (2008). Wikis: a collective approach to language production. *ReCALL*, *20*(1), 35–54.

Marsh, J. (2003). One-way traffic? Connections between literacy practices at home and in the nursery. *British Educational Research Journal*, *29*(3), 369–382. doi:10.1080/01411920301857

Moore, E., & Barbarin, O. A. (2003). Respecting the voices of parents: How the Spirit of Excellence Parent Empowerment Project connects with African American Parents. In J. Mendoza, L. G. Katz, A. S. Robertson, & D. Rothenberg (Eds.), Connecting with parents in the early years. Champaign, IL: University of Illinois at Urbana-Champaign, College of Education, Early Childhood and Parenting Collaborative.

National, P. T. A. (2000). Building successful partnerships: A guide for developing parent and family involvement programs. Bloomington, IN: National Education Services.

National Adult Literacy Agency. (2004). Working together. Approaches to family learning. Dublin: Author.

Noss, R., & Hoyles, C. (1996). Windows on Mathematical Meanings: Learning Cultures and Computers. Dordrecht: Kluwer Academic Publishers.

Papert, S. (1980). Mindstorms: children, computers, and powerful ideas. Brighton: Harvester Press.

Papert, S. (1996). The connected family: Bridging the digital generation gap. Atlanta, GA: Longstreet Press.

Stahl, G. (2006). Group Cognition: Computer Support for Collaborative Knowledge Building. Cambridge, MA: MIT Press.

van Groenestijn, M. (2007). Theory in MiA. In M. van Groenestijn, & L. Lindenskov (Eds.), Mathematics in Action, Communalities across Differences: A handbook for teachers in adult education (pp. 20-36). Netherlands: ALL Foundation.

van Groenestijn, M., & Lindenskov, L. (Eds.). (2007). Mathematics in Action, Communalities across Differences: A handbook for teachers in adult education. Netherlands: ALL Foundation.

Wenger, E. (1998). Communities of Practice: Leaning, Meaning, and Identity. Cambridge, UK: Cambridge University Press.

Wenger, E., McDermott, R., & Snyder, W. M. (2002). Cultivating communities of practice: A guide to managing knowledge. Boston: Harvard Business School Press

White, B., & Frederikson, J. (1998). Inquiry, modeling, and metacognition: Making science accessible to all students. *Cognition and Instruction*, *16*(1), 3–118. doi:10.1207/s1532690xci1601_2

Wilensky, U., & Stroup, W. (2002, April). *Participatory simulations: Envisioning the networked classroom as a way to support systems learning for all.* Paper presented at the annual meeting of the American Educational Research Association, New Orleans, LA.

Willis, J. (1998). Alternative instructional design paradigms: What's worth discussing and what isn't. *Educational Technology*, *38*(3), 5–16.

KEY TERMS AND DEFINITIONS

Grundtvig Training Course: An in-service training course for European adult educators.

Quality Assurance: A planned and systematic process which aims to ensure that a product or service provided by an organization is suitable for its intended purpose.

Mathematics Education: The practice of teaching and learning mathematics, as well as the field of scholarly research on this practice.

Science Education: The practice of teaching and learning science, as well as the field of scholarly research on this practice.

Distance Education: Education that takes place when the student and instructor are separated by physical space and/or time.

e-Learning: Web-based distance education

Blended Learning: Learning which combines online and face-to-face approaches.

ICT Mediated Instruction: Instruction delivered through a technological channel.

Didactical Approach: The teaching strategies and methods employed in instruction.

Chapter 11
Technology Enabled Education in Samoa:
Issues, Challenges, Strategies and Recommendations

Ioana Chan Mow
National University of Samoa, Samoa

ABSTRACT

Education is seen as one of the most important factors for poverty alleviation and economic growth in developing countries (UNDP 2005; UNESCO 2005; WSIS 2005) and the use of Information and Communication Technologies (ICTs) for dissemination of education is believed to have huge potential for governments struggling to meet a growing demand for education while facing an escalating shortage of teachers (UNESCO 2006 in Anderson, 2008). This case study examines technology enabled learning initiatives in education in Samoa, focusing on developments at a leading university in Samoa (hereafter referred to as the university) and the Ministry of Education Sports and Culture (MESC). The case study focuses on the current status of technology based learning in Samoa outlining the current initiatives addressing the core issues of social accessibility, technological adaptability, economic viability, and political agreeability towards providing education and development opportunities. The discussion includes an evaluation of the effectiveness of presently used technology/ technology mix used in e-learning and its effectiveness in facing the demands posed by Social, Technological, Economical and Political (STEP) factors. For each technology initiative, issues and challenges are discussed followed by solutions and recommendations for future action and direction. The case study also looks at various international partnerships/ collaboration fostered by NUS and MESC to facilitate and enhance access to education for students, thereby are considered as solutions to the challenges in implementing technology based learning. The discussion concludes with a set of recommendations for the future of technology enabled learning in Samoa.

DOI: 10.4018/978-1-61520-909-5.ch011

ORGANIZATION BACKGROUND

The University

The university referred to in this study was established in 1984 (NUS Corporate Plan, 2009) and comprises of two institutes, the Institute of Higher Education and the Institute of Technology. The Institute of Higher Education has five faculties: Business and Entrepreneurship, Arts, Science, Nursing and Health Science, and Education. The Institute of Technology is comprised of three Schools: Engineering, Maritime, Business Studies Tourism and Hospitality.

The university is not self-sufficient financially with the main source of revenue being an annual Government grant and tuition fees. The fact that the government grant has not increased despite an increasing student roll has meant that the University has had to operate under financial constraints. Hence the University needs to continue to find avenues to bridge the gap between the Government grant and funds required to deliver quality education to the increasing number of students as required to achieve their vision of excellence (NUS Corporate Plan 2009).

MESC

The Ministry of Education in Samoa (MESC) is responsible for policy, planning and research, corporate services, schools operations, curriculum development and assessment, sports, and culture. Primary education in Samoa extends through an eight-year cycle and is divided into lower primary (years 1-3), middle primary (years 4-6) and upper primary (years 7 and 8), corresponding to the 5 to 14 year-old age group (Chan Mow, Strigel & Vaa, 2007). Funding of schools is through partnership between government and communities, except for four senior colleges, which are fully government owned. The government provides salaries, stationery and curriculum whilst local communities, which mostly own the land, carry the costs of maintenance and facilities. Education is compulsory until year 8 or age 14. As of 2006, there were 131 preschools in the country in addition to the 208 primary and secondary schools. In 2006 there were 141 government primary schools, 13 mission primary schools, and six private primary schools. Mission schools are operated by a variety of church groups, including Roman Catholic, Baptist, Congregationalist, Methodist, Seventh Day Adventist, Mormon, and Bahai churches. The number of children in the education system is estimated at 54,743 (MESC Statistical Digest, 2007). Current figures show 39,578 students in primary schools.

Secondary Colleges operate from years 9 to 13 and are currently streamed, based on academic performance. Entrance to secondary level is determined by a national exam at the end of year 8. Secondary schools, which operate from years 9 to 12, currently follow a slightly different curriculum and are generally community-focused and built and managed by the districts. The number of children in the secondary school system is estimated at 15,165, with a total of 791 teachers teaching at this level (MESC Statistical Digest, 2007). Despite a marked improvement at the secondary level since 1996, still a large percentage of students do not continue from year 12 to 13. Key examinations for secondary education include the Samoa School Certificate taken at year 12 level and the Pacific Senior Secondary Certificate examinations at the year 13 level.

SETTING THE STAGE

ICT at the University

In 1989, technology based learning was still a distant dream yet to be realized at the university with major constraints being the lack of infrastructure, the high cost and poor quality of connectivity. For the university, perhaps the first breakthrough came as a result of the establishment of the first satellite dish which was operational at the university Malifa campus. This was a 2.5 metre dish donated by the Japanese government via PEACESAT and PICHTR (Pacific International Centre for Higher Technology and Research, in 1989 so that the university could have the capacity to be part of the PEACESAT (Pan Pacific Education and Communication Experiments by Satellite) network. This first satellite dish was a 2-way transmission dish but affording us with only audio conferencing capability. Activities or usage of the dish in these early days included the various meetings of the COPE consortium (a consortium of Pacific island states for the promotion of education in the Pacific- of which Samoa, American Samoa, Tonga, Cook Islands were members). Other activities included class exchanges for primary schools, medical consultations, data transfer for the fisheries division, and also the transfer of meteorological data.

In the year 2000, the university after an intensive campaign became the Point of presence of the then established SAS link or the Samoa-American Samoa link. The SAS link was made possible by a donation of unutilized telecommunication bandwidth between Samoa and American Samoa by the two telecom companies SamoaTel (on the Samoa side) and ASCTca (in American Samoa). This was made possible under an intergovernmental memorandum of agreement between the 2 Samoas.

The donated bandwidth of 15 channels under the SAS link was to enable distance learning for the university and telemedicine for Health. With the provision of bandwidth coupled with the university investment in videoconferencing equipment, and HDSL modems, the university was able to offer distance learning courses in Maths for Maths educators in American Samoa in 2003. The donated bandwidth also allowed free Internet access via the PEACESAT connection and the State of Hawaii Telehealth Access Network (STAN).

At that point in time, the first satellite dish which had suffered cyclone damage, was no longer operational. It was then decided that for purposes of robustness and redundancy, that there was a need to reactivate the satellite dish so that the university would have a backup and alternative communication pathway to the SAS link. Attempts to repair the 2.5 m dish were unsuccessful and this took place over a period of 4 years. Meanwhile, with the increase in number of students and staff, and with an increasing reliance on Internet access for email, and research, the need for reliable internet connections and the need for more bandwidth to operate both Internet and video conferencing became critical.

In 2005, the Japanese government donated a 3.7m dish with a 384kbps link to facilitate technology based learning and also email and Internet access for the university. The university faced problems when in 2006 after failing to apply for exemptions under community service obligations were asked by SamoaTel to pay for what was previously free under the SAS link agreement. Faced with issues of the financial costs of maintaining its communications link, the university explored other economically viable options. It was found that the cost of a dedicated satellite link through New Caledonia was a more cost effective option than the equivalent links through the local providers.

Currently ICT resources at the university include four computer laboratories, a network of some 220 stations, a 960 kb/sec off island digital link, the Samoa-American Samoa telecommunications link which provides Internet access, audio and video conferencing capability, and audio visual facilities with video and graphics production capability.

IT Strategic Plan at MESC

The Ministry of Education, Sports and Culture (MESC) has developed an Information Technology Strategic Plan 2000–2003 followed by the ICT Master Plan 2004-2007. These early plans focused on managing ICT to ensure the ministry meets the needs of stakeholders and the management and operation of an ICT system for both the ministry and the school system. Based on 19 key issues, these plans included Internet access for the ministry and schools, hardware/software, an ICT steering committee, and staff training. MESC has also launched a 10-year policy (2006-2015) which focuses on the promotion of basic ICT literacy and awareness for teachers and students, the development and upgrade of the MESC infrastructure and systems and the promotion of ICT-supported instruction.

In terms of technology utilization, MESC has mostly engaged in the use of traditional ICTs for education, such as its radio broadcasting, whilst the use of television and video in teaching is mostly limited to private schools. The Government of Samoa's involvement in provision of telephony to schools is in the form of the Institutional Strengthening Project, funded by Australian Agency for International Development (AusAid), to promote telephone communication for all schools. An estimated 59% of schools had telephone access (fixed or mobile) as of 2003 but the figures are now much higher with the introduction of Digicel and SamoaTel mobile services, which allowed many principals and others to utilize a cell phone for school purposes. As of 2003, 70% of schools had at least one computer at their disposal, and 46% of schools had access to a classroom/lab of computers. There is no direct government funding for provision of computers to schools. However, in 2003 a provision under the ADB-funded Education Sector Project, phase 1 (ESP I), equipped 13 schools (three secondary schools and 10 primary school) with at least one computer each.

TECHNOLOGY BASED INITIATIVES AT THE NATIONAL UNIVERSITY

The previous section has outlined the background in terms of technology utilization, management practices and issues within the university and MESC prior to the developments outlined as part of the IT initiatives described in this case study. The rest of the case study examines technology enabled learning initiatives in education in Samoa at the university and MESC. It looks at the current initiatives at both the university and MESC, examines issues and challenges in terms of technological and management concerns. Solutions put forward for resolving these issues are also discussed and finally recommendations for future action and direction.

Videoconferencing Courses

As mentioned earlier, the donated bandwidth of 15 channels which made up the SAS link was to enable distance learning for the university and telemedicine for Health. With the provision of bandwidth coupled with the university investment in videoconferencing equipment, and HDSL modems, the university was able to offer distance learning courses in Maths for Maths educators in American Samoa in 2003. The donated bandwidth also allowed free Internet access via PEACESAT (Pan Pacific Education and Communication Experiments by Satellite) connection and the STAN network.

A significant development in this area occurred in 2005-2006 with the Asia-Pacific Initiative (API), an international collaboration between 14 universities of which the university is part of. The main aim of the API initiative is expanding access by offering online course content on content areas identified as relevant and of value in the Asia- Pacific context. Since the Asia-Pacific region has been the scene of some major natural humanitarian disasters and this increasing vulnerability has made the ability to respond to these changes of critical importance. Hence the first courses offered and are still currently offered are Environmental Studies seminar series and Disaster management both at postgraduate level. These courses are offered via the use of video and teleconferencing (VTC) supplemented by the use of Moodle for hosting class lectures, discussion forums and an email helpdesk. The advantages of the API courses are many fold. The students can receive credits if enrolled at any of the partner universities. Students receive a certificate of completion at the end of the course. But more importantly, students get the opportunity to interact with some of the leading experts in the region and an international community of students with diverse backgrounds.

Virtual Classrooms

At the university, an important development was the setting up of the virtual classrooms which were first established in 2003 and currently supplement on-campus instruction. The virtual classrooms are hosted within the Moodle learner management system (LMS) (Chan Mow, 2008). The Moodle LMS is a computer supported collaborative learning environment based on principles of constructivism. There are 27 classes currently hosted in Moodle from the 5 faculties of the Institute of Higher Education (IHE).Current usage is mostly hosting of course notes in Word and Power point. The advantages of Moodle as an online learning environment are manifold. One of the limitations of online learning as compared to the face to face is the lack of social interactions. However, the collaborative nature of Moodle ensures social interactions of users through the use of chat rooms, bulletin boards and group discussions.

ITU and CISCO Networking

The university's CISCO academy was set up as part of CISCO and the International Telecommunication Union (ITU)'s Least Developed Countries (LDC) initiative to build capacity in least developed countries like Samoa. The importance of such an initiative was that the academy provided much needed training in technical skills to provide the technical skill base needed to support the national ICT initiatives. The CISCO academy was established in 2002 with the launch of the CCNA program and since its inception the academy has netted 294 enrolments between 2002 and 2005. CISCO academy programs utilize both online and face to face (the lectures and practicals are offered by tutors in face to face but the tutorials are conducted online and self-paced). One of the goals of the CISCO ITU LDC initiative is to promote female enrolments in technical courses. Hence discounted tuition and free transport were offered to female students as incentives in an attempt to boost female enrolments and improve access to technical training.

A major activity was the re-training of instructors in the revised CCNA curriculum. CCNA I and II instructor training was conducted in July 2006. Introduction of IT Essentials I and II into curricula began with ITU funded instructor training in December, 2006 and December 2008. In 2008 the re-launching of the CISCO academy also coincided with the initial offering of ITEssentials I and II which were introduced as prerequisites and feeder course for CCNA.

The Commonwealth of Learning

The use of strategic alliances for building capacity is key to promoting technology based learning and thereby establishes a resource base to face the demands posed by Social, Technological, Economical and Political (STEP) factors. One such alliance is through membership in the Commonwealth of learning. Through its membership the university has been able to participate in capacity building projects such as VUSSC, WikiPasifika and Learn4Content.

VUSSC

VUSSC stands for the Virtual University for Small States of the Commonwealth which is a network or consortium of states with the goal of collaborative course development processes for building educational courses and programmes for small island states of the Commonwealth. VUSCC was first conceived by Commonwealth Education Ministers when they met in Halifax, Canada in December 2000. The Commonwealth of Learning (COL) is facilitating the VUSCC initiative, with funding support from the Government of Singapore, The William and Flora Hewlett Foundation and the Commonwealth Fund for Technical Co-operation (CFTC).There are 28 of these states spanning Asia, Pacific Africa and the Caribbean (Chan Mow, 2008).

Content developed by VUSSC members can be shared under a Creative Commons licence. Specifically, VUSSC countries have chosen to focus on the development of postsecondary, skills-related courses in areas such as tourism, entrepreneurship, use of information and communications technologies (ICTs), life skills and disaster management (Dunlop, 2007). The VUSCC course materials are non-proprietary and readily adaptable to the specific context of each country. They can be used in the offering of credit-bearing qualifications as well as strengthening educational capacity and access in member countries.

Collaborative course development for VUSSC takes the form of "bootcamps". The bootcamps are immersion training workshops of almost three weeks duration where professional educators work together in teams to begin the creation of course materials and to learn a range of ICTs that can be applied and taught to others in their home countries. Four team leaders are chosen to represent each of the four regions of the Commonwealth and they attend an orientation workshop several months prior to the bootcamp. The first bootcamp was held in Mauritius in 2006 and since then, there have been other bootcamps in Singapore, Trinidad and Tobago, and Samoa.

FLOSS4EDU & WikiPasifika

Another initiative spearheaded by the Commonwealth of Learning is the promotion of the use of open source software via the FLOSS4Edu project promoting the use of Wikieducator, Open Office and Linux (Chan Mow, 2008). FLOSS4Edu (Free/Libre and Open Source Software for Education) is a rapidly growing Commonwealth initiative to tackle the dire shortage of free knowledge for education, and to build capacity in the use of free software tools for educators. WikiEducator's FLOSS4Edu project strives to build a thriving community of teachers sharing knowledge to widen access to quality learning opportunities.

A workshop in August 2007, funded by the Commonwealth of Learning in Wellington saw the launch of WikiPasifika the Pacific chapter of FLOSS4edu. WikiPasifika aimed towards building capacity focusing on the skills required for developing free content on WikiEducator so that participants can return to their home countries to present their own capacity building workshops; to introduce the range of free content resources and projects on WikiEducator which are freely available for use in facilitating capacity building workshops in country; to establish and launch the Pacific Chapter of the FLOSS4Edu project; to create the foundation for a community of support, during and after the workshop; to collaboratively build a strategy for growth and sustainability of the Pacific Chapter of the FLOSS4Edu project and to strengthen strategic networks in the Pacific region.

The compliance with licensing of proprietary software being a challenge in the under-resourced economies of small pacific islands, the capacity building in open source resources provides a feasible direction for widening access and provision of educational resources within the small island states of the Pacific.

Learn4Content

Another innovative Commonwealth of Learning (COL) project is the Learn4Content program in which teachers are given lessons in authoring tools such as Wikieducator in exchange for a free lesson which can be shared as part of Open Educational Resources (OERs).

- Facilitate at least one skills development workshop in each of the 53 states of the Commonwealth in the basic wiki editing required for free content development on WikiEducator;
- Train at least 2500 educators with a firm commitment to dedicate half of the workshops to building capacity among women in the developing world;
- Educators to produce at least 2 500 free content lessons for use in secondary schools, vocational education and formal tertiary education settings;
- Assist the English Wikipedia to improve the quality of existing articles that can be used for educational purposes before converting these encyclopedia articles into lessons for learners who don't have access to textbooks; and
- Build a thriving and sustainable network of educators collaborating on the development of free content for education.

COL's WikiEducator (www.wikieducator.org) is a website dedicated to the collaborative development of free content for education that anyone can modify and use. The strategy of the Learning4Content project is to scale up training and content development by networking with: COL's focal points in 48 of the 53 countries of the Commonwealth; teachers, trainers and lecturers in the Commonwealth; and members of the Freedom Culture, most notably the Wikipedia community. Progress is monitored on WikiEducator which tracks every edit on the website.

Two Learn4Content workshops were conducted in Samoa in 2008- 2009. The participants for these workshops were selected to ensure wide representation of the community and were from a range of institutions: the university, MESC, Samoa Qualifying Authority, Samoan Association of Trades and Vocational Training: SATVETI (Punaoa, Tesese, Don Bosco, Ulimasao), Samoa Primary school, and St Marys College. These workshops are expected to contribute to improving their repertoire of ICT skills, authoring skills, knowledge of Open Educational Resources and the Free and Open source movement, and associated concepts such as Creative Commons and issues such as the debate on quality of authoring. Such a collaboration and sharing of resources will ensure social accessibility and economic viability of this initiative.

Future plans at the university for furthering the wikicommunity in Samoa includes establishing a country chapter of Wikieducator, more wikitraining to expand the wiki user community and projects to promote the creation of more open educational resources (OERs).

TECHNOLOGY ENABLED LEARNING INITIATIVES OF MESC FOR SCHOOL EDUCATION

The integration of technology based learning into the school system in Samoa has been a slow process with many constraints and barriers slowing and hindering the process. The following are the main initiatives at MESC for integrating ICT into schools.

Radio Broadcasting

The MESC runs an education radio broadcasting service which has traditionally served primary schools and had served the country since 1940 when the unit was established. The unit has been engaged in a variety of donor-funded projects, mainly around teaching and learning materials, which provided additional textbooks and workbooks in relation to the radio broadcast. For example the unit has complemented the live broadcasting program with audio CDs and cassettes of archived programs. However, the broadcasting unit is aware that while the majority of primary schools in the country seem to regularly tune into the live program, the CDs are not optimally used (Chan Mow, Strigel & Vaa, 2007).

The advantage of radio broadcasting as a usable technology lies in the fact that it is sustainable and can be maintained at minimal cost and hence is economically viable within a developing country and third world settings. The ministry has recognized this and has plans of expanding and upgrading the radio broadcasting service under the ESPII project. A major component of this involves better accessibility through more efficient distribution of CDs/DVDs. Another interesting and related development to note is the use of radio frequency for community internet access, currently trialed under the SPC RICS project.

Samoa-SchoolNet

The Samoa School-Net and Community Access Pilot ("School-Net") project was aimed at piloting an appropriate model for introducing ICT in schools and also sought to extend this exposure to ICT to school communities to improve their knowledge and capacity to become productive members of the local communities. The project was implemented from March 2005 until December 2006. The goals of School-Net were to:

1. improve quality and efficiency of education;
2. enable access to global information;
3. enable increased sharing of information between schools and with communities; and
4. achieve the Government's Education for All and Millennium Development Goals for education (Chan Mow, Strigel & Vaa, 2007).

Five schools were selected to participate in the pilot: four government colleges, and one government primary school. Selection of these School-Net schools were based on such criteria as: accessibility rating as a pilot school, the existence of adjoining schools they could connect to, existing infrastructure conducive for connectivity, ability to meet recurrent costs, and commitment by school administrators and the community to the pilot project.

Activities in School-Net included:

- The provision of computer labs, Community Learning Centers (CLC), fully equipped with hardware and software (included pcs, Servers, video camera, printers, fax, web camera, photocopier, Internet access);
- The creation of a School-Net portal for hosting learning objects and e-resources;
- The provision of a training program in basic ICT skills, use of ICT hardware for "ICT administrators;
- The development and provision of training materials on basic applications, managing access through policies and regulations, business planning for managing the centers; and
- The provision of one year maintenance of School-Net equipment by a local vendor in terms of monthly routine system checks.

STEP-AP Study

In April 2006, a 21 month ADB funded regional study: "Study of Technology in Education and Its Potential to Reduce Poverty – Asia and the Pacific Region" (STEP-AP) was conducted in 3 developing countries: Samoa, Mongolia and Bangladesh. The study aimed at evaluating approaches to using ICT in education highlighting promising models of ICT integration and best practices; identifying drivers and barriers to successful ICT integration; and sharing lessons learned, with a specific focus on rural and remote areas (Chan Mow, Strigel & Vaa, 2007).

The STEP-AP study consisted of a combination of policy analysis, program evaluation (based on interviews and focus groups), and small-scale activities (professional development and provision of selected ICT resources) and piggy-backed on existing projects in each of the four participating countries. In Bangladesh and Nepal, those were projects focused on the use of ICT for teacher training. In Mongolia and Samoa, the task was to focus on projects introducing e-Resources (electronic teaching and learning materials) to better reach remote and isolated areas of the country with up-to-date teaching materials. The study featured three technical components: a) a Policy and strategy component (regional), b) an e-Resources component (Mongolia and Samoa), and c) an e-Teacher Training component (Nepal and Bangladesh).

Specifically, for Samoa, the study was to piggy back on the Samoa School-Net project and to implement study components one (policy and strategy) and two (e-Resources). The study in this context was not an extension for School-Net. The main goal of the Samoa component of this regional study was to strengthen and complement investments already done, while primarily aiming at studying the existing approaches and lessons learned (Chan Mow, Strigel & Vaa, 2007).

A number of activities were carried out guided by an initial site assessment and need analysis. These included (a) a one-day strategic planning workshop for participating principals, ICT administrators, and Peace Corps Volunteers (PCV) based at the School-Net schools; (b), a two-day strategic planning workshop for staff of the Curriculum Materials and Assessment Division (CMAD) at the Samoan Ministry of Education, Sports and Culture (MESC); (c), a five-week (35 hours) ICT training program for CMAD staff; and (d), moderate equipment procurement for CMAD. Six schools were selected to participate in the STEP-AP, the five original School-Net schools and one additional school, characterized by being an early ICT adopter school in the country.

On the whole, the study found that some of the approaches implemented have been successful, mostly at school level, in contributing to generating an enabling environment for ICT integration and change. However there were areas identified where approaches may need to be fine-tuned or changed to better meet local needs and educational development goals.

The study revealed that schools were very enthusiastic to be part of an ICT initiative, despite many issues and challenges. ICT administrators at the schools had shown keen ownership of the initiative and showed full commitment, often at considerable expense of personal time. Infrastructural issues facing schools included power outages and lack of telephone and Internet access, hindering effective use of ICT. Furthermore, schools had limited capacity to optimally use technology for teaching and learning, due to a lack of appropriate professional development. While basic computer skills had been developed by a number of teachers, they had to date not received sufficient training to use the technology for productivity or to enhance student learning. ICT administrators and principals identified the need for more support on technology management and organizational integration of ICT. Such support is needed in order to align the aims of ICT initiatives with overall school development objectives.

A small number of schools have implemented the community access part of School-Net. The rationale was that the community access and provision of technology-enhanced services would provide revenue critical to cover ongoing costs, such as toners and paper. Such costs are a major concern not only of school principals, but also of school committees. However, the lack of personnel to oversee the community access, coupled with external challenges, such as lack of after-hours public transport, have been critical barriers to further community, teacher and student access. Furthermore, schools were unclear about the ongoing support that they can expect from the government and other actors in the country.

In the area of policy and planning, national policies are already in place for the use of ICT in education. However, these need to be followed or supported by follow-up activities, such as targeted budget allocations, the alignment of school development strategies with national education development objectives, and the necessary organizational adjustments (distribution of roles and responsibilities) within government and other education stakeholders, are not yet fully implemented (Chan Mow, Strigel & Vaa, 2007).

CURRENT CHALLENGES FACING THE UNIVERSITY AND MESC AND SUBSEQUENT SOLUTIONS

The university and MESC have both faced many challenges in establishing technology based learning. The following sections outline these issues and challenges under the various initiatives followed by recently implemented and recommended solutions to these challenges.

Videoconferencing: Challenges and Issues

A number of issues and challenges have emerged in the offering of VTC courses. The main issue has been bandwidth constraints and the sustainability of its communications link. The university faced problems when in 2005 after failing to apply for exemptions under community service obligations were asked by SamoaTel to pay for what was previously free under the SAS link agreement. Faced with issues of the financial costs of maintaining its communications link, the university explored other economically viable options. It was found that the cost of a dedicated satellite link through New Caledonia was a more cost effective option than the equivalent links through the local providers.

As mentioned earlier, joining in the Asia Pacific Initiative was a strategic move to utilize collaborative course development in the Asia Pacific region for the provision of content for developing of faculty postgraduate programs. However, the need to boost enrolments in these courses calls for a more aggressive promotion campaign and incorporation into the postgraduate program.

Solutions and Recommendations

To resolve issues of bandwidth, a significant development was the donation by the Japanese government in 2005 of a satellite dish with a 128kb connection to the university for email, internet access and for provision of distance learning. This link was further upgraded in 2007 to 1 MB to accommodate for the demands of a growing university network and user base. Another issue in the offering of these VTC courses has been the reliability and quality of the VTC link which is also due to the bandwidth constraints.

Virtual Classrooms: Challenges and Issues

There are 27 classes currently hosted in the virtual classrooms and current usage is mostly in the hosting of course notes in Word and Power point. Unfortunately, the different features of the virtual classrooms are underutilized. For example, the use of bulletin boards, discussion forum, student web mail for running the helpdesk, and the use of chat rooms (Chan Mow 2008). Other issues include access, stability of infrastructure, and the need for training in the use of the learner management software.

A real issue in developing countries like Samoa is the prohibitive cost of proprietary software. The Moodle LMS is open source software hence ensuring that under-resourced institutions like the university can utilize the benefits and features of a learner management without having to pay exorbitant costs for proprietary LMS such as Blackboard and WebCT.

Evaluating the Virtual Classrooms

Simply creating online learning environments does not guarantee their effectiveness and hence the need for evaluation to inform further development. For the evaluation of effectiveness of online learning, the use of evidence based approaches such as the Triple P Framework as proposed by Ryba, Selby and Mentis (Ryba, Selby & Mentis 2001) is recommended.

The Triple P Framework evaluates online communities by: (a) documenting the views and experiences of students (Perceptions), (b) analyzing the content of interaction patterns of electronic contributions (Processes), and (c) verifying the products that result from the online learning process (Products).

In 2003 and 2004, the Triple P Framework was used as a basis for evaluating the virtual classroom for teaching computer programming (Chan Mow, 2006). Student perceptions were collected from a student questionnaire, (b) student interviews, and (c) log of student e-mails.

The products of online learning for this study are the e-mail messages and FAQs. Based on the Triple P Framework, contents of these products were categorized using Poole's (2000) method of coding students' participation and then analyzed using Salomon's 5 stage model, to evaluate the stage of growth, of the online community. According to Salomon (2000), there are 5 stages in the development of an online learning community. Stage one is when community members develop the motivation to access and use the web environment proficiently. Stage two is the establishment of online identities and the initiative to socialize with others online. Stage three is characterized by participants initiating the process of assisting and providing mutual support in information exchange. Stage four is characterized by course related group discussions; increased collaboration amongst members of the online community as they collaborate in online work. Finally, stage five, is characterized by the achievement of personal goals and an ability to reflect on the learning process. Analysis of the processes of online learning is linked to Poole's (2000) work of coding students' participation in an online course in which messages are categorized as one or more of the following: (a)Technical messages relating to the website and managing on-line learning (Stage one of Salomon's model - access & motivation); (b) Social – messages that are non-academic in nature (Stage two of Salomon's model - socialization); and (c) Coursework – information related to the course content and academic work (Stages three to five of Salomon's model - information exchange, knowledge construction and development)

Results of the analyses of the products of online learning indicated that the virtual classrooms at the university had proceeded to Stage 3 of the Triple P framework characterized by users involved in information exchange, knowledge construction and development.

A critical issue in the use of the virtual classrooms is access. With only 6 computer labs to service a student population of about 2000, access to computers and the network is a problem. Another problematic factor is the stability of the infrastructure. With frequent network outages and computers breaking down, this has meant disruptions and also discouragement on students wishing to utilise the online resources.

Another major aspect which needs addressing is that of training for staff and students. Research literature (Brace-Govan & Clulow, 2001) has indicated student difficulty in learning the software for online courses thus maintaining the need for provision of such training before utilizing the software. Hence, lecturers and students need to be trained in the use of Moodle (which hosts the virtual classrooms), basic file management skills, email usage and web navigation.

Yet another issue is the time intensive nature of usage of the virtual classrooms. The time demands of such activities as maintaining a student helpdesk is considerable and adds to what is already considered as excessive teaching loads. Thus, the main issues encountered in the implementation of the virtual classrooms are: a) access – which hinges on bandwidth and pc availability, b) the need for a stable infrastructure, c) the training of teachers and students in use of the Virtual Classrooms and not to mention d) the time intensive nature of such online activities.

Solutions and Recommendations

Solutions to the above mentioned issues include future plans for further development and expansion of the virtual classrooms include the training of teachers and students in the use of virtual classrooms and the training of teachers in pedagogical skills for technology integration into teaching. Plans also include the training in the use of authoring tools to develop learning objects for course content and to diversify course content by use of authoring tools for range of presentation forms for course content or learning objects.

Research suggests that it is the level of interaction amongst learners within a community of learners which facilitates the learning process (O'Donoghue et al., 2004). Hence, there is a need to promote interactions amongst community of learners through such strategies as reflection, the use of logs, discussions on topics, and through stimulation of critical inquiry. There is a need to encourage the use of the discussion forums, simulations, and the use of multi-agents. There is also a need to run email helpdesks for each of the courses to provide timely feedback and response to students.

The virtual classrooms have enhanced access and the quality of education through improved access to course notes, better communication between lecturer and students and amongst students, and through facilitation of more effective management of the classroom activities. Ongoing plans for further development and expansion of the virtual classrooms include: a) the training of teachers and students in the use of Virtual classrooms; b) training of teachers in pedagogical skills for technology integration into teaching; c) training in the use of authoring tools to develop learning objects for course content; and d) diversification of course content by use of authoring tools such as Webcom, EXE and Wikieducator (Chan Mow 2008).

ITU and CISCO Networking: Challenges and Issues

Most of the issues within the CISCO academy have had to do with sustainability and include: a) the cost of training instructors; b) the problem of retaining instructors and c) also of generating student clientele. There have also been management issues within the academy resulting in the relocation to within the Computing department. Yet another problem is the level of difficulty of CCNA, highlighting the need for an earlier course on basics i.e. IT Essentials. The CCNA curricula require a good command of English and this has been a stumbling block for most of our students.

Solutions and Recommendations

One of the major planned developments is for the university CISCO academy to become regional academy for ITE I and II. It is envisaged that this will be brought about by the establishment of local academies in selected secondary schools and tertiary institutions. Benefits of such a development will be its provision of capacity building for MESC ICT division, for the SchoolNet ICT administrators, for the ITU tele-centers and for all other National ICT initiatives, thus ensuring sustainability.

In 2008 the re-launching of the CISCO academy also coincided with the initial offering of

ITEssentials I and II which were introduced as prerequisites and feeder course for CCNA. The introduction of these feeder courses is to ensure steady enrolments for the CCNA courses thus improving the economic viability of the CISCO programs.

There are also plans to have the CCNA curricula integrated into the Computing BSc curriculum hopefully to improve relevance of the BSC program and to provide clientele to ensure the continuity of the CCNA program. The university CISCO academy has also reactivated its VUE online examination centre which will enable students to sit their final examinations for major certifications such as CCNA, A+, and MSCE locally and within the university.

MESC Broadcasting: Challenges and Issues

As mentioned earlier the main problem with the broadcasting unit has to do with the underutilization of CD ROMs which were developed as part of Educational Sector Project 1(ESPI) to enhance content by providing supplementary content on CD ROMs and with CD players distributed to schools. It is obvious that there should have been more training for teachers in the use of CD ROMs and better monitoring of the project to ensure better utilisation. Another issue with broadcasting is the need to upgrade and modernize its infrastructure.

Solutions and Recommendations

The value of broadcasting as a technology lies in the fact that is sustainable and in recognition of this MESC has plans to upgrade this as part of its ESPII project. The Educational Sector Project II (ESPII) initiative aims to consolidate on this by providing more content in the form of CD ROMs, use of the Internet to diversify content and also an improved broadcasting infrastructure

Samoa SchoolNet: Challenges and Issues

The main issues in the implementation of School-Net (SchoolNet Final Report, 2007) are as follows: specifically for the e-learning component, the main issue was the lack of access to the portal leading to the portal being under-utilized. Secondly the teachers were not familiar with the portal and hence not aware of its potential benefits as a tool and medium for teaching.

On the whole, issues with School-Net (School-Net Final Report, 2007) are as follows: Firstly, provision of IT equipment itself will not provide the solution to improving access to ICT in education and the wider community. A holistic and integrated approach is required, and needs to include infrastructure development, systems and procedures and capacity building – capacity building in schools, in CMAD and in local capacity in general (e.g., IT services).

Secondly, there needs to be a long term sustainable and integrated approach from the Government and the donors. Short term, ad hoc projects from donors working in isolation have little chance of success. Government, whilst showing a fair level of commitment to School-Net, needs to expand this commitment, in areas such as provision of human and budgetary resources, and fostering partnerships with the communities.

Solutions and Recommendations

Currently there are plans for extending and scaling up the project to include 30 school centers under the ADB funded ESPII project. The concern however is the need to perfect and adjust the pilot model taking into account lessons learnt from evaluations such as one conducted by the STEP-AP study on the School-Net project (refer to previous sections). Furthermore, School-Net shares the same goals as the ITU funded Fesootai centers which are now in 11 villages and collaboration between these two initiatives should provide mutual benefits (Chan Mow, 2008).

International Collaborations as Solutions to Issues in Technology Based Initiatives

Playing a major part in providing avenues for solutions to the many challenges are the various international partnerships/ collaboration fostered by the university and MESC to facilitate and enhance access to education for students. As Samoa is a small developing country with a fragile economy and mounting vulnerability due to its location and lack of resources, international collaboration and strategic alliances with better resourced institutions in progressing technology-enabled learning is seen as crucial in providing the way forward. For the university, links with the American Samoa government (SAS link), the Asia Pacific Initiative (API), the Government of Japan, the International Telecommunication Union (ITU), membership in the Commonwealth of Learning (COL) and the Virtual University of Small States of the Commonwealth (VUSSC), and the Learn4Content project have all contributed significantly to the developments of technology based learning at the university. At the Education ministry (MESC), various donor funding such as AUSAID, ADB funded SchoolNet, STEP-AP and ESPII have all made important and defining contributions to the integration of technology-based learning into schools.

SUMMARY AND CONCLUSION

This case study has outlined the various initiatives at both the university and MESC for establishing technology-based learning in Samoa. For each initiative, a discussion of challenges and issues in its implementation was then followed by solutions and recommended actions for coping and resolving the various challenges and issues.

Technology based learning in Samoa is still in its infancy stages. The lack of resources, due to a fragile economy, constraints such as lack of training, lack of access, poor infrastructure all point to the need for strategic alliances with better resourced countries and institutions. The promotion of the use of open source software such as Moodle, Wikieducator is to be encouraged and seen as the only way forward for small island nations such as Samoa struggling with the costs of licensing of proprietary software. There is also a need for establishing policy frameworks for technology based learning in Samoa to ensure initiatives are well planned and have the right educational principles underpinning them.

To conclude, the initiatives presented in this case study are just the beginning in the attempt to integrate technology based learning in Samoa. With more resources and better planning, technology based learning can develop into a feasible and sustainable avenue for accessing educational opportunities in the very near future.

REFERENCES

Brace-Govan, J. &., & Clulow, V. (2001). Comparing face-to-face with online: learners' perspective. *Academic Exchange Quarterly, 5*(4).

Chan Mow, I. T. (2001). The Samoa-American Samoa (SAS) Link – A case study in bridging the communications divide. In *Proceedings of the Pacific Regional Science Communication Forum*, FAO Conference Facility, Faculty of Science, The Australian National University, Canberra, August 2001.

Chan Mow, I. T. (2006). *The effectiveness of a cognitive apprenticeship-based learning environment (CABLE) in teaching computer programming.* Unpublished Doctoral dissertation, University of South Australia, Australia.

Chan Mow, I. T. (2008). Development of e-learning in education in Samoa: issues, challenges, strategies and recommendations for the way forward. In *Proceedings of PCF5 Conference*, University of London, UK. Retrieved from http://www.wikieducator.org/pcf5/Cross-Cutting_Themes

Chan Mow, I. T., Strigel, C., & Va'a, R. (2007). Provoking Change: Technology in Education Case Studies from Samoa (Samoa Country Report – Samoa). In Innovative Information and Communication Technology in Education and its Potential for Reducing Poverty in the Asia and Pacific Region (TA No. 6278-REG). Submitted to the Asian Development Bank, RTI International, Research Triangle Park, Manila.

Dunlop, C. (2007). *VUSSC Summary Evaluation Report*. Research and Evaluation Unit, Simon Fraser University, Vancouver.

MESC. (2006). Strategic policies and plan July 2006 – June 2015. Apia, Samoa: Author.

MESC. (2007). Education Statistical Digest. Apia, Samoa: Author.

Ministry of Education. Sports and Culture (MESC). (2004). ICT Master Plan 2004-2007: User policies, procedures and standards. Apia, Samoa: Author.

O'Donoghue, J., Singh, G., & Green, C. (2004). A Comparison of Advantages and Disadvantages of IT Based education and the Implications upon Students. *Interactive Educational Multimedia, 9*, 63-76. Retrieved June 2nd, 2005, from http://www.ub.es/multimedia/iem

Poole, D. (2000). Student participation in a discussion-oriented online course: A case study. *Journal of Research on Computing in Education, 22*(2).

Ryba. K., Selby, L., & Mentis, M. (2001). *Analysing the effectiveness of on-line learning found in communities*. [Electronic version]. Retrieved September 25, 2003, from http://www.ecu.edu.au/conferences/herdsa/main/papers/nonref/pdf/KenRyba.pdf

Salomon, G. (2000). E-Moderating: The key to teaching and learning online. London: Kogan Page.

SchoolNet Final Report. (2007). *Samoa Supporting the Samoa Schoolnet and Community Access Pilot Project* ADB TA No. 4305–SAM. Helsinki Consulting Group.

UNDP. (2005). Information and Communication Technology (ICT) for Development. New York: UNDP.

UNESCO. (2002). Information and Communication Technologies in Teacher education: A Planning Guide. Paris: UNESCO.

UNESCO. (2005). United Nations Decade of Education for Sustainable Development. Paris: UNESCO

ADDITIONAL READING

Alexander, S. (2001). E-learning developments and experiences. [from http://www.emerald-library.com/ft.]. *Education & Training, 43*(4/5), 240–248. Retrieved June 2, 2005. doi:10.1108/00400910110399247

Asia Development Bank Report. (2004). *Current Status and Trends of E-Learning.* Asia Development Bank, Manila.

Asia Development Bank Report. (2005). *Better Learning, Better Future: Education and Training Strategy for the Pacific.* Asia Development Bank, Manila.

Bracewell, R., & Laferriére, T. (1996). *The contribution of new technologies to learning and teaching in elementary and secondary schools.* Montreal, Quebec, Canada: Laval University and McGill University. Retrieved June, 3rd 2004 from http://www.tact.fse.ulaval.ca/fr/html/impactnt.html

Commonwealth of Learning. (2002). School Networking in Pacific Island States: An Environmental Scan and Plan for establishing School Nets in the Pacific Island States, Final Report. Vancouver, Canada.

SPAN Consultants. (2007). *Samoa National Teacher Development Framework (NTDF)*. Interim Report. ADB TA4738-SAM.

Crosta, L., & McConnell, D. (2005). Action Research and Tutoring in the Online Learning Community: New Implications for Adult Teaching and Learning. In *Proceedings of the 11th Cambridge International Conference on Open and Distance Learning,* Cambridge, UK, September 2005.

Esera, R. (2003). ICT desk study for Ministry of Education, Sports and Culture. Apia, Samoa. Asia Development Bank Final Report. (2008). Innovative Information and Communication Technology in Education and Its Potential for Reducing Poverty in the Asia Pacific Region. ADB Project Number: TA No. 6278-REG.

Gaskell, A., & Tait, A. (2007). What do we know about using new technologies for learning and teaching? A ten year perspective. In *Proceedings of the 12th Cambridge International Conference on Open and Distance Learning*, Cambridge, UK, September 2007.

Gouda, A., & Banks, F. (2005). Professional dignity and reforming teachers' practice: a case study of a distance learning network in Egypt. In *Proceedings of the 11th Cambridge International Conference on Open and Distance Learning,* Cambridge, UK, September 2005.

Government of Samoa. (2002). Samoa Information and Communication Technologies. Policy and Strategic Plan. Apia, Samoa.

Government of Samoa. (2005). Samoa National Strategic Plan (NSP) for ICT: Transforming government, business and civil society. Apia, Samoa.

Maxwell, I., Doherty, I., & Jones, N. (2005). E-Learning: Learning Led and Technology Enabled. In *Proceedings of the Second International Conference on eLearning for Knowledge-Based Society*, Bangkok, Thailand, August 2005.

Pouezevara, S., & Khan, R. (September 2007). *Innovative Information and Communication Technology in Education and its Potential for Reducing Poverty in the Asia and Pacific Region (TA No. 6278-REG): A Case Study of School based In-Service Teacher Training in Rural Bangladesh.* Submitted to the Asian Development Bank, RTI International, Research Triangle Park. Manila.

UNESCO. (2000). *Country Reports: EFA 2000 Assessment.* Apia, Samoa: Author. Retrieved from http://www2.unesco.org/wef/countryreports/home.html

KEY TERMS AND DEFINITIONS

Asia Pacific Initiative: An international collaboration between 14 universities of which the university is part of. The main aim of this initiative is expanding access by offering online course content on key content areas identified as relevant and of value in the Asia- Pacific context.

Virtual Classrooms: The virtual classrooms at the university are hosted within the Moodle learner management system (LMS). The Moodle LMS is a computer supported collaborative learning environment based on principles of constructivism.

FLOSS4Edu: FLOSS4Edu (Free/Libre and Open Source Software for Education) is a rapidly growing Commonwealth initiative to tackle the dire shortage of free knowledge for education, and to build capacity in the use of free software tools for educators. WikiEducator's FLOSS4Edu project strives to build a thriving community of teachers sharing knowledge to widen access to quality learning opportunities.

WikiPasifika: WikiPasifika is the Pacific chapter of FLOSS4edu. WikiPasifika aimed towards building capacity focusing on the skills required for developing free content on WikiEducator so that participants can return to their home countries to present their own capacity building workshops; to introduce the range of free content resources and projects on WikiEducator which are freely available for use in facilitating capacity building workshops in country; to establish and launch the Pacific Chapter of the FLOSS4Edu project; to create the foundation for a community of support, during and after the workshop; to collaboratively build a strategy for growth and sustainability of the Pacific Chapter of the FLOSS4Edu project and to strengthen strategic networks in the Pacific region.

Learn4Content: This is another innovative Commonwealth of Learning (COL) project in which teachers are given lessons in authoring tools such as Wikieducator in exchange for a free lesson which can be shared as part of Open Educational Resources (OERs).

SchoolNet: The Samoa School-Net and Community Access Pilot ("School-Net") project was aimed at piloting an appropriate model for introducing ICT in schools and also sought to extend this exposure to ICT to school communities to improve their knowledge and capacity.

STEP-AP Study: This is a 21 month ADB funded regional study: "Study of Technology in Education and Its Potential to Reduce Poverty – Asia and the Pacific Region" (STEP-AP) which was conducted in 3 developing countries: Samoa, Mongolia and Bangladesh. This study aimed at evaluating approaches to using ICT in education highlighting promising models of ICT integration and best practices; identifying drivers and barriers to successful ICT integration; and sharing lessons learned, with a specific focus on rural and remote areas.

VUSSC: This stands for the Virtual University for Small States of the Commonwealth which is a network or consortium of states with the goal of collaborative course development processes for building educational courses and programmes for small island states of the Commonwealth.

Chapter 12

Artifacts of Expansive Learning in Designing a Web-Based Performance Assessment System:

Institutional Effects of the Emergent Evaluative State of Educational Leadership Preparation in the United States

Hanne Mawhinney
University of Maryland College Park, USA

ABSTRACT

Recent evidence of the adoption of technologically mediated systems of knowledge management as part of the trend to accountability in the Institutions of Higher Education around the world has been widely disseminated in World Bank and UNESCO reports, and the effects of assessment driven accountability on preparation programs extensively debated in scholarly communities. Less scholarly attention has been paid to the institutional effects of the technology enhanced performance assessment evidentiary demands on university programs undergoing review by national accrediting bodies. The lack of scholarly attention is addressed by presenting a case study examining the institutional dynamics of accreditation review experienced by faculty in one department that offered graduate programs leading to certification for education leaders. Drawing from institutional analysis (Scott, 2008a, 2008b) a conceptual framework is established in a discussion of conditions of enactment of the regulative, normative and cognitive facets of the institutional dynamics evident in the implementation ecology of accountability systems. The case study analysis outlines four phases of development of the essential elements of a web-based assessment system, and describes the questions raised by faculty about performance evidence, the assessment of that evidence, and the nature of measures of program outcome effectiveness. Classic theories of organizations fail to fully explain the concerns and questions that were raised by faculty. In contrast, Engeström's (1999, 2001, 2008) theory of expansive learning grounded in Cultural Historical Activity Theory (CHAT) provides insights into faculty responses to questions raised by the criteria for program

DOI: 10.4018/978-1-61520-909-5.ch012

review established by the accrediting body. Artifacts of expansive learning evident in the development of a performance assessment system can be viewed as reflecting institutionalization of regulative, normative, and cognitive dimensions of the emergent evaluative state of leadership preparation around the world. Implications are suggested for understanding the development of information technology (IT) enhanced knowledge management systems (KMS).

INTRODUCTION

In the context of recent global economic volatility, many institutions of higher education (IHE) around the world are adapting to two significant trends of the past decade: 1) a turn to regulation and accountability (King, 2007, Shin & Harmon, 2009), and 2) technology-based socioeconomic and institutional changes (Dolata, 2009, Hage & Meuus, 2006). These two trends have had particular import for IHE that contribute to the preparation of professionals by offering programs of study leading to certification to meet the standards set by external accrediting bodies.

The first of these trends, the turn to regulation was evident over a decade ago. In an article documenting the changing face of accountability in higher education internationally that was leading to a new focus on monitoring and assessing institutional performance, Alexander (2000) observed

A new economic motivation is driving states to redefine relationships by pressuring institutions to become more accountable, more efficient, and more productive in the use of publicly generated resources. Earlier attempts by states to measure institutional efficiency and performance have generally been met with passive resistance or benign neglect in academic circles. Although this trend still prevails, an increasing number of educational leaders are now exhibiting awareness that the status quo is no longer a viable option for higher education. (p. 411)

As the millennium approached the accountability movement inundating many Organization of Economic Cooperation and Development (OECD) nations at that time was "premised on the perception that traditional measures of institutional performance and effectiveness such as peer review and market choice" were not sufficient indicators of institutional value (p. 414). This shift had its roots in the previous decade when governments in OECD nations across the globe became interested in performance funding and budgeting for higher education (Brennan & Shah, 2000; Burke & Serban, 1997; El-Khawas & Massey, 1996; Jongbloed & Koelman, 1996; Layzell, 1998; Peters, 1992; Piper & Issacs, 1992).

By 2000, researchers had begun to study the impact of the systems for the assessment of quality in higher education that had been established in nations around the world (Brennan & Shah, 2000). This research focused on rewards/incentives, policies/structures and cultures of institutions. For example in a study of quality assurance systems in IHE in 14 OECD countries, Brennan and Shah found that although "changing institutional policies and structures is a complex process", there was evidence of institutional changes impacting "structures and policies which were *fundamental* to the life and organisation of the institution, i.e. changing the balance of power and organisational values" (p. 340). Specifically they found evidence of a

shift in the distribution of power within higher education. This shift has favoured the institutional level at the expense of the basic unit. It has also tended to strengthen extrinsic over intrinsic values as both managerial and market concerns have acquired greater importance compared with disciplinary academic concerns. (p. 347)

Debates over the impact of what has come to be known as the "new managerialism" in higher education continued over the next decade. Researchers studying IHE in the UK, found evidence of several models of managerialism, including that of the learning organisation (Easterby-Smith *et al.*, 1999) in which there is "emphasis on cultural change, team-work, empowerment of employees and strategic scanning of the horizon" (Deem & Brehony, 2005, p. 225).

During this time a second and related trend in technology-based socioeconomic and institutional changes also impacted IHE. In the 1990s states and nations realized that to strengthen their competitive positioning they had to increase their involvement in the development of human capital and research through higher education. As Marshall (1995) observed, "In this more competitive world, dominated by knowledge-intensive technology, the keys to economic success have become human resources and more effective population systems, not possible new organizations of production, not natural resources and domestic economies of scale" (p. 53). Characteristics of what is now called a post-industrial era include increasing knowledge and competence, competitive and technological dynamics, and growing environmental complexity. Adapting to this context posed significant challenges to both private and public sector organizations. However, researchers following these trends reported a positive association between adaptability and innovativeness (Tuominen et al., 2003). By 2000 it was evident that organizations "seeking ways to manage their knowledge assets" were increasingly turning to information technology (IT) for solutions (Schultze & Boland, 2000, p. 193).

IHE around the world responded to this turn to IT in context of pressures for accountability and the "new managerialism" by ratcheting up the processes of incorporating technology-enhanced performance assessment processes into their knowledge management (KM) practices. As a result of this process we see the emergence of techno-wizards, by which I mean IHE where networked bundles of post-Web 2.0 adaptations are anticipating Web x.0 and second life technologies. As documented in the growing body of KM performance evaluation research there is some evidence that technological adaptations are transforming organizational practices long viewed as embedded in fragments of the medieval cultures from which modern IHE around the world have evolved (Chen & Chen, 2006). Indeed, with extensive investments in knowledge management systems (KMS) IHE and other organizations are now investigating how KM processes can best be organized to reap instrumental benefits. However, critics point out "most KM research, apart from being fragmented, overemphasizes knowledge creation and draws little attention to key intermediaries in the KM process" (Datta, 2007). Yet intermediaries become significant when we recognize that their involvement in the management of knowledge can have unintended consequences. As Schultz and Leidner (2002) note that "knowledge is a double-edged sword: while too little might result in expensive mistakes, too much might result in unwanted accountability" (p. 213). Indeed we do not have a good understanding of how organizational knowledge is related to organizational learning, in part because researchers have tended to focus on one or the other. Chiva and Alegre (2005) conclude that despite their implicit links, the two areas of literature they have produced have in the past been relatively unrelated. It is also clear that IHE around the world are adapting to advancements in ICTs in ways that require exploration of the links between organizational knowledge and organizational learning such as I undertake in this case study using Engeström's (1987, 2001, 2008) activity theoretical approach to understanding expansive learning associated with the IT enhanced performance assessment in IHE. In doing so I extend previous research on activity theory these arenas (see for example, Ditsa, 2003; Igira & Gregory, 2009; Roque & Figueiredo, 2006).

The need to explore the links between organizational learning and organizational knowledge is especially pressing in the context of the international trend for IHE to respond to accountability pressures (Brown, Desrosier & Edwards, 2009) by adopting newer assessment models that address complex learning outcomes and support measuring learning more authentically and providing alternatives to the conventional, test-based assessment models (Moallem, 2009, Juneau, 2008). The case study I present focuses specifically on the design and implementation of a new type of assessment, a kind of electronic or web portfolio (DiMarco, 2006; Wagner & Lamoureuz), that can be used in planning and formative evaluation (Ehrmann, 2006).

SETTING THE STAGE

In 1999 the Department of Education Leadership (EDEL) at a research intensive land grant university in a mid Atlantic state in the United States received the evaluation report of the Education Leadership Constituent Council (ELCC) on its Masters in School Leadership program. As the special professional association (SPA) designated by the National Council for Accreditation of Teacher Education (NCATE) to conduct accreditation reviews of professional certification programs, the ELCC had begun to revise its expectations to emphasize a standards-based curriculum with a focus on developing knowledge, skills and dispositions. With this charge, the ELCC began to seek evidence from programs seeking accreditation that students demonstrated competencies through completing performance activities associated with the 12 standards and over 100 indicators. The underlying focus taken by the ELCC evaluators of EDEL's program was on assessing evidence of student performances of activities reflecting competencies or skills associated with effective school leadership. In the initial review, evaluators did not find adequate evidence, with their concerns falling into two categories. First, the program included numerous electives, making it difficult to ensure that every student would experience each of the indicators. Second, the evaluators sought evidence of clearly defined student performance activities.

The EDEL faculty was initially surprised and puzzled, and the scope of weaknesses identified led them to question the relevance of this evaluation process. After much analysis and revision of approaches to linking fieldwork with coursework, the Department submitted its rejoinder report, along with two large binders providing examples of student work in the field associated with the indicators. At the heart of the revision was the development of a portfolio system which tracked students' fieldwork associated with performance activities. In addition the faculty developed evaluation rubrics for each performance activity. The rejoinder was accepted, and EDEL's report soon was used as an exemplar of competency-focused, performance-based learning.

In the fall of 2002 EDEL began preparations for a new NCATE accreditation review, one that required development of a performance assessment system and a system of monitoring program outcome effectiveness based the new ELCC (2002) standards for school building and school district leadership. The lessons gained in developing a portfolio system were useful; however, the challenges of creating a comprehensive performance system went well beyond those previously addressed. The faculty confronted questions such as: What counts as evidence of performance? What criteria should be used to examine that evidence? How can validity and reliability be ensured? How can the performance assessment system be used to create measures of program outcome effectiveness? How can a demonstration of dispositions be designed in a way that reflects the EDEL's commitments? The design of EDEL's web-based Performance Assessment System (WB-PAS) was a comprehensive response to these and other questions raised as part of the ELCC program review report. In August 2003, EDEL's programs were fully accredited without weaknesses noted by the ELCC. The design of EDEL's WB-PAS was recognized by the ELCC as offering evidence that the department's graduate programs leading to school building and school district leadership meet the standards for national recognition.

This case study is structured into four parts. In the first part, I begin with a brief overview of the conditions of enactment of the regulative, normative and cognitive facets of the institutional dynamics evident in what I have called elsewhere the implementation ecology of accountability systems. In the second part of the case study, I describe the four phases of design that resulted in the development of the essential elements of EDEL's WB- PAS, and the questions that were raised by faculty about performance evidence, the assessment of that evidence, and the nature of measures of program outcome effectiveness. In the third part of the case study, I consider how classic theories of organizations fail to fully explain the concerns and questions that were raised by faculty. In the fourth part of the case study, I explore how Engeström's (1999) theory of expansive learning provides insights into the ways in which EDEL has responded to these, and other questions raised by the ELCC/NCATE criteria for program review. In doing so, I consider how the artifacts of expansive learning evident in the development of EDEL's WB- PAS can be viewed as reflecting institutionalization of regulative, normative, and cognitive dimensions of the unique ELCC/NCATE accountability system of the state. I discuss how institutionalization, in this context of accountability is evident as the system concentrates the efforts of faculty and creates a context for deliberate intervention in the design and delivery of graduate programs leading to certification for school building and school district leadership roles. I conclude the case study by arguing that considering artifacts of expansive learning in the implementation ecology of accountability systems is useful in understanding the conditions of faculty engagement in active learning about, and innovation in aligning instructional practice, student performance activities, and assessments with standards for graduate programs for individuals seeking certification as school building and school district leaders. These arguments have broad implications for IHE around the world given the international trends to technology enhanced performance assessment as central to standards based professional preparation

CASE DESCRIPTION

Part 1: The Implementation Ecology of Accountability

The mid Atlantic state where the case study University is located requires that all programs leading to certification be accredited by NCATE. Its program approval is therefore contingent upon successful accreditation by NCATE and its SPAs, including the ELCC. In addition the state has adopted the School Leaders Licensure Assessment (SLLA) as a requirement for Administrator II (principal) certification in the state, establishing a cut score of 157. This means that candidates must complete Administrator I certification through an ELCC accredited MA program of preparation for school building leadership. However, the state does not at this point require that the SLLA for superintendents be taken for those seeking superintendents' certification in the state. In fact, the State Board of Education regulation on Superintendent certification allows candidates holding a masters degree, three years of successful teaching, and two years of administrative or supervisory experience, to apply for certification after completing a two-year program with graduate courses in administration and supervision.

Under the state's regulatory framework, therefore, the approval of programs leading to certification for school building or school district leadership is contingent upon their accreditation by the ELCC for NCATE. Departments seeking accreditation of programs preparing school building and school district leaders are thus regulated by NCATE and ELCC requirements that they develop plans for comprehensive assessment systems that include:

- detailed descriptions of plans for collecting, analyzing, summarizing and using candidate assessment information
- evaluation measures of outcomes that provide evidence of candidate proficiencies in professional, state and institutional standards
- clear communication of standards to candidates
- provisions for data collection to support accomplishment of program's mission

The Department had to meet these requirements because it offered two graduate degrees in Education Leadership for the candidates seeking certification, a Master of Arts (MA), and a Doctor of Education (Ed.D.). Overviews of both programs are provided in Appendix A.

Both programs were revised to meet these new requirements for accreditation through four phases, all framed within the implementation ecology of accountability. Phase one began in 1999 and resulted in directions for the development of the PAS from faculty evaluation of performance assessment processes underway at the time. Phase two began in 2002 and ended in January 2003. During that phase, EDEL faculty reached agreement on the design parameters of the PAS, including: a) the determination of an outcome expectation of demonstration of basic level of proficiency in the new ELCC standards for candidates completing the programs leading to certification for school building and school district leadership; b) choice of a web-based data management system; and c) the central importance of internships. During this phase the WB- PAS design parameters were determined, new courses were developed and existing courses were revised. After the design of the PAS was completed documentation of it prepared for the ELCC program review report. Phase three involved the development of the PAS into a web-based system with interfaces enabling candidates, faculty, coordinators, and field mentors to submit assessments of the performance of indicators by individual candidates. The PAS also enables compilation of data into individual candidate reports of Professional Growth Profiles and program evaluation reports that aggregate individual data at key transition points to serve as the foci for compilation and analysis of candidates' performance assessment data. The fourth phase, beginning in 2004 and continuing until 2010 has focused on refining the WB - PAS design for compiling individual candidate assessment data and for measuring program outcome effectiveness for program evaluation and improvement. The PAS design is intended enable EDEL faculty to:

- aggregate data to measure extent to which program outcome expectations of Basic Level of Proficiency have been met;
- evaluate program effectiveness in meeting NCATE program criteria for unacceptable, acceptable, and target levels, measure of program effectiveness;
- aggregate data to measure quality of field experiences and internships;
- develop the Quality Assurance Performance Assessment Process (QAPAP) required by the ELCC/NCATE review

In subsequent parts of this case study, I consider the artifacts of expansive learning during these four phases in the context of the institutionalization of regulative, normative, and cognitive dimensions of the state's ELCC/NCATE accountability system as it concentrates the efforts of faculty and creates a context for deliberate intervention. I refer to this context as reflecting the implementation ecology of accountability and have framed this conceptualization of institutional dynamics within the body of scholarship in institutional theory. Institutional theorists assume that organizations cannot be understood apart from their wider social and cultural contexts. I use Scott's (1995; 2008a, 2008b) definition of institution as a point of departure for the institutional dimensions of accountability systems:

Institutions consist of cognitive, normative, and regulative structures and activities that provide stability and meaning to social behavior. Institutions are transported by various carriers- cultures, structures, and routines-and they operate at multiple levels of jurisdiction. In this conception, institutions are multifaceted systems incorporating symbolic systems-cognitive constructions and normative rules- and regulative processes carried out through and shaping social behavior. Meaning systems, monitoring processes, and actions are interwoven. Although constructed and maintained by individual actors, institutions assume the guise of an impersonal and objective reality. (Scott, 1995, p. 33)

Scott (1995) observes that regulative, normative and cognitive systems have been separately emphasized by different social theorists, and argues that these varying emphases suggest that we can see each as a unique pillar of institutions. In his analysis the regulative, normative, and cognitive pillars are distinguishable across dimensions of the basis upon which compliance operates, the mechanisms and logic each uses, the indicators of their presence and the basis of legitimacy each incorporate. Scott's approach promises analytic clarity for those seeking to understand the nature of institutional dynamics under each pillar.

Such clarity must not come at the cost of capturing the kind of overlapping dynamics evident in the implementation of accountability systems such as is created by the ELCC/NCATE accreditation system. My orientation, therefore, also incorporates a more integrated conception of regulative, normative facets of institutions that contribute in interdependent and mutually reinforcing ways, to a powerful social framework. In taking this perspective I am guided by a more integrated conception of institutions offered by D'Andrade (1984). D'Andrade views institutions as over determined systems "in the sense that social sanctions, plus pressure for conformity, plus intrinsic direct reward, plus values, are all likely to act together to give a particular meaning system its directive force" (p. 98).

The case study analysis is premised on assumptions that organizational environments create the "infrastructures -regulative, normative, and cognitive- that constrain and support the operation of individual organizations. The formal structures of organizations are seen, at least in part, to represent theories of action that embody the prevailing cultural logics" Scott (1995, p. 151). Following Scott's (2008a, 2008b) arguments that all organizations are institutionalized, my description of EDEL's WB- PAS explores the nature of institutionalization of the accountability system created by the state by its mandating that graduate programs leading to certification for school building and school district leadership meet the ELCC/NCATE criteria for accreditation. I next consider the unique regulative, normative and cognitive infrastructures that are reflected in the EDEL PAS, and the institutional dynamics through which they were created during each of the four phases its development and design and implementation.

Part 2: Phases of Design and Development of Web-Based PAS

PHASE ONE: 1999 – 2002: Directions for PAS from Evaluation of Performance Assessment Processes

Viewed as a longer cycle of innovation, the first phase involved a process of revision and improvement that led EL faculty to design a comprehensive performance assessment system. It involved all faculty members working both together and alone to revise courses, design curriculum and design a performance assessment system to meet the requirements for accreditation established in the 2002 ELCC (and NCATE) standards. At several points during the process of design of the PAS, faculty met with officials of the State Department of Education, and consulted with the College of Education faculty responsible for NCATE review. The PAS was also designed to take into account the specific requirements for an Ed.D. in Education Leadership that was developed to respond to the need for school district leaders to acquire the knowledge and capabilities necessary to lead complex systems focused on improving student learning and outcomes for all students, through collaborative processes that motivate all constituents (teachers, principals, community members, policy makers and others).

EDEL's decision to initiate a process of broad consultation and begin comprehensive process of design coincided with the release of the 2002 ELCC Standards that now also include indicators for school district leadership. As a result, the design of the new Ed.D. benefited from faculty study of the ELCC standards and analysis of their implications for the development of the curriculum, course content, assignments, and internships. However, it was the significant change in ELCC's requirements for performance-based assessment evidence in program review reports that provided the impetus for EL faculty to design a performance assessment system that would provide candidates with formative and summative feedback, and that would enable faculty to analyze aggregated candidate data for program improvement. In designing the PAS, EDEL faculty also considered the lessons that they had learned from implementing a form of performance assessment of the internship and fieldwork of candidates seeking Administrator 1 (principal's) certification. These were candidates who had completed either an MA program in Education Leadership and Policy Studies or they were post Masters candidates who completed the set of 12-18 credits of course work from that MA program

Initial directions for the PAS, came from analysis of data on outcomes evident in MA candidate internship performance reports from the year's 1999- 2002. These performance reports had been designed to extend the work of the faculty in moving fully to a standards-based performance system that began in 1999 in which course revisions were made to show performances and assessments as part of a rejoinder report to ELCC. In 1999, following EDEL's successful rejoinder to the list of concerns by the ELCC, the Department revised its MA program to ensure that candidates met the Standard for Internships, and that courses addressed the knowledge, skills and dispositions associated with each of the 11 areas (the 12th area focused on the internship) covered by the 1995 ELCC Standards. Candidates were required to meet the performance expectations associated with each of the areas associated with the standards by completing assignments in courses that developed their knowledge of those areas, and by completing internships activities equivalent to six months of full time mentored fieldwork at several levels guided by the Internship Coordinator in collaboration with a field mentor.

In their tracking of all performance activities, candidates were required to identify the semester they completed the performance activity, the course or field experience with which it was associated, the faculty member/ instructor, and the field mentor who helped the candidate plan the performance activity, and who guided and assessed it. The Standard, area, and the indicator addressed by the performance activity, a summary of the information about the activity outlined in the memo, and the time that was spent on the activity were also included in the candidate's portfolio. The portfolio was presented to the Coordinator of Internships for review as evidence of meeting standards for school building leadership.

In January 2002, as part of the process of development of the PAS, data from summary tracking sheets and reflective memos of 18 candidates who met the requirements of demonstrating performances in each of the 11 areas covered by the 1999 Standards (nine MA and nine post masters course work candidates) were aggregated to assess whether the candidates had developed proficiencies set out in the standards. The data were organized around each standard, and a "crosswalk" was created that showed the relationship between the standard, area, indicator, total number of candidates submitting performances demonstrating proficiency in that indicator, and an example of the types of performance activities submitted, and the time that was spent on that example.

As specified by NCATE in its report on "aggregating data", the crosswalk aggregated data from the 18 individual performance reports to show that candidates who completed internship requirements submitted reflective memos describing performances covering all 11 areas of the 1999 Standards. The crosswalk displayed qualitative samples of the kinds of performances that were presented to demonstrate understanding of the different areas. The crosswalk also presented quantitative data summarizing the numbers of candidates who presented performances for each indicator. These data provided a representation of candidate proficiencies related to the standards in the sense that NCATE has specified: data represents candidate proficiencies across all the areas (domains) of the 1995 ELCC Standards, and the data is taken from all of the candidates who successfully presented portfolios as evidence of meeting the requirements for fieldwork. The crosswalk included identification of candidate performances related to specific indicators that provided inadequate evidence of proficiency. Data summarized in the crosswalk is supported by one full example of a candidate reflective memo in Figure 1.

PHASE TWO: January 2002 – January 2003: Faculty Agreements on Design Parameters of PAS

Faculty interpretations of the data presented in this measure of the outcome effectiveness of coursework and internship, and the performance assessment system itself, informed the design components developed for the WB- PAS. An example of the process of analysis is shown in Figure 1. As is shown, data were aggregated to assess whether the candidates had developed proficiencies set out in the standards. The data were organized around each standard, and a "crosswalk" was created that showed the relationship between the standard, area, indicator, total number of candidates submitting performances demonstrating proficiency in that indicator, and an example of the types of performance activities submitted, and the time that was spent on that example. Figure 1 provides a sample of the faculty analysis of the crosswalk data, and the implications for the criteria included in the outcome expectation for Basic Level of Proficiency and for the design of WB- PAS.

In particular, the data showed that candidates could easily identify and engage in performances related to the 11 areas of the 1995 ELCC Standards. Indeed it was clear that candidates were very appreciative of the way in which the internship had been designed using strategies that supported adult learning. The candidates took full advantage of the opportunities to select as a focus for their performance activities those indicators of standards of educational leadership that they felt best met their developmental needs (using

Figure 1. Crosswalk of summary data on effectiveness of MA program requirements for candidate demonstration of performances in each of the 12 areas of the 1999 ELCC standards for school building leaders

Examples taken from 18 students who completed their field experiences during a period when they were required to utilize NCATE standards in their portfolio development.

Area	Performance Indicator	Selected examples of Performances Submitted for Assessment by Candidates	Time spent on activity	Total number of candidates submitting performance
11. Education Law, Public Policy and Political Systems	11.1 Apply knowledge of federal and state constitutional, statutory, and regulatory provisions and judicial decisions governing education	Researched information on 504 federal law, state law, county policies. Discussed needs of staff with principal. Determined amount of information that could be shared in a day and what information was most important. Created overhead to emphasize important information and talking points. Presented in-service.	15 hours	10
	11.2 Apply knowledge of common law and contractual requirements and procedures in an educational setting	Reviewed code of student conduct with students, parents and staff. Applied knowledge of school district law in assessing infractions. Investigated and analyzed in depth background of infractions.	12hours	8
	11.3 Define and relate the general characteristics of internal and external political systems as they apply to school settings…	*Went to a board meeting and observed meeting. Wrote a paper on what I saw.*	*10 hours*	*3*
	11.4 Describe the process by which federal, state district and school-site policies are formulated, enacted, implemented and evaluated and develop strategies for influencing policy development	*Researched Goals 2000 and law surrounding the Goals 200. Interviewed state delegate.*	*10 hours*	*5*
	11.5 Make decisions based on the moral and ethical implications of policy options and political strategies	*No adequate examples*		*2*
	11.6 Analyze the major philosophical tenets of contemporary intellectual movements and analyze their effects on school contexts	Surveyed various school accountability practices, discussed experts' reactions to state, district and school accountability practices analyzed effects of accountability measures on learning outcomes.	15 hours	2
	11.7 Develop appropriate procedures and relationships for working with local governing boards…	*Went to a board meeting and wrote a paper on what I saw.*	*10 hours*	*2*

FACULTY ANALYSIS:

Program Strengths

- The number of candidates submitting performances that appropriately meet the intentions of the performance indicator 11.1 & 11.2, demonstrate that the program enables candidates to develop knowledge of how to analyze community and district power structures and identify major opinion leaders and their relationship to school goals.
- There is alignment of the level of cognitive complexity expected in indicators 11.1, 11.2 & 11.6 with the level of cognitive complexity demonstrated in the performance. Indicators calls for evidence of application of knowledge to practice, and performance provides that evidence and performance meets expectation for a field experience that involves sustained involvement with increasing levels of responsibility.

Program Weaknesses

- Performance examples for indicators 11.3 and 11.4, and 11.7 do not align well with the level of performance and proficiency called for in the indicators. Indicators suggest performances should demonstrate deeper understanding of the concepts and theories related to community, and show candidate's practices in demonstrating that understanding. Performances submitted do not do this.
- No adequate examples could be taken from the performances submitted by candidates demonstrating their capacity to make decisions based on the moral and ethical implications of policy options and political strategies.

Program Revisions:

- Faculty agree that the criteria for Basic Level of Proficiency (BLP) should be used to guide candidate performance activities to align with requirements of indicators, and that a common criteria for levels of proficiency should be used to guide evaluation of candidate performances, and suggest remediation plans where performances to not meet expectations
- Faculty agree that the criteria for BLP should include requirement to develop ethical platform on which to base decisions

Implications for Basic Level of Proficiency (BLP) and WB- PAS:

- BLP requires that candidates distinguish between awareness, understanding and capability activities, and that
- Criteria for performance assessment include: rudimentary, developing, proficient, and accomplished, and that
- The expectation is that candidates demonstrate proficient levels of awareness, understanding and capability. Rudimentary or developing levels will require remediation planning and resubmission of performance, and
- BLP requires that candidates: submit of an ethical platform in his her Professional Growth Plan developed by the conclusion of the program.

the parameters provided by the Department as a guide). The faculty concluded that this feature of candidate choice in selecting their developmental path should be further developed in the PAS.

However, the range of performances and the number of cases where inadequate evidence was presented confirmed the need for the PAS to include specifications of levels of performance activity, and levels of proficiency. For example, one candidate presented as evidence of indicator 11.7, which called for candidates to develop appropriate procedures and relationships for working with local governing boards, a performance showing that she/he had "gone to a board meeting and written a paper on what was seen." This could be considered adequate evidence of the candidate's awareness of how to develop those procedures, however, the indicator called for candidates to apply knowledge to practice and to actually develop appropriate procedures. It was apparent to faculty that without clear criteria for distinguishing types of performances, candidates could well be led to ignore the principle that the cognitive and skill demands of assessments should closely match expectations defined in standards. In this case, the candidate presented evidence of awareness when the indicator called for evidence of understanding or capabilities. This analysis led the faculty to discuss the need to distinguish between awareness, understanding and capability activities in designing a PAS that would meet the NCATE guideline that the cognitive and skill demands of assessments closely match expectations defined in standards.

Other examples in the crosswalk suggested that candidates lacked a clear sense of the level of proficiency that their performance should demonstrate. These cases were indicated in the crosswalk with the notation: *no adequate examples*. Faculty concluded that the PAS should meet the NCATE guideline that rubrics or criteria that define successful performance on assessments should be identified and clearly communicated to candidates, and used in evaluation of their work. The data in the crosswalk also revealed that candidates appreciated the opportunities to select their own developmental path. However, when individual tracking sheets were reviewed, it was evident that the candidates would have benefited from a clear understanding of the parameters of choices they could make in demonstrating that they had met the expectations of the Department. This analysis confirmed to the faculty the need to define clear outcome expectations that candidates can use to guide their selection of performance opportunities related to indicators of Standards. The outcome expectation that candidates completing programs leading to certification in school building or school district leadership demonstrate Basic Level of Proficiency (BLP) in ELCC standards was developed to address this and other requirements for the development of the kind of comprehensive performance assessment system called for by NCATE and ELCC.

The qualitative analysis of candidate's reflective commentaries in comparison to the documents presented as artifacts also revealed wide disparity in the capacity of candidates to articulate their dispositions toward students learning, and toward issues of diversity and equity. In some cases candidates presented as evidence of addressing issues of student learning, documentation of very managerial efforts they undertook with little consideration of the fundamental dispositions toward improving learning opportunities for all students that were central aspects of all the standards for educational leadership. The faculty concluded that more explicit means should be used to guide the development of candidates understanding of their own dispositions and their relationship to the ELCC standards. The faculty agreed that candidates should be provided with opportunities to formulate and examine an ethical platform upon which to rely on tough decisions.

Analysis of candidate performance evidence also revealed that few candidates had developed understanding of the role of school leaders in integrating technology throughout a school. There were few examples of performance activities that demonstrated even awareness of how educational leaders could ensure that curricular design, instructional strategies, and learning environments integrate appropriate technologies to maximize learning and teaching. Nor had candidates' submitted evidence of awareness of how educational leaders ensure the integration of technology to support productive systems for learning and administration, or use it to plan and implement comprehensive systems of effective assessment and evaluation. This finding was of particular concern to the faculty because the state had determined that beginning in 2004; principals would have to demonstrate proficiency in the Technology Standards for School Administrators (TSSA), developed by the Collaborative for Technology Standards for School Administrators. The faculty concluded that any outcome expectations that were developed should include proficiency in the TSSA Standards.

Figure 1 provides an example of faculty analysis of candidate performance evidence related to Standard 11 of ELCC's 1995 set of standards. It shows how this analysis helped faculty members determine program strengths, weaknesses and draw some implications for program revisions. The aggregated data presented in a summary table enabled the faculty to evaluate the effectiveness of the performance assessments used to guide MA candidates completing the requirements to demonstrate performances related to the 1995 ELCC Standards. This evaluation helped inform faculty debates and discussions about program revisions and new developments that were required to address the 2002 ELCC Standards, which included indicators to be met by candidates preparing for school district educational leadership. Central to the design of the PAS were the agreements reached by the EDEL faculty during the initial PAS design stage that began in January 2002. This design phase included extensive faculty discussions on alignment of course content with indicators of standards of school building and school district leaders, individual faculty member's analysis and revision or development of course content and assignments. Over the period of January to September 2002, EDEL faculty reached agreement on the following key elements of the PAS:

- The faculty members who teach in each program would align content, pedagogy and assignments with indicators of school building, or school district leadership.
- Their course assignments would provide bridging experiences for candidates between course content and the workplace that feature clinical exercises and/or field settings where appropriate.
- Their course assignments would also foster candidate development of:
    1. *Awareness*, defined as acquiring concepts, information, definitions, and procedures;
    2. *Understanding*, defined as interpreting knowledge to school environments, integrating concepts with practice, and using knowledge and skills in context; and
    3. *Capability*, defined as applying knowledge and skills to specific problems of practice.

Faculty agreed that

- the central goal of the MA and Ed.D. programs would be to promote an understanding of the connectedness of the various knowledge and skill areas of educational leadership by offering in several different courses many different kinds of performance activities focused on specific indicators of school building and district educational leadership.
- Candidates should be able to choose from a structured set of possible options the indicators that they wish to explore through performance activities that best meet their developmental needs, yet also meet the ELCC requirement that candidates demonstrate proficiencies across all Standards.
- The criteria defining the Basic Level of Proficiency (BLP) provided acceptable measures of candidate proficiency in indicators of educational leadership, and the BLP criteria defined acceptable levels of the outcome effectiveness of both programs.
- In order to develop reflective practices in school building and school district leaders, candidates would be required to prepare written reflections on the dispositions evident in the performance activities that they complete.
- Candidates would be given opportunities to develop and examine an ethical platform upon which to rely upon in making decisions.
- Candidates should demonstrate proficiency in TSSA standards.
- In order to increase the consistency, accuracy, fairness and credibility of assessments of candidate performances demonstrating awareness, understanding or capability in indicators of school building or school district leadership, a common evaluation

rubric would be used that distinguishes rudimentary, developing, proficient and accomplished levels.

Choice of a Web-Based Data Management System

The faculty reviewed the data management needs outlined by NCATE, and concluded that a web-based system would ensure that the Department had the data management capacity to retrieve candidate proficiency information easily quickly and frequently. It was agreed that the format developed for the web-based System would be guided by the four purposes of data management systems suggested by NCATE.

1. To provide evidence of program effectiveness, including important element of candidate competence for summative evaluation
2. To make summative judgments about candidate qualifications relative to a recommendations that the program must make about licensure
3. To make formative judgments about candidate progress, thus supporting advisement and instructional purposes, and
4. To review programs to determine whether the need for modifications is indicated.

In addition, the faculty reviewed the web-based Performance Assessment System developed by another department for teacher education candidates. The success of that web-based system led EDEL faculty to investigate the possibility of developing the PAS as a web-based system. Meetings the web designers from the University confirmed that the PAS could be developed as a web-based system that enabled:

a) candidates to track their own development of their Basic Level of Proficiency (BLP) during their program of study by using the system to show their current Professional Growth Profile;
b) candidates to create performance assessment instruments to submit along with performance evidence to reviewers for confirmation of self assessment, or for remediation planning at key transitions points of enrolment, pre-capstone, post-capstone and program completion; and
c) internship and program Coordinators to create measures of program outcome effectiveness for program improvement by aggregating individual candidate performance assessment data.

In addition, to the agreements noted above, the faculty agreed that although each course provided multiple opportunities for candidates to experience clinical exercises that bridged course content with workplace experiences of educational leaders, substantial, sustained, standards-based internship and field experiences that were planned and guided cooperatively should be a central feature of both programs. Moreover, the "internship" courses were able to provide points of data collection on the progress that candidates are making towards demonstrating Basic Level of Proficiency (BLP):

- as they enrolled in the program;
- while meeting indicators that understanding and capability type performances best met in fieldwork;
- as they prepare plans for capstone experiences;
- upon completion of capstone internships; and
- to submit a Professional Growth Portfolio to the Internship coordinator as evidence of Basic Level of Proficiency in the indicators of school building or school district leadership.

These points provided targets for tracking individual candidate development of BLP for the purposes of advisement, guidance and remediation.

WB- PAS Design Parameters

The agreements reached by faculty established the following parameters that guided the work of the EL coordinator and the team of University web designers in designing the WB- PAS:

1. The WB- PAS should be a candidate-friendly system using web-data base to demonstrate level of *proficiency* in three types of performances:

   Awareness: *Candidates demonstrate awareness of concepts, definitions and procedures:*

   Understanding: *Candidates demonstrate understanding by interpreting their knowledge to school environments, integrating concepts with practice, and using knowledge and skills in context.*

   Capability: *Candidates demonstrate capabilities by applying the knowledge and skills*
2. The WB- PAS should enable the Professional Growth Profile of candidates to be tracked, supported and refined as they develop and demonstrate levels of performance meeting the following criteria shown in Figure 2.

3. The WB- PAS should enable measurement of candidate performance against the Department's expectation that:
   - Candidates completing both MA and Ed.D programs in leadership will demonstrate through course assignments and ongoing and capstone internship experiences performance of leadership practices consistent with the Department's requirements for evidence of *Basic Level of Proficiency (BLP)* defined as:
     1. awareness at the proficient level in all indicators in Standards 1-6 of ELCC standards;
     2. understanding at the proficient level in one indicator within each element of Standards 1-6 of ELCC standards;
     3. capability at the proficient level in all indicators in one element within each of Standards 1-6;
     4. successful completion of elements of internship to meet ELCC Standard 7: substantial, sustained, standards- based, real settings, planned and guided cooperatively, for credit;
     5. demonstration of dispositions associated with narratives in each of the ELCC Standards 1-6 in the ethical platform submitted in the candidate's Professional Growth Plan upon conclusion of the program; and
     6. completion of a technology portfolio demonstrating:

     a) awareness at the proficient level of all indicators in TSSA Standards 1-6

     b) capability at the proficient level of one indicator in each of TSSA Standards 1-6.

PHASE THREE: January 2003 – Spring 2004: Web-Based PAS Development

The logic of the WB- PAS as it was developed becomes more evident when it is viewed as a web-based data management system in which candidates access an interface that allows them to prepare and submit performance assessments. The design logic of the WB- PAS is presented in a map of routes that candidates take to demonstrate BLP presented in Figure 3.

Figure 2.Criteria for developing and demonstrating the levels of performance

Awareness: of Concepts Definitions and procedures	*Rudimentary:* There is little or no evidence of awareness of concepts, definitions and procedures…	*Developing:* There is limited evidence of awareness concepts, definitions and procedures…	*Proficient* There is clear evidence of awareness of concepts, definitions and procedures…	*Accomplished* There is clear and consistent evidence of awareness of concepts, definitions and procedures
Understanding: demonstrated by candidates interpreting their knowledge to school environments, integrating concepts with practice, and using knowledge and skills in context	*Rudimentary:* There is little or no evidence of interpretation of knowledge to school environments, integrating concepts with practice, and using knowledge and skills in context	*Developing:* There is limited evidence of interpretation of knowledge to school environments, integrating concepts with practice, and using knowledge and skills in context	*Proficient* There is clear evidence of interpretation of knowledge to school environments, integrating concepts with practice, and using knowledge and skills in context	*Accomplished* There is clear and consistent evidence of interpretation of knowledge to school environments, integrating concepts with practice, and using knowledge and skills in context
Capabilities: demonstrated by applying the knowledge and skills	*Rudimentary:* There is little or no evidence of application of knowledge and skills to….	*Developing:* There is limited evidence of application of knowledge and skills to …	*Proficient* There is clear evidence of application of knowledge and skills to …	*Accomplished* There is clear and consistent evidence of application of knowledge and skills to ….

Figure 3. Candidate routes to demonstrating basic level of proficiency

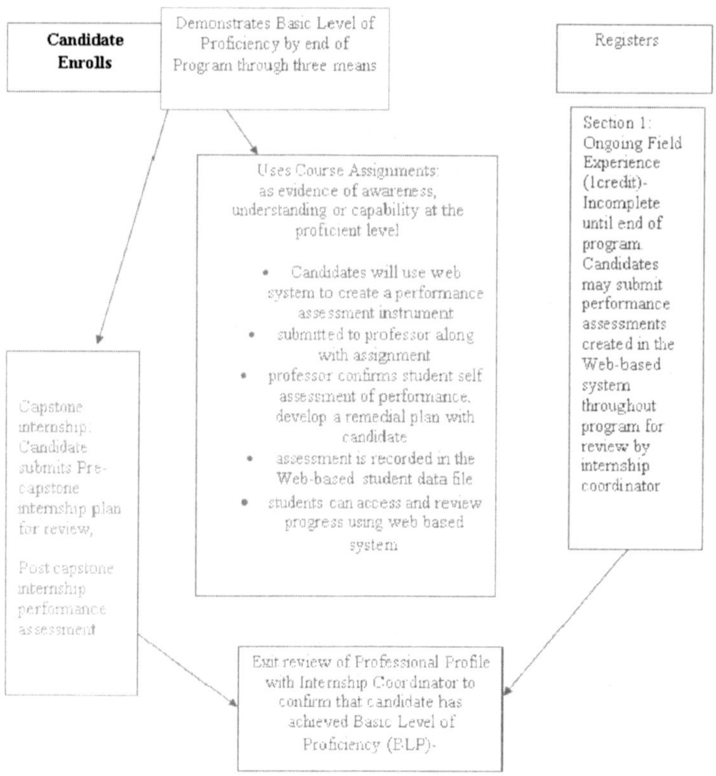

Key Transition Points as Foci for Compilation and Analysis of Performance Assessment Data

A key feature of EDEL's WB- PAS is the incorporation of performance assessment processes at transition points that occur when candidates enroll in, register for, or complete requirements of field experience courses. These field experiences include key transition points at which performance assessment data is submitted, complied and analyzed:

Upon Enrolment

Upon enrolment all candidates must register in Section 1 of a required field experience course. During this semester, candidates are introduced to the requirements for demonstrating BLP and are introduced to the PAS. During the first semester of registration in section 1 of these courses, candidates must submit an Internship Plan to the Internship Coordinator presenting their initial self audit of levels of awareness, understanding and capabilities in indicators of school building (MA), or school district (Ed.D.) leadership, and outlining plans for field-based experiences that will enable their development of proficiencies in those indicators and in indicators of TSSA standards. Individual candidate data in the Internship Plan is to be submitted to the WB-PAS. The WB-PAS database is accessible to individual candidates during their program, to Internship Coordinators, and to the Program Coordinator responsible for measuring program outcome effectiveness by aggregating individual Performance Profiles

During programs of study

Candidates may choose to submit courses assignments as evidence of performance related to indicators of school building or school district leadership during their preparation programs. It is also recommended that each semester while registered in Section 1 of field experience courses, candidates submit at least one performance activity demonstrating proficient levels of capability in an indicator that they have identified in the Professional Growth Profile to the Internship Coordinator for confirmation of self- assessment or for development of a remediation plan. In this way candidates can engage in the sustained, substantial, standards-based experiences in multiple settings that are the focus of indicators of ELCC Standards 1-6 and TSSA Standards 1-6.

Pre-Capstone Internship Plan Review

Candidates nearing the end of their programs register for Section 2 of their field experience course to complete a required Capstone Internship experience. Upon registration in this section, candidates must present pre- capstone internship plans to the Internship Coordinator for review. Candidates must complete the equivalent of six months of full time mentored internship experience. At the minimum the internship must include one semester of full time internship. Full time commitment to a capstone mentored internship is defined as the equivalent of full time academic study requiring 10 hours per week over 13 weeks. Additional internship activities must be planned cooperatively with the Internship Coordinator to ensure that the candidate completes the full requirement of six months of full time mentored internship experience. The Pre-Capstone Internship Plan includes the candidate's current Professional Growth Profile and a supporting commentary on how the capstone internship will enable the candidate to fulfill the requirements of Basic Level of Proficiency (BLP). The Internship Coordinator and the field mentor review the Pre-Capstone Internship Plan with the candidate and propose remedial activities if required for the candidate to fulfill requirements for BLP.

Post-Capstone Internship Performance Assessment

Candidates must submit post-capstone internship assessments providing performance evidence for assessment of proficiency level performances in capabilities associated with ELCC or TSSA Standards. Evidence includes an artifact accompanied by a reflective memo discussing the relationship of evidence to the criteria of Basic Level of Proficiency (BLP) addressed. Performance assessment must also include the candidate's current Professional Growth Profile and a supporting commentary on how the capstone internship enabled the candidate to fulfill the requirements of (BLP). Candidates submit a self-assessment of the Capstone Internship experience for review to both the site mentor and the Internship Coordinator. Candidates meet with reviewer(s) to discuss discrepant assessments and reach agreement on remediation plan.

Upon Completion of Requirements for Basic Level of Proficiency

Upon completion of the requirements for the outcome expectation of the MA or Ed.D. programs of demonstration of Basic Level of Proficiency (BLP) in indicators of school building or school district leadership, candidates must present a Professional Growth Portfolio to the Internship Coordinator for review. The Professional Growth Portfolio includes the following:

a. The candidate's PAS Professional Growth Profile;
b. A reflective memo explaining patterns of performance evident in the PAS Professional Growth Profile;
c. A sample of proficient performance in each standard demonstrating patterns described in the reflective memo;
d. A reflective memo describing how dispositions demonstrated in the performances inform the candidate's ethical platform for decision making; and
e. A Professional Growth Plan, outlining plans to extend levels of proficiency through ongoing development.

The Internship Coordinator confirms candidate self-assessment that the Professional Growth Portfolio demonstrates achievement of Basic Level of Proficiency. Discrepant assessment results in remediation plans.

Accomplished Level of Performance

Upon completion of requirements for Basic Level of Proficiency, candidates may also choose to submit additional evidence demonstrating their achievement of accomplished levels of performance in an ELCC standard. Candidates seeking commendation for achieving Accomplished Level of Performance in a Standard must demonstrate accomplished levels of capability in all indicators of all elements of the ELCC or TSSA standard when submitting their Professional Growth Portfolio for review.

PHASE FOUR: 2004-2009 Use and Revision of the Measurements of Program Outcome Effectiveness for Program Evaluation and Improvement Planning

The WB- PAS provides a means by which individual candidate performance assessment results can be aggregated for program improvement purposes. The program improvement processes that were designed included the creation of crosswalks showing the relationship of indicators of the ELCC standards for school building or school district leadership, candidates levels' of proficiency (rudimentary, developing, proficient, accomplished) in performances demonstrating awareness, understanding or capabilities. Faculty study the alignment of curriculum, instruction, assignments (assessments) with candidates' levels and types of performance in each indicator. The WB- PAS extends the process of measuring program outcome effectiveness that faculty used in examining the aggregation of data on performances submitted for assessment by MA and post masters course work candidates for Administrator I certification (described as part of the first phase). The detailed processes of analysis of aggregated quantitative and qualitative data presented in a crosswalk are used to measure program outcome effectiveness. However, the WB- PAS creates a more comprehensive system for use in measuring program outcome effectiveness for program evaluation and improvement planning by including the following components and processes:

1. Criteria are established for demonstrating Basic Levels of Proficiency in school building or school district leadership establish benchmarks for program outcome effectiveness;
2. Criteria are established for determining unacceptable, acceptable and target levels of candidate performance evidence of knowledge, skills and dispositions as specified by NCATE establish benchmarks for program outcome effectiveness;
3. Means have been developed for measuring candidates' levels of proficiency in all indicators at key transition points of entry, during the program, pre-capstone internship, post capstone internship, and program completion in the ongoing field experiences and capstone internship sections of both Master's and Doctoral field courses.
4. Methods of aggregating individual candidate data on levels of proficiency at these transition points have been designed that have enabled faculty to measure program outcomes in relation to criteria for BLP, and in relation to unacceptable, acceptable and target levels. Criteria and methods have been established for assessing the extent to which candidates' field and internship experiences are sustained, substantial, standard-based based, taking place in real setting, and planned and guided cooperatively; and
5. A quality assurance performance assessment process has been designed that enables faculty to assess the credibility of the PAS by determining the accuracy, consistency, fairness and avoidance of bias of the system.

Part 3: Conceptualizing Program Change from the Perspective of Organizational Theory

The ELCC requirements for program reviews reflect the kind of environmental demand that organizational theorists have variously interpreted to produce organizational responses. Yet, as I conclude in the following discussion, the theory of action evident in the ELCC/NCATE criteria for program review is not easily explained by organizational theories that have been widely used to study environmentally precipitated organizational change. Nevertheless, any effort to describe the processes by which a faculty member in a research intensive environment engages in the complex, and politically charged discussions of questions that touch on the heart of the scholarly enterprise must be conceptually framed to take into account the nature of the institutional dynamics at play when external control is exerted on organizational behavior. Researchers have considered these dynamics as reflective of processes of organizational adaptation in higher education that when focused on effectiveness may well elicit both conflict and consensus (Cameron, 1984;1986), but when they include institutional imperatives may also result in change (Kondakci & Van den Broeck, 2009)

Issues associated with adaptation to environmental pressures are, of course, among the classic concerns in organizational theory, one that has been explored through a number of conceptual lenses (Aldrich & Pfeffer, 1976; Tolbert & Zucker, 1983; Pfeffer, 1982, 1992). Most analyses of environmental demands emphasize change occurring through learning and adaptation, however; at least two alternative conceptions can be found in classic organizational theory. Population ecologists, for example, argue that change in populations of organizations occurs partly because of the operation of selection processes working on those organizations (Freeman & Hannan, 1989; Singh & Lumsden, 1990; Lemos, 2009). In one of the early efforts to explain this approach Hannan and Freeman (1977) noted, "Inertial pressures arise from both internal structural arrangements and environmental constraints... thus we should not presume that a course of action that is adaptive for a single organization facing some challenging environment will be adaptive for many competing organizations adopting a similar strategy" (pp. 931-932). Explanations of the particular responses to the questions faculty members faced when responding the requirements for program change precipitated by ELCC/NCATE standards and mandated accreditation by states could fruitfully be framed through the interpretive lens of population ecology. Certainly the conditions of accreditation faced by the "population of Colleges responding to state mandates, are consistent with those that Pfeffer (1982) described as amenable to analysis using population ecology where "selection processes and the competition among forms are general, not just mediated by market mechanisms but mediated by political mechanisms, social legitimacy, and so forth" (p. 192). For example, Abbott (2005) used ecological theory to study the links between professional and political ecologies associated with medical licensing and the professional and cases linking professional and university ecologies in fields of computer science, criminal justice and applied economies. Similarly Adams (2009) exploring the relationship between regulated professions and the state over time in Canada, found many more regulated professions had emerged by mid twentieth century.

Yet, departmental decision-making in universities and colleges is clearly a highly political process. Indeed, many critics argue that although departmental organizations are externally constrained, any effort to understand externally mandated program change must pay "greater attention to internal organizational political decision-making processes...[and must also take] the perspective that organizations seek to manage or strategically adapt to their environments' (Aldrich & Pfeffer, 1976, p. 79). Strategic adaptation to environmental pressures has been explored by resource dependency theorists, who claim that organizational behavior becomes externally influenced because the focal organization must attend to the demands of those in its environment that provide resources necessary and important for its continued survival (Pfeffer, 1982). State mandated accreditation by the ELCC/NCATE is a powerful external influence on Departments in publicly funded universities and colleges. Resource dependence theory, like population ecology, could be used to understand the forms and nature of organizational and interorganizational behaviors that have emerged as faculty members respond to the questions raised in responding to the ELCC/NCATE criteria for demonstrating program effectiveness. For example, exploring the international debates around the increasing permeation of business practices and private sector ideas and values in higher education Ntshoe (2004) used resource dependency theory in a case study revealing the influence of influences promoting the new managerialism in the University of Pretoria in South Africa. Similarly, Tabulawa's (2007) case study of the administrative/management restructuring exercise emphasizing effectiveness, quality and efficiency undertaken at the University of Botswana between 1998 and 2000 reflected the "reform fever currently gripping higher education institutions the world-over" (p. 457).

Notwithstanding the potential salience of conceptual guidance drawn from theories that focus on the influence of external controls on organizational decision making, any effort to understand program revision undertaken in response to ELCC/NCATE guidelines must also take into account the strategic responses of the department to the need for technological innovation.

To do so requires that we consider strategic response in light of organizations structural variables. Structural contingency theory, for example, draws attention to the influence of various contextual factors on the organizational structures that are adopted, thus recognizing that there are likely many ways of organizing, however, the way that is most effective depends on the context of the organization (Pennings, 1992). Thus, elements of size, "technology" and organizational environment have been explored in explaining the organization's structural variables. Critics, claim, however, that structural contingency theories neglect the importance of strategic choice (Eisenhardt &Zbaracki, 1992). Researchers have found that an organization's strategic orientation and its structures tend to adapt to each other (Miles, Snow & Pfeffer, 1974). Focusing on strategic choice draws attention to the ways in which the "linkage between environments and organizations are "diminished through the operation of perceptual mechanisms and the various biasing effects that occur in such perceptions" (Pfeffer, 1982, p. 161).

The processes of program revision precipitated by ELCC/NCATE review requirements can certainly be viewed as interpretive, not only in the sense implied by theories of strategic choice, but also by social constructivist views of the ways in which individual faculty behave. Theories framed from a social constructivist perspective are "essentially cognitive and social definitionist in nature" (Pfeffer, 1982, p. 209). There are, however, differences in among orientations to this perspective along a number of dimensions. Pfeffer notes,

one dimension, then, is the extent to which situations are considered unique or whether the theories strive for explanations of sense-making that generalize across contexts. Another dimension is the amount and kind of cognitive processing involved... A third dimension distinguishing among the theories is the extent to which they focus on cultural elements such as myths, symbols, settings, and vocabulary, as contrasted with more of an emphasis on quasi-rational causal cognitive work as the process by which explanations for situations are derived. (p. 211)

These differences point to the potential to adopt an "emergent, process-oriented focus on organizations incorporating elements of the social construction perspective without confining the analytic framework to the individual level and without relying as heavily on assumptions of cognition and intentional action." (p. 226). In the context of explaining faculty responses to questions raised by the ELCC/NCATE program review guidelines, there is utility in incorporating both aspects of structural effects and social reality construction in the ways used by institutionalization theorists (Meyer, Scott, Cole & Intili, 1978). Meyer and Rowan (1977) provide a now classic explanation of institutionalization and organizational structure,

.. . organizations are driven to incorporate the practices and procedures defined by prevailing rationalized concepts of organizational work and institutionalized in society.. . To maintain ceremonial conformity, organizations that reflect institutional rules tend to buffer their formal structures from the uncertainties of technical activities by becoming loosely coupled, building gaps between their formal structures and actual work activities. (pp. 340- 341)

Meyer and Rowan's analysis suggests that organizations are linked to their environments, but not in ways specified by population ecologists or by resource dependency theory. Pfeffer (1982) explains,

Because they are shared, institutionalized views in the environment about what organizations should look like and how organizational work should get performed, to maintain their legitimacy. .. organizations import the form, if not the substance, of these rules and incorporate them in their structure, rules, and reporting requirements. However, such rules and structures may have little to do with how the work can or should get performed; in fact there is little impact on task performance and the behavior of those organizational members who actually do the work. (p. 245)

Meyer and Rowan (1977) explained that decoupling might be useful to organizations because it enables work to be done according to localized judgments by those doing the work, while presenting an appearance of legitimated, rational organization of work. Meyer and Rowan's analysis focused on the ways in which schools resist evaluation. They argued that in the absence of a known technology of instruction, all that evaluation will do is to call into question the legitimacy of the structures and procedures in place. In their analysis, institutionalization occurs not because practices are technically sound, but rather because social expectations are that a good organization uses such practices.

Meyer and Rowan's analysis has, of course, become both well known and influential. Used as a framework for understanding the responses of faculty to ELCC/NCATE criteria for program review, their analysis would suggest that these responses may be efforts to provide the desired form of performance assessment, even incorporating the form into organizational structures, rules and reporting requirements. However, if Meyer and Rowan's analysis is correct, the substance of the ELCC/NCLB criteria for programs meeting standards for national recognition would have little impact on the behavior of faculty and students involved in graduate preparation. An analysis of such effects would be both theoretically and practically important. However, such an analysis would have to consider the claims of proponents of standards-based leadership practice who have argued that ELCC/NCATE indicators represent new "known's" of "effective" technology of school building and school district leadership. If we take into account Rowan's (1982) findings, institutionalization of the substance of standard-based performance and performance-based assessment specified by ELCC/NCATE may well occur if the associated technical procedures are highly certain and standards of evaluation are easy to formulate. Critics of the ELCC/NCATE criteria for programs seeking accreditation argue that neither of these conditions applies.

This analysis leaves us in a new kind of black box, one that fails to explain the effects of dialogue and engagement in critique of the kind precipitated as faculty members undergoing ELCC/NCATE review consider questions such as those explored by EDEL faculty; questions about performance evidence, the assessment of that evidence, and the nature of measures of program outcome effectiveness. These questions emerge in the intersection of the embedded context in which ELCC/NCATE reviews occur and the learning faculty members experience while engaged in dialogue and debate. These intersections are evident when we try to explain the responses of faculty to questions precipitated by their efforts to meet the criteria for the development of a valid and reliable performance assessment system designed to demonstrate the proficiency of candidates seeking certification for school building and school district leadership. They are highlighted in explanations of dialogic engagement by those who adopt sociocultural learning theories.

For example, Lave and Wenger (1991), Lave (1988), and Wenger (1998) formulated a theory of learning as a dimension of social practice that is distinct from conventional explanations which view learning as a process by which a "learner internalizes knowledge, whether "discovered," "transmitted," from others, or "experienced in interaction" with others" (Lave & Wenger, 1991, p. 47). In contrast to this conception of learning as process of internalization, "learning as increasing participation in communities of practice concerns the whole person acting in the world" (p. 49). The focus is consistent with a "theory of social practice which emphasizes the relational interdependency of agent and world, activity, meaning, cognition, learning, and knowing… [and which claims] that learning, thinking and knowing are relations among people in activity in, with, and arising from the socially and culturally structured world" (pp. 50-51).

Wenger (1998) notes these conceptions of learning derive from a related set of "activity theories" which focus on the structure of activities as historically constituted entities. Activity theories emerged in the 1920s and 1930s from the line of theorizing and research initiated by the founders of the cultural-historical school of Russian psychology, L.S. Vygotsky, A.N. Leont'ev, and A.R. Luria. Following this line of theorizing, Lave and Wenger (1991) describe learning as a social practice which involves an individual's participation in social communities, and implies "becoming able to be involved in new activities, to perform new tasks and functions, to master new understandings" (p. 53). Thus, activities, tasks, and functions are part of broader systems of relations that arise out of, and are reproduced by, social communities. Learning can therefore be conceived as an evolving form of membership in communities of practice. Researchers interested in learning as a necessary condition for improvement of instructional practice have found these conceptions of communities of practice useful. Wenger's (1998) theory has been used by a number of researchers interested in examining the issue of learning in the context of "sustaining the interconnected communities of practice through which an organization knows what it knows and thus becomes effective and valuable as an organization" (p. 8).

Other scholars use sociocultural theory to focus on activity theoretical-ideas from different perspectives. For example, Engeström (1999, 2001, 2008) explores innovative organizational learning through examinations of collaborative learning that produces new solutions, procedures, or the systemic transformations in organizational practices. In bringing activity theory to bear on analysis of organizational innovation, Engeström connects concepts of activity theory with organizational theories that have traditionally examined the ways individuals learn in organizational contexts. Organizational theories typically focus on organizational systems, structures, and politics, and on institutional forms of memory (Argyris & Schön, 1978; Senge, 1990; Brown & Duguid, 1991; Nonaka & Takeuchi, 1995). Engeström (1999, 2001, 2008) has shown how activity theory can provide a complementary but alternative approach to analyzing learning and problem solving in teams, a focus appropriate to exploring the dynamic conditions that are created as faculty respond to questions raised in meeting the criteria for ELCC/NCATE program review.

Part 4: Conceptualizing the Process of Expansive Learning

In exploring the enactment of these dynamic conditions I, therefore, find helpful the work by Engeström (1999, 2001, 2008) who views human cognition and behavior as embedded in collectively organized, artifact-mediated activity systems. Like other researchers studying ICT mediated organizational activities, my interest is in understanding the expansive learning in the context of technology adoption and use. The cultural-historical activity theory (CHAT) conceives human cognition and behavior as embedded in collectively organized, artifact-mediated activity systems (Leont'ev, 1978; Engeström, 1987, 1999; 2001, 2008; Cole & Engeström, 1993). Activities are social practices oriented to objects. Engeström (1999) cites Lektorsky (1984, p. 137) in explaining how an entity becomes an object of activity when it meets a human need.

A subject constructs the object, "singles out those properties that prove to be essential for developing social practice" using mediating artifacts that function as "forms of expression of cognitive norms, standards, and object-hypotheses existing outside the given individual (Lektorksy, 1984, p. 137). In this constructed, need–related capacity, the object gains motivating force that gives shape and direction to activity. (Engeström, 1999)

Objects in activity theory are distinct from goals attached to specific actions. Indeed goals do not explain the emergence of actions. Rather, following Weike's (1995) analysis of sense making in organizations, activity theory posits that goals and plans are formed and revised as individuals act, and become clearly specified only in retrospect. Engeström (1999) argues that an activity system constantly generates actions through which the object of the activity is enacted and reconstructed in specific forms and contexts but is never fully reached. The object of the activity system therefore often takes the form of problem finding and problem definition. Engeström (1999) suggests that although

mediating artifacts include tools and signs, both external implements and internal representations such as mental models ... it is not particularly useful to categorize mediating artifacts into external or practical ones, on the one hand, and internal or cognitive ones, on the other hand. These functions and uses are in constant flux and transformation occurs as the activity unfolds. An internal representation becomes externalized through speech, gesture, writing, manipulation of the material environment – and vice versa, external processes become internalized. Freezing or splitting these processes is a poor basis for understanding different artifacts. Instead, we need to differentiate between the processes themselves, between different ways of using artifacts. (p. 381)

Artifacts may be include those used to identify and describe objects ("what" artifacts), those used to guide and direct processes and procedures on, within, or between objects ("how" artifacts), those used to diagnose and explain the properties and behavior of objects ("why" artifacts), and those used to envision the future state or potential development of objects, including institutions and social systems ("where" artifacts). Significantly, artifact-mediated construction of objects "does not happen in a solitary manner or in harmonious unison. "It is a collaborative and dialogical process in which different perspectives and voices meet, collide, and merge (p. 382). In this conception, the often unsettled and conflicted relations between different positions and actors" are acknowledged as central feature of the context in which an activity system is created (p. 382).

Over the past decade Engeström (1999, 2001, 2008) has explored cases of "miniature cycles of innovative learning" that could potentially become expansive, while acknowledging that small cycles may remain isolated events, and that the "occurrence of a full-fledged expansive cycle typically requires concentrated effort and deliberate interventions" (1999, p. 385). His theory of expansive learning offers a conceptual lens drawn from activity theory that focuses on the interests that organizational learning theorists have in understanding the nature of innovative learning in organizations. Engeström describes his theory of expansive learning as based on the "dialectics of ascending from the abstract to the concrete" that occurs through specific "epistemic or learning actions." It begins with individuals questioning the accepted practice, and it gradually expands into a collective movement or institutionalization. The theory is related to Latour's (1987, 1988) actor-network theory in that "both regard innovations as stepwise construction of new forms of collaborative practice" (Engeström, 1999, p. 383). The ideal-typical sequence of epistemic actions in an expansive cycle include seven actions: questioning, historical analysis, actual empirical analysis, modeling the new solution, examining the new model, implementing the new model, reflecting on the process, consolidating the new practice (pp. 383-384).

At the heart of Engeström's (1999, 2001, 2008) theory of expansive learning, then, are sequences that reflect an ascent from the abstract to the concrete achieved through specific epistemic or learning actions. He argues that these actions, taken together, form an expansive cycle or spiral that follows an ideal-typical cycle best understood as "construction and resolution of successively evolving tensions or contradictions in a complex system that includes the object or objects, the mediating artifacts, and the perspectives of the participants" (1999, p. 384). Engeström has examined miniature cycles of learning that can be viewed as partially expansive beginning with actions of "questioning, criticizing, or rejecting some aspects of the accepted practice and existing wisdom" (p. 383). However, the theory has also been used to examine large-scale transformations in activity systems, spanning two or three years that while not common "typically requires concerted effort and deliberate interventions" (p. 385). This is the kind of transformation required in graduate programs leading to school building and school district leadership if they are to meet the ELCC/NCATE criteria for accreditation. Department's seeking accreditation must indeed make concerted effort and develop deliberate interventions if they are to meet those criteria.

In the case of EDEL, concerted effort occurred throughout the four phases that I previously described. Evident in those phases are artifacts that reflect resolutions and responses generated in debate and dialogue, through controversy and conflict, indeed through processes that Engeström terms negation. Typically these debates were triggered by deep questioning of the relevance and appropriateness of the ELCC standards, elements, and indicators, questions about the nature of a performance activity, and concerns about requirements that the Department develop a performance assessment system, and measure program outcome effectiveness. In the following discussion I highlight a few examples of the kinds of questioning, analysis, and modeling that occurred around these and other questions.

One of the ongoing discussions concerns the relevance of the standards, the appropriateness of indicators and performance assessments. Faculty wanted to know what, if any, relationship the ELCC standards had to the Department's mission. The "what" artifacts of this process of questioning are evident in interpretation of EDEL's goals in light of the purposes of the ELCC, described below in the commentary submitted to the ELCC outlining the Department's conception of the knowledge and skill base of education leadership, its philosophy for preparation, and its goals and commitments for MA and Ed.D. programs outlined in official documents that were revisited and considered during the initial phases of program review. These documents noted,

The Department seeks to develop educational leaders committed to using their knowledge of central concepts of leadership and appropriate tools of inquiry to ensure learning and success for all students. The Department is committed to fostering the development of knowledge, skills, and dispositions that will enable educational leaders to ensure that diverse students reach challenging learning goals and achieve their potentials. Consistent with the Conceptual Framework of the College of Education, the preparation of school and district level educational leaders is also grounded in the Department's commitment to research and inquiry, diversity, collaboration and technology.

Similar commitments were noted in the Department's *Introduction to the Prospective Applicant's Guide to Graduate Programs 2002-2003*:

The Department (EDEL) brings together people from diverse backgrounds and with diverse aspirations to form a community of learners committed to working on tough issues of education leadership, policy, and reform within a social context of conflict, diversity, and change. The

work undertaken in this community of learners rests on the fundamental belief that the goal of education is to promote the success of all students. The Department's work is based on the assumption that achieving this goal requires that students in graduate programs of preparation for educational leadership become reflective practitioners committed to fostering a democratic and just society. A central goal of these programs is to provide students with opportunities to examine the political and moral aspects of the practice of educational leadership.

Using Engeström's conception of epistemic actions, a critical aspect of the processes of expansive learning precipitated by the ELCC review involved faculty questioning the relevance of ELCC goals to those that had been developed through multiple debates among faculty across the department (as outlined above). Faculty questioned whether their goals were evident in the ELCC standards. The artifacts of the debates reflect the "what" kinds of concerns that Engeström suggests are used to identify and describe phenomenon. In this case faculty debates focused on whether the ELCC standards bore any identifiable relationship to the goals that they held for the programs. Artifacts of this process include the analysis that was undertaken of the Department's approach to developing reflective professionals as described in the *Prospective Applicant's Guide to Graduate Programs, 2002-2003*:

Students are encouraged to become actively involved in both cooperative and independent inquiry, involving critical thinking about complex problems and ideas... Every program in the Department offers a combined emphasis on scholarship and professional preparation, focusing on the connections between theory, research, and practice.

Examining ELCC standards and exploring how they related to Departmental goals also involved a second epistemic action; one that Engeström (1999) suggests focuses on analyzing the situation. He observes, "analysis involves mental, discursive, or practical transformation of the situation in order to find our causes and explanatory mechanisms" (p. 383). Debates among faculty focused took a "how" focus. Questions about how ELCC criteria would fit the Department's focus on critical thinking about problems and ideas led to examination of the focus of the ELCC standards while faculty were engaged in designing the new Ed.D. program for school district leaders. The year-long design process brought together key faculty members, two superintendents, and a student member in multiple meetings that focused on the content of the program, modes of delivery, and alignment with ELCC standards.

Notably these meetings moved back and forth between questioning and analysis. Because the design of the Ed.D. involved the development of new courses, questions about the relationship of theory, research and practice were relatively abstract. Yet the faculty also questioned practically, how the programs could be designed to meet the ELCC requirements that candidates have opportunities to demonstrate proficient performance in over 70 indicators.

While design of the Ed.D. was underway, review of the MA program leading to school building certification began. Faculty members responsible for courses in the program undertook an actual empirical analysis of the alignment of foci of courses with the ELCC indicators. Analysis revealed that course content and expectations mapped on to the ELCC indicators very well, but also actually reinforced, elaborated and extended the ideas framing the standards. Faculty who are committed to developing connections between theory, research and practice could see similar thrusts in the ELCC standards once analysis of alignment of indicators with their commitments to fostering these connections.

Figure 4 is an artifact of these processes of questioning and analysis that was submitted to the

Figure 4. Analysis of course content alignment with standard 1 indicators and overview of course assignments for MA courses

Standard 1 Elements & Indicators												Courses		Cognitive & Skill Demands of Performances		
1.1		1.2			1.3		1.4			1.5						
A	b	a	b	C	A	b	a	b	c	a	b	Course	Pg	AWARENESS	AWARENESS & UNDERSTANDING	AWARENESS, UNDERSTANDING & CAPABILITY
*		*		*			*			*		EDEL 715	9	Reading Reviews	Governing Board Paper	Political Analysis Paper
*												EDEL 730	10	Reading Reports	Curriculum Unit	
*												EDEL 719	11	Journals & Reflections	Portrait of Curriculum Leader, Reaction Paper & Critique, Curriculum Analysis, Plan, Reaction Paper	
*	*	*	*		*	*	*	*	*	*	*	EDEL 705	14	Team Presentations	Team Plan for Instructional Leadership, Individual Portfolio	Team Plan for Instructional Leadership in a 21st Century School, Reflective Journal
*	*	*			*		*				*	EDEL 701	16	Case Study Briefs	Case Study Briefs, Case Analyses	Case Development, School Improvement Plan Memo
*	*	*	*	*	*	*	*	*		*	*	EDEL 731	17	Learning Analysis	Learning Analysis Paper	Class Conference
			*					*				EDS 740	16	Assignments and Replications and Variations of Problems of Analysis		
*		*	*	*			*	*	*			EDEL 799	3			Activities specified in EDEL799Internship Performances
Total 1.1 activities		Total 1.2 activities			Total 1.3 activities		Total 1.4 activities			Total 1.5 activities		Courses contributing to Standard		Total number of types of awareness activities	Total number of types of understanding activities	Total number of types of capability activities
a	b	a	b	C	a	b	a	b	c	a	b					
7	3	5	4	3	3	2	5	4	2	3	3	8		7	12	6

ELCC as an indicator of excellence. The Figure reflects the analysis undertaken by individual faculty of the relationship between ELCC standards and indicators and their own conceptions of the qualities that courses leading to leadership in education should promote. This analysis revealed to faculty the shared conceptions of elements of leadership that should be emphasized (as noted in the number of courses that target similar indicators). Analysis confirmed that the MA program ensured that candidates gained understanding of the holistic nature of Standard 1 indicators through integrated curricula evident in the number of possible performance activities addressing each indicator that multiple courses have developed. It also revealed the extent to which the "work" of students in the courses provided multiple opportunities for students to bridge theory to practice through activities focused on developing:

a. awareness, through acquisition of concepts and information
b. understanding through the integration of concepts with practice and the use of knowledge in context and
c. capability through the application of knowledge and skills in a workplace environment.

As Engeström's theory suggests the epistemic actions of questioning, analysis and modeling, through the kind of charting that Figure 2 represents, did expand learning of the kind that supported subsequent innovations in design of the WB- PAS. Notably, the ELCC criteria that programs seeking accreditation have to meet pose challenges to existing institutional scripts. Indeed, they challenged faculty to consider the regulative, normative and cognitive dimensions of existing institutional practices.

Previously I noted the heuristic value of Scott's (1995, 2008a, 2008b) conception of institutions as multifaceted systems incorporating cognitive, normative and regulative pillars. Drawing from Scott I view these regulative, normative and cognitive elements not as separate pillars, but as dimensions of institutional arrangements that are enacted through different carriers: cultures, social structures, and routines. Table 1 illustrates these dimensions of institutional arrangements as adapted from Scott (1995, p. 52).

Table 1. Institutional Dimensions and carriers of culture, social structure, and routines [Adapted from Scott (1995, p. 52)]

Institutional Dimensions	Cultural Carriers	Carriers of Social Structure	Carriers of Routines
Regulative	Rules, laws	Governance systems, power systems	Protocols, standard procedures
Normative	Values, expectations	Regimes, authority systems	Conformity, performance of duty
Cognitive	Categories, typifications	Structural isomorphism, identities	Performance programs, scripts

The ELCC criteria call into question regulative, normative and cognitive aspects of institutional practices carried in cultures, social structures and routines. For example, ELCC criterion 4, 5 and 6 noted below led to questioning and analysis:

4. Programs include: (a) the acquisition of concepts and information, (b) the integration of concepts with practice and use of knowledge in context, and (c) the application of knowledge and skills in a workplace environment.
5. Bridging experiences are conducted between course content and the workplace that feature clinical exercises and/or field settings.
6. All candidates are required to have performance experiences in all standards as well as an extensive internship that requires the synthesis and application of appropriate knowledge and skills represented in the standards.

For EDEL faculty, these criteria caused debate and provoked analysis of the goals of the Department. An artifact of this "what" questioning led to a historical analysis of the *Prospective Applicant's Guide to Graduate Programs, 2002-2003*:

Students are encouraged to become actively involved in both cooperative and independent inquiry, involving critical thinking about complex programs and ideas... Every program in the Department offers a combined emphasis on scholarship and professional preparation, focusing on the connections between theory, research, and practice.

Further debate and analysis touched on regulative, normative and cognitive dimensions of institutional practices. The "epistemic actions" of questioning and analysis were less conflictual when focused on the normative dimensions carried in cultural values and expectations of the faculty concerning the links between theory-research-practice, as evidenced above in the Department's focus on connections between these. Similarly normative stances of faculty to the essential knowledge and skills of educational leadership, turned out upon analysis, to reflect a similar framework of essential knowledge and skills of educational leadership evident in the ELCC standards emphasizing the following:

- Leadership as collaborative, distributive practices focusing on a vision of learning shared by all;
- Leadership as consensus building;
- Leadership for accountability for learning processes and results;
- Leadership for collaboration with families and communities;
- Leadership for policy development;
- Leadership as moral and ethical agency.

These ELCC standards were mapped against the Department's philosophy that emphasizes the preparation of reflective practitioners of educational leadership. Further analysis in response to questions posed by the ELCC review revealed the alignment of the Department's philosophy to the Conceptual Framework of the College that NCATE specifies should be articulated. Consistent with the Conceptual Framework of the College of Education, the preparation of school and district level educational leaders is grounded in the Department's commitment to research and inquiry, diversity, collaboration and technology. These commitments are noted in the Department's *Introduction to the Prospective Applicant's Guide to Graduate Programs 2002-2003*:

The Department (EDEL) brings together people from diverse backgrounds and with diverse aspirations to form a community of learners committed to working on tough issues of education leadership, policy, and reform within a social context of conflict, diversity, and change.

Prompted by the ELCC reporting requirements, EDEL faculty agreed that the work undertaken in this community of learners rests on the fundamental belief that the goal of education is to promote the success of all students. The process of responding to the ELCC review led to discussion about the meaning of this goal, and a clarification that the department seeks to develop educational leaders committed to using their knowledge of central concepts of leadership and appropriate tools of inquiry to ensure learning and success for all students.

Questioning by faculty intensified, however, when regulative and cognitive dimensions of institutional practices were challenged by ELCC criteria for program accreditation. For example, faculty debated extensively about the appropriateness and feasibility of assessing student dispositions (as mandated by NCATE, not ELCC). Not only were "rules" seen as inappropriate, but also debates intensified around questions of how dispositions can be demonstrated and if they can, whether they should. The Department's response noted below reflects a degree of agreement among faculty about what constitutes an appropriate degree of regulative procedure and cognitive scripting.

The Department recognizes that dispositions reflect the "proclivities that lead us in one direction rather than another within the freedom of action that we have" (Perkins, 1995, p. 275).[1] Consistent with the view of NCATE, the Department recognizes that the development of appropriate professional dispositions can best be assessed along with performances associated with candidates' developing awareness, understanding and capabilities of, and practices in educational leadership. It also recognizes that while the ELCC Standards are presented as discrete, they reflect overlapping knowledge, skills and dispositions of educational leadership. Although dispositions are not directly identified in the ELCC Standards (2002), the Department considers the narrative descriptions of each of the Standards to reflect the dispositions stated directly in the Interstate School Leaders Licensure Consortium Standards for School Leaders.[2] Moreover, as previously noted, the Department agrees with NCATE's judgment that "dispositions are not usually assessed directly; instead they are assessed along with other performances in candidate's work with students families, and communities" (NCATE Standards, Chapter 2, p. 19). The Department has, therefore, adopted a philosophy of preparation that best supports the development of a holistic understanding of leadership practices.

The Department is committed to fostering and developing in candidate's dispositions associated with this framework. Dispositions are therefore seen as giving meaning to actions.[3] The goal of the programs is to provide opportunities for candidates to reflect on, and gain, a deeper understanding of the beliefs, values, and commitments that put meaning to the ELCC standards for educational leaders. Candidates are expected to explain in reflective memos presented at key transition points of entry, prior to and upon completion of capstone internship experiences, and upon completion of their programs, how their performance activities in coursework and in internship activities demonstrate dispositions outlined in the narratives describing each ELCC Standard.

I have highlighted some of the core debates that were precipitated by the ELCC review. Notably there is a clear congruence of a normative stance of EDEL to the values espouses in the ELCC goals, in the sense that Scott (1995, 2008a, 2008b) and other institutional theorists view as highly institutionalized contexts. It seems in that in the implementation ecology of accountability public sector institutions may engage in episodic actions leading to expansive learning around normative dimensions of the institutional context in which they are embedded. Practically, this means that faculty working together in the kind of program revision demanded by the criteria ELCC set for program accreditation may work from processes of critique and questioning that move toward innovative learning. Artifacts of this process are evident in the commentary on the alignment of EDEL goals with the ELCC standards. Thus, the department report to ELCC commented that faculty members,

are committed to fostering the development of knowledge, skills and dispositions that will enable educational leaders to ensure that diverse students reach challenging learning goals and achieve their potentials. The Department's work is based on the assumption that this requires that students in graduate programs of preparation for educational leadership become reflective practitioners committed to fostering a democratic and just society. A central goal of these programs is provide students with opportunities to examine the political and moral aspects of the practice of educational leadership.

This artifact reflects the potential for innovation as a collective achievement in the sense anticipated by Engeström. Innovative learning and knowledge creation does have a collaborative and constructive aspect. Yet, in the context of the implementation ecology facing Departments undergoing a state mandated accreditation review by the ELCC/NCATE, Engeström's assumptions about the nature of epistemic actions in an expansive learning cycle may underestimate the impetus and direction for action created by such a system of accountability. In the concluding part of this case study, I turn to consider the limitations and utility of looking at and for artifacts of expansive learning in the responses that the Department had to the ELCC/NCATE review.

CONCLUDING DISCUSSION: IMPLEMENTATION ECOLOGY OF ACCOUNTABILITY FRAMING EXPANSIVE LEARNING

The expansive cycle is helpful in understanding the problem finding and problem defining activities in which EDEL faculty engaged in responding to the requirements of the ELCC/NCATE program review. At the same time, Engeström's (1999, 2001, 2008) theory leaves open the questions about the kinds of concentrated effort and deliberate intervention that generates expansive learning. These are questions I have considered in studying the institutional dynamics of accountability (Mawhinney, 1995, 1998, 2003, Mawhinney & May, 2010). As a type of interpretive policy inquiry, my research has previously explored the interaction of regulative, normative and cognitive facets of accountability systems. I view these interactions as creating an implementation ecology in which individual agency by actors cannot be dismissed, despite the power of broad institutional scripts to define individual behavior. My interest is, therefore, in understanding the nature of agency of individual actors, in the implementation ecology created by accountability systems. I view implementation ecology as the particular conditions of legitimacy that frame the meaning of accountability systems for individuals in different organizations. Legitimacy is a dynamic condition reflecting the cultural alignment, normative support, and consonance with relevant rules that establishes the frame of agency for individual actors, and of course thereby underscores the potential enactment of power by actors and the conflict that can follow.

The phases of the process of design outlined in the previous part of this case study were marked by concerted efforts by the faculty to define the nature of the problem that the ELCC criteria posed, questioning, analysis, efforts to model possible designs, critical examination and testing of design elements, and currently implementing the PAS, while beginning to reflect on the process of design. In short, the process reflected at least the initial sequence of actions in what Engeström (1999, 2001, 2007, 2008) has called an expansive learning cycle. EDEL did receive ELCC approval of its programs leading to school building and school district leadership and in 2003 was awarded national recognition by that body. The WB- PAS was activated in 2005 and by 2010 over 200 MA and Ed.D. candidates had, or were using it for formative and summative feedback of their progress toward meeting the outcome criteria set by EDEL. As anticipated in the design of WBPAS, candidates view the WB- PAS a powerful form of personal knowledge management in the ways recently described by Agnihotri and Troutt (2009) in their study of effective technology utilization. Similarly, as intended in the design of the WB-PAS, the candidate performance data has proven to be a very useful mode of used by faculty members to reflect on program effectiveness. These reflective processes expanded the learning cycle begun as EDEL faculty designed responses to the ELCC criteria.

If Engeström is correct, reflective processes lead to consolidation of new practices, and indeed the processes prompted by WB-PAS have become embedded in EDEL's activity systems. This is, of course, the intended outcome of the ELCC/NCATE program review process, yet it is an outcome that many theories of organizational change would predict is problematic, if not unlikely. Although we have evidence of innovative learning in complex organizational contexts that suggests consolidation of new practice does occur in the context of expansive learning cycles from the work of Engeström (1999, 2001, 2007, 2008), and historically from Nonaka and Takeuchi (1995), Senge (1990), and Argyris and Schön (1978), critics argue that the transformation implied is highly constrained by social contexts and by issues of power and social antagonism (Avis, 2009). These are the issues that I have attempted to address by considering the implementation ecology that framed the expansive learning that took place in this case study. As I note next this framing highlights conflict and power in a way that addresses limitations of activity theory identified by Avis.

My purpose has been to discuss the processes by which EDEL faculty responded to the ELCC/NCATE criteria for accreditation. Although my descriptions of the problem finding and designing processes have been broad, I have shown artifacts of what Engeström (1999, 2001, 2008) has characterized as an expansive learning cycle. There is utility in examining the processes of responding to the ELCC/NCATE criteria as reflecting epistemic actions where conflict and debate productively accomplish progressive engagement of faculty in thinking about questions like those which preoccupied EDEL faculty: What counts as evidence of performance? What criteria should be used to examine that evidence? How can validity and reliability be ensured? How can the performance assessment system be used to create measures of program outcome effectiveness? How can a demonstration of dispositions be designed in a way that reflects the EDEL's commitments?

Expansive learning focuses on the "creation and practical application of powerful new concepts.. . [and] puts a lot of weight on the local discursive construction of shared object and intention in knowledge creation" (Engeström, 1999, p. 385). Appropriately for the purpose of exploring how faculty responded to the ELCC accreditation process, the theory also

emphasizes the central role of contradictions and debate in knowledge creation. The whole process is seen as energized and often radically refocuses by negation: questioning, criticizing, and even rejecting the accepted wisdom. (p. 385)

Negation is typically not viewed as resulting in innovation. Indeed, conventional views suggests that in the context of decision making in departments peopled by highly verbal, analytic, and principled individuals, such negation is more likely a constraint to change than an impetus for innovation. Yet there is growing evidence of the importance of critical questioning and rejection of conventional notions as triggering innovative learning. As Tjovold and Tjosvold (1994) point out there is utility in constructive controversy. Focusing on the positive potential of conflicts in organizational change makes a great deal of sense if we are to speak truth to the reality of the intense debates that are precipitated by the regulative thrust of the ELCC accreditation process.

Yet innovation has occurred as the different perspectives of faculty were brought to bear on defining problems, and in this process there is a "progression of collectively achieved actions" (Engeström, 1999, p. 401). My intention in this case study has been to offer both analytic and descriptive commentaries on how innovation has occurred as faculty responded to questions about what constitutes proficient practices by candidates for certification for school building and school district leadership during the four phases of development of EDEL's WB- PAS. My description of the features of EDEL's WB- PAS was, therefore, purposefully framed in an analysis of what Engeström calls "epistemic" actions that occurred in the four phases of its development and design. This is not to say that the conflicts and tensions created during the phases of program revision that I have previously outlined in this case study were fully or easily resolved sequentially. Many of the tensions continued throughout the processes of designing the WB- PAS, and continue now. This suggests a more constrained conclusion of the potential for expansive learning than is anticipated by Engeström when he observes, "the process of expansive learning should be understood as construction and resolution of successively evolving tensions or contradictions in a complex system that includes the object or objects, the mediating artifacts, and the perspectives of the participants" (1999, p. 384).

In other words, the analysis I have presented suggests that it may well be possible to have expansive learning under conditions of tension and contradiction, particularly in the context of the implementation ecology of accountability that public institutions face. Engeström's (1999, 2001, 2008) analysis is, of course, focused on innovative learning in work teams- where market forces are the drivers of organizational responsiveness. In contrast, the broad analysis I have presented here suggests that there is much to be learned about the nature of epistemic actions under the conditions of implementation ecology created in technology-mediated public sector accountability systems. Using these conceptual lenses, I have explained the artifacts of expansive learning evident in the key elements used in designing the EDEL, WB-PAS. Such artifacts provide new insights into the conditions that enhance the potential for faculty to design IT enhanced KMS that foster expansive learning. As a conceptual analysis of expansive learning the case study contributes to the new body of scholarship on the connections of activity theory to related theoretical traditions and provides new elaborations on institutional dynamics involved in the implementation ecology of accountability in the new IT-KMS in instructional environments (see for example, Elbanna, 2009). In sum, the case study I have presented here anticipates new directions in technological adaptability to emergent ICT innovations associated with Learning Management Systems (LMS) (Forment, Guerrero & Poch, 2010) by providing a glimpse into the directions now being taken in this fifth phase of development of the EDEL WB-PAS. As in previous phases, it enhances the emergent evaluative state of education leader preparation now common in countries around the world.

REFERENCES

Abbott, A. (2005). Linked ecologies: States and universities as environments for Professions. *Sociological Theory*, *23*(3), 245–274. doi:10.1111/j.0735-2751.2005.00253.x

Adams, T. L. (2009). The Changing Nature of Professional Regulation in Canada, 1867-1961. *Social Science History*, *33*(2), 217–243. doi:10.1215/01455532-2008-020

Agnihotri, R., & Troutt, M. D. (2009). The effective use of technology in personal knowledge management: A framework of skills, tools and user context. *Online Information Review*, *33*(2), 329–342. doi:10.1108/14684520910951249

Aldrich, H. E., & Pfeffer, J. (1976). Environments of organizations. In A. Inkeles, J. Coleman & N. Smelser (Eds.), Annual Review of Sociology, 40, 225-233.

Alexander, F. K. (2000). The changing face of accountability: Monitoring and assessing institutional performance in higher education. *The Journal of Higher Education*, *71*(4), 411–431. doi:10.2307/2649146

Argryis, C., & Schön, D. A. (1978). Organizational learning: A theory of action perspective. Reading, MA: Addison-Wesley.

Avis, J. (2009). Transformation or transformism: Engestrom's version of activity theory? *Educational Review*, *61*(2), 151–165. doi:10.1080/00131910902844754

Brennan, J., & Shah, T. (2000). Quality assessment and institutional change: Experiences from 14 countries. *Higher Education*, *40*, 331–349. doi:10.1023/A:1004159425182

Brown, G., Desrosier, T., & Edwards, D. (2009). Learning to work and working to learn: what we are learning and how technology and assessment can help. In V. C. X. Wang (Ed.), Handbook of Research on E-Learning Applications for Career and Technical Education: Technologies for Vocational Training (pp. 638-667). Hershey, PA: Information Science Reference.

Brown, J. S., & Duguid, P. (1991). Organizational learning and communities of practice: Toward a unified view of working, learning, and innovation. *Organization Science*, *2*, 40–57. doi:10.1287/orsc.2.1.40

Burke, J. C., & Serban, A. M. (1997). Performance funding and budgeting for public higher education: Current status and future prospects. Albany, NY: The Nelson Rockefeller Institute of Government, State University of New York.

Cameron, K. S. (1984). Organizational adaptation and higher-education. *The Journal of Higher Education*, *55*(2), 122–144. doi:10.2307/1981182

Cameron, K. S. (1986). Effectiveness as paradox - consensus and conflict in conceptions of organizational-effectiveness. *Management Science*, *32*(5), 539–553. doi:10.1287/mnsc.32.5.539

Chen, M. Y., & Chen, A. P. (2006). Knowledge management performance evaluation: a decade review from 1995 to 2004. *Journal of Information Science*, *32*(1), 17–38. doi:10.1177/0165551506059220

Chiva, R., & Alegre, J. (2005). Organizational learning and organizational knowledge - Towards the integration of two approaches. *Management Learning*, *36*(1), 49–68. doi:10.1177/1350507605049906

Cole, M., & Engeström, Y. (1993). A cultural-historical interpretation of distributed cognition. In G. Salomon (Ed.), Distribute cognition: Psychological and educational considerations. Cambridge, UK: Cambridge University Press.

D'Andrade, R. (1984). Cultural meaning systems. In R.A. Shweder & R.A. Levine (Eds.), Cultural theory: Essays on mind, self, and emotion (pp. 88-119). Cambridge, UK: Cambridge University Press.

Datta, P. (2007). An agent-mediated knowledge-in-motion model. *Journal of The Association For Information System*, *8*(5), 287–311.

Deem, R., & Brehony, K. J. (2005). Management as ideology: the case of 'new managerialism' in higher education. *Oxford Review of Education*, *31*(2), 217–235. doi:10.1080/03054980500117827

DiMarco, J. (2006). Web portfolios in the information society and future. In Web Portfolio Design and Applications (pp. 277-292), Hershey, PA: Idea Group Publishing.

Ditsa, G. (2003). Activity theory as a theoretical foundation for information systems research. In G. Ditsa, Information Management: Support Systems & Multimedia Technology (pp. 192-231), Hershey, PA: IRM Press.

Dolata, U. (2009). Technological innovations and sectoral change Transformative capacity, adaptability, patterns of change: An analytical framework. *Research Policy*, *38*(6), 1066–1076. doi:10.1016/j.respol.2009.03.006

Easterby-Smith, M., Burgoyne, J., et al. (Eds.). (1999) Organisational learning and the learning organisation. London: Sage.

Ehrmann, S. C. (2006). Electronic portfolio initiatives: A flashlight guide to planning and formative evaluation. In A. Jafari (Ed.), Handbook of Research on ePortfolios (pp. 180-193). Hershey PA: Idea Group Reference.

Eisenhardt, K. M., & Zbaracki, M. J. (1992). Strategic decision making. *Strategic Management Journal*, *13*, 17–37. doi:10.1002/smj.4250130904

El-Khawas, E., & Massey, W. F. (1996). Britain's performance-based system. In W. F. Massey (Ed.), Resource allocation in higher education (pp. 223-240). Ann Arbor, MI: The University of Michigan Press.

Elbanna, A. R. (2009). Actor-network theory in ICT research: A wider lens of enquiry. *International Journal of Actor-Network Theory and Technological Innovation*, *1*(3), 1–14.

Engeström, Y. (1987). *Learning by expanding: An activity-theoretical approach to developmental research.* Helskinki: Orienta-Konsultit.

Engeström, Y. (1999). Innovative learning in work teams: Analyzing cycles of knowledge creation in practice. In Y. Engeström, R.L. Miettinen & R.L. Punamäki (Eds.), Perspectives on activity theory. Cambridge, UK: Cambridge University Press.

Engeström, Y. (2001). Expansive learning at work: towards an activity theoretical reconceptualization. *Journal of Education and Work*, *14*(1), 133–156. doi:10.1080/13639080123238

Engeström, Y. (2008). Enriching activity theory without shortcuts. *Interacting with Computers*, *20*, 256–259. doi:10.1016/j.intcom.2007.07.003

Forment, M. A., Guerrero, M. J. C., & Poch, J. P. (2010). Towards mobile learning applications integration with learning management systems. In T. T. Goh (Ed.), Multiplatform E-Learning Systems and Technologies: Mobile Devices for Ubiquitous ICT-Based Education (pp. 182-194). Hershey, PA: Information Science Reference.

Freeman, J., & Hannan, M. T. (1989). Setting the record straight on organizational ecology - rebuttal to young. *American Journal of Sociology*, *95*(2), 425–439. doi:10.1086/229275

Hage, J., & Meuus, M. (Eds.). (2006). Innovation, Science, and Institutional Change. Oxford, UK: Oxford University Press.

Hannan, M. T., & Freeman, J. H. (1977). The population ecology of organizations. *American Journal of Sociology*, *82*, 929–964. doi:10.1086/226424

Igira, F. T., & Gregory, J. (2009). Cultural historical activity theory. In Y. Dwivedi, B. Lal, M. Williams, S. Schneberger & M. Wade (Eds.), Handbook of Research on Contemporary Theoretical Models in Information Systems (pp. 434-454). Hershey, PA: Information Science Reference.

Jongbloed, B., & Koelman, J. (1996). *Funding mechanisms for higher education: A five country based survey with special reference to performance-based funding approaches.* CHEPS working paper for Higher Education Council, National Board of Employment, Education and Training (NBEET), Canberra, Australia. Enschede, The Netherlands: Center for Higher Education Policy Studies, University of Twente.

Juneau, K. R. (2008). Varieties of authentic assessment. In L. Tomei (Ed.), Encyclopedia of Information Technology Curriculum Integration (pp. 936-942). Hershey, PA: Information Science Reference.

King, R. P. (2007). Governance and accountability in the higher education regulatory state. *Higher Education*, *53*, 411–430. doi:10.1007/s10734-005-3128-2

Kondakci, Y., & Van den Broeck, H. (2009). Institutional imperatives versus emergent dynamics: A case study on continuous change in higher education. *Higher Education*, *58*(4), 439–464. doi:10.1007/s10734-009-9204-2

Latour, B. (1987). Science in action: How to follow scientists and engineers through society. Cambridge, MA: Harvard University Press.

Latour, B. (1988). The pasteurization of France. Cambridge, MA: Harvard University Press.

Lave, J. (1988). Cognition in practice. Cambridge, UK: Cambridge University Press.

Lave, J., & Wenger, E. (1991). Situated learning: Legitimate peripheral participation. Cambridge, UK: Cambridge University Press.

Layzell, D. T. (1998). Linking performance to funding outcomes for public institutions of higher education: The U.S. *European Journal of Education*, *33*, 103–111.

Lektorksy, V. A. (1984). Subject, object, cognition. Moscow: Progress.

Lemos, J. (2009). In Defense of Organizational Evolution A Reply to Reydon and Scholz. *Philosophy of the Social Sciences*, *39*(3), 463–474. doi:10.1177/0048393109334582

Leont'ev, A. N. (1978). Activity, consciousness, and personality. Englewood Cliffs, NJ: Prentice Hall.

Marshall, R. (1995). The global jobs crisis. In Foreign policy: The U.N. in crisis. Washington, DC: The Carnegie Endowment for International Peace.

Mawhinney, H. B. (1995). New institutionalism and the reinvention of schools. *Journal of Education Policy*, *10*(5), 23–42. doi:10.1080/0268093950100504

Mawhinney, H. B. (1998). Patterns of social control in assessment practices in Canadian frameworks for accountability in education. *Educational Policy*, *12*, 98–109. doi:10.1177/0895904898012001007

Mawhinney, H. B. (2003, April). *Managing the institutional dynamics of accountability.* Paper presented to the annual meeting of the American Educational Research Association, Chicago, IL.

Mawhinney, H. B., & May, J. (2010). Localism, learning, and the pressures for accountability. In R.L. Crowson & E.B. Goldring (Eds.). The New Localism in American Education. A National Society for Studies in Education Yearbook. New York: Teachers College Record.

Meyer, J. W., & Rowan, B. (1977). Institutionalized organizations: Formal structure as myth and ceremony. *American Journal of Sociology*, *83*, 294–297.

Meyer, J. W., Scott, R. W., Cole, S., & Intili, J. K. (1978). Instructional dissensus and institutional consensus in schools. In M.W. Meyer & Associates (Eds.), Environments and organizations (pp. 233-263). San Francisco: Jossey-Bass.

Miles, R. E., Snow, C. C., & Pfeffer, J. (1974). Organization-environment: Concepts and issues. *Industrial Relations*, *13*, 244–264. doi:10.1111/j.1468-232X.1974.tb00581.x

Moallem, M. (2009). Assessment of complex learning outcomes in online learning environments. In P. Rogers, G. Berg, J. Boettcher, C. Howard, L. Justice, K. Schenk (Eds.), Encyclopedia of Distance Learning (2nd Ed.) (pp. 94-102). Hershey, PA: Information Science Reference.

Nonaka, I., & Takeuchi, H. (1995). The knowledge-creating company. How Japanese companies create the dynamics of innovation. New York: Oxford University Press.

Ntshoe, I. M. (2004). Higher education and training policy and practice in South Africa:Impacts of global privatisation, quasi-marketisation and new managerialism. *International Journal of Educational Development*, *24*(2), 137–154. doi:10.1016/j.ijedudev.2003.10.006

Peters, M. (1992). Performance and accountability in 'post-industrial society: The crises of British universities. *Studies in Higher Education*, *17*, 123–139. doi:10.1080/03075079212331382617

Pfeffer, J. (1982).Organizations and organizational theory. Boston: Pitman.

Pfeffer, J. (1992). Managing with Power: Politics and Influence in Organizations. Boston: Harvard Business School Press.

Piper, D. W., & Issacs, G. (1992). *Approaches to performance related funding for higher education in Europe and North America.* A Report for the Commonwealth Department of Employment, Education and Training. The Tertiary Education Institute, The University of Queensland, October, 1992.

Roque, L., & Figueiredo, A. D. D. (2006). Context engineering for learning: A sociotechnical approach. In A. Figueiredo & A. Afonso (Eds.), Managing Learning in Virtual Settings: The Role of Context (pp. 40-61). Hershey, PA: Information Science Publishing.

Rowan, B. (1982). Organizational structure and the institutional environment: the case of public schools. *Administrative Science Quarterly*, *27*, 259–279. doi:10.2307/2392303

Schultze, U., & Boland, R. J. (2000). Knowledge management technology and the reproduction of knowledge work practices. *The Journal of Strategic Information Systems*, *9*(2-3), 193–212. doi:10.1016/S0963-8687(00)00043-3

Schultze, U., & Leidner, D. E. (2002). Studying knowledge management in information systems research: Discourses and theoretical assumptions. *MIS Quarterly*, *26*(3), 213–242. doi:10.2307/4132331

Scott, W. R. (1995). Institutions and organizations. Thousand Oaks, CA: Sage.

Scott, W. R. (2008a). Institutions and organizations: ideas and interests (3rd ed.). Thousand Oaks, CA: Sage.

Scott, W. R. (2008b). Approaching adulthood: The maturing of institutional theory. *Theoretical Sociology*, *37*, 427–442. doi:10.1007/s11186-008-9067-z

Senge, P. M. (1990). The fifth dimension: The art and practice of the learning organization. New York: Doubleday.

Shin, J. C., & Harmon, G. (2009). New challenges for higher education: Global and Asia-Pacific perspectives. *Asia Pacific Education Review*, *10*(1), 1–13. doi:10.1007/s12564-009-9011-6

Singh, J. V., & Lumsden, C. J. (1990). Theory and research in organizational ecology. *Annual Review of Sociology*, *16*, 161–195. doi:10.1146/annurev.so.16.080190.001113

Tabulawa, R. (2007). Global influences and local responses: The restructuring of the University of Botswana, 1990-2000. *Higher Education*, *53*(4), 457–482. doi:10.1007/s10734-005-4832-7

Tjosvold, D., & Tjosvold, M. M. (1994). Cooperation, competition, and constructive controversy: Knowledge to empower self-managing work teams. In M. M. Beyerlein & D. A. Johnson (Eds.), Advances in interdisciplinary studies of work teams: Vol. 1. Theories of self-managing teams. Greenwich, CT: JAI Press.

Tolbert, P. S., & Zucker, L. G. (1983). Institutional sources of change in the formal structure of organizations: the diffusion of civil service reform, 1880–1935. *Administrative Science Quarterly*, *30*, 22–39. doi:10.2307/2392383

Tuominen, M., Rajala, A., Moller, K., & Anttila, M. (2003). Assessing innovativeness through organisational adaptability: A contingency approach. *International Journal of Technology Management*.

Wagner, M., & Lamoureux, E. (2006). Implementing an outcome-based assessment portfolio. In A. Jafari (Ed.), Handbook of Research on ePortfolios (pp. 539-550). Hershey, PA: Idea Group Reference.

Weike, K. (1995). Sense-making in organizations. Thousand Oaks, CA: Sage.

Wenger, E. (1998). Communities of practice. Learning, meaning, and identity. Cambridge, UK: Cambridge University Press.

ADDITIONAL READING

Baerentsen, K. B., & Trettvik, J. (2002). An activity theory approach to affordance. *Proceedings of the second Nordic conference on human-computer interaction table of contents Aarhus, Denmark* (pp. 51-60). New York: ACM Press.

Blackler, F., & Regan, S. (2009). Intentionality, Agency, Change: Practice Theory and Management. *Management Learning*, *40*(2), 161–176. doi:10.1177/1350507608101227

Bødker, S. (1996). Applying activity theory to video analysis: how to make sense of video data in HCI. In B. Nardi (Ed.), Context and consciousness. Activity theory and human computer interaction (pp. 147-174). Cambridge, MA: MIT Press.

de Leng, B. A., Dolmans, D. H. J. M., Jobsis, R., Muijtjens, A. M. M., & van der Vleuten, C. P. M. (2009). Exploration of an e-learning model to foster critical thinking on basic science concepts during work placements. *Computers & Education*, *53*(1), 1–13. doi:10.1016/j.compedu.2008.12.012

Engeström, Y. (2001). Making expansive decisions: an activity-theoretical study of practitioners building collaborative medical care for children. In C.M. Allwood & M. Selart (Eds.), Decision Making Social and Creative Dimensions. Dordrecht, The Netherlands: Kluwer.

Engeström, Y. (2006). From well-bounded ethnographies to intervening in mycorrhizae activities. *Organization Studies*, *27*(12), 1783–1793. doi:10.1177/0170840606071898

Engeström, Y., Kerosuo, H., & Ysajamaa, A. (2007). Beyond discontinuity - Expansive organizational learning remembered. *Management Learning*, *38*(3), 319–336. doi:10.1177/1350507607079032

Isssroff, K., & Scanlon, E. (2002). Using technology in higher education: An Activity Theory perspective. *Journal of Computer Assisted Learning*, *18*(1), 77–83. doi:10.1046/j.0266-4909.2001.00213.x

Jonassen, D. H., & Rohrer-Murphy, L. (1999). Activity theory as a framework for designing constructivist learning environments. *Educational Technology Research and Development*, *47*(1), 61–79. doi:10.1007/BF02299477

Kahveci, A., Gilmer, P. J., & Southerland, S. A. (2008). Understanding chemistry professors' use of educational technologies: An activity theoretical approach. *International Journal of Science Education*, *30*(3), 325–351. doi:10.1080/09500690601188638

Kaptelinin, V. (1996). Activity theory: implications for human-computer interaction. In B. Nardi (Ed.), Context and consciousness: activity theory and human-computer interaction (pp. 45-67). Cambridge, MA: MIT press.

Mwanza, D., & Engeström, Y. (2005). Managing content in e-learning environments. *British Journal of Educational Technology*, *36*(3), 453–463. doi:10.1111/j.1467-8535.2005.00479.x

Roth, W. M., & Lee, Y. J. (2007). Vygotsky's neglected legacy: Cultural-historical activity theory. *Review of Educational Research*, *77*(2), 186–232. doi:10.3102/0034654306298273

Schultze, U., & Stabell, C. (2004). Knowing what you don't know? Discourses and contradictions in knowledge management research. *Journal of Management Studies*, *41*(4), 549–573. doi:10.1111/j.1467-6486.2004.00444.x

Scott, W. R. (2004). Reflections on a half-century of organizational sociology. *Annual Review of Sociology*, *30*, 1–21. doi:10.1146/annurev.soc.30.012703.110644

Scott, W. R. (2005). Institutional theory: contributing to a theoretical research program. In K. G. Smith, & M. A. Hitt (Eds.), Great minds in management: The process of theory development. New York: Oxford University Press.

Stevenson, I. (2008). Tool, tutor, environment or resource: Exploring metaphors for digital technology and pedagogy using activity theory. *Computers & Education*, *51*(2), 836–853. doi:10.1016/j.compedu.2007.09.001

Uden, L., Valderas, P., & Pastor, O. (2008). An activity-theory-based model to analyse Web application requirements. Information Research, 13(2), AR 340.

Van Eijck, M., & Claxton, N. X. (2008). Rethinking the notion of technology in education: Techno epistemology as a feature inherent to human praxis. *Science Education*, 220–232.

Vygotsky, L. S. (1978). Mind and society. Cambridge, MA: Harvard University Press.

KEY TERMS AND DEFINITIONS

Activity Theory: or Formally Cultural Historical Activity Theory (CHAT): Conceives human cognition and behavior as embedded in collectively organized, artifact-mediated activity systems. Activities are social practices oriented to objects.

Artifacts: In CHAT Artifacts may include those used to identify and describe objects, those used to guide and direct processes and procedures on, within, or between objects, those used to diagnose and explain the properties and behavior of objects, and those used to envision the future state or potential development of objects, including institutions and social systems.

Expansive Learning Theory: Offers a conceptual lens drawn from activity theory that focuses on the interests that organizational learning theorists have in understanding the nature of innovative learning in organizations. Expansive learning begins with individuals questioning the accepted practice, and it gradually expands into a collective movement or institutionalization.

Epistemic Actions: Are learning actions that in an ideal expansive cycle include: questioning, historical analysis, actual empirical analysis, modeling the new solution, examining the new model, implementing the new model, reflecting on the process, consolidating the new practice.

Implementation Ecology: Created through the interactions of regulative, normative and cognitive facets of accountability systems. Creates the particular conditions of legitimacy that frame the meaning of accountability systems for individuals in different organizations.

Institutions: Consist of cognitive, normative, and regulative structures and activities that provide stability and meaning to social behavior. Institutions are transported by various carriers-cultures, structures, and routines-and they operate at multiple levels of jurisdiction.

Legitimacy: A dynamic condition reflecting the cultural alignment, normative support, and consonance with relevant rules that establishes the frame of agency for individual actors, and of course thereby underscores the potential enactment of power by actors and the conflict that can follow.

Performance Assessment System: A kind of Knowledge Management System (KMS) in which aggregations of assessments of proficiencies in the performances of specified activities are used for program improvement purposes.

ENDNOTES

1. David Perkins (1995). Outsmarting I.Q.: The Emerging Science of Learnable Intelligence. New York: The Free Press. Cited in: The Council of Chief State School Officers (1996). Interstate School Leaders Licensure Consortium, Standards for School Leaders. Washington, DC: CCSSO.
2. For example, the dispositions in ISLLC Standard I state that the administrator believes in, values and is committed to: the educability of all, a school vision of high standards of learning, continuous school improvement, the inclusion of all members of the school community, ensuring that students have the knowledge, skills and values needed to become successful adults, a willingness to continuously examine one's own assumptions, beliefs, and practices, doing the work required for high levels of personal and organizational performance. These stated dispositions match the narrative describing the ELCC Standard I: This standard addresses the need to prepare educational leaders who value and are committed to educating all students to become successful adults. Each educational leader is responsible for creating and articulating a vision of high standards for learning within the school or district that can be shared by all employees and is supported by the broader school community of parents and citizens. This requires that educational leaders be willing to examine their own assumptions, beliefs, and practices; understand and apply research; and foster a climate of continuous improvement among all members of the educational staff. Such educational leaders will commit themselves to high levels of personal and organizational

performance in order to ensure implementation of this vision of learning.

[3] The Council of Chief State School Officers (1996). Interstate School Leaders Licensure Consortium, Standards for School Leaders. (p. 8). Washington, DC: CCSSO

APPENDIX A

Master of Arts (MA) in Education Leadership Leading to Administrator I Certification

Candidates for the Master of Arts degree leading to Administrator I certification must complete a 39-credit program of study. The program includes course work and internship activities that enable candidates to develop knowledge, skills, and dispositions associated with all seven ELCC Standards, and with TSSA Standards. Courses offer opportunities for candidates to demonstrate the awareness, understanding, and capabilities associated with the Basic Level of Proficiency (BLP) that the Department expects candidates to demonstrate by completion of their program. The Department's philosophy of preparation emphasizes the use of bridging experiences between theory and practice. Many of these experiences are framed as course assignments, however, all candidates must also complete ongoing and capstone internships to meet the requirements of ELCC Standard 7 for substantial, sustained, standards-based, intern activities that take place in real settings and are planned and guided cooperatively. Candidates for the MA program also complete a seminar paper demonstrating their knowledge, skills and dispositions related to an element of one of the ELCC or TSSA Standards.

Post-Masters Coursework in the Master of Arts in Education Leadership for Administrator I Certification

In addition to those students enrolling in degree programs, a number of individuals also utilize a set of courses in EDEL's MA in Education Leadership to meet the special certification requirements for those holding Masters degrees in areas other than in Educational Leadership for Administrator I (leading to principal certification). These requirements were established by the state some years ago and remain in the state's regulations. Individual's who hold a Master's degree from an accredited institution and have at least 27 months (3 years) of satisfactory teaching experience may complete 18 credits of additional course work in the Master of Arts program in Education Leadership and submit transcripts directly to the State Department of Educationfor Administrator I certification review.

Doctor of Education. in Educational Leadership Leading to Superintendent Certification

The Ed.D in Leadership is designed to prepare educators for school district leadership positions. Graduates of the program are eligible to apply for superintendent certification. Candidates must have completed requirements for Administrator 1 Certification (school building leadership) prior to completion of this program. The program was designed in consultation with education leaders including superintendents in the state. It consists of coursework, performance assessments, a comprehensive examination, and a dissertation. The program is offered in both off campus cohorts and on campus, and is structured to enable students to complete course requirements in four years. Each of the program components is described below:

Course Work: Candidates will complete coursework that focuses on fostering and developing in candidates' dispositions, and awareness, understanding and capabilities associated with the ELCC

Standards for Educational Leadership. They will take a minimum of 30 credit hours in core courses, a minimum of 9 credit hours in research and analytic methods, a minimum of 6 credit hours in internship, and a minimum of 10 credit hours in dissertation research for a total minimum of 55 credit hours. Work in these areas is intended to enable candidates to improve their capacity to collect and analyze data, to apply theory and research to practice, and to engage in independent research on topics of particular interest to them as they complete the requirements for Basic Level of Proficiency in indicators of school district leadership.

Assessment of Performances Developing Proficiency in (ELCC) Indicators of School District Leadership: Candidates will use a web-based performance assessment system throughout their program of study to create individual electronic portfolios recording assessments of performance activities and demonstrating their development of BLP in indicators of school district leadership. This electronic system will allow candidates to show how their coursework activities, capstone internship, and field experiences fulfill the performance requirements of the program. The Internship Coordinator will monitor this portion of the program providing the candidates with consistent and focused attention on the integration of theory and practice.

Comprehensive Examination: The comprehensive exams are designed by faculty to help students make progress toward competing their dissertations. The comprehensive exams for this program will take the form of three substantive literature reviews in which candidates integrate information from courses and independent readings that they and their advisors have identified as critical to the development of their dissertations.

Doctoral Dissertation: Candidates will develop a theoretically anchored, carefully designed study of an important topic in education. They will work with their advisors to identify areas of special interest and to develop proposals for their studies. Candidates will work with their advisors and doctoral dissertation committee to complete this study.

Appendix B

ELCC Program Criteria

1. Curricula are designed in an integrated or problem-based mode to promote an understanding of the connectedness of the various knowledge and skill areas in educational leadership.
2. Instructional emphasis is placed on those methods and materials that anticipate learner performance in the workplace.
3. Appropriate adult learning strategies are broadly used.
4. Programs include: (a) the acquisition of concepts and information, (b) the integration of concepts with practice and use of knowledge in context, and (c) the application of knowledge and skills in a workplace environment.
5. Bridging experiences are conducted between course content and the workplace that feature clinical exercises and/or field settings.
6. All candidates are required to have performance experiences in all standards as well as an extensive internship that requires the synthesis and application of appropriate knowledge and skills represented in the standard.
7. Opportunities are provided for candidates to formulate and examine an ethical platform upon which to rely for tough decisions.

8. A quality assurance process is used for candidate preparation, including (a) plans for, and use of, multiple measures to capture various proficiencies of candidates called for in the standards, (b) plans and/or accomplishments under continuing efforts to assure credibility - accuracy, consistency, fairness, and avoidance of bias – of the assessment and evaluation system, and (c) plans for using, or regular use of, assessment results to evaluate and improve programs and teaching.
9. A program self-evaluation process that focuses on perceived program strengths and deviations for the ELCC standards.

Chapter 13
Beyond the Books:
Building Community and Promoting Student Retention in Online Learning Environments

Carolyn Stevenson
Kaplan University, USA

ABSTRACT

Retention of online students is a topic of special interest in higher education. Research shows that the highest percentage of students failing or withdrawing from classes occurs the first term. There is no panacea to retaining and motivating online students. A collaborative effort by instructors, administrators, and students is needed to promote student success the first term and beyond. Building community involves fostering relationships grounded in common interests and is critical to academic success and student retention. Student activities such as clubs and organizations create a bond between student and the institution. This case study will discuss strategies for retaining and motivating online students. Topics include: curriculum initiatives, student mentoring and peer coaching, academic services for poor-performing students, community building through online student activities and websites, promotion of socialization while learning at a distance, and ideas for working with faculty on promoting student success from admissions to graduation.

ORGANIZATION BACKGROUND

The virtual university described in this case, which was formed from three existing colleges, was founded in 1937. In November 2000, the name of the College was changed and became a University in 2004. The University offers online master's, bachelor's, and associate's degrees, as well as certificate programs. Graduates receive comprehensive education through disciplined, professional programs of instruction.

The University was founded to provide professional business training and has achieved this objective for over 70 years by keeping abreast of employment demands, employer needs, teaching methods, and the use of various educational resources and industry-standard technology and equipment.

DOI: 10.4018/978-1-61520-909-5.ch013

As stated in the University catalog, the University recognizes the worth and dignity of all people and is sensitive to the diversity of cultural and ethnic backgrounds represented in its student population. All students are encouraged to reach their potential within the framework of their individual needs, interests, and capabilities. The University employs instructional methods based on adult learning theory and is committed to the development of each student's intellectual, analytical, and critical thinking abilities. Teaching techniques encourage active student participation and may include group discussions and projects, laboratory work, simulations, demonstrations, field trips, guest speakers, and lectures.

The University catalog states that a strong emphasis is placed on ethics, accountability, professionalism, and the individual's commitment to pursuing lifelong personal and professional development. The University helps students reach their educational goals by providing them with the communication skills necessary to work successfully with clients and other professionals, offering courses that prepare them to successfully participate in society, equipping them with the business knowledge necessary to succeed in the "real world," and encouraging them to become involved in professional organizations that will promote their learning and professional skills.

As stated in the University catalog, the University's online platform is supported by a large farm of Web servers configured redundantly to generally assure uninterrupted, around-the-clock operation. Degree program and certificate courses are taught by qualified professors and administered by a unique high-performance, multi-user database management system. The attractively designed class pages encourage student involvement and interaction, and the system facilitates text-based class discussions based on professor commentaries, readings, Web field trips, and other assignments.

CASE DESCRIPTION

Technology Concerns

The major technology concerns are related to incorporating new media as a means for promoting student retention through community building activities. Use of podcasts, interactive presentations, and other collaborative tools such as Facebook and Twitter would allow additional means of communication for students not involved directly in a specific club or organization.

Emerging technologies that should be considered for this case include online collaborative spaces, mobile devices, and social networking tools. Webware suites such as Zoho Office (www.zoho.com) and Google Docs (www.Google.com) provide a way to offer collaborative content without software installation. Social networks such as Ning (www.ning.com) provide opportunities to share resources, exchange information, and provide an opportunity for socialization beyond the boundaries of the online classroom.

While a number of new media options exist, the challenge lies in training students, faculty, and student advisors on using the technology. Additionally, since the majority of the student population is adult learners, ease and promotion of use needs to occur.

Technology Components

At the present time, the major form of technology use for communicating in the student clubs and organizations is through the online platform. A separate "course" or student community site, has been established for each club and organization. Included in the student community site are: an announcement section for posting information and announcing upcoming events, an asynchronous discussion board area that allows discussion with other members, a live chat feature for hosting student-led meetings, and information on the organization, current topics, and careers in the discipline.

The student clubs and organizations also periodically host special conferences held via Adobe Connect which allow participants to hear the speaker as well as view PowerPoint presentations. Additionally, the interactive feature of Adobe Connect allows for participants to ask questions and discuss information via a live chat feature.

Management and Organizational Concerns

Successful student retention reaches beyond the blackboard, and involves recognizing students' individual learning styles and abilities; the special needs of adult learners such as balancing work and family issues, time management skills, and organizational skills; and providing resources within the curriculum to support the needs of online students. In addition to traditional core curriculum requirements, institutions of higher learning need to offer academic support services such as orientation seminars to help students engage in courses their first term. Additional student support services such as tutoring and mentoring also contribute to enhancing the first-term experience and to promotion of student success.

While reports reveal a trend in the growth in student enrollment in online learning degree programs, several studies have found that the retention rate for students learning in an online format is lower than students enrolled in traditional face-to-face degree programs (Nash, 2005; O'Brien & Reneer, 2002; Scalese 2001). Car (2000) also found that course completion rates in online courses were often 10-20 percentage points lower than that of traditional courses. One tool that may have been useful in identifying factors contributing to lower student retention rates in these cases would have been pre-admissions assessment testing. Pre-admissions assessment tests allow for identification of potential challenges contributing to academic success. Identifying these challenges early allows the opportunity to provide students with the support needed for academic success.

There have been several studies conducted on the need for pre-admissions testing for online students (Lozenzetti, 2005; Maki & Maki, 2003). Kidder (2004) found that 48% of faculty surveyed noted that pre-assessment of student's technological skills was not present, but that pre-assessment was important to academic success in online courses. Of the faculty surveyed, a total of 77% reported pre-assessment is important, while 29% reported that pre-assessment testing was used at their institutions (Maki & Maki, 2003).

A growing number of higher education institutions have seen the value of student community building and providing academic support and are devoting more resources to assist second-year students succeed on campus (Lipka, 2006). The researchers commented that the results of these initiatives are too new to effectively report on the impact on student retention. However, Azusa Pacific University reported that since implementing student support and activities, student retention from the sophomore to junior year did increase by 8%, up from 80% to 88% during the period 2000-2006 (Lipka, 2006).

Research conducted by Ackerman and Schibrowsky (2007) found that quality and availability of student support services influenced student decisions to purse degree completion. In their study, the researchers found that involvement in student activities linked them to the institution and to other students. These components increased student satisfaction and increased student persistence to graduation (Ackerman and Schibrowsky, 2007).

Although the above-mentioned research was based on information relating to traditional onground institutions, the concepts of building community, providing academic support, and connecting students to the institution relates to distance education. Students learning at a distance do not meet face-to-face with instructors and other students. Therefore, gaining a connection to the institution is critical to student success and persistence to gradation.

Despite the fact that students are at a distance, there are numerous student organizations that can be implemented based on interest and application to the specific degree program. Belonging to a student organization promotes leadership through officer positions, committee membership, and event planning. Student organizations also help create a bond with students having similar interests and strengths. Meetings for student activities can be held in teleconference format or in a student community classroom via live chat. Since implementation of the clubs and organizations offered by the University discussed in this case study are relatively new initiatives beginning in 2007, reporting on the full impact on student retention cannot be clearly defined. Additionally, it is difficult to quantify the impact of student involvement in community building and academic support initiatives. Since multiple retention efforts and community building programs are in place, contributing student success to one initiative or another cannot be qualified. Rather, it is through multiple initiatives, both social and academic, that assist in retaining students from admission to graduation.

COMMUNITY BUILDING AND RETENTION INITIATIVES

Academic Coaching and Peer Mentoring

Adult learners are challenged with balancing multiple responsibilities including work, family, social obligations, and college. While the online format offers students flexibility and convenience of access, instructors are faced with the challenges of promoting a sense of community to learners at a distance (Ammendolia 2006). Research from Smucny & Humber (2009) found that online students and faculty may feel isolated from the greater university community. To be academically successful, online students need to be technologically competent, require instructor and classmates' interaction, and need strong social support to attain their educational goals (Dabbagh 2007, Liu 2007, Seckel 2007). Providing this strong academic and social support can be a challenge when not meeting face-to-face. However, through employing community building initiatives such as those discussed in the following paragraphs can assist in improving connection to the university as well as assist in promoting student success.

Academic coaching and peer mentoring programs provide intensive coaching and mentoring in a student's first two terms at the University. The focus of these programs is to prepare students to be academically and personally self-sufficient, more adept at solving and preventing barriers to education, and to be better positioned for greater and consistent academic success as they move through the first two terms and into the remainder of the degree program. The ultimate measure of success is demonstration of a higher retention rate of students into their third term than is presently the case. A core element of the academic coaching program includes weekly conversations between coaches and students. Discussions center on the following areas:

- Learning about the student: motivation, goals, ambitions, barriers (real, perceived, and potential);
- Helping students navigate academic and other University-imposed expectations and deadlines. Devising time-management plans and other discipline-building tools and practices;
- Pre-empting barriers to progress through degree program, helping students to identify and implement solutions (ahead of time, as possible);
- Providing ongoing affirmations of student success, as well as firm guidance in areas of low performance.

Peer mentoring is a program offered by the University which provides first-term students with the opportunity to ask questions from a student who "has been through the process." Peer mentors participate in new student orientation training courses and live seminars. The peer mentor offers tips for surviving and thriving the first-term of college, time management skills, study skills, and organizational tips. Qualitative comments from peer mentors reveal that students often feel more comfortable discussing issues with peer mentors than with instructors. Since the peer mentor has had the authentic experience of pursing a college first-hand, other students feel a stronger connection to the peer mentor. In addition to academic concerns, students also discuss challenges faced by adult learners including balance work, college, and family; fears about returning to college after a number of years being out of school; and technology concerns related to learning at a distance.

Curriculum Initiatives

In addition to community building activities, academic support and curriculum initiatives should be in place to support academic readiness for college. Reaching beyond traditional core curriculum requirements, institutions of higher learning need to offer support services such as new student orientations to prepare students for their first term. Student support services such as tutoring and peer mentoring also contribute to enhancing the first-term experience and to promotion of retention.

Diversity in the level of student academic readiness is a challenge faced by the University. The student population is mainly adult learners that range from high-performing students to students academically challenged. In an effort to provide the most appropriate track for academic studies, pre-admissions testing was implemented in 2008. Prior to admissions into the University, students must take an entrance assessment based on a modified Wonderlic test. Cut-off scores were developed to ensure students meet a minimum score for admission into the University. Failure to meet this cut-off score results in denial for acceptance into the University.

Students meeting or exceeding the minimum cut-off scores for admission testing are placed into one of three tracks for academic study. These tracks are:

- Students falling into a low testing score range are placed into Foundation courses. Foundation courses are designed to assist students in strengthening their reading and writing skills.
- Students falling into a medium testing score range are placed into Traditional courses. The Traditional courses follow the sequence of first-term classes as outlined by the degree program.
- Students falling into a high testing score range are encouraged to participate in the Honors track. The Honors program provides a more academically rigorous approach to courses outlined by the degree program.

The following Foundations courses are available for students with low pre-admissions assessment scores:

- *Introduction to Reading Skills and Strategies:* Students will be introduced to reading techniques designed to increase comprehension and retention of informational texts. Students will develop a skills set to increase their vocabulary, word recognition, and contextual understanding. These skills will be introduced, implemented, and honed in this class so students can apply them to all future coursework increasing their reading effectiveness when reading scholastic material.
- *Introduction to Writing Skills and Strategies*: This course will review basic

skills in grammar and mechanics, spelling, and written expression in order to prepare students for success in College Composition I and subsequent courses. Students will be introduced to the writing process and will implement each step of the process, developing a personal writing process to fulfill specific writing tasks. In addition, students will examine the importance of peer review and revision in improving written expression.

- *Introduction to Math Skills and Strategies*: Students will review basic math skills and be introduced to foundational concepts in algebra. Students will develop a skills set to increase their understanding of mathematical operations and to increase their ability to solve problems accurately. These skills will be introduced, implemented, and honed in this class so students can apply them to all future coursework.

Academic Support

In addition to the Foundations courses, other retention efforts are in place to ensure academic readiness for college. Outreach to students is conduced by both instructors and advisors. Poor performing students develop a Student Personal Improvement Plan. This plan outlines strategies for succeeding in the course and describes the steps needed for improving class performance. Phone calls are made to both individuals and groups of students to discuss academic strategies and ways to promote strong academic performance.

The University provides an Academic Success Center (ASC). The ASC provides a network of support for students, including those identified as at risk of academic failure or in need of learner readiness support. The ASC encourages, guides, and supports all students—including those who may be struggling academically.

Online tutoring services, including live tutors, are available for all students. The Math Center has live tutors to help students with math related topics. For instance, there are Algebra modules so that students can practice algebra before beginning the Algebra class. Tutors are also available to assist students with thc modules.

The Writing Center has live tutors that can help students with papers for any class. Tutors are available for paper submission, correction, and general questions about the writing format used in classes.

The University also offers NetTutor and SmartThinking services as a means for providing additional academic support to students. NetTutor is available for some of the classes. The service has helpful sessions that run in conjunction with the lessons students learn each week. SmarThinking is a one-on-one session with a private tutor for some of the classes. Through SmarThinking, students may turn in papers for review, meet with a private tutor at the time of the student's choice, and have access to other information regarding support in classes.

Additional academic student support is available via the Online Library. The virtual library provides access to academic journals, articles, and eBooks. Also listed on the student portal are study tips and tools links designed to help students refresh their academic skills. For students with special needs, an Office of Disability Services is available to assist students with classroom support.

Honors Programs

An Honors Program is available for academically strong students. The School of Health Sciences and College of Arts and Sciences Honors Program contribute to excellence in education by enriching and enhancing the degree programs of qualified students. The Honors Program emphasizes critical thinking, leadership, and communication skills in both professional and academic arenas. To this end, the Honors Program promotes intellectual and personal development through curricular and co-curricular initiatives. Ultimately, the School of Health Sciences and College of Arts and Sciences Honors Program reflect the University's stated missions of commitment to general education, applied scholarship, and student-centered service and support.

Application to the School of Health Sciences and College of Arts and Sciences Honors Program is voluntary and qualification is based on evidence of academic achievement and leadership potential. The School of Health Science and College of Arts and Science Honors Program is an option for online students only.

Criteria for students to enter the Arts & Sciences Honors Program include the following:

- Arts & Health Sciences Major.
- Minimum 3.5/4.0 cumulative GPA.
- Candidates must maintain at least a cumulative GPA of 3.5 to remain in the Honors Program.
- Successful completion of an Honors Program application.
- Completion of 2nd term at the University.
- Honors students and candidates for the Honors Program must be in good standing with the University.
- Students reprimanded for an academic violation such as plagiarism, inappropriate behavior or communication will be immediately removed from the Honors Program.

In addition to academically challenging courses, there is a service component involved with the Honors Program. The service component of the School of Health Sciences and College of Arts and Sciences Honors Program provides students with valuable real-world experience and skills applications as they share their talents with others. Students participate in at least one service project per year.

Community Building through Online Clubs and Organizations

Creating online clubs and organizations helps to promote student collaboration and connectivity to both peers and the University. There are clubs and organizations designed specifically for Arts & Health Sciences students and University-wide clubs and organizations.

Additionally, a student website and other social networking tools can be used to foster community beyond the classroom. For example, the student community website provides students with an area for housing information ranging from career information to activities at the institution. Students can find interesting spotlights, feature articles and more information on clubs, conference calls, and events at the University by going to the "Arts and Sciences" Community Site.

Use of Second Life promotes community building through creating another means of student communication. Use of audio also creates a stronger connection between students. In Second Life, students can attend conferences on topics such as study skills, time management, and other academic and professional topics. Study sessions and real-time tutoring can also occur via this format.

Student organizations create a bond with students having similar interests and strengths. Meetings for student activities can be held via teleconference or in a student community classroom via live chat. The student community classrooms at the University provide a space for students to engage in dialog through discussion threads; provide information through a resources section; post announcements for upcoming events; and allow students to hold meetings via live chat. Following are a list of student online clubs and organizations offered by the University:

- *Book Club*: Students meet for discussions of bestselling books.

- *OWLS Roost*: A Non-Traditional Students Club.
- *Psychology Club*: Psychology students are eligible to participate in activities related to the field of Psychology.
- *ToastMasters*: Information about joining a local chapter to improve student public speaking skills.
- *Walking Club*: The U.S. Department of Health and Human Services offers a challenge to take steps toward improving physical and mental health. Students log in and track the number of steps taken in a day.
- *Educator's Club*: A club designed for student majoring in Educational Paraprofessional or Early Childhood Development programs.
- *Women in Communications*: A student chapter of the Association of Women in Communication, a national, professional organization. This club is open to Communication majors who meet specific eligibility requirements.
- *NCA Student Club*: Communication degree-seeking students are invited to join the University chapter of the National Communication Association Student Club.
- *AHDI*: The University Educational Chapter of AHDI is a Medical Transcription professional organization.

Student clubs and organizations link University students to peers that share their academic and career interests. Whether students are already involved or are just investigating some of the resources that the University offers, the mission is to expose students to numerous professional and social opportunities available as they strive to achieve the goal of academic success. Following is a list of clubs and organizations available to all University students.

- *Collegiate Entrepreneur's Organization*: The Collegiate Entrepreneurs' Organization informs, supports, and inspires college students to be entrepreneurial and seek opportunities through enterprise. This organization only accepts business students.
- *Association for Computing Machinery*: The Association for Computing Machinery is committed to advancing the skills of information technology professionals and students worldwide. This organization only accepts IT students.
- *Gamma Chi Theta*: Gamma Chi Theta is devoted to the furtherance of professionalism in all areas of business while instilling the value of community service through charitable endeavors.
- *Paralegal Club*: The University Paralegal Club offers professional development and networking opportunities, paralegal-based activities, and paralegal resources.
- *American Criminal Justice Association—Lambda Alpha Epsilon*: This national association is devoted to the furtherance of professionalism in all areas of criminal justice. Those who join receive memberships in the national association as well as the local chapter.
- *Student Accounting Association*: The University Student Accounting Association offers professional development and networking opportunities, accounting and financial-based activities, and accounting and financial news.
- *Ambassadors & Leaders*: The Ambassadors and Leaders Program provides students in the MBA and MSM program(s) to experience leadership experiences and personal growth through mentoring and representing the Graduate School to the public.

The University also offers a number of Honors Societies for students meeting eligibility requirements. The University strives to recognize outstanding students who excel academically; therefore, the University offers students the opportunity to join prestigious societies that promote academic achievement as well as active leadership. Following is a listing of University Honors Societies:

- *Alpha Beta Kappa Honor Society*: Alpha Beta Kappa is a national academic honor society that recognizes college students that have excelled in academics. Membership in the society is open to all students and by invitation only.
- *Golden Key International Honor Society*: Golden Key is an international academic honor society that recognizes and encourages scholastic achievement and active leadership among students from all academic disciplines. Membership in the society is by invitation only.
- *Sigma Beta Delta Honor Society*: Sigma Beta Delta is a national academic honor society that recognizes college students that have excelled in academics. Membership in the society is open to business students and by invitation only.
- *Kappa Lambda Honors Society in Paralegal Studies*: The Kappa Lambda Honors Society in Paralegal Studies is an exclusive University organization composed of legal studies students.
- *Kappa Delta Pi Honor Society*: Kappa Delta Pi Honor Society is open to students enrolled in the University's School of Teacher Education programs who meet the eligibility requirements.
- *Iota Sigma Tau*: Iota Sigma Tau is an honor society established by the University to recognize college students that have excelled in academics. Membership is open to IT students by invitation only.
- *Kappa Delta Pi Honors Society*: Kappa Delta Pi Honor Society – Alpha Epsilon Alpha Chapter 697 is open to students enrolled in the University's School of Teacher Education programs who meet the eligibility requirements.

Results

The initiatives discussed above are in a pilot stage and at the time of publication, the outcomes have not been fully analyzed but will be available in the near future. Additionally, it is difficult to point to one single factor in improving successful increase in retention. Preliminary data has shown both academic and student community initiatives positively affect student success.

CURRENT CHALLENGES FACING THE ORGANIZATION

In a virtual setting where students do not meet face-to-face, academic support services are more difficult to provide. However, with creative planning and efforts from all faculty, administrators, and other members of the online community, a sense of community can be fostered in the virtual learning setting.

Despite numerous outreach efforts and attempts to create a collaborative learning environment, overall retention rate at the University is still around 72%. There is no panacea for 100% student retention in an online setting. However, through community building efforts, outreach, academic support services, and innovative curriculum the University strives continuously to improve student success.

Another challenge facing the University is the adult learner population. On one hand, adult learners can be seen as focused, determined, and serious about achieving a college degree. On the other, adult learners often have additional responsibilities related to balancing work, family, and college. This "juggling act" can be stressful and affect strong academic performance.

The majority of students taking courses at a distance are adult learners, bringing with them a series of attributes and challenges that need to be discussed. The population of students discussed in this case is adult learners, with the average age of 35. Characteristics of the population include:

- Usually older
- Female
- Full time employees/caregivers
- Parents/grandparents
- Disabled
- Military
- Often do not have supportive environments
- May be first-generation college-bound
- May not have family support
- May have financial hardships

A survey of the students enrolled at the University found several challenges facing adult learners in a distance learning environment. Listed below are the top challenges faced by the student population:

- Balancing work and family issues
- Concern about financing education
- Poor time management skills
- Self-esteem issues related to returning to college and academic success
- Lack of support
- Anxiety related to being out of school for some time
- Technology-related fears
- Poor study skills/habits

The student demographics will continue to remain similar. While there are more "traditional age" (ages 18-22) students enrolling in the University, marketing efforts are geared toward the working adult. Although adult learners may not be seen as necessity a challenge to the University, efforts for engaging this population continue to be made.

SOLUTIONS AND RECOMMENDATIONS

Providing additional instruction in working with virtual teams is one recommendation for fostering collaboration at a distance. Be it in involvement in clubs or the classrooms, working collaboratively creates a stronger connection to the classroom and the University community. Additionally, skills learned while working in virtual teams reach beyond the classroom into the world of work.

Collaboration with others is part of living and working in the social world. Much of our daily communication occurs in groups such as our family, co-workers, friends, and classmates. Regardless of career choice, it is likely that students will spend a considerable part of their life and work collaborating with others. Virtual teams are growing in importance as companies become more geographically diverse and more employees are working in off-site locations. The key to successful virtual teams is learning to communicate effectively while working at a distance.

A short overview of business surveys reveals that teams may be one of the most often used communication methods within organizations.

- It is estimated that by 2010 over 75% of the U.S. workforce will work in teams of some sort (Shockley-Zalabak, 2006, p.202).
- A global, cross-functional team successfully designed the website for GE Global eX-change Services "so it would have the same simple, intuitive-looking feel in English, French, Spanish, German, and Italian (Williams, 2007, p.317). Today the website (gxs.com) is used successfully in 58 countries.
- Team suggestions at a Cleveland Maytag plant caused production to double, yearly production costs to drop by $7 million, and required on-hand inventory to drop by a $10 million (Williams, 2003).

- Rubbermaid created 20 cross-functional teams of five to seven people to develop new products. In one year the teams developed over 365 new products. The problem now is not finding innovative products ideas, but deciding which new product ideas to select (Jones, 2007).
- At Honeywell's Industrial Automation and Control plant in Phoenix, Arizona, quality control decision by employee teams lowered defect rates by 70% (Daft and Marcic, 2006).
- Florida Power & Light Company used teams to guild a nuclear power plant in an unbelievably fast six years. For example, because of the work teams, "a slip-forming technique was developed for pouring concrete around the clock, allowing the 3-foot thick, 190-foot-tall concrete shell to be finished in just 17 days, compared with a year for other power companies" (Daft, 1995, pp. 199-200).

Effective and appropriate communication is vital to working in virtual teams. Listed below are a few strategies for promoting effective communication in both the classroom as well as in student clubs and organizations:

- *Channels for Communication*: Communication systems need to be established that encourage ideas, questions, and concerns to be directed to the team members. Methods for virtual communication in teams include email, instant messenger, discussion forums, Web-based meetings (such as through Adobe Connect), blogs, live chats, and teleconferencing.
- *Virtual team member roles*: A virtual team needs to be organized around a set of team roles and responsibilities. Roles need to be created that address both the talent and interest of the team members. The roles must also take into account the work distribution by each member. An equal amount of work and responsibility needs to be established among the various roles.
- *Clear instructions*: One of the challenges for individuals working in virtual teams is the anxiety often associated with group work. A student may have had negative experiences working in groups and teams and bring this anxiety in the project. It is important to clearly provide instructions for group roles which outline a timeline for completion and expectations so that members of the group will understand the steps required for completion of the project and a reassurance of equal distribution of the workload.
- *Managing conflict*: Conflict is sure to arise in virtual teams. Guidelines need to be established within the virtual teams for working with group members when conflict occurs. At appropriate times, the group leader may be required to intervene to resolve group conflict.
- *Communicate respect*: Communicate respect to each other by acknowledging group members comments. Provide a direct response elaborating on what someone else has said. Be polite and let everyone talk during live chats. Take turns sharing information. The group leader should ask if the team is ready to move on to a new topic and wait for acknowledgement.
- *Stay on topic during group chats*: When the group members stay on the subject at hand it refrains from the possibility of miscommunication. The designated agenda items can also be covered in a timely manner.
- *Be an active listener*: Listen actively and pay attention to the conversation at hand. It is important to remain open-minded and respect everyone's ideas.
- *Ensure all voices are heard*: During an online discussion, one detrimental group

practice is when one participant dominates the conversation. This does not allow for proper group dynamics since participation is not balanced. If one person controls the group it becomes a biased project. When each person in a group agrees to unite and work together, the group becomes perhaps the most effective force it can be--a team.

As our global workplace is becoming increasing smaller and more diverse, more organizations are incorporating virtual teams into their work groups. As such, it is critical that students have prior knowledge working in virtual teams before entering the workplace. A sense of community needs to be embraced following the guidelines of effective communication to ensure that every voice is heard in the virtual team.

Upon review of the success factors related to community building and retention, the data is not complete. The majority of the activities, student support services, and outreach efforts are slightly over two years running. Building a sense of community does foster connection to the University and to other students. It is through a combination of efforts that the University strives to not only attract talent, but retain students from the admissions point to degree completion. It is recommended that community building activities remain in place and additional qualitative and quantitative data be gathered.

REFERENCES

Ackerman, R., & Schibrowsky, J. (2007). A business marketing strategy applied to student retention: A higher education initiative. *Journal of College Student Retention*, *9*(3), 307–356. doi:10.2190/CS.9.3.d

Ammendolia, M. A. (2006 June). The Instructor's Challenge: Helping Newbies. *Online Classroom,* 1-8.

Carr, S. (2000). As distance education comes of age, the challenge is keeping the students. *The Chronicle of Higher Education*, A39.

Dabbagh, N. (2007). The Online Learner: Characteristics and Pedagogical Implications. *Contemporary Issues in Technology & Teacher Education*, *7*, 217–226.

Daft, R. I. (2006).Understanding management (5th ed.). Mason, OH: Thompson South-Western.

Jones, G. R. (2007). Introduction to Business: How companies create value for people. New York: McGraw-Hill.

Kidder, M. L. (2004). Institutional elements that encourage or discourage the implementation of on-line classes in Illinois community colleges (Doctoral dissertation, Northern Illinois University, 2004). *Dissertation Abstracts International-A 65,* (05). (UMI No. 3132423).

Lipka, S. (2006). After the freshmen bubble pop: More colleges try to help their sophomores thrive. *The Chronicle of Higher Education*, *53*(3), A34.

Lorenzetti, J. P. (2005). Secrets of online success: Lessons learned from community colleges. *Distance Education Report*, *9*(11), 3–6.

Maki, R. H., & Maki, W. S. (2003). Prediction of learning and satisfaction in web-based and lecture courses. *Journal of Educational Computing Research*, *28*, 197–219. doi:10.2190/DXJU-7HGJ-1RVP-Q5F2

Seckel, S. (2007). Characteristics and Responsibilities of Successful e-Learners. *Journal of Instruction Delivery Systems*, *21*, 22–26.

Shockley-Zalabak, P. (2006). Fundamentals of organizational communication (6th ed.). Boston, MA: Allyn & Bacon.

Smucny, D.A., & Humber, K. (2009). Building Global Community for Online Students and Faculty. *Footnotes, 37*(3).

Williams, C. (2003). Management (2nd ed.). Mason, OH: South-Western.

Williams, C. (2007). Management (4th ed.). Mason, OH: South-Western.

ADDITIONAL READING

Andrews, H. (2003). Higher education studies, reports, and surveys in the SREB States. Atlanta, GA: Southern Regional Educational Board. (ERIC Document Reproduction Service No. ED481866).

Ashby, C. M. (2003). *College completion: Additional efforts could help education with its completion goals*. Report to congressional requesters (Report No. GAO-03-568). Washington, DC: General Accounting Office. (ERIC Document Reproduction Service No. ED478814).

Bailey, T., Alfonso, M., Calcagno, J. C., Jenkins, D., Kienzl, G., & Leinbach, T. (2004). Improving student attainment in community colleges: Institutional characteristics and policies. New York, NY: Community College Research Center, Teachers College, Columbia University. (ERIC Document Reproduction Service No. ED 484346).

Bailey, T., Calcagno, J. C., Jenkins, D., Kienzl, G., & Leinbach, T. (2005). The effects of institutional factors on the success of community college students. New York, NY: Community College Research Center, Teachers College, Columbia University. (ERIC Document Reproduction Service No. ED484345).

Battaglini, J. K. (2004). Retention and graduation rates at Maryland public four-year institutions. Annapolis, MD: Maryland Higher Education Commission. (ERIC Document Reproduction Service No. ED484153).

Belch, H. A. (2004). Retention and students with disabilities. *Journal of College Student Retention Research Theory and Practice*, *6*, 3–22. doi:10.2190/MC5A-DHRV-1GHM-N0CD

Drouin, M. A. (2008). The relationship between students' perceived sense of community and satisfaction, achievement, and retention in an online course. *The Quarterly Review of Distance Education*, *9*(3), 267–284.

Dunn, H., & Mays, A. (2004). Improving student success, not just increasing retention rates. *Community College Times*, *16*(24), 7.

Fetzner, M. J. (2003). Institutional support for online faculty: Expanding the model. In J. Bourne & J. C. Moore (Eds.), Elements of Quality Online Education: Practice and Direction (Vol. 4, pp. 229 – 244).

Gaide, S. (2004). Community college identifies student expectations as key element in online retention. *Distance Education Report*, 4 – 6.

Habley, W. R. (2000). Current practices in academic advising. In V. N. Gordon, W. R. Habley et al. (Eds.), Academic advising: A comprehensive handbook (pp. 35-43). San Francisco, CA: Jossey-Bass.

Kidder, M. L. (2004). Institutional elements that encourage or discourage the implementation of on-line classes in Illinois community colleges (Doctoral dissertation, Northern Illinois University, 2004). *Dissertation Abstracts International-A 65* (05). (UMI No. 3132423).

Kuh, G. D., & Love, P. G. (2000). A cultural perspective on student departure. In J.M. Braxton (Ed.), Reworking the student departure puzzle (pp. 196-213). Nashville, TN: Vanderbilt University Press.

Light, R. J. (2001). Making the most of college: Students speak their minds. Cambridge, MA: Harvard University Press.

Liu, S., Gomez, J., Khan, B., & Yen, C. (2007). Toward a learner-oriented community college online course dropout framework. *International Journal on E-Learning*, *6*(4), 519–542.

Lotkowski, V. A., Robbins, S. B., & Noeth, R. J. (2004). The role of academic and non-academic factors in improving college retention. Washington, DC: ACT policy report. (ERIC Document Reproduction Service No. ED485476).

Martinez, P. (2001). Improving student retention and achievement: What do we know and what do we need to find out? LSDA Reports. London, England: Learning and Skills and Development Agency. (ERIC Document Reproduction Service No. ED465898).

Moore, J. C., Sener, J., & Fetzner, M. (2006 July). Getting Better: ALN and Student Success. *Journal of Asynchronous Learning Networks (JALN), 10*(3). Retrieved April 6, 2009, from http://www.sloanc.org/publications/jaln/v10n3/v10n3_6moore_member.asp

Rendon, L. I., Jalomo, R. E., & Nora, A. (2000). Theoretical considerations in the study of minority student retention in higher education. In J. M. Braxton (Ed.), Reworking the student departure puzzle (pp. 127-153). Nashville, TN: Vanderbilt University Press.

Shea, P., Li, C. S., Swan, K., & Pickett, A. (2005). Developing learning community in online asynchronous college courses: The role of teaching presence. [JALN]. *Journal of Asynchronous Learning Networks*, *9*(4).

Swail, W. S., Redd, K. E., & Perna, L. W. (2003). Retaining minority students in higher education: A framework for success. San Francisco: Jossey-Bass.

Warburton, E. C., Bugarin, R., & Nunez, A. M. (2001). Bridging the gap: Academic preparation and postsecondary success of first-generation students. *Education Statistics Quarterly*, *3*, 73–77.

KEY TERMS AND DEFINITIONS

Adult Learner: College students beyond the traditional ages of 18-22 years old charged with balancing work, family, college, or other responsibilities.

Community Building: Creating connection to the University through academic and social initiatives, both inside and outside the classroom.

Foundations Courses: Courses designed to provide instruction on basic reading, writing, and math skills.

Online Learning: Education obtained at a distance via use of technology and classroom instruction.

Student Retention: Persistence of college students from admissions through degree completion.

Virtual Teams: Groups of individuals working in a professional or academic setting as a team set out to achieve common goals or completion of a project.

Chapter 14
Challenges in Aligning Pedagogical Practices and Pupils' Competencies with the Information Society's Demands:
The Case of Norway

Hans Christian Arnseth
University of Oslo, Norway

Ove E. Hatlevik
University of Oslo, Norway

ABSTRACT

The authors discuss why it seems to be difficult to change educational practices in ways that put them in alignment with the competencies needed in a networked society and global economy. During the past decade most developed countries have invested heavily in improving education with ICT. However, these efforts' effects have not met people's high expectations. The authors provide insights into the complexities involved in changing institutional practices and argue that using new technologies to make learning and teaching active, innovative and productive must be cultivated over time. Furthermore, change requires a systemic perspective because multiple factors interact to determine what actually happens in classrooms. Teachers' competencies are particularly crucial. Furthermore, ambitious plans setting out new goals for students' learning need to be matched with assessment practices that assess the skills we want to develop in students.

INTRODUCTION

During the past couple of decades, the emergence of ICT and the Internet have contributed to transforming how we organise and carry out our work, our shopping, our play and leisure activities, and our communication with friends and family. Even more important than these changes, at least for our argument, are the transformations of how

DOI: 10.4018/978-1-61520-909-5.ch014

we organise, access and share information and knowledge. Obviously, these changes pose some very important challenges as to how we organise teaching and learning in schools. In this chapter, we discuss how national educational policy addresses these challenges and examine how schools as historical institutions in society have taken up and responded to these policies that deal with ICT's implementation in teaching and learning.

The Norwegian Ministry of Education and Research (NMER) has invested quite extensively in implementing ICT in schools, particularly during the past decade. The government has devised several national plans and put a significant amount of money into developing pedagogical practices and pupils' ICT skills. Furthermore, the average pupil per computer ratio in Norwegian schools is very low. In most upper secondary schools, students even have access to their own laptop. Having said that, the uptake of ICT in schools and its effect on pupils' learning have not met society's high expectations (Arnseth, et al., 2007). Our aim is to discuss and provide some explanations for why this might be the case. Our main argument is that ICT's introduction poses some challenges to institutionalised traditions of teaching, learning and managing knowledge, traditions that it is important to be aware of in order to integrate ICT into teaching and learning. These historically developed traditions for organising teaching and learning impact how we make sense of ICT and incorporate it into pedagogical practices.

There are several explanations for teachers' reluctance to take up ICT and use it as part of their pedagogies. A particularly popular one seems to be that teachers and schools as institutions are conservative and resist change. In our view, more interesting explanations than this one emerge if we zoom in on the interface between the abilities the technology makes available and the characteristics of teachers' and learners' actual practices (Arnseth & Ludvigsen, 2006). If we do this, we can come up with highly interesting and useful explanations of how teachers make sense of ICTs as learning tools.

However, how teachers can incorporate ICTs into their pedagogy to make learning better or more effective than it currently is is only half the story when it comes to national educational policy on ICT and education. Just as important as this issue are issues of how ICTs require and demand the development of new competencies and literacies, from technical skills to complex cognitive skills regarding, for instance, learners' abilities to find, compare and evaluate information on the Internet.

During the past five years, the issue of digital literacy or digital competencies, which is the term policy documents use, has become central to our national policy agenda. The remaining part of this chapter uses these two terms interchangeably. This refocusing of attention regarding ICT and education means that ICT is not just a means for making education effective or productive, even though the national agenda by no means excludes these issues. Instead, using, knowing about and making critical judgements about ICT applications and sites have become ends in their own right.

In Norway, digital literacy has become one of five generic skills and competencies that are to be implemented across the different subjects in the national curriculum. Despite this, the curriculum does not clearly define what digital literacy is, or how it should be elaborated, described and assessed. There is also considerable room for teachers to interpret how to elaborate and incorporate digital literacy into their pedagogical practice. In this chapter we discuss both how ICT is conceived with regard to pedagogies, that is, how teachers can use ICT as part of their strategies for teaching the curriculum to their students, and the issue of digital literacy as a generic skill that pupils need to learn.

The policy developments mentioned above also have been mirrored by a substantial research agenda. Several national and international surveys have been conducted, several case studies of innovative technologies have been conducted and design-based research has been promoted and supported in order to generate context-sensitive models for effectively and productively using ICT for learning. The National Network for IT Research and Competence in Education has, for the most part, coordinated these efforts. Lately this organisation also has been working on establishing models and practices for assessing pupils' digital literacy using various research methodologies. In collaboration with researchers at the faculty of education, the National Network for IT Research and Competence in Education has started developing multiple-choice formats, but is also looking into making complex assessment tools for researching pupils' digital literacy. The use of multiple-choice forms of assessment has been tested in the municipality of Oslo (Hatlevik & Arnseth, 2009).

In this chapter we discuss how research can contribute to our gaining knowledge of how teachers and learners can use ICT productively, and we also discuss how assessment could work as a driver of change regarding teachers' pedagogies and organisational development in general. To provide insights into these issues, we draw together important research findings and bring in our experiences with devising assessment tools that enable us to establish valid and reliable measures of pupils' levels of digital literacy or competency. Taken together, we hope that these discussions will provide some useful knowledge regarding the relationship between national policies and local practices. To be able to provide excellent opportunities for developing pupils' skills with and knowledge of ICT, something which, in our view, is necessary in order to prepare them to participate in an information society and knowledge economy, it is necessary to focus on the interface between policy and practice. In our view, this can help devise effective policies, and it enhances the likelihood that practitioners will find policy efforts meaningful, realistic and possible to implement in regard to the local circumstances in which they operate.

Before we introduce and discuss relevant research findings and experiences regarding these issues, we need to provide some background information about the Norwegian educational system, to enable interested readers to make sense of the discussion and the research results reported.

BACKGROUND

Of a population of about 4.5 million people, about 607,500 pupils attended public primary and lower secondary schools during the 2006–2007 school year (NMER, 2007). Lower and secondary education lasts for 10 years and children generally start school the year they turn six. Few pupils in Norway attend private education, about 10,000 during this same school year. The approximate numbers of schools and teachers are 3100 and 64,000, respectively. Furthermore, about 180,000 pupils attend public upper secondary schools, and the number of pupils in private alternatives is about 14,000 at this level. There are approximately 450 upper secondary schools and about 23,000 teachers at this level. Norway has a national educational policy by which the government define the goals and decide on a national framework for the educational sector. "National standards are ensured through legislation, regulations, curricula and framework plans" (NMER, 2007, p. 6).

Norway has a national curriculum and introduced a new national curriculum in 2006. Here specific competence goals are devised in each subject, competencies that children should master at certain stages of their education. What is interesting about the reform is that it introduces five basic and generic skills that should permeate and be adapted across all subjects. These skills are that pupils should be able to read, express themselves orally, express themselves in writing, develop numeracy and use digital tools.

What concerns us here is digital tools' integration into pedagogy and pupils' ability to use digital tools across subjects. Although these have been important goals on the national policy agenda for several years, their uptake among teachers and learners has been slow. Before we discuss this issue in detail, however, we need to look into how this topic emerged in the national policy agenda.

As in most developed countries, ICT for learning emerged as an important topic in the mid-90s with the Internet's advent and spread. Before that, ICT was used sparsely and mostly for teaching pupils to master simple programming skills. To facilitate ICT's introduction into education in order to make it innovative and to prepare pupils for a high tech society, the ministry took certain steps. It started working on developing a national strategy in the early '90s. The result was a national plan for ICT in education that ran from 1996–1999. In this early phase, it seems reasonable to claim that there was a certain focus on the technology itself, on devising courses for teachers and on developing technological infrastructures. In addition, the ministry also initiated efforts to develop new digital learning resources (see Erstad, 2005). Toward 2000 it became clear that the ministry had neglected the challenges with integrating ICT into pedagogy during this early phase. The next plan, from 2000–2003, was directed toward the pedagogical challenges involved in utilising ICT, and how ICT could facilitate innovative pedagogical practices characterised by active inquiry, collaboration and the use of modern ICT-tools.

The last national plan, or, to be precise, programme for ICT in education, went from 2004–2008, and was termed the "Plan for Digital Competence". The programme noted 4 different areas as particularly important: 1) developing infrastructure and services; 2) developing teachers' competencies; 3) developing digital learning resources, curricula and pedagogies; and 4) research and development. This plan continues along the lines devised in the previous one, focusing on ICT's pedagogical use, on developing teachers' competencies, and on infrastructure and assessment. In addition, this plan emphasises the challenges that ICT implies for what pupils need to know. We recognise that ICT changes how we gain information, evaluate information and collaborate with others, and that schools need to take these issues into account. This is why the focus on developing pupils' digital literacy and competencies became so important during the past five years. With the focus on digital literacy, however, we do not see ICT only as a means for teaching and learning subjects. ICT is also transforming these subjects and is becoming a topic of study in its own right. That is to say, students need to develop critical skills concerning how they should understand, for example, the Internet as a place to be, how they should behave ethically and so forth. Issues regarding critically evaluating knowledge available on the Internet through, for instance, Wikipedia, also have become crucial during the past decade.

In addition, ICT is used extensively for sharing experiences, ideas and knowledge about how to use ICT for learning and planning across all levels of the educational system, for instance, in communication between school leaders and teachers, between local municipalities and school leaders, and between teachers within and across different schools and geographic locations. The past few years also have seen an increased focus on developing adequate digital learning resources. However, this remains perhaps one of the biggest challenges regarding ICT's implementation. Challenges limit how new business models can be developed concerning, for instance, publishers' role in producing digital content.

According to Krumsvik, ICT gained "momentum and became a formal part of the subject curricula" (Krumsvik, 2008, p. 9) in primary, secondary and upper secondary education through the reforms in the middle of the '90s. Curricula require and promote ICT's use; however, they say very little about how teachers should use ICT to develop learners' skills and knowledge.

This is partly because teachers have considerable freedom when choosing their instructional methods as long as they reach the goals formulated in the curriculum. Still, these goals as they are formulated in the curriculum are by no means clear to teachers; therefore it remains very much up to them what they do and how they do it. As mentioned above, digital literacy has become one of the generic skills and competencies that are to be implemented across the different subjects in the national curriculum. In practice, pupils need to be able to use and master ICT in its own right. Then learners can use ICT to learn their subjects. Skills using ICT, and skills in and knowledge of the subjects, also develop in tandem as learners traverse the educational system.

Nevertheless, making sense of what digital literacy is in practice is a challenge for teachers. What digital literacy is, what the goals for pupils' competence are, how teachers should assess it and how they should teach their pupils are by no means clear to teachers.

The distance between ambitious visions and goals formulated in policy documents and schools' abilities to change and implement ICT in practice is also substantial. This is not particularly surprising, but it is important to examine in detail why it is the case. Furthermore, even though the ministry regularly provides national assessments in addition to heightening teachers' awareness of formative and summative assessments, no national attempts have been made to develop assessment strategies and practices regarding the notion of digital literacy or competencies. We know that assessment practices are crucial drivers of change, and that this might be a way of increasing the quantity and quality of ICT use in Norwegian schools.

SETTING THE STAGE

Traditionally, the Norwegian educational system has been a comprehensive school system with a centralised structure and a strong emphasis on equity and universal access to schooling. From the mid '90s onward, ideals and concepts from New Public Management (NPM) (e.g., accountability and quality assurance systems) have influenced how the Norwegian educational system has been reformed and organised. NPM has become "one of the dominant paradigms for public management across the world" (McLaughlin & Osborne, 2002:1). There are different definitions of NPM (Schedler and Proeller, 2002), but they have some common features when adapted to an educational context. NPM underpins the importance of output measures (statistical indicators), autonomy for educational institutions, little direct control from government, internal systems and, frequently, controls made by outside agencies. However, the recently increased emphasis on accountability and assessments are part of a European trend toward deregulating education, by which governments have reduced their direct controls "in order to support greater autonomy, flexibility, and diversity at the institutional level" (Brennan & Shah, 2000:336).

Overall, the educational system seems to use a combination of central and local decision-making. On one hand, the national government (i.e., the Norwegian Ministry of Education and Research) decides the educational sector's goals and framework. On the other hand, local authorities have a central role in planning, budgeting and administrating schools. There is a centralised developed curriculum, a subject syllabus, national assessments in the middle of semesters and examinations operating in combination with the possibility for local governments to the give the curriculum a local aspect.

The Norwegian Ministry of Education and Research emphasises that education for all is a "basic precept of Norwegian educational policy" (2007). All children from 6–18 years old have a right to attend public schools without paying any fees. Primary school (grades 1–7) and lower secondary school (grades 8–10) are compulsory for Norwegian children. All 5th and 8th grade pupils are tested with national assessments in reading, mathematics and English. Results from national tests are used to compare schools and municipalities. Test results show substantial variation between counties and municipalities. Research has demonstrated a clear and consistent relationship between pupils' performance and their family's socioeconomic status.

Upper secondary education offers different educational programmes, which can lead "to admission to higher education, to vocational qualifications or to basic skills" (Norwegian Ministry of Education and Research, 2007). All young people (between 16 and 19 years old) can apply for admission to at least three different educational programmes, and they have the right to attend one of them. Almost 90% of pupils start upper secondary education. Studies show that 57% of pupils who started upper secondary education in 2001 completed it within a normal time. However, there are differences between general studies (74–77% completed) and vocational studies (38–40% completed).

THE NORWEGIAN EDUCATIONAL SYSTEM FROM AN INTERNATIONAL COMPARATIVE PERSPECTIVE

International comparative studies (e.g., PISA and TIMSS) show that Norwegian pupils are performing below the average score of OECD countries in reading, mathematics and science. Norwegian pupils' competence in these three subjects also has decreased from 2000–2006 (The Norwegian Directorate for Education and Training, 2007). An evaluation in the Global Information Technology Report 2008–2009 from The World Economic Forum (Dutta & Mia, 2009) on the quality of education in mathematics and science ranks Norway 56th out of 134 countries. We will not go into why this might be the case. It primarily serves as a backdrop for our argument regarding the slow uptake of ICT and the problems teachers have with implementing ICT into productive pedagogical practices that improve pupils' learning.

Results from the PISA 2006 study show that almost all Norwegian pupils (15 years old) have access to computers at school. Further, Norwegian pupils do have a high level of self-confidence in ICT and a rather advanced use of ICT as measured by PISA (Kjærnsli, Lie, Olsen & Roe, 2007). Lately, Norway ranks eighth out of 134 countries in the Global Information Technology Report 2008–2009 (Dutta & Mia, 2009).

Norway ranks 10th out of 134 countries regarding access to the Internet. The Norwegian Directorate for Education and Training (2007) reports that the computer density has increased in Norway; moreover, this measure differs between the compulsory school level (grades 1–10) and upper secondary school. In 2008 there were 6.4 pupils per computer in primary school, 4.2 pupils per computer in lower secondary school (90% of the computers in primary and lower secondary schools are connected to the Internet) and 1.9 pupils per computer in upper secondary school (96% of the computers are connected to the Internet).

During the past few years, several Norwegian schools have been participating in the eTwinning project (www.etwinning.net). This is a promising project that enables schools in 32 European countries to work together using ICT. Schools (working with pupils between the ages of 3 and 20) can have short- or long-term partnerships in any subject area. Hopefully, participating in eTwinning can enhance ICT competencies and increase cultural awareness and motivation.

To summarise, it seems reasonable to claim that modern ICT tools permeate Norwegian society, and that access to ICT in Norwegian schools is also high compared to other countries. Furthermore, principles concerning equity in access to education are important. Having said that, the potential exists to use ICT to improve learning, as the international studies referred to above indicate. In addition, research demonstrates that despite the access to ICT, pupils and teachers can use computers much more effectively and productively than they currently are.

THE USE OF ICT IN SCHOOLS: WHAT DO NATIONAL SURVEYS TELL US?

The ITU monitor is a national survey aiming at collecting data from a representative selection of pupils, teachers and school leaders in Norwegian schools. The ITU monitor was conducted in 2003, 2005, 2007 and 2009. It has longitudinal parts (e.g., time spent at school with computers and time spent at home with computers), but it also has undergone several revisions to incorporate new trends and knowledge demands (moving from time spent on a specific technology toward developing competence in using technology). In 2007 the notion of digital literacy was surveyed using a self-assessment format, and in 2009 digital literacy was measured using a multiple-choice format. In this chapter we refer to the findings from the ITU monitor's 2007 and 2009 surveys, each of which covers more than 2500 pupils (seventh grade, ninth grade and upper secondary level 2), 350 teachers and 250 school administrators.

The 2007 ITU monitor's findings reveal how the aspects of digital literacy that we, inspired by the educational testing service (ETS, 2001), termed *integrate and create*, were related to grades in some subjects (reading, social science and English), family background and a motivational approach to mastering skills and knowledge. Preliminary findings from the 2009 survey reveal that pupils' digital competence is related to grades in five different subjects (reading, mathematics, social science, science and English), family's background, motivational approach to mastering skills and knowledge and the school they attend. The results show a clear relationship between pupils' digital competence and their family's background, e.g., as the national assessments (of subjects as reading, mathematics, etc.) found previously.

The 2007 ITU monitor show that teachers (in all three grades) use computers more for "administrative tasks and preparatory and follow-up work than for teaching" (Arnseth et al., 2007, p. 91). A comparison of the 2007 and 2005 ITU monitors shows that teachers in all three grades increased their use of ICT for administrative tasks (Erstad et al., 2005). Moreover, ninth grade and second year upper secondary school teachers reported an increased use of computers for teaching from 2005–2007. When comparing teachers from different grades, it seems that teachers from level 2 (upper secondary school) are using computers in their teaching "far more extensively than do teacher in the two low grades" (Arnseth et al., 2007, p. 91). The results show that pupils in compulsory schools spend less time on computers (both at home and at school) than pupils from upper secondary school. Therefore, the survey's findings (from both teachers and pupils) consistently show that ICT is used and integrated more frequently in learning and teaching activities in upper secondary school (level 2) than in other grades.

One important issue concerns whether teachers have learned how to use ICT, and if they can use it when teaching a subject or monitoring a pupil's project. The results from the 2007 ITU monitor (and the 2009 ITU monitor's preliminary findings support this) show substantial differences between schools when it comes to teachers' use of ICT, and substantial variations in teachers' digital competences. These findings emphasise the importance of taking teachers' competences into account when trying to increase Norwegian pupils' digital competence and digital literacy. It also underlines the importance of training teachers and implementing ICT when teachers are learning to teach during their training. Teachers' integration and use of ICT for instruction have been too unsystematic and not satisfactorily grounded in the practices of teacher training.

DEVELOPMENT OF DIGITAL COMPETENCIES IN TEACHERS AND STUDENT TEACHERS

The IEA SITES 2006 study was an international project involving schools and teachers from more than 20 countries (Law, Pelgrum & Plomp, 2008). It focused on how schools and teachers organise their teaching, what ICT facilities schools provide, how teachers use ICT in their pedagogical practice and the problems and obstacles teachers experience in relation to technology. Experiences from the SITES study help us to decide how to integrate ICT as part of the systemic changes in how schools carry out their business. The study points out some of the same weaknesses we identified above, that is, the asymmetry between systemic issues and how teaching and learning are actually realised in classrooms. What teachers and learners do in classrooms is insufficiently grounded in common plans and strategies for using ICT to develop pupils' skills and competencies. The SITES study's results show that access is improving, but that schools differ significantly in this regard (Erstad & Quale, 2008). Access differs between basic education and upper secondary schools, teacher education is struggling to meet the new national curriculum's requirements and the use and implementation of ICT show considerable variation between subjects. All in all, these findings strengthen our arguments that ICT's use and implementation are too unsystematic, and the formulations of digital literacies in subjects are too vague. This means that teachers face significant challenges regarding how they should use ICT to make pupils' learning more productive and effective than it currently is.

One important issue is how teachers experience the development of own competencies in the use of ICT. The ITU monitors include questions about teachers' opinions of the benefits they get from various skill development strategies (presented in Figure 1).

More teachers are attending external courses in 2009 (74%) than did in 2007 (59%). However, the percentage of teachers who feel that they gained some benefit from external courses decreased from 30.5% in 2007 to 25.7% in 2009. The schools have to improve the match between their competencies' aim, the external courses selected and the teachers' need for development.

These findings (presented in Figure 1) underpin some of the difficulties that arise when trying to develop digital competence among teachers, and

Figure 1. Teachers' opinion of the benefits they feel they have gained from various types of skills development strategies (Source: ITU monitor 2009)

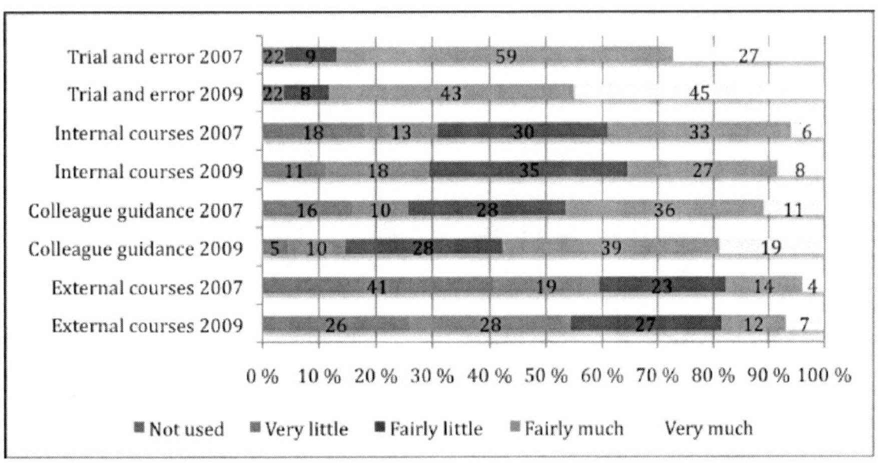

they also show the importance of strategically developing teachers' competencies. Results from the ITU monitor 2009 (Figure 1) show that teachers report they have gained the most benefit from informal and unorganised activities (e.g., trial and error and colleague guidance) when developing their own competencies in the use of ICT. Almost 90% of the teachers feel that they have benefited from trial and error in 2009.

There are several weaknesses to using informal activities to develop teachers' competence in the use of ICT. First, informal learning might lead to a privatised use of ICT in education. Second, teachers might forget or ignore some important issues because informal learning is often unorganised. Third, informal learning depends on competent colleagues or a competent environment; otherwise misunderstandings and wrong procedures can be reproduced without being revealed or questioned (Billett, 2001). Erstad & Quale (2008) argue that teacher education is still struggling to meet the new national curriculum's requirements.

Hetland and Solum (2008) have conducted a study to identify the strategies selected to enhance digital competence among student teachers. Their study combines a survey of 20 Teacher Training Institutions (higher education) and a qualitative approach to four selected institutions. The results indicate that the Teacher Training Institutions have insufficient knowledge-based digital practice to meet the demand for digital competencies. The report states that Teacher Training Institutions do not meet the new curriculum's demands. Hetland and Solum (2008) have identified two different strategies among these institutions. First, they emphasise using ICT as digital tools for teaching and learning; and second, they use ICT to change how teaching and learning activities are organised. One major obstacle in the current teacher training is the lack of emphasis on how student teachers can use the available technology to change or develop the practices of teachers and pupils. Therefore, these findings call into question whether student teachers are prepared to use computers adaptively and creatively in their forthcoming teaching.

The problem with teacher training is a systemic one, and considerably impacts what happens in classrooms. First, we cannot expect teachers who are not digitally literate to teach pupils how to search for information, evaluate information and use complex simulations to enhance their understanding of science. Second, teachers who use ICT tools in class depend too much on trial and error as a strategy for gaining knowledge of and competence with how ICT should be used. This is a significant problem on both a systemic and practical level. One issue is that policymakers have no means or criteria to decide how ICT should be used. Another is that through trial and error, teachers might develop strategies that are, at worst, simply wrong, and at best, unproductive and unsystematic.

PUPILS' USE OF COMPUTERS AND THEIR DIGITAL LITERACY

When comparing pupils' use of ICT at school, we find major differences between primary, lower secondary and upper secondary school pupils. The results from 2007 and 2009 show that pupils in upper secondary school spend much more time at their computer doing schoolwork (both at home and at school). In 2007 the difference between upper secondary and the other schools was smaller than in 2005. However, findings from 2009 show that the gap is larger than in both 2005 and 2007. Another interesting finding is that pupils in upper secondary school managed to integrate ICT as part of their learning activities combined with the use of a variety of digital tools to a larger extent than did pupils in primary and lower secondary school.

However, indications of mere use, in terms of hours spent on computers, cannot be taken for granted as indicators of what pupils are doing or learning when they use a computer. In our view, this depends on how learners use computers, and how teachers scaffold this use. If computers are used badly, the amount of use can negatively impact pupils' performance. For instance, findings from PISA ICT 2003 (OECD, 2006) show that pupils with a highly frequent use of ICT performed lower in reading and mathematics than moderate users of ICT.

However, preliminary analysis from the ITU monitor 2009 of the relationship between school performance (i.e., marks), time on computers and digital competence (measured by a multiple-choice test) show: 1) a linear relationship between grades and digital competence, and 2) a non-linear relationship between grades and time spent on computers. When relating time on computers with performance, we find a similar pattern as in the PISA ICT 2003. However, when adding an assessment measuring digital competence, we find a moderate correlation (Pearson's r = 0.35) between grades and digital competence. Figure 2 shows how the average marks of five subjects relate to time spent on computers at school and digital competence.

We want to underline two important issues. First, national and international surveys often use time spent on computers at school or at home as an indicator of access to computers. This is perfectly legitimate, but time spent on a computer does not equal access to knowledge or proficiency. For example, pupil A can spend 11 hours per week playing a game or browsing the Internet, with only a surface learning orientation; and pupil B can spend 11 hours per week playing different games and browsing the Internet trying to answer various questions. Both spend 11 hours per week on a computer, but they have different experiences and learning trajectories. Second, education can use ICT productively or unproductively, depending on the goals for an activity. Therefore, it is necessary to move toward a clear understanding of how pupils use ICT and computers for learning, and how teachers use them for teaching. Research also needs to emphasise the interface between the skills and abilities the technology makes available and the characteristics of learners' and teachers' practices (Arnseth & Ludvigsen, 2006).

Figure 2. Relation between standardised average marks (Reading, Mathematics, Social Science, Science and English) and the use of computers and digital competence (Source: ITU monitor 2009)

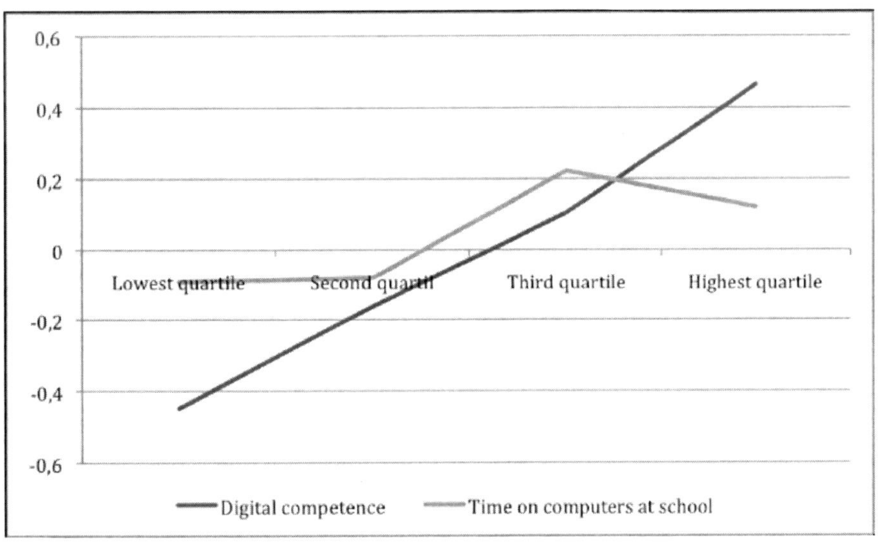

QUALITATIVE STUDIES OF ICT'S USE AND DEVELOPMENT OF PUPILS' DIGITAL LITERACY

In order to get a comprehensive picture of the obstacles and opportunities teachers and learners face when they attempt to use ICT in their learning and to develop their skills and competencies, it is necessary to combine quantitative surveys with detailed case studies.

Providing a thorough account of all the different case studies conducted of learning with ICT in Norway is beyond the scope of this chapter. Instead we try to highlight some of the interesting findings in regard to our topic. We mentioned above that one of the reasons teachers and pupils do not use ICT extensively and productively is that they have problems making sense of the technology, including how they can use the technology to carry out their projects. Instead, their use of technology becomes instrumental in that teachers, for instance, often tell pupils to simply find information on the Internet (see Rasmussen, 2005). In such a practice, the Internet becomes simply a source of information, a way of using the Internet similar to how pupils use textbooks. In these practices, ICT is more or less adopted to fit what teachers already have done with other types of tools (Arnseth, 2004). Thus, ICT does not become part of the innovative pedagogical practices that we know from previous research are productive for pupils' learning (Bransford, Brown & Cocking, 2000).

Studies also demonstrate that teachers have problems providing adequate feedback and scaffolding to pupils when they are solving problems or performing other types of tasks with ICT. That is, even though teachers instruct pupils what to do and how to do it, they do not provide feedback *just in time* when pupils are engaged in their activities (Furberg & Arnseth, 2009). Furthermore, we also have reason to believe that, in their instruction, teachers focus on technical tasks and a procedural approach to knowledge and problem solving (Krange, 2008). This is also the case when it comes to pupils' digital literacy. Thus, teachers inadequately scaffold pupils when they are searching for information, for instance, or when they use simulations of complex scientific phenomena. We have inadequate information about why this is the case. First, these are aspects of educational practices that were introduced long before ICT came along, so they strongly resist change (see Cuban, 1986, 2001). Second, the problem might be that student teachers do not learn how to provide feedback to pupils that fosters deep learning.

Aggregated results from a range of qualitative studies called PILOT (Erstad, 2004) demonstrate that schools that provide for systemic changes also use ICT more productively than other schools do in terms of pedagogy. Systemic change means that schools have clear and articulated goals and strategies for how to achieve them. They can see how successfully implementing and using ICT depend on a whole range of variables that have to do with technological infrastructure, teachers' competencies, access to resources and so forth (Erstad, 2004). Results from the ITU monitor 2009 show that many schools are starting to take these complex issues into account, but that many schools still have a long way to go.

But just as interesting as infrastructure, teachers' competencies and assess to learning resources are issues regarding teachers' scaffolding strategies and assessment. Regarding developing pupils' understanding and skills, we know that scaffolding and assessment are absolutely crucial. Furthermore, we also know that assessment is a substantial driver of change. Naturally, teachers and pupils are concerned with what they are assessed on, and they coordinate their activities in ways that enable them to manage their accountabilities toward those standards. This also makes it crucial to be aware of how we assess pupils' learning. We might argue that what is good for pupils' learning is not necessarily what the government needs to be able to manage the school system. For instance, to focus only on what we can measure using national or international tests as a benchmark for what pupils are supposed to learn and know is problematic for several reasons. These test are not particularly suited for assessing complex or creative skills, which we believe are crucial in the information society. Thus, large-scale assessment needs to be combined with local and formative needs, and to fit individual pupils' learning trajectories.

When we have been developing multiple-choice tests of digital literacy for the municipality of Oslo, we have been very concerned with emphasising these issues in our feedback to teachers and pupils (Arnseth & Hatlevik, 2009). We emphasised that teachers should use the pupils' test scores as a resource. They should be a starting point for a conversation with pupils during which teachers can ask additional questions and use these questions as diagnostic tools for assessing what pupils know in regard to digital literacy. Such tests can be very useful resources for teachers, but teachers should not treat them as if they tell the whole story about what the pupils know or have mastered in terms of knowledge and skills. In addition, such tests can provide teachers with information regarding how to identify and describe digital literacy. But, in the same vein, they should not conceive this in a technical fashion, i.e., teachers should not become instrumental. On the contrary, teachers should identify and describe digital literacy and use large scale assessments as a resource for developing local pedagogy.

CONCLUSION

In this chapter we have attempted to address issues regarding the use of ICT for developing both pupils' expertise in their, subjects and their digital literacy. We have provided research findings on how much Norway's pupils and teachers use ICTs; but more importantly, we have discussed findings beyond these simple indicators. We need to understand how schools use ICT, what pupils master in terms of skills and knowledge and how teachers can facilitate this learning and mastery in classrooms on a systemic level. We have discussed and provided explanations of why teachers are struggling with using ICT productively and effectively, on both local and systemic levels. On a local level, we believe that teachers do not master or have sufficient access to strategies and pedagogies for using ICT productively. They have problems making sense of the curriculum and adequately translating what it states into pedagogical practice. Teachers need help and support with this work and with specifying and elaborating the curriculum's abstract goals and aims.

On a systemic level, there are still problems with coordinating different factors so that they push in the same direction. We know that institutions that have clear plans and goals, adequate infrastructure and support and spaces for sharing knowledge and expertise are much more successful than institutions that use ad hoc strategies. To increase Norwegian pupils' mastery of knowledge and skills with and about ICT, we believe it is particularly crucial to focus on teachers' assessment and scaffolding strategies. But of course, we cannot believe that teachers will develop these strategies only through trial and error. They need adequate institutional backing and teacher training that focus explicitly on these issues.

REFERENCES

Arnseth, H. C. (2004). *Discourse and artefacts in learning to argue. Analysing the practical management of computer supported collaborative learning*. University of Oslo: Faculty of education.

Arnseth, H. C., & Hatlevik, O. E. (2008). Vurdering av digital kompetanse [Assessment of digital literacy]. *Nordic journal of digital literacy, 3*(4), 285-293.

Arnseth, H. C., Hatlevik, O. E., Kløvstad, V., Kristiansen, T., & Ottestad, G. (2007). ITU Monitor 2007. Skolens digitale tilstand 2007. Oslo: Universitetsforlaget.

Arnseth, H. C., & Ludvigsen, S. R. (2006). Approaching institutional contexts: Systemic versus dialogic research in CSCL. *International Journal of Computer-Supported Collaborative Learning*, *1*, 167–185. doi:10.1007/s11412-006-8874-3

Billett, S. (2001). Learning in the workplace. Strategies for effective practice. Crows Nest, Australia: Allen & Urwin.

Brennan, J., & Shah, T. (2000). Quality assessment and institutional change: Experiences from 14 countries. *Higher Education*, *40*, 331–349. doi:10.1023/A:1004159425182

Cuban, L. (1986). Teachers and machines. The classroom use of technology since 1920. New York: Teachers College Press.

Cuban, L. (2001). Oversold & underused. Computers in the classroom. Cambridge, MA: Harvard University Press.

Dutta, S., & Mia, I. (2009). *The Global Information Technology Report 2008-2009. Mobility in a Networked World.* World Economic Forum.

Erstad, O. (2004). Piloter for skoleutvikling. Oslo: Unipub AS

Erstad, O. (2005). Digital kompetanse i skolen – en innføring. Oslo: Universitetsforlaget.

Erstad, O., & Quale, A. (2008). National Policiees and Practices on ICT in Education: Norway. In T. Plomp, R. E. Anderson, N. Law & A. Quale (Eds.), Cross-National Information and Communication Technology (pp. 551-567). Charlotte, NC: IAP

Furberg, A., & Arnseth, H. C. (2009). Reconsidering conceptual change from a socio-cultural perspective: analyszing students' meaning making in genetics in collaborative learning activities. *Cultural Studies of Science Education*, *4*, 157–191. doi:10.1007/s11422-008-9161-6

ITU (Network for IT Research and Competence in Education). (2009). ITU monitor 2009. Oslo: ITU.

Kindergarden to Adult Education. Downloaded May 6, 2009, from http://www.utdanningsdirektoratet.no/Brosjyrer/_english/Education-in-Norway-From-Kindergarten-to-Adult-Education/

Kjærnsli, M. Lie, S., Olsen, R. V., & Roe, A. (2007). Tid for tunge løft norske elevers kompetanse i naturfag, lesing og matematikk i PISA 2006. Oslo: Universitetsforlaget.

Krange, I. (2008). *Computer-based 3D models in science education. Studying artefacts and students' knowledge constructions.* University of Oslo: Faculty of Education.

Krumsvik, R. (2008). Educational technology, epistemology and discourses in curricula in Norway. *US-China Education Review*, *5*, 1–17.

Law, N., Pelgrum, W. J., & Plomp, T. (2008). Pedagogy and ICT use in schools around the world. Findings from the IEA SITES 2006 study. Hong Kong: Springer.

Rasmussen, I. (2005). *Project work and ICT. Studying learning as participation trajectories.* University of Oslo: Faculty of Education.

Schedler, K., & Proeller, I. (2002). The New Public Management: a perspective from mainland Europe. In K. McLauglin, S. P. Osborne & E. Ferlie (Eds.), New Public Management. Current trends and future prospectives (pp. 163-180). Oxon, UK: Routledge

The Norwegian directorate for Education and Training. (2007). *The Education mirror.* Oslo: Author.

The Norwegian Ministry of Education and Research (NMER). (2007). *Education – from*

ADDITIONAL READING

Becta. (2006). *The Becta review 2006*. Retrieved August 9, 2007, from http://partners.becta.org.uk/upload-dir/downloads/page_documents/research/The_Becta_Review_2006.pdf

Bereiter, C. (2002). Education and mind in the knowledge age. Mahwah, NJ: Lawrence Erlbaum Associates.

Bransford, J. D., Brown, S. L., & Cocking, R. R. (2000). How people learn. Brain, mind, experience and school. Washington, DC: National academy press.

Castells, M. (1996). The information age: economy, society and culture. Oxford, UK: Blackwell.

Collins, A. (2001). The balance between task focus and understanding focus: Education as apprenticeship versus education as research. In T. Koschmann, R. Hall & N. Miyake (Eds.), CSCL 2. Carrying forward the conversation. Mahwah, NJ: Lawrence Erlbaum.

Crook, C., & Light, P. (2002). Virtual society and the cultural practice of study. In S. Woolgar (Ed.), Virtual Society? Technology, Cyberbole, Reality. Oxford: Oxford University Press.

Educational testing service. (2001). *Digital transformation. A framework for ICT literacy. A report of the international literacy panel.* Downloaded August 8, 2007, from http://www.ets.org/Media/Tests/Information_and_Communication_Technology_Literacy/ictreport.pdf

Erstad, O. (2008). Changing Assessment Practices and the Role of IT. In J. Voogt & G. Knezek (Eds.), International Handbook of Information Technology in Primary and Secondary Education (pp. 181–194). Dordrecht: Springer.

Eshet-Alkalai, Y. (2004). Digital literacy: A conceptual framework for survival skills in the digital era. *Journal of Educational Multimedia and Hypermedia, 13*(1), 93–106.

Grossen, M. (2000). Institutional framings in thinking, learning and teaching. In H. Cowie & G. van der Aalsvoort (Eds.), Social interaction in learning and instruction. Amsterdam: Pergamon.

Hewitt, J. (2001). From focus on tasks to a focus on understanding: The cultural transformation of a Toronto classroom. In T. Koschmann, R. Hall & N. Miyake (Eds.), CSCL 2. Carrying forward the conversation. Mahwah, NJ: Lawrence Erlbaum.

Huberman, A. M., & Miles, M. B. (1984). Innovation up close: How school improvement works. New York: Plenum press.

Koschmann, T. (1996). Paradigm shifts and instructional technology: An introduction. In T. Koschmann (Ed.), CSCL: Theory and practice of an emerging paradigm. Mahwah, NJ: Lawrence Erlbaum.

Kress, G. (2003). Literacy in the new media age. London: Routledge.

Lankshear, C., & Knobel, M. (2006). Digital literacy and digital literacies: Policy, pedagogy and research considerations for education. *Nordic journal of digital literacy, 1*(1), 12–24.

Linnakylä, P., Lie, S., Roe, A., & Universitetet i Oslo Institutt for lærerutdanning og skoleutvikling. (2003). *Northern lights on PISA unity and diversity in the Nordic countries in PISA 2000*. Oslo: Department of Teacher Education and School Development.

Littleton, K., & Light, P. (Eds.). (1999). Learning with computers. Analysing productive interaction. London: Routledge.

O'Donell, A. M., Hmelo-Silver, C. E., & Erkens, G. (Eds.). (2006). Collaborative learning, reasoning, and technology. Mahwah, NJ: Lawrence Erlbaum Associates.

OECD. (2005). Are students ready for a technology-rich world? What PISA studies tell us. Paris: Author.

OECD. (2007). PISA 2006. Science competencies for tomorrow. Paris: Author.

Olson, D. R. (2003). Psychological theory and educational reform. How school remakes mind and society. Cambridge, UK: Cambridge University Press.

Ottestad, G. (2008). Schools as Digital Competent Organizations: Developing Organisational Traits to Strengthen the Implementation of Digital Founded Pedagogy. *International Journal of Technology. Knowledge and Society*, *4*(4), 10.

Ottestad, G., & Quale, A. (2008). Trends in Instructional Infrastructure. In T. Plomp, R. E. Anderson, N. Law & A. Quale (Eds.), Cross-National Information and Communication Technology (pp. 41–65). Charlotte, NC: IAP.

Schauble, L., & Glaser, R. (Eds.). (1996). Innovations in learning. New environments for education. Mahwah, NJ: Lawrence Erlbaum Associates.

Schofield, J. W. (1995). Computers and classroom culture. New York: Cambridge University Press.

The Cognition and Technology Group at Vanderbilt. (1997). The Jasper Project. Lessons in curriculum, instruction, assessment, and professional development. Mahwah, NJ: Lawrence Erlbaum.

Wasson, B., Ludvigsen, S., & Hoppe, U. (Eds.). (2003). Designing for change in networked learning environments. Dordrecht: Kluwer academic press.

Weinberger, D. (2007). Everything is miscellaneous. The power of the new digital disorder. New York: Times Books.

KEY TERMS AND DEFINITIONS

Assessment: Usually divided into formative and summative assessment. Formative assessments are evaluations designed to improve the outcome when a student is engaged in an activity. Summative assessment are evaluations of a product of an activity such as an essay or an exam paper.

Curriculum: A document laying out the content, goals and objectives of education, including how teachers make sense of the document and realise it in their classroom.

Digital Literacy: People's competencies in accessing, evaluating and producing digital content.

ICT (Information and Communication Technology): A range of technologies for gathering, storing, retrieving, processing, analysing and transmitting information.

ICT Infrastructure: The computer hardware, wires, hubs, protocols, servers, systems software and so on which provide the foundation for the use of various types of applications.

Institutional Change: How institutions, which are stable ways of organising specific activities and tasks in a society, change over time.

Pedagogy: The methods, strategies and reflections teachers engage in when planning, performing and reflecting on their teaching.

Chapter 15
Collaborative Learning Experiences in Teaching of e-Business Management

Wael Assaf
Scuola Superiore ISUFI - University of Salento, Italy

Gianluca Elia
Scuola Superiore ISUFI - University of Salento, Italy

Ayham Fayyoumi
Scuola Superiore ISUFI - University of Salento, Italy

Cesare Taurino
Scuola Superiore ISUFI - University of Salento, Italy

ABSTRACT

In the context of the e-Business Management Section (eBMS) of the Scuola Superiore ISUFI at University of Salento (Italy), the case of the International Master in e-Business Management (IMeBM) is discussed here which is aimed to contribute pragmatically to create e-Business Capabilities in Mediterranean Countries. This chapter presents the results obtained in the Laboratory Phase of the first two years of Master's editions, i.e. 2006 and 2007 editions. This phase has been designed on blended (on-line and off-line) learning experience. Specifically, it has been structured by mixing the delivery of some Web learning courseware with face-to-face meetings with mentors and e-Business experts. The technological platform designed, developed and adopted for the Web learning activities is called the "Virtual eBMS" that represents the collaborative learning environment of the Mediterranean School. The pedagogical approach adopted by the School, named ("Learning-in-Action") together with some considerations on the effectiveness and the implications of the Problem-Based Learning (PBL) strategy are also deliberated upon. It also presents how the whole case of the International Master in e-Business Management generated intellectual capital assets, described in terms of Human Capital (competences developed in the e-Business context), Social Capital (networks and cooperation with local institutions and companies) and Structural Capital (research projects).

DOI: 10.4018/978-1-61520-909-5.ch015

ORGANIZATION BACKGROUND

The e-Business Management Section (eBMS) of the Scuola Superiore ISUFI is an interdisciplinary department focused on Digital, Organizational and Strategic Innovation, with a specific focus on Mediterranean area. In 2004, the school conceived and launched a challenging project aimed to create the "Mediterranean School of e-Business Management", a network-based organization constituted by competence centers in Southern Mediterranean Countries. Each center is specialized in developing qualified human capital and in promoting new projects for diffusing strategic, digital and organizational innovation, to support the modernization of traditional productive industries (Agro industry, Tourism and Cultural Heritage, Handicrafts), Public Administration, as well as of high-tech sectors (Aeronautics, Aerospace, Electronics, Software and Automotive) and Public Administration.

The official start-up of the project was in 2004. Today, besides the Italian node of the network, represented by the Euro Mediterranean Incubator (www.ebms.it), there are three more active competence centres in:

- Morocco, in partnership with Al Akhawayn University;
- Jordan, in partnership with The University of Jordan;
- Tunisia, in partnership with Technopole El-Gazala of Tunisi and the sponsorship of the Tunisian Ministry of ICT.

SETTING THE STAGE

Economic and social development is strongly related to the development of human capital, which is related to education (ESCWA, 2005). Recent studies published by the World Economic Forum, INSEAD and World Bank document reflects the connection amongst Human Capital assets, Innovation capabilities and e-Readiness index, in the perspective of the richness of a Country.

Through education and training, countries are able to improve the skills of their citizens, and their national innovation systems. In this framework, a nation's human capital becomes fundamental for the success of the country, if efforts are-to be connected, to develop skilled human capital so as to increase the digital literacy penetration. In this context the Middle East and North Africa (MENA) countries have been able to expand their education and training systems and succeeded in narrowing gender, rural and socio economic gaps in access to schooling and training resources. However, the fact remains that only few countries in the MENA region have developed effective learning programs. Education systems in most MENA countries provide limited opportunities for individuals to gain more skills and acquire more knowledge after completing their formal education (World Bank, 2003).

Derived from the necessities of the MENA countries in this area and the expertise in reforming human capital creation processes required for the digital and knowledge based economy, the Mediterranean School of e-Business Management was created to represent a cluster of research centers, which seek to distribute innovative practices in traditional institutions and emerging sectors among the networked countries. This network aims to improve the knowledge exchange flow and sharing of expertise among its members along with other local entities; and facilitates and supports the diffusion of strategic, digital and organizational innovation within private and public institutions.

In this conceptual framework, this chapter attempts to describe the empirical results obtained during the e-Business laboratory phase of international edition of master level program in e-Business Management, in terms of e-Business Capabilities developed within the laboratory activities.

The general objective of the entire Master is to develop the professional profile of *Digital and Organizational Innovation Engineers* who are able to conceive, design, and diffuse e-Business solutions, with integrated competences related to business management and ICT management.

The learning strategy followed in the International Master Program is the "Learning-in-Action" approach that integrates content related to business management and ICT management, combines and integrates practical experience and theoretical knowledge, and involves students in research activities with local and international companies and institutions. With this learning approach, the teacher acts as a mentor and introduces students to the relevant issue and problems while creating the context of the training and activities to facilitate an autonomous learning process. Moreover, students work in laboratories where they can experience applications, tools and methodologies related to digital and organizational innovation in the various fields (Tourism, Agro Business, Web-Learning and New Product development) (See Table 1).

During the learning activities, learners are given access to a library that contains the reference manuals for each of the Master's building blocks, a repository of case studies and reports, multimedia materials consisting of DVDs from prestigious international universities, as well as interactive courses, web-learning paths and web-seminars. This is has been made possible because of the Virtual eBMS, a virtual global learning environment. This learning environment for virtual collaboration represents a transversal asset for the other programs and activities as well (See Figure 1).

CASE DESCRIPTION

The Problem-Based Learning Approach for Creating Human Capital

Researchers have indicated that the current management education does not prepare students for the realities of business life (Bailey et al., 2005). Indeed, the traditional business school pedagogy has focused mainly on:

1. Transferring the content of disciplines, considering the student as a recipient of learning. According to Fekula (1994), "In the face of certainty, course content is both necessary and sufficient; however, when faced with uncertainty, course content, though necessary, is insufficient. To be effective in a world of uncertainty, students must learn to learn"
2. A body of knowledge to be taught very theoretically, disconnected from the student needs, and that is delivered exactly in the same way to all the students and without considering their previous experience.

In few words, the current management education system is not able to accommodate the needs of the business for which knowledge has to be quickly and directly applicable to specific problems. These considerations require new pedagogical approach-

Table 1. The learning in action approach

Learning in Classroom	To Learning in Action
Learners as students in classroom	Learners as "knowledge workers"
Learning is faculty-driven	Learning is self managed
Faculties are teachers	Faculty as mentors
Learning is passive	Learning is interactive
Modules structure is 'functional'	Modules structure is multidisciplinary
Activities take place in classrooms	Activities take place in research laboratories
Assessment based on grades	Assessment based (mainly) on results or innovations
Structured curricula based on disciplines	Dynamic patterns based on the solutions to develop
Local educational experience	Global cross-cultural educational experience

Figure 1. The VeBMS supporting different programs and activities

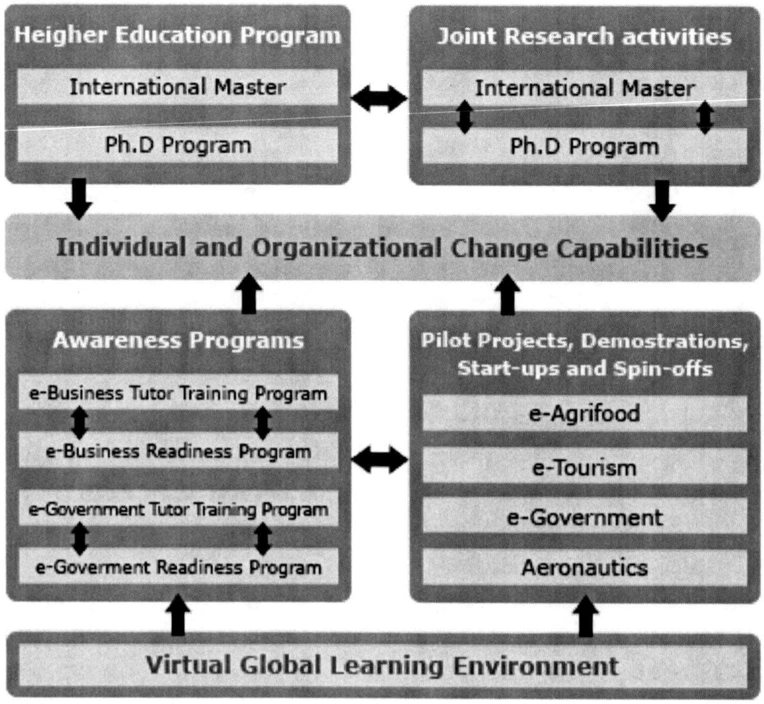

es, based on a fundamental rethinking of learning methods, from *course-based*, *one-to-many* and *off-line* provisioning to *application-based*, *peer-to-peer* and *online* interactions (Romano et al., 2005). With this new approach, learners should be allowed to learn at their own rhythm or in a self-paced way and to become responsible for their learning process, which happens 'in action', rather than in 'classroom'. This entails a substantial shift from traditional, course-based learning approaches to context-aware, just-in-time, individualised learning strategies and processes (Secundo & Passiante, 2007), in which the problem becomes the overall context of the learning process. It is crucial, in this scenario, to adopt a learning methodology that is mainly based on problem definition and problem solving, with which the learner can autonomously acquire the necessary amount of knowledge to face and solve specific problems and, as a consequence, can improve his/her competences and skills.

An educational approach, the so called Problem Based Learning (PBL), provides support to faculty members to develop a new learning style based on the integration and use of three different learning methods, such as the development of internships and mentorships, the introduction of case studies and skills workshops, as well as the experimentation of other instructional innovations. This approach uses a prototypical, real-world problem as the focus for student-centred active learning.

In PBL, students learn by solving problems and reflecting on their experiences. PBL is well suited to help students become active learners because it situates learning in real-world problems and makes students responsible for their learning (Hmelo-Silver, 2004). It has a dual emphasis on helping learners develop strategies and construct knowledge (Collins et al., 1989; Kolodner et al., 1996). PBL has the following two distinct goals:

- to learn a required set of competencies or objectives
- to develop problem-solving skills that are necessary for lifelong learning (Engel, 1991).

According to PBL, a problem (not flat lessons, exercises or other structured material) is assigned to the learner, and the learner has to autonomously search all the information he needs to solve that problem. In this way the learner has a proactive role in his own learning experience and becomes responsible for his competences growth.

The PBL approach followed in this experimental case has mainly the following features:

- *A cross-disciplinary approach:* According to Meier et al. (1996), students taught within the lecture-based disciplinary system typically have not been able to solve problems that require them to make connections and use relationships between concepts and content. In contrast, cross-disciplinary teaching starts with a topic, theme, problem or project that requires active student participation and knowledge of multiple disciplines in order to reach a resolution. Cross-disciplinary teaching uses relevant applications that motivate students to search for needed facts.
- *Teacher as mentor and learning facilitator:* The PBL requires changes in the way teachers plan instruction, direct learning, transmit knowledge, oversee instruction and assess learning (Gordon et al., 2001; Maxwell et al., 2001). In lecture-based instruction, teachers are in control and are the 'experts' dispensing knowledge. In PBL, teachers select the problem, present it to the students and then provide direction for student research and inquiry. Teachers behave as facilitators (mentors), and the students are the main actors of the problem-solving process.
- *Action-oriented/experiential learning:* Action learning approach relies on application in which the learning link between cognition and action is genuine, pure and direct. Kolb (1984) defined learning as "a process whereby knowledge is created through the transformation of experience". The students learn through experience and active involvement. Moreover, experiential learning promotes the activation of prior knowledge as new knowledge and its reconstruction as new knowledge is integrated into existing schemata.
- *Unstructured problems:*Peterson (2004) describes the workplace as an environment where 'problems are ill-structured, ambiguous, messy, complex, and most often do not have one correct answer that can be found at the end of the book in the answer key'. Such opportunities would be served using a problem-based approach that is unique and challenging for both faculty and students. However, the development of a problem and how to solve it are often more critical than its solution, which is frequently a matter of experimental skill. Unlike the presented problem, a discovered problem is a situation in which the problem itself has not been formulated but must be identified, and a method for reaching a solution and even the nature of a satisfactory solution are yet unknown.

'Virtual eBMS': A Web-Based System Supporting the PBL Approach

A critical element in the change toward the adoption of the PBL approach is the recognition of the need to redesign and integrate the traditional business curricula and to create new knowledge architectures supporting problem-solving methodology and inquiring learning. With the progressive diffusion of Information and Communication Technology (ICT), web-based learning and knowledge management environments provide both collaborative and self-paced learning services with empowered functionalities that conventional face-to-face classroom could not provide.

Starting from this consideration, and taking into account the importance of the PBL methodology for creating human capital in the emerging competitive environment, the 'Virtual eBMS' system has been designed and developed. This chapter, therefore, describes a web-based environment, named 'Virtual eBMS', conceived to support the research and the educational activities of the school researcher and students. Such a complex and innovative technology platform integrates three subsystems of Knowledge Management, Project Management and Web Learning. The Web Learning subsystem has been awarded in 2006 in Denver (Colorado, USA) the International "Brandon Hall Research" prize in the category "Learning Technology", whereas the Knowledge Management subsystem was recognized as a result of excellence within the Program PON 2000-2006. In particular, the Web Learning subsystem aimed at facilitating and practicing the PBL methodology for creating business leaders, and used for the development and the delivery of complex and interdisciplinary curricula related to technology management and business management domains, for Master and PhD students as well as for enterprises executives and managers.

The 'Virtual eBMS', a complex platform has been designed and developed in collaboration with some leading international industrial partners and stakeholders to support all academic, education, research and project activities in the school. The VeBMS is an integrated Web Learning and Knowledge Management solution, consisting in the design and implementation of innovative technological models and tools for Web Learning and in the management of individual and organizational knowledge. Beside the integration of web learning and knowledge management system components, some innovative approaches has been defined and adopted such as the design of taxonomies of interdisciplinary competences, the design and implementation of services and tools enabling collaborative learning and "just-in-time" learning, the design and creation of interactive and multimedia learning paths, as well as the design and monitoring of on-line learning experiences.

Before starting the design phase of the 'Virtual eBMS', the team project conducted a deep analysis of the educational and research activities and practices at the school, in order to gather the required information to set up a complete and efficient platform useful for the delivery of effective online learning patterns. The system has been created by integrating different market products and some components developed ad hoc; in particular, at the base of the knowledge management, project management and the web learning system integration process, there is the use of open-source, Linux and Java-based technologies.

The Web Learning subsystem offers the following categories of services:

- *Skill Gap Analysis and Competence Profile Management*, to manage the different competency profiles within a project team or learning community;
- *Structured Learning Program Management*, for realizing structured *on line* learning paths;
- *Unstructured Learning Program Management*, to "self-create" non-predefined learning paths in the perspective of *just-in-time* learning;
- *Tracking and Reporting*, to monitoring the performance of a learning path; and
- *Recommendation Engine*, to suggest new learning modules and resources corresponding to a given competency level to achieve based on personal interests and preferences.

These services operate on the following categories of content:

- *Competence Taxonomy*, the backbone of the system with a three-level taxonomy: *"Knowledge Domain Level"*, *"Competence Level"* and *"Learning Objective Level"*;
- *Competence Profiles*, the profiles managed by the system through a punctual monitoring of competency levels achieved and gaps to fill;
- *SCORM objects*, the traditional learning modules realized according to SCORM standards;
- *Multimedia Knowledge Objects* (MKO), aggregation of different types of files (e.g. pdf, word, power point, excel), coming from the Knowledge Management subsystem; and
- *Multimedia Learning Modules* (MLM), the key objects of learning paths created according to a *Problem Based Learning* strategy (See Figure 2).

Related to the Knowledge Management subsystem, the main classes of services provided are the following:

- *Document Management*, to manage the entire lifecycle of documents, including the aspects of workflow to support process automation;
- *Content Management*, to manage news, bookmarks and posts on electronic blackboards;
- *e-Library*, to manage physical and digital library resources (e-book, CDs, DVD, videos);
- *Search and Retrieval*, to retrieve resources stored in the knowledge base of the system. There are different typologies of search available that leverage on both syntactic and semantic features of a text: searches based on tags added in the cataloguing phase (*metadata search*), searches of keywords contained in the text (*text-based search*), and searches based on the navigation of domain taxonomies (*taxonomy-oriented search*), and searches based on graphical navigation of conceptual maps (*knowledge map*);

Figure 2. The dynamic interactions among classes of services and types of content.

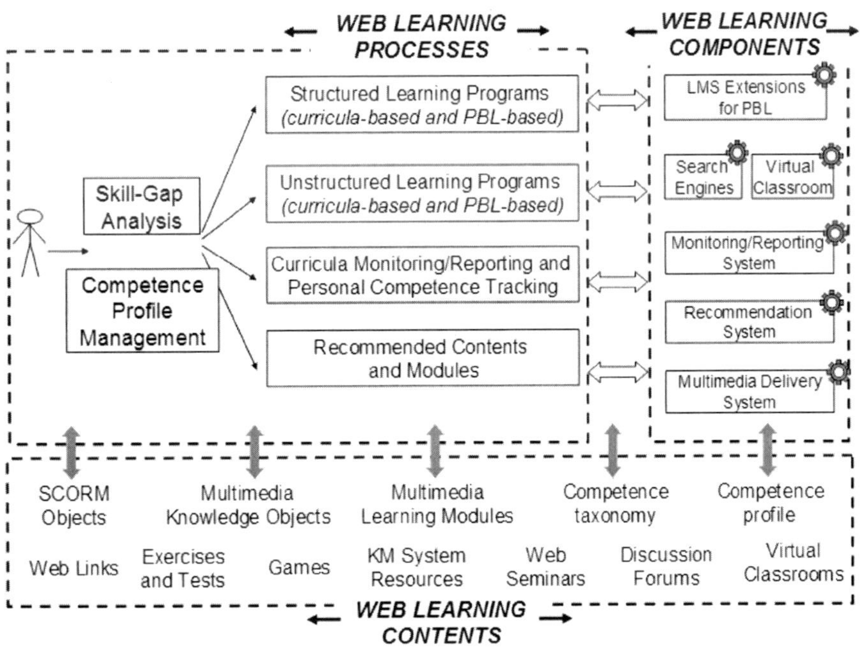

- *Community*, to facilitate the emergence and creation of communities of practice aimed at exchanging experiences, project knowledge, and ideas. Individual and group chat, thematic forums, areas for sharing knowledge and exchanging documents, spaces for collaborative job and virtual meeting all contribute to build the area dedicated to the life of communities;
- *Web Mining*, to retrieve knowledge useful for system's users. Internal and external knowledge sources, also available on the web, are periodically tagged and catalogued, to be found in the research phase; and
- *Recommendation Engine*, to suggest news, documents and references to experts useful to deepen a topic, to solve a problem, or to execute a task.

The Project Management subsystem provides users with a set of functionalities useful for a flexible and integrated management of projects. Among the distinguishing features of this system, two aspects are particularly innovative:

- *Document Management service*, to maximize the effectiveness in managing a project (both in terms of reusing documents contained in the knowledge base and in the perspective of automatically enriching the base at the end of project activities); and
- *Web Learning subsystem* to leverage on project tasks in terms of the same competencies and skills which build up the taxonomy of competencies contained in the Web Learning subsystem (this allows an optimized allocation of human resource and the involvement of profiles more suitable to executing a specific activity, and it also enables the planning of personal competency development plans inspired to a *project-based learning strategy*).

The following services build up the Project Management subsystem:

- *Phase and Activity Management*, for structuring a project in terms of phases and activities. Each activity is then associated to a manager of the preparation and submission of a deliverable.
- *Workflow Definition*, to manage and automatically orchestrate the workflow of project documents, including their review and final approval.
- *Reporting*, to provide the project manager with integrated snapshots, both synthetic and analytic, on the progression of a project, possible delays, milestones and deliverables, and the responsibilities of single phases and activities; and
- *Recommendation Engine*, to suggest and provide "*just-in-time*" learning paths useful to execute a project task in case the owner does not possess the competency profile suitable to effectively execute the task.

The integrated Web Learning, Knowledge Management and Project Management systems are backed by a multimedia infrastructure for the acquisition, processing, storage and delivery of multimedia content. The infrastructure is constituted by a high resolution *fixed acquisition system*, a *mobile acquisition system*, an *automatic acquisition system* based on sensors, a 4-terabyte *storage system*, a *post-production system*, a *streaming system* to broadcast content, and a *documents scanning system*. The system also provides instruments for the semi-automatic translation of content into other languages (including Arabic).

Developing E-Business Capabilities

The International Program in eBusiness Management

The mission of the IMeBM Program is to prepare outstanding people in leading Business Innovations based on the use of ICTs. The aim is to create business Engineers and Change Managers capable to identify and exploit the distinctive potential of the new ICTs for reconfiguring traditional business contexts, which we refer as e-Business capabilities. This program is aimed to organize in mobility between Italy and the Southern Mediterranean Countries and is offered on annual basis, full–time, for a total of 1940 hours and is devoted to people graduated in Business, Engineering or Computer Science coming from Italy, Morocco, Tunisia, Jordan, Egypt and other Southern Mediterranean Countries.

As for the case analysis, we observed the IMeBM community, while taking part in it, from January 2006 till January 2008. During the observation time, more than 20 learners coming from Mediterranean countries have been involved in the two cycles of the IMeBM program. According to the methodology chosen, researchers and executive staff actively participated in the program meetings, activities, projects and learning processes. Weekly, questionnaires and daily informal meeting for evaluating students' satisfaction on learning processes were developed for these students. Monthly meeting and focus group with partners was realized in order to focus on the learning strategy with the current results of the learning patterns.

The Program Approach for Creating e-Business Capabilities

e-Business Capabilities represent an evolution of traditional management education in the 21st Century (Romano et al., 2001), and can be developed integrating management studies with technological ones. The basic principles of the IMeBM for business leaders' creation are illustrated as follows:

- *Profile:* The overall aim of is to create outstanding people defined as *change managers and business engineers* able to ideate, design and develop complex e-Business solutions in the changing scenario of the digital economy. This is a multidisciplinary profile pursued through the creation of trans-disciplinary competences profiles able to identify the distinctive potential of emerging technologies and finding the right matching with hidden business needs, integrating both technological and business knowledge (Secundo and Passiante, 2007).
- *Content:* A trans-disciplinary approach characterizes this program. Knowledge coevolves with the context of application, dynamically and beyond the contribution of any single discipline. The focus will increasingly be an integrated offering of various disciplinary fields, through integrative modular program design, rather than offering semester length courses in particular specialist topics such as marketing, finance, accounting...etc. (Lorange, 2005).
- *Learning approach:* As stated before, the *Learning in action* strategy lies at the center of the Mediterranean School business leaders' creation process: the learning process is triggered by a number of activities beyond the classroom, supported by experiential laboratories in which participants think, work and learn together how to invent new ICT-based business solutions. Learning does not occur in theory-driven, discipline-based ways, rather it occurs from everyday experience when people act in order to solve a problem and/or to achieve a goal. The logic is reversed: application and experience are not means to

learn, but ends from which learning originates, in a process that relies on a series of trials/experiences, observation, reflection, and systematization (Secundo and Passiante, 2007).

- *Strategy:* Cross cultural educational experience, with people coming from different countries. Lectures and seminars are held by faculty coming from different Universities and Business Schools located in Europe, USA and Euro-Mediterranean countries and from an International Networking of Academic and Industrial Partners.

The Laboratory in Practice for Developing e-business Capabilities

Within the IMeBM, activities take place beyond classroom, in the research and development laboratories. Laboratory represents the "learning environment" of all the student activities that bring to the development of innovative e-Business models and solutions in some business contexts, like Agri-food, Tourism, New Product Development and e-Government. The dominant philosophy is that students learn best when they are experimenting, interpreting, and learning through discovery while setting the pace of their own learning. Thus, the learning strategy becomes more experiential-oriented and based on simulations, projects, action-learning exercises with unpredictable outcomes, discussions and independent learning (Baets & van der Linden, 2003). The *Laboratory Phase* is based on the previous stated principles. Figure 3 shows the integrated view of the e-Business design laboratory phases.

The laboratories activities of the IMeBM 2006 and 2007 editions have been organized into three main phases:

- *Phase 1: e-Business Design (in Italy. Duration: 7 weeks)*. The activities of this phase aim to provide participants with a set of competencies related to the benefits

Figure 3. The phases of the laboratory experience

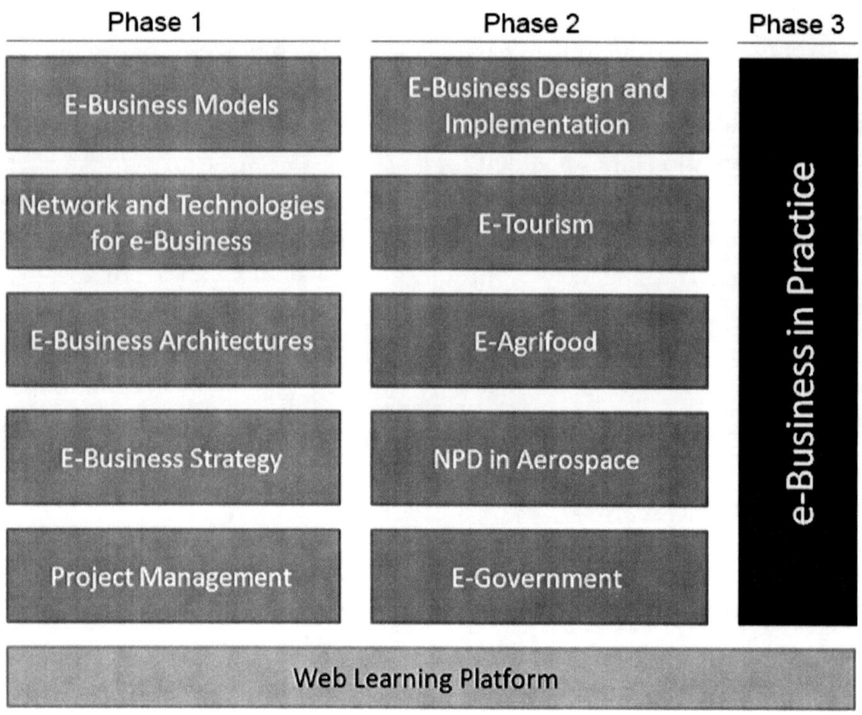

deriving from the application of ICTs to business as well as to the methodologies supporting business and organizational change. Moreover, students will be provided with a methodology for the implementation of organizational change through the ICT-driven innovation of business processes. The competencies to acquire in this phase are preliminary to the activities for the experimentation of the following step, and consisting of ICT-based applications for the innovative management of traditional business domains. The competences to acquire during this phase are related to: e-Business models, Network and Technologies for e-Business, e-Business Architecture, e-Business strategy and Project Management.

- *Phase 2: e-Business Implementation (in Italy. Duration: 7 weeks).* The activities of this phase are focused on the application of methodologies and tools to verify in "action" the benefits deriving from the e-Business applications in some traditional industries. This phase is characterized by the adoption of a "Project based" learning strategy. Participants, divided up into four groups, are involved in different applicative learning activities related to the Innovative management of Agri-Food Value chain, Tourist destinations, New Product development in aerospace industry and e-Government. The projects developed within the experiential laboratories serve as the "central core" of the learning program, by which the knowledge and skills learned are put in practice.
- *Phase 3: e-Business in practices (in Morocco, Tunisia and Jordan. Duration: 10 weeks).* This phase is characterized by the analysis and contextualization of e-business models and solutions developed during the phase2 to firms operating in the Mediterranean area. Getting involved into complex projects and real issues is the ultimate learning experience. Participants may contextualize the e-Business capabilities with a company that corresponds to a field of interest or specialization area pre-existing within phase2 and represents a variety of industry including Agri-food, Tourism, software companies and other types.

The three phases of the laboratory have been supported by the use of a web learning platform allowing the experimentation of a blended learning experience for the development of e-Business capabilities.

Web Learning Platform Supporting the Development of e-business Capabilities

During all the phases of the laboratory, a blended (on-line and off-line) learning experience on the topic of e-Business was designed and developed. The laboratory's experience was structured according to the delivery of some Web learning courseware, mixed with face-to-face meetings with mentors and e-Business experts. The technological platform adopted for the Web learning activities was the 'Virtual eBMS'.

With respect to the two Master's editions, the 2006 edition was much more focused on face-to-face seminars with some use of CD, DVD, and web learning courses. The 2007 edition was more focused on the use of online web learning modules and face to face seminars delivered to a target of 14 young talents coming from Morocco, Tunisia and Jordan, especially for a period of 9 weeks during spring 2007.

Moreover, by using collaborative synchronous and asynchronous tools, like chat, threaded discussion forum, e-mail, as well as workspaces for document management and sharing, learners could spread and share their personal learning and professional experiences, by discussing and facing in a collaborative environment the main issues related to e-Business. Furthermore, the availability of different ways of knowledge delivery (use of multimedia presentations, Web resources, knowledge objects, SCORM objects), jointly with collaboration tools such as: chat, forum and shared notes (Figure 4) can provide the means for learners to decide how to better personalize their experience based on their learning style, in order to maximize the effectiveness of their learning experience (Elia et al, 2006).

To increase effectiveness of the learning experience, Master fellows were organized in workgroups and were assigned some specific project-work related to e-Business design, e-Business strategies and e-Business technologies. Specifically, the following case studies were selected and assigned: eBay, eLance, Alibaba, Dell, and Expedia. The expected deliverable for project works was a report structured according to a specific template; some of the main elements of this template were the identification of the main company advantages from the Internet revolution; Classification of the case within the landscape of e-Business; Description of the related e-Business model; Identification of the characterizing e-business model components according to the Afuah and Tucci (2001) framework; Description of the company's value chain in terms of primary and support activities; and the identification of the main technology and e-commerce features characterizing the case.

Figure 4. The structure of the learning module of the 'virtual eBMS' system

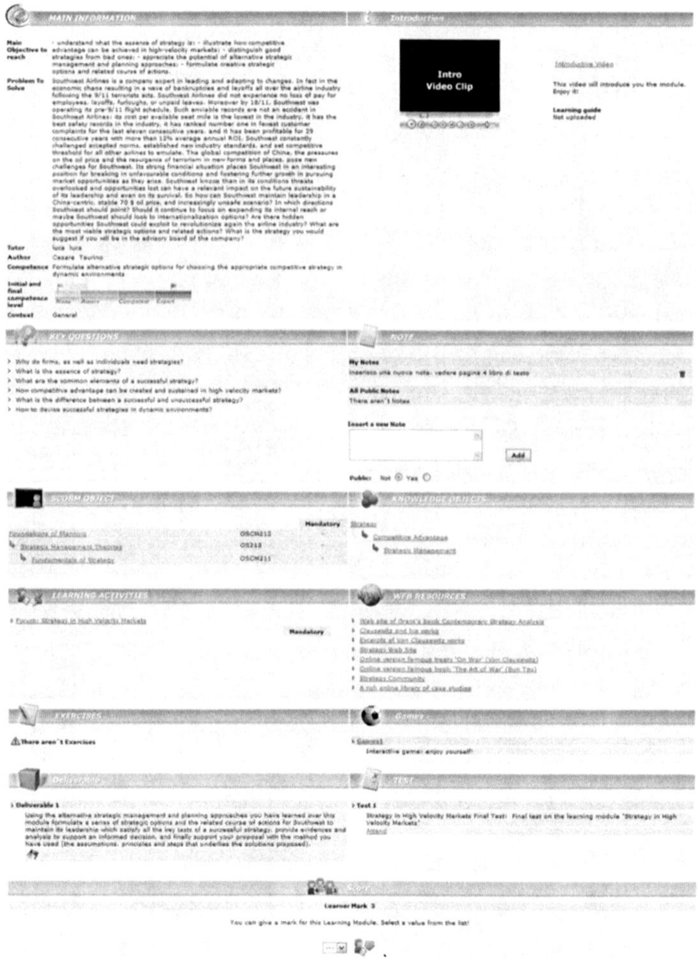

The project and reports were assigned in order to allow fellows put in practice the theoretical knowledge on e-Business they acquired during the Web Learning courses fruition (knowledge application). From the other side, the deliverable related to each project work allowed learners to extract the main theoretical concepts on e-Business they need in order to have a deep understanding of the knowledge domain they were analyzing (knowledge identification) (Pawlowsky, 2001).

During the laboratory an efficient tutorship activity was conducted to provide learners with online support, both from a technological point of view – for technical issues and troubles related to the use of the Virtual eBMS Web Learning platform, and from the content point of view – to explain or clarify some doubts related to the knowledge domain to analyze. The learning pattern designed for the experimentation was organized around six question-oriented learning modules (Table 2).

Master fellows learning activities were monitored and tracked by the Virtual eBMS Web Learning system; periodically, a list of reports containing the main information related to learner activities were automatically generated by the system.

RESULTS

To conclude the presentation of above described experimentation, here the results obtained from the two editions of the program are shown in terms of e-Business Capabilities developed during all the three phases of the e-Business Design Laboratory. During all the three phases, human capital (competences developed in the e-Business context), Social Capital (networks and cooperation with local institutions and companies) and Structural Capital (innovation projects) have been created. In order to highlight the distinctive features of each laboratory phase, the results will be described as follow:

- the *Human Capital* developed will be presented mainly referring to phase1 (e-Business design), since phase1 is the more theoretical one, with the aim to develop basically the human capital dimension (basic capabilities on e-Business);
- the *Structural Capital* will be described mainly referring to phase2 (e-Business Implementation), since phase2 is conceived more practically, oriented to develop and configure the structural capital dimension (research and innovation projects); and
- the *Social Capital* will be described mainly referring to phase3 (e-Business in practices), since phase3 aims basically to expand the Social Capital dimension (cooperation and relationship with Mediterranean companies and institutions).

Concerning the *Human Capital* dimension, in *Phase1 i.e. e-Business Design*, 20 students have been involved (35% coming from Morocco, 48% coming from Jordan and 17% coming from Tunisia). More than 15 mentors and speakers mostly coming from Europe, North-America, and testimonials have been involved in face-to-face seminars. During this phase, master students learning activities were monitored and assessed; periodically, a set of reports containing the main information related to learner activities were generated by the master's coordinator and mentors.

Table 2. The learning pattern designed for the experimentation

1. e-Business: how to face challenges related to technological change?
2. Which applications and technologies for e-Business?
3. How to implement CRM in an enterprise?
4. How to set up and manage Supply Chain Management and e-Procurement services in an enterprise?
5. Why and how to guarantee e-Commerce Security?
6. How to build a successful e-Commerce business case?

The students' final evaluation made by the mentor was based on the following elements:

- Results of learners' intermediate test structured according to a set of single choice, multiple choice, matching questions, as well as true/false questions;
- Results of learners' final test structured as the intermediate test; and
- Assessment of the deliverables related to the project assigned.

These three elements have had a different weight on the final evaluation, according to the following percentages: 20% for the intermediate test, 50% for the final test, and 30% for the project deliverable. The mentor assigned a specific score, from 0 (poor) to 5 (excellent) to both the two tests and the deliverable. The final results of each learner are shown in Table 3.

As shown in Table 3, the final average score for the initiative is 3.78 on a maximum of 5 points; therefore we can consider the final results as fulfilling in respect to the objective of the laboratory experience. Furthermore, the application of a list of questionnaires in two different phases (during and at the end) of the learning experience provided some useful learners feedback in order to perform a qualitative and quantitative evaluation of the overall experimentation, from four different points of view:

Table 3. Final evaluation of students involved in the Phase 1 of the e-business design laboratory

Learner	**Intermediate Test** *(min 0 – max 5)* *(weight 20%)*	**Final Test** *(min 0 – max 5)* *(weight 50%)*	**Report** *(min 0 – max 5)* *(weight 30%)*	**Final Score**
Learner 1	4	2.67	4.5	3.49
Learner 2	4.08	3	4.2	3.58
Learner 3	4.5	3.92	4	4.06
Learner 4	4	4	4.5	3.35
Learner 5	3.83	3.25	4.25	3.67
Learner 6	4.42	3.92	5	4.34
Learner 7	3.58	2.75	4	3.29
Learner 8	3.67	4.17	4.5	4.17
Learner 9	3.92	3.25	4.25	3.68
Learner 10	3.83	3.17	5	3.85
Learner 11	3.67	2.5	4	3.18
Learner 12	4	4.42	5	4.51
Learner 13	2.5	3	4	3.20
Learner 14	3.42	3	4	3.38
Learner 15	3.62	3.2	4.5	3.67
Learner 16	3.32	3.4	4.25	3.64
Learner 17	3.83	3.92	4	3.93
Learner 18	3.42	3.2	4	3.48
Learner 19	4.08	4.42	5	4.52
Learner 20	3.92	3.16	4.75	3.79
Average Score	**3.78**	**3.42**	**4.39**	**3.78**

- Contents (the logic architecture of the initiative);
- Organizational aspects (the quality and the effectiveness of tutorship);
- Technology (the level of usability of the system); and
- Learner Satisfaction (learner expectations, knowledge acquired, competencies reached).

By analyzing the gathered data it is possible to conclude that such a learning experience was useful and effective also from the learner perspective, as shown in the following graphs (Figure 5, Figure 6, Figure 7, and Figure 8).

The e-Business capabilities created during Phase1 have also contributed to develop the *Structural capital* – what is usually defined as projects, software and databases during Phase2. These act at the same time as enabling factors (since structural capital is generated for matching projects' requirements) and as catalysts of the learning-in-action environment of the IMeBM. The projects' development, then, reinforces the dynamics of interactive learning which constitute the core mission of the Med School. Finally, the Phase3 contributed to create the *Social capital* in terms of relationship and partnerships with local institutions and companies located in Morocco, Jordan and Tunisia where the students spent this phase contextualizing the e-Business models and solutions developed during the previous phases. We refer at first to the agreement with 15 companies and institutions (35% in Morocco, 48% in Jordan and 17% in Tunisia) in the field of Tourism, ICT, Agrifood, Government and Aerospace in which the Master's students spent the phase3 of the Laboratory. In particular, in Morocco the 20% of companies belong to Agrifood, 20% to aerospace, 30% to tourism and 30% to governmental institutions; in Jordan the 50% of companies belong to software and ICT industry, 20% to governmental institutions, 15% to tourism and 15% to telecommunication industry. In Tunisia, the 20% of companies belonged to Agrifood, 30% to aerospace, 20% to tourism and 30% to governmental institutions.

Figure 5. Content: Logical sequence of the learning material

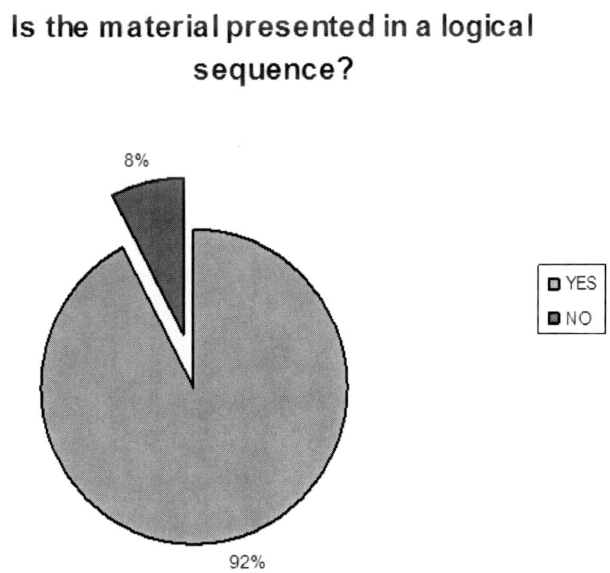

Figure 6. Tutorship: Tutor problem-solving ability

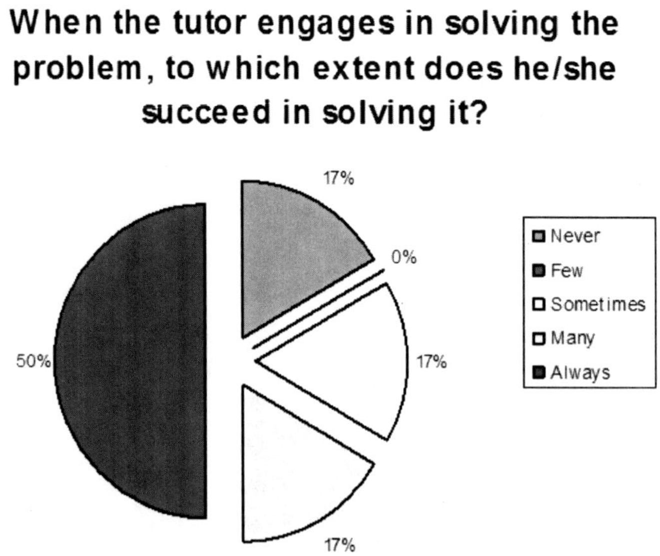

Figure 7. Technology: Number of platform bugs/faults/blocks

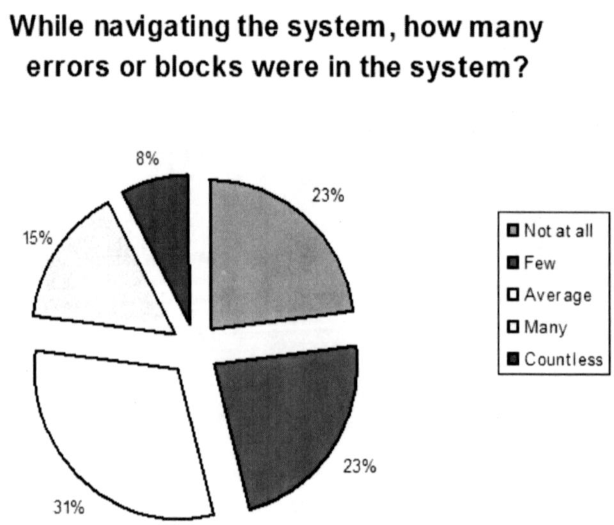

CHALLENGES AND FUTURE DIRECTIONS

Referring to the two IMeBM editions (2006 and 2007), the three phases of the laboratory (for a total of 24 weeks) significantly contributed to develop Human Capital (competences developed in e-Business issues, topics and contexts), Social Capital (networks and cooperation with Mediterranean institutions and companies) and Structural Capital (research and innovation projects). So, especially through the laboratory phase and more

Figure 8. Learner: Knowledge acquired

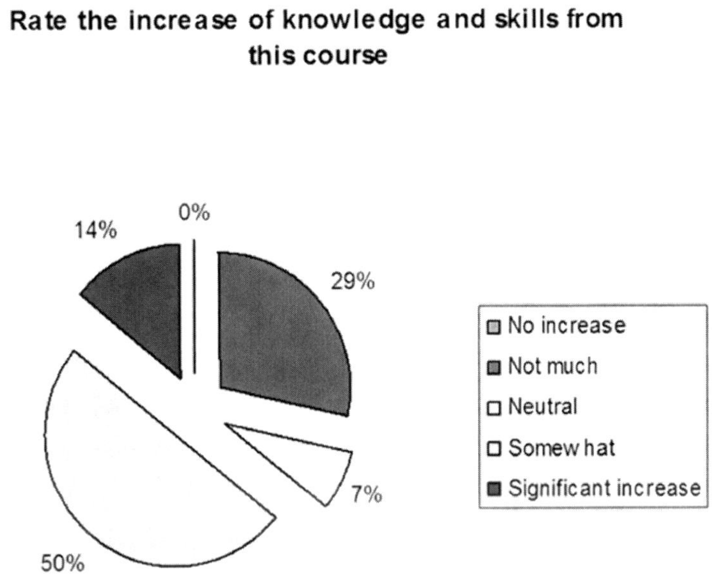

in general through the entire IMeBM program, e-Business capabilities have been created in 20 young talents. They represent the first nucleus of people to activate the diffusion of organizational and digital innovation to modernize traditional and emerging industries in Mediterranean Countries.

However, the adaptation of acceptance of some learners to rely on a virtual learning environment for attaining the knowledge and create competences is still an issue that is challenging when thinking to move completely online. Moreover, dealing with technology requires the organization to cope with new advancements of technology and software and technical upgrades.

In addition, the future development of our work will be focused on the activation of similar and complementary initiatives within the Mediterranean School institutional framework, by involving all the managerial levels to promote and diffuse at large scale the e-Business capabilities and practices that represent the real strategic and sustainable lever to leapfrog Mediterranean Countries in the Digital and Knowledge Economy.

REFERENCES

Afuah, A., & Tucci, C. L. (2001). Internet Business Models and Strategies: Text and Cases. New York: McGraw-Hill/Irwin.

Baets, W. R. J., & Van der Linden, G. (2003). Virtual Corporate Universities: A Matrix Of Knowledge And Learning For The New Digital Dawn. Norwell, MA: Kluwer.

Bailey, J., Sass, M., Swiercz, P. M., Seal, C., & Kayes, D. C. (2005). Teaching with and through teams: Student-written, instructor-facilitated case writing and the signatory code. *Journal of Management Education*, *29*(1), 39–59. doi:10.1177/1052562904269641

Collins, A., Brown, J. S., & Newman, S. E. (1989). Cognitive apprenticeship: Teaching the crafts of reading, writing, and mathematics. In L. B. Resnick (Ed.), Knowing, Learning, and Instruction: Essays in Honor of Robert Glaser (pp. 453–494). Hillsdale, NJ: Lawrence Erlbaum.

Economic and Social Commission for Western Asia (ESCWA). (2005). *Information Society Indicator.* New York: United Nations. Retrieved April 13, 2009, from http://www.escwa.org.lb/information/publications/edit/upload/ictd-05-1.pdf

Elia, G., Secundo, G., & Taurino, T. (2006). Towards unstructured and just-in-time learning: the Virtual eBMS e-learning system. In Proceedings of m-ICTE2006 - Current Developments in Technology-Assisted Education (Vol. 2, pp.1067–1072).

Engel, C. (1991). Not just a method but a way of learning. In D. Boud & G. Feletti (Eds.), The challenge of problem-based learning (pp. 23-33). New York: St. Martin's Press.

Fekula, M. J. (1994). Information and uncertainty as strange bedfellows: A model and experiential exercise. *Developments in Business Simulation and Experiential Learning, 21*, 133–136.

Gordon, P., Rogers, A., & Comfort, M. (2001). A taste of problem-based learning increases achievement of urban minority middle-school students. *Educational Horizons, 79*(4), 171–175.

Hmelo-Silver, C. E. (2004). Problem-based learning: what and how students learn? *Educational Psychology Review, 16*(3), 235–266. doi:10.1023/B:EDPR.0000034022.16470.f3

Kolb, D. A. (1984). Experiential learning: Experience as the source of learning development. Upper Saddle River, NJ: Prentice-Hall.

Kolodner, J. L., Hmelo, C. E., & Narayanan, N. H. (1996). Problem-based learning meets case-based reasoning. In D. C. Edelson, & E. A. Domeshek (Eds.), *Proceedings of ICLS 96* (pp. 188–195). Charlottesville, VA: AACE.

Lorange, P. (2005). Strategy means choice: also for today's business school! *Journal of Management Development, 24*(9), 783–790. doi:10.1108/02621710510621295

Maxwell, N., Bellisimo, Y., & Mergendoller, J. (2001). Problem-based learning: Modifying the medical school model for teaching high school economics. *Social Studies, 92*(2), 73–78. doi:10.1080/00377990109603981

Meier, S., Hovde, R., & Meier, R. (1996). Problem solving: Teachers' perceptions, content area models, and interdisciplinary connections. *School Science and Mathematics, 96*(5), 230–237.

Pawlowsky, P. (2001). The treatment of organisational learning in management science. In M. Dierkes, et al. (Eds.), Handbook of organisational learning and knowledge (pp. 62-88). New York: Oxford University Press.

Peterson, T. O. (2004). So you're thinking of trying problem based learning? Three critical success factors for implementation. *Journal of Management Education, 28*(5), 630–647. doi:10.1177/1052562904267543

Romano, A., Elia, V., & Passiante, G. (Eds.). (2001). Creating Business Innovation Leadership. An Ongoing Experiment, The e-Business Management School at ISUFI. Naples: Edizioni Scientifiche Italiane.

Romano, A., Passiante, G., Petti, C., & Secundo, G. (2005). Creating Human capital suitable for leading the XXI century organizations. In *Proceedings of the 11th International Conference on Industrial Engineering and Engineering Management*, Northeastern University, Shenyang, China.

Secundo, G., & Passiante, G. (2007). An innovative approach to creating business leaders: evidence from a case study. *International Journal of Management in Education, 1*(3), 214–230. doi:10.1504/IJMIE.2007.015122

Secundo, G., & Passiante, G. (2007). Innovative practices in human capital creation: the eBMS case. In *Proceedings of 28th McMaster World Congress*, Hamilton Convention Centre, Canada.

World Bank. (2003). *Lifelong Learning in the Global Knowledge Economy: Challenges for Developing Countries*. Retrieved April 13, 2009, from http://siteresources.worldbank.org/INTLL/Resources/Lifelong-Learning-in-the-Global-Knowledge-Economy/lifelonglearning_GKE.pdf

ADDITIONAL READING

Armstrong, A., & Hagel, J. (1995). Real Profits from Virtual Communities. *Mc Kinsey Quarterly*, *3*, 127–141.

Augar, N., Raitman, R., Lanham, E., & Zhou, W. (2006). Building Virtual Learning Communities. In Z. Ma (Ed.), Web-based Intelligent e-Learning Systems: Technologies and Applications (pp. 72-100). Hershey, PA: Idea Group.

Bonett, M. (2001). Personalization of web services: opportunities and challenges. *ARIADNE*, 28. Retrieved April 13, 2009, from http://www.ariadne.ac.uk/issue28/personalization/

Cha, S., & Joung, Y. (2001). Managing Personal Data in the Age of Customization Services. *International Association for Computer Information Systems*, *2*, 50–56.

Chen, C., Lee, H., & Chen, Y. (2005). Personalized e-learning system using item response theory. *Computers & Education*, *44*, 237–255. doi:10.1016/j.compedu.2004.01.006

Coakes, E., & Clareke, S. (2006). Encyclopaedia of communities of practice in information and knowledge management. Hershey, PA: Idea Group Reference.

Cohen, D., & Prusak, L. (2001). In Good Company: How Social Capital Makes Organizations Work. Boston, MA: Harvard Business School Press.

Collison, C. (1999). Connecting the new organization. How BP Amoco encourages post-merger collaboration. *Knowledge Management Review*, *7*(2), 12–15.

Dagger, D., Vincent, W., & Owen, C. (2003). Towards anytime, anywhere Learning: The Role and Realization of Dynamic Terminal Personalization in Adaptive eLearning. In D. Lassner & C. McNaught (Eds.), *Proceedings of World Conference on Educational Multimedia, Hypermedia and Telecommunications 2003* (pp. 32-35). Chesapeake, VA: AACE

Dasgupta, S. (2006). Encyclopaedia of virtual communities and technologies. Hershey, PA: Idea Group Reference.

Davenport, T., & Prusak, L. (1998). Working Knowledge. How organization manage what they know. Boston, MA: Harvard Business School Press.

De Bra, P., Stash, N., & De Lange, B. (2003). AHA! Adding Adaptive Behaviour to Websites. In *Proceedings of NLUUG*. Ede, The Netherlands: De Reehorst.

Denman-Maier, E. (2004). Intercultural Factors in Web-based Training Systems. *Journal of Universal Computer Science*, *10*(1), 90–104.

Figallo, C. (1998). Hosting Web Communities: Building relationships, increasing customer loyalty, and maintaining a competitive advantage. New York: Wiley Computer Publishing.

Gloor, P. (2005). Swarm creativity: Competitive advantage through collaborative innovation networks. New York: Oxford University Press, Inc.

Hardaker, G., & Smith, D. (2002). e-learning communities, virtual markets and knowledge creation. *European Business Review*, *14*(5), 342–350. doi:10.1108/09555340210444194

Henderson, A. (2003), The E-Learning Question and Answer Book: A Survival Guide for Trainers and Business Managers (1st Ed). NY: AMACOM/ American Management Association.

Horton, W., & Horton, K. (2003). E-learning Tools and Technologies: A consumer's guide for trainers, teachers, educators, and instructional designers. Indianapolis, IN: Wiley Publishing.

Igbaria, M., Shayo, C., & Olfman, L. (1998). Virtual societies: their prospects and dilemmas. In J. Gackenbach (Ed.), Psychology and the Internet (pp. 227-250). San Diego, CA: Academic Press.

Jonassen, D., Howland, J., Moore, J., & Marra, R. M. (2003). Learning to solve problems with technology: A constructive perspective (2nd Ed.). Upper Saddle River, NJ: Person Education.

Kim, A. (2000). Community building on the web: secret strategies for successful online communities. Berkeley, CA: Peachpit Press.

Lave, J., & Wenger, E. (1991). Situated Learning: Legitimate Peripheral Participation. Cambridge, UK: Cambridge University Press.

Lewis, D., & Allan, B. (2005). Virtual Learning Communities: A Guide for Practitioners. Berkshire, UK: Open University Press.

Lundvall, B. (2000). *The Learning Economy: some implications for the Knowledge Base of health and education systems, OECD* (pp. 125-141). Retrieved April 13, 2009, from http://www.gbv.de/dms/goettingen/312704216.pdf

Maier, R. (2002). Knowledge Management Systems - Information and communication technologies for Knowledge Management. Heidelberg: Springer-Verlag.

McDermott, R. (1999). Learning across teams: the role of communities of practice in team organizations. *Knowledge Management Review*, *8*, 32–36.

Morrison, D. (2003). e-Learning Strategies: How to get implementation and delivery right first time. Chichester, UK: Wiley.

Najjar, J., Duval, E., & Wolpers, M. (2006). Towards Effective Usage-Based Learning Applications: Track and Learn from User Experience(s). In *Proceedings of the Sixth International Conference on Advanced Learning Technologies – ICALT'06*, Kerkrade, Netherlands (pp. 1022- 1024).

Nonaka, I., & Konno, N. (1998). The concept of 'Ba': building a foundation for knowledge creation. *California Management Review*, *40*(3), 40–54.

Nonaka, I., Toyama, R., & Konno, N. (2000). SECI, Ba and Leadership: a Unified Model of Dynamic Knowledge Creation. *Long Range Planning*, *33*, 5–34. doi:10.1016/S0024-6301(99)00115-6

OECD. (2006). *Athabasca University: A case study in Open Educational Resources Production And Use in Higher Education In Canada.* Prepared for the Canadian Council on learning. Retrieved April 13, 2009, from http://www.oecd.org/dataoecd/61/45/37647739.pdf

Park, I., & Hannafin, M. J. (1993). Empirically-based guidelines for the design of interactive multimedia. *Educational Technology Research and Development*, *41*(3), 63–85. doi:10.1007/BF02297358

Piskurich, G. (2003). The AMA Handbook of E-Learning: Effective Design, Implementation, and Technology Solutions. New York: AMACOM.

Riecken, D. (2000). Personalized views of personalization. *Communications of the ACM*, *43*(8), 26–28. doi:10.1145/345124.345133

Rosenberg, M. (2001). e-Learning - Strategies for Delivering Knowledge in the Digital Age. New York: McGraw-Hill.

Rosenberg, M. (2006). Beyond e-learning: approaches and technologies to enhance organizational knowledge learning, and performance. San Francisco, CA: Pfeiffer.

Saint-Onge, H., & Wallace, D. (2003). Leveraging communities of practice for strategic advantage. Heinemann, Germany: Butterworth.

Sergiovanni, T. (2000). The Lifeworld of Leadership: Creating Culture, Community, and Personal Meaning in Our Schools. San Francisco, CA: Jossey Bass.

Teece, D. J., & Pisano, G. (1994). The Dynamic Capabilities of Firms: An Introduction. *Industrial and Corporate Change*, *3*(3), 537–556. doi:10.1093/icc/3.3.537-a

Volpentesta, A., Frega, N., & Filice, G. (2004). Early steps toward an e-learning community at the University of Calabria. In *Proceedings of ED-MEDIA World Conference on Educational Multimedia, Hypermedia & Telecommunications*, 21-26 giugno 2004, Lugano, Swiss (pp.5102-5107).

Wenger, E. (1998). Community of Practice: Learning, Meaning and Identity. Cambridge, UK: Cambridge University Press.

Wenger, E., McDermott, R., & Snyder, W. (2002). Cultivating communities of practice: a guide to managing knowledge (1st Ed.). Boston, MA: Harvard Business School Press.

Wenger, E., & Snyder, W. (2000, January-February). Community of Practice: the Organizational Frontier. *Harvard Business Review*, 139–145.

Xu, D., Wang, H., & Wang, M. (2005). Conceptual Model of Personalized Virtual Learning Environments. *Expert Systems with Applications*, *29*(3), 525–534. doi:10.1016/j.eswa.2005.04.028

Zack, M. H. (1999). Developing a Knowledge Strategy. *California Management Review*, *41*(3).

KEY TERMS AND DEFINITIONS

Problem Based Learning (PBL): A learning approach founded on the usage of real-world problems and projects to develop competencies and skills "on the job". In PBL, learners learn by solving problems and reflecting on their experiences.

Skill Gap Analysis: A technique used for understanding the missing skills that people need but don't have to perform their activities effectively. Skill Gap Analysis helps organizations in refining and defining the skills they need.

Knowledge Domain: The knowledge domain refers to the content of a particular field of knowledge.

Competence Level: A learning experience referred to the level of expertise a learner has reached in regard to a specific knowledge area. A competence corresponds to the ability of the learner to be able to analyze a specific problem, to understand the reference context, and to find a rational solution for the problem.

Learning Objective: A learning objective is a clear specification of a measurable behavioural outcome of learning. It is also used during the evaluation of learning effectiveness. In the eBMS vision, there is a one-to-one relationship between the learning objectives and the tasks that a knowledge worker has to perform during his research and/or project activities; i.e. a knowledge worker has to acquire just the right knowledge he needs (and therefore he has to reach a specific learning objective) in order to fill a skill gap and to correctly solve a specific problem or a specific activity of a more complex project.

Multimedia Knowledge Objects: An object composed of a single document or a collection of documents. Each file composing the object is in its native format (such as text, graphics, image, presentation, audio, video, etc.).

Web Mining: A technique used to extract useful information from the data gathered from the web, and then using this data to generate value for the organization; i.e: better understanding consumers' behaviors.

e-Library: A collection of organized materials that are stored in digital formats and accessible over a network. In the e-library, materials can be retrieved by using keyword, author name, subject or other searches.Modoloreet aciduis sequat lan eu faccum duipit, sis dolor alisis augue verostionsed.

Chapter 16
A Framework to Analyze Teaching-Learning Objects (T-LO):
A Case Study of a Didactic Module

Ingrid Kleist Clark Nunes
Santa Catarina Federal University, Brazil

Elena Maria Mallmann
Santa Maria Federal University (UFSM), Brazil

ABSTRACT

The pedagogical mediation in Distance Education (DE) is sustained by hypermediatic didactic materials, which are marked by principles of autonomy, interaction, interactivity, motivation and cooperation. The main thought in this article is to know if the developed Teaching-Learning Objects (T-LO) are potentially meaningful answering these principles. The planning and elaboration of the T-LO are highlighted processes in Brazil. Therefore, the authors present the conceptual singularities of the T-LO; the Instructional Design (ID) processes and the importance of the Instructional Project (IP) elaboration to guarantee a meaningful potentiality of the T-LO. As a research result, the authors center attention on the contribution of a framework (called the T-LO List), which is used to analyze the T-LO developed, implemented, and evaluated in a specific context of a didactic module elaboration. In conclusion, it is important to realize that the usage of a framework to analyze the T-LO can orient theoretical methodological steps of planning, developing, implementing, observing, reflecting, and re-planning, all carried out by multidisciplinary teams.

ORGANIZATION BACKGROUND

The systematization of the analysis, descriptions and reflections in the presented case are results of researches that have been performed by the authors during several years (Mallmann, 2008; Nunes, 2008) These researches have always been linked with the teacher, tutor and Instructional Design (ID) activities in multidisciplinary teams of Distance Education (DE) at the Santa Catarina Federal University, in Brazil. This is a public institution of learning, research and extension activities and, since 1960,

DOI: 10.4018/978-1-61520-909-5.ch016

which offers graduation and post-graduation courses. The organization also develops research and extension projects within the scope of international, national and regional scenarios.

In Brazil, the actual scenario of DE is marked by investments of public institutions of higher education in their course offers. The creation of the "Universidade Aberta do Brazil" (UAB) – Brazil Open University -, in 2006, is an important event in their political proposals (financial issues, organization of multidisciplinary teams, how to manage the institution, the academic and pedagogical issues). The UAB proposes innovation through the collaborative integration with federal, state and municipal systems, consolidating partnerships and strategies to offer demanding courses.

The expansion of the process of offering DE courses has caused innovations and urgencies in the elaboration processes and in the usage of hypermedia and printed didactic materials; between them we have the Teaching-Learning Objects(T-LO). In this scenario, focus of our research is the development of methodological strategies to analyze the meaningful potentiality of the T-LO in the pedagogical mediation at distance. The steps and results of the process of a framework for analyzing a specific didactic module are discussed in detail in the case description.

SETTING THE STAGE

The principle of action-reflecting-action sustaining the teaching-research activities during the cyclic steps of planning, implementation, observation, evaluation and re-planning is shown in Figure 1 which makes a link with our functions like teachers, instructional designers and tutors in distance courses.

The organization of multidisciplinary teams to produce hypermedia and printed didactic materials is still a recent phenomenon in Brazil, especially in public and higher education. The insertion of Teaching-Learning Virtual Environments (T-LVE) and the T-LO in pedagogical mediation, to speed up autonomy, cooperation and interaction, has produced innovation in the teaching-learning process for universities.

Therefore, our teacher and research activities have been guided by the development of strategies, methodologies and technologies that can contribute in team management. This also can contribute to answer some challenges caused by course structure, financial issues, technological issues, epistemological and pedagogical principles, all related with the T-LO elaboration process for distance courses (Mallmann, 2008; Nunes, 2008).

Figure 1. Article structure. (© 2009, Ingrid Kleist Clark Nunes and Elena Maria Mallmann. Used with permission.)

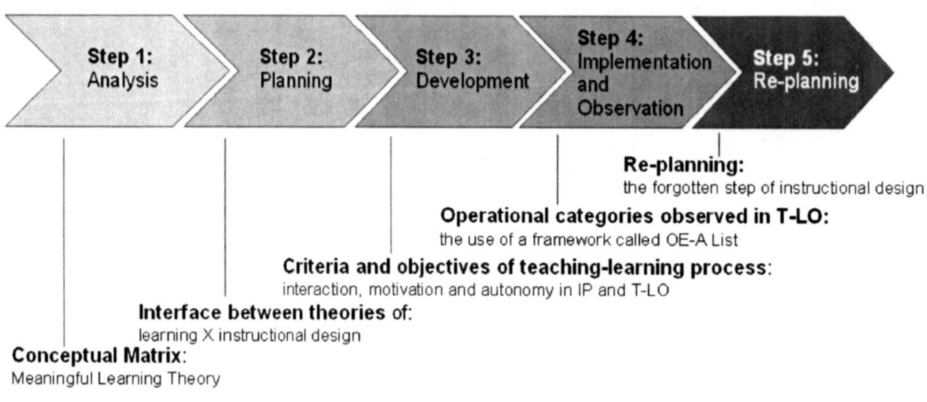

Beyond the framework development to analyze the T-LO potentiality, which is going to be detailed in the "case description" section; we are going to contribute in two ways:

a) the conceptual production about theories and ID functions in multidisciplinary teams. We present the concept "designer of mediation" (Mallmann, 2008) referenced in the purpose of Actor-Network Theory (ANT). This definition shows a meaning of a "problem-solving process", which is coherent with the cyclical principle of the "action-reflecting-action" and also includes the re-planning step as an essential step in the mediation design. With this idea, the mediation design expands the comprehension beyond the prescriptive functions of the "ID theories" and the technical activities of the instructional designer work realized in the T-LO production steps; and
b) the elaboration of a check-list (called Perfo_List) to manage the retrospective and prospective actions in multidisciplinary teams which produce didactic materials for DE (Mallmann, 2008).

CASE DESCRIPTION

Technology and Conceptual Concerns

The T-LO are didactic materials, which always have a specific educational function. Therefore, there is a different concept recognized internationally with the term "learning objects":

Learning objects are elements of a new type of computer-based instruction grounded in the object oriented paradigm of computer science. [...] This is the fundamental idea behind learning objects: instructional designers can build small (relative to the size of an entire course) instructional components that can be reused a number of times in different learning contexts [...] learning objects are generally understood to be digital entities deliverable over the Internet, meaning that any number of people can access and use them simultaneously (as opposed to traditional instructional media, such as an overhead or video tape, which can only exist in one place at a time) (Willey, 2000, p. 3-4).

Besides objectifying the approach of a concept, the meaningful potentiality of the T-LO turns possible establishing "a solid connection between the concepts that the students already know and those that it is pretended to teach". An object to be called as "teaching-learning" has always to be presented in a specific course, and contextualize a determined learning path, defined pedagogical intention,and outline assumptions in view of a given specific Instructional Project (IP) (Nunes et al., 2007, p. 4). This definition also differs from the Learning Technology Standards Committee (LTSC), which describes Learning Objects (LO) as "any entity, digital or not digital, which can be used for learning, education and training" (Draft Standard for eXtensible Markup Language (XML) Binding for Learning Object Metadata Model (LOM), 2003).

The potentiality of the LO organized at the SCORM development model like an instructional technology is important in the pedagogical mediation, but this potentiality will never be established without any balanced effort between areas of technology, curriculum, design and learning theories. We can say that the **T-LO** comprehend a specific educational function (the mediation) as a didactic material, mainly when these objects are planned and elaborated by the teacher and multidisciplinary teams under the light of principles of pedagogy, technology and specific contents.

Regardless of the technical and financial issues, we can't forget the main role of the T-LO in the didactic module investigated in this case which is to speed up the teaching-learning process meaningfully. During the description of this case, we trace the outline of what was considered as meaningful potentiality.

Management and Organizational Concerns

Facing this conceptual panorama, several issues have permeated the investigation process and the reflection about the T-LO as hypermediatic didactic materials for pedagogic mediation in DE. For example, how didactic materials such as T-LO can be potentially meaningful in DE?

We find that the different experiences in multidisciplinary teams show that even if the principles are being presented in a planned way in a specific IP, it doesn't mean that the T-LO are contemplated with these principles or that there is a relevant result for the course. Beyond that, we also cannot guarantee that the T-LO and IP are retrospectively evaluated to generate re-planning for the T-LO and the entire course. In this manner, it is important to investigate an IP mainly in its steps of elaboration and evaluation because it can or cannot have their relevance to produce T-LO.

To answer this question, there is a need for a better understanding of their organization and programming, both in IP and T-LO, making the usage of theoretical-methodological elements which are essential with reference to instructional projects during the Teaching-Learning Object planning and development steps.

Methodologically, this article is organized through investigations, which were done by the authors about the steps of planning, developing, implementing, observing, reflecting, and redesigning in the multidisciplinary teams (See Figure 1).

The conceptual contribution in this article is the result of concrete experiences in distance courses as teachers, instructional designers and tutors and the learning acquired with researches about the didactic materials elaboration process (Mallmann, 2008; Nunes, 2008). To explain each one of the steps represented in Figure 1, we have chosen a specific didactic module which was developed over the years of 2006, 2007 and 2008. It also has been observed, in our experiences and researches, that other productions had the same conceptual organization as instructional designers. The choice of this module is justified by the use of its IP as a reference for the development of a framework to analyze each Teaching-Learning Object.

Step 1: Conceptual Matrix

The elaboration of T-LO created a challenge for the definition of a conceptual matrix that theoretically sustains the procedures and the analysis of this kind of didactic material. In this manner, the best choice for the studied case was the Meaningful Learning Theory (Ausubel; Novak; Hanesian, 1978). This conceptual choice was realized mainly because this theory helps in the identification of the T-LO meaningful potentiality (Mallmann, 2008; Nunes, 2008). Therefore, we discuss about the conceptual categories, which are prioritized for the activities development, and also present how we achieve some evidence of the T-LO meaningful potentiality using the operational categories listed in the framework.

In line with Holmberg (1995), the learning has not to be known like a "passive process", which means having the learner as a "teaching object" and as a person that just receives information in the teaching-learning process. That is also in line with the concept of the Meaningful Learning Theory chosen to sustain the elaboration of the didactic module. The teaching-learning is an "active process", the learners interpret the information and try to associate it with their knowledge already acquired and to place the information in their previous cognitive structure (1995, p. 32). In Ausubel's theory (Ausubel, 2000; Ausubel, 1978) we can say that the meaningful learning occurs in DE if the didactic materials present didactic-methodological strategies and when have learner activities that promote the interconnection of new concepts with concepts already known by the students or concepts already presented before in the course.

The conceptual matrix of the meaningful learning reasons related to the teaching-learning process of IP and T-LO for the didactic module is being studied here. With these postulates, allied with Holmberg (1995) contributions, we can say that the didactic materials like the T-LO are co-responsible for the meaningful learning success (Ausubel; Novak; Hanesian, 1978). Furthermore, we consider that Ausubel's thoughts and contributions could have a decisive importance in the learning structure in DE courses (Holmberg, 1995).

The assimilation, according to Ausubel (Ausubel, 2000; Ausubel, 1978), is responsible to the memorization and longevity of the ideas learned meaningfully and to contribute as how the knowledge is organized in the cognitive structure. The possibility of the new learning material discrimination and of the prior concepts of learned discrimination in the cognitive structure is one of the main variables in the meaningful learning and retention (Ausubel; Novak; Hanesian, 1978, p. 153).

To get meaningful learning, the teaching has to be structured with the "subsumptions" which are known as fundamental elements for assimilation to the new presented information. Subsumptions are concepts existing in the cognitive structure of the learner and can make a relationship with new concepts that have to be learned. To have the success of this assimilation, it is necessary to use "advance organizers" in the didactic materials working as "conceptual links" present in the new content that will be assimilated by the learner. These organizers have to facilitate the connection between the new content and the subsumptions. Therefore, presence of the advance organizers in didactic materials is important. In DE, they are presented as strategies created in T-LO content which allow this connection with the subsumptions (Nunes, 2008).

For occurrence of the meaningful learning, beyond the subsumptions and advance organizers, the conceptual hierarchies also have to be considered, because they are the logical form of organization of the information. Therefore, we cannot deny that the conceptual hierarchies and the content sequencing are important for the teaching-learning process, because in this theory this process only occurs when there is an interaction between the existing learner knowledge with the new information that has to be assimilated (Ausubel; Novak; Hanesian, 1978).

On the basis of these theoretical assumptions, under the light of the existing advance organizers and conceptual hierarchies, we explored the reality of convergence of the observable categories between IP and T-LO. These observable categories are found in IP and T-LO through an exploratory analysis process. The content organization, like an example of this conceptual blueprint, has to use the advance organizers linked with the existing subsumptions in the cognitive structure of the learner. Therefore, we also looked for evidence for use of this appropriate theory in the IP proposal and consequently in the T-LO.

In the following section, each one of the organizational postulates observed in the steps of didactic modules elaboration (planning, development, implementing, observing, reflecting and re-planning) on the basis of Meaningful Learning Theory is discussed and explored during the framework systematization which were made for the T-LO analysis.

- **Progressive differentiation**: this postulate explains when content is developed with subjects organized as general to specific, which means that the content is progressively differentiated, in "decreasing order" of the "inclusiveness". The meaningful learning is enhanced when we use the beginning sequence with inclusive concepts and then present concepts which are less inclusive (Ausubel, 2000, p. 164);

- **Integrative reconciliation**: to have similarities, meaningful differences and also reconcile inconsistencies, content has to be explicitly explored to establish some relationship between the ideas. That also has to be considered in the contents organized in parallel, without a hierarchical sequencing. Even though the contents and subjects are separated in the material organization, an advance organizer has to clearly and precisely design the main similarities and differences between the new concepts and subordinated principles to be learned, on one side, and, on the other side, between similar ideas established in the cognitive structure" (Ausubel; Novak; Hanesian, 1978, p. 163);
- **Sequential organization**: this principle is based on the vantages of the "sequential" and "natural" "dependencies" between the components division of one discipline. The comprehension of a subject presupposes "prior comprehension of another topic related". Therefore, the possibility of subjects organization in accordance with these sequential dependencies make the meaningful learning an "its own right realization" (Ausubel; Novak; Hanesian, 1978, p. 163-164); and
- **Consolidation**: this postulate states that to guarantee the learner's readiness (maturity: the existence of advance organizers in their cognitive structure) to the new subject, it has to be a consolidation step with the prior lessons. The consolidation is obtained with the "confirmation, correction, clarification, differential practice" and revision during the "repetitive exposure", with feedback, to the learning material (Ausubel; Novak; Hanesian, 1978, p. 165).

One of the principles which we have observed during the steps of T-LO production is the possibility of using the advance organizers, the progressive differentiation, the integrative reconciliation, the sequential organization and the consolidation in the T-LO, independently of the subject complexity related with the learner's cognitive structure. For each one of these postulates, the learner can use the prior concepts (subsumptions), which also can be related with a determined new subject. The possibility of considering these subsumptions to speed up the meaningful learning exists through the usage of analogies for connecting with the new subject. It means that even a determined group of learners has never known or listened about the new content; we consider that their members will have subsumptions in their cognitive structures (that can be considered at the teaching-learning moment).

Step 2: Interface between Theories

To elaborate the T-LO potentially meaningful, it is not just enough to know what makes up the teaching-learning movement, what kind of components have the possible strategies to structure this process and what makes up these objects (Nunes, 2008,). Therefore, it is necessary to align the Meaningful Learning Theory with the instructional theories which can offer theoretic-methodological and coherent support to comprehend the meaningful potentiality in T-LO.

The **ID** theories are prescriptive and look for clarifying as how to construct the teaching-learning process (Reigeluth, 1999). This "how to construct" the teaching-learning creates a meeting point with Meaningful Learning Theory categories, which are chosen to comprehend the meaningful potentiality of T-LO inside of a specific didactic module. Reigeluth (1983) describes the appearance of ID like a linking science, which means that ID is a science, which looks for the connection between learning theory and educational practice.

The ID theories are important and became relevant for planning and elaboration of T-LO. An ID theory, when it explains instructional strategies and proposal models, helps to improve the consistency and support to the relationship between IP and T-LO elaboration.

In view of our conceptual building, concerning hypermedia didactic materials and comprehending them as teaching objects, as learning objects and their mediator characteristics (with teacher and learners), we also expanded our conceptual comprehension about theories and concepts of design. Therefore, the concept of "mediation design" (Mallmann, 2008) referenced in the Actor-Network Theory (ANT) acquires the means of the "problem-solving process" which is coherent with the cyclical principle of the action-reflecting-action. This means that the process of didactic materials elaboration, especially the T-LO elaboration, cannot lose the re-planning step. This step is important especially because of the retrospective (evaluation of T-LO) and prospective characteristics of T-LO (reorganization using the evaluation evidence oriented by pedagogical, technological principles and specific content).

For the DE, it is necessary to know how and when we have to use and structure the T-LO, it is also necessary to comprehend basic aspects of the planning and specific aspects of Design. Ausubel, Novak and Hanesinan (1978), wrote about the planning step – which is one of the steps realized during the design of the IP –, explaining that "arbitrary decisions" in the content sequencing, realized during the course planning, can change the teaching-learning movement and results into de-motivation.

This idea presents the importance of the comprehension and connection between the theories: learning theory, design theories and DE theory. From that connection, it is also important to comprehend the planning processes which are necessary to structure a course that use all these theories. In agreement with Holmberg (1995), these thoughts establish the processes of distance education, bringing up the "personality development" and the "problem resolution" like an academic exercise. The building of these processes needs planning that has to be "useful" (p. 36).

The IP is the concrete planning, it is the physical document which describes all the pedagogical and technical defined details and which guide the materials elaboration (aiming materials that have a specific function during the mediation teaching- learning process). This kind of a document, mainly the one that was analyzed in this case, has to offer orientation for the T-LO development and for their didactic-methodological strategies to speed up the pedagogical mediation during the entire course. We present at this sequencing the IP structure which has been used by us during the experiences as instructional designers in multidisciplinary teams (See Figure 2).

Reigeluth (1999a) used the concept of IP for understanding it as a set of "instruction methods". Under our thoughts, which are supported by theoretical principles of mediation, we are in favor of the project elaboration as a fundamental step to specify how, where and when to use the T-LO in a determined course. We believe that here is a possibility to speed up the meaningful learning.

It is also important to highlight that the IP elaboration has been considered as a responsibility of the instructional designer. Even though the instructional designer is responsible for registering this process; it is important to highlight the fundamental existence of the co-authors from a teacher/specialist of the subject. This is because of the fact that the instructional designer is the IP author, but the content author is the specialist. Without content, it does not have the IP. Therefore, the functions of each one of the members of the multidisciplinary teams are important (Nunes, 2008).

The comprehension of the relationship between the Mediation Design and IP document, as the understanding of the practical aspects of the design theories facilitated the selection moments of the observable operational categories (didactic-methodological elements) included in T-LO.

Figure 2. Copy of "Concepts used in the elaboration of the T-LO List". (© 2008, Ingrid Kleist Clark Nunes. Free translation. Used with permission)

STEP PRESENTED IN INSTRUCTIONAL PROJECT	DESCRIPTION AND FUNCTION OF THE STEP	ELABORATI ON STEP	WHO PARTICIPATED?
Course Conceptual Map (CCM)	Transmitting the comprehension of the general content of the course.	The end of context analyses	Instructional designer; and e-learning manager (specialist).
Teaching Plan (TP)	Contains the general goals, the general content sequencing and the general description of activities.	Start of planning	Instructional designer; and subject specialist.
Conceptual Map of Teaching-Learning Object (CMT-LO)	Contains a comprehension of the course specific content; in this case a CMT-LO for each one of those nine T-LO was elaborated.	During the planning	Instructional designer; and subject specialist.
T-LO Plan (T-LOP) and *Storyboards*	Contains all the sequences of the specific content, the language adaptation and the step-by-step of Teaching-Learning Object.	Between planning and development	Instructional designer, specialist, writer and graphic designer.

Step 3: Criteria and Objectives of Teaching-Learning Process

To construct an analysis methodology, that could identify some indicators of IP use relevance in relation with T-LO elaboration, we identified some observable operational categories. These categories converge with the ideas presented in the Meaningful Learning Theory (Ausubel), in two ID theories (Elaboration Theory from Reigeluth (1983, 1999b) and ARCS Model from Keller (1983, 1987)) and in a DE theory (Transactional Distance Theory from Moore (2002)).

Within the study of these theories and our focus on the analysis of IP and T-LO, we identified the necessity of building a check-list, which was the inspiration to construct the framework of analysis called the T-LO List. But, to use a framework like this one, and if it has to be effective, mainly when we are talking about education, it was necessary to thoroughly establish the criteria and objectives of the teaching-learning process that orientated the didactic module elaboration.

In this case, we have considered that the T-LO can be potentially meaningful if it presents indicators or evidence of cognitive interaction (Ausubel, 1978: Ausubel 2000) in their observed operational categories. The cognitive interaction was considered a relevant conceptual category in this work, just because it is present in the teaching-learning IP proposals for the didactic module analyzed.

For Ausubel (2000), the motivation has an important role in the teaching-learning process. The concept of motivation has to cover the idea that the meaningful learning suffers from external and internal influences by the learner, enhancing or not the relationship between the prior knowledge and the new information in their cognitive structure. Therefore, these relationships need to be inserted to a matrix with "intentions, purposes and expectations" of the learner (Salvador, 2000, p. 383).

The motivation can be "a mediator of individual learning" (Maier, Prange & Rosenstiel, 2003). It can give "one position of when and how, what and which level of success one person learns in a determined educational and occupational context" (Nunes, 2008, p. 92). Even though the teaching-learning process is not directly connected with motivation actions but these actions can promote the meaningful potentiality of the T-LO.

It occurs because the motivation component is the cognitive impulse which is "potentially more important and stable" as considered by Ausubel, Novak and Hanesian (1978). This impulse is what wakes up the desire of the learning process. Furthermore, it is task oriented, making the learning a success and its "own reward", leaving any other external influence of acceptation. Even though the learning does not depend on the motivators actions in the teaching, the motivation has to be considered in the planning of the T-LO to promote meaningful potentiality of the learning in this kind of didactic material.

There is causal and reciprocal relationship between the learning and the motivation. When an individual learns, he or she becomes motivated to learn more by his or hers own learning process. Therefore, the more appropriated "level" to "activate the motivation" to learn consists in concentrating on the cognitive aspects of the learning. In this way the motivation by cognitive impulse can be developed (Ausubel; Novak; Hanesian, 1978) and enhanced in the T-LO.

The conception of the meaningful potentiality proposed in the IP of the didactic module investigated cannot be summarized just by the cognitive interaction and motivation. Therefore, we also have explored the Transactional Distance Theory of Moore (2002) as a DE theory to complement the analysis indicators of the third and last conceptual category: the autonomy.

It is necessary that learners gain autonomy related with their own learning, administrate their own study hours, know how to select the contents of their interest, participate in the activities, independently of time or place (Kenski, 2005, p. 3).

This last category has the link with Ausubel's (2000) description when he defines, among orientations presented previously, that the potentially meaningful didactic materials has to present a concern with the erroneous conception of the learners and has to allow a fast correction. In this case, we can say that an observable operational category could be identified by the didactic-methodological elements that enhance the autonomy.

As an example, we can see the didactic-methodological elements of the kind of feedback (conceptual answer specific of an activity) encountered in the analyzed didactic module. When the feedback messages present assimilative questions, which require the learner to make choices or to answer by words, we can consider that as evidences of the autonomy promotion.

To achieve this goal, beyond the comprehension, the motivation concepts and cognitive interaction, presented previously; we have studied the Transactional Distance Theory (Moore, 2002) which describes the autonomy and another important issue of DE. Moore considers that in DE the learner needs to be responsible for these choices and decision making about the study strategies and actions. In any distance course, independently of the number of the qualified instructions and orientations, if there is no dialogue – intentional and guided dialogue to"improve the comprehension by the learner" –, the learners have to be capable to make decisions by themselves, they have to know how to make the most of their lessons (2002, p. 5).

The absence of this dialogue is one of the conditions considered by the author, which increases the "transactional distance". The lesser the dialogue was between the teacher/tutor and the learner, the bigger will be the "transactional distance" between them and the greater will be the autonomy of the learner(Moore, 2002, p. 5). The analyzed didactic module in this case does not compose this dialogue between teacher and learner.

When the learner is a crucial actor in the "transaction of the teaching–learning", in agreement with Moore (2002), the potential he has of autonomous learning becomes a promotion to the reduction of the transactional distance between learner and content in any course. The T-LO are no-human actors or mediators (Latour, 2001) in the transaction or in the teaching-learning movement, representing an interactive role to this process. The T-LO need to be potentially meaningful to promote this interaction relationship with the subject to be learned and for reduction of the transactional distance between learner and content.

On the basis in evidence found during our involvement as teachers, instructional designers and tutors in DE courses, allied to researches developed about the elaboration process of didactic materials and their role in pedagogical mediation in distance courses, we have chosen as meaningful potentiality category of analysis of the T-LO: a) cognitive interaction (David Ausubel and Charles Reigeluth); b) motivation (John Keller) and c) autonomy (Michael Moore).

Step 4: Operational Categories Observed in T-LO

To explore these concepts which enhance the teaching-learning process, in observable elements or characteristics of T-LO, we defined different operational categories detailed in the building of the framework called the T-LO List.

To improve the choice of observable operational categories (or also called didactic-methodological elements), which may be evidence of cognitive interaction in the observed and analyzed objects, we used highlighted aspects presented at Elaboration Theory of Reigeluth (1999b, 1983). This theory suggests a logical sequencing of contents and consolidation like Ausubel's (2000, 1978) proposes. The Elaboration Theory explains different methods of "how" content has to be organized. The key idea is based on the building of a meaningful context for the learner.

Reigeluth (1999a, 1999b, 1992, 1983) guides, by practical examples, that content has to be first presented in a general manner and later on to be detailed layer upon layer, time to time. These detailed layers have to increase the level of complexity, inserting with recalls of content, which is linked with the general or the simplest idea presented previously. The final result of this didactic-methodological strategy and their complexity, required by the entire content of the course will be achieved by the learner.

In describing the theory, which presents an explanation of "how an instruction model is organized", Reigeluth and Stein (1983) proposes seven strategic components based on Ausubel's (2000, 1978) postulates:

- model of "simple-to-complex sequence";
- "learning prerequisite sequences";
- "summarizers";
- "synthesizers";
- "analogies";
- "cognitive-strategy activators";
- "learner-control format" (p.342).

Even though the Elaboration Theory and its strategic components also have a relationship with the motivation concept, during the research development, we needed to look for other "molecular" theories which could explore this different category. Therefore, for analysis of the motivation category, we have chosen the theory presented in ARCS Model of Keller (1983).

Keller (1983), on the theory development of Motivational Design of Instruction, had chosen four criteria which enhance learner motivation by didactic materials: Interest, Relevance, Expectancy and Satisfaction. Later, the author redesigned his theory which resulted in the development of ARCS Model. Keller (1987) stated that motivation speeds up the learning by didactic materials and these ones have to be concerned with the categories below:

- Learner ATTENTION: to promote attention and curiosity of the learner, to stimulate the perception;
- RELEVANCE of the content for the learner: to establish a link between instruction and learner's requirements and realities, to promote choice, to be concerned with learner experiences;

- Learner CONFIDENCE: to develop confidence by learner's success, to support learner's expectations, to allow that learners believe in their own learning capabilities, to consider pre-requisites, to offer feedbacks, to allow learner's control; and
- Learner SATISFACTION: to administer the management of content review and evaluation, by extrinsic and intrinsic form for the learner; to maintain coherence with the initial course proposal, and to recognize learner's efforts.

On the basis of these concepts, it is possible to choose some strategies that didactic materials have to use. In this case, these strategies we preferred to choose from the subdivision of each one of the four conceptual categories of the model in many observable didactic-methodological elements. These strategies defined the operational categories which were chosen for the composition of the T-LO List.

In order to reach operational categories of autonomy concept, which was the third conceptual category of analysis, we used some indicators of the Transactional Distance Theory (Moore, 2002). In this theory, the author considers that the course structure is a qualitative variable and also important to reduce the transactional distance in DE promoting autonomy.

When the Transactional Distance Theory refers to organization and requirements, that a course must include, the ideas converge with other ideas that were already reviewed in this case by Reigeluth (1999b, 1983) and Keller (1987, 1983). The theory of Moore (2002) recommends that DE courses use the structure called "educational processes" and these processes could be adapted for the didactic module studied in this matter:

- presentation;
- support for learner motivation;
- stimulus for critical analysis;
- assistance and guidance;
- organization of: practice, application, test and evaluation; and
- organization of learner knowledge construction (p. 4).

Figure 3. Copy of "Initial step of the T-LO List construction: evaluated concepts". (© 2008, Ingrid Kleist Clark Nunes. Free translation. Used with permission)

AUTONOMY Transactional Distance	Presentation
	Stimulus of Critical Analysis
	Assistance and Guidance
	Administration and Tests of Learning
MOTIVATION (ARCS) Cognitive Impulse	Attention Promotion
	Relevance Demonstration
	Confidence Promotion
	Satisfaction Stimulation
COGNITIVE INTERACTION Elaboration Theory	Progressive Differentiation / Sequencing Model
	Harmony and Integrative Reconciliation / Prerequisites
	Consolidation / Summary
	Learner Control
	Cognitive-Strategy Activator

To construct the T-LO List, we used as a base these studied theories and some previously observed operational categories in the T-LO. In this manner, we developed a frame of conceptual categories with some operational indicators to define what would be the through categories to be observed (See Figure 3).

From this prior definition of conceptual categories that would be observed in IP and T-LO, we analyzed the IP proposal developed on the basis of meaningful learning for a specific didactic module. The analyzed IP defined how the didactic-methodological elements (specific functionalities present in the nine T-LO of the didactic module) would be developed and presented during the course. We identified some relevant conceptual categories from analysis of the description of these elements. The writings below, present some examples of didactic-methodological elements proposed in the IP of this case:

Character

- Function and categories: as the character had the intention in the specific IP to demonstrate how the subject might be useful, beginning from its relevance concept, considered as fundamental in accordance with Keller (1983) theory and his ARCS (1987) Model, we considered that this instructional element was aimed to use the conceptual category of motivation (Nunes, 2008).

Attention Frame

- Function and categories: this instructional element was proposed in IP looking to promote the learners curiosity; interest and attention. Therefore, as the character, this element also represents motivation category because it used more than one of the ARCS Model subcategories (Nunes, 2008).

Vantages Frame

- Function and categories: just like the character, this element was aimed to explicit the content's relevance for the prior cognitive structure of the learner. In this manner, and beyond the motivation category, the cognitive interaction category of Ausubel (1978, 2000) was used, also presented in the Elaboration Theory of Reigeluth and Stein (1983). That could be considered because the main objective of the element was to present the content linked with concepts that the learner already knows and concepts that the learner is still acquiring (Nunes, 2008).

Transition Messages Between Challenges

- Function and categories: these messages are aimed to stimulate the learner's confidence, also presented in ARCS Model of Keller (1987), before the "challenge" activity. As the former element, this one also is aimed to use the learner's control in view of proposed exercises (recommended in the Elaboration Theory of Reigeluth (1983)). Furthermore, the element used the autonomy category in their objectives by assistance and guidance, recommended in the Transactional Distance Theory of Moore (2002) (Nunes, 2008).

Lesson Finalization Messages

- Function and categories: in the IP proposal, these messages are aimed to promote the learner's satisfaction between each finishing phase of the didactic module. This element shows the intentionality of using one more characteristic of ARCS Model of Keller (1987), because it is aimed to present coherence between the different phases.

> And also, if the "Lesson finalization messages" recall some contents previously presented (consolidation), this element can contemplate characteristics of a cognitive interaction category (Nunes, 2008).

Beyond the conceptual subcategories of Keller (1987), presented in didactic-methodological elements as a suggestion of observable operational categories, other conceptual subcategories of Elaboration, Meaningful Learning and Transactional Distance Theories could be observed. As an example, we can present the subcategories: "progressive differentiation" and "sequential organization". These ones were presented as a general form in the didactic module, more than in each proposal of T-LO separately.

Technology Components

After the definition of different parameters and indicators, on the basis of the exploratory analysis realized in IP and conceptual categories, we constructed the detailing of the T-LO List. For the composition of the T-LO List a spreadsheet editor program was used, because it was considered an appropriate system for the needs of this composition process. One of the needs is the development of an own technological tool to analyze the T-LO and implement the conceptual building to generate indicators of eventual re-planning. These research requirements were also the accounting data, so we used different formulas, always referred to in the principles and chosen categories.

On the basis of the tool detailing, we could realize a qualitative analysis of the T-LO observable categories that were present in the didactic module. To evaluate each object, we divided them into three kinds: C – Content Presentation, E – Practical Exercise and T – Assimilation Test. For the didactic-methodological elements evaluated inside of each kind of the T-LO, we described observations and considerations in the spreadsheet of the T-LO List. In Figure 4, we present two examples of didactic-methodological elements that were analyzed and previously proposed in IP (mainly inside of the T-LO of the C kind).

We also could explore, if the specific didactic module presents the need for evidence of meaningful potentiality proposed in the IP. During the findings and counting of the evidence in the T-LO List, we have realized adjustments in the tool and improved the measure form: if one object is or not potentially meaningful under the light of the priority categories. It is important to highlight that we divided the analysis in three question groups to facilitate the framework building and filling.

Figure 4. Copy of didactic-methodological elements (attention frame and character) of a teaching-learning object called "First Lesson". (© 2008, Ingrid Kleist Clark Nunes. Used with permission)

These groups helped to identify how many observable categories each object had on the basis of the theoretical scopes: autonomy; motivation and cognitive interaction.

Step 5: Re-Planning and the Results

The needs experienced as teachers, tutors and designers in multidisciplinary teams involved directly with the steps of elaboration, implementing, evaluation and re-planning the didactic materials generated the requirement of the construction of a tool that would conceive the indicators of the potentiality of the T-LO in pedagogical mediation. The expectation for the development and application of the framework represents the contribution as an element that strengthens the retrospective and prospective stages of the multidisciplinary teams, with the re-planning representing a situation that requires organization and systematization of curricular knowledge and didactic-methodological elements to improve the coherence with pedagogical, technological and specific contents carrying principles. The use of the T-LO List may indicate which action is to be taken after implementing a course. It also helps in the identification of the relevance of an IP elaborated for the course and developed based on the analysis of the meaningful potentiality of each T-LO.

This case is a special example of the establishment of the relationship between theory and practice, as it made it possible to tie our experience with the development of the methodological tool, and at the same time, to build and improve our conceptual matrix with regard to the learning theories and to the design itself. Beginning with the use of a framework in the didactic mode we were able to arrive at a structured evaluation of the T-LO, which did not exist before in the context of the present work. The study went far beyond the exploitation of data, as a reflective context was organized that furnished retrospective and prospective stages on the potentiality of materials elaborated, as well as on the performance of each of the professionals involved in the multidisciplinary team. Furthermore, was it possible to improve some theoretical parameters that should be considered in the process of elaboration of didactic materials and that aim to establish a meaningful teaching-learning mode in DE? The parameters analyzed in each Teaching-Learning Object for the category of autonomy are summarized in Figure 5.

The T-LO List made it possible that aspects of the teaching-learning process, taken in consideration in the elaboration of the T-LO and consequently of the IP, became models of operational categories and can be used in the planning of other didactic models, which also aim to reach meaningful learning. From the point of verifying the adherence of the T-LO to the proposed IP it was possible to realize the completion of the detailed framework of the T-LO List. Confer another table completed with the framework of the T-LO List for analysis of the motivation of the didactic mode (See Figure 6).

As an example of data completed in the T-LO List framework, in Keller's (1983) light, we have **"promotion of confidence".** It has to be coherent with the IP proposal and present in the objectives of each didactic-methodological element, so as to enhance the learning. In agreement with the author, the establishment of the "sense of responsibility" in the learner will require a relation of compromise generated by the motivation coming through the success of the learning process in line with the learner's effort. This success is only feasible, when the content is clearly outlined and coherent with its objectives.

It is necessary to explain that the T-LO List is a tool built in accordance with the principle of action-reflecting-action and is placed in a move constant of evaluation and re-planning as a possibility to always improve the comprehension of the stages for elaboration of didactic materials, functions and obligations of the different profes-

Figure 5. Copy of "Questions to analyze the category of autonomy". (© 2008, Ingrid Kleist Clark Nunes. Free translation. Used with permission)

	EVALUATED CONCEPTS	ANSWER THE QUESTIONS BELOW FOR EACH TEACHING-LEARNING OBJECT:	IMPORTANT ORIENTATIONS TO ANSWER THE QUESTIONS:
AUTONOMY Transactional Distance	Presentation	How many text presentations (at the library or TL-O content) or animation presentation the Teaching-Learning Object has been presented at its content?	Add / count only if the communication means used are suitable for the amount of the content.
	Stimulus of Critical Analysis	Has some Teaching-Leaning Object questioning demonstrated intentionality to promote critical thoughts of the learner (how many questionings)?	Analyze parts of the content that contain questions that enable the learner to think critically. Judge if it has the necessary intentionality (count how much / answer the columns beside).
	Guidance and Assistance	Has the analyzed Teaching-Learning Object offered any information, by visual / textual way, about tools that enable the learner to call in assistance or guidance (how many)?	Add / count any visual or textual element that has the intention to help the learner for assistance or guidance for the learning.
	Administration and Test of Learning	Is there any activity that proposes tests of content assimilation or evaluation of the studied subject?	Add / count just the questions that result in assimilations with the previous content and activities that direct the learner to make the choices or answer by words.

Figure 6. Copy of "Questions to analyze the category of motivation". (© 2008, Ingrid Kleist Clark Nunes. Free translation. Used with permission)

	EVALUATED CONCEPTS	ANSWER THE QUESTIONS BELOW FOR EACH TEACHING-LEARNING OBJECT:	Important orientation to answer the questions:
MOTIVATION (ARCS) Cognitive Impulse	Attention Promotion	How many instructional elements of the ATTENTION kind has the Teaching-Learning Object? How many instructional elements promote the learner perception or curiosity?	Count the ATTENTION frames that really have the intention to promote the learner curiosity or perception. If the Teaching-Learning Object is one of the kinds of E or T, count the instructional elements that have the same intention in it.
	Relevance Demonstration	How many instructional elements of the ADVANTAGES kind has the Teaching-Learning Object? How many instructional elements promote the relevance of the content to the learner?	Count the ADVANTAGES frames that really have the intention to promote the relevance of the content to the learner. If the Teaching-Learning Object is one of the kinds of E or T, count the instructional elements that have the same intention in it.
	Confidence Promotion	Has the Teaching-Learning Object clarity in its goals and organization? If the Teaching-Learning Object does not have explicit goals, is it consistent with the initial purpose?	1 = YES / 0 = NO Choose 1 only when the Teaching-Learning Object is consistent with the initial purpose.
	Satisfaction Stimulation	How many messages connected with the acknowledgment of the learner effort has the Teaching-Learning Object? How many examples can stimulate the learner satisfaction?	The *feedback messages*, of the assimilated questions, have to be counted when the learner effort is acknowledged in the Teaching-Learning Object. Examples about the content (that increases the satisfaction) also have to be counted.

sionals composing a multidisciplinary team, as well as the strengthening of the levels of comprehension and conceptual construction with regard to a meaningful potentiality in pedagogical mediation of DE. Furthermore, it is necessary to take into consideration pedagogical, technological and specific content principles for each situation.

The intentionality of each didactic methodological element, which will have to be present in the IP, is not only important for an analysis of the meaningful potentiality of the T-LO, but also is to constitute a part of its own content (See Figure 7)

"The learner must know the structure of the course organized for his or her learning program(order of contents, activities, evaluation, timing, etc.), so that he or she may implement the passage with full control"(Reigeluth and Stein 1983, p. 362). Therefore, it is important that the IP has the intentionality of each learning program well defined and outlined.

CURRENT CHALLENGES FACING THE ORGANIZATION

One of the major challenges of the research and development process for the T-LO List was to contemplate the indicator elements of the re-planning phases for the T-LO produced. In using the tool in the T-LO analysis comparatively to projects initially elaborated for the guidance of these production stages, the existence of initially unforeseen situations and components in the storyboards was perceived. This means that the principle of action-reflecting-action during the elaboration of didactic materials is present in the activities implemented by the designers of mediation. This explains itself through the components of the proper T-LO.

The elaborated framework was based on some principles and categories of the design theories, as well as the theories of the learning program, which at the moment of application for analysis of the potentiality of the T-LO reflect the interferences in the orientation of the designer of the mediation. By the analysis of the T-LO through the application of the framework it is perceived that at the end of each Teaching-Learning Object there exist didactic methodological elements as motivators for learning, feedback texts and interrogations. This fact instigates interactivity, special mentions of the relevance of some concepts, among others, and which were not necessarily foreseen in the initial project.

Figure 7. Copy of "Questions to analyze the category of cognitive interaction". (© 2008, Ingrid Kleist Clark Nunes. Free translation. Used with permission)

	EVALUATED CONCEPTS	ANSWER THE QUESTIONS BELOW, FOR EACH TEACHING-LEARNING OBJECT:	IMPORTANT ORIENTATION TO ANSWER THE QUESTIONS:
COGNITIVE INTERACTION Elaboration Theory	Progressive Differentiation / Sequencing Model	Is the Teaching-Learning Object content sequence organized to change from general to specific detail? Is the conceptual hierarchy properly structured and convergent with the other Teaching-Learning Object?	1 = YES / 0 = NO Only answer "YES" if the Teaching-Learning Object is coherent with the questions. In the case that the Teaching-Learning Object is one of the kinds of T or E, just answer the second question.
	Harmony and Integrative Reconciliation / Prerequisites	Is there evidence of substantive or inclusive concepts? Which means that the Teaching-Learning Object has concepts and proposals that consolidate the main subject of the Teaching-Learning Object, are there concepts that have the power to explain (allow relationship among pieces of knowledge)?	1 = YES / 0 = NO / IT IS NOT APPLIED This evaluation **is not applied** if the Teaching-Learning Object is one of the kinds E or T.
	Consolidation / Summary	Does there exist some summary or activity that stimulates reflection (recall) about the previously presented content? How many?	Count the summary and the recall messages that have relationship with the previous content presented in the Teaching-Learning Object before. The biggest Teaching-Learning Object has to have 1 recall and 1 summary at least. This evaluation **isn't applied** for the Exercise (E) or Test (T) Teaching-Learning Object.
	Learner Control	How many *links* (calls/messages) present the Teaching-Learning Object to the next activities? (activities orientation, time orientation etc)	Take account of the screens that represent content milestones in the course. The last screens, for example, were programmed in PI to make these *links*.
	Cognitive-Strategy Activator	How many diagrams, images and/or visual elements promote an interaction with the content (with the internal cognitive structure of the learner)?	Take account of the images/diagrams that promote an identification with the reality known by the learner, do not count the repetitive images.

Therefore, one of the major challenges during the development of the T-LO List was selecting principles and categories that could contemplate the indicators of the re-planning stage of a Teaching-Learning Object at the time of its analysis. Thus, it appears to us that there was a meaningful advancement in the tool built; beyond the analysis of the potentiality of the T-LO in the pedagogical mediation it extends its contribution in explaining the implications of the work of observing, evaluating and orienting by the designer of mediation in the phases of re-planning the didactic materials.

SOLUTIONS AND RECOMMENDATIONS

The T-LO List is a result of a concrete study by the authors in the process of didactic materials elaboration to inspire pedagogic mediation in DE. This concrete experience as instructional designers has sustained the investigation, reflections and methodological strategies worked out in order to improve the steps of: planning, developing, implementation, observation, reflection and re-planning.

We highlight that the utilization of a framework to analyze the T-LO, makes it possible to identification the meaningful potentiality in the pedagogic mediation. It further evidences the importance of the mediation designer's work in observing, registering, evaluation and orientation of the productive stages of the T-LO. The development of tools like the T-LO List may be useful in improving the work of multidisciplinary teams, so as to contemplate principles like autonomy, interaction, interactivity and cooperation in hypermediatic materials important in any pedagogical situation for DE.

This case study will contribute within the international community in many ways:

a. the expansion of conceptual discussion about the ID and the hypermedia materials in DE;
b. the publication of research realized in Brazil with regard to the renovation of the theory of functions and implications in the mediation design;
c. the presentation of a concrete methodological strategy which allows the systematization of the operational activities of each one of the steps of T-LO production in multidisciplinary teams;
d. the systematization of an organized strategy such as an interface check-list between learning theories, design theories and distance education theories.

Although sincere efforts were made in realizing the five steps performed, in the way that knowledge is acquired in scientific studies, there is still much to be investigated on this theme. Thus, it is hoped that this study may disseminate and contribute in part with the work of teams involved with the elaboration of didactic materials for different formats of DE courses. We are also hopeful that this study will be an incentive to reflect on the importance of improving the next IP, and, as a consequence, the teaching-learning in DE.

REFERENCES

Ausubel, D. P. (2000). The Acquisition and Retention of Knowledge: A Cognitive View. Holanda: Kluwer Academic Publishers.

Ausubel, D. P., Novak, J. D., & Hanesian, H. (1978). Psicologia educacional. Rio de Janeiro: Interoamericana.

Draft Standard for eXtensible Markup Language (XML) Binding for Learning Object Metadata Model (LOM). (2003). Learning Technology Standards Committee (LTCS). Retrieved March 5, 2006, from http://www.cs.kuleuven.ac.be/~erikd/LOM/20030214/ballot.pdf

Holmberg, B. (1995). Theory and Practice of Distance Education. London: Routledge.

Keller, J. M. (1983). Motivational Design of Instruction. In C. M. Reigeluth (Ed.), Instructional Design Theories and Models: An Overview of their Current Status (pp. 383-42). Hillsdale, NJ: Lawrence Erlbaum.

Keller, J. M. (1987). Development and Use of the ARCS Model of Motivational Design. [from http://www.eric.ed.gov]. *Journal of Instructional Development, 10*(3), 2–10. Retrieved September 5, 2008. doi:10.1007/BF02905780

Kenski, V. M. (2005). Das salas de aula aos ambientes virtuais de aprendizagem. In *Brazilian Association of Distance Education (ABED).* Retrieved September 7, 2006, from http://www.abed.org.br/congresso2005/por/pdf/030tcc5.pdf

Latour, B. (2001). A esperança de Pandora. Bauru, SP: EDUSC.

Maier, G. W., Prange, C., & Rosenstiel, L. (2003). Psychological Perspectives of Organizational Learning. In M. Dierkes et al., Handbook of Organizational Learning and Knowledge (pp. 14-34). Oxford, UK: Oxford University Press.

Mallmann, E. M. (2008). *Mediação pedagógica em educação a distância: cartografia da performance docente no processo de elaboração de materiais didáticos*. Thesis (Doctor in Education), Santa Catarina Federal University, Florianópolis.

Mallmann, E. M., & Nunes, I. K. C. (2008). The potentiality of the Teaching-Learning Objects (T-LO) and Teaching-Learning Virtual Environments (T-LVE). In *International Journal of Emerging Technologies in Learning (iJET), 3*(4). Retrieved October 13, 2008, from http://www.i-jet.org

Moore, M. G. (2002). Teoria da Distância Transacional. (W. Azevedo, Trans.). In D. Keegan (Ed.), *Theoretical Principles of Distance Education* (pp. 22-38). London: Routledge. Retrieved May 15, 2006, from http://www.abed.org.br/publique

Nunes, I. K. C. (2008). *PROJETO INSTRUCIONAL: sua relevância no desenvolvimento de Objetos de Ensino–Aprendizagem.* Dissertation (Master in Education), Santa Catarina Federal University, Florianópolis. Retrieved March 10, 2009, from http://www.tede.ufsc.br/teses/PEED0672-D.pdf

Nunes, I. K. C., Mallmann, E. M., Catapan, A. H., & Roncarelli, D. (2007, September). *The Meaningful Potentiality of the Teaching-Learning Objects (T-LO) elaborated with the Interactive Tools: Lesson (Module of Moodle) and Articulate (integrated to Power Point).* Paper presented at the International Conference on Interactive Computer Aidded Blended Learning (ICBL), Brazil, Florianópolis.

Reigeluth, C. M. (1983). Instructional Design: What is it and Why is it? In C. M. Reigeluth (Ed.), Instructional Design Theories and Models: An Overview of their Current Status (pp. 3-30). Mahwah, NJ: Lawrence Erlbaum.

Reigeluth, C. M. (1992). Elaborating the Elaboration Theory. Educational Technology Research & Development. Mahwah, NJ: Lawrence Erlbaum.

Reigeluth, C. M. (1999). What is Instructional Design Theory and How is it Changing? In C. M. Reigeluth (Ed.), Instructional Design Theories and Models: A New Paradigm of instructional Theory. Mahwah, NJ: Lawrence Erlbaum.

Reigeluth, C. M. (1999a). What is Instructional Design Theory and How is it Changing? In C. M. Reigeluth (Ed.), Instructional Design Theories and Models: A New Paradigm of instructional Theory. Mahwah, NJ: Lawrence Erlbaum.

Reigeluth, C. M. (1999b). The Elaboration Theory: Guidance for Scope and Sequence Decisions. In C. M. Reigeluth (Ed.), Instructional Design Theories and Models: A New Paradigm of Instructional Theory. Mahwah, NJ: Lawrence Erlbaum.

Reigeluth, C. M., & Stein, F. S. (1983). The Elaboration Theory of Instruction. In C. M. Reigeluth (Ed.), Instructional Design Theories and Models: An Overview of their Current Status (pp. 375-379). Mahwah, NJ: Lawrence Erlbaum.

Wiley, D. A. (2000). Connecting Learning Objects to Instructional Design Theory: A Definition, a Metaphor, and a Taxonomy. In D. A. Wiley (Ed.), *The Instructional Use of Learning Objects*. Retrieved May 5, 2007, from http://reusability.org/read/chapters/wiley.doc

ADDITIONAL READING

Clark, D. (2005). *Training Handbook*. Big Dog ISD Page. Retrieved March 10, 2009, from http://www.nwlink.com/~donclark/

Mallmann, E. M. (2008). *Mediação pedagógica em educação a distância: cartografia da performance docente no processo de elaboração de materiais didáticos*. Thesis (Doctor in Education), Santa Catarina Federal University, Florianópolis. Retrieved May 10, 2009, from http://www.tede.ufsc.br/teses/PEED0664-T.pdf

Mallmann, E. M., & Nunes, I. K. C. (2008). The potentiality of the Teaching-Learning Objects (T-LO) and Teaching-Learning Virtual Environments (T-LVE). In International Journal of Emerging Technologies in Learning iJET, 3(4).

Mallmann, E. M., Nunes, I. K. C., Catapan, A. H., & Roncarelli, D. (2006, May). *Pedagogical Mediation and Virtual Environments of Teaching-Learning*. Paper presented at the 22 World Conference of Distance Education - ICDE.

Novak, J. D. (1998). Learning, Creating and Using Knowledge: Concept Maps as a Facilitative Tools in Schools and Coorporations. London: Lawrence Erlbaum Associates.

Nunes, I. K. C. (2008). *PROJETO INSTRUCIONAL: sua relevância no desenvolvimento de Objetos de Ensino−Aprendizagem*. Dissertation (Master in Education), Santa Catarina Federal University, Florianópolis. Retrieved March 10, 2009, from http://www.tede.ufsc.br/teses/PEED0672-D.pdf

Nunes, I. K. C., Mallmann, E. M., Catapan, A. H., & Roncarelli, D. (2007, September). *The meaningful potentiality of the Teaching-Learning Objects (T-LO) elaborated with the interactive tools: Lesson (Moodle module) and Articulate Presenter (authoring tool)*. Paper presented at the International Conference on Interactive Computer Aided Blended Learning (ICBL). Kirchengasse: International Association of Online Engineering.

Nunes, I. K. C., & Vaz, A. F. (2006). Centro de Formação Continuada de Professores: Experienciando a Educação a Distância. *Extensio*, *3*, 1–11.

Romisowski, H. P. (2001). *Avaliação no design e desenvolvimento de multimídia educativa: estratégia de apoio ou parte do processo?* Rio de Janeiro: TTS. Retrieved March 20, 2005, from http://www.miniweb.com.br/top/Jornal/artigos/Artigos/avaliacao_design.html

Wiley, D. A. (2000). Connecting Learning Objects to Instructional Design Theory: A Definition, a Metaphor, and a Taxonomy. In D. A. Wiley (Ed.), *The Instructional Use of Learning Objects*. Retrieved March 5, 2007, from http://reusability.org/read/chapters/wiley.doc

KEY TERMS AND DEFINITIONS

Teaching-Learning Virtual Environments (T-LVE): Are online systems to manage the teaching-learning process, they are customized and directed in accordance with pedagogic principles.

Instructional Design (ID): Is the process of planning, organizing and creating instructional strategies for the development of didactic materials, mainly of the T-LO.

Elaboration/Building: This study represents the practice of the more abstract creation or building of something. In this case the elaboration represents in a general way the constructions of ideas realized during a planning, or, still before, of an action of planning.

Framework: May signify different meanings, but in this study it is utilized to build a supporting structure used to construct an analysis of T-LO within a set of theoretical concepts that constitute a way of viewing the contents.

Feedback: A term used in the elaboration of didactic materials to represent an instructional element, which gives a conceptual return for a determined activity realized in the T-LVE or in the LMS. Normally, there is an explicative text of a previously learned content; it may also mean a text especially elaborated for a given learner.

Learning Management System (LMS): This is the definition used for systems developed by programmers and that make it possible to administer the learning program (control of registers, types of accounts, tutor, teacher, learner, administrator, visitor, etc.), control of costs.

Teaching-Learning Objects (T-LO): T-LO are always contained in a specific course, present at a special moment on the learning trail, with its pedagogic intentionality defined, objectives well outlined with regard to a given Instructional Project.

Teaching Plan (TP): In this study the TP is a part of a document (part of the Instructional Project (IP) that contains the general objectives, the sequence of the contents and of the activities proposed during the process of Instructional Design (ID).

Instructional Project (IP): This is a document of reference that should contemplate an instructional model composed of an assembly of instructional methods. The model should specify: how, where and when to use the T-LO in a given course, which means in the case of this study than the IP is the materialization of the work realized for the Instructional Design (ID).

Plan of the OE-A: This is a document or part of a document (part of the IP), which details the specific content, the manner in which the adaptation of the language should be worked in the instructional design and, step-by-step, how each object (T-LO) should be presented (storyboards).

Assimilative Questions: Questions that oblige the learner to make choices or to reply in words.

Storyboard: Outlines that explain step-by-step, in a detailed manner, how the animations or virtual activities should be presented, which means, canvas after screens.

Screens: Stages of lessons that are so defined, whenever the learner clicks on the link called "continue" to proceed on the trail of the lesson.

Chapter 17
Enculturation of the Utilization of Learning Management System:
The Experience of Universiti Putra Malaysia

Aida Suraya Md. Yunus
Universiti Putra Malaysia, Malaysia

Hamidah Meseran
Universiti Putra Malaysia, Malaysia

Zaidan Abdul Wahab
Universiti Putra Malaysia, Malaysia

ABSTRACT

Universiti Putra Malaysia's (UPM) vision is to become a university with international repute. The Strategic Plan Document 2001- 2010 includes a goal for the university to be fully wired through ICT in enhancing research, extension work, professional service, strengthening teaching and learning environment and enhancing the culture of ICT in supporting teaching and learning. Two strategies were drawn; namely (i) implement the use of one learning management system (LMS) and (ii) enhance competency of academic staff in using the LMS. It has been a practice that each faculty decides on a platform for implementing e-Learning. However, the use of various LMSs had created difficulties in the sharing of integrated database, continuous monitoring of the effectiveness of the e-Learning system, and depository of e-Learning resources in the UPM's knowledge repository. This paper reports on UPM's experience in adapting the use of LMS from the early 1990s until today.

ORGANIZATION BACKGROUND

Achieving the standard of a world class university is a common concern among universities in developed and developing countries. Universiti Putra Malaysia (UPM)'s vision is to become a university with international repute. From its humble beginnings in 1971, UPM has continued to develop and has become one of the distinguished universities in the region. Commencing as an agricultural-based university, UPM has expanded its frontiers in various

DOI: 10.4018/978-1-61520-909-5.ch017

disciplines such as engineering, medical sciences, pure sciences, economics, management, education, languages, communication and other fields. These fields have synergized and complemented the university's focal area, namely, agro-bio, which encompasses related areas of agriculture and science. The field of tropical agriculture has gained the most prominence. Today, the university has gained international reputation among international students and scholars from fifty nine different nations and has become an acclaimed international institution of higher learning in the region. The staff of UPM is committed towards excellence through the inculcation of quality culture in teaching, research and professional service, and to fulfill the expectations of its clients (http://www.upm.edu.my/?kat=D&aktvt=).

On October 11, 2006, four Malaysian universities were announced as research universities; Universiti Putra Malaysia, Universiti Sains Malaysia, Universiti Malaya and Universiti Kebangsaan Malaysia. This was an initiative by Malaysian Ministry of Higher Education (MOHE) to appoint and to award recognition to universities who have met the benchmark set by MOHE. The vision of a research university expands existing philosophies and good practices to enhance overall education system and contribute to nation building. A research university seeks to actively participate in new adventures of ideas, experiment with innovative methods, and take intellectual initiatives to further discover and expand the frontiers of knowledge. The mission of a research university is to be an engine of growth of the nation where scholars and students exchange ideas as well as conduct research in a conducive environment that nurtures exploration and creativity discover knowledge and create wealth, leading towards an improved quality of life. The goals of the research university include to be a leader in innovation, to produce Nobel Prize winners, to produce world class research outputs, to be a center of excellence in prioritized areas of the nation, to generate high impact research publications, to secure research funds from industry; to attract and to graduate students of high standard, and to attract the best brains for teaching and research.

With its current focus on expanding research work, innovations, and commercialization of research products, UPM takes several measures to ensure that the developments towards research do not in any way impede its reputation as an institution that strives on maintaining and enhancing good teaching. UPM strives to provide better access to lecture materials to on-campus students as well as the off-campus students or students enrolled for the distance learning programs. Thus, UPM shares the vision on the need to extend teaching and learning beyond the physical border of the university and the accessibility of conducting face-to-face teaching. The Strategic Plan Document 2001- 2010 (Revised 2007) (Universiti Putra Malaysia, 2008) includes the goal that the university is to be fully wired through information communication technology (ICT) in enhancing research, extension work, professional service, strengthening teaching and learning environment and enhancing the culture of ICT in supporting teaching and learning. To meet the objective pertaining to the enculturation of ICT in teaching and learning, two strategies were drawn; namely (i) implement the use of one learning management system (LMS) and (ii) enhance competency of academic staff in using the LMS. Actions to be taken include increasing the quality of training for both academic and non-academic staff and to reward staff who creates ICT innovations in e-Learning.

The University offers a wide range of programs at both the undergraduate and postgraduate levels across sixteen faculties and nine research institutes. Current enrolment of students for both undergraduates and postgraduates is close to 18,000 with a total of about 2500 academic staff. For a Malaysian university, this number of students is almost the largest. With such diverse offerings of programs to such a large number of students, the University ensure that the quality of education is maintained.

Of fundamental importance to the University is the performance of its students and the quality of teaching and learning it provides.

Over the years, the University has seen positive changes in the use of technology in teaching. Some 15 years back, the use of white board and overhead projectors was a common sight among the lecturers and during tutorial classes. During this time many of the teaching strategies and pedagogical methods were implemented through the use of those teaching technologies. With the advent of personal computers in early 1980s and the internet in early 1990s there had been a progressive change in the teaching landscape in the university especially in the 1990s where the University had began embarking in serious efforts to enhance the university's ICT infrastructures. In line with the improvements in ICT infrastructures, positive policy on usage and support on ICT were put in place and this has spurred renewed interests among academic staff to use ICT in both their work and teaching. In some faculties, recognition in the form of certificates or awards is given to staff members who had demonstrated effective implementation of ICT in their teaching. In the last few years, recipients of the Vice-Chancellor Fellowship for Teaching were avid users of ICT since innovation in teaching and learning is one of the main criteria used in selecting the winners. The winners were those who had put in tremendous efforts in developing online materials to enhance their teaching, which was complemented by good teaching based on evaluation of their Deans, peers and above all, their students.

SETTING THE STAGE

ICT Utilization in Teaching and Learning

To realize the strategy on the integration of ICT use in the curriculum, it is stated that the university should continue to develop its e-learning environment, enhancing and leveraging on the latest offerings from various e-learning technologies. One of the important and positive decisions made by the university in 2008 was the initiative to integrate disparate learning management systems (LMSs) used by the faculties into one e-learning platform for the whole university.

LMS is an educational process that leverages on the opportunities of digital technologies for delivering contents, assessing learners' competences and for enhancing interaction among learners and between tutors and learners. e-Learning is the delivery of education and training courses over the Internet and/or Intranets. It can be defined as a mixture of content (on-line courses or courseware) and communication (reaching online, emails, discussion, forums). Online courses may involve a blend of both online and offline activities. The degree to which e-learning is made up of online, offline content and communication is dependent on factors such as the suitability of the subject to be offered online, characteristics of the learner group and educational needs.

LMS is viewed by the university as a strategy that can help instructors reach out to students and thus enhances teaching and learning. It supports the heavy schedule of the instructors in maintaining a balance between conducting excellent teaching and doing excellent research and writing. It is also viewed as a way to enhance communication between student and student and students with their instructors. The challenge is to get all lecturers/instructors to develop their learning content using LMS; and for them to adopt only one LMS for use in UPM.

UPM deems the use of a uniform LMS for the entire campus as necessary since it will be able to provide integrated database and systematic sharing of learning contents between all lecturers/instructors. Maintenance and monitoring of system can be also done much efficiently. With one LMS use, content sharing can be done between academics within the institution and outside the institution. The cost for the university to maintain the infrastructure and infostructure would also be much lesser.

The decision to change to another LMS was also experienced by Central Queensland University (CQU) in Australia. The university "was forced to replace existing university wide LMS software". In early 2002, staff were informed that the current version of the LMS then used would not be supported after 2003 since both versions of the LMS would involve increase in cost and allocation of resources to support the change. The CQU experience shows that migration to another LMS had major consequences for academic, administration, technical and multimedia development staff (Sturgess & Nouwens, 2004). The overdependence on a particular LMS software was earlier raised by Owens (1998) when he questioned on how responsive can a socio-technical system be to changes in the external environment if it becomes tied to an LMS and the vendor's development of the LMS is not in the direction that the institution desires to go. This is so true since most commercialized LMSs are not customized to suit the needs of an institution. In the migration to another LMS, Chapman (2003) had raised concerns on the difficulty in transferring content from one LMS to another due to conflicting data types. Although there are many contemplated setbacks that must be resolved in the introduction of a new LMS and many resistances in its implementation, UPM had considered all the consequences and the decision to adopt a university wide system is considered timely and may be the better solution in the long run.

CASE DESCRIPTION: INTEGRATION OF LMS IN TEACHING AND LEARNING

The evolution of ICT utilization, specifically LMS utilization in UPM discussed in this chapter is based on three quite distinct phases; (i) Familiarization Phase, (ii) Enculturation Phase, and (iii) Enhancement Phase. The technology, management and organizational concerns are discussed in each of these phases.

The Familiarization Phase (Early 1990s – 2004)

Alongside the advancement of the technology of computers, computing and especially the internet in the 1990s, academic staff slowly embraces the idea of the use of ICT in their teaching. The overhead transparencies started to diminish and slowly being replaced by electronic presentations, mainly Power Point. By end of 1990s, almost all main lecture rooms were equipped with liquid crystal display (LCD) projectors. Price of the LCD projectors was getting more affordable, and the size was getting smaller. The LCD projectors were getting to be portable.

In 2002 to 2003, the ICT policy was drafted and implemented soon after it was approved by the university management. It was launched on 3rd January 2003. The ICT policy was formulated in relation to the university's strategic plan on use of ICT through e-University. The ICT policy document contains several other policies, such as ICT Management Policy, Knowledge Management Policy and e-Learning Policy. The e-Learning policy imposes on the use of a common platform for e-Learning, sharing of integrated database, continuous monitoring of the effectiveness of the e-Learning system, providing online access for all academic course materials, evaluation of students and instructors' competencies in e-Learning, and depository of e-Learning resources in the UPM's knowledge repository.

The development of web-based learning materials was monitored by the respective faculties, in terms of quantity of content but not the quality of content. The e-Learning policy states that academic staffs are to provide at least 40% of course materials online for students' access. Some faculties give recognition to academic staff who develop web-based teaching materials, in terms of points in the yearly appraisal of staff. The university also awards staff for ICT innovations in learning.

Center of Knowledge Management was given the responsibility in managing and depositing intellectual properties of students and staffs in UPM's knowledge repository. It stresses on knowledge sharing, to be benefited by all parties in UPM. Part of the knowledge to be deposited is the web-based teaching and learning materials contributed by academic staff.

The e-Learning policy also imposes on the sharing of integrated databases. During this phase, separate databases were used by the bursary, Department of Students Affairs, Department of Academic Affairs, and Students Information System (for online registration, dropping and adding of courses, and keying in students grades).

Academic staffs in UPM have various information technology and communication (ICT) competencies. Some staff was quite apprehensive towards the use of computers in teaching such as the use of presentation and graphics tools or having to attend courses on development of web-based teaching and learning materials. However, many staff was then starting to see the importance of having a repository of their lecture materials online.

At about this time, vendors were storming the various faculties with solutions for their online teaching and learning. LMSs such as Blackboard, Learning Space and Keleidoscope were viewed by a group of e-Learning experts in UPM to evaluate their potential for adoption. The faculties were then given the liberty to select and purchase any LMS that fulfill the needs of their e-Learning agenda. Apart from purchasing, some faculties outsourced the development of a customized LMS that can meet their requirements. Although UPM was quite open with faculties' decision to purchase commercially-produced LMS, academic staff was also encouraged to develop LMS for use in UPM and could eventually be introduced to the other universities.

Five major LMSs were used in UPM by different groups of users. Among the LMSs, the most widely accepted was e-SPRINT (Sistem Pengurusan Rangkaian Integrasi Nota Kuliah Atas Talian mod Elektronik) (was later referred to as e-SPRINT Version1). The online instructional delivery system developed to provide sustainable and scalable software for lecturers to create, manage and deploy online courses, was developed and implemented since year 2000. More than half of the academic staff was given training in the use of e-SPRINT. Each academic staff was allocated 15 Mb of storage space for their e-learning content. The Sun Enterprise 3500 server has a storage capacity of 64 Gb for each of the four hard disks (64 Gb x 4) and 4 Gb RAM. Besides the storage provided in the e-SPRINT server, staff could also upload their web-based materials in their faculty's server, by just making a link to their e-SPRINT website. The LMS and faculties that were adopting its use are as shown in Table 1.

Upon purchase of the LMS and some training, staff were given the task to develop their e-Learning content for their course. Some universities in the region even hired a team of instructional designers and programmers to develop online materials using the LMS that was adopted. However, UPM had decided that we must build our expertise and that we cannot lose the technology. Thus, academic staff were encouraged to design, develop, manage and update the online materials themselves. A two-days training session got them started on getting their courses online. The computer center provided technical support team that can be contacted to cater for any problems that the staff might encounter once the training session is over.

To enhance the efforts in emerging the web-based teaching and learning culture in UPM during this phase, it was acceptable if an academic staff only provides lecture materials consisting of text only, which is not interactive, and without any hyperlinks to other web sites. The university does not critically evaluate the web-based learn-

Table 1. LMSs Used in several faculties in UPM

LMS	Website	Faculties
e-SPRINT	http://eSPRINT.upm.edu.my/	Faculty of Science and Environmental Studies Faculty of Agriculture Faculty of Veterinary Medicine Faculty of Educational Studies Faculty of Forestry
Web Ed	http://webed.eng.upm.edu.my/webed/	Faculty of Engineering
Virtual Class	http://csnotes.upm.edu.my/kelasmaya/web.nsf	Faculty of Economics and Management
e-Pembelajaran	http://www.fbmk.upm.edu.my/ccms/	Faculty of Modern Languages and Communication
Nota Kuliah Online	http://www.food.upm.edu.my/kuliah/kuliahonline.htm	Faculty of Food Science and Technology

ing materials developed by our academic staffs in terms of interactivity, ability to explain beyond chalk-and-talk, motivation, instructional design, and appeal.

e-SPRINT was developed in the year 2000 by a group of researchers from the Institute of Multimedia and Software. The research was funded by UPM's Short-Term Research Grant. It was developed using PERL (Practical Extraction and Report Language) and supported by standard flat files in Linux/UNIX environment. The objective of this system is to establish a system that acts as a one-stop teaching and learning resource centre for students and lecturers. The e-SPRINT prototype was successfully developed in which it took into account the aspects of data flow, database design, process design, navigation and interface design. The web based application was used by the lecturers to organize the learning materials, whereby the students used it in order to access lectures notes; news updates of courses and to have online discussions. The interface design of the e-SPRINT prototype does not contain oversized graphic elements and it also has simple navigation to simplify the usage.

e- SPRINT was meant to cultivate the culture of digitized lecture notes management. The five main modules of e-SPRINT were developed to address most of the users' requirements. Listed below are some of the guidance characteristic in developing the modules and feature of e-SPRINT (Sidek et al., 2006):

- Full implementation in the Malaysian national language, the Bahasa Melayu;
- Easy maintenance of contents;
- Easy access points for students;
- Secured;
- Easy to use application;
- Direct upload facilities for various file formats;
- Required minimal ICT related skills; and
- Interactive system.

The features highlighted above are addressed in the development of the five main modules namely the News, Lecture Notes, Tutorials, Forums and Students.

1. **News** – Official communication channel meant for instructors to post notices and messages pertaining to courses taught.
2. **Lecture Notes** – A module for lecturers to post and edit lecture notes. Lecturers can also include brief information about the course such as course outline, list of lecture topics, schedules, references and further readings, methods of assessment and contact information.
3. **Tutorials** – A module for putting tutorial materials online.
4. **Forum** – A tool to allow two-way communication between lecturers and students as well as among students themselves.

5. **Student** – A module for lectures to post lists of students, continuous assessment marks, and tutorial/laboratory groupings.

The Study

Readiness of academic staff to use the e-SPRINT prototype was gathered through a survey (Sidek et al., 2007a). Targeted sample was active users of e-SPRINT. Ninety-five lecturers were identified and given the questionnaire. The aspects surveyed were their attitude, the interface design and navigation, skill in using the technology and their fields of expertise. The reliability of the Likert-Scale questionnaire was high with Alpha Cronbach coefficient of 0.91. As many as 80% (n = 76) of the targeted sample responded. Their age ranges from 24 to 57 years (mean = 36.95, sd = 8.48) and majority (59.2%) of the respondents had a Masters degree, 35.2% with doctoral degrees and 5.6% was a Bachelor degree holder. It was found that lecturers were positive towards new changes that were happening especially in the campus ICT development. Overall, on a five-point scale, it was found that respondents' attitude towards the use of e-SPRINT was high (mean = 4.03, sd = .76). Likewise, for technology skill (mean = 4.19, sd = 0.85) and field of expertise (mean = 4.07, sd = 0.93). The respondents perception was also positive on the needs of LMS (mean = 4.12, sd = 0.80) and Learning Contents Management System (mean = 4.11, sd = 0.80) in their effort towards e-Learning accomplishment.

The lecturers' perception towards the e-SPRINT prototype showed that they were really positive about the LMS and they agreed with the interface design and navigation with mean scores of more than 3.50 for each of the items given. Respondents agreed with the e-SPRINT interface design which was simple with clear-cut text presentation (mean = 4.10, sd = 0.77), unambiguous icons or graphics (mean = 4.14, sd = 0.64), instructions that were easy to follow (mean = 4.10, sd = 0.68) and ease in exploring e-SPRINT (mean = 4.10, sd = 0.79). The survey also found that more than 40 lecturers (53%) updated their online lectures notes at least once a week.

The e-SPRINT prototype that was developed fulfilled the requirements of the user (mean = 3.35, sd=0.93). For the purpose of organizing the learning resources through e-SPRINT, respondents also agreed that it was easy to upload (mean = 3.69, sd = 0.82) and to download (mean = 3.70, sd = 0.80) the teaching documents. In conclusion, respondents agreed that the e-SPRINT prototype which contains minimal modules was simple to use (mean = 4.04, sd = 0.79) and it matched the ICT competency of lecturers and students (Sidek et al., 2007a).

In another study, students who were active users of the online course developed using e-SPRINT were asked to indicate their preference of the modules provided in the online course. The students enrolled in the Bioindustrial Microbiology (BIP3501) course preferred the lectures notes module (72%), followed by the info/news updates module (15%) and tutorial activities (10%). On the other hand, students who were in the Semiconductor Devices (PHY4202) course were more interested in accessing the info/news updates (40%), as compared to lectures notes (36%) and forum (22%). The difference in the patterns of preference for a particular module was apparently due to the learning method adapted for the course PHY4202, which was more student centered while the course BIP3501 was more teacher centered, thus it explained on BIP3501 students' dependency on the lecture notes.

e-SPRINT Version 1 has gained several recognitions such as the Gold Medal and Jury Recommendation at the UPM Research and Innovative Exhibition in 2002, a Silver Medal award at the Malaysian Science and Technology Expo in 2002. The application was also ranked as the top ten best innovation by Malaysian Administrative Modernisation and Management Planning Unit (MAMPU's) 'Anugerah Perdana Teknologi Maklumat' in 2004.

Enculturation Phase (2005 – 2008)

The use of various LMSs in one organization create difficulties in the sharing of integrated database, continuous monitoring of the effectiveness of the e-Learning system, providing online access for all academic course materials, and depository of e-Learning resources in the knowledge repository. Although the use of a common platform for e-Learning was specifically stated in the e-Learning policy, it could not be enforced onto the staff. They did not view LMS as a solution to a more effective teaching, were not ready to migrate to a new LMS, were already familiar and have grown accustomed to the LMS that they were currently using.

Sidek (2004) found that less than 60% of the academic staff was using the system, and this was due to their lack of awareness on the LMS provided, lack of enforcement by the university and inability of the provided LMS to create richness in presentations. In order for staff to incorporate the use of such a system, they have to see the need and the advantage of its use. It has to be user friendly, easy to manage and ease them of the workload of teaching and consulting with students. In juggling between teaching, research, publication and extension work, the academic staff were not willing to put in the time to develop online lessons using the LMS.

Sidek's (2004) AIPA Report for MAMPU suggested that there were some issues that need to be resolved on the use of e-SPRINT Version 1. It was found that there was a need for a systematic database to store lecture notes and a platform for knowledge sharing among students and lecturers. Among the other problems identified were: (i) lack of application development documentation and the absence of any system development methodology during the system development phase; (ii) problems in maintaining the application, and (iii) difficulties in monitoring students' academic performance.

Having secured a grant from the Ministry of Science and Technology, a group of researchers of the Institute of Multimedia and Software, one of the research institutes in UPM at that time, started work on improving the currently used LMS, e-SPRINT Version 1, to meet the university's specific academic and administrative needs. In May 2003, a workshop attended by Deputy Deans (Academic) was held to gather requirements for the new e-SPRINT.

Apart from the workshop, findings of the surveys on e-SPRINT Version 1 were also used as a basis in the development of e-SPRINT Version 2. e-SPRINT Version 2 was ready for deployment in 2005 (Sidek et al., 2007b). The home-grown LMS was to provide a platform for developing web-based teaching and learning materials that would enable staff who might just have bare ICT competency, to upload their teaching materials. A systematic and holistic approach adapting proper system methodology was planned for the application development to fulfill the teaching and learning requirements of UPM. The system was able to integrate with the other systems used in students' management, such as course registration. It was fully web-based, multimedia rich content development environment, and used the web 2.0 technology. It was developed as open source environment architecture for multi format operating systems using PHP, Java Script, HTML with MySQL as the Database engine.

The e-SPRINT Version 2 added new features as compared to the earlier version. The 15 functionalities are as follows:

- **Module 1** Student List
- **Module 2** Course Material
- **Module 3** Assignment
- **Module 4** Download Software
- **Module 5** Teaching Assessment
- **Module 6** Student Attendance
- **Module 7** Group Discussion
- **Module 8** Chat Room

- **Module 9** Quiz Online
- **Module 10** Group Discussion
- **Module 11** My Favourites
- **Module 12** Calendars and Activities
- **Module 13** Marks and Results
- **Module 14** My Blog
- **Module 15** Help/Ask Questions

The MySQL database was heavily used for the development of e-SPRINT Version 2, while the development tools used were HTML, PHP, JavaScript, unified modeling language (UML) and Visio Pro. Object-oriented design was used in developing the application as the method which leads to software architectures based on the objects every system or subsystem manipulates (rather than the function it is meant to ensure). The functionalities of e-SPRINT Version 2 is illustrated in the following Figure 1 (Institute of Multimedia and Software, 2002).

Screen shots of some of the modules are as follows:

Module 1 - Student List

The module displays list of student names by course (Figure 2).

Figure 1. Functionalities of e-SPRINT version 2

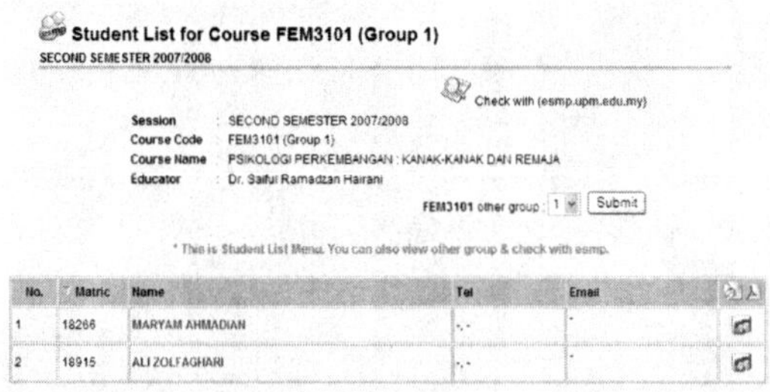

Figure 2. Screen for module 1 – student list

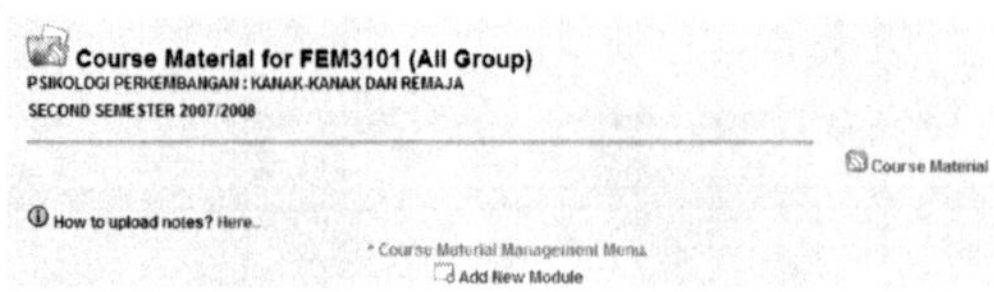

Figure 3. Screen for uploading course materials management

Module 2 - Course Material

The module allows developers of learning content to upload, to add chapters/modules and submodules as shown in Figures 3 and 4.

Module 3 - Assignment

The module allows learners to upload and to view assignments that have been submitted by the other students enrolled in the courses (Figures 5 and 6).

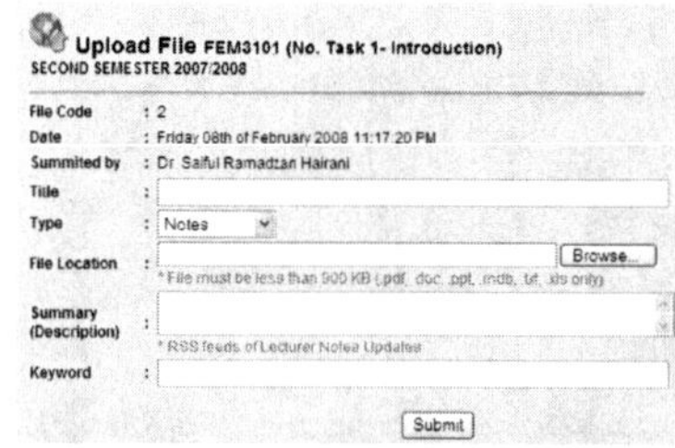

Figure 4. Screen for uploading course materials

Module 4 - Download Software

The module allows users to download tools for teaching and learning as shown in Figure 7.

Module 5 - Teaching Assessment

Students are required to assess their instructors at the end of the semester. Teaching assessments of the instructors can be done by the student online using this system, as shown in Figure 8.

Although e-SPRINT Version 2 was very well received by majority of the staff, it was not SCORM compliance. In March 2008, the university management approved on outsourcing an LMS that is SCORM compliance and can be customized for UPM based on its user requirements. The user requirements were identified through a workshop involving all deans of faculties. To facilitate identification of the user requirements, the deans were introduced to all the major LMSs that were used in UPM. This brings us to the current phase of LMS implementation in UPM, the introduction of PutraLMS.

Figure 5. Screen for assignment

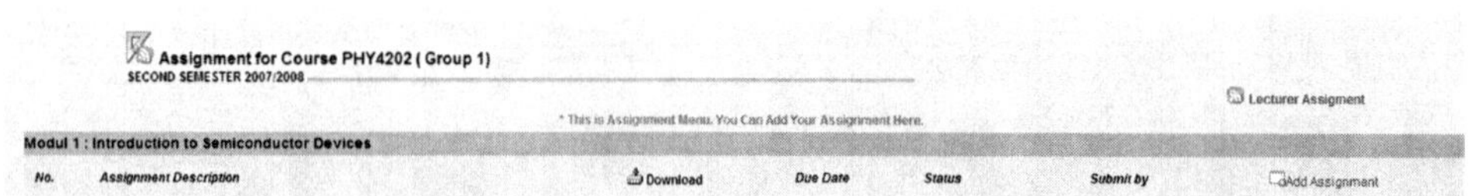

Figure 6. Screen to view assignments uploaded

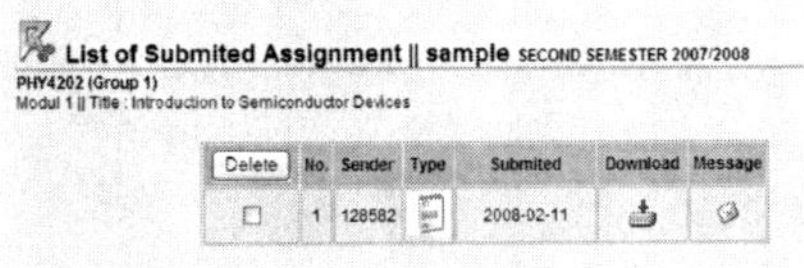

List of Submited Assignment || sample SECOND SEMESTER 2007/2008
PHY4202 (Group 1)
Modul 1 || Title : Introduction to Semiconductor Devices

Delete	No.	Sender	Type	Submited	Download	Message
	1	128582		2008-02-11		

The Enhancement Phase (2009 onwards)

In 2008, the University Management has mandated the Centre for Academic Development (CADe) to plan, design and develop a full feature, SCORM compatible and visually attractive e-learning platform. The new LMS, named PutraLMS, was developed and deployed to fullfill the following objectives:

1. To enhance the effectiveness of teaching and learning activities through the use of a common e-learning platform;
2. To introduce a single integrated databases of learning contents which are shareable among UPM's educators and experts;
3. To facilitate effective and systematic system maintenance and improvement of the learning management system running on a common e-learning paltform; and
4. To fullfil the University's vision of producing quality graduates who are competative, ethical and has the ability to progress and excel through life long learning.

The new LMS, the PutraLMS, was launched in a grand affair by the Deputy Minister of Higher Education in April 2009. The new LMS application was motivated by the need to enhance the

Figure 7. Screen to view list of free downloadable software

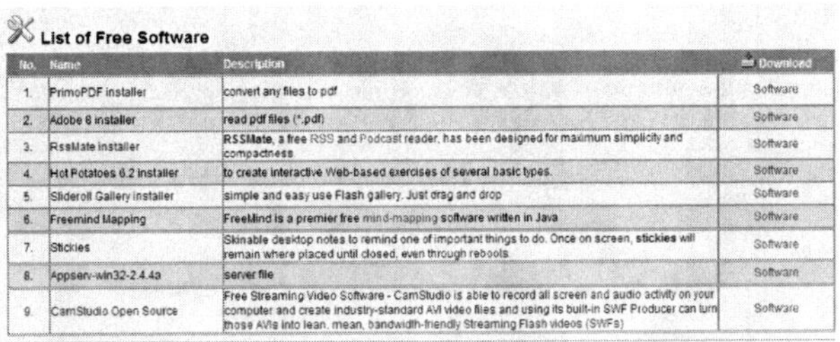

List of Free Software

No.	Name	Description	Download
1.	PrimoPDF installer	convert any files to pdf	Software
2.	Adobe 8 installer	read pdf files (*.pdf)	Software
3.	RssMate installer	RSSMate, a free RSS and Podcast reader, has been designed for maximum simplicity and compactness	Software
4.	Hot Potatoes 6.2 installer	to create interactive Web-based exercises of several basic types.	Software
5.	Slideroll Gallery installer	simple and easy use Flash gallery. Just drag and drop	Software
6.	Freemind Mapping	FreeMind is a premier free mind-mapping software written in Java	Software
7.	Stickies	Skinable desktop notes to remind one of important things to do. Once on screen, stickies will remain where placed until closed, even through reboots	Software
8.	Appserv-win32-2.4.4a	server file	Software
9.	CamStudio Open Source	Free Streaming Video Software - CamStudio is able to record all screen and audio activity on your computer and create industry-standard AVI video files and using its built-in SWF Producer can turn those AVIs into lean, mean, bandwidth-friendly Streaming Flash videos (SWFs)	Software

Figure 8. Screen to view students' assessment of the course instructor

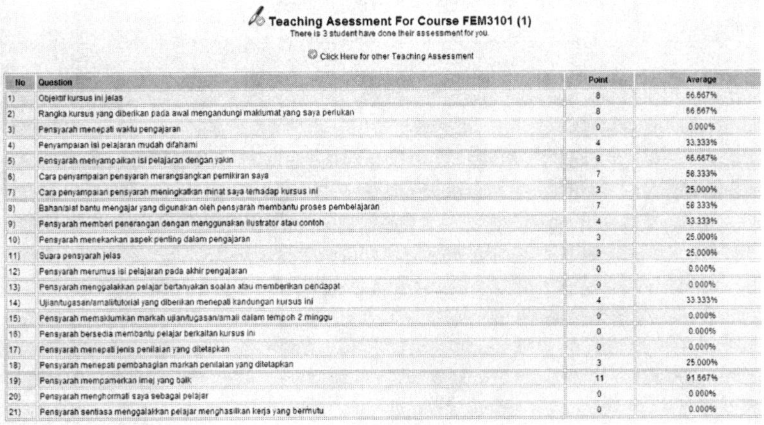

Teaching Asessment For Course FEM3101 (1)
There is 3 student have done their assessment for you.
Click Here for other Teaching Assessment

No	Question	Point	Average
1)	Objektif kursus ini jelas	8	66.667%
2)	Rangka kursus yang diberikan pada awal mengandungi maklumat yang saya perlukan	8	66.667%
3)	Pensyarah menepati waktu pengajaran	0	0.000%
4)	Penyampaian isi pelajaran mudah difahami	4	33.333%
5)	Pensyarah menyampaikan isi pelajaran dengan yakin	8	66.667%
6)	Cara penyampaian pensyarah merangsangkan pemikiran saya	7	58.333%
7)	Cara penyampaian pensyarah meningkatkan minat saya terhadap kursus ini	3	25.000%
8)	Bahan/alat bantu mengajar yang digunakan oleh pensyarah membantu proses pembelajaran	7	58.333%
9)	Pensyarah memberi penerangan dengan menggunakan ilustrator atau contoh	4	33.333%
10)	Pensyarah menekankan aspek penting dalam pengajaran	3	25.000%
11)	Suara pensyarah jelas	3	25.000%
12)	Pensyarah merumus isi pelajaran pada akhir pengajaran	0	0.000%
13)	Pensyarah menggalakkan pelajar bertanyakan soalan atau memberikan pendapat	0	0.000%
14)	Ujian/tugasan/amali/tutorial yang diberikan menepati kandungan kursus ini	4	33.333%
15)	Pensyarah memaklumkan markah ujian/tugasan/amali dalam tempoh 2 minggu	0	0.000%
16)	Pensyarah bersedia membantu pelajar berkaitan kursus ini	0	0.000%
17)	Pensyarah menepati jenis penilaian yang ditetapkan	0	0.000%
18)	Pensyarah menepati pembahagian markah penilaian yang ditetapkan	3	25.000%
19)	Pensyarah mempamerkan imej yang baik	11	91.667%
20)	Pensyarah menghormati saya sebagai pelajar	0	0.000%
21)	Pensyarah sentiasa menggalakkan pelajar menghasilkan kerja yang bermutu	0	0.000%

Table 2. Functionalities of PutraLMS

Module	Functions
Discussion Forum	• Area where instructors and students • Conduct discussion and information exchange • Follow and response to discussion threads shown on the screen • Uploading files.
File Exchange	• Students could upload assignments and other files types to be accessed by the instructor or students, as well as downloading files sent by other users. • Authorization is given only to registered courses.
Internet e-mail	• Students/Instructor could send e-mail to instructor and individual student or group of students within a course.
Online notes / assignment question	• Instructor could upload lecture notes. • Instructor could view and update lecture notes which is not active in a particular semester. • Instructor could also download notes/assignments.
Laboratory report/assignment	• Allow students to send in reports/assignments online.
Calendar / Progress Review	• Scheduled activities and time tabling for exams/tests are recorded/displayed. • Date dues and progress tracking are also recorded/displayed. This information could be shared with instructor and group of students.
Work Offline	• Allow both students and instructor to download notes and work offline.
Group Work/ Creation of Student Community/Group	• Facility to create group among students. • Students could work within their group or under the supervision of an instructor.
Authentication	• User Authentication system must allow password to be changed by the users themselves. Password problems should be referred to the system administration at the faculty level or computer centre. Password is sent via email.
Teaching plan online (Learning Outcomes & Soft Skills)	• Teaching plan and teaching methods • Support for course/lesson Learning Outcomes and Soft Skills.
Content Security	• Uploaded information must be secured.
Class management	• Facility to prepare class attendance sheet, logging of attendance, detail monitoring and reporting of student attendance throughout the semester.
Course Management	• Facility to both uploading and downloading course materials or notes.
Instructor Help Desk (manual)	• Online help manual for users.
Student Tracking	• Ability to monitor and track students' to the courses.
Content Reusability (RLO) and Content Sharing	• Shareable of content/information within a subject. There is no need to prepare the same content repeatedly.
Instructional Standards Compliance (SCORM)	• The system has to conform to SCORM 2004 standard.
Facilitate activities among students (tutor management)	• A facilitator manages a number of tutors
Teaching Assessment	• Teaching assessment on the instructor by the registered students.
Self-assessment/ improvement/ reflection	• Assessment on each section of course content that help students' understanding of a particular topic. • Reflection on a particular topic, e.g. questions and quiz.
Choice of template/ Customized Look & Feel	• Ability to change color theme of the application. • Limited/minimum change on the visual placements of the screen components.
Video/audio streaming	• Able to use video/audio to allow a variety of teaching methods.
Student Biodata	• Brief students' biodata for reference. • Able to update from time to time.

continued on following page

Table 2. continued

Module	Functions
Automated Testing and Scoring	• Keeping score for each tests and exams • Processing the grade • Students could see only their own marks/grade. • Instructors could see overall students' mark/grade.
Real-time chatting	• Realtime discussion on a variety of topics.
Multilingual	• Choices of popular world languages. • Interpreting facility.
Course Authorization	• Authorization is given to other user to access fail or course content on a web page. • Authorization is from the course coordinator.
Wiki – wikipedia	• Students' reference materials
Blog	• Blogging area
Net meeting	• A platform where interaction/discussion could be done between users living in disparate location.

features according to user satisfaction and the latest requirements from UPM lecturers. Sophisticated reporting provides a wealth of data about student activities that can be used for review and assessment. It also incorporates enhanced features such as online quizzes, and video conferencing.

Since 2008, the university had to impose stricter policy for purchase of hardware and software. A newly setup committee, under the InfoComm Development Center (iDEC) was given the responsibility to screen proposals for purchase of ICT equipments and software from all entities within UPM. Thus, this will make it easier to for CADe to push for the idea of one LMS for all in UPM.

Apart from the five LMSs that have been used by lecturers from the different faculties, Moodle was also getting to be popular among some staff. Although one-LMS utilization had been a standing agenda since early 2003, the policy was not realized due to rejection by staff who resist the migration to another LMS. It meant learning a new technology, a new software. It meant a struggle to transfer their learning contents from the previously used LMS. With the unending work of the academic world, this appeared as something very tedious, time consuming and a total waste of time. They were not willing to reinvent the process of developing their online learning contents. Serious monitoring and measures need to be undertaken so that everyone adopts only one system. Apart from that, technical help must be provided to help staff migrate from their previous system. The Center for Academic Development (CADe) of UPM is given the task to train and provide the support for the staff.

There are about 30 functionalities present in the PutraLMS that has been suggested and implemented. The funtionalities are shown in the following Table 2.

The decision to add the functionalities or course modules was to fulfill the current needs of delivery system required by UPM's academic staff. With the 30 functionalities packaged in the PutraLMS, the system provides a sophisticated platform for the enhancement of teaching and learning. The main screen of the PutraLMS is shown in Figures 9 and 10.

CURRENT CHALLENGES FACING THE ORGANIZATION

UPM has gone through several phases in its deployment of LMS in teaching and learning. LMS is viewed as a solution for teaching especially in a vast research university as UPM. Adopting one LMS will allow content sharing among academic

Figure 9. Main screen of PutraLMS

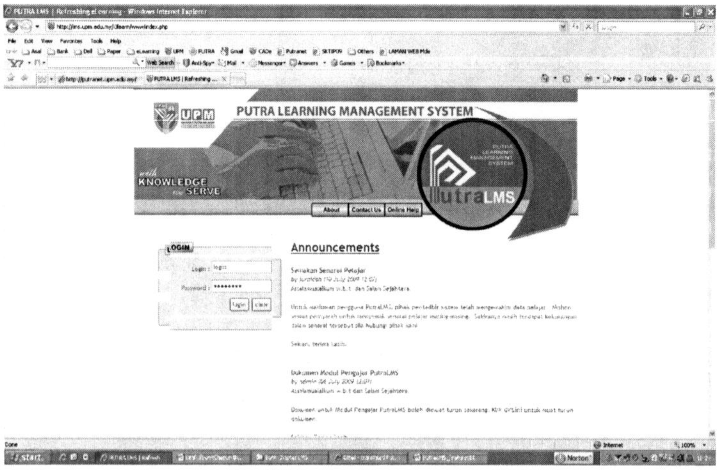

Figure 10. Modules of PutraLMS

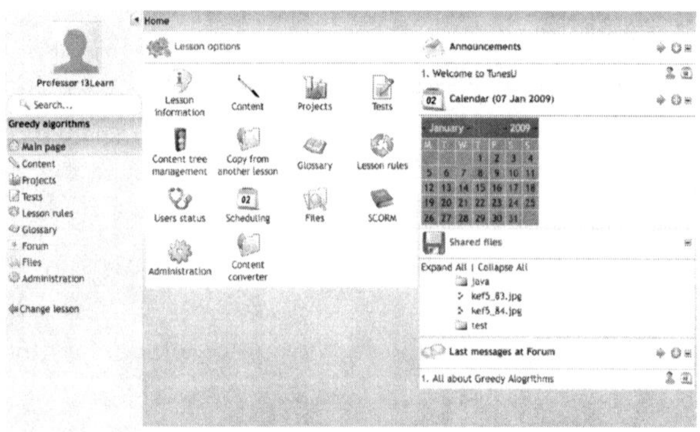

staff within and outside of the university. It will also ensure that lecture materials of retiring professors are well archived for future references. The use of multiple LMSs is difficult to maintain and a single database for lecture materials cannot be created. Furthermore, proper technical support could not be provided since each LMS and its server was maintained separately by the different entities within the university. Thus, it may incur more cost in maintaining the infrastructure and infostructure of LMSs. The use of multiple LMSs had also made it difficult to provide the technical support that is needed since no entity within the university was entrusted with this responsibility.

As it moves from the familiarization phase to the enhancement phase, several challenges have been identified. Among the challenges are as follows:

1. to get all lecturers/instructors to develop their learning content using LMS;
2. to get all lecturers/instructors to adopt only one LMS for use in UPM.
3. to get students to fully utilize the system.
4. to train non-ICT inclined users.
5. to provide endless support for learning content developers.
6. to develop a user friendly system.
7. to develop a one-stop solution for e-Learning.

8. to enhance infrastructure and info structure and ICT-related facilities throughout campus and residential dormitories.

UPM deems the use of a uniform LMS for the entire campus as necessary since it will be able to provide integrated database and systematic sharing of learning contents between all lecturers/instructors. Maintenance and monitoring of system can be also done much efficiently.

SOLUTIONS AND RECOMMENDATIONS

Capper (2001), Farrell (2001) and Jackson and Jones (2001) had identified three main factors that contribute to an organization's readiness in adopting e-Learning; (i) people, (ii) place, and (iii) resources. They posited that commitment and skill of the people as very important. Commitment of key decision makers is critical since the decision on investment in e-Learning much depends on their beliefs and concerns. To implement e-Learning through the use of LMS also requires skill of the people; including project managers, instructional developers, multimedia, graphics and system experts. Place refers to flexibility and the infrastructure provided, whilst resources refers to the organization's readiness to provide the funds and knowledge of decision makers on what the e-Learning options are and the impact of e-Learning.

UPM's leadership has always shown strong commitment on the establishment and enhancement of the culture of e-Learning through the use of LMS. The ICT policy was put in place, and the strategic plan is inline with the policy. The establishment of the Division of Teaching and Learning Technology under the Center of Academic Development (CADe) shows the commitment of the organization. Lead by a Deputy Director (Teaching and Learning Technology), the division has five system analysts and a few programmers to ensure that the development and deployment of the newly launched PutraLMS will be integrated in the teaching and content developers are fully supported in their effort to put up their online lessons. The center also has the support of deans of faculties. Decisions such as the user requirements for the new PutraLMS was tabled and decided upon by the deans. Besides indentifying the user requirements, CADe runs system testing to ensure the system fulfills the user requirements, conduct training for all academic staff and technical support staff (IT personnel of faculties), and provide continuous technical support (help desk etc.). Upon full adoption of the LMS, CADe is to conduct impact studies on the effectiveness of the LMS based on the perspectives of lecturers and students, prepare report regarding LMS use for the University Management and may make suggestion to top management regarding the inclusion of development of online lessons as part of the annual appraisal of lecturers.

Apart from the establishment of a specific division under CADe to take the responsibility of enculturation of LMS use among the lecturers, another center which has long been established, renamed as InfoComm Development Center (iDEC) from its previous name, Computer Center, is given the responsibility to maintain and enhance the infrastructure and infostructure to support the use of ICT in teaching and learning, specifically the use of LMS.

Apart from people skill provided by CADe and iDEC, UPM has also identified key personnel from the faculties to provide the support to realize our vision to be a fully wired university where the use of LMS for e-Learning is fully explored and supported. Academics from the Faculty of Educational Studies provide advise and training for instructional design of online lessons. Faculty of Computer Science and Faculty of Engineering provide advise regarding the technicalities in supporting LMS use. These academics are in constant collaboration with CADe and iDEC on several matters.

Training on the use of LMS is fully the responsibility of CADe under its other divison, Teaching and Learning. Series of training has been conducted for the training of earlier LMSs adopted and now training for the introduction and use of the newly launched PutraLMS is being planned. It is hoped that all academic staff will be trained by middle of 2010. Apart from the academic staff, IT personnel from each faculty will also be trained as they can provide immediate support to the staff in the faculties.

CADe is the reference center for all teaching and learning initiatives in UPM. The center's director is part of the University Senate and principal officers of UPM. CADe is also the secretariat for the University's Teaching and Learning committee. Thus, any development in teaching and learning can easily be channeled through the various committees and meetings. With such support and commitment from the University Management, the full utilization of PutraLMS will be realized.

REFERENCES

Capper, J. (2001). E-Learning growth and promise for the developing world. *TechKnowLogia*, *2*(2), 7–10.

Farrell, G. (2001). *The changing faces of virtual education*. Vancouver, Canada: The Commonwealth of Learning. Retrieved October 26, 2006, from http://wwww.col.org/virtualed/

Institute of Multimedia and Software. (2002). User Manual for Online Lecture Application. Serdang: UPM.

Jackson, G. B., & Jones, J. (2001). Web-based simulations for science and mathematics instruction. *TechKnowLogia*, *2*(2), 39–41.

Owens, R. G. (1998). Organisational behaviour in education (6th ed.). Boston, MA: Allyn & Bacon.

Sidek, A. A. (2004). AIPA report for MAMPU. Public Service Department, Kuala Lumpur.

Sidek, A. A. Md.Yunus, A. S., Bakar, K., Meseran, H. (2006). *Design and development of learning management system - A case of eSPRINT*. Poster presentation at the 15th International World Wide Web Conference, Scotland, May 22-26. Retrieved May 23, 2009, from http://www.ra.ethz.ch/CDstore/www2006/devel-www2006.ecs.soton.ac.uk/programme/files/pdf/p223.pdf

Sidek, A. A. Md.Yunus, A. S., Bakar, K., Wong, S. L., & Meseran, H. (2007b). Development and implementation of e-SPRINT: Lecture notes management system implementation at Universiti Putra Malaysia. In A. A. Sidek (Ed.), Design and development of management system at UPM (pp. 1 – 4). Serdang: Center for Academic Development, Universiti Putra Malaysia.

Sidek, A. A., Meseran, H., Jabar, M., & Sidek, Z. Md.Yunus, A. S., Bakar, K., & Wong, S. L. (2007a). The experience of the e-SPRINT: Lecture notes management system implementation at Universiti Putra Malaysia: A case study. In A. A. Sidek (Ed.), Design and development of management system at UPM (pp. 97 – 103). Serdang: Center for Academic Development, Universiti Putra Malaysia.

Sturgess, P., & Nouwens, F. (July 2004). Evaluation of online learning management systems. *Turkish Online Journal of Distance Education, 5*(3). Retrieved July 20, 2009, from http://tojde.anadolu.edu.tr/tojde15/articles/sturgess.htm

The Mind of the Vice Chancellor. (n.d.). Accessed on June 20, 2009, from http://www.upm.edu.my/?kat=D&aktvt=.

Universiti Putra Malaysia. (2008). *The Strategic Plan Document 2001- 2010 (Revised 2007)*. Serdang: Author.

ADDITIONAL READING

Abdullah, I. Md.Yunus, A. S., Sidek, A. A., & Matthews, R. (2007). Integrating learning style with e-learning instructional design: A formative evaluation. In A. A. Sidek (Ed.), Design and development of learning management system at Universiti Putra Malaysia. (pp. 49 – 65) Serdang: Centre for Academic Development.

Alias, N. A., & Zainuddin, A. M. (2005). Innovation for better teaching and learning: adopting the learning management system. *Malaysian Online Journal of Instructional Technology (MOJIT), 2*(2), 27-40. Retrieved June 20, 2009, from http://pppjj.usm.my/mojit/articles/pdf/August05/03-Article-037-NorAziah-UiTM%20version%20 2%5B1%5D.pdf

Kalnins-Cole, T., & Peters, D. (2007). Towards an accessible learning management system. *International Journal of Continuing Engineering Education and Lifelong Learning, 17*(1), 84–96. doi:10.1504/IJCEELL.2007.013232

Low, A. L., Low, K. L. T., & Koo, V. C. (2003). Multimedia learning systems: A future interactive educational tools. *The Internet and Education, 6*, 25–40. doi:10.1016/S1096-7516(02)00160-4

Lu, E. J., & Chen, Y. H. (2006). Design of a delegable SCORM conformant learning management system. *Journal of Computer Assisted Learning, 22*(6), 423–436. doi:10.1111/j.1365-2729.2006.00189.x

Merino, P. J. M., Kloos, C. D., Seepold, R., & Garcia, R. M. C. (2006). Rating the importance of different LMS functionalities. In *Proceedings of the 36th Annual Frontiers in Education Conference,* San Diego, California, 27-31 October (pp. 13-18).

Meseran, H., & Jabar, M. Sidek, A. A., Rahiman, A., Sharif, K., Md. Yunus, A. S., Sulaiman, M. A. H., & Selamat, M. H. (2007). Design of interactive web-based instructional system: A methodology approach in system development. In A. A. Sidek. (Eds\.), Design and development of learning management system at Universiti Putra Malaysia (pp. 21 – 27), Serdang: Centre for Academic Development.

Othman, S. A. S., Atan, H., & Kooi Guan, C. (2005). The Open University Malaysia Learning Management System: A study of interaction in the asynchronous forum board. *International Journal of Instructional Technology and Distance Learning, 2*(11). Retrieved July 9, 2009 from http://itdl.org/journal/nov_05/article01.htm

Picciano, A. G. (2002). Beyond student perceptions: issues of interaction, presences and performance in an online course. *Journal of Asynchronous Learning Networks, 6*(1), 21–40.

Saade, R. G., & Huang, Q. (2008). Prototyping a learning management system for Higher Education. In *Proceedings of the Informing Science & IT Conference (I*n*SITE 2008).* Retrieved July 9, 2009 from http://proceedings.informingscience.org/InSITE2008/InSITE08p155-165Saade461.pdf

Saba, F. (2008). Learning management systems of the future: A theoretical framework and design. *MERLOT Journal of Online Learning and Teaching, 4*(2). Retrieved July 9, 2009 from http://jolt.merlot.org/vol4no2/saba0608.htm

Sidek, A. A. Md. Yunus, A. S., Abdullah, I., Bakar, K., & Meseran, H. (2004). Challenges in implementing e-SPRINT: e-learning system at UPM. In *Proceedings of the National Seminar on e-Learning,* Penang, 7 – 9 June.

Sidek, A. A., Jabar, M., Meseran, H., & Selamat, M. H. Md. Yunus, A. S. (2005). Design and development of KM based learning content management system for e-SPRINT. *Paper presented in the International Conference on Knowledge Management, Kuala Lumpur.*

Sidek, A. A., Jabar, M., Meseran, H., Selamat, M. H., & Md. Yunus, A. S. (2007). Design and development of KM based learning management system for e-SPRINT. In A. A. Sidek (Ed.), Design and development of learning management system at Universiti Putra Malaysia (pp. 15 – 20). Serdang: Centre for Academic Development, Universiti Putra Malaysia.

Sidek, A. A., & Loong, C. F. Md. Yunus, A. S., Bakar, K., Meseran, H. (2007). Design and development of online quiz using the open source system. In A. A. Sidek (Ed.), Design and development of learning management system at Universiti Putra Malaysia. (pp. 105 – 115). Serdang: Centre for Academic Development, Universiti Putra Malaysia.

Sidek, A. A., Meseran, H., Jabar, M., & Sidek, Z. Md. Yunus, A. S., Bakar, K. (2005). The Experience of the e-SPRINT - Lecture notes management system implementation at Universiti Putra Malaysia: A case study. In *Proceedings of the Brunei International Conference on Engineering and Technology (BICET 2005),* Brunei Darussalam, 15-18 August. Chapman, B. (2003). *LCMS report: Comparing analysis of enterprise Learning Content Management Systems.* Sunnyvale, CA: Brandon-Hall. Colazzo, L., & Molinari, A. (2005). Building, Testing and Assessing a Learning Management System. *Journalof Computing and Information Technology, 13*(1), 25-41.

Tsukahara, W., Anma, F., Nakayama, K., & Okamoto, T. (2007). A development of learning management system for the practice of e-Learning in Higher Education. Boston: Springer.

Whelan, R., & Bhartu, D. (2007). Factors in the deployment of a learning management system at the University of the South Pacific. In *Proceedings of the ASCILITE Conference* (pp. 1053-1062). Retrieved July 9, 2009, from http://www.ascilite.org.au/conferences/singapore07/procs/whelan.pdf

KEY TERMS AND DEFINITIONS

Learning Management System: An e-learning system that organizes and administers instructor-facilitated courses.

Information Sharing: Platform where e-learning knowledge are shared among students and lecturers.

Knowledge Repository: Location for storage of e-learning materials.

Integrated Database: Systematic and meaningful structure of shareable related data.

Continues Monitoring: Maintaining an ongoing observation on all aspects of e-learning system.

e-Learning Resources: Various types of curricula materials that are easily accessible in electronic forms.

ICT Culture: Widespread and pervasive use of communication and computer related technologies in a community.

Online Courses: Courses or lecture notes designed to be posted online.

e-Learning: Delivery of education and training courses over the Internet and/or Intranets, a mixture of content (online courses or courseware) and communication (reaching online, emails, discussion, forums).

Chapter 18
Technology-Assisted Reading: Challenges and Opportunities in a Developing Country

Gerda van Wyk
Reading Zone and University of Johannesburg, South Africa

Arno Louw
Reading Zone and University of Johannesburg, South Africa

ABSTRACT

This chapter presents the findings of a comparison between two different computer reading programmes with the aim of compiling a minimum set of requirements for such a programme in a third world educational environment. It further examines the challenges, benefits and limitations of implementing technology assisted reading on a wide scale. The results of this study are used to formulate strategies to best obtain results in reading difficulties. Consequently, reading difficulties are a world- wide problem and therefore require new and innovative ideas to be effectively addressed. Moreover, reading difficulties do not exist in isolation, and should be addressed in small groups with a holistic approach to ensure the best chance of successfully addressing the problem. The facilitator – learner ratio is important to ensure individual attention to learners. The flexibility and adaptability of the software are therefore important aspects during software implementation. When deciding on effective reading software, the applicability of assistive technology as part of an intervention strategy in reading difficulties should be considered as the most important aspect.

BACKGROUND

It has been well documented in academic literature that South African learners are amongst the poorest in the world (Van Wyk & Louw, 2008:[online]). The poor level of reading skills across the world is a daunting phenomenon. Van Wyk and Louw (*op. cit.*) reported their research results on technology assisted reading for learners in South Africa in 2008, and concluded that computer based reading programmes play an important role in the improvement of reading skills for young learners. Learners identify with the electronic medium and it can therefore be utilised to re-create a love for reading.

However, a third world country faces many challenges in addressing reading difficulties as so

DOI: 10.4018/978-1-61520-909-5.ch018

many factors play a role in introducing Reading interventions. These include poverty and lack of financial and structural resources, lack of computer literacy in learners and teachers and high crime rates which increase the costs to safeguard computer laboratories. Furthermore, government education departments place restrictions on the software to be installed at schools according to their own standards. Experts in the field of technology assisted reading are seldom part of decision making in terms of the reading software to be implemented. It is nevertheless a fact that technology is the medium of instruction for the future and should be utilised within the limitations it presents. However, reading difficulties do not exist and cannot be treated in isolation and any intervention programme should therefore be holistic in nature.

FOLLOW-UP RESEARCH

Van Wyk and Louw envisaged follow–up research in the efficacy of different computer reading programmes with the aim of compiling a minimum set of requirements for such a programme in a third world educational environment. Furthermore, this paper will present the findings of a study that was collected over a period of two years and reflects the reading results of learners who followed two different computer reading programmes over a period of seven months each. Moreover, this paper aims to examine the challenges, benefits and limitations of implementing technology assisted reading programmes on a wide scale. It will also include the results of a research study where technology was used as an aid with other intervention strategies. This study will include qualitative as well as quantitative data. The results of this study will be used to formulate strategies to best obtain results in reading difficulties. The obstacles will be identified and conclusions will be drawn as practical and usable solutions.

The lack of reading skills in higher education in South Africa often discards reading difficulties as the reason for unsuccessful studies. Strategies and the use of modern technologies attempt to bridge the gap in academic literacy. In this regard, we will draw on the work of Siragusa, Dixon and Dixon, who state that: "The development of effective online learning environment that meet these pedagogical needs require the application of appropriate instructional design principles. The literature suggests that there are gaps between the bodies of knowledge relating to learning theories, instructional design principles and student learning in higher education" (Siragusa, Dixon & Dixon, 2007,pp.923).

ASSISTIVE TECHNOLOGY AS A PART OF READING INTERVENTIONS

The Landmark College (2006:[online]) proposes a strategy for the initiation of technology assistive reading for learners. These strategies largely impose interventions from stakeholders. These stakeholders mainly include a teacher that provides space for learning, the computer software as well as the reading material (Pearson, Ferdig, Blomeyer and Moran (2005:2). The recommended strategy is:

- The appropriate learning material must be selected;
- Learners skim through the text after the purpose and steps of skimming have been explained ;
- Main topics and sub-topics are highlighted with respective colours, copy and pasted, and read from a new document. However, the author claims that this can only be performed if the related software allows for this function;
- The content information is then processed by asking the following questions:
    - What is the main idea?
    - What are the sub-topics?
    - What questions will you expect to be answered in the reading?

However, we argue that the technology used for assisting reading in South Africa, is demographically bound and should rather have a single selected reading assisting program that is generic in its nature. In choosing assistive technology as aid in reading, different factors should be considered, of which the technologies' effectiveness in accomplishing the primary purpose of use is the most important. (Raskind, 2006:[online]). As reading difficulties do not exist in isolation and struggling readers differ extensively in terms of the degree and nature of their reading difficulties, the support of assistive technology should be able to address these differences. Closely associated with online reading and technologies and computer-based reading programmes, Coiro (2003:[online]) refers to Allington (2001), Keene and Zimmermann (1997), and Robb (2000) and prominently states that: "These shallow, random, and often passive interactions with text are in direct contrast to the active, strategic, and critical processes of constructing meaning now being proposed by instructional leaders and supported by 25 years of reading research." Investigating the effect of technology on reading performance, Pearson, Ferdig, Blomeyer and Moran (2005:2) attempted to determine if digital technologies have an effect on the acquisition of advanced reading skills. The same authors suggest (*op. cit.*) advanced reading skills to be:

- Comprehension;
- Metacognition;
- Strategy use; and
- Motivation and Engagement.

To promote higher-order thinking in technology assisted environments, the instructional strategies used must make connections between new skills and information. New, meaningful knowledge should be acquired to utilize metacognitive thinking skills. "Students may be required to learn a set of principles within a discipline area and integrate previously learned knowledge with new knowledge by employing techniques such as advanced organisers, worked-out examples, and elaborative questions" (Siragusa, Dixon & Dixon, 2007, pp.923-924). Subsequently, the underlying pedagogical philosophy for integrating prior knowledge with existing knowledge towards acquiring new reading skills, is based on a continuum. This continuum ranges from instructivist/behaviourist approaches on the one end, to constructivist/cognitive learning on the other end.

Pearson, *et. al.* (2005, pp.2) further explain their purpose to have been the identification of "technical and contextual factors associated with effective interventions." In this paper, we would like to add the purpose of adaptability and flexibility as well as feedback provided by the reading software, which should be factors added to effective technology assisted reading.

METHODOLOGY

Three types of analyses can be performed in meta-analysis of computer assistive reading technologies on middle-school level (Pearson, *et. al.*, 2005, pp.11-12). These strategies are:

- Statistics from a variety of reading software can be combined and overall tested for statistical significance.
- Investigation on heterogeneity and publication bias of the size of the effect.
- Comparisons of the extent to which studies feature such as population served or instructional focus, "moderated to the effect on outcome measures" (Pearson, *et. al.*, 2005, pp.11).

We argue that the effectiveness of the two programmes compared in this paper, is dependent on quantitative as well as qualitative analysis. Furthermore, we agree with the authors' findings that:

there may be a trade-off between statistical power and experimental precision; that is, it may be easier for researchers to maintain a high degree of fidelity to treatment in smaller studies because of the greater manageability prospects;

Technologies that were created by a research team had a much larger effect size than those technologies either adapted from the commercial market or those that merely used the technology as a delivery system. In addition, those created by researchers tended to have a clear theoretical focus that was matched by assessments employed by the team, and

Studies that used some sort of correlated design (pre-tests used as covariates for post-tests or repeated measures designs in which the same subjects cycle through different interventions) are more likely to find reliable differences between interventions than an independent group designs (Pearson, et. al.,2005, pp.19).

Hence, we present statistics (given as tables) as well as qualitative involvement such as feedback from the actual learners who participated in the research. For this research, data was collected in a lower to middle class primary school with mother tongue learners in Johannesburg, South Africa. Reading on both programs was compulsory and learners could participate with their parents' consent. Reading results of learners from grade two to grade seven were used to compare the two reading programmes over a period of seven months on each program. Learners were actively involved in hourly sessions on a weekly basis. No scheduled reading sessions were held during school holidays. The qualitative aspect of the study was included to specifically focus on what the learners experienced despite their reading results. For the qualitative aspect, the feedback of learners who participated on both the programs was included. These learners' actual reading results were not included in the study.

All variables such as personal interventions and additional activities were kept the same for both groups on Program A and on Program B, however, no control was possible over different teacher's approaches in the class as well as parents involvement at home.

The two programs did not run simultaneously. Program A was implemented in 2007 for approximately 7 months, from April to October and Program B was implemented in 2008 from April to October. Data were therefore collected over a period of 14 months.

DEVELOPMENTAL STAGES OF THE STUDY

The study consisted of four stages namely:

Stage 1: The Pre-Reading Assessment

Assessment procedures for both groups were identical irrespective of the programme they followed.

The identical standardised scholastic reading test was utilised that provided information on reading speed, comprehension, vocabulary and typical reading mistakes. An additional standardised spelling test was used in order to also assess the spelling skills of the learners. The tracking of eye movements by means of moving a pencil horizontally and vertically and towards learners' eyes, formed part of the assessment. Any irregular eye movements, discomfort or pain were noted, duly reported and recommendations for an appointment with an optometrist were made when necessary.

No learners were assessed electronically as to ensure that the lack of computer skills does not negatively impact on their assessment results. (Foxcroft and Roodt 2005, pp.183).

To ensure that data could be scientifically compared, the final results were calculated as the mean over all sessions attended as this was the procedure followed for Program A. The reasoning behind not doing a post assessment was to be able to measure growth and actual mastery of the reading task over a short period of time.(Van Wyk & Louw; 2008).

Stage 2: The Reading Intervention

All learners were placed on the programme with compulsory attendance for at least 16 sessions of 45 minutes each. Learners started at different times during the two seven month periods. No reading sessions took place during school holidays.

Learners were familiarized with the both programs before commencement through the use of the electronic assessment on Program A and the first reading lesson on program B as Program B did not offer an assessment function. The first session served therefore as an introduction as well as an opportunity to assess the learners' mouse skills.

A standard reading session throughout both seven month periods contained the following elements. The order in which the elements (activities) were presented may have differed.

Spelling Test

On Program A the spelling words were flashed on the screen and the learner had to type the word on the computer. The learner could simultaneously hear the word over the microphone and had the opportunity to replay the auditory function. Flashing speed gradually increased automatically with every session.

Spelling words on Program B were flashed on the screen and the learner had to type the word on the computer. No opportunity was provided to relook or listen to the word, should the learner have missed the flashed word. The speed increment on program B was manually adjusted.

Both programs provided immediate feedback on responses entered through animated figures.

Reading Speed and Comprehension Test

Program A: Reading content on the screen was to be read and the computer calculated the reading speed in words per minute. Immediate feedback of reading speed was provided to the learner in terms of an automatically generated graph. A comprehension test immediately followed with a function where the learner could revisit the text.

Program B: A specific lesson could be chosen and was to be read from the computer screen. On completion the computer automatically calculated the reading speed in words per minute with immediate feedback in terms of a number of words per minute. After feedback a comprehension test automatically followed with feedback after completion in terms of a percentage achieved. The learner had no opportunity to revisit the text when doing the comprehension test.

Contained Reading Exercises

On Program A, a contained reading exercise automatically followed the comprehension test, with the contained speed automatically determined and generated according to the achievement on the comprehension test. After completing the comprehension test the automated session expired.

The contained reading exercises promoted the following aspects:

- reduce the duration of fixation on a word;
- improve the recognition span to a minimum of eleven characters.
- improve the fluency of the eye in moving from left to right.

After completion of the comprehension test on Program B, the learner or facilitator could manually choose from seven different contained reading exercises. Contained speed is manually adjusted. Immediately after the contained reading exercise, the same comprehension test followed. Learners were encouraged to redo the comprehension test if they obtained below 70% for the first attempt. This was done to compensate for the fact that the learners could not revisit the text when doing the comprehension test the first time as the learners on Program A were the opportunity to do.

The same aspects as in program A were promoted during the contained reading exercises, however more options are available in terms of minimum characters for improving eye span, foreground and background reading and more aggressive techniques in terms of reducing the duration of fixation and improving fluency in eye movements.

Language Skills

Grammar related questions formed part of the comprehension test on program A. Program B offered many application exercises and games to improve grammar and vocabulary.

Visual Exercises

Program A provided very limited exercises to improve visual accuracy or memory and an additional program was used to encompass vision as part of the Reading intervention. Program B provided practical application exercises to engage with, in order to improve visual accuracy, visual memory and eye span.

Personal Interventions as a Part of the Programme

Research indicates that failure or achievement is often based on person's perceptions of abilities and not determined by ability itself. Poor readers lack self confidence as a result of negative experiences in class and at home causing dislike in reading and an unwillingness to engage in reading activities (Van Wyk & Louw; 2008). They very often based their own perception of their reading abilities on the feedback from others. For this reason the facilitators created a positive and non threatening environment during reading sessions. Personal engagement with learners, encouragement and support were regarded as just an important aspect of the Reading intervention strategy. Acknowledgement on all levels (behaviour, manners, friendliness etc) formed part of an attempt to improve the self esteem of the learners.

Competition between readers was discouraged but taking responsibility to improve oneself was encouraged. Both programs provided immediate feedback on all responses entered which was seen as an important factor in keeping learners motivated.

Soft reading with minimum movement of the head was encouraged and the facilitator provided techniques for the memory of the spelling of difficult words and provides continuous information on spelling rules.

Learners were encouraged to make use of the different games and application exercises after completing their formal reading session. Learners were allowed to choose the applications themselves. However, if it was felt that learners repeatedly only choose specific applications they were encouraged to try other applications as well.

Grade two and three learners were expected to engage in the games where letters and sounds were identified and words recognized.

Parents and teachers formed part of the reading team providing the support, encouragement and time the learners needed. Parents and teachers were invited to discuss their concerns and involvements on a regular basis with the facilitator.

Stage 3: Qualitative Feedback from Learners and Facilitator

A short interview was held with learners who had exposure to both programs regarding their reading experience over the seven month period with specific reference to the aspects in both the reading programs that assisted them or added value to their reading achievements.

The feedback from the facilitator in terms of the effectiveness of different aspects was incorporated as a valuable and important input from a different perspective.

Stage 4: Comparison of Assessment Results with Mastering of the Reading Skill

At the end of the seven months period, the average score of every learner in terms of reading speed, comprehension and spelling were compared against the learner's initial assessment results. This was done within each group during the data gathering period. This enables the researcher to assess the mastering of reading skills on both programs.

All the above results for learners on the two separate programmes were then compared in an attempt to compare the effectiveness of the two programs as an aid in Reading intervention.

Three assumptions are applicable:

- *Assumption 1*: A significant difference in the reading results on both programs when compared to the initial assessment results will indicate the importance of technology as aid in Reading interventions
- *Assumption 2*: A significant difference in the reading results of learners when mastering of the reading skill on the two programs is compared will indicate the importance of the different applications and functions of a specific software program in Reading intervention.
- *Assumption 3*: No significant differences between the reading results of learners when mastering of the reading skill on the two programs are compared will indicate that the different applications and functions of the software are not meaningful contributory factors in the achievement of reading results.

RESULTS AND DISCUSSION

In comparing any results it should be kept in mind that there are many aspects that influence achievement in general and that also applies to reading achievement. Such factors are, for example, cognitive abilities of learners, the level of commitment, motivation and interest as well as concentration and nutrition. The support from parents and teachers also plays a role in achievement. The researchers had no control over these factors although they attempt to compromise possible negative influences by setting a positive and caring atmosphere during the sessions.

Reading results were compared in terms of three assessed reading functions namely reading speed, Reading comprehension and spelling. The average reading results at completion of the 16 sessions over seven months for every grade on both programs were compared with the average initial assessment results for every grade before commencement on both programs.

The first table (Table 1) reflects the results in reading speed, measured in words per minute. The expected level of reading speed indicates the standard norms for different grades according to Taylor, S., Frackenpohl, H and Pettee, J.L. (1960) and is accepted worldwide.

Reading speed is seen as an important aspect in Reading interventions as well as in a learning environment as it impacts on comprehension and impacts on completion of tasks within a time limit such as in a test- situation.

Reading Speed

According to the results in Table 1, the average improvement of reading speed on program A was 53,5 words per minute and on program B, 60 words per minute. The difference of 6,5 words per minute in favour of program B can be seen as

Table 1. Reading speed

		Program A			Program B		
Grade	Expected Level of reading speed Per grade **wpm**	Average Reading speed at assessment **wpm**	Average Reading speed after 15 sessions **wpm**	Average Improvement in Reading speed **wpm**	Average Reading speed at assessment **wpm**	Average Reading speed after 15 sessions **wpm**	Average improvement In reading speed **wpm**
2	80	25	51	26	18	58	40
3	115	40	95	55	31	93	62
4	158	38	96	58	52	112	6o
5	173	72	142	70	105	192	87
6	185	76	147	71	108	153	45
7	195	80	121	41	83	148	65
Total				53,5			60

insignificant. However, a significant improvement is noticed on both programmes in comparison to the assessment results, indicating that the software played a significant role as an aid in the improvement of reading speed. It is worth noting that the reading speed for all the grades improved.

Comprehension

Comprehension forms a crucial aspect in the reading activity as it reflects the level of insight a learner shows in the content of the written word. Comprehension plays a major role in academic success from primary school to tertiary level. The level of comprehension is one of the indicators of academic achievement at tertiary level.

Table 2 reflects the achievement in comprehension assessment on both programs in comparison with the initial assessment.

The results shown in Table 2 were greatly influenced by the grade 4 group on program A, who achieved very poorly on the assessment. One learner achieved 0% and two learners obtained

Table 2. Comprehension

Program A			Program B		
Average Achievement in comprehension at assessment %	Average Achievement in comprehension after 16 sessions %	Average Improvement in comprehension %	Average Achievement in comprehension at assessment %	Average Achievement in comprehension after 16 sessions %	Average Improvement in comprehension %
39	81	42	42	82	40
61	81	20	69	76	7
19	84	65	50	78	28
49	75	26	62	77	15
54	79	25	64	85	21
46	74	28	50	85	35
		34,3			24,3

13% during the assessment. The assessment results on program B were in general higher allowing less room to achieve to the maximum.

According to the achievement results when compared with the assessment results an improvement of 24% to 34% were obtained. This can be regarded as a significant improvement in comprehension over seven months. The difference between program A and program B is 10% in favour of program A. In interpreting these results it should be kept in mind that the learner on Program A could revisit the text, while the learners on program B did the comprehension test twice because they were not offered the opportunity to revisit the text. It can therefore be assumed that on Program B learners had to rely on memory as well in order to complete the comprehension test.

Spelling

Spelling forms an integral part of the reading activity and is therefore regarded as part of the assessment. Spelling skills allow the learner to accurately communicate his or her thoughts in writing which is to be read by another person.

Spelling results are reflected in Table 3 for both programs and in comparison with the initial assessment results.

The results indicate an overall average improvement on both programs of 27% to 38% which can be regarded as remarkable over a period of seven months. The difference in achievement between program A and program B is 11.5% in favour of program A.

Program A differ significantly from program B in the spelling aspect as program A allows the learner to also listen repeatedly to the flashed spelling word where on Program B, the word is flashed only once. This resulted in learners who did not recognize the flashed word immediately not to be able to make any response or making a knowingly wrong response to enable the program to progress.

The assumption can be made that the sound feature significantly contributed to the improved spelling achievement of learners.

Qualitative Feedback from the Facilitator in Comparing Program A and Program B

In addressing reading difficulties, the choice of a suitable computer program is an important aspect. (Van Wyk & Louw: 2008) The authors suggested that a list of criteria should be compiled as a set of minimum requirements. With possibilities of

Table 3. Spelling

	Program A			Program B		
Grade	Average Achievement in spelling at assessment %	Average Achievement in spelling after 15 sessions %	**Average Improvement in spelling on %**	Average Achievement in spelling at assessment %	Average Achievement in spelling after 15 sessions %	**Average Improvement in spelling on %**
2	67	86	**19**	45	81	**36**
3	32	87	**55**	45	81	**36**
4	23	88	**65**	35	73	**38**
5	45	79	**34**	62	77	**15**
6	52	83	**31**	72	82	**10**
7	56	85	**29**	47	76	**29**
Total			**38,8**			**27, 3**

criteria in mind, this study compared the two programs in terms of five factors of difference between Program A and Program B. These factors were identified on the strength of the literature study as well as the expertise of the facilitator and researcher in engaging with the programs for several months.

The five factors of comparison are:

- The flexibility and adaptability of the programs

This factor refers to the level of which the facilitator has access to change settings or content on the program in order to enhance the Reading intervention. It also refers to the user friendliness of the programs from the perspective of the learner as well as the facilitator.

"Instructional design decisions can influence different learning strategies" (Siragusa, Dixon & Dixon, 2007, pp. 928). The same authors also explain that: "Observational strategies may include observing students as they study..." and elaborate that another pedagogical dimension is identified. They suggest that the dimension for the development of learning strategies ranges from teacher guided to student guided and can also be seen as ranging from teacher developed to student developed. Thus, the intended strategy envisaged from the reading facilitator can ideally develop to an interventional strategy prompted by the learner.

Consequently, the content given to the learner is not fixed, except for the exclusive age of the learner participating in the online program. Therefore, learners may either seek for other learning material (not provided by the program or suggested by the facilitator) or "...assist with solving a particular problem through applying the concepts learner" (Siragusa, Dixon & Dixon, 2007, pp.929). Hence, learning material can either be found by the learner as enrichment material or can be suitably integrated by the facilitator. The same authors describe this pedagogical dimension as *content guided learning strategies* which range from non-existent to integral to the learning process.

Complementing the pedagogical dimensions discussed earlier, is another dimension for flexibility of a computer-supported environment such as the ecology of the learning program environment. This dimension is dubbed: *Study flexibility – when, where, what pace* by the same authors. They explain that the "amount of flexibility allowed for students to study when, where and at what pace required may be presented along a dimension". Subsequently, this dimension ranges from teacher determined to student controlled.

We argue that if content guided learning strategies exist, guided by a facilitator, then student learning strategies also exist as emerged from the explanations in the preceding paragraphs. We further agree, though not intentional to the learners, that there are automated interactive activities. These automated activities can be at substantive level and practical levels "... propose an approach and programme for development of an online learning ecology" (Louw, 2008, pp.299). Thus, the automated learning activity ranges on a continuum from non-existent to integral.

- Applicable associations

Applicable associations refer to what every program offer in terms of applying newly learned knowledge (for example vocabulary) and what type of learning opportunities does every program offer in repetition of newly learned knowledge to ensure storing of information in the long term memory.

- Teacher and learner control

The study investigated how the level of control, from both facilitator and learner, towards the software program influence the reading experience and reading results of learners and the experience of the facilitator. (Also compare the previous paragraph on *content guided learning strategies* and *study flexibility*).

- Possibilities for Reading interventions.

This factor refers to the opportunities that both programs provide in terms of a successful Reading intervention

- Accommodating learning styles of the different learners

The two programs are compared as to the way in which different learning styles are accommodated with specific reference to visual, auditory and kinaesthetic learning styles (See Table 4).

The Advantages and Disadvantages of the Above Factors

Factors are discussed from the facilitator's point of view in terms of their advantages and disadvantages and the value these specific factors add to the reading experience as an intervention in improving reading skills.

Table 4. Comparison between Program A and Program B regarding the five factors

Comparison of Factors	*Program A*	**Program B**
Flexibility and adaptability	•This program is fully automated • limited or no access to settings such as speed settings • The program always runs in the same sequence of activities to enable the program to generate a useful report at the end of the session. The learner cannot quit or redo any part without exiting completely. • Able to upload MSWord text with none of the functions of the program to be applicable. •The facilitator is not able to address any technical problems •Technical support not easily available • Technical support costly	•All functional settings operates manually •Allowing the facilitator to make changes in terms of reading speed, flash speed, changing spelling words, comprehension questions, content of applications etc. •All functions applied on newly uploaded lessons. •Changes can also be made by learners who have advanced computer skills • Technical support is easily available (telephonically) allowing the facilitator to address technical problems in the centre. • Technical support available at no cost • Access to change colour and font.
Applicable associations	•No applicable associations are available	• Games allowing the learner to apply newly learned vocabulary in practical ways. •Games allowing learners to practice sentence construction and grammar related aspects. • Definitions and explanations of words
Teacher and learner control	• Teacher control over the program is limited as the program is automated. •Teacher is allowed access to adapt reading speed and level of reading. •Learners have no control over the running of the program.	•Teacher is in full control of the program and has access to all settings. •Learners have limited access to settings • Learners with advanced technological skills can easily change settings in the program. • Learners can choose between the different application exercises.
Possibilities for Reading interventions	• Basic Reading assessment in terms of reading speed, comprehension and spelling. • Intervention in terms of speed, comprehension and spelling and limited grammar related aspects. • Three automatic contained reading exercises. •No visual accuracy, visual perception or visual memory exercises.	• No Reading assessment. • Interventions in terms of reading speed, comprehension and spelling. • six to seven contained reading exercises • Visual accuracy and visual memory exercises. • Applications allowing interventions in terms of specific reading difficulties. • Learners with specific visual difficulties can be accommodated.
Learning styles	• Selective auditory functions. • Visual feedback in terms of an animated character.	• Ample visual material is provided for the visual learner. • Auditory feedback in terms of sounds

The Flexibility and Adaptability of the Programs

Program A

Program A is fully automated which allows limited to no access for the facilitator to manipulate the program in addressing the individual needs of every learner. Because the program always runs the same sequence for every lesson, learners get bored after a couple of sessions and loose interest in the programme with a downwards spiral in achievement after 15 sessions. No additional fun activities are available to counteract the boredom aspect.

As the programming for automated reading programs is much more complicated, technical problems cause many frustrations for facilitators and learners alike and solutions to these problems are not easily or cheaply available. If technical problems occur, learners are unable to exit the program due to "hanging" which often results in a zero score for tests during that session.

Although the program allows the facilitator to upload a word document, none of the functions are applicable on this document, making it a useless feature and nothing more than reading a normal word document or a document from paper format.

The advantage of the automated program is that learners have no access to speed settings. This will especially be true in a larger group where the facilitator will not be able to set the speed for every individual learner which might result is slowing down the progress.

Program B

The functional settings are done by hand and therefore allow the facilitator to adapt the settings according to the needs of every learner. The Reading intervention can thus be focused on every individual learner in the group. This is however not possible in a larger group as the facilitator will not be able to change the settings for every learner without additional help. In allowing younger learners to change their own settings endangers their progress as they are tempted to take the easy and fast way out. Facilitators will also not be able to keep track of progress during a session which might lead to a scenario of remedy rather than intervention. This also applies to learners with advanced computer skills who find ways to change their settings without the facilitator's knowledge and slowing their own progress.

The program allows the uploading of new reading material with all built in software functions to automatically be available as applications. This allows the facilitator to enrich the learning experience for learners when selected reading material slots in with the relevant school topics of learners.

More learners with specific problems can be accommodated on program B because of the access to change the foreground and background colours, the font sizes and types as to suit individual preferences or visual sensitivities.

As access is allowed to already existing reading material, the facilitator may include or change existing comprehension questions to encompass deeper insight and different levels of comprehension.

Applicable Solutions

Program A

As no applicable associations on program A are available there is no fun in learning and learners are easily bored. Furthermore, this does not allow the learner to apply newly learned knowledge in practical ways and no opportunity is available for repetition to allow newly learned information to take place.

Program B

This program provides the learner with a couple of games to apply their newly learned vocabulary in practical ways and to ensure their understanding and recognition of new words. These games are entertaining as well as educational and provide a stimulating learning experience with little chance of boredom. Learners are allowed to choose the games for every lesson. The program also provides a facility where the facilitator can identify keywords from reading content and then upload definitions, explanations, images and additional information about the words.

Application exercises for sentence construction and grammar related exercises such as idioms, synonyms antonyms plurals, opposites etc. are also provided.

For the younger learner exercises are available to identify letters and sounds in words as well as building words from clues provided.

Teacher and Learner Control

Program A

Teacher control over the program is extremely limited allowing access to the adaption of automated speed increments if necessary. From an advantage point of view it makes facilitating quite easy but not necessarily effective. Because the program adjust settings automatically the facilitator does not need to adjust the settings for every learner allowing more free time to observe the learners performance and intervene on a personal level. Should larger groups of learners be considered, this program will definitely be more effective. On the other hand, not being able to choose specific techniques or adapting flash speed for example, does not allow the facilitator to manipulate the program to focus the Reading intervention for every individual learner.

Learners and facilitators have to live with mistakes on the program as it is not possible to fix mistakes causing learners to be negative when wrong marks are assigned for correct responses. Mistakes will only be rectified when a next upgrade is available at a specific cost.

The fact that learners have no control or access to settings can also be viewed as positive and negative. From an advantage point of view are learners not able to jeopardise their own progress by changing speed settings to finish the session in the shortest possible time, however not being able to have choices regarding activities allow little challenges and creativity in the learning process.

Program B

Being in full control of the program allows the facilitator to manipulate the software to the advantage of every individual learner. However from an administrative point of view it places a heavy additional load on the facilitator as it is necessary to record all changes to settings for every learner during every session to enable the facilitator to plan the intervention tailor-made for every learner. To ensure progress this program should not be used in larger groups without additional help.

Learners have limited access to settings yet learners with slightly advanced computer skills can easily change settings in the program which might be detrimental to their progress.

Possibilities for Reading interventions

Program A

The program offers a basic Reading assessment in terms of reading speed, comprehension and spelling. However, literature indicates that Reading assessment on a computer does not provide valid information regarding the reading skills as different factors influence the assessment such as level of computer literacy, mouse skills, anxiety because of first time computer reading etc.

The program offers intervention in terms of speed, comprehension and spelling and limited grammar related aspects as grammar related questions form part of the comprehension test but no grammar related activities are provided.

The program offers three automatic techniques in term of reading speed intervention with no choice to the facilitator in the technique to be introduced. No visual accuracy, visual perception or visual memory exercises form part of this program.

In summary it could be concluded that the automated program offers limited possibilities for Reading intervention as the software cannot be manipulated to address the individual causes for reading difficulties but is generically applied to all learners irrespective of individual reading problems

Program B

This program offers substantially more possibilities for Reading intervention as it allows the facilitator to manipulate the functions and settings by hand to accommodate specific reading difficulties of individual learners. Not only is intervention possible in terms of reading speed, comprehension and spelling, but also in terms of visual perception and memory. As this program offers a couple of reading techniques the suitable technique can be chosen to address very specific problems such as eye span, crossing the visual midline and fluency of reading. Some techniques are also more aggressive in obtaining results. Learners with visual sensitivities can also be accommodated because of access to settings.

It should however be stressed again that individually focused Reading interventions that make use of technology as assistance will be implemented with difficulty in larger groups.

Learning Styles

Program A

This program offers the opportunity to listen to the text being read while following the text simultaneously allowing the auditory learner an advantage. This feature is also very helpful for second language readers.

Hardly any visual material forms part of this program. Only feedback is provided in terms of a graph and a little animated character who dances or cries depending on the accuracy of the learner's response.

Program B

Ample visual material is provided for the visual learner with hardly any provision made to accommodate the auditory learner except for feedback in terms of "sounds from visuals".

The fact that both programs are computer based provide opportunity for the kinaesthetic learner to engage in the reading activity, yet program B offers additional applications in the forms of games which also provide good learning experience for the kinaesthetic learner.

Qualitative Feedback from Learners

According to the qualitative feedback received from learners who participated on both programs, it is evident that:

- Learners prefer the software which offers application activities (games) where they can apply newly learned words and skills;
- The automated program offered too little variety causing learners to be bored;
- Although learners preferred shorter reading content, they appreciated a wider variety of reading material;
- Sound was not regarded as a contributing factor to achieving success on the reading program by the older learners;
- All learners agreed that reading on both programs assisted them in improving their reading skills; and
- Learners agreed that the facilitator's attitude towards them played an important role in their success and in their level of motivation and participation.

"Students are increasingly expecting more reliable and valid assessment with prompt feedback on their performance" (Siragusa, Dixon & Dixon, 2007, pp.931). The authors go on and explain that "The amount and type of feedback students require will vary depending upon student need and level of engagement with the learning materials." Related to technology assisted reading, we agree with the authors that another pedagogical dimension for *feedback* should be claimed.

CONCLUSIONS

Additional Aspects that Impact on the Success of Technology Assisted Reading Programs

Assessment Opportunities

Literature indicates that Reading assessments on the computer pose certain difficulties such as the level of computer literacy of learners, familiarity with technology etc. From a Reading intervention point of view, computer assessments do not provide the necessary information as to the causes of reading difficulties and can therefore only partly be used as a tool to plan an intervention strategy in reading difficulties. Many difficulties cannot be assessed on a computer.

Pathing

The computer offers limited intervention possibilities in addressing the causes of reading difficulties. The path of Reading intervention will be prescribed by the functions of the software and will be limited to addressing problems where the specific functions can be utilized as a remedy to such difficulties. Furthermore an automated computer program offers very limited pathways for Reading interventions as the software cannot be manipulated to address the individual needs of learners. (Also compare the paragraphs on *content guided strategies, flexibility* and *learner control*).

Time

As learners in developing countries who do not reading their mother tongue present with serious difficulties in reading, enough time should be provided to catch up with serious backlogs in reading. It was also experienced that the achieved levels of reading drops during school holidays when learners do not enter in reading activities. Learners should be encouraged to actively read during school breaks to keep reading momentum

Positive Reinforcement

Positive reinforcement as part of the software seems to play an important role in the levels of motivation of learners. However, the positive feedback from the computer program is short-lived and forgotten by the time the learner leaves the room. It is therefore seen as of utmost importance to strengthen the self image of learners to aid in reading difficulties. Reading tasks should be chosen to ensure growth and achievement and should gradually increase in difficulty. Demotion on the reading program as a result of the assessment is seen as a positive intervention strategy, as the reading material is then not a daunting task.

Economic Implications

Economic implications are also seen as an important aspect in the choice of reading software. Fully automated programs are expensive and the technological assistance is equally expensive and often not readily available. Without the technical support on hand, computer aided programs cause major frustrations. Furthermore, the financial implications of maintenance of the hardware, safeguarding the computers from criminals pose serious financial implications for schools in a lower economic environment. License fees and upgrades on the software also pose financial implications.

Sound

Sound and the opportunity to listen to reading material read by mother tongue speakers provide learners, who read in a second language, the opportunity to listen to the correct pronunciations and provide a richer reading experience especially from the point of view that language is primarily learned from listening. The same can be argued for visual images as the second language reader can match words with pictures which enhance the understanding of newly learned words. The conclusion can therefore be made that a successful reading program should accommodate different learning styles. A recent announcement explains that:

"Based on two years of research, the Tune to Reading singing software program helps students improve all five areas of reading: phonetic awareness, phonics, fluency, vocabulary and comprehension... [the software] uses its real time pitch tracking and speech recognition technology to create products for an increasing wide range of educational purposes" (newsblaze.com).

Small Groups

As classes in developing countries are often large and individual attention to learners a rare commodity, Reading interventions should take place in smaller groups to ensure individual attention, a focused approach to individual learners according to the assessment results. Reading in large groups can only be successful with additional help. It is also not possible to address individual needs in large groups. Using software in large groups can therefore be compared with a hit and run approach.

In conclusion, achieving success in a reading program depends on a combination of factors and cannot be ascribed to one or two single aspects within the program. Reading difficulties do not exist in isolation and therefore a holistic approach is the only way to achieve significant results. Software programs therefore can only be used as a tool to be manipulated in order to achieve the desired reading outcomes.

REFERENCES

Coiro, J. (2003). *Reading comprehension on the Internet: Expanding Our Understanding of Reading comprehension to Encompass New Literacies*. Retrieved March 25, 2008, from http://www.readingonline.org/electronic/rt/2-03_Column/index.html

Davies, C., Foxcroft, C., Griessel, L., & Tredoux, N. (2005). Computer-based and Internet-delivered assessment. In C. Foxcroft & G. Roodt (Eds.), An introduction to psychological assessment in the South African context. Cape Town, South Africa: Oxford University Press.

Landmark College - Institute for Research and Training. (2006). *Effective Strategies Using Technology for Reading comprehension*. Available at: http://www.landmark.edu/institute/assitive_technology/reading_strategies.html. Retrieved on 1 May 2008.

Louw, T. A. (2008). *Online Learning Ecologies: Towards Supporting Teachers of Information Technology for the New Curriculum.* Unpublished doctoral thesis. University of Johannesburg, South Africa.

News Blaze Realtime News. (2006, March 15). *Singing A New Tune: Technology Boosts Student Reading comprehension*. Retrieved May 27, 2008, from http://newsblaze.com/story/2006315001436nnnn.nb/topstory.html

Pearson, P. D., Ferdig, R. E., Blomeyer, R. L., & Moran, J. (2005). The Effects of Technology on Reading Performance in the Middle-School Grades: A Meta-Analysis With Recommendations for Policy. Learning Point Associates.

Siragusa, L., Dixon, K. C., & Dixon, R. (2007). Designing quality e-learning environments in higher education. In Proceedings of ascilite Singapore 2007 (pp. 923-935).

Taylor, S., Frackenpohl, H., & Pettee J.L. (1960). *Grade level norms for the components of the fundamental reading skills* [Internal document].

Van Wyk, G., & Louw, A. (2008). Technology-Assisted Reading for Improving Reading Skills for young South African Learners. *Electronic Journal of e-Learning, 6*(3). Retrieved from http://www.ejel.org/issue-current.htm

ADDITIONAL READING

Butler, Y. G. (2004). How to make sense of word meanings in context: Meaning-making skills among young readers of English. In Y. Oshima-Takane, Y. Shirai, & H. Shirai (Eds.), Studies in Language Sciences (Vol. 3, pp. 139-154). Tokyo: Kuroshio Publishing.

Butler, Y. G., & Gutierrez, M. B. (2003). Learning climates: A case of 4th grade students in an English-only district in California. *Bilingual Research Journal, 27*(2), 207–224.

Dowsing, R. D. (1998). *Flexibility And The Technology Of Computer-Aided Assessment*. Retrieved from http://www.ascilite.org.au/conferences/wollongong98/asc98.../dowsing.pdf

FamilyEducation.com. (2009). *Top 10 Ways to Improve Reading Skills*. Retrieved from http://school.familyeducation.com/reading/cognitive-development/38329.html

International Reading Association. (1999-2000). *Reading Online - Formative Assessment of Reading comprehension by Computer: Advantages and Disadvantages of the Accelerated Reader Software. Inc*. Retrieved from http://www.readingonline.org/critical/topping/

Jimenez, R. T., Garcia, G. E., & Pearson, P. D. (1996). The reading strategies of bilingual Latina/o students who are successful English readers: Opportunities and obstacles. *Reading Research Quarterly, 31*(1), 90–112. doi:10.1598/RRQ.31.1.5

Koda, K. (2005). Insights into second language reading: A cross-linguistic approach. Cambridge, UK: Cambridge University Press.

Natural Language Engineering archive. (2006 December). *Reading comprehension tests for computer-based understanding evaluation*. Natural Language Engineering, 12(4), 2006. Retrieved from http://portal.acm.org/citation.cfm?id=1181161

Rapid Intellect Group. (2006). Cognitive factors in children's L1 and L2 reading. *Academic Exchange Quarterly*. Retrieved from http://www.thefreelibrary.com/Cognitive+factors+in+children's+L1+and+L2+reading-a0146219118

Science Daily. (2009). *Music Education Cab Help Children Improve Reading Skills*. Retrieved from http://www.sciencedaily.com/releases/2009/03/090316075843.htm

Smith, F. (1994). Understanding Reading. Hillsdale, NJ: Lawrence Erlbaum.

Stanovich, K. E. (1980). Towards an interactive-compensatory model of individual differences in the development of reading fluency. *Reading Research Quarterly, 15*, 32–71. doi:10.2307/747348

University of Connecticut. (2008). *Reading comprehension*. The Literacy Web at UConn, Neag School of Education. Retrieved from http://www.literacy.uconn.edu/compre.htm

KEY TERMS AND DEFINITIONS

Reading: Reading is a cognitive process which entails decoding symbols to make and build meaning, also known as *Reading comprehension*. Clues are used within context to identify and make meaning of unknown words. Once meaning is made from words, it is integrated into an existing framework of knowledge or schema known to the reader.

Reading Comprehension: This implies the level of understanding of a piece of writing. Proficiency of a reader is dependent on the ability to recognise words quickly and effortlessly – difficulty with recognising words places too much processing capacity on recognising individual words to such extend that the ability to comprehend is impaired. Researchers are of opinion that the younger a child can decode words as part of the reading process, the better their comprehension become. Phonics accompanies the decoding of words by means of sound. Within the social cognitive theory, learners are encouraged to read independently to become autonomic readers who comprehend what they read.

Reading Speed: According to various resources, the best explanation we could find accumulated in Wikipedia and we regard this as fairly accurate. Rates of reading, measured in *words per minute* [wpm], include reading for memorization; reading for learning; reading for comprehension; and skimming. Reading for comprehension is the essence of the daily reading of most people. Skimming is for superficially processing large quantities of text at a low level of comprehension (below 50%).

Technology-Assisted Reading: Reading that is assisted by technology such as the computer. Independence of the person is promoted as he or she is enabled to perform the reading process they were formerly unable to accomplish, or had great difficulty to accomplish. This is achieved by enhancements related to changed methods of interaction with the computer and reading software.

Computer-Based Reading: Often the medium of instruction is through computer technology, particularly involving digital technologies. Computer-based reading can be defined as: reading pedagogy empowered by digital technology. In most instances, face-to-face (F2F) interaction is complemented by computer-learner interaction.

Reading Intervention: Actions which are taken during the process of technology-assisted reading are known as *Reading interventions*. The reading instructor, in collaboration with computer-based reading software, takes actions during the process of enhancing reading abilities of learners. The interventions often include activities targeted at vocabulary, comprehension, narrative ability, reading speed, selection of associative reading material, pathing of the computer program, and customised flexibility and adaptability of the computer program. Interventions take place on a frequent basis either by interaction with computer and interaction with the reading instructor.

Teacher and Learner Control: The chosen route, taken by a learner through a range of (commonly) e-learning activities, which allows them to build knowledge progressively. With learning pathways, the control of choice moves away from the tutor to the learner. "The sequence of intermediate steps from preconceptions to target model form what Scott (1991) and Niedderer and Goldberg (1995) have called a ***learning pathway***. For any particular topic, such a pathway would provide both a theory of instruction and a guideline for teachers and curriculum developers" (Clement, 2000)."Interactive courseware aids learners to access information and tools by which they can construct personalized transitions between the information to be accessed and their own cognitive structures. The process of navigation enables learners to experience the content of interactive courseware. Learning pathways also reveal the learning trails while learners traverse any interactive environment. Since learners have unique knowledge structures based upon their experiences and abilities, the ways that they choose to access, interact, and interrelate messages in interactive courseware also vary. Studies on pathways help us to explore and explain human behaviors during learning processes" (Jih, 1996). (Wikipedia, 2009)

Programme Flexibility: The design of software (as a part of software engineering) claims *flexibility* as an attribute to the design of a software system. Flexibility refers to how the system can adapt when external changes occur. Within context of this article, flexibility is the ability of the related computer reading software to be able to respond to potential internal changes (within the program, e.g. different reading material) and external changes (e.g. more or less vocabulary can be added and reading speed might be increased). This directly influences the value of delivery of the software system. Thus, flexibility can pose both risk and opportunity.

Programme Adaptability: The term "**adaptability**" characterizes a computer system that empowers end-users without or with limited programming skills to customise or tailor this computer system according to their individual or environment-specific requirements. Such adaptable systems allow for fast adaptations to dynamically changing requirements by letting the end-users put their domain-specific expertise to the task of system customisation. After the user identified a change of her needs, she is enabled to manually adapt the system's features. This approach provides adaptation methods and programming tools that are under the control of the user instead of the system. Therefore, adaptable systems enable users to override certain functions or correct decisions if the system's model of the user or the environment and the reality mismatch (e.g. refinement of preferences, change of modality) (Wikipedia, 2009).

Positive Reinforcement: In operant conditioning, within context of this article, *Positive reinforcement* is a reaction (response) from the computer software that gives added value to a new stimulus immediately following a response. For example, when a learner correctly gives a synonym for a specific word, the software gives feedback as sound and maybe another synonym as to motivate the learner to even do better. This is according to *behaviourism and operant conditioning* in learning theorised by B.F. Skinner.

Reading Assessment: As with any type of assessment, Reading assessment is very vast to define. However, a Reading assessment framework can be used as to give a layout of the elements which constitute the framework. These elements are used together to be able to formulate a complete assessment of a learner's reading progress and enhanced capabilities. These elements are: Reading comprehension, Language comprehension, Decoding, Background knowledge, Linguistic knowledge, Phonology, Semantics, Syntax, Cipher knowledge, Lexical knowledge, Phoneme awareness, Knowledge of the alphabetic principle, Letter knowledge, and Concepts about print.

Chapter 19
Application of E-Learning in Teaching:
Learning and Research in East African Universities

Michael Walimbwa
Makerere University, Uganda

ABSTRACT

The challenges of an increasingly borderless world, as seen in the advancements in information technology, have brought reform in universities and re-conceptualized what constitutes learning, teaching, and research. E-learning is often implemented as a response to increasing educational demand and an increasingly networked community. E-learning is considered as an interactive means to provide an alternative environment that stimulates practical learning and equips learners with the skills to manage technological change and innovations. This chapter evaluates the initial phase of e-learning, the importance of a rightful attitude, context, and instructional design in digital learning environments in Makerere University, Uganda, University of Nairobi, Kenya and University of Dar es Salaam, Tanzania. The increase in enrollment in these universities brings in many challenges in service provision, negatively affecting instruction, learning, assessment and research services. A crisis-solving approach is presented as stimulating a creative context for the meaningful introduction of e-learning. It is also discussed whether the environment created so far through computer-mediated learning motivates institutions to integrate e-learning further. The sample involved instructors and learners from three universities in three different countries of Eastern Africa. Findings conclude that an e-learning environment must be introduced by creating relevant awareness to change attitude and empower users with an authentic approach without too much technological complexity. Review of curriculum, assessment and training around e-learning environments are also imperative as these interrelated factors form part of the e-learning process.

DOI: 10.4018/978-1-61520-909-5.ch019

ORGANIZATION BACKGROUND

Some of the problems in higher education of countries of Eastern Africa are the huge numbers of learners and fewer instructors that eventually affect the quality of teaching, learning and research. There have been attempts to tackle some of these major problems by the introduction of e-learning through integration of information and communication technology (ICT) into teaching, learning and research situations. E-learning, begun with the use of radios and television sets in instruction followed by the instructor led systems (audio) where cassettes were recorded for learners to use independently with minimum help of the teachers. In all these phases, there was support of printed media to enable independent and self-paced learning on the side of the learner. In East African universities, e-learning is a recent technological initiative, which started with few computers and basic networks. Makerere University, Universities of Nairobi and Dar es Salaam were connected to an internet service provider (ISP) that enabled them to periodically download e-mails. These Universities, with little knowledge of the potential of e-mail in instruction and limited networks left internet service to the wits of a few individuals, who later abandoned it (Tusubira, 2002).

The three universities share a common context of location in Eastern Africa and have a common challenge of increasing education demands amidst limited resources. During colonial days, these three were constituent colleges of the University of London, specialized in some programs. For instance, students who wanted to do law in East Africa would go to the University of Dar es Salaam as it was not offered in either of the two. In 1963, the three universities became constituent colleges of the University of East Africa: Makerere University College in Uganda, University of Dar es salaam in Tanzania and Nairobi University College in Kenya. Since then, these Universities have grown in terms of student intake, academic units and academic programs. Naturally, the numbers were manageable then, and quality training was guaranteed. Makerere University, which had less than 5,000 students in 1990, had increased this enrolment to 30, 000 students by 2005. There were equivalent increments in student enrolment at universities of Nairobi and Dar es Salaam to 20,000 and 16,000 respectively. With the large number of students, traditional modes of teaching became quite limiting, compelling the universities into innovations to ensure quality service. From analogue file management system of large box files with immense papers, there was a dig through the digital world of computing and networking as innovations. In these universities, using ICT is so popular now that it has a Swahili language name, TEHEMA: "*technologia, ehabari mawasiliano*"

SETTING THE STAGE

Computers, multimedia (mm), interactive databanks and communication platforms in e-learning stirs expectation of the potential of ICT in education. Institutions of learning embarked on connections to the internet, formulation of ICT policy master plans and acquisition of learning management systems (LMS) sometimes called learning platforms. Meanwhile, there was demarcation of e-learning centers and intensive set up of other appropriate facilities for e-learning. It was felt that ICT in education have the potential to increase not only the effectiveness of the educational process but also its overall efficiency whether in terms of classroom activities or administration (Omwenga, 2003). Jonassen (2001) asserts that e-learning conforms to constructivism- a teaching and learning paradigm that allows one to learn what they want, at their own pace and to construct knowledge in a social environment. Jonassen describes a constructivist-learning situation as:

- *Active:* where students are able to meaningfully process their own information into valuable personal and social knowledge.

- *Cumulative:* where new learning bases and builds on prior learning; why personal experiences are a good basis for instruction.
- *Integrative:* where learners elaborate on new knowledge and inter relate it with their current knowledge, just to suit the knowledge into prior knowledge.
- *Reflective:* where learners consciously reflect on what they know and need to learn. This is a basis for transfer of learning and situational or practical learning.
- *Goal directed and intentional:* where learners subscribe to goals of learning; enabling focus on ideas that fascinate learners most.

Deriving from constructivism, Omwenga (2003) presents five modes of using ICT in technology enhanced learning environment (TEL) as:

- *Support mode:* This is aimed at increased accuracy and enhancing presentation of work. Tools for use in this mode include word processing, PowerPoint, computer aided design and desktop publishing among others.
- *Exploration and control:* Learners are able to explore, examine, experiment with and build situations. Simulations, expert systems and statistical packages are mostly used for this purpose in TEL.
- *Tutorial mode*: Information is presented at an appropriate level and pace giving learners an opportunity for feedback on progress.
- *Resource mode*: Technology is used to access information and other resources whether online through internet or offline through CDs and other software.
- *Link mode*: Communication between individual learners and instructors, examples of e-mails, net meetings and video conferencing.

Notably however, these modes are not exclusive of each other, they tend to be blended for effectiveness.

Constructivism is a teaching and learning paradigm in which people are assumed to act interactively and socially to create knowledge. Methodologies of instruction are being recast to leverage new learning media and honor multiple e-learning styles to fit learning situations. Ravenscroft (2001), in a study, remarks that most TEL initiatives have been technology-led rather than theory-led. Leading thinkers from both within and outside academia are exploring radically different approaches to teaching and learning based on theory; e-learning, among them.

In Africa, information and communication technology use in educational environment is far from being fully realized as in many incidences, there are a number of encumbrances. In a research done by Karen (2008), in several African primary schools, there was an interesting finding about information and communication use. Most of the schools surveyed reported no functioning computers, and no internet. Interestingly, the report indicates that contacts between African and United Kingdom schools were by e-mails mostly. This study though done in primary schools has an implication on higher education as it is the products of primary schools that end up in Universities. But it is interesting to say on this basis that the will to use ICT is there though with limitations.

Curran (2004) makes interesting conclusions that indicates that universities adopted a strategy of e-learning due to their inherent characteristic of adaptability in use and flexibility in application. Though Curran's study was done in European environment, it informs this study that the major reason why a strategy for e-learning is taken is because of flexibility, if things don't work, there is a lot of freedom to do something else. There is no use clinging on a strategy that is failing in a given context just because it worked in another context. In certain situations, the integration of ICT in teaching and learning has failed because of the implementers attempting the *"Everest syndrome"*.

In a study in an African context, Van Der Merwe (2004) describes the salient issues in a technology enhanced learning environment summarized on Table 1.

Table 1. E-Learning tools used in teaching and learning

TEL "tool"	Uses and advantaged	Principle for good teaching
COMMUNICATION		
Homepage	Good way of introducing instructors to students, last minute changes can be made, other resources.	Student-instructor contact
Bulletin board or discussion tool (asynchronous)	One-to-many communication moderated discussions, anonymous interaction, debate, peer assessment, group work, searches, introvert students get involved, more writing by students, attachments can be posted	Student-instructor contact, cooperation among students.
Chat rooms (synchronous)	One-to-many communication, brainstorm, virtual office hours, immediate feed back	Cooperative learning, gives prompt feed back
Calendar	Posting of target dates, reminders, last minute changes, full calendar available with dates of activities	Emphasizes time on task, communicates high expectations.
E-mail	One-to-one and one-to-many communication, private communication, reminders of specific dates, personal motivation, groupwork, searchable medium, documents can be sent as attachments	Student-Lecturer contact, cooperation among students
TOOLS FOR AVAILABILITY AND ENRICHMENT OF CONTENT		
Content module: linked pages	Gives the feeling of flow, easier navigation, can add video, audio, graphics	Encourage active meaning
Self assessments	Students asses their own knowledge of the subject, instructors can include detailed feedback, tests can be repeated until students are sure that they mastered it, drilling is good for memory.	Encourages active learning, gives prompt feedback
Hyperlinks and references	Gives links to other pages which can be interactive and credit to referred to material	Encourages active learning, respects diverse ways of learning
Syllabus (course content folders)	Gives a description of the module content, lecturer information, outcomes, textbooks and expectations	Emphasizes time on task, student-lecturer contact
STUDENT ACTIVITY AND STUDY TOOLS		
Search facility	Students can find material electronically	Encourages active learning, respects diverse talents.
Grade tool	Students get their marks rapidly and can determine if they have to put in more effort for a module	Gives prompt feedback (depends on what and how much is made available), high expectations
Help files	Explains to students what is necessary to be successful	Encourages active learning, gives prompt feedback
ASSESSMENT TOOLS		
Quizzes: Timed, Randomized and multiple	Formative / summative assessment, immediate feedback. Students must have mastered the work to complete it in the set time. Students get different sets of questions, generated randomly from the database	Encourages active learning, Expectations, emphasizes time on task, gives prompt feedback, Diverse learning.
Assignment tools	Students can submit assignments electronically, grade assignments and the grades and feedback are immediate	Emphasizes time on task, gives prompt feedback
Group projects	Gives students the opportunity to help each other as they become aware of each other's strengths and weakness, prepares students for future jobs, in which group work is becoming vital.	Cooperative learning

Adapted from Van Der Merwe (2004) Evaluating the integration of ICT into teaching and learning activities at a South African higher education institution, p. 124-126.

Multimedia refers to text, sound, graphics, animations, imaging, and spatial modeling into computer systems. Multimedia involves the integration of more than one medium into a form of communication. E-learning and communication theory combines for effectiveness. With the surfacing of computers into education, multimedia has been strengthened and is popular. Multimedia holds a special place in technology enhanced learning because as Jonassen (2001) argues, it attracts and holds attention. A multimedia computer is able to capture sound and video. High-resolution monitors, sound cards and increase in random access memory (RAM) and processing speed of personal computers, can be exploited to transform teaching and learning environments. Multimedia may be very useful where learners use multitasking, but not every learner can be able to do this.

Jonassen (2001) further states that past research has proved that multiple-channel and complimentary channels improve e-learning situations while information from different channels which are inconsistent worsens a learning situation. This compares with the position of Mayer (2001), Clarke and Mayer (2003) as cited in Merrill (2005) who contends that when a presentation contains three elements: graphics audio and visual, there is a decrease in learning. Nevertheless, the integration of multimedia as a tool in e-learning is very vital to enhance instruction and learning situations as long as it is carefully used, given the fact that it goes far beyond what could be possible in a normal face-to-face lecture room situation.

However, Merrill (2005) is critical of designed e-learning materials, saying most so called e-learning materials are merely information transferred to the Internet without appropriate demonstration, practice, feedback, and learner guidance. This is what I call using ICT to give learners *electronic notes*, instead of enabling them to learn at ease. He hastens to add that the letter *'e'* in e-learning has to be replaced with *enervative, endless* or *empty* learning meaning that many of the designed e-learning materials available weakens or destroy the capacity of learning. Merrill is critical of e-learning material because they are designed badly. Though Merrill makes this comment, it should be noted that the beginning phase of e-learning in is characterized by this, so no university should despair that their materials are in this start at the beginning. This is a very big leap forward.

CASE DESCRIPTION

The initial days of the use of ICT in instruction were filled with excitement and prophecies about the great potential and improvement in education (Alessi and Trollip 2001). The same was felt at the three universities under this study. This projection has not been realized, many years down the road and one wonders why. Challenges as understanding, change of attitude and training are still prevalent (Omwenga, Waema and Wagacha, 2004). The persistence of these challenges and ignorance about ICT in education hinders any real utilization of e-learning as a resource that facilitates educational environments (Fonseca, 2001). These issues made this research inevitable. The three universities have heavily invested in e-learning infrastructure in the initial phases; this case study looks into the benefits being realized, if not then why?

The Study

The present study in an attempt to evaluate e-learning for teaching, learning and research in three universities was conducted with the following objectives:

1. To identify the features of e-learning in the universities;
2. To describe the utilization of features of e-learning; and
3. To outline the attitude towards the use of e-learning in teaching and learning.

Evaluation approach as a research design was used because the aim of this research was to study the practice of e-learning in its natural setting in order to interpret it in terms of the meaning people accord to it. The required data mainly concerned actions and feelings about the practice, usage and attitude to a digital learning environment (DLE). The data required was for evaluating practice that made a qualitative design suitable. Data relating to e-learning was collected from Makerere, Nairobi and Dar es Salaam universities. The universities are chosen purposively, to enable a baseline for Makerere University's e-learning project and make the study a comparative one. Additionally, all the three universities were engaged in piloting e-learning at different levels, introduction, implementation and evaluation. The target population was faculty students and instructors (under-graduate and post-graduate).

Purposive sampling was considered because e-learning is a pilot project thus few students and instructors are deeply involved and the characteristics of e-learning practice and indicators needed to be studied intensively. The respondents needed to be reached by discussion groups, observation, and interviews that required a small sample size as the purposive research required only those respondents with relevant data.

The collection of data was done using instruments: observation checklists, structured interviews and focus group discussion guides. Observation enabled the researcher to get first hand information through personal experience. Focused group discussions enabled the researcher to participate in live discussions while noting attitudes and opinions of the respondents. Interviews enabled in-depth examination the practice of e-learning in Makerere, Dar es Salaam and Nairobi universities. The discussions were held because it was vital to facilitate informants' interaction and therefore generate a wider response, while directly observing group reactions and feelings. Focused group discussions consisted of 20 students each, 5 focus group discussions from Makerere, and two for each of the universities of Dar es Salaam and Nairobi respectively. This technique helped in getting data faster by way of brainstorming.

Structured interviews and focus group discussions involved intensive probing questions using a structured guide to reinforce group discussions and get information from instructors. Participant observation and checklists helped the researcher get and record rightful data from the practical ground. The researcher made observation tours of Nairobi and Dar es Salaam universities and e-learning centers during data collection. Observation checked inter-rater agreement and inter-rater reliability because of poor observation sometimes.

Secondary data was used as universities had extensive documents, some of them posted on the university websites and e-learning platforms. Many other publications from textbooks, journals, magazines and compact disc read only memory (CD-ROM) were studied and analysis of the same done (Jansen and Vithal, 2005).

The findings of the study are summarized below under broad headings of Features of e-learning, Utilization of e-learning, and Attitudes towards use of e-learning.

Features of E-Learning

Computing history of learners and instructors in all the three selected institutions is average. Most of the respondents had used computers for more than two years. The instructors had used computers in daily work while the students used them while being taught, most of them during high school. This has made the introduction of technology enhanced a little easy as the struggle to train in basic computer may be sidelined. Computer literacy is high, with the highest literacy noted at the University of Nairobi. There were therefore not many courses organized as induction into e-learning for students. For instructors, there are several induction and refresher courses in e-learning. Sometimes, it is easy for both students and instructors to find their own way into e-learning. Most of the users said that they learnt how to use the electronic platforms by themselves, but sometimes only after a very limited induction. In fact some of the students access internet from mostly other places outside the university internet cafes.

There is use of various computer applications in the design of e-content with macromedia ™ and Microsoft office ™ often being used in all the institutions. Macromedia is software that is used to design e-content in hypertext markup language (HTML). This enables instructors to create hyperlinks to content outside the designed content to enable further self discovery and learning. Microsoft office™ is used very frequently though respondents were not conscious that they were using the software in almost all the daily routines. For instance, you would find an instructor with several presentations in power point, or students with a number of typed course works, but when you ask them of the software they use in their digital learning environments, they would say, they have none.

E-learning platforms exist in all the universities, Moodle for Makerere, Blackboard ™ and WebCT™ for Dar es Salaam and Wedusoft ™ for Nairobi with the internet as electronic learning platforms in the institutions. Makerere, had Kewl™ and Blackboard ™ at the beginning but has now opted for Moodle which is open source. Most of the features as described in the Table 1 given earlier are existent on the platforms. The features make the learning environment highly engaging and interactive both in synchronous and asynchronous ways.

Internet connection exists with the intranets though the access points and facilities are still inadequate. Nonetheless, these universities have tried their best to increase access points. In Makerere University for example, there is wireless in several places and in many lecturer rooms and offices, there are access points. Network plans like the one given in the Figure 1 have been a very salient feature in the introduction of e-learning. None of the universities could have gone any step without such plans.

In all the universities, there has been a complete digitization of libraries. Students can research online as the universities have been able to get journals, books and other literature, which they have subscribed to and can be accessed by students. The University of Nairobi had been able to do this with support of AVIOR, a Belgian support organization. By the time of this write up, the University of Nairobi had over 20,000, Dar es Salaam 25,000 and Makerere had 19,000 journals they could access. Research literature

Figure 1. Network plans at Makerere University

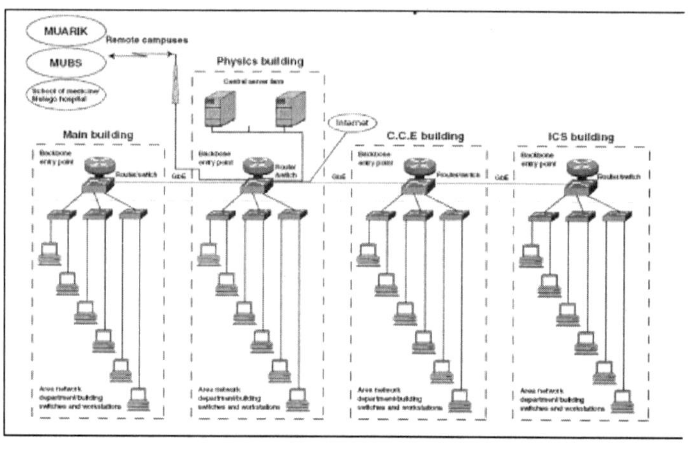

is more up to date and global compared to the earlier times.

Utilization of E-Learning

Findings on the utilization of e-learning in the three universities relate to technology concerns, technology components, management and organization. To design e-content materials instructors utilize the features of e-learning existent in the universities in e-learning. The design skills are provided in the several e-learning workshops. At the University of Nairobi, all courses on the electronic learning platform are a property of the university. The University of Nairobi, among the three universities had the best (as rated by the researcher) management of the technology they had, where the University of Dar es salaam had the best organization of the technology. At the University of Dar es salaam, there was a very well organized e-learning unit under the University computing center, but Makerere was only trying to put in place such a unit.

Instructors need enough time to concentrate on the design of e-content though this time is hard to be availed to them by the institutions. The conventional teaching methodologies are equally demanding for the time that would have been used to design e-content. Even if there was enough time, the change is so fast in technology. The trap has always been to change with the technological change and pay little attention to the real pedagogic issues and needs required in using technology in education. The management of time to engage in e-learning and to teach is clashing. E-learning at this level is used as a supplement to traditional methods of instruction best described as blended learning approaches. Makerere University learning platforms had more e-content courses than the other institutions though the quality of these courses was still low with little or no interactivity in most of them being electronic lecture notes and Microsoft PowerPoint™ slide shows. The courses at the universities of Nairobi and Dar es Salaam were better compared to those of Makerere. This variation may be because of the deliberate e-content design workshops at these universities. Naturally, Makerere has a lesson to learn from this as it had no deliberate e-content design workshops. Though the institutions evidently had some e-learning equipment that could produce quality multimedia e-content, multimedia content was not common, because they require more time and technicality to make. The quality of technology to produce and deliver quality multimedia is limited. Currently broadband that has increased the internet bandwidth all over East Africa has come and universities are attempting to increase on their bandwidth. Before, to download only a small image would take too long or sometimes, it would time out because of the bandwidth. This had been a major bottleneck for the universities to effectively implement e-learning.

Effective administration and support enhances the use of technology enhanced learning. There was some evidence of effective administration and support. At Makerere, the support team did not ably handle the e-learning user demands. As stated before, Makerere was at the beginning phase of piloting e-learning. However, many things have drastically changed for the better and now there is an established e-learning unit only awaiting senate to discuss and pass a policy for its total implementation. There are student internet kiosk attendants for the effective management and delivery of e-learning. Though, more is needed for the efficiency of this system.

E-learning takes place through effective communication where an instructor is at one end and the student at another; able to interact in a virtual way just like they were more or less face-to-face. Instructors need time wherever they are to communicate to their students in both, asynchronous and synchronous ways. Instructors did not report effective communication and its use in e-learning because on many occasion, they did not create enough time to communicate with their students. Students on the other hand were more enthusiastic in communication as they would chat with each other, send emails, and join discussion forums, activities that they instructors had created for them. This comes about because in Makerere for instance, though wiring has done up to offices, very little attempts have been made to put computers in them. In most occasions, staffs who are interested in e-learning have had to buy their own computers. This has been detrimental to the pace of e-learning. On all the main university intranets of Nairobi, Dar es Salaam and Makerere nonetheless, there are a number of issues related to announcements, jobs and other important announcements. Related to this communication, of later, some of the faculties at Makerere University have established state of art video conferencing facilities that will facilitate real time technology enhanced learning.

Attitude towards Use of E-Learning

It was rather difficult to get a general attitude towards the operation of e-learning in all the three institutions, as it required more time than the research had. Nevertheless, some instructors see technology enhanced learning replacing face-to-face sessions and some students use e-learning to dodge face-to-face sessions. At the University of Nairobi, an instructor asked, if e-learning will not take away all students from the lecture room as they would have all they need in terms of notes, assignments and coursework. This comes because of the factor that most instructors do upload all the notes they would have given in class. It would not be appropriate for one to upload the notes that the students will have in class, as this will not make any big difference between technology enhanced learning and electronic notes. It requires time to put notes design materials for uploading in a right format. E-learning would appropriately be a blended instructional method. This is the reason why some instructors have avoided getting involved in electronic instruction as they are used to face-to-face instruction. E-learning is viewed as demanding considerable amount of time for one to make an effective contribution or use of it.

The presence of multimedia and interactive content in e-learning enables users to formulate a different perception about e-learning. Most of those who are not very conversant with computer use feel that e-learning is very complicated and needs very high intelligence for success. This may be the case but what is basic is, one should leave programming for computer scientists and look at the potential of multimedia in instruction. All that is needed are only the basics, which bring in the fact that there is need for teamwork in e-learning between computer scientist, administrators, teachers etc. The kind of support and administration in an e-learning environment also gives users a platform for different attitudes.

There are different motivational factors for engagement in e-learning both intrinsic and extrinsic in all the institutions. But the operational initiation of e-learning has an impact on its success. The universities are using a top-down approach and in this way, those who engage in e-learning might feel that it is imposed on them. On the contrary, if a bottom-up approach is used, it will bring in more ownership of the technology enhanced learning initiative. These approaches serve as either intrinsic or extrinsic motivators.

Users in all the three universities saw many benefits in e-learning including the ability to access advanced content, availability of content all the time, independent study and more effective communication. All these have changed and shaped the way institutions deliver and package their services now. For example, the University of Nairobi had a completely digitized library during the time of this research. The Universities of Makerere and Dar es Salaam have since then also embarked on digitizing their libraries (this publication has been done when the digitization is also complete), where catalogues, journal books and most services are becoming digital. All these bring in the perception that e-learning solves all the problems which of course is not true. General comments indicated that in e-learning, users go for learning aspects including interactivity in e-content and the potential to improve teaching not technological issues.

Challenges of participation in e-learning exist in all the universities that included limited accessibility due to limited access points, high degree of computer illiteracy among both staff and students, incoherent policies for e-learning, and the need for mindset change among them. These are very limiting factors in the e-learning pilot given the fact that they relate to psychological orientation. Issues of computers being expensive can be solved by getting a few finances but issues of mindset are too personal. It is hoped that all institutions will try to engage in some sensitization to create awareness in ICT use.

CONCLUSION

Technology enhanced learning in the universities of Dar es Salaam, Makerere and Nairobi is here to stay. It is an evolving and gradual process. It has just started and has not yet reached the climax and users have a lot of expectations from e-learning. The universities are aware of this fact that the e-learning will not replace face-to-face teaching and learning but will be a complementary and blended aspect of learning in which learners have a diversity of media in learning. Users need patience with e-learning because it has just started and is not going to perform miracles. It is a journey. We can equate the introduction of e-learning in these institutions to a newly born baby, it is breast fed, and it sits, crawls, walks and one time it will run. The following are generic conclusions that may be generalized to all institution at the beginning of an e-learning journey

- There are scanty but clear indications of e-learning in the universities of Nairobi, Dar es Salaam and Makerere as seen from the infrastructure available. There is internet connection, learning platforms, and e-content so far designed and developed. There is also a potential skill in users in the operation of e-learning. However, in all the universities, e-learning demand is outgrowing supply if measures are not taken to curtail this.
- There is utilization of e-learning infrastructure in instruction, learning and research in the universities of Dar es Salaam, Makerere and Nairobi. Utilization of e-learning has been the design of e-content, provision and search for content in a given course unit with little emphasis on the pedagogic issues. The potential of e-learning in instruction learning and research is therefore yet to be fully tapped. Technological and managerial concerns related to e-learn still prevails in these universities.
- Nevertheless, there is generally a very positive attitude towards technology enhanced learning in all the three institutions. Students, instructors and other administrators concur that e-learning presents a choice for them to operate in an environment they like best. Knowledge about many aspects of e-learning is still limited for some misconceived reasons. This hinders the real utilization of e-learning in teaching, learning and research.

In the Universities of Makerere, Nairobi and Dar es Salaam, based on the earlier discussions, the following specific conclusions can be obtained relating to the practice of e-learning:

- E-learning is clearly taking shape in institutions where there exists computer infrastructure, intranet, internet, learning platforms, e-learning policies and e-content course materials.
- E-learning in its first phase is being used for distribution of content though there is an apparent move towards more interactive materials

- Students need effective communication and guidance from instructors concerning aspects of content in an e-learning environment
- E-learning use has not realized its full potential
- There is general satisfaction among users with regard to the use of e-learning in teaching and learning. This is supported by the fact that there is more strong agreement with perceived advantages and disagreement with disadvantages of e-learning.
- The potential benefits of e-learning in teaching and learning manifest but do not reflect in most instructors due to lack of course redesign.
- Motivators into participation in e-learning are intrinsic: teaching and learning issues (such as increased benefit to students).
- There is effective team management and administration of e-learning infrastructure.

RECOMMENDATIONS

On the basis of the findings of this project, in order to improve on the practice and enable change of attitudes towards the practice of e-learning, the following recommendations may be considered;

- Get more computers connected to the internet and liberalize accessibility in the institutions. In some e-learning centers there was evidence of numerous computers but with very few connected to the internet. This limits the number of access terminals for e-learning.
- Better infrastructure: computers, printers, e-learning centers, networks for more practice and utilization in e-learning.
- Greater sensitization about the practice of e-learning is called for to make it more popular among all participants in the selected institutions.
- Develop a curriculum in e-content development similar to that used by the case with the University of Nairobi.
- Regular training and workshops should be encouraged to popularize e-learning amongst users in Nairobi, Makerere and Dar es Salaam Universities. In these workshops however, aspects of learning and effective communication and not technology should emphasized.
- Specialized training in design of instructional materials. Many of the instructors are not teachers by training thus needing pedagogic training to make more appropriate instructional material in all the three universities. The capacity to exploit e-learning depends on users' skills.
- Increased bandwidth in all the three universities as the networks are still slow.
- Improve the kind of support given in e-learning centers, particularly in Makerere University though it may be applicable in all the three institutions. Learners complained about the technical support people and uncooperative end user personnel. This necessitated that people apt in use of ICT but with some background pedagogic training can do a better job than computer technicians in e-learning.

REFERENCES

Bullen, M., & Janes, D. P. (Eds.). (2007). Making the transition to e-learning. British journal of educational technology, 38(4), 762-762.

Curran, C. (2004). Strategies for e-learning in Universities. *CSHE Research and occasional paper series: CSHE.7.04.* Retrieved from http://ishi.lib.berkeley.edu/cshe/

Fonseca, C. (2001). Fallacies and objectives regarding the uses of new technologies in education. *Prospects*, *31*(3), 399–413.

Jonassen, D. H. (2001). Computers in the Classroom Minds for critical thinking. Upper Saddle River, NJ: Merrill.

Merrill, M. D. (2002). First principles of instruction. *Educational Technology Research and Development*, *50*(3), 43–59. doi:10.1007/BF02505024

Mutula, S. (2002). E-learning initiatives at the University of Botswana: challenges and opportunities. *Journal of Campus-wide Information Systems*, *19*(3), 99–109. doi:10.1108/10650740210431916

Omwenga, E. I. (2003). *Modeling and analyzing a computer mediated learning Infrastructure*. Unpublished Doctoral Thesis, University of Nairobi, Nairobi, Kenya.

Omwenga, E. I., Waema, T. M., & Wagacha, P. W. (2004). A model for introducing and implementing E-learning for delivery of educational content within the African context. [AJST]. *African Journal of Science and Technology*, *5*(1), 34–46.

Van Der Merwe, A. (2004). *Evaluating the integration of ICT into teaching and learning activities at a South African higher education institution*. Unpublished Doctoral Thesis, University of Stellenbosch, Cape Town, South Africa.

Walimbwa, M. (2007). *E-learning practices in teaching, learning and research at the universities of Makerere, Nairobi and Dar es Salaam*. Unpublished M.Ed Dissertation, Makerere University, Kampala.

ADDITIONAL READING

Alessi, S., & Trollip, S. (2001). Multimedia for learning: methods and development (3rd Ed.). Boston: Allyn and Bacon.

Arsham, H. (2002). Impact of the internet on learning and teaching. *USDLA Journal, 16*(3), 9-20. Retrieved from http://www.usdla.org/html/journal/MAR02_Issue/article01.html

Delvin, M. (2002). *Introduction. In The Internet and the University: 2001 Forum*. Forum for the Future of Higher Education, Aspen Symposium.

Karen, E. (2008). North South School Partnerships: Learning from schools in the UK, Africa and Asia. London: Institute of Education.

Laurillard, D. (2002). *Rethinking teaching for the knowledge society. In The Internet and the University: 2001 Forum*. Forum for the Future of Higher Education, Aspen Symposium.

Luhanga, M. L., et al. (2003). Strategic Planning and Higher Education Management in Africa: The University of Dar Es Salaam Experience. Dar es Salaam: Dar es Salaam University Press Ltd.

Makerere University. (2009). Retrieved from http://www.mak.ac.ug

McPherson, M. (Ed.). (2005). Developing innovation in e-learning: lessons to be learned. *British Journal of Educational Technology*, *36*(4), 585–586. doi:10.1111/j.1467-8535.2005.00548.x

Omwenga, E. I. (2003). *Modeling and analyzing a computer mediated learning Infrastructure*. Unpublished PhD Thesis, University of Nairobi, Nairobi, Kenya.

Omwenga, E. I., Waema, T. M., & Wagacha, P. W. (2004). A model for introducing and implementing E-learning for delivery of educational content within the African context. [AJST]. *African Journal of Science and Technology*, *5*(1), 34–46.

Picciano, A. (2002). Beyond student perceptions: issues of interaction, presence and performance in an online course. *Journal of Asynchronous Learning Networks (JALN)* *6*(1). Retrieved from http://www.aln.org/publications/jaln/vn1/

Ravenscroft, A. (2001). Designing e-learning interaction in the 21st century: revisiting and rethinking the role of theory. *European Journal of Education*, *36*(2), 133–156. doi:10.1111/1467-3435.00056

Republic of Uganda. (2002). National information and communication technology policy. Kampala Uganda.

Rogers, M. O. (1995). Diffusion of innovations (4th Ed.). New York: Free Press

Surry, D. W., & Farquhar, J. D. (1997). Diffusion Theory and Education Technology. *Journal of Instructional Science and Technology*, *2*(1), 24–36.

Taskforce on Higher Education and Society. (2000). Higher education in developing countries, peril and promise. Washington DC: World Bank publication.

Tusubira. (2002). *Supporting universities' ICT developments: the Makerere university experience.* A paper presented at CODESRIA general Assembly 8 – 12 Dec 2002.

UNESCO. (2002). Information, Communication Technology in Education. A curriculum for schools and programme for teacher development. Paris: UNESCO.

University of Dar es Salaam. (n.d.). Retrieved from http://www.udsm.ac.tz

University of Nairobi. (n.d.). Retrieved from http://www.uonbi.ac.ke

Van Der Merwe, A. D. (2004). *Evaluating the integration of ICT into teaching and learning activities at a South African higher education institution.* Unpublished PhD Thesis, University of Stellenbosch, Cape Town, South Africa.

Wayne, M. (2005). Can You Lead from Behind? Critical Reflections on the Rhetoric of E-learning, Open Distance Learning, and ICTs for Development in Sub-Saharan Africa (SSA). In A. Carr-Chellman (Ed.), Global Perspectives on E-learning. Rhetoric and Reality (pp. 222-240). Thousand Oaks, CA: Sage Publications.

Wischhhusen, M., et al. (2003). Applied Information and Communication Technology. Oxford, London: Heinemann Educational Publishers.

World Bank. (2000). Higher Education in developing countries, Peril and promise. Washington DC: World Bank publication.

World Bank. (2002) Constructing knowledge societies: New challenges for tertiary institutions. Washington DC: World Bank publication.

KEY TERMS AND DEFINITIONS

Attitude: The feeling towards e-learning. This feeling comes either before or after engaging in e-learning.

Blended Learning: Learning which is delivered using a mixture of both traditional methods like lecturers and technology enhanced instruction.

E-Learning/ Technology Enhanced Learning: The delivery of learning, training or education program by electronic means. It involves the use of a computer or other electronic device in a way to provide learning material.

E-Content: Materials that have been transformed from those that are delivered in the normal lecture room, to those that are highly interactive and allows self paced learning.

Digital Environment: A situation where there are electronic devices being used in instruction, leaning and research.

TEHEMA: Is a Kiswahili acronym (*technologia ehabari mawasiliano*) for Information and Communication Technology.

Multimedia: The act of a lesson integrating audio-visual and video interactions to make learners more engaged in a study.

Intranet: Is a local area network, where a university can use the available computers to access information from within the campus.

Compilation of References

Aalto, P., & Jalava, M. (1995). Implementing experiences from small-scale courses to large education systems. In F. Lockwood (Ed.), Open and Distance Learning Today (pp. 255-264). London: Routledge.

AARNET home page. (2009). Accessed May 10, 2090, from http://www.aarnet.edu.au/aarnet3.aspx

Abbott, A. (2005). Linked ecologies: States and universities as environments for Professions. *Sociological Theory*, *23*(3), 245–274. doi:10.1111/j.0735-2751.2005.00253.x

Abbott, C. (2007). E-inclusion: Learning Difficulties and Digital Technologies, REPORT 15: FUTURELAB SERIES, Kings College, London.

Abdullah, I. Md.Yunus, A. S., Sidek, A. A., & Matthews, R. (2007). Integrating learning style with e-learning instructional design: A formative evaluation. In A. A. Sidek (Ed.), Design and development of learning management system at Universiti Putra Malaysia. (pp. 49 – 65) Serdang: Centre for Academic Development.

Abramson, M., Bird, J., & Stennet, A. (1996). Introduction. In M. Abramson, J. Bird, & A. Stennet (Eds.), Further and higher education partnerships: The future for collaboration (pp.1-3). Buckingham, UK: Open University Press.

Accino Domínguez, J. A. (2002). Un entorno de componentes para enseñanza virtual basado en software libre. *Novatica*, *156*, 55–60.

Ackerman, R., & Schibrowsky, J. (2007). A business marketing strategy applied to student retention: A higher education initiative. *Journal of College Student Retention*, *9*(3), 307–356. doi:10.2190/CS.9.3.d

ACOLAD. (2006). Retrieved from http://www.paris4.sorbonne.fr/e-cursus/texte/acolad.htm

Adam, M., Maxwell, G. A., Pooran, J., & Scott, B. (1999). *South East Asian Students Learning Styles*. Paper presented at the CHME Hospitality Research Conference, Surrey, pp. 9-21.

Adams, T. L. (2009). The Changing Nature of Professional Regulation in Canada, 1867-1961. *Social Science History*, *33*(2), 217–243. doi:10.1215/01455532-2008-020

Adei, S. (2004). Overview of university level education in Africa. In M. Beebe, K. Kouakou, B. Oyeyinka-Oyelaran & M. Rao (Eds.), Africa Dot Edu: IT Opportunities and Higher Education in Africa (pp. 90). New Delhi: Tata McGraw-Hill Publishing Company Limited.

Adekanmbi, G. (1998). Development orientation of distance education programmes in Africa: A preliminary submission. *Ghana Educational Media and Technology Association (GEMTA). Journal*, *2*, 59–70.

Adekanmbi, G. (2002). A comment on the education and training of distance education practitioners in Africa. Open and Distance Learning Association of Australia (ODLAA) Papers, (pp. 1-11).

Adekanmbi, G. (2004). Collaborative strategies for implementing continuing education programmes in Botswana. In D. Sanders & K. Brosnan et al. (Eds.), Learning transformations: Changing learners, organizations and communities (pp. 87-95). London: FACE.

Adekanmbi, G. (2007). Quantitative aspirations, qualitative considerations and technological imperatives: Collaborating for progress in African distance education. *Journal of Sociology and Education in Africa*, *6*(1), 1–12.

Adekanmbi, G. (2008). The neo liberal ideology and the future of higher education in Africa: Lessons for Nigeria. The Second Annual Professor (Mrs) Grace Mbipom Foundation Lecture, University of Calabar, Nigeria, 4 June 2008.

Aderinoye, R. (1992). *Retention and failure in distance education: the experience of the National Teachers' Institute, (NTI) Kaduna*. Unpublished Doctoral Thesis, University of Ibadan, Nigeria.

African Economic Outlook. (2009). *Niger: Innovation and ICT*. Retrieved from http://africaeconomicoutlook.org/en/countries/west Africa/niger/

Afuah, A., & Tucci, C. L. (2001). Internet Business Models and Strategies: Text and Cases. New York: McGraw-Hill/Irwin.

Agnihotri, R., & Troutt, M. D. (2009). The effective use of technology in personal knowledge management: A framework of skills, tools and user context. *Online Information Review*, *33*(2), 329–342. doi:10.1108/14684520910951249

Agyeman, O. T. (2007). *Survey of ICT and Education in Africa. Niger country report*. Retrieved from http://www.infodev.org

Aitmatov, G. (2006). *Ve Ha Yom Einenu Cale (The day lasts more than a hundred years)*. (D. Marcon & A. Porat, Trans.). Tel-Aviv: Am-Oved.

Aldrich, H. E., & Pfeffer, J. (1976). Environments of organizations. In A. Inkeles, J. Coleman & N. Smelser (Eds.), Annual Review of Sociology, 40, 225-233.

Alessi, S., & Trollip, S. (2001). Multimedia for learning: methods and development (3rd Ed.). Boston: Allyn and Bacon.

Alexander, F. K. (2000). The changing face of accountability: Monitoring and assessing institutional performance in higher education. *The Journal of Higher Education*, *71*(4), 411–431. doi:10.2307/2649146

Alexander, S. (2001). E-learning developments and experiences. [from http://www.emerald-library.com/ft.]. Education & Training, 43(4/5), 240–248. Retrieved June 2, 2005. doi:10.1108/00400910110399247

Algonquin College. (1996). *Learning styles*. Retrieved August 28, 2003, from Algonquin College Website: http://www.algonquinc.on.ca/edtech/gened/styles.html

Alias, N. A., & Zainuddin, A. M. (2005). Innovation for better teaching and learning: adopting the learning management system. *Malaysian Online Journal of Instructional Technology (MOJIT)*, *2*(2), 27-40. Retrieved June 20, 2009, from http://pppjj.usm.my/mojit/articles/pdf/August05/03-Article-037-NorAziah-UiTM%20version%202%5B1%5D.pdf

Alsunbul, A. (2001). Education in the Arab world in the outset of the third millenium. Alxandria, Egypt: University Library.

Altbach, P. (2008). Globalization and forces for change in higher education. *Industry and Higher Education*, *50*(Winter), 2.

American Association for the Advancement of Science. (2004). Science & Everyday Experiences: A Parent Educator Manual. Washington, DC: Delta Research & Educational Foundation

Amey, M., Eddy, L., & Ozaki, C. (2007). Demands for partnership and collaboration in higher education: A model. *New Directions for Community Colleges*, *139*, 5–14. doi:10.1002/cc.288

Ammendolia, M. A. (2006 June). The Instructor's Challenge: Helping Newbies. *Online Classroom*, 1-8.

Anderson, J. R. (2000). Learning and memory. New York, NY: Wiley & Sons.

Andrews, H. (2003). Higher education studies, reports, and surveys in the SREB States. Atlanta, GA: Southern Regional Educational Board. (ERIC Document Reproduction Service No. ED481866).

Andrews, T., & Daly, C. (2008). Using Moodle, an open source learning management system, to support a national teaching and learning collaboration. In *Proceedings of the 19th Conference of the Australasian Association for Engineering Education*, Yeppoon, Australia.

Andrews, T., & Lind, G. (2007). Evaluation and assessment of problem-based and case-based learning in the

Mining Education Australia (MEA) collaborative initiative. In *Proceedings ATN Assessment and Evaluation Conference,* QUT, Brisbane.

Aparicio, P., & Castán, J. Mª, Espluga, C.Mª, Gallardo, E., Guitart, L., Miravitlles, P., Nuñez, A., Rimbau, E., Triadó, X.Mª., & Viu, M. (2004). *Desarrollo de casos audiovisuales para el aprendizaje en organización de empresas.* Paper presented at III Congreso Internacional de Docencia Universitária e Innovación (CIDUI), Gerona, Spain.

Ardichvili, A., Page, V., & Wentling, T. (2003). Motivation and barriers to participation in virtual knowledge-sharing communities of practice. *Journal of Knowledge Management, 7*(1), 64–77. doi:10.1108/13673270310463626

Argryis, C., & Schön, D. A. (1978). Organizational learning: A theory of action perspective. Reading, MA: Addison-Wesley.

Armstrong, A., & Hagel, J. (1995). Real Profits from Virtual Communities. *Mc Kinsey Quarterly, 3,* 127–141.

Arnseth, H. C. (2004). *Discourse and artefacts in learning to argue. Analysing the practical management of computer supported collaborative learning.* University of Oslo: Faculty of education.

Arnseth, H. C., & Hatlevik, O. E. (2008). Vurdering av digital kompetanse [Assessment of digital literacy]. *Nordic journal of digital literacy, 3*(4), 285-293.

Arnseth, H. C., & Ludvigsen, S. R. (2006). Approaching institutional contexts: Systemic versus dialogic research in CSCL. *International Journal of Computer-Supported Collaborative Learning, 1,* 167–185. doi:10.1007/s11412-006-8874-3

Arnseth, H. C., Hatlevik, O. E., Kløvstad, V., Kristiansen, T., & Ottestad, G. (2007). ITU Monitor 2007. Skolens digitale tilstand 2007. Oslo: Universitetsforlaget.

Arntzen, J. (2007). Mentoring information and communication technologies within teacher education: Synthesizing Research Practice with Research Literature. In C. Montgomerie & J. Seale (Eds.), *Proceedings of World Conference on Educational Multimedia, Hypermedia and Telecommunications 2007* (pp. 2383-2386). Chesapeake, VA: AACE.

Arntzen, J., Krug, D. H., & Wen, Z. (2008). ICT literacies and the curricular conundrum of calling all complex digital technologies Tools. *International Journal of Educational Development, 4*(4).

Arsham, H. (2002). Impact of the internet on learning and teaching. *USDLA Journal, 16*(3), 9-20. Retrieved from http://www.usdla.org/html/journal/MAR02_Issue/article01.html

Ashby, C. M. (2003). *College completion: Additional efforts could help education with its completion goals.* Report to congressional requesters (Report No. GAO-03-568). Washington, DC: General Accounting Office. (ERIC Document Reproduction Service No. ED478814).

Asia Development Bank Report. (2004). *Current Status and Trends of E-Learning.* Asia Development Bank, Manila.

Asia Development Bank Report. (2005). *Better Learning, Better Future: Education and Training Strategy for the Pacific.* Asia Development Bank, Manila.

Aspects of information and communications technology integration. (2009). Retrieved June 5, 2009, from http://www.bced.gov.bc.ca/perf_stands/icti/content.php?page=aspectsict

AUFP4. (n.d.). *Programme « Technologies de l information et de la communication et appropriation des savoirs » de l Agence universitaire de la Francophonie.* Retrieved from http://www.auf.org/programmes/ programme4/

Augar, N., Raitman, R., Lanham, E., & Zhou, W. (2006). Building Virtual Learning Communities. In Z. Ma (Ed.), Web-based Intelligent e-Learning Systems: Technologies and Applications (pp. 72-100). Hershey, PA: Idea Group.

Australian Bureau of Statistics. (2008). *Year Book Australia.* Retrieved May 10, 2009, from http://www.abs.gov.au/AUSSTATS/abs@.nsf/7d12b0f6763c78caca257061001cc588/76282812C4583EB5CA2573D20010CC8A?opendocument

Ausubel, D. P. (2000). The Acquisition and Retention of Knowledge: A Cognitive View. Holanda: Kluwer Academic Publishers.

Ausubel, D. P., Novak, J. D., & Hanesian, H. (1978). Psicologia educacional. Rio de Janeiro: Interoamericana.

Avis, J. (2009). Transformation or transformism: Engestrom's version of activity theory? *Educational Review, 61*(2), 151–165. doi:10.1080/00131910902844754

Ayoubi, R. M., & Al-Habaibeh, A. (2006). An investigation into international business collaboration in higher education organizations. *International Journal of Educational Management, 20.* Retrieved 18 May 2009 from http://www.emeraldinsight.com/Insight/ViewContentServlet?Filename+Published

Bacon, S., & Dillion, T. (2007). *Opening education: The potential of open source approaches for education.* Future Lab. Retrieved May 5, 2009, from http://www.futurelab.org.uk

Baerentsen, K. B., & Trettvik, J. (2002). An activity theory approach to affordance. *Proceedings of the second Nordic conference on human-computer interaction table of contents Aarhus, Denmark* (pp. 51-60). New York: ACM Press.

Baets, W. R. J., & Van der Linden, G. (2003). Virtual Corporate Universities: A Matrix Of Knowledge And Learning For The New Digital Dawn. Norwell, MA: Kluwer.

Bailey, J., Sass, M., Swiercz, P. M., Seal, C., & Kayes, D. C. (2005). Teaching with and through teams: Student-written, instructor-facilitated case writing and the signatory code. *Journal of Management Education, 29*(1), 39–59. doi:10.1177/1052562904269641

Bailey, T., Alfonso, M., Calcagno, J. C., Jenkins, D., Kienzl, G., & Leinbach, T. (2004). Improving student attainment in community colleges: Institutional characteristics and policies. New York, NY: Community College Research Center, Teachers College, Columbia University. (ERIC Document Reproduction Service No. ED 484346).

Bailey, T., Calcagno, J. C., Jenkins, D., Kienzl, G., & Leinbach, T. (2005). The effects of institutional factors on the success of community college students. New York, NY: Community College Research Center, Teachers College, Columbia University. (ERIC Document Reproduction Service No. ED484345).

Baker, D., Street, B., & Tomlin, A. (2002). *Understanding relationships between home and school numeracy practices: Examples from the field.* Paper presented at AERA Annual Conference, New Orleans, April 1-5.

Bandura, A. (1965). Influence of model's reinforcement contingencies on the acquisition of imitative responses. *Journal of Personality and Social Psychology, 1*, 589–595. doi:10.1037/h0022070

Bandura, A. (1995). Self-efficacy in changing societies. Cambridge, UK: Cambridge University Press.

Bandura, A. (1997). Self-efficacy: The exercise of control. New York: W.H. Freeman.

Barab, S. A., & Duffy, T. (2000). From Practice Fields to Communities of Practice. In D. Jonassen, & S. M. Land (Eds.), Theoretical Foundations of Learning Environments (pp. 25-56). Mahwah, NJ: Lawrence Erlbaum Associates.

Barab, S. A., Makinster, J. G., Moore, J. A., & Cunningham, D. J. (2001). Designing and Building an On-line Community: The Struggle to Support Sociability in the Inquiry Learning Forum. *Educational Technology Research and Development, 49*(4), 71–96. doi:10.1007/BF02504948

Barolli, L., Koyama, A., Durresi, A., & De Marco, G. (2006). A web-based e-Learning Efficiency by Stimulating Learner's Motivation. *Information Systems Frontiers, 8*, 297–306. doi:10.1007/s10796-006-9004-5

Barron, P. E. (2002). Providing a More Successful Education Experience for Asian Hospitality Management Students Studying in Australia: A Focus on Teaching and Learning Styles. *Journal of Teaching in Travel & Tourism, 2*(2), 63–88. doi:10.1300/J172v02n02_04

Bateson, G. (1991). A Sacred Unity. In Donaldson (Ed.), Further Steps to an Ecology of Mind. HarperCollins Publishers.

Battaglini, J. K. (2004). Retention and graduation rates at Maryland public four-year institutions. Annapolis, MD: Maryland Higher Education Commission. (ERIC Document Reproduction Service No. ED484153).

Bawden, D. (2001). Information and digital literacy: A review of concepts. *The Journal of Documentation*, *57*(2), 218–259. doi:10.1108/EUM0000000007083

Becker, H. J. (2000). *Findings from the teaching, learning and computing survey: Is Larry Cuban right?* Retrieved May, 8, 2009, from http://www.crito.uci.edu/tlc/findings/ccsso.pdf

Becta. (2001). *ImpaCT2 – Emerging Findings from the Evaluation of the Impact of Information and Communications Technologies on Pupil Attainment.* Retrieved from http://www.becta.org.uk/research/reports/impact2

Becta. (2006). *The Becta review 2006.* Retrieved August 9, 2007, from http://partners.becta.org.uk/upload-dir/downloads/page_documents/research/The_Becta_Review_2006.pdf

Belawati, T., & Zuhairi, A. (2007). The Practice of a Quality Assurance System in Open and Distance Learning: A case study at Universitas Terbuka Indonesia (The Indonesia Open University). *The International Review of Research in Open and Distance Learning, 8*(1), 1-15. Retrieved July 29, 2007, from http://www.irrodl.org/index.php/irrodl/article/view/340/782

Belch, H. A. (2004). Retention and students with disabilities. *Journal of College Student Retention Research Theory and Practice*, *6*, 3–22. doi:10.2190/MC5A-DHRV-1GHM-N0CD

Beniest, J., Vandenbosch, T., & Drame Yaye, A. (2008). *E-Learning for Agriculture and Natural Resources Management Education: Some Experiences and Future Directions.* Paper presented at the Second Symposium of ANAFE on Mainstreaming Climate Change into Agricultural Education: Tools, Challenges and Perspectives, Lilongwe, Malawi.

Ben-Zvi, D. (2007). Using Wiki to promote collaborative learning in statistics education. *Technology Innovations in Statistics Education, 1*(1), Article 4. Retrieved May, 3, 2009, from: http://repositories.cdlib.org/uclastat/cts/tise/vol1/iss1/art4

Bereiter, C. (2002). Education and mind in the knowledge age. Mahwah, NJ: Lawrence Erlbaum Associates.

Beuchot, A., & Bullen, M. (2005). Interaction and interpersonality in online discussion forums. *Distance Education*, *26*(1), 67–87. doi:10.1080/01587910500081285

Biggs, J. B. (1999). Teaching for quality learning at university: What the student does. Buckingham, UK: Society for Research in Higher Education and Open University Press.

Billett, S. (2001). Learning in the workplace. Strategies for effective practice. Crows Nest, Australia: Allen & Urwin.

Birt, D., Krug, D. H., & Sheridan, M. (1997). Earthly matters: Learning occurs when you hear the grass singing. *Art Education*, *50*(6), 6–14. doi:10.2307/3193682

Black, A. L., & Halliwell, G. (2000). Assessing practical knowledge: How? Why? *Teaching and Teacher Education, 16*, 103–115. doi:10.1016/S0742-051X(99)00045-1

Blackler, F., & Regan, S. (2009). Intentionality, Agency, Change: Practice Theory and Management. *Management Learning*, *40*(2), 161–176. doi:10.1177/1350507608101227

Bladt, K. (2006). It-støttet undervisning udvikler børns selvværd og fremmer inklusion [ICT supported teaching develops childrens self esteem and promote inclusion]. *Kognition & Pædagogik*, *61*(16), 56–69.

Bladt, K. (2008). It-støttet undervisning fremmer ligeværdig deltagelse [ICT supported education promotes equal participation]. *Viden om læsning, 3*, 16-19.

Boaz, M., Elliott, B., Foshee, D., Hardy, D., Jarmon, C., & Olcott, D. (1999). Teaching at a distance: A handbook for instructors. Mission Viejo, CA: League for Innovation in the Community College.

Bødker, S. (1996). Applying activity theory to video analysis: how to make sense of video data in HCI. In B. Nardi (Ed.), Context and consciousness. Activity theory and human computer interaction (pp. 147-174). Cambridge, MA: MIT Press.

Boekaerts, P., Pintrich, R., & Zeidner, M. (2000). (Eds.), Handbook of self-regulation. San Diego, California: Academic Press.

Boettcher, J. (1999). Another look at the tower of WW-Webble. *Syllabus Magazine*, *13*(3), 50–52.

Boles, K., & Troven, V. (1996). Teacher leaders and power: Achieving school reform from the classroom. In G. Moller and M. Katzenmeyer (Eds.). Every Teacher as a Leader, New Directions for School Leadership, No. 1, Fall 1996. San Francisco, CA: Jossey-Bass.

Bonett, M. (2001). Personalization of web services: opportunities and challenges. *ARIADNE,* 28. Retrieved April 13, 2009, from http://www.ariadne.ac.uk/issue28/personalization/

Bonk, C. J., & Graham, C. R. (Eds.) (2006). Handbook of Blended Learning: Global Perspectives, Local Designs. San Francisco, CA: Pfeiffer Publishing.

Bonk, C. J., & King, K. S. (1998). Electronic collaborators: Learner-centered technologies for literacy, apprenticeship, and discourse. Mahwah, NJ: L. Erlbaum Associates.

Boswell, C., & Cannon, S. (2005). New horizons for collaborative partnerships. *Online Journal of Issues in Nursing*, *10*(1), 75–80.

Bottomly, J. (2005). Recionfiguring Institutional strategies for flexible learning and deliver. In V. Jackupec & J. Garrick (Eds.), Flexible learning, human resource and organisational development: Putting theory to work. London: Routledge.

Boud, D., Cohen, R., & Sampson, J. (1998). Peer learning and assessment. *Assessment & Evaluation in Higher Education*, *24*(4), 413–426. doi:10.1080/0260293990240405

Bourne, J. R., McMaster, E., Reiger, J., & Campbell, J. O. (1997). Paradigms for on-line learning: A case study in the design and implementation of an asynchronous learning networks (ALN) course. *Journal of Asynchronous Learning Networks*, *1*(2), 38–56.

Brace-Govan, J. &., & Clulow, V. (2001). Comparing face-to-face with online: learners' perspective. *Academic Exchange Quarterly, 5*(4).

Bracewell, R., & Laferriére, T. (1996). *The contribution of new technologies to learning and teaching in elementary and secondary schools.* Montreal, Quebec, Canada: Laval University and McGill University. Retrieved June, 3rd 2004 from http://www.tact.fse.ulaval.ca/fr/html/impactnt.html

Bradley, D., & Bradley, M. (1984). Problems of Asian Students in Australia: Language, Culture and Education. Canberra: Department of Education and Youth Affairs.

Bransford, J. D., Brown, S. L., & Cocking, R. R. (2000). How people learn. Brain, mind, experience and school. Washington, DC: National academy press.

Bregar, L., Ograjensek, I., & Bavdaz, K. (2002). Statistical Education and the Workplace: Present State of Affairs and Future Challenges. In B. Phillips (Ed.), *Proceedings of the Sixth International Conference on Teaching Statistics (ICOTS6).* Cape Town, South Africa: IASE.

Brennan, J., & Shah, T. (2000). Quality assessment and institutional change: Experiences from 14 countries. *Higher Education*, *40*, 331–349. doi:10.1023/A:1004159425182

Brightman, H. (n.d.). *GSU master teacher program: On learning styles.* Retrieved July 3, 2003, from Georgia State University Website: http://www.gsu.edu/~dschjb/wwwmbti.html

Brown, G., Desrosier, T., & Edwards, D. (2009). Learning to work and working to learn: what we are learning and how technology and assessment can help. In V. C. X. Wang (Ed.), Handbook of Research on E-Learning Applications for Career and Technical Education: Technologies for Vocational Training (pp. 638-667). Hershey, PA: Information Science Reference.

Brown, J. S., & Duguid, P. (1991). Organizational learning and communities of practice: Toward a unified view of working, learning, and innovation. *Organization Science*, *2*, 40–57. doi:10.1287/orsc.2.1.40

Brown, M., & Long, P. (2006).Trends in Learning Space Design. In D. Oblinger (Ed.), *Learning Spaces*. Retrieved April 15, 2007, from www.educause.edu/learningspaces.

Brown, R. E. (2001). The process of community building in distance learning classes. *Journal of Asynchronous Learning Networks*, *5*(2), 18–35.

Bruns, A., & Humphreys, S. (2007). Building Collaborative Capacities in Learners: The M/Cyclopedia Project Revisited. In *Proceedings of International Symposium on Wikis*, Montréal, Canada.

Building student ICT in teacher education expertise. Retrieved June 8, 2009, from http://www.uoregon.edu/~moursund/ICT-planning/building-expertise.htm

Bullen, M., & Janes, D. P. (Eds.). (2007). Making the transition to e-learning. British journal of educational technology, 38(4), 762-762.

Burgos, D., & Corbalan, G. (2006). Modelado y uso de escenarios de aprendizaje en entornos b-learning desde la práctica educativa. En *III Jornadas Campus Virtual*, September, Madrid (Spain), University Complutense of Madrid. Retrieved June 30th, 2006, from http://dspace.learningnetworks.org

Burgos, D., Tattersall, C., & Koper, R. (2005). Utilización de estándares en el aprendizaje virtual. En II Jornadas Campus Virtual, May 2005. Madrid: Universidad Complutense de Madrid

Burke, J. C., & Serban, A. M. (1997). Performance funding and budgeting for public higher education: Current status and future prospects. Albany, NY: The Nelson Rockefeller Institute of Government, State University of New York.

Butler, K. (1987). Learning and teaching style: In theory and practice. Columbia, CT: The Learner's Dimension.

Butler, Y. G. (2004). How to make sense of word meanings in context: Meaning-making skills among young readers of English. In Y. Oshima-Takane, Y. Shirai, & H. Shirai (Eds.), Studies in Language Sciences (Vol. 3, pp. 139-154). Tokyo: Kuroshio Publishing.

Butler, Y. G., & Gutierrez, M. B. (2003). Learning climates: A case of 4th grade students in an English-only district in California. *Bilingual Research Journal*, *27*(2), 207–224.

Butler-Williams, L. A., & Kpo, W. (1990). *A Study of Teachers' Attitudes toward School Reform.* Paper presented at the Annual Meeting of the American Educational Research Association, Boston, MA.

Cabinet du Premier Ministre. (2003). *Ministère des Enseignements Secondaires et Supérieur, de la Recherche et de la Technologie*. Document portant Politique Nationale d'Enseignement Supérieur et de Recherche au Niger.

Caladine, R., Andrews, T., Tynan, B., Symth, R., & Vale, D. (in press). New communications Options: A renaissance in IP use. In Veletsianos, G. (Ed.), Using Emerging Technologies in Distance Education. Athabasca, Canada: Athabasca University Press.

Calder, J. (1994). Programme Evaluation and Quality. London: Kogan Page.

Cameron, K. S. (1984). Organizational adaptation and higher-education. *The Journal of Higher Education*, *55*(2), 122–144. doi:10.2307/1981182

Cameron, K. S. (1986). Effectiveness as paradox - consensus and conflict in conceptions of organizational-effectiveness. *Management Science*, *32*(5), 539–553. doi:10.1287/mnsc.32.5.539

Canadian Teachers' Federation. (2003). *An investigation of the integration of information and communication technology into Canadian schools and classrooms.*

Canfield, A., & Lafferty, J. (1976). Learning style inventory. Detroit, MI: Humanics Media.

Capper, J. (2001). E-Learning growth and promise for the developing world. *TechKnowLogia*, *2*(2), 7–10.

Carliner, S., & Shank, P. (2008). The e-leraning handbook. San Francisco: Pfeiffer.

Carr, S. (2000). As distance education comes of age, the challenge is keeping the students. *The Chronicle of Higher Education*, A39.

Carter, S. (2002). The Impact of Parent/Family Involvement on Student Outcomes: An Annotated Bibliography of Research during the Past Decade. Eugene, OR: Consortium for Appropriate Dispute Resolution in Special Education.

Carter, S. (2003). Educating Our Children Together: A Sourcebook for Effective Family-School-Community Partnerships. Consortium for Alternative Dispute Resolution in Special Education (CADRE).

Carver, C. S., Scheier, M. F., & Weintraub, J. K. (1989). Assessing coping strategies: A theoretically based approach. *Journal of Personality and Social Psychology*, *56*(2), 267–283. doi:10.1037/0022-3514.56.2.267

Castells, M. (1996). The information age: economy, society and culture. Oxford, UK: Blackwell.

Castells, M. (2000). Materials for an exploratory theory of the network society. *The British Journal of Sociology*, *51*(1), 5–24. doi:10.1080/000713100358408

Castells, M. (2001). The Internet Galaxy: Reflections on the Internet, Business and Society. London: Oxford University Press.

Castro, E. (2004). Manual del Profesor de Moodle. Retrieved from http://download.moodle.org/docs/teacher-Cole, J. (2006). *Using Moodle. Teaching with the Popular Open Source Management System.* Retrieved October 19, 2006, from http://docs.moodle.org/en/Using_Moodle_book

Cha, S., & Joung, Y. (2001). Managing Personal Data in the Age of Customization Services. *International Association for Computer Information Systems*, *2*, 50–56.

Chale, E. M. (1992). Application and cost effectiveness of distance education in teacher preparation: A case study of Tanzania. In P. Murphy and A. Zhiri (Eds.), Distance Education in Anglophone Africa (pp.123-136). Washington, DC: The World Bank.

Chan Mow, I. T. (2001). The Samoa-American Samoa (SAS) Link – A case study in bridging the communications divide. In *Proceedings of the Pacific Regional Science Communication Forum*, FAO Conference Facility, Faculty of Science, The Australian National University, Canberra, August 2001.

Chan Mow, I. T. (2006). *The effectiveness of a cognitive apprenticeship-based learning environment (CABLE) in teaching computer programming.* Unpublished Doctoral dissertation, University of South Australia, Australia.

Chan Mow, I. T. (2008). Development of e-learning in education in Samoa: issues, challenges, strategies and recommendations for the way forward. In *Proceedings of PCF5 Conference*, University of London, UK. Retrieved from http://www.wikieducator.org/pcf5/Cross-Cutting_Themes

Chan Mow, I. T., Strigel, C., & Va'a, R. (2007). Provoking Change: Technology in Education Case Studies from Samoa (Samoa Country Report – Samoa). In Innovative Information and Communication Technology in Education and its Potential for Reducing Poverty in the Asia and Pacific Region (TA No. 6278-REG). Submitted to the Asian Development Bank, RTI International, Research Triangle Park, Manila.

Chapman, B. (2003). *LCMS report: Comparing analysis of enterprise Learning Content Management Systems.* Sunnyvale, CA: Brandon-Hall.

Chen, C., Lee, H., & Chen, Y. (2005). Personalized e-learning system using item response theory. *Computers & Education*, *44*, 237–255. doi:10.1016/j.compedu.2004.01.006

Chen, H. (2001). Parents' attitudes and expectations regarding science education: Comparisons among American, Chinese-American, and Chinese families. *Adolescence*, *36*, 305–313.

Chen, M. Y., & Chen, A. P. (2006). Knowledge management performance evaluation: a decade review from 1995 to 2004. *Journal of Information Science*, *32*(1), 17–38. doi:10.1177/0165551506059220

Chichering, A. W. (1981). The Modern American College: Responding to the New Realities of Diverse Students and a Changing Society. San Francisco: Jossey-Bass.

Chism, N. (1998). Preparing graduate students to teach: Past, present, and future. In M. R. Clarke (Ed.), *A primer in diffusion of innovation theory.* Retrieved April 20, 2009, from http://www.anu.edu.au/people/Roger.Clarke/SOS/InnDiff.html

Chism, N. (2008). Faculty at the Margins: New Directions for Higher Education. San Francisco: Jossey-Bass.

Chism, N., Lees, N., & Evenbeck, S. (2002, Summer). Faculty development innovation for teaching. *Liberal Education*, *88*(3), 34–41.

Chiva, R., & Alegre, J. (2005). Organizational learning and organizational knowledge - Towards the integration of two approaches. *Management Learning*, *36*(1), 49–68. doi:10.1177/1350507605049906

Chou, C. C. (2001). Formative evaluation of synchronous CMC systems for a learner centered online course. *Journal of Interactive Learning Research*, *12*(2/3), 170–188.

Chua, A., & Lam, W. (2007). Quality assurance in online education: The Universitas 21 Global approach. *British Journal of Educational Technology*, *38*(1), 133–152. doi:10.1111/j.1467-8535.2006.00652.x

Civil, M. (2002). Everyday Mathematics, Mathematicians' Mathematics, and School Mathematics: Can We Bring Them Together? In M. Brenner & J. Moschkovich (Eds.), Everyday and academic mathematics in the classroom. Journal of Research in Mathematics Education Monograph #11 (pp. 40-62). Reston, VA: NCTM.

Civil, M., & Andrade, R. (2002). Transitions between home and school mathematics: rays of hope amidst the passing clouds. In G. de Abreu, A.J. Bishop, & N.C. Presmeg (Eds.), Transitions between contexts of mathematical practices (pp. 149-169). Dordrecht: Kluwer.

Clark, D. (2005). *Training Handbook*. Big Dog ISD Page. Retrieved March 10, 2009, from http://www.nwlink.com/~donclark/

Claxton, C., & Murrell, P. (1987). *Learning styles: Implications for improving educational practices*. ASHE-ERIC Higher Education Report No. 4.

Coakes, E., & Clareke, S. (2006). Encyclopaedia of communities of practice in information and knowledge management. Hershey, PA: Idea Group Reference.

Cohen, D., & Prusak, L. (2001). In Good Company: How Social Capital Makes Organizations Work. Boston, MA: Harvard Business School Press.

Coiro, J. (2003). *Reading comprehension on the Internet: Expanding Our Understanding of Reading comprehension to Encompass New Literacies*. Retrieved March 25, 2008, from http://www.readingonline.org/electronic/rt/2-03_Column/index.html

Colazzo, L., & Molinari, A. (2005). Building, Testing and Assessing a Learning Management System. *Journalof Computing and Information Technology, 13*(1), 25-41.

Cole, J. (2006). *Using Moodle. Teaching with the Popular Open Source Management System.* Retrived October 19, 2006, from http://docs.moodle.org/en/Using_Moodle_book

Cole, M., & Engeström, Y. (1993). A cultural-historical interpretation of distributed cognition. In G. Salomon (Ed.), Distribute cognition: Psychological and educational considerations. Cambridge, UK: Cambridge University Press.

Collazos, C. Guerrero, L., Pino, J., Ochoa, S., & Stahl G. (2006). A Model and a Game for Investigating and Designing Collaborative Learning Environments. In *Proceedings of 8th International Symposium on Computers in Education*, SIIE'06, León, Spain.

Collier, S., Weinburgh, M., & Rivera, M. (2004). Infusing Technology Skills into a Teacher Education Program: Change in Students' Knowledge About and Use of Technology. *Journal of Technology and Teacher Education*, *12*(3), 447–468.

Collins, A. (2001). The balance between task focus and understanding focus: Education as apprenticeship versus education as research. In T. Koschmann, R. Hall & N. Miyake (Eds.), CSCL 2. Carrying forward the conversation. Mahwah, NJ: Lawrence Erlbaum.

Collins, A., Brown, J. S., & Newman, S. E. (1989). Cognitive apprenticeship: Teaching the crafts of reading, writing, and mathematics. In L. B. Resnick (Ed.), Knowing, Learning, and Instruction: Essays in Honor of Robert Glaser (pp. 453–494). Hillsdale, NJ: Lawrence Erlbaum.

Collison, C. (1999). Connecting the new organization. How BP Amoco encourages post-merger collaboration. *Knowledge Management Review*, *7*(2), 12–15.

Commission of the European Communities. (2002). *European benchmarks in education and training: follow-up to the Lisbon European Council.* COM(2002) 629 final, Brussels, Belgium. Retrieved June 2008, from http://ec.europa.eu/education/policies/2010/doc/bench_ed_trai_en.pdf

Commission of the European Communities. (2007). *A Coherent Framework of Indicators and Benchmarks for Monitoring Progress Towards the Lisbon Objectives in Education and Training.* Retrieved February 2008, from http://eur lex.europa.eu/LexUriServ/site/en/com/ 2007/com2007_0061en01.pdf

Commonwealth of Learning and the VUSSC government interlocutors. (2007). *A business strategy for the Virtual University for small states of the Commonwealth (2007– 2013).* Retrieved June 7, 2009, from http://www.col.org/sitecollectionDocument/VUSSC.Business_Plan_20070220.doc

Commonwealth of Learning. (1995). Directory of courses and materials for training in distance education. Vancouver: Commonwealth of Learning.

Commonwealth of Learning. (2002). School Networking in Pacific Island States: An Environmental Scan and Plan for establishing School Nets in the Pacific Island States, Final Report. Vancouver, Canada: Author.

Connolly, W. E. (1974). Essentially Contested Concepts in Politics. In W.E. Connolly (Ed.), The Terms of Political Discourse (pp. 10-44). Lexington, MA: Heath.

Cook, K. (2000). Computer conferencing really makes the Web interactive. In E. J. Leach (Ed.), A collection of practices from the league's conference on information technology. Mission Viejo, CA: League for Innovation in the Community College.

Corey, E. R. (1996). The use of cases in management education. Teaching note 9-376-240. Harvard Business School.

Council of the European Union. (2004, February 26). *Joint Interim Report of the Council and the Commission on the implementation of the Detailed Work Programme.* Retrieved from http://europa. eu.int/comm/education/policies/2010/doc/jir_council_final.pdf

Courant, C., & Griffiths, R. (2006). Software and collaboration in higher education: A study of open source software. *Online report.* Retrieved from http://www.ithaka.org/saved-pages/strategic-services/oss/OOSS_Report_FINAL.pdf

Covarrubia, J. (2000). Family literacy: Sharing classrooms with parents. *Principal*, *80*(1), 44–45.

Crawford, K. (2004). E-Learning and Activity: Supporting Communication, Cooperation and Co-Invention. In *Proceedings of the 2nd IEEE Workshop on Wireless and Mobile Technologies in Education (WMTE '04).* JungLi, Taiwan: IEEE Computer Society.

Creswell, J. (1998). Qualitative inquiry and research design. Thousand Oaks, CA: Sage.

Crook, C., & Light, P. (2002). Virtual society and the cultural practice of study. In S. Woolgar (Ed.), Virtual Society? Technology, Cyberbole, Reality. Oxford: Oxford University Press.

Crosta, L., & McConnell, D. (2005). Action Research and Tutoring in the Online Learning Community: New Implications for Adult Teaching and Learning. In *Proceedings of the 11th Cambridge International Conference on Open and Distance Learning,* Cambridge, UK, September 2005.

Crosthwaite, C. (2006). *Team projects: facilitating successful student teams and project centred learning.* Presentation to MEA staff, Brisbane, 14th July.

Crosthwaite, C., & Cameron, I. (2006). Changing a culture: Project centered curriculum, creativity, challenge, change: partnerships in engineering education. In *Proceedings 17th Conference of the Australasian Association of Engineering Education (AAEE)*, Auckland, New Zealand.

Cuban, L. (1986). Teachers and machines. The classroom use of technology since 1920. New York: Teachers College Press.

Cuban, L. (2001). Oversold & underused. Computers in the classroom. Cambridge, MA: Harvard University Press.

Cuban, L. (2001). Why are most teachers infrequent and restrained users of computers in their classrooms? In J. Woodward & L. Cuban (Eds.), Technology curriculum and professional development. Thousand Oaks, CA: Corwin Press.

Curran, C. (2004). Strategies for e-learning in Universities. *CSHE Research and occasional paper series: CSHE.7.04.* Retrieved from http://ishi.lib.berkeley.edu/cshe/

Curry, L. (1990). A critique of the research on learning styles. *Educational Leadership, 48*, 50–56.

D'Andrade, R. (1984). Cultural meaning systems. In R.A. Shweder & R.A. Levine (Eds.), Cultural theory: Essays on mind, self, and emotion (pp. 88-119). Cambridge, UK: Cambridge University Press.

Dabbagh, N. (2007). The Online Learner: Characteristics and Pedagogical Implications. *Contemporary Issues in Technology & Teacher Education, 7*, 217–226.

Daft, R. I. (2006).Understanding management (5th ed.). Mason, OH: Thompson South-Western.

Daft, R. L. (2003). Organizational theory and design 8 Ed. Boston: South Western College Publishing.

Dagger, D., Vincent, W., & Owen, C. (2003). Towards anytime, anywhere Learning: The Role and Realization of Dynamic Terminal Personalization in Adaptive eLearning. In D. Lassner & C. McNaught (Eds.), *Proceedings of World Conference on Educational Multimedia, Hypermedia and Telecommunications 2003* (pp. 32-35). Chesapeake, VA: AACE

Daniel, J. (2005). Open and distance learning in Africa. In 15 CCEM mid-term review for Africa and Europe, Freetown, Sierra Leone, 14 November 2005.

Daniel, J., & Menon, M. (2005). *ODL and ICTs for teacher development in Sub-Saharan Africa: The experience of the Commonwealth of Learning.* Retrieved 12 November, 2005, from http://www.col.org/speeches/JD_0509BOCODOL.htm

Daniel, J., & West, P. (2008). *The virtual university for small states of the Commonwealth: What is it for? How is it doing? Where is it going?* Retrieved June 7, 2009, from http://www.col.org/resources/speeches/2008presentations/2008-VUSSC/Pages/articleVUSSC.aspx

Darling-Hammond, L., Banks, J., Zumwalt, K., Gomez, L., Gamoran Sherin, M., Griesdorn, K., & Finn, L.-E. (2005). Educational goals and purposes: Developing a curricular vision for teaching. In L. Darling-Hammond & J. Bransford (Eds.), Preparing teachers for a changing world (pp. 169-200). San Francisco, CA: Jossey-Bass.

Dasgupta, S. (2006). Encyclopaedia of virtual communities and technologies. Hershey, PA: Idea Group Reference.

Datta, P. (2007). An agent-mediated knowledge-in-motion model. *Journal of The Association For Information System, 8*(5), 287–311.

Davenport, T., & Prusak, L. (1998). Working Knowledge. How organization manage what they know. Boston, MA: Harvard Business School Press.

Davies, C., Foxcroft, C., Griessel, L., & Tredoux, N. (2005). Computer-based and Internet-delivered assessment. In C. Foxcroft & G. Roodt (Eds.), An introduction to psychological assessment in the South African context. Cape Town, South Africa: Oxford University Press.

Davis, J., & Davis, A. (1998). *Effective training strategies: A comprehensive guide to maximizing learning in organizations.* San Francisco: Berrett-Koehler Publishers. Denzine, G. (n.d.). *The existence of learning styles: Myth or reality.* Retrieved September 17, 2003, from http://star.ucc.nau.edu/~dlk/Learn.styles.html

De Bra, P., Stash, N., & De Lange, B. (2003). AHA! Adding Adaptive Behaviour to Websites. In *Proceedings of NLUUG.* Ede, The Netherlands: De Reehorst.

De Laat, M., & Lally, V. (2004). It's not so easy: Researching the complexity of emergent participant roles and awareness in asynchronous networked learning discussions. *Journal of Computer Assisted Learning, 20,* 165–171. doi:10.1111/j.1365-2729.2004.00085.x

de Laet, M., & Mol, A. (2000). The Zimbabwe Bush Pump: Mechanics of a Fluid Technology. *Social Studies of Science, 30*(2), 225–263. doi:10.1177/030631200030002002

de Leng, B. A., Dolmans, D. H. J. M., Jobsis, R., Muijtjens, A. M. M., & van der Vleuten, C. P. M. (2009). Exploration of an e-learning model to foster critical thinking on basic science concepts during work placements. *Computers & Education, 53*(1), 1–13. doi:10.1016/j.compedu.2008.12.012

Debande, O., & Ottersten, E. K. (2004). Information and communication technologies: A tool for empowering and developing the horizon of the learner. *Higher Education Management and Policy, 16*(2), 31–61. doi:10.1787/hemp-v16-art15-en

Deem, R., & Brehony, K. J. (2005). Management as ideology: the case of 'new managerialism' in higher education. *Oxford Review of Education, 31*(2), 217–235. doi:10.1080/03054980500117827

Deleuze, G., & Guattari, F. (1987). A thousand plateaus: Capitalism and schizophrenia. Minneapolis, MN: University of Minneapolis Press.

Delvin, M. (2002). *Introduction. In The Internet and the University: 2001 Forum.* Forum for the Future of Higher Education, Aspen Symposium.

Denman-Maier, E. (2004). Intercultural Factors in Web-based Training Systems. *Journal of Universal Computer Science, 10*(1), 90–104.

Denzin, N. (1996). The facts and fictions of qualitative inquiry. *Qualitative Inquiry, 2*(2), 230–241. doi:10.1177/107780049600200207

Denzin, N. (2004). The war on culture, the war on truth. *Cultural Studies Critical Methodologies, 4*(2), 137–142. doi:10.1177/1532708603256627

Department for International Development. (2009). *Imfundo: Partnership for IT in education.* Retrieved September 20, 2009, from http://imfundo.digitalbrain.com/imfundo/

Désilets, A., & Paquet, S. (2005). Wiki as a tool for web-based collaborative story telling in primary school: A case study. In *EdMedia 2005, World Conference on Educational Multimedia, Hypermedia & Telecommunications,* Montréal, Québec, Canada. June 27-July 2, 2005.

Dexter, S. L., Anderson, R. E., & Becker, H. J. (1999). Teachers' views of computers as catalysts for changes in their teaching practice. *Journal of Research on Computing in Education, 31*(3), 221–239.

Diaz, D. P. (2000a). *Comparison of student characteristics, and evaluation of student success. In an online health education course.* Unpublished doctoral dissertation, Nova Southeastern University, Fort Lauderdale, Florida

Diaz, D. P., & Cartnal, R. B. (1999). Students' learning styles in two classes: Online distance learning and equivalent on-campus. *College Teaching, 47*(4), 130–135. doi:10.1080/87567559909595802

DiCamillo, M. P. (2001). Parent Education as an Essential Component of Parent Involvement Programs. In D. B. Hiatt-Michael (Ed.), Promising Practices for Family Involvement in Schools (pp. 153-183). Greenwich, CT: Information Age Publishing.

Dille, B., & Mezack, M. (1991). Identifying predictors of high risk among community college telecourse students.

American Journal of Distance Education, *5*(1), 24–25. doi:10.1080/08923649109526729

DiMarco, J. (2006). Web portfolios in the information society and future. In Web Portfolio Design and Applications (pp. 277-292), Hershey, PA: Idea Group Publishing.

Ditsa, G. (2003). Activity theory as a theoretical foundation for information systems research. In G. Ditsa, Information Management: Support Systems & Multimedia Technology (pp. 192-231), Hershey, PA: IRM Press.

Dobson, I. R., Sharma, R., & Calderon, A. J. (1998). *The Comparative Performance of Overseas and Australian Undergraduates*. Paper presented at the 12th Australian International Education Conference, Canberra, 3-18.

Dolata, U. (2009). Technological innovations and sectoral change Transformative capacity, adaptability, patterns of change: An analytical framework. *Research Policy*, *38*(6), 1066–1076. doi:10.1016/j.respol.2009.03.006

Doolan, M., Hilliard, A., & Thorton, H. (2006). Collaborative Learning: Using technology for fostering those valued practices inherent in constructive environments in traditional education. *Journal for the Enhancement of Learning and Teaching*, *3*(2), 7–17.

Dooley, B. (2006). *Open Source E-Learning: Alternatives to Proprietary Tools, Systems and Courseware.* Brandon Hall Research. Retrieved March 10, 2008, from http://www.brandon- hall.com/publications/opensource/opensource.shtml

Downey, D. B. (2005). When Bigger is Not Better: Family Size, Parental Resources, and Children's Educational Performance. *American Sociological Review*, *60*, 746–761. doi:10.2307/2096320

Downey, S., Wentling, R. M., Wentling, T., & Wadsworth, A. (2005). The Relationship between National Culture and the Usability of an E-learning System. *Human Resource Development International*, *8*(1), 47–64. doi:10.1080/1367886042000338245

Downing, K. (2001). Information Technology, Education and Health Care: constructivism in the 21st Century. *Educational Studies*, *27*(3), 229–235. doi:10.1080/03055690120076510

Downing, K. J., & Shin, K. (2006, November). *Developing metacognition with LASSI online.* Paper presented at International Conference of the Asia-Pacific Educational Research Association, Hong Kong Institute of Education, Hong Kong.

Downing, K., Chan, S.-W., Downing, W. K., Kwong, T., & Lam, T. F. (2008). Measuring gender differences in cognitive functioning. *Multicultural Education & Technology Journal*, *2*(1), 4–18. doi:10.1108/17504970810867124

Downing, K., Ho, R., Shin, K., Vrijmoed, L., & Wong, E. (2007). Metacognitive development and moving away. *Educational Studies*, *33*(1), 1–13. doi:10.1080/03055690600850347

Downing, K., Kwong, T., Chan, S., Lam, I., & Downing, W. K. (2009). Problem-based learning and the development of metacognition. *Higher Education*, *57*(5), 609–621. doi:10.1007/s10734-008-9165-x

Downing, K., Lam, T., Kwong, T., Downing, W. K., & Chan, S. (2007). Creating interaction in online learning: a case study. *ALT-J*, *15*(3), 201–215. doi:10.1080/09687760701673592

Dowsing, R. D. (1998). *Flexibility And The Technology Of Computer-Aided Assessment*. Retrieved from http://www.ascilite.org.au/conferences/wollongong98/asc98.../dowsing.pdf

Draft Standard for eXtensible Markup Language (XML) Binding for Learning Object Metadata Model (LOM). (2003). Learning Technology Standards Committee (LTCS). Retrieved March 5, 2006, from http://www.cs.kuleuven.ac.be/~erikd/LOM/20030214/ballot.pdf

Drouin, M. A. (2008). The relationship between students' perceived sense of community and satisfaction, achievement, and retention in an online course. *The Quarterly Review of Distance Education*, *9*(3), 267–284.

Dryburgh, H. (2002). Learning computer skills. *Canadian Social Trends*, *64*(4), 20–24.

Dunlop, C. (2007). *VUSSC Summary Evaluation Report.* Research and Evaluation Unit, Simon Fraser University, Vancouver.

Dunn, H., & Mays, A. (2004). Improving student success, not just increasing retention rates. *Community College Times, 16*(24), 7.

Dunn, R. (2000). Learning styles: Theory, research, and practice. *National Forum of Applied Educational Research Journal, 13*(1), 3–22.

Dunn, R., & Griggs, S. (1998). Learning styles: Link between teaching and learning. In R. Dunn, & S. Griggs (Eds.), Learning styles and the nursing profession (pp. 9-23). New York: NLN Press.

Dutta, S., & Mia, I. (2009). *The Global Information Technology Report 2008-2009. Mobility in a Networked World.* World Economic Forum.

Dwairy, M. A. (2006). Counseling and psychotherapy with Arab and Muslims: A culturally sensitive approach. New York: Teachers College Press.

Dyson, A. (1999). Inclusion and Inclusions: Theories and discourses in inclusive education. In H. Daniels & P. Garner (1999), World yearbook of education 1999: Inclusive education (pp. 36-54). London: Kogan Page.

Dziuban, C., Moskal, P., Juge, F., Truman, B., Sorg, S., & Hartman, J. (2002, February 15). *Developing a web-based instructional program in a metropolitan university.* Paper presented at University of Central Florida.

Easterby-Smith, M., Burgoyne, J., et al. (Eds.). (1999) Organisational learning and the learning organisation. London: Sage.

Eastmond, D. (2000). Realizing the promise of distance education in low technology countries. *ETR & D, 48*(2), 100–111. doi:10.1007/BF02313405

Easton, G. (1992). Learning from case studies. London: Prentice Hall.

Economic and Social Commission for Western Asia (ESCWA). (2005). *Information Society Indicator.* New York: United Nations. Retrieved April 13, 2009, from http://www.escwa.org.lb/information/publications/edit/upload/ictd-05-1.pdf

Educational testing service. (2001). *Digital transformation. A framework for ICT literacy. A report of the international literacy panel.* Downloaded August 8, 2007, from http://www.ets.org/Media/Tests/Information_and_Communication_Technology_Literacy/ictreport.pdf

Egan, M. W., Sebastian, J., & Welch, M. (1991, March). Effective television teaching: Perceptions of those who count most...distance learners. *Proceedings of the Rural Education Symposium, Nashville*, TN. (ERIC Document Reproduction Service No. ED 342 579).

Egelund, N. (2004). Specialpædagogisk praksis – indspil og udspil (Special needs pedagogic practice). København: Danmarks Pædagogiske Universitets Forlag.

Eggan, P., & Kauchak, D. (2004). Educational Psychology: Windows on Classrooms. 7th Ed. Upper Saddle River, NJ, Merrill Prentice Hall.

Ehrmann, S. C. (2006). Electronic portfolio initiatives: A flashlight guide to planning and formative evaluation. In A. Jafari (Ed.), Handbook of Research on ePortfolios (pp. 180-193). Hershey PA: Idea Group Reference.

Eilam, B. (2002). Passing Through Western-Democratic Teacher Education: The Case of Israeli Arab Teachers. *Teachers College Record, 104*(8), 1656–1701. doi:10.1111/1467-9620.00216

Eisenhardt, K. M., & Zbaracki, M. J. (1992). Strategic decision making. *Strategic Management Journal, 13*, 17–37. doi:10.1002/smj.4250130904

Eisner, E. W. (2002). The arts and the creation of mind. New Haven and London: Yale University Press.

Elbanna, A. R. (2009). Actor-network theory in ICT research: A wider lens of enquiry. *International Journal of Actor-Network Theory and Technological Innovation, 1*(3), 1–14.

eLearning Africa. (2005). *1st International conference on ICT for development, education and training, UNCC, Addis Ababa, Ethiopia May 24-26, 2006.* Retrieved 12

November, 2005, from http://www.elearning-africa.com/conference.php

Elia, G., Secundo, G., & Taurino, T. (2006). Towards unstructured and just-in-time learning: the Virtual eBMS e-learning system. In Proceedings of m-ICTE2006 - Current Developments in Technology-Assisted Education (Vol. 2, pp.1067–1072).

El-Khawas, E., & Massey, W. F. (1996). Britain's performance-based system. In W. F. Massey (Ed.), Resource allocation in higher education (pp. 223-240). Ann Arbor, MI: The University of Michigan Press.

Elliott, A. (2001). Introduction. In M. Richards, A. Eliot, V. Woloshyn, & C. Mitchell (Eds.), Collaboration uncovered: the forgotten, the assumed, and the unexamined in collaborative education. Westport, CT: Bergin and Garvey.

Elluminate. (n.d.). Retrieved May 5, 2009, from http://www.elluminate.com

Emerson, R., Fretz, R., & Shaw, L. (1995). Writing ethnographic fieldnotes. Chicago: University of Chicago Press.

Emig, J. (1977). Writing as a mode of learning. *College Composition and Communication*, *28*(2), 122–128. doi:10.2307/356095

Engel, C. (1991). Not just a method but a way of learning. In D. Boud & G. Feletti (Eds.), The challenge of problem-based learning (pp. 23-33). New York: St. Martin's Press.

Engeström, Y. (1987). *Learning by expanding: An activity-theoretical approach to developmental research.* Helskinki: Orienta-Konsultit.

Engeström, Y. (1999). Innovative learning in work teams: Analyzing cycles of knowledge creation in practice. In Y. Engeström, R.L. Miettinen & R.L. Punamäki (Eds.), Perspectives on activity theory. Cambridge, UK: Cambridge University Press.

Engeström, Y. (2001). Expansive learning at work: towards an activity theoretical reconceptualization. *Journal of Education and Work*, *14*(1), 133–156. doi:10.1080/13639080123238

Engeström, Y. (2001). Making expansive decisions: an activity-theoretical study of practitioners building collaborative medical care for children. In C.M. Allwood & M. Selart (Eds.), Decision Making Social and Creative Dimensions. Dordrecht, The Netherlands: Kluwer.

Engeström, Y. (2006). From well-bounded ethnographies to intervening in mycorrhizae activities. *Organization Studies*, *27*(12), 1783–1793. doi:10.1177/0170840606071898

Engeström, Y. (2008). Enriching activity theory without shortcuts. *Interacting with Computers*, *20*, 256–259. doi:10.1016/j.intcom.2007.07.003

Engeström, Y., Kerosuo, H., & Ysajamaa, A. (2007). Beyond discontinuity - Expansive organizational learning remembered. *Management Learning*, *38*(3), 319–336. doi:10.1177/1350507607079032

Epper, R. M., & Bates, A. W. (2001). Teaching faculty how to use technology: Best practices from leading institutions. Westport, CT: American Council on Education and Oryx Press.

Epstein, J. L., Sanders, M. G., Simon, B. S., Salinas, K. C., Rodriguez Jansorn, N., & Van Voorhis, F. L. (2002). School, family, and community partnerships. Your handbook for action (2nd ed.). Thousand Oaks, CA: Corwin Press.

EQUELLA. (n.d.). Retrieved May 5, 2009, from http://www.thelearningedge.com.au/products.php

Erstad, O. (2004). Piloter for skoleutvikling. Oslo: Unipub AS

Erstad, O. (2005). Digital kompetanse i skolen – en innføring. Oslo: Universitetsforlaget.

Erstad, O. (2008). Changing Assessment Practices and the Role of IT. In J. Voogt & G. Knezek (Eds.), International Handbook of Information Technology in Primary and Secondary Education (pp. 181–194). Dordrecht: Springer.

Erstad, O., & Quale, A. (2008). National Policiees and Practices on ICT in Education: Norway. In T. Plomp, R. E. Anderson, N. Law & A. Quale (Eds.), Cross-National Information and Communication Technology (pp. 551-567). Charlotte, NC: IAP

Ertmer, P. A. (1999). Addressing first- and second-order barriers to change: Strategies for technology integration. *Educational Technology Research and Development*, *47*(4), 47–61. doi:10.1007/BF02299597

Esera, R. (2003). ICT desk study for Ministry of Education, Sports and Culture. Apia, Samoa. Asia Development Bank Final Report. (2008). Innovative Information and Communication Technology in Education and Its Potential for Reducing Poverty in the Asia Pacific Region. ADB Project Number: TA No. 6278-REG.

Eshet-Alkalai, Y. (2004). Digital literacy: A conceptual framework for survival skills in the digital era. *Journal of Educational Multimedia and Hypermedia*, *13*(1), 93–106.

Ethel, R. G., & McMeniman, M. M. (2000). Unlocking the knowledge in action of an expert practitioner. *Journal of Teacher Education*, *51*(2), 87–102. doi:10.1177/002248710005100203

European Commission, Directorate-General for Education and Culture. (2004). *Working Group D 'Mathematics, Science and Technology'Objective 1.4 Increasing recruitment to scientific and technical studies Interim report.* Retrieved from http://ec.europa.eu/education/policies/2010/doc/math2004.pdf

Evans, T. (1994). Understanding Learners in Open and Distance Education. London: Kogan Page.

Eysenck, H. J. (1959). Manual of the Maudsley Personality Inventory. London: University of London Press.

Eysenck, H. J. (1963). On the dual nature of extraversion. *The British Journal of Social and Clinical Psychology*, *2*, 46.

Eysenck, H. J., & Eysenck, S. B. G. (1991). Manual of the Eysenck Personality Scales (EPS Adult). London: Hodder and Stoughton.

FamilyEducation.com. (2009). *Top 10 Ways to Improve Reading Skills*. Retrieved from http://school.familyeducation.com/reading/cognitive-development/38329.html

Farabaugh, R. (2007). 'The Isle is Full of Noises': Using Wiki Software to Establish a Discourse Community in a Shakespeare Classroom. *Language Awareness*, *16*(1), 41–56. doi:10.2167/la428.0

Farrell, G. (2001). *The changing faces of virtual education.* Vancouver, Canada: The Commonwealth of Learning. Retrieved October 26, 2006, from http://wwww.col.org/virtualed/

Farrell, G. (Ed.). (2003). A virtual university for small states of the Commonwealth. Vancouver, Canada: The Commonwealth of Learning.

Fekula, M. J. (1994). Information and uncertainty as strange bedfellows: A model and experiential exercise. *Developments in Business Simulation and Experiential Learning*, *21*, 133–136.

Felder, R. (1993). Reaching the second tier: Learning and teaching styles in college science education. *Journal of College Science Teaching*, *23*(5), 286–290.

Felder, R., & Silverman, L. (1988). Learning styles and teaching styles in engineering education. *English Education*, *78*(7), 674–681.

Feltovich, P. J., Spiro, R. J., Coulson, R. L., & Feltovich, J. (1996). Collaboration Within and Among Minds: Mastering Complexity, Individually and in Groups. In T. Koschmann (Ed.), CSCL: Theory and practice of an emerging paradigm (pp. 25-44). Mahwah, NJ: Lawrence Erlbaum Associates, Publishers.

Fetzner, M. J. (2003). Institutional support for online faculty: Expanding the model. In J. Bourne & J. C. Moore (Eds.), Elements of Quality Online Education: Practice and Direction (Vol. 4, pp. 229 – 244).

Figallo, C. (1998). Hosting Web Communities: Building relationships, increasing customer loyalty, and maintaining a competitive advantage. New York: Wiley Computer Publishing.

Flecha, R. (2000). Sharing words: Theory and practice of dialogic learning. Lanham, MA: Rowman & Littlefield Publishers.

Flick, U. (1998). An introduction to qualitative research. Thousand Oaks, CA: SAGE Publications.

Florian, L., & Hegarty, J. (Eds.). (2004). ICT and Special Educational Needs: a Tool for Inclusion. Maidenhead: Open University Press.

Fonseca, C. (2001). Fallacies and objectives regarding the uses of new technologies in education. *Prospects*, *31*(3), 399–413.

Forment, M. A., Guerrero, M. J. C., & Poch, J. P. (2010). Towards mobile learning applications integration with learning management systems. In T. T. Goh (Ed.), Multi-platform E-Learning Systems and Technologies: Mobile Devices for Ubiquitous ICT-Based Education (pp. 182-194). Hershey, PA: Information Science Reference.

Foucault, M. (1982). The subject and power. *Critical Inquiry*, *8*(4), 777–795. doi:10.1086/448181

Freedman, E., & Montgomery, J. F. (1994). Parent Education and Student Achievement. *Thrust for Educational Leadership*, *24*, 40–44.

Freeman, J., & Hannan, M. T. (1989). Setting the record straight on organizational ecology - rebuttal to young. *American Journal of Sociology*, *95*(2), 425–439. doi:10.1086/229275

Fullan, M. (1993). Change forces: Probing the depths of educational reform. Bristol, PA: Falmer Press.

Furberg, A., & Arnseth, H. C. (2009). Reconsidering conceptual change from a socio-cultural perspective: analyszing students' meaning making in genetics in collaborative learning activities. *Cultural Studies of Science Education*, *4*, 157–191. doi:10.1007/s11422-008-9161-6

Gaide, S. (2004). Community college identifies student expectations as key element in online retention. *Distance Education Report*, 4 – 6.

Gallardo, E., Aparicio, P., & Triadó, X. (2008). *Adapting an audiovisual case methodology to a virtual campus in business organization lessons.* Paper presented at INTED 08. International Technology, Education and Development Conference, València, Spain.

Galy, K. A., & Dane, E. (2005). *Obstacles et solutions à l appropriation des NTICs au Sud: leçons sur l expérience de l Université Abdou Moumouni du Niger.*

Gandell, T., Weston, C., Finkelstein, A., & Weiner, L. (2000). Appropriate use of the web in teaching higher education. In B.L. Mann (Ed.), Perspectives in web course management (pp. 61-68). Toronto: Canadian Scholar's Press.

Gardner, H. (1993). Multiple intelligences: The theory in practice. New York: Basic.

Gardner, H. (2000). Intelligence reframed: Multiple intelligences for the 21st century. New York: Basic.

Garrison, D. R., & Anderson, T. (2003). E-learning in the 21st century: A framework for research and practice. London: Routledge Falmer.

Garrison, D. R., & Kanuka, H. (2004). Blended learning: Uncovering its transformative potential in higher education. *The Internet and Higher Education*, *7*(2), 95–105. doi:10.1016/j.iheduc.2004.02.001

Garrison, R., & Vaughan, N. (2008). Blended learning in higher education. San Francisco: Jossey Bass.

Gaskell, A., & Tait, A. (2007). What do we know about using new technologies for learning and teaching? A ten year perspective. In *Proceedings of the 12th Cambridge International Conference on Open and Distance Learning*, Cambridge, UK, September 2007.

Gatlif, B., & Wendel, F. (1998). Inter-institutional collaboration and team teaching. *American Journal of Distance Education*, *12*(1), 26–37. doi:10.1080/08923649809526981

Geertz, C. (1973). The Interpretation of Cultures. NY: Basic books.

Gibson, C. C., & Graff, A. O. (1992). Impact of adult's preferred learning styles and perception of barriers on completions of external baccalaureate degree programs. *Journal of Distance Education*, *VII*(1), 39–51.

Gilbert, P. K., & Dabbagh, N. (2005). How to structure online discussions for meaningful discourse: A case study. *British Journal of Educational Technology*, *36*(1), 5–18. doi:10.1111/j.1467-8535.2005.00434.x

Gloor, P. (2005). Swarm creativity: Competitive advantage through collaborative innovation networks. New York: Oxford University Press, Inc.

Goodison, T. A. (2002). Learning with ICT at primary level: pupils' perceptions. *Journal of Computer Assisted Learning, 18*, 282–295. doi:10.1046/j.0266-4909.2002.00240.x

Goodlad, J. I. (1990). Places where teachers are taught. San Francisco: Jossey Bass.

Gordon, P., Rogers, A., & Comfort, M. (2001). A taste of problem-based learning increases achievement of urban minority middle-school students. *Educational Horizons, 79*(4), 171–175.

Gordon, S., Petocz, P., & Reid, A. (2007). Tools, artefacts, resources and pedagogy—stories of international statistics educators. In P. L Jeffery (Ed.), *Australian Association for Research in Education 2006 Conference Papers*, AARE, Adelaide. Retrieved March 25, 2008 from http://www.aare.edu.au/06pap/gor06358.pdf Gray, B. (2004). Informal Learning in an Online Community of Practice. *Journal of Distance Education, 19*(1), 20-35.

Gouda, A., & Banks, F. (2005). Professional dignity and reforming teachers' practice: a case study of a distance learning network in Egypt. In *Proceedings of the 11th Cambridge International Conference on Open and Distance Learning,* Cambridge, UK, September 2005.

Governer issues executive order supporting digital literacy efforts in California (2009). Retrieved June 8, 2009, from http://www.ictliteracy.info/Executive%20 Order%20S-06-09.htm

Government of Samoa. (2002). Samoa Information and Communication Technologies. Policy and Strategic Plan. Apia, Samoa.

Government of Samoa. (2005). Samoa National Strategic Plan (NSP) for ICT: Transforming government, business and civil society. Apia, Samoa.

Grady, D. B. (2003). Mapping online discussions with lexical scores. *Journal of Interactive Learning, 14*(2), 209–229.

Graham, C. R. (2005). Blended learning systems: Definition, current trends, and future directions. In C. J. Bonk, & C. R. Graham (Eds.). Handbook of blended learning: Global perspectives, local designs (pp. 3-21). San Francisco, CA: Pfeiffer.

Greening, T. (1998). Building the constructivist toolbox: An exploration of cognitive technologies. *Educational Technology, 38*(2), 23–35.

Gregorc, A. (1985). An adult's guide to style. Columbia, CT: Gregorc Associates, Inc.

Gregorc, A. (1998). Mind Styles Model: Theory, Principles and Practice. Columbia, CT: Gregorc Associates, Inc.

Grossen, M. (2000). Institutional framings in thinking, learning and teaching. In H. Cowie & G. van der Aalsvoort (Eds.), Social interaction in learning and instruction. Amsterdam: Pergamon.

Grundy, J. (2002 December). Flexible learning and the flexible worker [White Paper]. London: British Telecom.

Habley, W. R. (2000). Current practices in academic advising. In V. N. Gordon, W. R. Habley et al. (Eds.), Academic advising: A comprehensive handbook (pp. 35-43). San Francisco, CA: Jossey-Bass.

Hage, J., & Meuus, M. (Eds.). (2006). Innovation, Science, and Institutional Change. Oxford, UK: Oxford University Press.

Hall, A. (2006). Who's learning? Responding to the needs of a culturally diverse world of online learners. In *Proceedings of the 23rd annual ascilite conference,* The University of Sydney.

Hanna, E., Donald, , & Latchem, C. (2002). Beyond national borders: Transforming higher education institutions. *Journal of Studies in International Education, 6*, 115–133. doi:10.1177/1028315302006002003

Hannafin, M. J., & Land, S, M. (1997). The foundations and assumptions of technology-enhanced student-centered learning environments. *Instructional Science, 25*, 167–202. doi:10.1023/A:1002997414652

Hannafin, M. J., Hannafin, K.M., & Land, S, M., & Oliver, K. (1997). Grounded practice and the design of constructivist learning environments. *Educational Technology Research and Development*, *45*(3), 101–117. doi:10.1007/BF02299733

Hannan, M. T., & Freeman, J. H. (1977). The population ecology of organizations. *American Journal of Sociology*, *82*, 929–964. doi:10.1086/226424

Hardaker, G., & Smith, D. (2002). e-learning communities, virtual markets and knowledge creation. *European Business Review*, *14*(5), 342–350. doi:10.1108/09555340210444194

Harman, G. (2000). Quality assurance in higher education. Bangkok: Ministry of University Affairs & UNESCO PROAP.

Harris, W. J. A. (1971). Education by post (England). In O. Mackenzie & E.L. Christensen (Eds.), The changing world of correspondence study (pp. 299-302). University Park, PA: Pennsylvania State University Press.

Haven, D., & Nielsen, H. (2004). *Ordblindhed - Rapport over spørgeskemaundersøgelsen: Kommunale tilbud til ordblinde elever* [Dyslexia – Report from the survey: municipal offers to dyslexic students]. Dansk Videnscenter for Ordblindhed, Virum 2004. Retrieved January 20, 2009, from http://www.dvo.dk/fileadmin/lavervi/publik/pprrapport/index.html

Hayes, N. (2002). Managing Teams. A strategy for success. Cengage Learning EMEA.

Heidegger, M. (1996). Being and Time. (J. Stambaugh trans.). Albany, NY: State University of New York Press.

Heinich, R., Molenda, M., Russell, J., & Smaldino, S. (2002). Instructional media and technologies for learning, 7th Ed. Columbus, OH: Prentice-Hall.

Heinze, A., & Procter, C. (2004). Reflections on the use of blended learning. In *Conference Proceedings Education in a Changing Environment,* 13Th-14th September, 2004. Retrieved April, 30, 2009, from http://www.ece.salford.ac.uk/proceedings/papers/ah_04.rtf

Helleve, I. (2007). In an ICT-based teacher-education context: why was our group 'the magic group? *European Journal of Teacher Education*, *30*(3), 267–284. doi:10.1080/02619760701486118

Henderson, A. (2003), The E-Learning Question and Answer Book: A Survival Guide for Trainers and Business Managers (1st Ed). NY: AMACOM/American Management Association.

Henderson, A., & Mapp, K. L. (2002). A new wave of evidence: The impact of school, family, and community connections on student achievement. Austin, TX: National Center for Family and Community Connections with Schools.

Henri, F., & Pudelko, B. (2003). Understanding and analysing activity and learning in virtual communities. *Journal of Computer Assisted Learning*, *19*, 474–487. doi:10.1046/j.0266-4909.2003.00051.x

Herbet, N. (2006, September). *Peer Assessment: is it fair?* Paper presented at Uniserve Science Assessment Symposium Proceedings, The University of Sydney.

Herrmann, N. (1988). The creative brain. Lake Lure, NC: Brain Books.

Hewitt, J. (2001). From focus on tasks to a focus on understanding: The cultural transformation of a Toronto classroom. In T. Koschmann, R. Hall & N. Miyake (Eds.), CSCL 2. Carrying forward the conversation. Mahwah, NJ: Lawrence Erlbaum.

Hill, J. (1971). Personalized education programs: Utilizing cognitive style mapping. Bloomfield Hills, MI: Oakland Community College.

Hmelo-Silver, C. E. (2004). Problem-based learning: what and how students learn? *Educational Psychology Review*, *16*(3), 235–266. doi:10.1023/B:EDPR.0000034022.16470.f3

Hodge, B. J., Anthony, W. P., & Gales, L. M. (2002). Organizational Theory. A Strategic Approach. Upper Saddle River, NJ: Prentice Hall Inc.

Holmberg, B. (1995). Theory and Practice of Distance Education. London: Routledge.

Holmgaard, A. (2004). Hvordan blev inklusion til rummelighed? – en analyse af rummelighedsbegrebets oprindelse (How inclusion became spaciousness). *Psykologisk Paedagogisk Rådgivning*, 2.

Honey, P., & Mumford, A. (1986). The Manual of Learning Styles. Maidenhead: Peter Honey Publications

Honey, P., & Mumford, A. (2000). The Learning Styles Questionnaire. Maidenhead: Peter Honey Publications

Horton, W., & Horton, K. (2003). E-learning Tools and Technologies: A consumer's guide for trainers, teachers, educators, and instructional designers. Indianapolis, IN: Wiley Publishing.

Hoyles, C., Wolf, A., Molyneux-Hodgson, S., & Kent, P. (2002). Mathematical Skills in the Workplace. Final report to the Science, Technology and Mathematics Council. London: Institute of Education.

Hron, A., & Friedrich, H. F. (2003). A review of web-based collaborative learning: factors beyond technology. *Journal of Computer Assisted Learning*, *19*, 70–79. doi:10.1046/j.0266-4909.2002.00007.x

http://www.auf.org (n.d.).

http://www.refer.ne (n.d.).

Huberman, A. M., & Miles, M. B. (1984). Innovation up close: How school improvement works. New York: Plenum press.

Hughes, J. (2005). The Role of Teacher Knowledge and Learning Experiences in Forming Technology-Integrated Pedagogy. *Journal of Technology and Teacher Education*, *13*(2), 277–302.

Huntsinger, C. S., Jose, P. E., & Ching, W. D. (1994). *Ethnic differences in early math learning: A comparison of Chinese-American and Caucasian-American families.* Presented at the Annual Symposium of the Jean Piaget Society, Chicago, IL. (ERIC Document Reproduction Service No. 375940).

Hwang, W. Y., & Wang, C. Y. (2004). A study of learning time patterns in asynchronous learning environments. *Journal of Computer Assisted Learning*, *20*, 292–304. doi:10.1111/j.1365-2729.2004.00088.x

Igbaria, M., Shayo, C., & Olfman, L. (1998). Virtual societies: their prospects and dilemmas. In J. Gackenbach (Ed.), Psychology and the Internet (pp. 227-250). San Diego, CA: Academic Press.

Igira, F. T., & Gregory, J. (2009). Cultural historical activity theory. In Y. Dwivedi, B. Lal, M. Williams, S. Schneberger & M. Wade (Eds.), Handbook of Research on Contemporary Theoretical Models in Information Systems (pp. 434-454). Hershey, PA: Information Science Reference.

InfoDev. (2009). *Quick guide: ICT and education at DFID.* Retrieved 07 June, 2009, from http://74.125.77.132/search?q=cache:i8YkiIxFsaIJ:www.infodev.org/en/Publication.146.html

Information and communications technology integration performance standards. (n.d.). Retrieved June 5, 2009, from http://www.bced.gov.bc.ca/perf_stands/icti/content.php?page=overview

Institute of Multimedia and Software. (2002). User Manual for Online Lecture Application. Serdang: UPM.

International Reading Association. (1999-2000). *Reading Online - Formative Assessment of Reading comprehension by Computer: Advantages and Disadvantages of the Accelerated Reader Software. Inc.* Retrieved from http://www.readingonline.org/critical/topping/

ipeer. (n.d.) Retrieved July 17, 2008, from http://ipeer.apsc.ubc.ca/home/

Isaacs, S., Broekman, I., & Mogale, T. (2004). Contextualizing Education in Africa: the role of ICTs. In T. James (Ed.), Information and communication technologies for development in Africa: Volume 3, Networking institutions of Learning --SchoolNet (Vol. 3, pp. 1-23). Ottawa, Canada: CODESRIA/IDRC.

Isssroff, K., & Scanlon, E. (2002). Using technology in higher education: An Activity Theory perspective. *Journal of Computer Assisted Learning*, *18*(1), 77–83. doi:10.1046/j.0266-4909.2001.00213.x

Ite, U. (2004). *Return to sender: using the African intellectual disapora to establish academic links.*

ITU (Network for IT Research and Competence in Education). (2009). ITU monitor 2009. Oslo: ITU.

ITU, International Telecommunications Union. (2007). *Measuring Village ICT in Sub-Saharan Africa*. Retrieved December 11, 2007, from http://www.itu.int/ITU-D/ict/statistics/material/Africa_Village_ICT_2007.pdf

Jackson, G. B., & Jones, J. (2001). Web-based simulations for science and mathematics instruction. *TechKnowLogia*, *2*(2), 39–41.

Jackupec, V., & Garrick, J. (Eds.). (2000). Flexible learning, human resource and organisational development: Putting theory to work. London: Routledge.

Jacobson C., Heindorff H., & Björn, M. (2007). *ICT in Teaching.* WR06 Report of CallDysc Project: Växjö University.

Jimenez, R. T., Garcia, G. E., & Pearson, P. D. (1996). The reading strategies of bilingual Latina/o students who are successful English readers: Opportunities and obstacles. *Reading Research Quarterly*, *31*(1), 90–112. doi:10.1598/RRQ.31.1.5

JISC. (2006). *Shibboleth: Connecting People and Resources Briefing* (version 2). Retrieved July 17, 2008, from http://www.jisc.ac.uk/publications/publications/pub_shibboleth.aspx.

Jonassen, D. H. (2001). Computers in the Classroom Minds for critical thinking. Upper Saddle River, NJ: Merrill.

Jonassen, D. H., & Rohrer-Murphy, L. (1999). Activity theory as a framework for designing constructivist learning environments. *Educational Technology Research and Development*, *47*(1), 61–79. doi:10.1007/BF02299477

Jonassen, D., Howland, J., Moore, J., & Marra, R. M. (2003). Learning to solve problems with technology: A constructive perspective (2nd Ed.). Upper Saddle River, NJ: Person Education.

Jones, G. R. (2007). Introduction to Business: How companies create value for people. New York: McGraw-Hill.

Jongbloed, B., & Koelman, J. (1996). *Funding mechanisms for higher education: A five country based survey with special reference to performance-based funding approaches.* CHEPS working paper for Higher Education Council, National Board of Employment, Education and Training (NBEET), Canberra, Australia. Enschede, The Netherlands: Center for Higher Education Policy Studies, University of Twente.

Juma, M. N. (2006). Kenyatta University-African Virtual University, Kenya. In D. Antoni (Ed.), The virtual university: Models and messages/ lessons from case studies. Paris: UNESCO.

Juneau, K. R. (2008). Varieties of authentic assessment. In L. Tomei (Ed.), Encyclopedia of Information Technology Curriculum Integration (pp. 936-942). Hershey, PA: Information Science Reference.

Kadijevich, Dj., & Haapasalo, L. (2008). Factors that influence student teachers' interest to achieve educational technology standards. *Computers & Education*, *50*(1), 262–270. doi:10.1016/j.compedu.2006.05.005

Kahveci, A., Gilmer, P. J., & Southerland, S. A. (2008). Understanding chemistry professors' use of educational technologies: An activity theoretical approach. *International Journal of Science Education*, *30*(3), 325–351. doi:10.1080/09500690601188638

Kalnins-Cole, T., & Peters, D. (2007). Towards an accessible learning management system. *International Journal of Continuing Engineering Education and Lifelong Learning*, *17*(1), 84–96. doi:10.1504/IJCEELL.2007.013232

Kaptelinin, V. (1996). Activity theory: implications for human-computer interaction. In B. Nardi (Ed.), Context and consciousness: activity theory and human-computer interaction (pp. 45-67). Cambridge, MA: MIT press.

Kapur, D. M., & Crowley, M. (2008). *Beyond the ABCs: Higher Education and Developing Countries.* Working paper Number 139, February 2008, Center for Global Development.

Karagiorgi, Y., & Charalambous, K. (2006). ICT in-service training and school practices: in search for the impact. *Journal of Education for Teaching*, *32*(4), 395–411. doi:10.1080/02607470600981995

Karen, E. (2008). North South School Partnerships: Learning from schools in the UK, Africa and Asia. London: Institute of Education.

Kavanaugh, A., Carroll, J. M., Rosson, M. B., Zin, T. T., & Reese, D. D. (2005). Community networks: Where offline communities meet online' [Electronic Version]. *Journal of Computer-Mediated Communication, 10*. Retrieved June 2008 from http://jcmc.indiana.edu/vol10/issue4/kavanaugh.html

Kawatchi, P. (2008). Future Directions for Distance Education 'Researching and Promoting Access to Education and Training. In The Role of Distance Education and e-Learning in Technology-Enhanced Environments' EDEN / UNESCO 5th Research Workshop: Plenary Session Paris. Retrieved July11, 2009, from AJDE2008_Kawachi_EDEN.pdf

Kay, R. H. (2006). Developing a comprehensive metric for assessing discussion board Effectiveness. *British Journal of Educational Technology, 37*(5), 761–783. doi:10.1111/j.1467-8535.2006.00560.x

Kayler, M., & Weller, K. (2007). Pedagogy, Self-Assessment, and Online Discussion Groups. *Educational Technology & Society, 10*(1), 136–147.

Keats, D. (2003). Collaborative Development of Open Content: A Process Model Potential for African Universities. *First Monday, 8*(2). Retrieved May 2, 2008, from http://firstmonday.org/issues/issue8_2/keats/index.html

Keeton, C. L. (2000). *Institutional structures that influence faculty to participate in distance education*. Dissertation Abstracts International, A-61 (10), 3840. (UMI No. AAT 9993226).

Kellaghan, T., Sloane, K., Alvarez, B., & Bloom, B. S. (1993). Home Environment & School Learning: Promoting Parental Involvement in the Education of Children. San Francisco: Jossey-Bass.

Keller, J. M. (1983). Motivational Design of Instruction. In C. M. Reigeluth (Ed.), Instructional Design Theories and Models: An Overview of their Current Status (pp. 383-42). Hillsdale, NJ: Lawrence Erlbaum.

Keller, J. M. (1987). Development and Use of the ARCS Model of Motivational Design. [from http://www.eric.ed.gov]. *Journal of Instructional Development, 10*(3), 2–10. Retrieved September 5, 2008. doi:10.1007/BF02905780

Kennard, C. (2007). Wiki Productivity and Discussion Forum Activity in a Postgraduate Online Distance Learning Cours. In C. Montgomery C., & J. Seale (eds.), *Proceedings of World Conference on Educational Multimedia, Hypermedia and Telecommunications 2007*. Chesapeake, VA: AACE.

Kennedy, G. J. (2005). Peer assessment in group projects: Is it worth it*? Proceedings of the Seventh Australian Conference on Computing Education*. Newcastle, Australia.

Kenski, V. M. (2005). Das salas de aula aos ambientes virtuais de aprendizagem. In *Brazilian Association of Distance Education (ABED)*. Retrieved September 7, 2006, from http://www.abed.org.br/congresso2005/por/pdf/030tcc5.pdf

Kezar, A. (2005). Redesigning for Collaboration within Higher Education Institutions. *Research in Higher Education, 46*(7), 831–860. doi:10.1007/s11162-004-6227-5

Kidd, T., & Song, H. (2007). Handbook of research on instructional systems and technology. Hershey, PA: IGI Global.

Kidder, M. L. (2004). Institutional elements that encourage or discourage the implementation of on-line classes in Illinois community colleges (Doctoral dissertation, Northern Illinois University, 2004). *Dissertation Abstracts International-A 65,* (05). (UMI No. 3132423).

Kilpatrick, S., Field, J., & Falk, I. (2003). Social capital: an analytical tool for exploring lifelong learning and community development. *British Educational Research Journal, 29*(3), 417–433. doi:10.1080/01411920301859

Kim, A. (2000). Community building on the web: secret strategies for successful online communities. Berkeley, CA: Peachpit Press.

Kindergarden to Adult Education. Downloaded May 6, 2009, from http://www.utdanningsdirektoratet.no/

Brosjyrer/_english/Education-in-Norway-From-Kindergarten-to-Adult-Education/

King, R. (1996). Competition or co-operation? In *Universities in the Twenty-first Century, Education in a Borderless World Conference*, Singapore, 13-14 August, IDP Education Australia.

King, R. P. (2007). Governance and accountability in the higher education regulatory state. *Higher Education, 53*, 411–430. doi:10.1007/s10734-005-3128-2

Kinyanjui, P. (1992). The organization of teacher training at a distance with particular reference to Kenya. In P. Murphy and A. Zhiri (Eds.), Distance education in Anglophone Africa: Experience with secondary education and teacher training (pp. 117-122). Washington, DC: The World Bank.

Kirsh, D. (2000). A few thought on cognitive overload. *Intellectica, 30*, 19–53.

Kjærnsli, M. Lie, S., Olsen, R. V., & Roe, A. (2007). Tid for tunge løft norske elevers kompetanse i naturfag, lesing og matematikk i PISA 2006. Oslo: Universitetsforlaget.

Koda, K. (2005). Insights into second language reading: A cross-linguistic approach. Cambridge, UK: Cambridge University Press.

Kolb, D. (2000). Facilitator's Guide to Learning. Philadelphia: Hay Group Transforming Learning.

Kolb, D. (2007). Kolb Learning Style Inventory. Philadelphia: Hay Group Transforming Learning.

Kolb, D. A. (1984). Experiential learning: Experience as the source of learning development. Upper Saddle River, NJ: Prentice-Hall.

Kolb, D. A. (1993). LSI-IIa: Self scoring inventory and interpretation booklet. Boston: McBer & Company.

Kolodner, J. L., Hmelo, C. E., & Narayanan, N. H. (1996). Problem-based learning meets case-based reasoning. In D. C. Edelson, & E. A. Domeshek (Eds.), *Proceedings of ICLS 96* (pp. 188–195). Charlottesville, VA: AACE.

Kondakci, Y., & Van den Broeck, H. (2009). Institutional imperatives versus emergent dynamics: A case study on continuous change in higher education. *Higher Education, 58*(4), 439–464. doi:10.1007/s10734-009-9204-2

Korthagen, F., & Brouwer, N. (2005). Can teacher education make a difference? *American Educational Research Journal, 42*(1), 153–224. doi:10.3102/00028312042001153

Korthagen, F., & Kessels, J. P. A. M. (1999). Linking theory and practice: Changing the pedagogy of teacher education. *Educational Researcher, 28*, 4–17.

Koschmann, T. (1996). Paradigm shifts and instructional technology: An introduction. In T. Koschmann (Ed.), CSCL: Theory and practice of an emerging paradigm. Mahwah, NJ: Lawrence Erlbaum.

Koschmann, T. D., Myers, A. C., Feltovich, P. J., & Barrows, H. S. (1994). Using technology to assist in realizing effective learning and instruction: A principled approach to the use of computers in collaborative learning. *Journal of the Learning Sciences, 3*(3), 227–264. doi:10.1207/s15327809jls0303_2

Kotsik, B., & Tokareva, N. (2007). UNESCO IITE Contribution to e-Inclusion Policy Development for Education of Students with Disabilities. In *The first International Conference on ICT & Accessibility*, Hammamet, Tunesia. Retrieved January 20, 2009, from http://www.esstt.rnu.tn/utic/tica2007/index96b6.html?pId=5

Krange, I. (2008). *Computer-based 3D models in science education. Studying artefacts and students' knowledge constructions.* University of Oslo: Faculty of Education.

Kress, G. (2003). Literacy in the new media age. London: Routledge.

Krug, D. (2006). Seeds of possibility: Mentoring K-7 educators' ICT ecology of cognition. Social Sciences and Humanities Research Council.

Krug, D. H, & Arntzen, J. (2009). *Seeds of Possibility: Timeline of research activities.*

Krug, D., Echols, F., Wynston, G., & Seeds Graduate Mentors (2005-06). *Report: The Seeds of Possibility: Integrating ICT into the Teacher Education Two-year Elementary Program.* Faculty of Education Dean's

Learning Technology Funds, The University of British Columbia. 1-12.

Krumsvik, R. (2008). Educational technology, epistemology and discourses in curricula in Norway. *US-China Education Review*, *5*, 1–17.

Kuh, G. D., & Love, P. G. (2000). A cultural perspective on student departure. In J.M. Braxton (Ed.), Reworking the student departure puzzle (pp. 196-213). Nashville, TN: Vanderbilt University Press.

Lakoff, G. (1988). Cognitive Semantics. In U. Eco, M. Santambrogio & P. Violi (Eds.), Meaning and mental representations. Bloomington: Indiana University Press.

Lally, V., & Barrett, E. (1999). Building a learning community on-line: Towards socio academic interaction. *Research Papers in Education*, *14*(2), 147–163. doi:10.1080/0267152990140205

Landmark College - Institute for Research and Training. (2006). *Effective Strategies Using Technology for Reading comprehension*. Available at: http://www.landmark.edu/institute/assitive_technology/reading_strategies.html. Retrieved on 1 May 2008.

Lankshear, C., & Knobel, M. (2006). Digital literacy and digital literacies: Policy, pedagogy and research considerations for education. *Nordic journal of digital literacy, 1*(1), 12–24.

Latour, B. (1987). Science in action: How to follow scientists and engineers through society. Cambridge, MA: Harvard University Press.

Latour, B. (1988). The pasteurization of France. Cambridge, MA: Harvard University Press.

Latour, B. (2001). A esperança de Pandora. Bauru, SP: EDUSC.

Latour, B., & Woolgar, S. (1979). Laboratory Life: the Social Construction of Scientific Facts. Los Angeles, CA: Sage.

Laurillard, D. (2002). *Rethinking teaching for the knowledge society. In The Internet and the University: 2001 Forum*. Forum for the Future of Higher Education, Aspen Symposium.

Lave, J. (1988). Cognition in practice. Cambridge, UK: Cambridge University Press.

Lave, J., & Wenger, E. (1991). Situated Learning: Legitimate Peripheral Participation. Cambridge, UK: Cambridge University Press.

Law, N., Pelgrum, W. J., & Plomp, T. (2008). Pedagogy and ICT use in schools around the world. Findings from the IEA SITES 2006 study. Hong Kong: Springer.

Lawrence, P. R. (1953). The preparation of Case Material. In K. R. Andrews (Ed.), The Case Method of Teaching Human Relations and Administration (p.215). Cambridge, MA: Harvard University Press.

Layzell, D. T. (1998). Linking performance to funding outcomes for public institutions of higher education: The U.S. *European Journal of Education*, *33*, 103–111.

Lectopia homepage. (n.d) Retrieved May 5th 2009 from http://lectopia.com.au.

Lee, H., & Lawson, A. (2002). What do the faculty think? The importance of concerns analysis in introducing technological change. *To Improve the Academy, 20,* 150-161.

Lee, W. O. (1999). The Cultural Context for Chinese Learners: Conceptions of Learning in the Confucian Tradition. In D.A Watkins & J.B. Biggs (eds.), The Chinese Learner: Cultural, Psychological and Contextual Influences (pp. 22-42). Hong Kong: Centre for Comparative Research in Education/Camberwell, Victoria: Australian Council for Educational Research.

Leinhardt, G., Young, K. M., & Merriman, J. (1995). Integrating professional knowledge: The theory of practice and the practice of theory. *Learning and Instruction*, *5*, 401–408. doi:10.1016/0959-4752(95)00025-9

Lektorksy, V. A. (1984). Subject, object, cognition. Moscow: Progress.

Lemos, J. (2009). In Defense of Organizational Evolution A Reply to Reydon and Scholz. *Philosophy of the Social Sciences*, *39*(3), 463–474. doi:10.1177/0048393109334582

Leont'ev, A. N. (1978). Activity, consciousness, and personality. Englewood Cliffs, NJ: Prentice Hall.

Leuf, B., & Cunningham, W. (2001). The Wiki Way: Collaboration and Sharing on the Internet. Reading, MA: Addison-Wesley.

Levinsen, K. (2005). Virtuel Uddannelsespraksis. Master i IKT og Læring - et casestudie i hvordan proaktiv proceshåndtering kan forbedre praksis i virtuelle læringsmiljøer [Virtual educational practice. Master in ICT and Learning – a case study of how proactive process management may improve practice in virtual learning environments]. Copenhagen: Samfundslitteratur.

Lewin, K. M. (2000). New technologies and knowledge acquisition and use in developing countries. *Compare*, *30*(3), 313–321. doi:10.1080/713657464

Lewis, D., & Allan, B. (2005). Virtual Learning Communities: A Guide for Practitioners. Berkshire, UK: Open University Press.

Lieberman, A. (2000). Networks as learning communities-Shaping the future of teacher development. *Journal of Teacher Education*, *51*(3), 221–227. doi:10.1177/0022487100051003010

Light, R. J. (2001). Making the most of college: Students speak their minds. Cambridge, MA: Harvard University Press.

Lim, C. P., & Khine, M. S. (2006). Managing teachers' barriers to ICT integration in Singapore schools. *Journal of Technology and Teacher Education*, *14*(1), 97–125.

Linnakylä, P., Lie, S., Roe, A., & Universitetet i Oslo Institutt for lærerutdanning og skoleutvikling. (2003). *Northern lights on PISA unity and diversity in the Nordic countries in PISA 2000*. Oslo: Department of Teacher Education and School Development.

Lipka, S. (2006). After the freshmen bubble pop: More colleges try to help their sophomores thrive. *The Chronicle of Higher Education*, *53*(3), A34.

Littlejohn, A. H., & Stefani, L. J. (1999). Effective use of communication and information technology: bridging the skills gap. *ALT-J*, *7*(2), 66–76. doi:10.1080/0968776990070208

Littlejohn, A. H., Stefani, L. J., & Sclater, N. (1999). Promoting effective use of technology, the pedagogy and the practicalities: a case study. [Oxford CTISS.]. *Active Learning*, *11*, 27–30.

Littleton, K., & Light, P. (Eds.). (1999). Learning with computers. Analysing productive interaction. London: Routledge.

Liu, S., Gomez, J., Khan, B., & Yen, C. (2007). Toward a learner-oriented community college online course dropout framework. *International Journal on E-Learning*, *6*(4), 519–542.

Lockwood, F. (2005). Quality Assurance and Evaluation (Overview Essay 4). H804 Implementing Online, Open and Distance Learning. Milton Keynes: The Open University.

Lorange, P. (2005). Strategy means choice: also for today's business school! *Journal of Management Development*, *24*(9), 783–790. doi:10.1108/02621710510621295

Lorenzetti, J. P. (2005). Secrets of online success: Lessons learned from community colleges. *Distance Education Report*, *9*(11), 3–6.

Lorsbach, A. W., & Jinks, J. L. (1999). Self-efficacy theory and learning environment research. *Learning Environments Research*, *2*, 157–167. doi:10.1023/A:1009902810926

Lotkowski, V. A., Robbins, S. B., & Noeth, R. J. (2004). The role of academic and non-academic factors in improving college retention. Washington, DC: ACT policy report. (ERIC Document Reproduction Service No. ED485476).

Louw, T. A. (2008). *Online Learning Ecologies: Towards Supporting Teachers of Information Technology for the New Curriculum*. Unpublished doctoral thesis. University of Johannesburg, South Africa.

Low, A. L., Low, K. L. T., & Koo, V. C. (2003). Multimedia learning systems: A future interactive educational tools. *The Internet and Education*, *6*, 25–40. doi:10.1016/S1096-7516(02)00160-4

Lu, E. J., & Chen, Y. H. (2006). Design of a delegable SCORM conformant learning management system. *Journal of Computer Assisted Learning, 22*(6), 423–436. doi:10.1111/j.1365-2729.2006.00189.x

Luhanga, M. L., et al. (2003). Strategic Planning and Higher Education Management in Africa: The University of Dar Es Salaam Experience. Dar es Salaam: Dar es Salaam University Press Ltd.

Lunds, A. (2008). Wikis: a collective approach to language production. *ReCALL, 20*(1), 35–54.

Lundvall, B. (2000). *The Learning Economy: some implications for the Knowledge Base of health and education systems, OECD* (pp. 125-141). Retrieved April 13, 2009, from http://www.gbv.de/dms/goettingen/312704216.pdf

Lyndsay, G. (2006). Using Wikis in schools. *Futurelab innovation in education.* Retrieved May, 3, 2009, from http://www.futurelab.org.uk/resources/documents/discussion_papers/Wikis_in_Schools.pdf

Mackintosh, W. (2005). Can you lead from behind? Critical reflections on the rhetoric of e-learning, open distance learning and, ICTs for development in Sub-Saharan Africa (SSA). In A. A. Carr-Chellman (Ed.). Global Perspectives on e- learning: Rhetoric and reality (pp.222-240). Thousand Oaks, California: SAGE Publications.

Maeroff, G. I. (2003). A classroom one: How online learning is changing our schools and colleges. New York: Palgrave Macmillan.

Maier, G. W., Prange, C., & Rosenstiel, L. (2003). Psychological Perspectives of Organizational Learning. In M. Dierkes et al., Handbook of Organizational Learning and Knowledge (pp. 14-34). Oxford, UK: Oxford University Press.

Maier, R. (2002). Knowledge Management Systems - Information and communication technologies for Knowledge Management. Heidelberg: Springer-Verlag.

Makerere University. (2009). Retrieved from http://www.mak.ac.ug

Maki, R. H., & Maki, W. S. (2003). Prediction of learning and satisfaction in web-based and lecture courses. *Journal of Educational Computing Research, 28*, 197–219. doi:10.2190/DXJU-7HGJ-1RVP-Q5F2

Malik, N. (2005). Framework of Collaborative Research and Development on Distance Learning Technology for Asia. In *Proceedings, 19th AAOU Annual Conference.* Jakarta: Indonesia.

Malinski, R. M. (2000). An examination of the experiences which university teachers have in the process of incorporating computer-mediated instruction techniques into their courses. *Dissertation Abstracts International, A-61*(06), 2270. (UMI No. AAT NQ50018).

Mallmann, E. M. (2008). *Mediação pedagógica em educação a distância: cartografia da performance docente no processo de elaboração de materiais didáticos.* Thesis (Doctor in Education), Santa Catarina Federal University, Florianópolis. Retrieved May 10, 2009, from http://www.tede.ufsc.br/teses/PEED0664-T.pdf

Mallmann, E. M., & Nunes, I. K. C. (2008). The potentiality of the Teaching-Learning Objects (T-LO) and Teaching-Learning Virtual Environments (T-LVE). In *International Journal of Emerging Technologies in Learning (iJET), 3*(4). Retrieved October 13, 2008, from http://www.i-jet.org

Mallmann, E. M., Nunes, I. K. C., Catapan, A. H., & Roncarelli, D. (2006, May). *Pedagogical Mediation and Virtual Environments of Teaching-Learning.* Paper presented at the 22 World Conference of Distance Education - ICDE.

Management, R. (2006). *E-learning Nordic 2006.* Retrieved from:http://www.skolutveckling.se/it_i_skolan/undersokningar_rapporter/enordic2006/

Management, R. (2006). *E-learning Nordic 2006: Impact of ICT on Education.* Retrieved February 2008, from http://wwwupload.pls.ramboll.dk/eng/Publications/PublicAdministration/StudyOnInnovative-learningEnvironments.pdf

Marincovich, M., Prostko, J., & Stout, F. (Eds.). The professional development of graduate teaching assistants. Bolton, MA: Anker.

Marsh, J. (2003). One-way traffic? Connections between literacy practices at home and in the nursery. *British Educational Research Journal*, *29*(3), 369–382. doi:10.1080/01411920301857

Marshall, C., & Rossman, G. B. (1995). Designing qualitative research. Thousand Oaks, CA: Sage.

Marshall, R. (1995). The global jobs crisis. In Foreign policy: The U.N. in crisis. Washington, DC: The Carnegie Endowment for International Peace.

Martin, J. (2006). *Manual del Profesor de Moodle 1.5.* Retrieved from http://www.lasalle.es/descargas/ManualMoodle2006.zip

Martinez, P. (2001). Improving student retention and achievement: What do we know and what do we need to find out? LSDA Reports. London, England: Learning and Skills and Development Agency. (ERIC Document Reproduction Service No. ED465898).

Mavrotheris, E., Meletiou-Mavrotheris, M., & Maouri, C. (2004). Towards a More Constructive Use of Technology in Mathematics and Science. In *Proceedings of the 1st International Conference on Information & Communication Technologies.*

Mawhinney, H. B. (1995). New institutionalism and the reinvention of schools. *Journal of Education Policy*, *10*(5), 23–42. doi:10.1080/0268093950100504

Mawhinney, H. B. (1998). Patterns of social control in assessment practices in Canadian frameworks for accountability in education. *Educational Policy*, *12*, 98–109. doi:10.1177/0895904898012001007

Mawhinney, H. B. (2003, April). *Managing the institutional dynamics of accountability.* Paper presented to the annual meeting of the American Educational Research Association, Chicago, IL.

Mawhinney, H. B., & May, J. (2010). Localism, learning, and the pressures for accountability. In R.L. Crowson & E.B. Goldring (Eds.). The New Localism in American Education. A National Society for Studies in Education Yearbook. New York: Teachers College Record.

Maxwell, I., Doherty, I., & Jones, N. (2005). E-Learning: Learning Led and Technology Enabled. In *Proceedings of the Second International Conference on eLearning for Knowledge-Based Society*, Bangkok, Thailand, August 2005.

Maxwell, N., Bellisimo, Y., & Mergendoller, J. (2001). Problem-based learning: Modifying the medical school model for teaching high school economics. *Social Studies*, *92*(2), 73–78. doi:10.1080/00377990109603981

Mayer, R. E. (1999). Designing instruction for constructivist learning. In C.M. Reigeluth (Ed.), Instructional design theories and models (pp 141-159). Mahwah, NJ: Lawrence Erlbaum.

Mayer, R. E. (2002). The promise of educational psychology: Teaching for meaningful learning (Vol. 2). Upper Saddle River, NJ: Prentice Hall.

Mayer, R. E., & Moreno, R. (2003). Nine ways to reduce cognitive load in multimedia learning. *Educational Psychologist*, *38*(1), 43–52. doi:10.1207/S15326985EP3801_6

Mayes, J. T. (2001). Quality in an e-University. *Assessment & Evaluation in Higher Education*, *26*(5), 465–473. doi:10.1080/02602930120082032

McConnell, D. (2000). Implementing Computer Supported Cooperative Learning. London: Kogan Page.

McCurdy, S., & Schroder, R. (2006). Achieving Diversity Through Online inter-institutional collaborations. *Journal of Asynchronous Learning Networks*, *10*(1).

McCutcheon, G. (2001). Developing the curriculum: Solo and group deliberation. Troy, NY: Educator's International Press, Incorporated.

McDermott, R. (1999). Learning across teams: the role of communities of practice in team organizations. *Knowledge Management Review*, *8*, 32–36.

McGregor, D. (1967). The professional manager. New York: McGraw-Hill.

McNaught, C., & Lam, P. (2005). Building an evaluation culture and evidence base for e-learning in three

Hong Kong universities. *British Journal of Educational Technology, 36*(4), 599–614. doi:10.1111/j.1467-8535.2005.00538.x

McPherson, M. (Ed.). (2005). Developing innovation in e-learning: lessons to be learned. *British Journal of Educational Technology, 36*(4), 585–586. doi:10.1111/j.1467-8535.2005.00548.x

Means, B. (2008). Technology's role in curriculum and instruction. In M. Connelly, F.H. He, & J. Phillion (Eds.), The Sage handbook of curriculum and instruction. Thousand Oaks, CA: Sage Publications, Inc.

Measuring the information society: The ICT development index. (2009). Geneva, Switzerland: International Telecommunications Union.

Meier, S., Hovde, R., & Meier, R. (1996). Problem solving: Teachers' perceptions, content area models, and interdisciplinary connections. *School Science and Mathematics, 96*(5), 230–237.

Merino, P. J. M., Kloos, C. D., Seepold, R., & Garcia, R. M. C. (2006). Rating the importance of different LMS functionalities. In *Proceedings of the 36th Annual Frontiers in Education Conference,* San Diego, California, 27-31 October (pp. 13-18).

Merrill, M. D. (2002). First principles of instruction. *Educational Technology Research and Development, 50*(3), 43–59. doi:10.1007/BF02505024

MESC. (2006). Strategic policies and plan July 2006 – June 2015. Apia, Samoa: Author.

MESC. (2007). Education Statistical Digest. Apia, Samoa: Author.

Meseran, H., & Jabar, M. Sidek, A. A., Rahiman, A., Sharif, K., Md. Yunus, A. S., Sulaiman, M. A. H., & Selamat, M. H. (2007). Design of interactive web-based instructional system: A methodology approach in system development. In A. A. Sidek. (Eds\.), Design and development of learning management system at Universiti Putra Malaysia (pp. 21 – 27), Serdang: Centre for Academic Development.

Meshar-Tal, H., & Tal-el-Hasid, E. (2006). Collaborative assignments in Wiki-based environment academic courses. *Al Ha Gova, 6*, 44–47.

Meyer, J. W., & Rowan, B. (1977). Institutionalized organizations: Formal structure as myth and ceremony. *American Journal of Sociology, 83*, 294–297.

Meyer, J. W., Scott, R. W., Cole, S., & Intili, J. K. (1978). Instructional dissensus and institutional consensus in schools. In M.W. Meyer & Associates (Eds.), Environments and organizations (pp. 233-263). San Francisco: Jossey-Bass.

Meyer, K. A. (2003). Face-to-face versus threaded discussions: The role of time and higher order thinking. *Journal of Asynchronous Learning Networks, 7*(3), 55–65.

Meyer, O., & Thille, C. (2006). Developing Statistical Literacy across Social, Economic and Geographical Barriers Using a Stand-Alone Online Course. *Proceedings of the 7th International Conference on Teaching Statistics.* Retrieved January 2007 from http://www.stat.auckland.ac.nz/~iase/publications/17/ 6C3_MEYE.pdf

Middendorf, J. K. (1998). A case study in getting faculty to change. In M. Kaplan (Ed.), To Improve the Academy (Vol. 17, pp. 203-224).

Miles, R. E., Snow, C. C., & Pfeffer, J. (1974). Organization-environment: Concepts and issues. *Industrial Relations, 13*, 244–264. doi:10.1111/j.1468-232X.1974.tb00581.x

Miller, R. (2009). The Benefits of E-portfolios for Students and Faculty in Their Own Words. *Peer Review, 11*(1). Retrieved May 5, 2009, from http://www.aacu.org/peerreview/pr-wi09/pr-wi09_benefits.cfm

Mills, S. J., Yanes, M. J., & Casebeer, C. M. (2009). Perceptions of distance learning among faculty of a college of education. *MERLOT Journal of Online Learning and Teaching, 5*(1), 19–28.

Minerals Council of Australia national Tertiary Education Taskforce. (1998). *Back From the Brink: Reshaping Minerals Tertiary Education.* Discussion paper, February 1998.

Ministry of Education. Sports and Culture (MESC). (2004). ICT Master Plan 2004-2007: User policies, procedures and standards. Apia, Samoa: Author.

Mishra, P., Koehler, M., & Zhao, Y. (2007). Faculty development by design: integrating technology in higher education. Charlotte, NC: Information Age Publishing.

Moallem, M. (2009). Assessment of complex learning outcomes in online learning environments. In P. Rogers, G. Berg, J. Boettcher, C. Howard, L. Justice, K. Schenk (Eds.), Encyclopedia of Distance Learning (2nd Ed.) (pp. 94-102). Hershey, PA: Information Science Reference.

Molist, M. (2006). Institutos y universidades apuestan por la plataforma libre de 'e-learning' Moodle. *EL PAÍS*. Retrieved from http://www.elpais.es/articulo/portada/Institutos/universidades/apuestan/plataforma/libre/e-MOODLE. (n.d.). Retrieved from http://moodle.org/

Montgomery, C. J. (1999). Faculty attitudes toward technology-based distance education at the University of Nevada, Las Vegas. *Dissertation Abstracts International, A-60*(09), 3222. (UMI No. AAT 9946518).

Moodle statistics. (2008). Retrieved May 18, 2009, from http://moodle.org/stats/

Moodle. (n.d.). Retrieved May 18, 2009, from http://moodle.org/.

Moore, E., & Barbarin, O. A. (2003). Respecting the voices of parents: How the Spirit of Excellence Parent Empowerment Project connects with African American Parents. In J. Mendoza, L. G. Katz, A. S. Robertson, & D. Rothenberg (Eds.), Connecting with parents in the early years. Champaign, IL: University of Illinois at Urbana-Champaign, College of Education, Early Childhood and Parenting Collaborative.

Moore, J. C., Sener, J., & Fetzner, M. (2006 July). Getting Better: ALN and Student Success. *Journal of Asynchronous Learning Networks (JALN), 10*(3). Retrieved April 6, 2009, from http://www.sloanc.org/publications/jaln/v10n3/v10n3_6moore_member.asp

Moore, M. G. (2002). Teoria da Distância Transacional. (W. Azevedo, Trans.). In D. Keegan (Ed.), *Theoretical Principles of Distance Education* (pp. 22-38). London: Routledge. Retrieved May 15, 2006, from http://www.abed.org.br/publique

Moran, L., & Mugridge, I. (Eds.). (1993). Collaboration in distance education: International case studies. New York: Nicholas Publishing.

Morgan, M. (2004). *Notes towards a Rhetoric of Wiki*. Paper presented at CCCC 2004, San Antonio TX. Retrieved May, 3, 2009, from: http://mcmorgan.org/academics/papers_and_presentations/notes_towards_a_rhetoric_of/

Morrison, D. (2003). e-Learning Strategies: How to get implementation and delivery right first time. Chichester, UK: Wiley.

Moursand, D., & Bielefeldt, T. (1999). Will new teachers be prepared to teach in a digital age? International Society for Technology in Education & Milken Exchange on Education Technology, U.S.A.

Muirhead, B. (2001). Enhancing social interaction in computer-mediated distance education, *United States Distance Learning Association Ed at a Distance Magazine and Ed Journal, 15*(40). Retrieved April 3, from: www.usdla.org/html/journal/APR01_Issue/article02.html

Muirhead, B. (2007). Integrating Creativity into Online University Classes. *Educational Technology & Society, 10*(1), 1–13.

Murton, T., & Hyams, J. (1970). *Accomplices to the Crime: the Arkansas Prison Scandal* Publisher: Grove Press, Inc.

Mutula, S. (2002). E-learning initiatives at the University of Botswana: challenges and opportunities. *Journal of Campus-wide Information Systems, 19*(3), 99–109. doi:10.1108/10650740210431916

Mwanza, D., & Engeström, Y. (2005). Managing content in e-learning environments. *British Journal of Educational Technology, 36*(3), 453–463. doi:10.1111/j.1467-8535.2005.00479.x

Myers, I. (1976). *Introduction to type*. Gainesville, FL: Center for the Application of Psychological Type.

Nasmith, G., Schultz, A., & Williams, T. (n.d.). *Thinking styles and impact on military leadership practices.* Retrieved July 1, 2006, from Canadian Defence Academy Website: http://www.cda-acd.forces.gc.ca/cfli/engraph/research/pdf/47.pdf

Naidoo, V. (April 2003). *ICT in education policy- Reflecting on key issues.* Paper presented at the Pan-African workshop focusing on using ICT to support the education systems in Africa, organized by the Ministry of Education (Botswana), SchoolNet and Commonwealth of Learning in partnership with other agencies, Gaborone, Botswana.

Najjar, J., Duval, E., & Wolpers, M. (2006). Towards Effective Usage-Based Learning Applications: Track and Learn from User Experience(s). In *Proceedings of the Sixth International Conference on Advanced Learning Technologies – ICALT'06*, Kerkrade, Netherlands (pp. 1022- 1024).

Nash, S. S. (2004). New quality benchmarks for online courses: Meshing technology and conceptual underpinning. In *Selected Papers from the Fifteenth International Conference on College Teaching and Learning,* Jacksonville, Fl., U.S.A. 29th March-2nd April 2004 (pp. 195-222).

National Adult Literacy Agency. (2004). Working together. Approaches to family learning. Dublin: Author.

National, P. T. A. (2000). Building successful partnerships: A guide for developing parent and family involvement programs. Bloomington, IN: National Education Services.

Natural Language Engineering archive. (2006 December). *Reading comprehension tests for computer-based understanding evaluation.* Natural Language Engineering, 12(4), 2006. Retrieved from http://portal.acm.org/citation.cfm?id=1181161

Netspot homepage. (n.d.). Retrieved May 5, 2009, from http://www.netspot.com.au/moodle.htm

News Blaze Realtime News. (2006, March 15). *Singing A New Tune: Technology Boosts Student Reading comprehension.* Retrieved May 27, 2008, from http://newsblaze.com/story/2006315001436nnnn.nb/topstory.html

Nicol, D. J., Minty, I., & Sinclair, C. (2003). The social dimensions of online learning. *Innovations in Education and Teaching International, 40*(3), 270–280. doi:10.1080/1470329032000103807

Nonaka, I., & Konno, N. (1998). The concept of 'Ba': building a foundation for knowledge creation. *California Management Review, 40*(3), 40–54.

Nonaka, I., & Takeuchi, H. (1995). The knowledge-creating company. How Japanese companies create the dynamics of innovation. New York: Oxford University Press.

Nonaka, I., Toyama, R., & Konno, N. (2000). SECI, Ba and Leadership: a Unified Model of Dynamic Knowledge Creation. *Long Range Planning, 33*, 5–34. doi:10.1016/S0024-6301(99)00115-6

Noss, R., & Hoyles, C. (1996). Windows on Mathematical Meanings: Learning Cultures and Computers. Dordrecht: Kluwer Academic Publishers.

Novak, J. D. (1998). Learning, Creating and Using Knowledge: Concept Maps as a Facilitative Tools in Schools and Coorporations. London: Lawrence Erlbaum Associates.

Ntshoe, I. M. (2004). Higher education and training policy and practice in South Africa:Impacts of global privatisation, quasi-marketisation and new managerialism. *International Journal of Educational Development, 24*(2), 137–154. doi:10.1016/j.ijedudev.2003.10.006

Nunes, I. K. C. (2008). *PROJETO INSTRUCIONAL: sua relevância no desenvolvimento de Objetos de Ensino–Aprendizagem.* Dissertation (Master in Education), Santa Catarina Federal University, Florianópolis. Retrieved March 10, 2009, from http://www.tede.ufsc.br/teses/PEED0672-D.pdf

Nunes, I. K. C., & Vaz, A. F. (2006). Centro de Formação Continuada de Professores: Experienciando a Educação a Distância. *Extensio, 3*, 1–11.

Nunes, I. K. C., Mallmann, E. M., Catapan, A. H., & Roncarelli, D. (2007, September). *The meaningful potentiality of the Teaching-Learning Objects (T-LO) elaborated with the interactive tools: Lesson (Moodle module) and*

Articulate Presenter (authoring tool). Paper presented at the International Conference on Interactive Computer Aided Blended Learning (ICBL). Kirchengasse: International Association of Online Engineering.

Nwuke, K. (2003). Higher education, economic growth, and information technology in Africa: some challenges and issues. In Beebe, M., Kouakou, K., Oyeyinka-Oyelaran, B. & Rao, M. (Eds.), Africa Dot Edu: IT opportunities and higher education in Africa (pp.17-42). New Delhi: Tata McGraw-Hill Publishing Company Limited.

O'Donell, A. M., Hmelo-Silver, C. E., & Erkens, G. (Eds.). (2006). Collaborative learning, reasoning, and technology. Mahwah, NJ: Lawrence Erlbaum Associates.

O'Donoghue, J., Singh, G., & Green, C. (2004). A Comparison of Advantages and Disadvantages of IT Based education and the Implications upon Students. *Interactive Educational Multimedia, 9*, 63-76. Retrieved June 2nd, 2005, from http://www.ub.es/multimedia/iem

Oduaran, A., & Bhola, H. (2006). Widening access to education as social policy: essays in honor of Michael Omolewa. Dordrecht: Springer.

OECD. (2005). Are students ready for a technology-rich world? What PISA studies tell us. Paris: Author.

OECD. (2006). *Athabasca University: A case study in Open Educational Resources Production And Use in Higher Education In Canada.* Prepared for the Canadian Council on learning. Retrieved April 13, 2009, from http://www.oecd.org/dataoecd/61/45/37647739.pdf

OECD. (2007). *Giving knowledge for free: The emergence of open educational resources.* Website. Retrieved July 10, 2008, from http://213.253.134.43/oecd/ pdfs/browseit/9607041E.pdf

OECD. (2007). PISA 2006. Science competencies for tomorrow. Paris: Author.

Olson, D. R. (2003). Psychological theory and educational reform. How school remakes mind and society. Cambridge, UK: Cambridge University Press.

Omolewa, M. (1978). Oxford University Delegacy of Local Examinations and Secondary School Education in Nigeria, 1929-1937. *Journal of Educational Administration and History, 10*(2), 39–44. doi:10.1080/0022062780100205

Omolewa, M. (1982). Historical antecedents of distance education in Nigeria, 1887-1960. *Adult Education in Nigeria, 7*(December), 7–26.

Omwenga, E. I. (2003). *Modeling and analyzing a computer mediated learning Infrastructure.* Unpublished Doctoral Thesis, University of Nairobi, Nairobi, Kenya.

Omwenga, E. I., Waema, T. M., & Wagacha, P. W. (2004). A model for introducing and implementing E-learning for delivery of educational content within the African context. [AJST]. *African Journal of Science and Technology, 5*(1), 34–46.

Onikama, D. L., Hammond, O. W., & Koki, S. (1998). Family Involvement in Education: A Synthesis of Research for Pacific Educators. Honolulu, HI: Pacific Resources for Education and Learning.

Organisation for Economic Co-operation and Development. (2005). E-learning in tertiary education: Where do we stand? Paris: OECD.

Organization for Economic Cooperation and Development. (2007). Qualification Systems: bridges to lifelong learning. Paris: OECD.

Ostroff, F. (1999). The horizontal organization. New York: Oxford University Press.

Othman, S. A. S., Atan, H., & Kooi Guan, C. (2005). The Open University Malaysia Learning Management System: A study of interaction in the asynchronous forum board. *International Journal of Instructional Technology and Distance Learning, 2*(11). Retrieved July 9, 2009 from http://itdl.org/journal/nov_05/article01.htm

Ottestad, G. (2008). Schools as Digital Competent Organizations: Developing Organisational Traits to Strengthen the Implementation of Digital Founded Pedagogy. *International Journal of Technology. Knowledge and Society, 4*(4), 10.

Ottestad, G., & Quale, A. (2008). Trends in Instructional Infrastructure. In T. Plomp, R. E. Anderson, N. Law & A. Quale (Eds.), Cross-National Information and Communication Technology (pp. 41–65). Charlotte, NC: IAP.

Owens, R. G. (1998). Organisational behaviour in education (6th ed.). Boston, MA: Allyn & Bacon.

Pacific University. (2002). *Learning, technology and educational transformation: Examining the ed. tech. metamorphosis: Emerging butterfly or deleterious root worm?* Berglund Center Summer Institute. Retrieved April 26, 2009, from http://education.ed.pacificu.edu/bcis/workshop/adoption.html

Panitz, T. (1996). A definition of Collaborative versus Cooperative learning. *Deliberations.* Retrieved May 18, 2009, from http://www.londonmet.ac.uk/deliberations/collaborative-learning/panitz-paper.cfm

Papert, S. (1980). Mindstorms: children, computers, and powerful ideas. Brighton: Harvester Press.

Papert, S. (1996). The connected family: Bridging the digital generation gap. Atlanta, GA: Longstreet Press.

Park, I., & Hannafin, M. J. (1993). Empirically-based guidelines for the design of interactive multimedia. *Educational Technology Research and Development, 41*(3), 63–85. doi:10.1007/BF02297358

Parker, K. R., & Chao, J. T. (2007). Wiki as a teaching tool. *Interdisciplinary Journal of Knowledge and Learning Objects, 3.* Retrieved May 1, 2009, from http://www.scribd.com/doc/167120/Wiki-as-a-Teaching-Tool

Past experience is invaluable for complex decision making, brain research shows (2009). Retrieved June 8, 2009, from http://www.sciencedaily.com/releases/2009/05/090513130930.htm

Patton, M. Q. (1990). Qualitative evaluation and research methods. London: Sage.

Paulsen, M. B., & Smart, J. C. (2001). *The finance of higher education: Theory, research, policy & practice.* New York: Agathon Press. Personality Pathways. (n.d.). *What is your Myers-Briggs Personality Type?* Retrieved July 3, 2003, from http://www.personalitypathways.com/type_inventory.html

Pauwels, A. (2007). Collaborative Structural Reform Research Project: Innovative approaches to the provision of Languages other than English in Australian Higher Education. *DASSH.* Retrieved May 20, 2008, from http://www.dassh.edu.au/casr/casr_projects.html

Pawlowsky, P. (2001). The treatment of organisational learning in management science. In M. Dierkes, et al. (Eds.), Handbook of organisational learning and knowledge (pp. 62-88). New York: Oxford University Press.

Pearson, P. D., Ferdig, R. E., Blomeyer, R. L., & Moran, J. (2005). The Effects of Technology on Reading Performance in the Middle-School Grades: A Meta-Analysis With Recommendations for Policy. Learning Point Associates.

Pelgrum, W. J. (2001). Obstacles to the integration of ICT in education: Results from a worldwide educational assessment. *Computers & Education, 37,* 163–178. doi:10.1016/S0360-1315(01)00045-8

Peters, M. (1992). Performance and accountability in 'post-industrial society: The crises of British universities. *Studies in Higher Education, 17,* 123–139. doi:10.1080/03075079212331382617

Peterson, T. O. (2004). So you're thinking of trying problem based learning? Three critical success factors for implementation. *Journal of Management Education, 28*(5), 630–647. doi:10.1177/1052562904267543

Pfeffer, J. (1982).Organizations and organizational theory. Boston: Pitman.

Pfeffer, J. (1992). Managing with Power: Politics and Influence in Organizations. Boston: Harvard Business School Press.

Piaget, J. (1977). The development of thought: Equilibrium of cognitive structures. New York: Viking Press.

Picciano, A. G. (2002). Beyond student perceptions: issues of interaction, presences and performance in an online course. *Journal of Asynchronous Learning Networks, 6*(1), 21–40.

Piper, D. W., & Issacs, G. (1992). *Approaches to performance related funding for higher education in Europe and North America.* A Report for the Commonwealth Department of Employment, Education and Training. The Tertiary Education Institute, The University of Queensland, October, 1992.

Piskurich, G. (2003). The AMA Handbook of E-Learning: Effective Design, Implementation, and Technology Solutions. New York: AMACOM.

Plante, J., & Beattie, D. (2004). Connectivity and ICT Integration in Canadian Elementary and Secondary Schools: First Results from the Information and Communications Technologies in Schools Survey, 2003-2004. Ottawa: Statistics Canada.

Polycom home page. (2009). Retrieved May 4, 2008, from http://www.polycom.com/products/index.html.

Ponte, J. P. (2001). Investigating in Mathematics and in Learning to Teach Mathematics. In F. L. Lin & T J. Cooney (Eds.), Making Sense of Mathematics Teacher Education (pp. 53-72). Dordrecht: Kluwer.

Poole, D. (2000). Student participation in a discussion-oriented online course: A case study. *Journal of Research on Computing in Education, 22*(2).

Poole, D. M. (2000). Student participation in a discussion oriented online course: a case study. *Journal of Research on Computing in Education, 33*(2), 162–177.

Potential for African Universities. *First Monday*, 8 (2). Retrieved May 2, 2008, from http://firstmonday.org/issues/issue8_2/keats/index.html.

Pouezevara, S., & Khan, R. (September 2007). *Innovative Information and Communication Technology in Education and its Potential for Reducing Poverty in the Asia and Pacific Region (TA No. 6278-REG): A Case Study of School based In-Service Teacher Training in Rural Bangladesh.* Submitted to the Asian Development Bank, RTI International, Research Triangle Park. Manila.

Premier's Technology Council: 10th report. (2007 September). Vancouver, BC: Premier's Technology Council.

Prensky, M. (2001). Digital Natives, Digital Immigrants. *On the Horizon, 9*(5). Lincoln, NE: NCB University Press.

Programme for International Student Assessment. (2000). Retrieved January 20, 2009, from http://www.sfi.dk/sw198.asp

Pujol, i Fons. (1981). *Los métodos en la enseñanza universitaria.* Pamplona, Spain: Eunsa.

Race, S. P. (2001). Instructional technology preparation of pre-service teachers at Widener University: A descriptive case study (Pennsylvania). *Dissertation Abstracts International, A-60*(10), 3962. (UMI No. AAT 3003357).

Ramirez, M., & Castenada, A. (1974). Cultural democracy, bidognitive development, and education. New York: Academic Press.

Rapid Intellect Group. (2006). Cognitive factors in children's L1 and L2 reading. *Academic Exchange Quarterly.* Retrieved from http://www.thefreelibrary.com/Cognitive+factors+in+children's+L1+and+L2+reading-a0146219118

Rasmussen, I. (2005). *Project work and ICT. Studying learning as participation trajectories.* University of Oslo: Faculty of Education.

Ravenscroft, A. (2001). Designing e-learning interaction in the 21st century: revisiting and rethinking the role of theory. *European Journal of Education, 36*(2), 133–156. doi:10.1111/1467-3435.00056

Ravid, G. (2006). Wiki: New challenges in higher education. [Hebrew]. *Al Ha Gova, 6*, 40–43.

Ravid, G., Kalman, Y., & Rafaeli, M. S. (2008). Wikibooks in higher education: Empowerment through online distributed collaboration. *Computers in Human Behavior, 24*(5), 1913–1928. doi:10.1016/j.chb.2008.02.010

Read, B. (2005). Romantic poetry meets 21st century technology. *The Chronicle of Higher Education, 51*(45).

Reed, G., Cooper, J., & Young, L. (2007). A partnership in flux: The demise of a program. *New Directions for Community Colleges, 139*, 79–90. doi:10.1002/cc.295

Rees, W. D., & Porter, C. (2008). Skills of Management. Cengage Learning EMEA.

Refer. (2006). Retrieved from http://www.refer.ne

Reigeluth, C. M. (1983). Instructional Design: What is it and Why is it? In C. M. Reigeluth (Ed.), Instructional Design Theories and Models: An Overview of their Current Status (pp. 3-30). Mahwah, NJ: Lawrence Erlbaum.

Reigeluth, C. M. (1992). Elaborating the Elaboration Theory. Educational Technology Research & Development. Mahwah, NJ: Lawrence Erlbaum.

Reigeluth, C. M. (1999). What is Instructional Design Theory and How is it Changing? In C. M. Reigeluth (Ed.), Instructional Design Theories and Models: A New Paradigm of instructional Theory. Mahwah, NJ: Lawrence Erlbaum.

Reigeluth, C. M. (1999b). The Elaboration Theory: Guidance for Scope and Sequence Decisions. In C. M. Reigeluth (Ed.), Instructional Design Theories and Models: A New Paradigm of Instructional Theory. Mahwah, NJ: Lawrence Erlbaum.

Reigeluth, C. M., & Stein, F. S. (1983). The Elaboration Theory of Instruction. In C. M. Reigeluth (Ed.), Instructional Design Theories and Models: An Overview of their Current Status (pp. 375-379). Mahwah, NJ: Lawrence Erlbaum.

Rendon, L. I., Jalomo, R. E., & Nora, A. (2000). Theoretical considerations in the study of minority student retention in higher education. In J. M. Braxton (Ed.), Reworking the student departure puzzle (pp. 127-153). Nashville, TN: Vanderbilt University Press.

Republic of Uganda. (2002). National information and communication technology policy. Kampala Uganda.

Rick, J., & Guzdial, M. (2006). Situating CoWeb: a scholarship of application. *International Journal of Computer-Supported Collaborative Learning, 1*(1), 89–115. doi:10.1007/s11412-006-6842-6

Riding, P. (2002). On-line teacher communities and continuing professional development. *Teacher Development, 5*(3).

Ridley, D. R., & Sammour, H. Y. (1996). Viable alternative means of instructional delivery: Online courses as an alternative teaching method. *College Student Journal, 30*, 337–339.

Riecken, D. (2000). Personalized views of personalization. *Communications of the ACM, 43*(8), 26–28. doi:10.1145/345124.345133

Robbins, S. P. (2003). Organizational Behaviour. Upper Saddle River, NJ: Pearson Education.

Robertson, M., & Collins, A. (2003). OPEN SOURCE INITIATIVE (OSI). The Open source definition: The video role model as an enterprise teaching aid. *Education+Training, 45*(6), pp. 331-340. Retrieved from http://www.opensource.org/docs/definition.php

Robertson, T. J., & Klotz, J. (2004). How can instructors and administrators fill the missing link in online instruction. *Online Journal of Distance Learning Administration, 5*(4). Retrieved April 3, 2007 from http://www.westga.edu/~dist ance/ojdl a/winter54 /roberson54.htm

Robinson, B. (1995). Research and Pragmatism in Learner Support. In F. Lockwood (Ed.), Open and Distance Learning Today (pp. 221-231). London: Routledge.

Robson, J. (2000). Evaluating On-line Teaching. *Open Learning, 15*(2), 151–172. doi:10.1080/713688394

Rogers, M. O. (1995). Diffusion of innovations (4th Ed.). New York: Free Press

Rogers, P. L. (2000). Barriers to adopting emerging technologies in education. *Journal of Educational Computing Research, 22*(4), 455–472. doi:10.2190/4UJE-B6VW-A30N-MCE5

Romano, A., Elia, V., & Passiante, G. (Eds.). (2001). Creating Business Innovation Leadership. An Ongoing Experiment, The e-Business Management School at ISUFI. Naples: Edizioni Scientifiche Italiane.

Romano, A., Passiante, G., Petti, C., & Secundo, G. (2005). Creating Human capital suitable for leading the XXI century organizations. In *Proceedings of the 11th International Conference on Industrial Engineering and Engineering Management*, Northeastern University, Shenyang, China.

Romisowski, H. P. (2001). *Avaliação no design e desenvolvimento de multimídia educativa: estratégia de apoio ou parte do processo?* Rio de Janeiro: TTS. Retrieved

March 20, 2005, from http://www.miniweb.com.br/top/Jornal/artigos/Artigos/avaliacao_design.html

Roque, L., & Figueiredo, A. D. D. (2006). Context engineering for learning: A sociotechnical approach. In A. Figueiredo & A. Afonso (Eds.), Managing Learning in Virtual Settings: The Role of Context (pp. 40-61). Hershey, PA: Information Science Publishing.

Roschelle, J. (1995). *What should collaborative technology be? A perspective from Dewey and situated learning.* Available online at: ACM Digital Library http://portal.acm.org/ dl.cfm?collportal&dl ACM&CFID 28918368&CFTOKEN 76631710 (accessed 5 October 2004).

Rosenberg, M. (2001). e-Learning - Strategies for Delivering Knowledge in the Digital Age. New York: McGraw-Hill.

Rosenberg, M. (2006). Beyond e-learning: approaches and technologies to enhance organizational knowledge learning, and performance. San Francisco, CA: Pfeiffer.

Ross, J. A. (1994). *Beliefs that make a difference: The origins and impacts of teacher efficacy.* Paper presented at the Annual meeting of the Canadian Association for Curriculum Studies.

Roth, W. M., & Lee, Y. J. (2007). Vygotsky's neglected legacy: Cultural-historical activity theory. *Review of Educational Research, 77*(2), 186–232. doi:10.3102/0034654306298273

Rourke, L., & Kanuka, H. (2007). Barriers to online critical discourse. *IJCSCL, 2*(1), 105–126.

Rowan, B. (1982). Organizational structure and the institutional environment: the case of public schools. *Administrative Science Quarterly, 27*, 259–279. doi:10.2307/2392303

Rowntree, D. (2005). Designing ODL Courses and Programmes (Overview Essay 2). H804 Implementing Online, Open and Distance Learning. Milton Keynes: The Open University.

Rustemier, S. (2002). *Inclusion Information Guide.* Retrieved January 20, 2009, from http://inclusion.uwe.ac.uk/csie/studnts02.htm

Ryba. K., Selby, L., & Mentis, M. (2001). *Analysing the effectiveness of on-line learning found in communities.* [Electronic version]. Retrieved September 25, 2003, from http://www.ecu.edu.au/conferences/herdsa/main/papers/nonref/pdf/KenRyba.pdf

Rychen, D., & Salganik, L. (2003). Key Competencies for a Successful Life and Well-Functioning Society. Cambridge, MA: Hogrefe & Huber.

Saade, R. G., & Huang, Q. (2008). Prototyping a learning management system for Higher Education. In *Proceedings of the Informing Science & IT Conference (InSITE 2008).* Retrieved July 9, 2009 from http://proceedings.informingscience.org/InSITE2008/InSITE08p155-165Saade461.pdf

Saba, F. (2008). Learning management systems of the future: A theoretical framework and design. *MERLOT Journal of Online Learning and Teaching, 4*(2). Retrieved July 9, 2009 from http://jolt.merlot.org/vol4no2/saba0608.htm

Saint, W. (1999). Tertiary distance education and technology in sub-Saharan Africa. Washington, DC: The World Bank.

Saint-Onge, H., & Wallace, D. (2003). Leveraging communities of practice for strategic advantage. Heinemann, Germany: Butterworth.

Salmi, J. (2000). Tertiary Education in the Twenty-first Century: Challenges and Opportunities. The World Bank Latin America and Caribbean Regional Office.

Salmon, G. (2001, February). *Psychological and Group Learning Perspectives.* Paper presented at the E-Learning Conference, London.

Salomon, G. (2000). E-Moderating: The key to teaching and learning online. London: Kogan Page.

Salomon, G., & Perkins, D. N. (1998). Individual and social aspects of learning. *Review of Research in Education, 23*, 1–24.

Saltiel, I. M., Sgroi, A., & Brockett, R. G. (1998). (Eds.). The power and potential of collaborative learning partnerships. San Francisco: Jossey-Bass Publishers.

Saperas, E. (1998). Manual básico de teoría de comunicación. Barcelona, Spain: CIMS.

Schallert, D. L., & Reed, J. H., & D-Team, T. (2003). Intellectual, motivational, textual, and cultural considerations in teaching and learning with computer-mediated discussion. *Journal of Research on Technology in Education, 36*(2), 103–118.

Schauble, L., & Glaser, R. (Eds.). (1996). Innovations in learning. New environments for education. Mahwah, NJ: Lawrence Erlbaum Associates.

Schechter, C. (2005). Communal deliberation: The art of learning schools. *International Journal of Educational Management, 19*(3), 197–206. doi:10.1108/09513540510590986

Schedler, K., & Proeller, I. (2002). The New Public Management: a perspective from mainland Europe. In K. McLauglin, S. P. Osborne & E. Ferlie (Eds.), New Public Management. Current trends and future prospectives (pp. 163-180). Oxon, UK: Routledge

Schneider, D. K., & Synteta, P. Frété, C., & Girardin, S. (2003). Conception and implementation of rich pedagogical scenarios through collaborative portal sites: Clear focus and fuzzy edges. *Paper presented at ICOOL – International Conference on Open and Online Learning, University of Mauritius*. Retrieved May, 3, 2009, from: http://tecfa.unige.ch/proj/seed/catalog/docs/icool03-schneider.pdf

Schneider, R. (2009). Examining the Instructional Design of a Technology Enhanced Course for New Mentor Teachers. *Journal of Technology and Teacher Education, 17*(1), 85–107.

Scho¨n, D. A. (1987) *Educating the reflective practitioner*, San Francisco, CA: Jossey-Bass.

Schofield, J. W. (1995). Computer and classroom culture. New York: Cambridge University Press.

SchoolNet Africa. (2007). *African education knowledge warehouse*. Retrieved on July 20, 2009, from http://www.schoolnetafrica.org/english/index.htm

SchoolNet Final Report. (2007). *Samoa Supporting the Samoa Schoolnet and Community Access Pilot Project* ADB TA No. 4305–SAM. Helsinki Consulting Group.

Schultze, U., & Boland, R. J. (2000). Knowledge management technology and the reproduction of knowledge work practices. *The Journal of Strategic Information Systems, 9*(2-3), 193–212. doi:10.1016/S0963-8687(00)00043-3

Schultze, U., & Leidner, D. E. (2002). Studying knowledge management in information systems research: Discourses and theoretical assumptions. *MIS Quarterly, 26*(3), 213–242. doi:10.2307/4132331

Schultze, U., & Stabell, C. (2004). Knowing what you don't know? Discourses and contradictions in knowledge management research. *Journal of Management Studies, 41*(4), 549–573. doi:10.1111/j.1467-6486.2004.00444.x

Schunk, D. H. (2000). Learning Theories: An Educational Perspective (3rd edition). Upper Saddle River, NJ: Merrill.

Schunk, D. H., & Zimmerman, B. J. (1998). (Eds.). Self-regulated learning and performance. Hillsdale, N.J.: Lawrence Earlbaum Associates.

Schutz, A., & Abbey, S. (2001). Collaborative mentoring: insights from a university research centre. In M. Richards, A. Elliott, V. Woloshyn, & C. Mitchell (Eds.), Collaboration uncovered: the forgotten, the assumed, and the unexamined in collaborative education (pp.219-235). Westport, CT: Bergin and Garvey.

Science Daily. (2009). *Music Education Cab Help Children Improve Reading Skills*. Retrieved from http://www.sciencedaily.com/releases/2009/03/090316075843.htm

Scott, W. R. (1995). Institutions and organizations. Thousand Oaks, CA: Sage.

Scott, W. R. (2004). Reflections on a half-century of organizational sociology. *Annual Review of Sociology, 30*, 1–21. doi:10.1146/annurev.soc.30.012703.110644

Scott, W. R. (2005). Institutional theory: contributing to a theoretical research program. In K. G. Smith, & M. A. Hitt (Eds.), Great minds in management: The process of theory development. New York: Oxford University Press.

Scott, W. R. (2008a). Institutions and organizations: ideas and interests (3rd ed.). Thousand Oaks, CA: Sage.

Scott, W. R. (2008b). Approaching adulthood: The maturing of institutional theory. *Theoretical Sociology*, *37*, 427–442. doi:10.1007/s11186-008-9067-z

Seabolt, B., & Arends, B. (2000). *Remaining real in a virtual world.* Retrieved April 3, 2007, from http://www.web ct.com/service/viewcontentframe?contentID=2385857&pageName=index.html

Seckel, S. (2007). Characteristics and Responsibilities of Successful e-Learners. *Journal of Instruction Delivery Systems*, *21*, 22–26.

Secundo, G., & Passiante, G. (2007). An innovative approach to creating business leaders: evidence from a case study. *International Journal of Management in Education*, *1*(3), 214–230. doi:10.1504/IJMIE.2007.015122

Secundo, G., & Passiante, G. (2007). Innovative practices in human capital creation: the eBMS case. In *Proceedings of 28th McMaster World Congress*, Hamilton Convention Centre, Canada.

Seely Brown, J. (1999). *Learning, working and playing in the digital age: Creating learning ecologies.* Retrieved June 8, 2009, from http://serendip.brynmawr.edu/sci_edu/seelybrown/

Selinger, M. (2002). *Education and skills development in sub-Saharan Africa.* Paper presented at the ASET Conference on Untangling the Web: Establishing Learning Links, 7-10th July, Melbourne, Australia.

Selwyn, N. (2000). Creating a 'connected' community? Teachers use of an electronic discussion group. *Teachers College Record*, *102*(4), 750–778. doi:10.1111/0161-4681.00076

Selwyn, N., Gorard, S., & Furlong, J. (2006). Adult learning in the digital age. London and New York: Routledge.

Senge, P. M. (1990). The fifth dimension: The art and practice of the learning organization. New York: Doubleday.

Sergiovanni, T. (2000). The Lifeworld of Leadership: Creating Culture, Community, and Personal Meaning in Our Schools. San Francisco, CA: Jossey Bass.

Sharp, H., Rogers, Y., & Preece, J. (2007). Interaction Design: Beyond Human-Computer Interaction. Chichester, UK: John Wiley & Sons Ltd.

Shea, P., Li, C. S., Swan, K., & Pickett, A. (2005). Developing learning community in online asynchronous college courses: The role of teaching presence. [JALN]. *Journal of Asynchronous Learning Networks*, *9*(4).

Sheehy, K. (2005). ICT and Special Educational Needs: a Tool for Inclusion. *British Journal of Learning Disabilities*, *33*(4), 206–207. doi:10.1111/j.1468-3156.2005.00366.x

Shibboleth. (2008). Retrieved July 17, 2008, from http://shibbbboleth.internet2.edu/

Shin, J. C., & Harmon, G. (2009). New challenges for higher education: Global and Asia-Pacific perspectives. *Asia Pacific Education Review*, *10*(1), 1–13. doi:10.1007/s12564-009-9011-6

Shockley-Zalabak, P. (2006). Fundamentals of organizational communication (6th ed.). Boston, MA: Allyn & Bacon.

Shrestha, G. (2000). Utilization of information and communications technology for education in Africa. Addis Ababa, Ethiopia: UNESCO, IICBA.

SICNF. (2004). *Les enjeux de la Société de l□Information □ le dispositif du Campus numérique*. Présentation du CNF de Niamey aux différents publics cibles. Retrieved from http://ftp.refer.ne/Documents/CNFNy/CNFNy_presentation-2004-02-11_html/presentation.html

Sidek, A. A. (2004). AIPA report for MAMPU. Public Service Department, Kuala Lumpur.

Sidek, A. A. Md. Yunus, A. S., Abdullah, I., Bakar, K., & Meseran, H. (2004). Challenges in implementing e-

SPRINT: e-learning system at UPM. In *Proceedings of the National Seminar on e-Learning*, Penang, 7 – 9 June.

Sidek, A. A. Md.Yunus, A. S., Bakar, K., Meseran, H. (2006). *Design and development of learning management system - A case of eSPRINT.* Poster presentation at the 15th International World Wide Web Conference, Scotland, May 22-26. Retrieved May 23, 2009, from http://www.ra.ethz.ch/CDstore/www2006/devel-www2006.ecs.soton.ac.uk/programme/files/pdf/p223.pdf

Sidek, A. A. Md.Yunus, A. S., Bakar, K., Wong, S. L., & Meseran, H. (2007b). Development and implementation of e-SPRINT: Lecture notes management system implementation at Universiti Putra Malaysia. In A. A. Sidek (Ed.), Design and development of management system at UPM (pp. 1 – 4). Serdang: Center for Academic Development, Universiti Putra Malaysia.

Sidek, A. A., & Loong, C. F. Md. Yunus, A. S., Bakar, K., Meseran, H. (2007). Design and development of online quiz using the open source system. In A. A. Sidek (Ed.), Design and development of learning management system at Universiti Putra Malaysia. (pp. 105 – 115). Serdang: Centre for Academic Development, Universiti Putra Malaysia.

Sidek, A. A., Jabar, M., Meseran, H., Selamat, M. H., & Md. Yunus, A. S. (2007). Design and development of KM based learning management system for e-SPRINT. In A. A. Sidek (Ed.), Design and development of learning management system at Universiti Putra Malaysia (pp. 15 – 20). Serdang: Centre for Academic Development, Universiti Putra Malaysia.

Sidek, A. A., Meseran, H., Jabar, M., & Sidek, Z. Md. Yunus, A. S., Bakar, K. (2005). The Experience of the e-SPRINT - Lecture notes management system implementation at Universiti Putra Malaysia: A case study. In *Proceedings of the Brunei International Conference on Engineering and Technology (BICET 2005),* Brunei Darussalam, 15-18 August.

Sidek, A. A., Meseran, H., Jabar, M., & Sidek, Z. Md.Yunus, A. S., Bakar, K., & Wong, S. L. (2007a). The experience of the e-SPRINT: Lecture notes management system implementation at Universiti Putra Malaysia: A case study. In A. A. Sidek (Ed.), Design and development of management system at UPM (pp. 97 – 103). Serdang: Center for Academic Development, Universiti Putra Malaysia.

Silverman, R. (Producer), & Rosenberg, S. (Director). (1980). *Brubaker* [Motion Picture]. USA: Fox.

Silvernail. (2004). *The impact of Maine's One-to-One Laptop Program on Middle School Teachers and Students.* University of Southern Maine. Retrieved from http://www.usm.maine.edu/cepare/Reports/MLTI_Report1.pdf

Simpson, O. (2002). Supporting students in online, open and distance learning. London and New York: Taylor and Francis Group.

Sinclair, G. McClaren, & Griffin, M. (2006). *E-learning and beyond: A discussion paper prepared as part of the Campus 2020 process for the British Columbia Ministry of Advanced Education.* Retrieved June 8, 2009, from www.aved.gov.bc.ca/campus2020/documents/e-learning.pdf

Singh, J. V., & Lumsden, C. J. (1990). Theory and research in organizational ecology. *Annual Review of Sociology, 16*, 161–195. doi:10.1146/annurev.so.16.080190.001113

Siragusa, L., Dixon, K. C., & Dixon, R. (2007). Designing quality e-learning environments in higher education. In Proceedings of ascilite Singapore 2007 (pp. 923-935).

Slack, J. D. (1996). The theory and method of articulation in cultural studies. In D. Morley & K.-H. Chen (Eds.), Stuart Hall: Critical dialogues in cultural studies. New York: Taylor & Francis.

Slavin, R. E. (1996). Research for the future: Research on cooperative learning and achievement: What we know, what we need to know. *Contemporary Educational Psychology, 21*, 43–69. doi:10.1006/ceps.1996.0004

Smith, F. (1994). Understanding Reading. Hillsdale, NJ: Lawrence Erlbaum.

Smith, M. S., & Casserly, C. M. (2006). The promise of open educational resources. *Change*, *38*(5), 8–17. doi:10.3200/CHNG.38.5.8-17

SMSI. (2003). *Sommet Mondial sur la Société de l Information, première phase*, Genève, 10-12 décembre 2003. Retrieved from http://www.itu.int/wsis/index-fr.html

Smucny, D.A., & Humber, K. (2009). Building Global Community for Online Students and Faculty. *Footnotes, 37*(3).

Son, J. (2002). Online discussion in a CALL course for distance language teachers. *CALICO Journal, 20*(1), 127–144.

Sorg, S., Truman, B., Dziuban, C., Moskal, P., Hartman, J., & Juge, F. (2002, February 15). *Faculty development learner support, and evaluation in Web-based programs*. Paper presented at University of Central Florida.

Souder, W. E. (1993). The effectiveness of traditional vs. satellite delivery in three management of technology master's degree programs. *American Journal of Distance Education, 7*(1), 37–53. doi:10.1080/08923649309526809

SPAN Consultants. (2007). *Samoa National Teacher Development Framework (NTDF)*. Interim Report. ADB TA4738-SAM.

Spiro, R. J., Feltovich, P. J., Jacobson, M. J., & Coulson, R. L. (1991). Cognitive flexibility, constructivism, and Hypertext. Hillsdale, NJ: Lawrence Erlbaum Associates.

Stahl, G. (2006). Group Cognition: Computer Support for Collaborative Knowledge Building. Cambridge, MA: MIT Press.

Stanovich, K. E. (1980). Towards an interactive-compensatory model of individual differences in the development of reading fluency. *Reading Research Quarterly, 15*, 32–71. doi:10.2307/747348

State of e-learning in Canada. (2009). Ottawa, ON: Canadian Council on Learning.

Statement, S. (1994). Retrieved January 20, 2009, from http://www.inclusion.com/artsalamanca.html

Stein, R., & Short, P. (2001). Collaboration in Delivering Higher Education Programs: Barriers and Challenges. *The Review of Higher Education, 24*(4), 417–435. doi:10.1353/rhe.2001.0010

Stevenson, I. (2008). Tool, tutor, environment or resource: Exploring metaphors for digital technology and pedagogy using activity theory. *Computers & Education, 51*(2), 836–853. doi:10.1016/j.compedu.2007.09.001

Stoner, J., Daniel, R., & Gilbert, Jr. (1999). *Management 6 Ed.* Upper Saddle River, NJ: Prentice Hall.

Strieter, L., & Blalock, L. B. (2006). Journey to successful collaborations. *Journal of Extension, 44* (1). Retrieved May 4, 2008, from http://www.joe.org/joe/2006february/tt4p.shtml

Stuhr, P., Krug, D. H., & Scott, A. P. (1995). Partial tales of three translators: An essay. *Studies in Art Education, 37*(1), 29–46. doi:10.2307/1320490

Sturgess, P., & Nouwens, F. (July 2004). Evaluation of online learning management systems. *Turkish Online Journal of Distance Education, 5*(3). Retrieved July 20, 2009, from http://tojde.anadolu.edu.tr/tojde15/articles/sturgess.htm

Sumara, D. J. (2002). Why reading literature in school still matters. Mahwah, NJ: Lawrence Erlbaum Associates.

Surry, D. W., & Farquhar, J. D. (1997). Diffusion Theory and Education Technology. *Journal of Instructional Science and Technology, 2*(1), 24–36.

Swail, W. S., Redd, K. E., & Perna, L. W. (2003). Retaining minority students in higher education: A framework for success. San Francisco: Jossey-Bass.

Swedish National Agency for School Improvement. (2008). *Effective use of ICT in schools Analysis of international research. Retrieved from*http://www.skolutveckling.se

Tabulawa, R. (2007). Global influences and local responses: The restructuring of the University of Botswana, 1990-2000. *Higher Education, 53*(4), 457–482. doi:10.1007/s10734-005-4832-7

Tan, M. (1997). Multi-agent reinforcement learning vs. cooperative agents In M. N. Huhns & M. P. Singh (Eds.), Readings in Agents (pp. 487). San Francisco: Morgan Kaufmann.

Tapscott, D. (1998). Growing up digital: The rise of the net generation. New York: McGraw-Hill.

Taskforce on Higher Education and Society. (2000). Higher education in developing countries, peril and promise. Washington DC: World Bank publication.

Taylor, S., Frackenpohl, H., & Pettee J.L. (1960). *Grade level norms for the components of the fundamental reading skills* [Internal document].

Teece, D. J., & Pisano, G. (1994). The Dynamic Capabilities of Firms: An Introduction. *Industrial and Corporate Change*, *3*(3), 537–556. doi:10.1093/icc/3.3.537-a

Terrell, S. R., & Dringus, L. (2000). An investigation of the effect of learning style on student success in an online learning environment. *Journal of Educational Technology Systems*, *28*(3), 231–238. doi:10.2190/R53M-BVBD-UGV5-77EH

Tetler, S. (2000). Den inkluderende skole – fra vision til virkelighed (The inklusive school – from vision to realization). København, Danmark: Nordisk Forlag A/S.

Tettey, W. (2006). Staff retention in African universities: elements of a sustainable strategy. Washington DC: The World Bank.

The Cognition and Technology Group at Vanderbilt. (1997). The Jasper Project. Lessons in curriculum, instruction, assessment, and professional development. Mahwah, NJ: Lawrence Erlbaum.

The Mind of the Vice Chancellor. (n.d.). Accessed on June 20, 2009, from http://www.upm.edu.my/?kat=D&aktvt=.

The Norwegian directorate for Education and Training. (2007). *The Education mirror.* Oslo: Author.

The Norwegian Ministry of Education and Research (NMER). (2007). *Education – from*

The School of Mining Engineering. *UNSW home page.* (2009). Retrieved May 4, 2009, from http://www.mining.unsw.edu.au/index.html

The University of New South Wales. (2006). Application for a CASR grant. Implementation of Mining Education Australia.

Thinkquest. (2002). *About SchoolNet Africa.* Retrieved November 14, 2005, from http://www.thinkquestafrica.org/about_sna.shtm

Thomas, J. (1996). Distance education for refugees: The experience of using distance and open learning with refugees in Africa, 1980-1995 with guidelines for action and a directory of information. Cambridge, UK: International Extension College.

Thompson, E. (2004). Life and mind: From autopoiesis to neurophenomenology. A tribute to Francisco Varela. *Phenomenology and the Cognitive Sciences*, *3*, 381–398. doi:10.1023/B:PHEN.0000048936.73339.dd

Thompson, E. (2007). Empathy and enculturation Mind in life: Biology, phenomenology and the sciences of the mind. Boston: Harvard University Press.

Thompson, M. M. (1998). Distance learners in higher education. In C. Gibson (Ed.), Distance learners in higher education: Institutional responses for quality outcomes (pp. 9-24). Madison, WI: Atwood.

Thorpe, M. (2005). Preparing for course development in ODL (Overview Essay 3). H804 Supporting Learners in ODL Systems. Milton Keynes, UK: The Open University.

Thorpe, M., & Pettit, J. (2001). Choices and costs for course designers. H804 Implementing Online, Open and Distance Learning. Milton Keynes, UK: The Open University.

Tileston, D. W. (2005). Ten Best Teaching Practices: How Brain Research, Learning Styles, and Standards Define Teaching Competencies. Tyler, TX: Corwin Press.

Tjosvold, D., & Tjosvold, M. M. (1994). Cooperation, competition, and constructive controversy: Knowledge to empower self-managing work teams. In M. M. Beyerlein & D. A. Johnson (Eds.), Advances in interdisciplinary studies of work teams: Vol. 1. Theories of self-managing teams. Greenwich, CT: JAI Press.

Tolbert, P. S., & Zucker, L. G. (1983). Institutional sources of change in the formal structure of organizations: the diffusion of civil service reform, 1880–1935. *Administrative Science Quarterly*, *30*, 22–39. doi:10.2307/2392383

Toren, Z., & Iliyan, S. (2008). The problems of the beginning teacher in the Arab schools in Israel. *Teaching and Teacher Education*, *24*, 1041–1056. doi:10.1016/j.tate.2007.11.009

Trentin, G. (2009). Using Wiki to evaluate individual contribution to collaborative learning projects. *Journal of Computer Assisted Learning*, *25*, 43–55. doi:10.1111/j.1365-2729.2008.00276.x

Triadó, X. (2008). El aprendizaje en ciencias sociales mediante el uso de casos audiovisuales. Un instrumento de aprendizaje, motivación y mejora de la comprensión conceptual. *Revista Didáctica, Innovación y Multimedia. Núm 11*. Retrieved from http://dewey.uab.es/pmarques/dim/revistaDIM11/revcentro1.htm

Triadó, X. (2008). El uso de casos audiovisuales como instrumento de aprendizaje, motivación y mejora de la comprensión educativa en el ámbito de las ciencias sociales. *Revista de Innovación e Investigación Educativa*, *18*, 213–222.

Triadó, X. (2008). Revista Didáctica, Innovación y Multimedia. Núm 11. *El aprendizaje en ciencias sociales mediante el uso de casos audiovisuales. Un instrumento de aprendizaje, motivación y mejora de la comprensión conceptual.* Retrieved from http://dewey.uab.es/pmarques/dim/revistaDIM11/revcentro1.htm

Tripathi, P., & Mukerji, S. (2008). Access and equity to education in India through synergy of conventional and ODL systems: A step towards democratization of education. *Open Praxis*, *9*(9). Retrieved 20 June, 2008, from http:// www.distanceandaccesstoeducation.org/contents/OP2008-IGNOU.pdf

Tsukahara, W., Anma, F., Nakayama, K., & Okamoto, T. (2007). A development of learning management system for the practice of e-Learning in Higher Education. Boston: Springer.

Tuominen, M., Rajala, A., Moller, K., & Anttila, M. (2003). Assessing innovativeness through organisational adaptability: A contingency approach. *International Journal of Technology Management*.

Turkle, S. (1996). Life on the screen. Cambridge, MA: MIT Press.

Tusubira. (2002). *Supporting universities' ICT developments: the Makerere university experience.* A paper presented at CODESRIA general Assembly 8 – 12 Dec 2002.

Tynan, B., & Smyth, R. (Eds.). (2007). Collaborations to offer small courses forum, final report. University of New England.

Uden, L., Valderas, P., & Pastor, O. (2008). An activity-theory-based model to analyse Web application requirements. Information Research, 13(2), AR 340.

Undervisningsministeriet. (2003). *Skolens rummelighed - fra idé til handling* [The spacious school – from idea to action]. Retrieved January 20, 2009, from http://pub.uvm.dk/2003/rummelighed/

Undervisningsministeriet. (2004). OECD-rapport om grundskolen i Danmark – 2004. [OECD- Report on the primary school in Denmark]. *Uddannelses-styrelsens temahæfteserie,* 5. Retrieved January 20, 2009, from http://pub.uvm.dk/2004/oecd/

Undervisningsministeriet. (2005). *National handlingsplan for læsning* [National plan of action for reading]. Retrieved January 20, 2009, from http://www.uvm.dk/05/documents/national_handlingsplan.pdf

UNDP. (2005). Information and Communication Technology (ICT) for Development. New York: UNDP.

UNESCO. (2000). *Country Reports: EFA 2000 Assessment.* Apia, Samoa: Author. Retrieved from http://www2.unesco.org/wef/countryreports/home.html

UNESCO. (2002). Information, Communication Technology in Education. A curriculum for schools and programme for teacher development. Paris: UNESCO.

UNESCO. (2005). Global education digest. Montreal: UNESCO Institute for Statistics.

UNESCO. (2005). United Nations Decade of Education for Sustainable Development. Paris: UNESCO

UNESCO. (2006). Education for all global monitoring report. Paris: UNESCO.

Universiti Putra Malaysia. (2008). *The Strategic Plan Document 2001- 2010 (Revised 2007).* Serdang: Author.

University of Connecticut. (2008). *Reading comprehension.* The Literacy Web at UConn, Neag School of Education. Retrieved from http://www.literacy.uconn.edu/compre.htm

University of Dar es Salaam. (n.d.). Retrieved from http://www.udsm.ac.tz

University of Nairobi. (n.d.). Retrieved from http://www.uonbi.ac.ke

Unwin, T. (2005). Partnerships in development practice: Evidence from multi-stakeholder ICT4D partnerships practice in Africa. Paris: UNESCO.

Valiathan, P. (2006). *Blended learning models.* Retrieved April 3, 2007 from http://www.learningcircuits.org/2002/aug2002/valiathan.html

Van Der Merwe, A. (2004). *Evaluating the integration of ICT into teaching and learning activities at a South African higher education institution.* Unpublished Doctoral Thesis, University of Stellenbosch, Cape Town, South Africa.

Van Eijck, M., & Claxton, N. X. (2008). Rethinking the notion of technology in education: Techno epistemology as a feature inherent to human praxis. *Science Education,* 220–232.

van Groenestijn, M. (2007). Theory in MiA. In M. van Groenestijn, & L. Lindenskov (Eds.), Mathematics in Action, Communalities across Differences: A handbook for teachers in adult education (pp. 20-36). Netherlands: ALL Foundation.

van Groenestijn, M., & Lindenskov, L. (Eds.). (2007). Mathematics in Action, Communalities across Differences: A handbook for teachers in adult education. Netherlands: ALL Foundation.

Van Maanen, J. (1988). Tales of the field: On writing ethnography. Chicago: University of Chicago Press.

Van Wyk, G., & Louw, A. (2008). Technology-Assisted Reading for Improving Reading Skills for young South African Learners. *Electronic Journal of e-Learning, 6*(3). Retrieved from http://www.ejel.org/issue-current.htm

Varela, F. J. (1992). Ethical know-how: Action, wisdom and cognition. Stanford, CA: Stanford University Press.

Varela, F. J., Thompson, E., & Rosch, E. (1991). The embodied mind: Cognitive science and human experience. Cambridge, MA: The MIT Press.

Varghese, N. (Ed.). (2006). Growth and expansion of private higher education in Africa. Paris: International Institute for Educational Planning (IIEP).

Vgotsky, L. (1978). Mind in Society. London: Harvard University Press.

Volet, S. E., & Renshaw, P. (1999). Chinese Students at an Australian University: Adaptability and Continuity. In D. A. Watkins & J. B. Biggs (Ed.), The Chinese Learner: Cultural, Psychological and Contextual Influences (pp. 205-220). Hong Kong: Centre for Comparative Research in Education/Camberwell, Victoria: Australian Council for Educational Research.

Volpentesta, A., Frega, N., & Filice, G. (2004). Early steps toward an e-learning community at the University of Calabria. In *Proceedings of ED-MEDIA World Conference on Educational Multimedia, Hypermedia & Telecommunications,* 21-26 giugno 2004, Lugano, Swiss (pp.5102-5107).

VUSSC. (2009). *A virtual university for small states of the Commonwealth (VUSSC).* Retrieved on 24 July 2009 from http://www.vussc.info/

Vygotsky, L. S. (1978). Mind in society: The development of higher psychological processes. Cambridge, MA: Harvard University.

Vygotsky, L. S. (1986). Thought and language. Cambridge MA.: MIT Press.

Wagner, M., & Lamoureux, E. (2006). Implementing an outcome-based assessment portfolio. In A. Jafari (Ed.),

Handbook of Research on ePortfolios (pp. 539-550). Hershey, PA: Idea Group Reference.

Walimbwa, M. (2007). *E-learning practices in teaching, learning and research at the universities of Makerere, Nairobi and Dar es Salaam.* Unpublished M.Ed Dissertation, Makerere University, Kampala.

Wang, L. C., & Beasley, W. (2008). The wiki as a Web 2.0 tool in education. *International Journal of Technology in Teaching and Learning, 4*(1), 78–45.

Wang, X., Dannenhoffer, J., Davidson, B., & Spector, J. (2005). Design Issues in a Cross-Institutional Collaboration on a Distance Education Course. *Distance Education, 26*(3), 405–423. doi:10.1080/01587910500291546

Warburton, E. C., Bugarin, R., & Nunez, A. M. (2001). Bridging the gap: Academic preparation and postsecondary success of first-generation students. *Education Statistics Quarterly, 3*, 73–77.

Wasson, B., Ludvigsen, S., & Hoppe, U. (Eds.). (2003). Designing for change in networked learning environments. Dordrecht: Kluwer academic press.

Watson, R. T., Boudreau, M.-C., York, P. T., Greiner, M., & Wynn, D. E. (2008). Opening the classroom. *Journal of Information Systems Education, 19*(1). Retrieved May, 3, 2009, from: http://202.116.45.198/kcyjxl/jxtj/pdf/9/3.Opening%20the%20Classroom.pdf

Wayne, M. (2005). Can You Lead from Behind? Critical Reflections on the Rhetoric of E-learning, Open Distance Learning, and ICTs for Development in Sub-Saharan Africa (SSA). In A. Carr-Chellman (Ed.), Global Perspectives on E-learning. Rhetoric and Reality (pp. 222-240). Thousand Oaks,CA: Sage Publications.

Web, P. *A.* (n.d). Retrieved May 4, 2009, from http://webpaproject.lboro.ac.uk/

Weike, K. (1995). Sense-making in organizations. Thousand Oaks, CA: Sage.

Weinberger, D. (2007). Everything is miscellaneous. The power of the new digital disorder. New York: Times Books.

Welcome to the BC College of Teachers. (2009). Retrieved June 5, 2009, from http://www.bcct.ca/

Wenger, E. (1998). Communities of practice - Learning, meaning, and identity. Cambridge, UK: Cambridge University Press.

Wenger, E., & Snyder, W. (2000, January-February). Community of Practice: the Organizational Frontier. *Harvard Business Review*, 139–145.

Wenger, E., McDermott, R., & Snyder, W. (2002). Cultivating communities of practice: a guide to managing knowledge (1st Ed.). Boston, MA: Harvard Business School Press.

West, P. G. (2007). The virtual university becomes a reality. *Educational Technology, 67*(6), 38–40.

Wheeler, D. A. (2007). *Why Open Source Software / Free Software (OSS/FS, FLOSS, or FOSS)? Look at the Numbers!* Retrieved July 17, 2008, from http://www.dwheeler.com/oss_fs_why.html

Wheeler, S. (2009). Using Wikis to promote quality learning in teacher education. *Learning, Media and Technology, 34*(1), 1–10. doi:10.1080/17439880902759851

Wheeler, S., Yeomana, P., & Wheeler, D. (2008). The good, the bad and the wiki: Evaluating student-generated content for collaborative learning. *British Journal of Educational Technology, 39*(6), 987–995. doi:10.1111/j.1467-8535.2007.00799.x

Whelan, R., & Bhartu, D. (2007). Factors in the deployment of a learning management system at the University of the South Pacific. In *Proceedings of the ASCILITE Conference* (pp.1053-1062). Retrieved July 9, 2009, from http://www.ascilite.org.au/conferences/singapore07/procs/whelan.pdf

White, B., & Frederikson, J. (1998). Inquiry, modeling, and metacognition: Making science accessible to all students. *Cognition and Instruction, 16*(1), 3–118. doi:10.1207/s1532690xci1601_2

Wickstrom, C. D. (2003). A funny thing happened on the way to the forum. *Journal of Adolescent & Adult Literacy, 46*(5), 414–423.

Wiersema, N. (2000). How does Collaborative Learning actually work in a classroom and how do students react to it? A Brief Reflection. *Deliberations*. Retrieved June 11, 2008, from http://www.londonmet.ac.uk/deliberations/collaborative-learning/wiersema.cfm

Wikipedia. (2007). *Digital divide*. Retrieved December 11, 2007, from http://en.wikipedia.org/wiki/Digital_divide

Wilensky, U., & Stroup, W. (2002, April). *Participatory simulations: Envisioning the networked classroom as a way to support systems learning for all.* Paper presented at the annual meeting of the American Educational Research Association, New Orleans, LA.

Wiley, D. (2007). *On the sustainability of open educational resource initiatives in higher education.* OECD Publication: Center for Educational Research and Innovation CERI. Retrieved 20 June, 2008, from http://www.oecd.org/dataoecd/ 33/9/38645447.pdf

Wiley, D. A. (2000). Connecting Learning Objects to Instructional Design Theory: A Definition, a Metaphor, and a Taxonomy. In D. A. Wiley (Ed.), *The Instructional Use of Learning Objects*. Retrieved May 5, 2007, from http://reusability.org/read/chapters/wiley.doc

Willey, K., & Freeman, M. (2006). Improving teamwork and engagement: the case for self and peer assessment. *Australasian Journal of Engineering Education, 2.* Retrieved from http://www.aaee.com.au/journal/2006/willey0106.pdf

Willey, K., & Gardner, A. P. (2008). *Improvements in the self and peer assessment tool SPARK: do they improve learning outcomes?* Paper presented at ATN Assessment Conference 2008: Engaging Students in Assessment, University of South Australia, Adelaide.

Willey, K., & Gardner, A. P. (2008). *Using self and peer assessment for professional and team skill development: do well functioning teams experience all the benefits?* Paper presented at ATN Assessment Conference 2008: Engaging Students in Assessment, University of South Australia, Adelaide.

Willey, K., & Gardner, A. P. (2008). Using self assessment to integrate graduate attribute development with discipline content delivery. In *Proceedings of the 36th Annual Conference of SEFI*. SEFI 36th Annual Conference. Denmark:Aalborg.

Willey, K., & Gardner, A. P. (2009 July). *Investigating the capacity of self and peer assessment to engage students and increase their desire to learn*. Paper presented at SEFI 37th Annual Conference, Rotterdam, The Netherlands.

Willey, K., & Gardner, A. P. (2009). *Self and Peer Assessment: A Necessary Ingredient in Developing and Tracking Students' Graduate Attributes*. Paper presented at Research in Engineering Education Symposium, Queensland, Australia.

Willey, K., & Gardner, A. P. (2009, July). *Changing Student's Perceptions of Self and Peer Assessment.* Paper presented at Research in Engineering Education Symposium, Queensland, Australia.

Williams, C. (2007). Management (4th ed.). Mason, OH: South-Western.

Williams, J., Clegg, P., & Dulaney, E. (2005). *The Advantages of Adopting Open Source Software.* Retrieved July 17th 2008, from http://www.informit.com/articles/article.aspx?p=376255

Willis, J. (1998). Alternative instructional design paradigms: What's worth discussing and what isn't. *Educational Technology, 38*(3), 5–16.

Wilson, T. (2008). New ways of mediating learning: Investigating the implications of adopting open educational resources for tertiary education at an institution in the United Kingdom as compared to one in South Africa. *International Review of Research in Open and Distance Learning, 9*(1), 1-4. Retrieved, June 20, 2009, from Jhttp://www.irrodl.org/index.php/irrodl/article/view/485/1000

Wimba. (n.d.). Retrieved May15, 2009, from http://www.wimba.com/

Wischhhusen, M., et al. (2003). Applied Information and Communication Technology. Oxford, London: Heinemann Educational Publishers.

Wong, D. (2008). Online distance learning provides additional learning opportunities and improves the socioeconomic status of working adults in Malaysia. *Asian Journal of Distance Education, 6*(1), 5-14. Retrieved from www.AsianJDE.org/2008v6.1.Wong.pdf

Wood, J. (1997). Staff development for the virtual campus: a matter of teacher's first re-skilling as learners? Presented at Alt C, University of Wolverhampton.

Woodrow, M., & Thomas, L. (2002). Pyramids or spiders? Cross-sector collaboration to widen participation, learning from international experiences. In L. Thomas, M. Cooper, & J. Quinn (Eds.), Collaboration to widen participation in higher education (pp. 3-28). Stoke on Trent: Trentham Books.

World Bank. (2000). Higher Education in developing countries, Peril and promise. Washington DC: World Bank publication.

World Bank. (2002) Constructing knowledge societies: New challenges for tertiary institutions. Washington DC: World Bank publication.

World Bank. (2003). *Lifelong Learning in the Global Knowledge Economy: Challenges for Developing Countries.* Retrieved April 13, 2009, from http://siteresources.worldbank.org/INTLL/Resources/Lifelong-Learning-in-the-Global-Knowledge-Economy/lifelonglearning_GKE.pdf

World Bank. (2006). Annual Report: Health, Nutrition and Population.

Wright, C. (2007, June 15). *Educational technology conferences for 2007-2008.*

Xu, D., Wang, H., & Wang, M. (2005). Conceptual Model of Personalized Virtual Learning Environments. *Expert Systems with Applications, 29*(3), 525–534. doi:10.1016/j.eswa.2005.04.028

Yildiz, S., & Bichelmeyer, B. A. (2003). Exploring electronic forum participation and interaction by EFL speakers in two web-based graduate-level courses. *Distance Education, 24*(2), 175–193. doi:10.1080/0158791032000127464

Yukselturk, E., & Top, E. (2006). Reconsidering online course discussions: A case study. *Journal of Educational Technology Systems, 34*(3), 341–367. doi:10.2190/6GQ8-P7TX-VGMR-4NR4

Zack, M. H. (1999). Developing a Knowledge Strategy. *California Management Review, 41*(3).

Zaharna, R. S. (1995). Understanding cultural preferences of Arab communication patterns. *Public Relations Review, 21*(3), 241–255. doi:10.1016/0363-8111(95)90024-1

Zeichner, K., & Liston, D. (1998). Reflective teaching. NJ: Lawrence Erlbaum.

Zeleza, P., & Olukoshi, A. (Eds.). African universities in the twenty-first century Vol. 1. Dakar, Senegal: CODESRIA.

Zondiros, D. (2008). Access, inequality and exclusion. *European Journal of Open, Distance and E-Learning.* Retrieved from http://www.eurodl.org/index.php?keyword=distance%20education&article=302

Zondiros, D. (2008). Online, distance education and globalisation: Its impact on educational access, inequality and exclusion. *European Journal of Open, Distance and E-Learning, 1* (January to June). Retrieved June 25, 2009, from http://www.eurodl.org/materials/special/2008/Dimitris_Zondiros.htm

Zywno, M. (2003). A contribution to validation of score meaning for Felder-Soloman's index of learning styles. In *Proceedings of the 2003 American Society for Engineering Education Annual Conference & Exposition.*

About the Contributors

Siran Mukerji is Jawahar Lal Nehru scholar for her doctorate in HRD and also has Masters in Distance Education and Public Administration. She has been International Research Fellow of Open University Business School (2009), Open University, UK. She was associated with Arab Open University Saudi Arabia Branch for three years as a faculty member in Business Administration and co edited teaching case books and contributed articles in standard national and international journals and also presented papers in national and international conferences. Her current research interests are Performance management and HRM in open and distance learning institutions. She is a member of review committees of a number of international conferences / journals. In her parent institution IGNOU, India, she is Assistant Director.

Purnendu Tripathi, an International Research Fellow of Open University Business School (2009), Open University, UK, is Ph.D. in Management, with Masters in Distance Education also. He was associated with Arab Open University Saudi Arabia Branch for three years as a faculty member in Business Administration. In his parent institution IGNOU, India, he is Assistant Director. He has co edited teaching case books and contributed articles in standard national and international journals and presented papers in national and international conferences. He is a member of review committees of a number of international conferences and journals. His current research interest is Academic Program Life Cycle (APLC) and Educational Marketing.

* * *

Gbolagade Adekanmbi has Ph.D. in Adult Education, specialising in Principles and Methods of Adult Education, with a focus on distance education. From 1987, he taught courses in adult education at the University of Ibadan and joined the Centre for Continuing Education (CCE) University of Botswana in 1995. His research interests include trends in distance education development in Africa, continuing education, self directed learning and biographies in adult education. He has published articles in the *FID Review*, *Open Learning* and the *Journal of the African Association for Literacy and Adult Education*, among others. He is currently the Acting Director, Centre for Continuing Education, University of Botswana.

Trish Andrews is currently working as a senior researcher on a national distance learning project has worked in the field of higher education for over fifteen years. She has considerable experience in the areas of open, distance, flexible and blended learning. She has extensive experience in supporting innovative curriculum development with a particular focus on integrating technologies into higher education programs. Trish has worked on national curriculum development projects and been awarded several educational development and research grants including current ALTC grants in the area of rich media and learning spaces. Dr. Andrews has published widely in the area of educational innovation.

Pilar Aparicio, a PhD in Business Administration, is Senior Lecturer at the University of Barcelona (Spain). Her research interests are organizational service business and the entrepreneurship. She has published several articles in both national and international academic journals. At the same time she is involved in some consultancy projects, most of which are related to the improvement of education quality, although has interest in other fields, mainly at health organizations.

Hans Christian Arnseth is an associate professor at the Institute of Educational research, University of Oslo. In 2004 he earned his PhD in education at the same university. He has published several articles and book chapters on topics to do with ICT and learning and the use of computer games and simulations for learning. He coordinates the phd-program at the Institute of educational research, and is involved in several research projects to do with learning, identity and new media. His research explores computer-supported collaborative learning, computer gaming, simulations and learning, and analyses of students' and teachers' classroom interaction.

Jenny Arntzen is a graduate student at the University of British Columbia in the Faculty of Education, Department of Curriculum and Pedagogy. She is currently working on completing her PhD program. She has a Master of Arts degree in Technology Studies Education (2007). Ms. Arntzen's research investigates the cultural formations of ICT and pedagogy perspectives. She is interested in the role institutions play in forming, and being formed by, participant experiences. Her research involves asking how learning occurs as phenomenological processes of empathy, enculturation and the formation of consciousness in institutionalized settings. She is particularly interested in the role ICT social learning cultures will play in educational institutions.

Wael Assaf is a research fellow in e-Learning at the e-Business Management Section (eBMS) of the Scuola Superiore ISUFI – University of Salento (Italy). After receiving his bachelor's degree in Management Information Systems (MIS) from Jordan, he pursued his higher education studies in Italy and obtained a master's degree in "Business Innovation Leadership". His research studies are focused on Web-Learning, particularly in the context of Mediterranean countries. He is also working at the e-Business Management Competence Centre (eBMCC) - the Jordanian node of the "Mediterranean School of e-Business Management".

Bopelo Boitshwarelo, PhD in Education with specialization in Instructional Technology and Flexible Learning is coordinating the development and delivery of distance education programs and training of academic staff in the area of Instructional design for e-learning at the Centre for Continuing Education at the University of Botswana. His research interests are online communities of practice, blended learning, course design and development, quality assurance issues in online learning and the use of activity theory in learning settings.

Kevin J Downing is Convenor of the Institutional Analysis Group at City University of Hong Kong. He has experience of teaching in the UK, Hong Kong, Mainland China, Singapore, Malaysia, Romania, Latvia and France and is a Chartered Psychologist and Chartered Scientist and Associate Fellow of the British Psychological Society. He has substantial published work in the field of psychology, education, social work and criminology and is editor of Health Education Abstracts, and a member of the editorial boards of Educational Studies, British Journal of Community Justice, and International Journal of Fashion Design, Technology and Education. Dr. Downing was awarded the City University of Hong Kong Teaching Excellence Award for his contribution to the development of blended learning with the innovative use of technology. He is also recipient of the prestigious International Award for Innovative use of Technology in Teaching and Learning conferred in the USA.

Amal Elasri is Associated Teacher at the University of Barcelona, Spain. She has Business Administration degree from the University of Barcelona.

Gianluca Elia is an Assistant Professor at the University of Salento (Italy) and he is strongly involved in the educational and research activities of Scuola Superiore ISUFI (www.ebms.it). His research interests concern "Learning, Innovation and Value Network" field, with a specific focus on innovative methodologies, strategies and tools enhancing collaborative learning. He is also the coordinator of the "Mediterranean School" initiative, a program launched by ISUFI in Southern Mediterranean Countries. Dr. Elia had a major role in the design and implementation of the "Virtual eBMS", a technology platform integrating knowledge management and web learning applications. This platform was awarded the "Brandon Hall Research" prize in learning technology in 2006.

Ayham Fayyoumi: is a post-doc researcher at Scuola Superiore ISUFI, University of Salento. His research interests concern "Learning, Innovation and Value Network" field, with a specific focus on innovative training programs design and evaluation, and he is involved in some research activities related to e-Business, e-Learning Evaluation, e-Content Development, and Learning Communities. He is also in charge of the e-Business Management Competence Centre (eBMCC), which represents the Jordanian node of the "Mediterranean School" initiative; a program that aimed at creating a network of Competence Centres specialized in Digital, Organizational and Strategic Innovation.

Ove Edvard Hatlevik is a researcher at the Network for IT Research and Competence in Education (ITU), University of Oslo. In 2006 he earned his PhD in education at the same university. He has published reports and articles on topics to do with learning, motivation and the use of ICT. His research explores the design and use of feedback in digital learning resources, and how to use various forms of assessments (e.g. multiple-choices, written text) to identify digital competencies of students and teachers.

Natalia Jaría is Assistant Teacher at the University of Barcelona, Spain. She has Business Administration degree and Research Master degree from the University of Barcelona. Her research is focused on organizational service business and the entrepreneurship. She has published several articles in both national and international academic journals. At the same time she is involved in some consultancy projects, most of them related with the improvement on quality education.

Don Krug is a Professor in the Faculty of Education at the University of British Columbia in the Department of Curriculum & Pedagogy and a faculty associate with the Institute for Computing, Information & Cognitive Systems (ICICS), Media and Graphics Interdisciplinary Centre and Centre for Digital Media at UBC. From 1993-2002, he taught at The Ohio State University and held associate faculty appointments with the Advance Computing Center for Art and Design and the Center for Folklife Studies. He was a Fulbright Award recipient in 2000-2001. Dr. Krug's research investigates how best to develop, design, and use digital media in face-to-face, hybrid, and online learning environments, whether it is a K–16 classroom, an online university course, or professional development seminar. His research involves asking critical questions about the social-cultural conditions of using ICT in education to ensure that human interaction remains part of the process of curriculum and pedagogy.

Karin Tweddell Levinsen is an associate professor in online education at university level at the Danish School of Education at Aarhus University. She is a member of the internationally acknowledged Research Programme on Digital Media and ICT in a Learning Perspective. Currently her research is focused on both university pedagogy and ICT and ICT and learning in the primary school. Of special interest is the implementation of ICT support for children with reading and writing difficulties. Dr. Levinsen has many years of experience as a professional user centred design developer of digital educational solutions, and she has been in the field since the two-screen solution and the laserdisc. Simultaneous with her professional carrier, she has kept contact with the research community and taught at several Danish Universities, including the Danish IT-University.

Arno Louw obtained a Higher Education Diploma (1994) at the University of Pretoria specialising in Computer Science, Mathematics, Biology, Music and Drama. He has a BEd (Hons) in Computer-based Education from RAU and a MEd in 2002. In 2009, he got his DEd degree from the University of Johannesburg in which his research focused largely on the online professional development of IT educators in South Africa. He lectured Computer Science, IT and CAT at Vorentoe High School, RAUCALL and at the University of Johannesburg. He is a certified WebCT/Blackboard trainer (2006). Dr. Louw is currently an instructional designer at UJ responsible for the professional development of lecturers.

Elena Maria Mallmann, Doctor in education, Master and Graduated in Pedagogy. Presently she is Professor at the Department of School Administration of the Santa Maria Federal University, Rio Grande do Sul, Brazil. She has experience in the area of Education, with emphasis in "teaching-learning", working mainly with the following themes: pedagogic mediation, distance education, developing teachers, didactic material, dialogical-problem solving, education in science and technology, instructional design, creation of teaching-learning virtual environments, as well as establishing policies and administration of educative modalities. Electronic address to access to Curriculum Vitae: http://lattes.cnpq.br/4353719005526350

Robson Marinho is Associate Professor of Leadership and the Coordinator of the Higher Education Administration graduate programs at Andrews University. His professional background includes university teaching and academic administration, including being the Dean of the Graduate School at University of Santo Amaro, in São Paulo, Brazil. With experience in online learning and instructional technology, he has done research in faculty development in this area. As a writer, Dr. Marinho is co-author of the Portuguese book Liderança: uma Questão de Competência (Leadership: A Matter of Competency), and was the founding editor of Estudos em Liderança (Leadership Studies), an academic journal in Brazil. He also serves on the editorial board for both The International Journal of Servant Leadership and *The Journal of Applied Christian Leadership.* He has a PhD in Higher Education Administration from Indiana University at Bloomington, USA.

Efstathios Mavrotheris is the Head of the ICT Division at the Open University of Cyprus. He has extensive experience in managing applied research programs in the USA and in Europe. His work includes the assessment of emerging technologies and their introduction into commercial products and services; the design and development of innovative platforms and environments for e-learning; and the employment of contemporary pedagogical methodologies and state of the art technologies for the development of ICT-enhanced programs for Science, Statistics, Mathematics and Engineering Education. He has participated in numerous EU funded projects dealing with ICT applications in education under the Grundtvig, Socrates Minerva, Comenius, Leonardo da Vinci, and Eureka Programs.

Hanne B. Mawhinney, Ph.D. is an associate professor in the Department of Education Leadership, Higher Education and International Education. She coordinates the Organizational Leadership and Policy Studies Program Area and teaches courses in education leadership, organizational theory, education governance and change, and qualitative research methods. Her research broadly explores the organizational dynamics of change and the politics of education governance at local, state, national, and international levels. She has presented over 130 papers at refereed national and international conferences Dr. Mawhinney serves on the editorial boards of several national and international journals, and is currently Co Chair of the Maryland Professional Development Advisory Council and is a Commissioner on the Maryland Civic Literacy Commission, and is a member of the Steering Committee of the Education Leadership Constituent Council of the National Council for Accreditation of Teacher Education.

Maria Meletiou-Mavrotheris is an Associate Professor at the European University Cyprus, and Director of the Research Laboratory in ICT-Enhanced Education. She has a Ph.D. in Mathematics Education (University of Texas, 2000), an M.Sc. in Statistics (University of Texas, 1994), an M.Sc. in Engineering (University of Texas, 1998), an M.A. in Open and Distance Learning (Open University, 2008), a B. A. in Mathematics (University of Texas, 1993), and Teacher's Diploma in Elementary Education (Pedagogical Academy of Cyprus, 1990). Her research interests focus on the educational applications of advanced eLearning technologies in Mathematics, Statistics, Science, and Engineering. Dr. Meletiou-Mavrotheris has been involved, in the capacity of coordinator or research collaborator, in numerous locally or EU-funded projects exploring the utilization of open and distance education environments in formal education systems (at the elementary, secondary, or higher education level), as well as in adult education and vocational training.

Hamidah Meseran holds a Diploma in Computer Science from MARA University of Technology. Her Bachelor and Master Degrees in Computer Science are from Universiti Putra Malaysia. She was appointed as a Computer Programmer at Computer Center, University Putra Malaysia in 1986 and was promoted to System Analyst (now known as Information Technology Officer) in 1999. She has vast experience as project manager in the development of e-learning system. She has authored numerous publications, conference papers and poster presentations related to e-learning both at national and international levels. She is currently the Head of Technology in Teaching and Learning Division, Centre for Academic Development (CADe) UPM.

Ioana Chan Mow is currently the Dean of the Faculty of Science at the National University of Samoa. She is an educationist and a specialist in educational technology and information science, with interests in e-learning and computer programming learning environments. She is currently a lecturer in the computing department at the National University of Samoa. Dr. Mow holds a bachelor's degree in science from Otago University, New Zealand and a Diploma in Information Science from Massey University, New Zealand. She also has a master's degree in Educational Computing and a PhD from the University of South Australia.

Ingrid Kleist Clark Nunes, Master in Education, Graduation in Pedagogy and Technical Course in Informatics, studying mainly research in education and communication. Presently, she works as HR Analyst in one of the major Glass Industries of Brazil. She has experience in Internal Communication, Corporative Education, Training of Human Resources, specializing in the Development of People and Talents Management. She has also worked as an instructional designer and coordinator of Distance Education Projects for different organizations. Electronic address to access Curriculum Vitae: http://lattes.cnpq.br/3541030095398563

Yael Poyas (PhD) is a senior lecturer at Oranim Academic College of Education, and a senior lecturer at Haifa University in Israel. She served as the Rector of Oranim College for ten years and was the Head of the M.Ed program of Interdisciplinary Teaching of the Humanities in the Faculty of Graduate Studies. In addition, Dr. Poyas is a teacher educator in the Faculty of Education at Haifa University, where she has developed the Methodology Courses for teaching Hebrew Literature. Her fields of interest are the instruction of Literature and teacher education. Her publications focus on learning with multimedia and with cognitive aspects of teachers' behaviors in the course of learning with video-cases. Presetnly her focus of study is on the impact of Wiki environments on academic and social achievements of students in teacher education programs.

Carolyn Stevenson holds a Bachelor of Arts degree in English, Master of Arts degree in Communications, and a Doctor of Education degree with an emphasis in Educational Leadership and Organizational Change. She has over 13 years teaching and administrative experience in higher education, including ten years experience in online education. She is currently a full-time faculty member for the Communication Department at Kaplan University and has been working for the university since 2004. Her recent publications include serving as a co-author for the textbook, Technical Writing, published in 2008 by Kaplan Publishing.

Cesare Taurino: After a Degree in Computer Science Engineering, Eng. Cesare Taurino started his professional experience as a Research Fellow at the e-Business Management Section of Scuola Superiore ISUFI (University of Salento). His research is focused on emerging trends, methodologies and technologies for web learning, including the implication of semantic web paradigm. As a responsible of the Web Learning Lab of the eBMS, he's involved in the management, customization and administration of the eBMS Web Learning platform, as well as in the creation of learning contents delivered through the platform.

Xavier M. Triadó is PhD in Business Administration and has a degree in Economics by the University of Barcelona, Spain. He is deputy director of Science of Education Institute, at the University of Barcelona and Professor of Management and Organizational Behaviour, and Director of the master's degree in Sport Business Management. His research focuses on services management and entrepreneurship. He has published several articles in national and international academic journals. At the same time he is involved in some consultancy projects, at service and sports business management. He works to analyze and to improve the quality of teaching at higher education system, and research at universities.

Zaidan Abdul Wahab has Master degree in Solid State Physics from the University of Iowa, USA and Ph.D in Materials Science. His research interest is in thermal properties measurements of materials. He has conducted consultancy works for the Ministry of Education Malaysia and private software (Education) industry in the areas of multimedia Physics teaching module development. He is a member of the Institute of Physics Malaysia, American Association of Physics Teachers and a life member of the Malaysian Association of Solid State Sciences. Dr. Zaidan has served as Deputy Director of Institute of Software Development, Post Graduate Coordinator, Head of Physics Department and Deputy Dean (Development) Faculty of Science. Presently he is Deputy Director (Technology in Teaching & Learning) for the Centre for Academic Development (CADe) UPM.

Michael Walimbwa is an Assistant Lecturer at the Department of Curriculum, Teaching and Media, Makerere University School of Education, Kampala. He has Masters Degree in Education (Information and Communication Technology). He is a teacher trainer, with keen interest in Educational Technology as it evolves, now focusing on how technology is transforming Education systems the world over through e-learning, mlearning, etc. He has a Certificate in Education for Sustainable Development (ESD). His research interests include technology integration in education to achieve sustainable educational development.

Gerda van Wyk obtained a B. Soc. Sc. – Hons in Psychology from the University of the Free State, South Africa. She practiced as a psychometrist for almost 20 years at various renowned educational institutions in South Africa. She is a distinguished academic researcher in the field of technology-assisted reading and is the founder of Reading Zone, a young and dynamic company specializing in reading interventions and the upliftment of reading skills of learners and students. She is involved as an evaluator of technology assisted learning material and projects at the University of Johannesburg, South Africa.

Aissetou Drame Yaye holding a BSc in Forestry, a distance learning Masters in Using ICTs in Education and a PhD in Entomology, has rich experience in agroforestry and entomology. She worked as a Forest Engineer at the FAO Forest Management project of PREVINOBA in Senegal from 1986 to 1987 followed by being a Training expert in Entomology in the Department of Crop Protection of the Regional training Centre (AGRHYMET) of the Interstate Committee against Drought in the Sahel (CILLS), Niger. She has been in the Capacity Building Centre of the PAGT (Projet d'Appui a la Gestion des Terroirs) in Niger as its Director. Dr. Yaye was also a Research Fellow in ICRISAT Centre, Niger. From 2000 to 2007, she was actively involved in teaching and research as a Lecturer of Forestry and Entomology at the Faculty of Agriculture of the Abdou Moumouni University (UAM) in Niger. Since November 2007, she is Executive Secretary of ANAFE, Kenya.

Aida Suraya Md. Yunus has doctoral degree in Mathematics Education from the University of Malaya. She was appointed as a lecturer with University Putra Malaysia in 1984 and was promoted to Associate Professor in 2001. She has been involved in research and consultancy works, both nationally and internationally in the area of mathematics education. She is an associate researcher at the Institute of Mathematical Research (INSPEM) and the National Higher Education Research Institute. She was the Head, Department of Science and Technical Education, Faculty of Educational Studies in June 2006 – Jan 2009, Deputy Director (Policy and Quality), Center for Academic Development (CADe) UPM in Feb 2009 and Director, CADe from March 2009 until present.

Index

L

M

N

O

P

Q

R

S

Z